KT-195-686

Web Database Applications
with PHP and MySQL

Other resources from O'Reilly

Related titles

Programming PHP	Learning PHP 5
PHP Pocket Reference	MySQL Pocket Reference
PHP Cookbook	Managing and Using MySQL
JavaScript and DHTML Cookbook	MySQL Cookbook
	High Performance MySQL
Cascading Style Sheets	Upgrading to PHP 5

oreilly.com

oreilly.com is more than a complete catalog of O'Reilly books. You'll also find links to news, events, articles, weblogs, sample chapters, and code examples.

oreillynet.com is the essential portal for developers interested in open and emerging technologies, including new platforms, programming languages, and operating systems.

Conferences

O'Reilly brings diverse innovators together to nurture the ideas that spark revolutionary industries. We specialize in documenting the latest tools and systems, translating the innovator's knowledge into useful skills for those in the trenches. Visit *conferences.oreilly.com* for our upcoming events.

Safari Bookshelf (*safari.oreilly.com*) is the premier online reference library for programmers and IT professionals. Conduct searches across more than 1,000 books. Subscribers can zero in on answers to time-critical questions in a matter of seconds. Read the books on your Bookshelf from cover to cover or simply flip to the page you need. Try it today with a free trial.

SECOND EDITION

Web Database Applications
with PHP and MySQL

Hugh E. Williams and David Lane

O'REILLY®

Beijing · Cambridge · Farnham · Köln · Paris · Sebastopol · Taipei · Tokyo

Web Database Applications with PHP and MySQL, Second Edition

by Hugh E. Williams and David Lane

Copyright © 2004, 2002 O'Reilly Media, Inc. All rights reserved.
Printed in the United States of America.

Published by O'Reilly Media, Inc., 1005 Gravenstein Highway North, Sebastopol, CA 95472.

O'Reilly books may be purchased for educational, business, or sales promotional use. Online editions are also available for most titles (*safari.oreilly.com*). For more information, contact our corporate/institutional sales department: (800) 998-9938 or *corporate@oreilly.com*.

Editor:	Andy Oram
Production Editor:	Darren Kelly
Cover Designers:	Ellie Volckhausen and Emma Colby
Interior Designer:	Melanie Wang

Printing History:

March 2002:	First Edition.
May 2004:	Second Edition.

RepKover™   This book uses RepKover™, a durable and flexible lay-flat binding.

ISBN: 0-596-00543-1
[M]   [1/06]

Table of Contents

Preface

There are lots of PHP and MySQL resources. So why did we decide to add this book to the market? We made the decision after we started teaching graduate students how to program with PHP in 1999. We found that the PHP and MySQL manuals, as well as most books, train people to use particular tools. But almost no resources explained the principles of programming for the Web. We realized that Web administrators and programmers needed to know more than what PHP functions to use and how to write SQL queries. That's where this book comes in: it'll help you learn about web database development, as well as understand the principles.

This book explains what to do and why, along with how it's done in PHP and MySQL. You'll find information here that you won't find elsewhere. Hopefully, you'll use this knowledge with whatever web tools you choose in the future. But you'll also learn about the breadth and depth of PHP and MySQL. When you finish this book, you'll be able to build an online store, a portal, or a content management system.

What This Book Is About

This book is for developers who want to build database applications that are integrated with the Web. We show you the principles and techniques for developing small- to medium-scale web database applications that store, manage, and retrieve data. The architecture we describe is a successful framework for applications that can run on modest hardware and process more than a million hits per day.

We show you all of the critical tasks you need to know to build successful web software. We cover programming fundamentals for the Web. We show you the principles and practice of working with databases using the SQL query language. We teach you about tracking users with sessions, securing an application, separating presentation from code, writing database-independent code, writing reports, adding error handling, and advanced object-oriented and database topics.

An important feature of this book is our case study, *Hugh and Dave's Online Wines*. It's a complete but fictional online retail store that illustrates how most of the techniques described in the book can be put together to build a real application. The winestore application allows users to browse and search a database of wines, add items to a shopping cart, manage their membership, and purchase wines. It has all the basic security, user-tracking, and error-handling features of a real-world application. It features a medium-size database that we use in querying examples throughout the book.

We use Open Source software, and we show you how to use it on Unix-based platforms such as Linux and Mac OS X, and under Microsoft Windows 2000, 2003, and XP. Our database server is MySQL, a system known for its suitability to applications that require speed but low resource overheads. Our scripting language is PHP, which is best known for its function libraries that interact with more than 15 relational database systems, the web environment, and many other services. Apache is our web server of choice, but most other web servers can be used successfully with MySQL, PHP, and this book.

What You Need to Know

This book is about understanding and developing application logic that brings databases and the Web together. We introduce database systems over the course of the book, but our discussions don't replace a book or class dedicated to relational database theory, or a book about a specific relational database system such as MySQL. Likewise, we assume you're already familiar with the Web. We don't delve deeply into the three key web protocols, HTML, HTTP, and TCP/IP.

You don't need to know how to program to use this book, but you do need to understand basic HTML. Our introduction to PHP doesn't assume you are familiar with web scripting or are a programmer, but we do assume you understand the basic HTML constructs and are familiar with the popular web browsers. If you can use a text editor to author an HTML document that contains a form and a table, you have sufficient HTML skills to use this book. It's the principles of structure in the markup process that are important, not the attractiveness or usability of the presentation in the web browser.

You don't need a detailed understanding of relational databases to use this book, but a working knowledge is helpful. We present the relational database theory needed for developing simple applications, and we cover many other basic concepts, including how to tell when a database is the method of choice to store data, the database query language SQL, and a case study that models system requirements and converts the model to a database design. This book isn't a substitute for the many good resources on database theory. However, it's enough to begin developing the underlying databases for many web database applications.

We briefly introduce web servers and networking in Chapter 1 and provide additional material in Appendix B. Both web servers and networking are important to a web database application but aren't the focus of this book. We present enough information to set up a web server and to understand how it fits in the architecture of a web database application. For many applications, this is sufficient. Likewise, we present sufficient detail so that you will understand what networking and network protocol issues impact web database application design.

How This Book Is Organized

There are 20 chapters and 8 appendixes in this book. Chapters 1 to 5 introduce web database applications, PHP, MySQL, and SQL:

Chapter 1, *Database Applications and the Web*
> Discusses the three-tier architecture commonly used in web database applications, and how data is exchanged between browsers and servers. It introduces PHP and MySQL, and discusses when and why databases are used on the Web. The features of MySQL 4.1 and PHP5 are introduced.

Chapter 2, *The PHP Scripting Language*
> Introduces the PHP scripting language. It covers programming in PHP and discusses the basic programming constructs, variables, types, functions, and techniques.

Chapter 3, *Arrays, Strings, and Advanced Data Manipulation in PHP*
> Explains the intermediate level features of PHP, including how to work with arrays, strings, and times and dates. The chapter is illustrated with many short examples that show how each technique is used in practice.

Chapter 4, *Introduction to Object-Oriented Programming with PHP 5*
> Shows you how to use the basic object-oriented (OO) features of PHP4 and PHP5, and explains why OO programming is popular and becoming important in PHP. A more advanced discussion of the new OO features in PHP5 is presented in Chapter 14, but this chapter gives you all the knowledge you need to work with the PEAR packages that are discussed in Chapter 7.

Chapter 5, *SQL and MySQL*
> Introduces MySQL and how to interact with it using the SQL query language. The focus of the chapter is an example-driven section on querying, and we illustrate it using examples from the online winestore's database. We also introduce you to the basics of creating, deleting, and updating data and databases. A more advanced discussion of the features of MySQL 4.1 is presented in Chapter 15, but the basics discussed in this chapter are sufficient for you to work with all of the material up to Chapter 13 and with the online wines case study in Chapters 17 to 20.

Chapters 6 to 11 cover the principles and practice of developing web database application logic.

Chapter 6, *Querying Web Databases*

Introduces connecting to MySQL with PHP. We explain the querying process used in most interactions with MySQL and present examples that use the PHP MySQL library functions. We show how user data is encoded, sent in requests from a web browser to a web server, and decoded for processing in PHP. We discuss the security implications in processing user data and show steps to secure interactive querying systems. Our discussions are supported by short examples that show you how to build simple query modules.

Chapter 7, *PEAR*

Discusses the PEAR package repository. Packages are source code modules that can be used in your code and save you from reinventing widely used concepts. PEAR includes over 100 packages for tasks as diverse as date and time manipulation, security, networking, and database access, and this chapter shows you how to install and upgrade them. The chapter focuses on a templates package—a useful tool for separating HTML from code—and another for database abstraction. Both packages are used in later chapters to develop robust, reusable code.

Chapter 8, *Writing to Web Databases*

Covers writing data to web databases. There are several reasons why writing data is different from reading it and that's why it isn't discussed in Chapter 6. For example, reloading or printing a page from a web browser can cause data to be written to a database more than once. Multiple users accessing the same database introduces other problems, such as data unexpectedly being changed by one user while it's being read by another. We discuss how to solve problems related to the nature of the Web and multiple users. We illustrate the principles with a case study example of collecting form data from a user and saving it in a database.

Chapter 9, *Validation with PHP and JavaScript*

This chapter is related to Chapter 8 and presents the principles and techniques for user input validation. We show you techniques such as how to validate dates, credit card numbers, and phone numbers, and explain how to use these in error-checking modules that are scalable and practical for web database applications. We also introduce client-side, browser-based JavaScript and show you how to use it for common tasks including user input validation in the web browser.

Chapter 10, *Sessions*

Covers the principles of adding session management to web database applications. Session management allows the interactions between a user and the application to be related so that, for example, a user can log in and log out of an application and be guided through a series of steps in a process. We show how PHP manages sessions and illustrate the techniques with a case study of managing error feedback to users. We also discuss when and when not to use sessions, and how to configure PHP's session handler so it's secure and scalable.

Chapter 11, *Authentication and Security*

Discusses web security and authentication. We show how PHP can be used for basic authentication, how databases can be used to manage users, and why you might need to secure communications with the secure sockets layer (SSL). The case study is a reusable authentication module with login, logout, and password change features.

Chapters 12 to 15 discuss tasks and techniques you'll need when you're building a real-world application or deploying an application to users.

Chapter 12, *Errors, Debugging, and Deployment*

Error handling and debugging are the focus of this chapter. We discuss the types of errors that can occur in PHP and show you how to identify the source of common programming errors that cause these problems. We then show you how to write your own error handler that can be integrated into an application, and how to trigger your own errors when you need them. Adding a custom error handler gives a professional finish to an application.

Chapter 13, *Reporting*

Discusses reporting for the Web and what solutions work in PHP. The focus is producing PDF (Adobe Portable Document Format) reports using a popular PHP PDF library, and we illustrate the techniques with several examples. The chapter concludes with a function reference for the class we use.

Chapter 14, *Advanced Features of Object-Oriented Programming in PHP 5*

This chapter shows you the advanced features of PHP5's object-oriented programming model. We extend the discussion in Chapter 4, and show you how to build and reuse classes, and how to write powerful OO applications. The chapter concludes with a case study that shows how all of the features can be used together to build a complex and powerful class hierarchy.

Chapter 15, *Advanced SQL*

This chapter shows you the advanced features of MySQL 4.1. It extends the discussion in Chapter 5, and shows you how to write complex queries, manipulate data in complex ways, manage users, and tune your database and MySQL server.

Chapters 16 to 20 present and outline the winestore case study that shows how most of the techniques discussed in the book are put together to build an application. The outlines aren't comprehensive: we assume you've read the book and understand the principles of developing web database applications.

Chapter 16, *Hugh and Dave's Online Wines: A Case Study*

Explains the structure of the winestore application and discusses how the principles shown in earlier chapters are put together to build a real-world application that is flexible, robust, secure, and scalable. It also shows how the scripts work together through figures and explanations. We also explain how we've developed classes and functions for general-purpose tasks, and we list the code of all of the reusable components.

Chapter 17, *Managing Customers*

Presents the code for customer management in the winestore. We list the scripts for collecting, validating, and modifying customer details, and show how new accounts are created.

Chapter 18, *The Shopping Cart*

Presents the code for the shopping cart at the winestore. The shopping cart is stored in a database and each user's cart is tracked using the session techniques from Chapter 10. The cart module allows a user to view her cart, add items to the cart, update item quantities, delete items, and empty the cart.

Chapter 19, *Ordering and Shipping at the Online Winestore*

Presents the code for the ordering and shipping modules of the winestore. The ordering process shows how complex database processing is used to convert a shopping cart into a customer order. We also show how to validate credit card details, send an email confirmation of the order to the user, and show the confirmation as an HTML page.

Chapter 20, *Searching and Authentication in the Online Winestore*

Concludes the winestore application by presenting the user authentication and searching modules. The user authentication module is almost identical to the one in Chapter 11. The searching and browsing module shows how to develop a component that presents a large number of results in separate pages and how to use previous and next functionality to move between the pages.

There are eight appendixes to this book:

Appendix A, *Linux Installation Guide*

A guide to installing the Apache web server, PHP, and MySQL on Linux platforms. Installation instructions change as software changes over time, so the latest version of this appendix can be downloaded at *http://www.webdatabasebook.com/install-guides*.

Appendix B, *Microsoft Windows Installation Guide*

A guide to installing the Apache web server, PHP, and MySQL on Microsoft Windows platforms. Installation instructions change as software changes over time, therefore the latest version of this appendix can be downloaded at *http://www.webdatabasebook.com/install-guides*.

Appendix C, *Mac OS X Installation Guide*

A guide to installing the Apache web server, PHP, and MySQL on Mac OS X platforms. Installation instructions change as software changes over time, so the latest version of this appendix can be downloaded at *http://www.webdatabasebook.com/install-guides*.

Appendix D, *Web Protocols*

> Describes the workings of the Web and explains how the HTTP protocol is used to transfer data between browsers and servers.

Appendix E, *Modeling and Designing Relational Databases*

> Contains a case study that models the system requirements for the winestore using entity-relationship database modeling. It shows how this model can be converted to a design. It also details the SQL statements used to create the winestore database.

Appendix F, *Managing Sessions in the Database Tier*

> An extension of Chapter 10, this appendix shows how the default PHP method for session handling (which uses disk files) can be moved into a database.

Appendix G, *Resources*

> Lists useful resources, including web sites and books containing more information on the topics presented throughout this book.

Appendix H, *The Improved MySQL Library*

> A guide to PHP's new improved MySQL library, and how it makes use of the new features of MySQL 4.1.

How to Use This Book

This book is designed as a tutorial-style introduction to web database applications. To begin, read Chapter 1 for an overview of the architecture and tools that are used in this book.

If you haven't installed the Apache web server, the PHP scripting engine, or the MySQL database management system (or you're not sure you've got the latest software), then follow the instructions in Appendix A, Appendix B, or Appendix C, depending on the platform you are using. They also show how the examples used in this book can be downloaded and installed locally. We recommend downloading the code and databases used in this book, as they will help you understand the concepts as they are presented.

Chapter 2 and Chapter 5 are designed as introductions to PHP and SQL, respectively. Read them both for an introduction to the key tools, and before you read Chapter 6 and later chapters. Chapter 3 and Chapter 4 provide more detail on PHP and are structured by topic. You can read them as tutorials or use them as references for functions or concepts.

Chapters 6 through 13 are tutorial-style chapters that follow through the principles and practice of web database applications, and include annotated function references and short case study examples to illustrate the concepts. Chapters 6 through 11 describe the basic principles and components and should be read sequentially. When you've read these chapters, you're ready to start building your own applications. If you're using MySQL 4.1, then after you've read Chapter 6, read Appendix H for more information on PHP's new improved MySQL function library.

Chapter 12 introduces writing custom error handlers that will aid your debugging and add robustness to your application when it's deployed. Chapter 13 focuses on developing printable reports using Adobe's PDF format. By the conclusion of Chapter 13, you should be a master of the principles of developing web database applications.

Chapter 14 and Chapter 15 contain advanced topics. These rely on concepts from the earlier chapters and give you complete skills for building sophisticated applications using advanced programming and database techniques. You can reserve these optional chapters for later, when you get interested in advanced web development. You don't need to read these chapters to understand our sample application in Chapters 16 to 20.

Chapters 16 to 20 present and briefly discuss complete scripts for the online winestore case study. The scripts show how the techniques from Chapter 2 to Chapter 12 are applied in practice and, as such, are most useful after mastering the content of the earlier chapters. The material in these later chapters is most useful when the example application has been downloaded and installed on a local server, allowing the scripts to be modified and tested as the chapters are read.

Appendix D and Appendix E are also in a tutorial style. We recommend Appendix D if you are interested in or are unfamiliar with the web environment and its underlying protocols. Appendix E is a brief introduction to entity-relationship modeling for databases and shows the steps we took in designing the winestore database. We recommend reading Appendix E after completing Chapter 5.

Conventions Used in This Book

The following conventions are used in this book:

Italic

> Used for program names, URLs, and database entities, and for new terms when they are defined.

Constant width

> Used for code examples, functions, statements, and attributes, and to show the output of commands.

Constant width italic

> Used to indicate variables within commands and functions.

Constant width bold

> Used to indicate emphasis in program code.

This icon designates a note, which is an important aside to the nearby text.

This icon designates a warning relating to the nearby text.

Using Code Examples

All the code in this book is available for download from *http://www.oreilly.com/ catalog/webdbapps2*. See the file *readme.txt* in the download for installation instructions.

This book is here to help you get your job done. In general, you may use the code in this book in your programs and documentation. You do not need to contact us for permission unless you're reproducing a significant portion of the code. For example, writing a program that uses several chunks of code from this book does not require permission. Selling or distributing a CD-ROM of examples from O'Reilly books *does* require permission. Answering a question by citing this book and quoting example code does not require permission. Incorporating a significant amount of example code from this book into your product's documentation *does* require permission.

We appreciate, but do not require, attribution. An attribution usually includes the title, author, publisher, and ISBN. For example: "*Web Database Applications with PHP and MySQL*, Second Edition, by Hugh E. Williams and David Lane. Copyright 2004 O'Reilly Media, Inc., 0-596-00543-1."

If you feel your use of code examples falls outside fair use or the permission given above, feel free to contact us at *permissions@oreilly.com*.

How to Contact Us

Please address comments and questions concerning this book to the publisher:

O'Reilly Media, Inc.
1005 Gravenstein Highway North
Sebastopol, CA 95472
(800) 998-9938 (in the United States or Canada)
(707) 829-0515 (international or local)
(707) 829-0104 (fax)

There is a web page for this book, which lists errata, examples, or any additional information. You can access this page at:

http://www.oreilly.com/catalog/webdbapps2

To comment or ask technical questions about this book, send email to:

bookquestions@oreilly.com

For more information about books, conferences, Resource Centers, and the O'Reilly Network, see the O'Reilly web site at:

http://www.oreilly.com

The authors can be reached at:

hugh@hughwilliams.com
dave@inquirion.com

Web Site and Code Examples

Code examples from this book, data used to create the online winestore database, and the completed winestore application can be found at this book's web site, *http://www.webdatabasebook.com*.

Acknowledgments

We thank our technical reviewers, Donal Ellis, Kimberlee Jensen, Caryn-Amy King, S.M.M. (Saied) Tahaghoghi, and Harry Williams for their time, patience, and care in helping us improve this book. We also thank our editor, Andy Oram. Most of what's new and fresh about this edition exists because Andy's pushed, helped, and encouraged us to deliver the best book we could. Thanks Andy, it's been fun!

Hugh thanks Selina and Lucy. Seline, thanks for being patient while I write, write, write. Lucy, you're not quite as patient, but you're lovely. And to Mum and Dad for starting it all: thanks Dad for building the Dick Smith 2650, and thanks Mum for encouraging me to sit in front of it and its successors!

Dave thanks Louise, Beth, and Will for putting up with yet another project. Lou, I can't thank you enough for your friendship, encouragement, and support. Thanks Beth for recycling chapter drafts and decorating my office with paintings and drawings; and thanks Will for finding the platypus.

We acknowledge the support of our employer, RMIT University. Hugh thanks the School of Computer Science and Information Technology, and Dave thanks InQuirion Pty. Ltd.

CHAPTER 1

Database Applications and the Web

Most of the services we enjoy on the Web are provided by web database applications. Web-based email, online shopping, forums and bulletin boards, corporate web sites, and sports and news portals are all database-driven. To build a modern web site, you need to develop a database application.

This book presents a highly popular, easy, low-cost way to bring together the Web and databases to build applications. The most popular database management system used in these solutions is MySQL, a very fast and easy-to-use system distributed under an Open Source license by its manufacturer, MySQL AB. We discuss MySQL in detail in this book.

With a web server such as Apache (we assume Apache in this book, although the software discussed here works with other web servers as well) and MySQL, you have most of what you need to develop a web database application. The key glue you need is a way for the web server to talk to the database; in other words, a way to incorporate database operations into web pages. The most popular glue that accomplishes this task is PHP.

PHP is an open source project of the Apache Software Foundation and it's the most popular Apache web server add-on module, with around 53% of the Apache HTTP servers having PHP capabilities.[*] PHP is particularly suited to web database applications because of its integration tools for the Web and database environments. In particular, the flexibility of embedding scripts in HTML pages permits easy integration of HTML presentation and code. The database tier integration support is also excellent, with more than 15 libraries available to interact with almost all popular database servers. In this book, we present a comprehensive view of PHP along with a number of powerful extensions provided by a repository known as PEAR.

---

[*] From the Security Space web server survey, Apache module report, *http://www.securityspace.com/s_survey/ data/index.html* (1 December 2003).

Apache, MySQL, and PHP can run on a wide variety of operating systems. In this book, we show you how to use them on Linux, Mac OS X, and Microsoft Windows.

This is an introductory book, but it gives you the sophisticated knowledge you need to build applications properly. This includes critical tasks such as checking user input, handling errors robustly, and locking your database operations to avoid data corruption. Most importantly, we explain the principles behind good web database applications. You'll finish the book with not only the technical skills to create an application, but also an appreciation for the strategies that make an application secure, reliable, maintainable, and expandable.

The Web

When you browse the Web, you use your web browser to request resources from a web server and the web server responds with the resources. You make these requests by filling in and submitting forms, clicking on links, or typing URLs into your browser. Often, resources are static HTML pages that are displayed in the browser. Figure 1-1 shows how a web browser communicates with a web server to retrieve this book's home page. This is the classic two-tier or client-server architecture used on the Web.

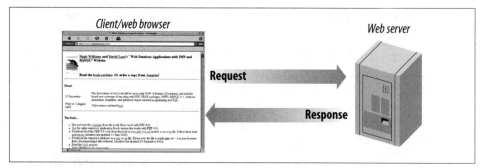

Figure 1-1. A two-tier architecture where a web browser makes a request and the web server responds

A web server is not sophisticated storage software. Complicated operations on data, done by commercial sites and anyone else presenting lots of dynamic data, should be handled by a separate database. This leads to a more complex architecture with three-tiers: the browser is still the client tier, the web server becomes the middle tier, and the database is the third or database tier. Figure 1-2 shows how a web browser requests a resource that's generated from a database, and how the database and web server respond to the request.

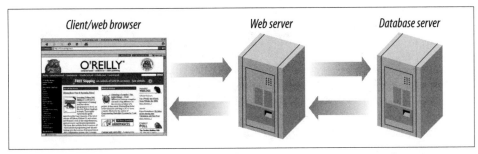

Client/web browser   Web server   Database server

Figure 1-2. A three-tier architecture where a web browser requests a resource, and a response is generated from a database

Three-Tier Architectures

This book shows you how to develop web database applications that are built around the *three-tier architecture* model shown in Figure 1-3. At the base of an application is the *database tier,* consisting of the *database management system* that manages the data users create, delete, modify, and query. Built on top of the database tier is the *middle tier*, which contains most of the application logic that you develop. It also communicates data between the other tiers. On top is the *client tier*, usually web browser software that interacts with the application.

The three-tier architecture is conceptual. In practice, there are different implementations of web database applications that fit this architecture. The most common implementation has the web server (which includes the scripting engine that processes the scripts and carries out the actions they specify) and the database management system installed on one machine: it's the simplest to manage and secure, and it's our focus in this book. With this implementation on modern hardware, your applications can probably handle tens of thousands of requests every hour.

For popular web sites, a common implementation is to install the web server and the database server on different machines, so that resources are dedicated to permit a more scalable and faster application. For very high-end applications, a cluster of computers can be used, where the database and web servers are replicated and the load distributed across many machines. Our focus is on simple implementations; replication and load distribution are beyond the scope of this book.

Describing web database applications as three-tier architectures makes them sound formally structured and organized. However, it hides the reality that the applications must bring together different protocols and software, and that the software needs to be installed, configured, and secured. The majority of the material in this book discusses the middle tier and the application logic that allows web browsers to work with databases.

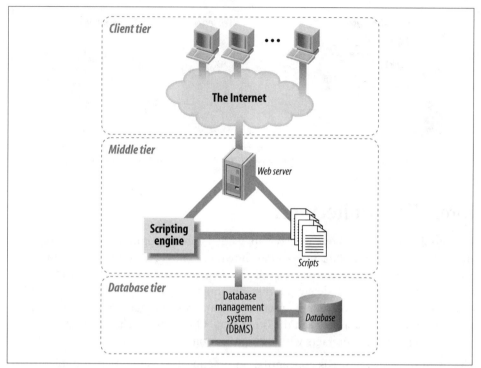

Figure 1-3. The three-tier architecture model of a web database application

HTTP: the Hypertext Transfer Protocol

The three-tier architecture provides a conceptual framework for web database applications. The Web itself provides the protocols and network that connect the client and middle tiers of the application: it provides the connection between the web browser and the web server. HTTP is one component that binds together the three-tier architecture.

HTTP allows resources to be communicated and shared over the Web. Most web servers and web browsers communicate using the current version, HTTP/1.1. A detailed knowledge of HTTP isn't necessary to understand the material in this book, but it's important to understand the problems HTTP presents for web database applications. (A longer introduction to the underlying web protocols can be found in Appendix D.)

HTTP example

HTTP is conceptually simple: a web browser sends a *request* for a resource to a web server, and the web server sends back a *response*. For every request, there's always one response. The HTTP response carries the resource—the HTML document, image, or output of a program—back to the web browser.

An HTTP request is a textual description of a resource, and additional information or *headers* that describe how the resource should be returned. Consider the following example request:

```
GET /~hugh/index.html HTTP/1.1
Host: goanna.cs.rmit.edu.au
From: hugh@hughwilliams.com (Hugh Williams)
User-agent: Hugh-fake-browser/version-1.0
Accept: text/plain, text/html
```

This example uses a GET method to request an HTML page */~hugh/index.html* from the server *goanna.cs.rmit.edu.au* with HTTP/1.1. In this example, four additional header lines specify the host, identify the user and the web browser, and define what data types can be accepted by the browser. A request is normally made by a web browser and may include other headers.

An HTTP response has a response code and message, additional headers, and usually the resource that has been requested. Part of the response to the request for */~hugh/index.html* is as follows:

```
HTTP/1.1 200 OK
Date: Thu, 04 Dec 2003 04:30:02 GMT
Server: Apache/1.3.27 (Unix)
Last-Modified: Fri, 21 Nov 2003 22:26:07 GMT
ETag: "a87da0-2128-3fbe90ff"
Accept-Ranges: bytes
Content-Length: 8488
Content-Type: text/html

<!DOCTYPE HTML PUBLIC
                    "-//W3C//DTD HTML 4.0 Transitional//EN"
                    "http://www.w3.org/TR/html4/loose.dtd">
<html>
<head>
...
```

The first line of the response tells the browser that the response is HTTP/1.1 and confirms that the request succeeded by reporting the response code 200 and the message OK. In this example, seven lines of additional headers identify the current date and time, the web server software, the last date and time the page was changed, an entity tag (ETag) that is used for caching, an instruction to the browser on how to request part of the document, the length of the response, and the content type. After a blank line, the resource itself follows, and we've shown only the first few lines. In this example the resource is the requested HTML document, */~hugh/index.html*.

State

Traditional database applications are *stateful*. Users log in, run related transactions, and then log out when they are finished. For example, in a bank application, a bank teller might log in, use the application through a series of menus as he serves customer requests, and log out when he's finished for the day. The bank application has state: after the teller is logged in, he can interact with the application in a structured way using menus. When the teller has logged out, he can no longer use the application.

HTTP is *stateless*. Any interaction between a web browser and a web server is independent of any other interaction. Each HTTP request from a web browser includes the same header information, such as the security credentials of the user, the types of pages the browser can accept, and instructions on how to format the response. The server processes the headers, formulates a response that explains how the request was served, and returns the headers and a resource to the browser. Once the response is complete, the server forgets the request and there's no way to go back and retrieve the request or response.

Statelessness has benefits: the most significant are the resource savings from not having to maintain information at the web server to track a user or requests, and the flexibility to allow users to move between unrelated pages or resources. However, because HTTP is stateless, it is difficult to develop stateful web database applications: for example, it's hard to force a user to follow menus or a series of steps to complete a task.

To add state to HTTP, you need a method to impose information flows and structure. A common solution is to exchange a token or key between a web browser and a web server that uniquely identifies the user and her *session*. Each time a browser requests a resource, it presents the token, and each time the web server responds, it returns the token to the web browser. The token is used by the middle-tier software to restore information about a user from her previous request, such as which menu in the application she last accessed.

Exchanging tokens allows stateful structure such as menus, steps, and workflow processes to be added to the application. They can also be used to prevent actions from happening more than once, time out logins after a period of inactivity, and control access to an application.

Thickening the Client in the Three-Tier Model

Given that a web database application built with a three-tier architecture doesn't fit naturally with HTTP, why use that model at all? The answer mostly lies in the popularity and standardization of web browsers: any user who has a web browser can use the web database application, and usually without any restrictions. This means an application can be delivered to any number of diverse, dispersed users who use any platform, operating system, or browser software. This advantage is so significant that our focus in this book is entirely on three-tier solutions that use a web browser as the client tier.

Web browsers are *thin clients*. This means almost no application logic is included in the client tier. The browser simply sends HTTP requests for resources and then displays the responses, most of which are HTML pages. This thin client model means you don't have to build, install, or configure the client tier, but that you do need to build almost all of your application to run in the middle tier.

You can thicken the client tier to put more work on the browser. Using popular technologies such as Java, JavaScript, and Macromedia Flash, you can develop application components that process data independently of the web server or preprocess data before sending it to the server.

JavaScript is particularly good for many tasks because it's easy to use, open source, and built into all popular browsers (although users can turn it off). It's often used to validate data that's typed into forms before it's sent to the server, highlight parts of a page when the mouse passes over, display menus, and perform other simple tasks. However, it's limited in the information it can store and it can't communicate with a database server. Therefore, although you shouldn't depend on JavaScript to do critical tasks, it's useful for preprocessing and it's another important technology we discuss in Chapter 7.

The Middle Tier

The middle tier has many roles in a web database application. It brings together the other tiers, drives the structure and content of the data displayed to the user, provides security and authentication, and adds state to the application. It's the tier that integrates the Web with the database server.

Web servers

There are essentially two types of request made to a web server: the first asks for a file—often a static HTML web page or an image—to be returned, and the second asks for a program or script to be run and its output to be returned. We've shown you a simple example previously in this chapter, and simple requests for files are further discussed in Appendix D. HTTP requests for PHP scripts require a server to run PHP's Zend scripting engine, process the instructions in the script (which may access a database), and return the script output to the browser to output as plain HTML.

Apache is an open source, fast, and scalable web server. It can handle simultaneous requests from browsers and is designed to run under multitasking operating systems such as Linux, Mac OS X, and Microsoft Windows. It has low resource requirements, can effectively handle changes in request loads, and can run fast on even modest hardware. It is widely used and tested. The current release at the time of writing is 2.0.48.

Conceptually, Apache isn't complicated. On a Unix platform, the web server is actually several running programs, where one coordinates the others and doesn't serve requests itself. The other server programs notify their availability to handle requests to the coordinating server. If too few servers are available to handle incoming requests, the coordinating server may start new servers; if too many are free, it may kill spare servers to save resources.

Apache's configuration file controls how it listens on the network and serves requests. The server administrator controls the behavior of Apache through more than 150 directives that affect resource requirements, response time, flexibility in dealing with request load variability, security, how HTTP requests are handled and logged, how scripting engines are used to run scripts, and most other aspects of its operation.

The configuration of Apache for most web database applications is straightforward. We discuss how to install Apache in Appendixes A through C, how to hide files that you don't want to serve in Chapter 6, and the features of a secure web server in Chapter 11. We discuss the HTTP protocol and how it's implemented in Appendix D. More details on Apache configuration can be found in the resources listed in Appendix G.

Web Scripting with PHP

PHP is the most widely supported and used web scripting language and an excellent tool for building web database applications. This isn't to say that other scripting languages don't have excellent features. However, there are many reasons that make PHP a good choice, including that it's:

Open source
> Community efforts to maintain and improve it are unconstrained by commercial imperatives.

Flexible for integration with HTML
> One or more PHP scripts can be embedded into static HTML files and this makes client tier integration easy. On the downside, this can blend the scripts with the presentation; however the template techniques described in Chapter 7 can solve most of these problems.

Suited to complex projects
> It is a fully featured object-oriented programming language, with more than 110 libraries of programming functions for tasks as diverse as math, sorting, creating PDF documents, and sending email. There are over 15 libraries for native, fast access to the database tier.

Fast at running scripts
> Using its built-in Zend scripting engine, PHP script execution is fast and all components run within the main memory space of PHP (in contrast to other scripting frameworks, in which components are in distinct modules). Our experiments suggest that for tasks of at least moderate complexity, PHP is faster than other popular scripting tools.

Platform- and operating-system portable
> Apache and PHP run on many different platforms and operating systems. PHP can also be integrated with other web servers.

A community effort
> PHP contains PEAR, a repository that is home to over 100 freely available source code packages for common PHP programming tasks.

At the time of writing, PHP4 (Version 4.3.3) was the current version and PHP5 was available for beta testing (Version 5.0.0b2). The scripts in this book have been developed and tested using PHP4, and testing on PHP5 has identified a few limitations. This book describes both versions of PHP: in particular, you'll find a discussion of new object-oriented PHP5 features in Chapter 14. When a feature is only available in PHP5, we tell you in the text. When a PHP4 script or feature doesn't work on PHP5, we explain why and predict how it'll be fixed in the future; it's likely that almost all scripts that run under PHP4 will run under PHP5 in the future.

PHP is a major topic of this book. It's introduced in Chapters 3 through 5, where we discuss most of the features of the core language. PHP libraries that are important to web database application development are the subject of Chapters 6 and 8 through 13. PHP's PEAR package repository is the subject of Chapter 7. An example PHP application is the subject of Chapters 16 to 20. Appendixes A through C show how to install PHP. Other pointers to web resources, books, and commercial products for PHP development are listed in Appendix G.

A technical explanation of the new features of PHP5 is presented in the next section. If you aren't familiar with PHP4, skip ahead to the next section.

Introducing PHP5

PHP4 included the first release of the Zend engine version 1.0, PHP's scripting engine that implements the syntax of the language and provides all of the tools needed to run library functions. PHP5 includes a new Zend engine version 2.0, that's enhanced to address the limitations of version 1.0 and to include new features that have been requested by developers. However, unlike the changes that occurred when PHP3 became PHP4, the changes from PHP4 to PHP5 only affect part of the language. Most code that's written for PHP4 will run without modification under PHP5.

In brief, the following are the major new features in PHP5. Many of these features are explained in detail elsewhere in this book:

New Object Model
> Object-oriented programming (OOP) and the OOP features of PHP5 are discussed in detail in Chapter 14. PHP4 has a simple object model that doesn't include many of the features that object-oriented programmers expect in an OOP language such as destructors, private and protected member functions and variables, static member functions and variables, interfaces, and class type hints. All of these features are available in PHP5.

The PHP5 OOP model also better manages how objects are passed around between functions and classes. Handles to objects are now passed, rather than the objects themselves. This has substantially improved the performance of PHP.

Internationalization
Support for non-Western character sets and Unicode. This is discussed in Chapter 3.

Exception Handling
New try...catch, and throw statements are available that are aimed at improving the robustness of applications when errors occur. These are discussed in Chapter 4. There's also a backtrace feature that you can use to develop a custom error handler that shows how the code that caused an error was called. This feature has been back-ported into PHP4 and is discussed in Chapter 12.

Improved memory handling and speed
PHP4 was fast, but PHP5 is faster and makes even better use of memory. We don't discuss this in detail.

New XML support
There were several different tools for working with the eXtensible Markup Language (XML) in PHP4. These tools have been replaced with a single new, robust framework in PHP5. We don't discuss XML support in this book.

The Improved MySQL library (mysqli)
A new MySQL function library is available in PHP5 that supports MySQL 4. The library has the significant feature that it allows an SQL query to be prepared once, and executed many times, and this substantially improves speed if a query is often used. This library is briefly described in Chapter 6, and is the source of many of the PHP4 and PHP5 compatibility problems described throughout in this book.

You can find out more about what's new in PHP5 from *http://www.zend.com/zend/ future.php*.

The Database Tier

The database tier stores and retrieves data. It's also responsible for managing updates, allowing simultaneous (*concurrent*) access from web servers, providing security, ensuring the integrity of data, and providing support services such as data backup. Importantly, a good database tier must allow quick and flexible access to millions upon millions of facts.

Managing data in the database tier requires complex software. Fortunately, most database management systems (DBMSs) or servers are designed so that the software complexities are hidden. To effectively use a database server, skills are required to design a database and formulate queries using the SQL language; SQL is discussed in Chapter 5. An understanding of the underlying architecture of the database server is unimportant to most users.

In this book, we use the *MySQL* server to manage data. It has a well-deserved reputation for speed: it can manage many millions of facts, it's very scalable, and particularly suited to the characteristics of web database applications. Also, like PHP and Apache, MySQL is open source software. However, there are downsides to MySQL that we discuss later in this section.

The first step in successful web database application development is understanding system requirements and designing databases. We discuss techniques for modeling system requirements, converting a model into a database, and the principles of database technology in Appendix E. In this section, we focus on the database tier and introduce database software by contrasting it with other techniques for storing data. Chapters 5 and 15 cover the standards and software we use in more detail.

There are other server choices for storing data in the database tier. These include search engines, document management systems, and gateway services such as email software. Our discussions in this book focus on the MySQL server in the database tier.

Database Management Systems

A database server or DBMS searches and manages data that's stored in databases. A database is a collection of related data, and an application can have more than one database. A database might contain a few entries that make up a simple address book of names, addresses, and phone numbers. At the other extreme, a database can contain tens or hundreds of millions of records that describe the catalog, purchases, orders, and payroll of a large company. Most web database applications have small- to medium-size databases that store thousands, or tens of thousands, of records.

Database servers are complex software. However, the important component for web database application development is the applications interface that's used to access the database server. For all but the largest applications, understanding and configuring the internals of a database server is usually unnecessary.

SQL

The database server applications interface is accessed using SQL. It's a standard query language that's used to define and manipulate databases and data, and it's supported by all popular database servers.

SQL has had a complicated life. It began at the IBM San Jose Research Laboratory in the early 1970s, where it was known as *Sequel*; some users still call it Sequel, though it's more correctly referred to by the three-letter acronym, SQL. After almost 16 years of development and differing implementations, the standards organizations ANSI and ISO published an SQL standard in 1986. IBM published a different standard one year later!

Since the mid-1980s, three subsequent standards have been published by ANSI and ISO. The first, SQL-89, is the most widely, completely implemented SQL in popular database servers. Many servers implement only some features of the next release, SQL-2 or SQL-92, and almost no servers have implemented the features of the most recently approved standard, SQL-99 or SQL-3. MySQL supports the entry-level SQL-92 standard and has some proprietary extensions.

Consider an SQL example. Suppose you want to store information about books in a library. You can create a table—an object that's stored in your database—using the following statement:

```
CREATE TABLE books (
   title char(50),
   author char(50),
   ISBN char(50) NOT NULL,
   PRIMARY KEY (ISBN)
);
```

Then, you can add books to the database using statements such as:

```
INSERT INTO books ("Web Database Apps", "Hugh and Dave", "123-456-N");
```

Once you've added data, you can retrieve facts about the books using queries such as the following that finds the author and title of a book with a specific ISBN:

```
SELECT author, title FROM books WHERE ISBN = "456-789-Q";
```

These are only some of the features of SQL, and even these features can be used in complex ways. SQL also allows you to update and delete data and databases, and it includes many other features such as security and access management, multiuser transactions that allow many users to access the same database without corrupting the data, tools to import and export data, and powerful undo and redo features.

SQL is discussed in detail in Chapters 5 and 15.

Why use a database server?

Why use a complex database server to manage data? There are several reasons that can be explained by contrasting a database with a spreadsheet, a simple text file, or a custom-built method of storing data. A few example situations where a database server should and should not be used are discussed later in this section.

Take spreadsheets as an example. Spreadsheet worksheets are typically designed for a specific application. If two users store names and addresses, they are likely to organize data in a different way and develop custom methods to move around and summarize the data. The program and the data aren't independent: moving a column might mean rewriting a macro or formula, while exchanging data between the two users' applications might be complex. In contrast, a database server and SQL provide data-program independence, where the method for storing the data is independent of the language that accesses it.

Managing complex relationships is difficult in a spreadsheet or text file. For example, consider what happens if we want to store information about customers: we might allocate a few spreadsheet columns to store each customer's residential address. If we were to add business addresses and postal addresses, we'd need more columns and complex processing to, for example, process a mail-out to customers. If we want to store information about the purchases by our customers, the spreadsheet becomes wider still, and problems start to emerge. For example, it is difficult to determine the maximum number of columns needed to store orders and to design a method to process these for reporting. In contrast, databases are designed to manage complex *relational* data.

A database server usually permits multiple users to access a database at the same time in a methodical way. In contrast, a spreadsheet should be opened and written only by one user; if another user opens the spreadsheet, she won't see any updates being made at the same time by the first user. At best, a shared spreadsheet or text file permits very limited concurrent access.

An additional benefit of a database server is its speed and scalability. It isn't totally true to say that a database provides faster searching of data than a spreadsheet or a custom filesystem. In many cases, searching a spreadsheet or a special-purpose file might be perfectly acceptable, or even faster if it is designed carefully and the volume of data is small. However, for managing large amounts of related information, the underlying search structures allow fast searching, and if information needs are complex, a database server should optimize the method of retrieving the data.

There are also other advantages of database servers, including data-oriented and user-oriented security, administration software, portability, and data recovery support. A practical benefit of this is reduced application development time: the system is already built, it needs only data and queries to access the data.

Examples of when to use a database server

In any of these situations, a database server should be used to manage data:

- There is more than one user who needs to access the data at the same time.
- There is at least a moderate amount of data. For example, you might need to maintain information about a few hundred customers.
- There are relationships between the stored data items. For example, customers may have any number of related invoices.
- There is more than one kind of data object. For example, there might be information about customers, orders, inventory, and other data in an online store.
- There are constraints that must be rigidly enforced on the data, such as field lengths, field types, uniqueness of customer numbers, and so on.
- New or consolidated information must be produced from basic, related information; that is, the data must be queried to produce reports or results.
- There is a large amount of data that must be searched quickly.

- Security is important. There is a need to enforce rules as to who can access the data.
- Adding, deleting, or modifying data is a complex process.
- Adding, deleting, and updating data is a frequent or complex process.

Examples of when not to use a DBMS

There are some situations where a relational DBMS is probably unnecessary or unsuitable. Here are some examples:

- There is one type of data item, and the data isn't searched. For example, if a log entry is written when a user logs in and logs out, appending the entry to the end of a simple text file may be sufficient.
- The data management task is trivial and accessing a database server adds unnecessary overhead. In this case, the data might be coded into a web script in the middle tier.

The MySQL server

MySQL has most of the features of high-end commercial database servers, including the ability to manage very large quantities of data. Its design is ideally suited to managing databases that are typical of most web database applications. The current version at the time of writing is MySQL 4.1.

The difference between MySQL and high-end commercial servers is that MySQL's components aren't as mature. For example, MySQL's query evaluator doesn't always develop a fast plan to evaluate complex queries. It also doesn't support all of the features you might find in other servers: for example, views, triggers, and stored procedures are planned for future versions. There are other, more minor limitations that don't typically affect web development. However, even users who need these features often choose MySQL because it's free. (Contrary to popular belief, since 2002, MySQL has supported nested queries, transactions, and row (or record) locking.)

MySQL is another major topic of this book. It's introduced in Chapter 5, and used extensively in examples in Chapters 6 through 8 and 11 and 12. Advanced MySQL features are a subject of Chapter 15. An example application that uses PHP and MySQL is the subject of Chapters 16 through 20. Appendixes A through C shows how to install MySQL and selected MySQL resources are listed in Appendix G.

A technical explanation of the features of MySQL 4 is presented in the next section. If you aren't familiar with MySQL, skip ahead to the next section.

Introducing MySQL 4

MySQL 4 is a major new release that includes important features that have been added since MySQL 3.23. The current version, MySQL 4.1, supports a wide range of

SQL queries, including joins, multi-table updates and deletes, and nested queries. At present it supports most features of the SQL 92 standard, and its aim is to fully support SQL 99.

The MySQL server supports several table types that allow a wide range of choice in your applications of locking techniques, transaction environments, and performance choices. It also has good tools for backup and recovery. MySQL is a powerful, fully-featured DBMS that's commercially supported by the company MySQL AB.

In detail, the following are the major features of MySQL 4. Many of these features are explained in detail elsewhere in this book:

Nested query and derived table support
> Sub-queries are new in MySQL 4.1. This allows you to use the SQL statements EXISTS, IN, NOT EXISTS, and NOT IN, and it also allows you to include a nested query in the FROM clause that creates a derived table. UNION was introduced in MySQL 4.0. All of these are discussed in detail in Chapter 15.

Internationalization
> MySQL 4.1 now supports Unicode, allowing you to develop applications that don't use Western languages. We don't discuss MySQL's use of Unicode in this book, but we do discuss PHP's Unicode support in Chapter 3.

Query caching
> MySQL 4.0 introduced a query cache that stores the most-recent results of queries, and intelligently delivers these as answers to identical future queries. We show you how to use this feature in Chapter 15. We explain other speed improvements in the same chapter.

Transaction-safe InnoDB tables
> The InnoDB table type was included as a built-in module in MySQL 4.0. InnoDB supports transactions, and allows you to decide whether to commit or rollback a set of writes to the database. It also supports checkpointing, which is used by MySQL to get the database into a known state after a crash or serious error. We explain the advantages and disadvantages of InnoDB in Chapter 15.

Full text searching
> MySQL 4 introduced new methods for fast searching of text and a form of search engine-like ranking. We don't discuss this in the book.

MySQL 4 resources are listed in Appendix G.

CHAPTER 2

The PHP Scripting Language

This chapter is the first of three that focus on the PHP scripting language. This chapter describes the PHP language basics. Chapter 3 describes PHP's support for arrays, strings, and other data types, and Chapter 4 introduces object-oriented programming in PHP.

If you're familiar with any programming language, PHP should be easy to learn. If you have done no programming before, the pace of this chapter may be brisk but should still be manageable. PHP has a syntax similar to JavaScript, which many web designers have learned; both languages hark back to the classic C and Perl languages in syntax.

The topics covered in this chapter include:

- PHP basics, including script structure, variables, supported types, constants, expressions, and type conversions
- Condition and branch statements supported by PHP, including if, if...else, and the switch statements
- Looping statements
- User-defined functions

We conclude the chapter with a short example that puts many of the basic PHP concepts together.

Introducing PHP

The current version of PHP is PHP4 (Version 4.3.4). PHP5 is available for beta testing at the time of writing as Version 5.0.0b3. We discuss both versions in this chapter.

PHP is a recursive acronym that stands for *PHP: Hypertext Preprocessor*; this is in the naming style of *GNU*, which stands for *GNU's Not Unix* and which began this odd trend. The name isn't a particularly good description of what PHP is and what it's commonly used for. PHP is a scripting language that's usually embedded or combined with the HTML of a web page. When the page is requested, the web server executes the PHP script and substitutes in the result back into the page. PHP has many excellent libraries that provide fast, customized access to DBMSs and is an ideal tool for developing application logic in the middle tier of a three-tier application.

PHP Basics

Example 2-1 shows the first PHP script in this book, the ubiquitous "Hello, world." It's actually mostly HTML; the PHP is embedded near the end.

Example 2-1. The ubiquitous Hello, world in PHP

```
<!DOCTYPE HTML PUBLIC "-//W3C//DTD HTML 4.01 Transitional//EN"
                  "http://www.w3.org/TR/html401/loose.dtd">
<html>
<head>
  <meta http-equiv="Content-Type" content="text/html; charset=iso-8859-1">
  <title>Hello, world</title>
</head>
<body bgcolor="#ffffff">
  <h1>
  <?php
    print "Hello, world";
  ?>
  </h1>
</body>
</html>
```

When requested by a web browser, the script is run on the web server and the resulting HTML document sent back to the browser and rendered as shown in Figure 2-1.

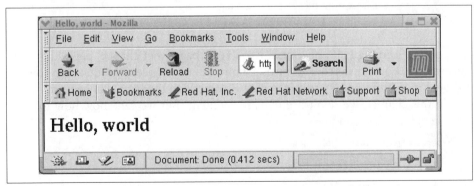

Figure 2-1. The output of Example 2-1 shown in the Netscape browser

Example 2-1 illustrates the basic features of a PHP script. It's a mixture of HTML—in this case it's mostly HTML—and PHP code. The PHP code in this example:

```
<?php
  print "Hello, world";
?>
```

simply prints the greeting, "Hello, world."

The PHP script shown in Example 2-1 is rather pointless: we could simply have authored the HTML to include the greeting directly. Because PHP integrates so well with HTML, using PHP to produce static sequence of characters is far less complicated and less interesting than using other high-level languages. However, the example does illustrate several features of PHP:

- A block of PHP code is embedded within HTML using the begin and end tags `<?php` and `?>`. Other begin and end tag styles can also be used, such as the HTML style that is used with JavaScript or other embedded scripts: `<script language="PHP">` and `</script>`. There's also a shorter style `<?` and `?>`. For consistency, we use only the `<?php` and `?>` style in this book.

- Whitespace has no effect, except to aid readability for the developer. For example, the PHP could have been written succinctly as `<?php print "Hello, world";?>` with the same effect. Any mix of whitespace characters—spaces, tabs, carriage returns, and so on—can be used to separate PHP statements.

- A PHP script is a series of statements, each terminated with a semicolon. Our simple example has only one statement: `print "Hello, world";`. PHP script can be anywhere in a file and interleaved with any HTML fragment. While Example 2-1 contains only one statement within one set of `<?php` and `?>` tags, statements can be distribute code across multiple blocks of code.

- When PHP script is run, each block of code, including the start and end script tags `<?php` and `?>` is replaced with the output of the block.

 When we present a few lines of code that are sections of larger scripts, we usually omit the start and end tags.

The point of learning PHP, of course, is to create pages that change, pages that contain dynamic content derived from user input or a database. The first step toward that goal is to introduce a *variable*, which is something that can change from run to run. In this chapter, we don't use dynamic content. But we can show how to set a variable to a string as follows:

```
<?php $outputString = "Hello, world"; ?>
```

And then rewrite our script as follows:

```
<?php print $outputString; ?>
```

Because $outputString has been set to Hello, world, that string is printed as part of the surrounding HTML page.

The freedom to interleave blocks of PHP statements with HTML is one of the most powerful features of PHP. A short example is shown in Example 2-2; the variable $outputString is initialized before the start of the HTML document, and later this variable is output twice, as part of the <title> and <body> elements. We discuss more about variables and how to use them later in this chapter.

Example 2-2. Embedding three blocks of code in a single document

```
<?php $outputString = "Hello, world"; ?>
<!DOCTYPE HTML PUBLIC "-//W3C//DTD HTML 4.01 Transitional//EN"
                      "http://www.w3.org/TR/html401/loose.dtd">
<html>
<head>
  <meta http-equiv="Content-Type" content="text/html; charset=iso-8859-1">
  <title><?php print $outputString; ?></title>
</head>
<body bgcolor="#ffffff">
  <h1><?php print $outputString; ?></h1>
</body>
</html>
```

The flexibility to add multiple blocks of PHP to HTML can also lead to unwieldy, hard-to-maintain code. Care should be taken in modularizing code and HTML; we discuss how to separate code and HTML using templates in Chapter 7.

Creating PHP scripts

A PHP script can be written using plain text and can be created with any text editor, such as the Unix editors *joe*, *vi*, *nedit*, Emacs, or *pico*, or a Microsoft Windows editor such as Notepad or WordPad. There are also several special-purpose PHP programming editors available, and a well-maintained list of these can be found at *http://phpeditors.linuxbackup.co.uk/*.

If you save a PHP script in a file with a *.php* extension under the directory configured as Apache's document root, Apache executes the script when a request is made for the resource. Following the installation instructions given in Appendixes A through C, the document root on a Unix machine is:

    /usr/local/apache/htdocs/

and in a Microsoft Windows environment:

    C:\Program Files\EasyPHP1-7\www\

Consider what happens when the script shown in Example 2-1 is saved in the file *example.2-1.php* in the document root directory and you view the file in a Web browser on the same machine. Apache—when configured with the PHP module—executes the script when requests to the URL *http://localhost/example.2-1.php* are made.

If you are working on a Unix host, and directory permissions don't permit creation of files in the document root, it's also possible to work in your user home directory. If the installation instructions in Appendixes A through C have been followed, a directory can be created beneath your Unix home directory and the permissions set so that the directory is readable by the web server. You can do this by running a terminal window and typing the following after the shell prompt (shown here as a %):

```
% mkdir ~/public_html
% chmod a+rx ~/public_html
```

The example file can then be created with the filename:

```
~/public_html/example.2-1.php
```

The file can then be retrieved with the URL *http://localhost/~user/example.2-1.php*, where *user* is the user login name.

You can insert any of the code in this chapter into that file, or another one of your choice, and see what's displayed by calling it up in a browser as we have shown.

Comments

Comments can be included in code using several styles used by high-level programming languages. This includes the following styles:

```
// This is a one-line comment

#  This is another one-line comment style

/* This is how you
   can create a multi-line
   comment */
```

Outputting data with echo and print

The print statement used in Example 2-1 and Example 2-2 is frequently used and can output any type of data. The echo statement can be used for the same purpose. Consider some examples:

```
print "Hello, world";

// echo works just the same
echo "Hello, world";

// numbers can be printed with echo too
echo 123;

// So can the contents of variables
$outputString = "Hi!";
echo $outputString;
```

The difference between print and echo is that echo can output more than one parameter, each separated by a comma. For example, echo can print a string and an integer together in the one message:

```
// prints "The answer is 42"
echo "The answer is ", 42;
```

The print and echo statements are also often seen with parentheses:

```
echo "hello";

// is the same as
echo ("hello");
```

Parentheses make no difference to the behavior of print. However, when they are used with echo, only one output parameter can be provided.

The echo and print statements can be used for most tasks and can output any combination of static strings, numbers, arrays, and other variable types discussed later in this chapter. We discuss more complex output with *printf()* in the next chapter.

String Literals

One of the most common tasks in a PHP script is to output literal sequences of characters to create messages, headings, and other text that appear on HTML pages. A literal sequence of characters—a *string literal* or simply a *string*—can be included in a PHP script using quotation characters. PHP can create double- and single-quoted string literals:

```
print 'This works';
print "just like this.";
```

Because quotation marks are used to mark the start and end of strings, a quotation mark that is actually part of a string must be marked in some way. Marking a character so that it is treated as a normal character, instead of being part of the PHP syntax, is called *escaping*. Quotation marks can be escaped by putting a backslash before them:

```
print "This string has a \": a double quote!";
print 'This string has a \': a single quote!';
```

A simple alternative to including quotation marks in a string is to switch to the single-quotation style:

```
// And here are some strings that contain quotes
print "This string has a ': a single quote!";
print 'This string has a ": a double quote!';
```

To include a backslash character in a double-quoted string, use the escaped sequence \\. Tab, newline (line break), and carriage-return characters can be included in a double-quoted string using the escape sequences \t, \n, and \r, respectively. Inserting the white space characters \t, \n, and \r is often useful to make output more readable, however as HTML, white space is generally disregarded.

Unlike many other languages, PHP allows newline characters to be included directly in a string literal. The following example shows the variable $var assigned with a string that contains a newline character:

```
// This is Ok. $var contains a newline character
$var = 'The quick brown fox
        jumps over the lazy dog';
```

This feature is used in later chapters to construct SQL statements that are easier to read in the PHP source code, for example:

```
$query = "SELECT max(order_id)
            FROM orders
            WHERE cust_id = $custID";
```

Variable substitution

Variable substitution provides a convenient way to embed data held in a variable directly into string literals. PHP examines, or *parses*, double-quoted strings and replaces variable names with the variable's value. The following example shows how:

```
$number = 45;
$vehicle = "bus";
$message = "This $vehicle holds $number people";

// prints "This bus holds 45 people"
print $message;
```

PHP interprets the $ and the following non-space characters as the name of a variable to insert. To include the dollar signs in a double-quoted string you need to escape the variable substitution meaning with the backslash sequence \$.

When the name of the variable is ambiguous, braces {} can delimit the name as shown in the following example:

```
$memory = 256;

// No variable called $memoryMbytes
// Sets $message to "My computer has  of RAM"
$message = "My computer has $memoryMbytes of RAM";

// Works: braces are used delimit variable name
// Sets $message to "My computer has 256Mbytes of RAM"
$message = "My computer has {$memory}Mbytes of RAM";
```

When the string literal containing the characters $memoryMbytes is parsed, PHP tries to substitute the value of the nonexisting variable $memoryMbytes. Braces are also used for more complex variables, such as arrays and objects:

```
print "The array element is {$array["element"]}.";
print "Mars is {$planets['Mars']['dia']} times the diameter of the Earth";
print "There are {$order->count} green bottles ...";
```

We explain arrays in the next chapter and objects in Chapter 4.

We recommend using the braces syntax when including variables in string literals. It makes your code more readable, and saves you the trouble of remembering to escape characters.

Single-quoted strings aren't parsed in the same way as double-quoted strings for variable substitution. For example, the characters $vehicle and $number aren't substituted in the following fragment of code:

```
$number = 45;
$vehicle = "bus";

// prints "This $vehicle holds $number people"
print 'This $vehicle holds $number people';
```

Character encoding

When a PHP script is executed, the PHP engine starts by reading the script from a file. A file is simply a sequence of characters than are interpreted by PHP as statements, variable identifiers, literal strings, HTML, and so on. To correctly interpret these characters, PHP needs to know the *character encoding* of the file. Put more simply, PHP needs to know what each 8-bit sequence that makes up a character means.

In many cases, you won't need to worry about character encoding. By default PHP reads the characters encoded to the ISO-8859-1 standard—a standard that is equivalent to 7-bit ASCII for the first 127 characters. The ISO-8859-1 encoding standard—also known as Latin-1 encoding—uses the next 128 characters to represent characters used in Western European languages. By default PHP scripts can include ISO-8859-1 characters directly, as the following fragment demonstrates:

```
$gesprächsnotiz =
    "von Paulus Esterházy und Markus Hoff-Holtmannus";
```

The ä and á characters in the previous example are represented by the 8-bit sequences 11100100 and 11100001—the 228th and 225th characters from ISO-8859-1.

Sometimes, it's not convenient to work with non-7-bit ASCII characters in an editor environment. Indeed, some programs can only handle 7-bit ASCII and ignore *high-bit* characters—characters with a leading "1". You can include high-bit characters using an escape sequence to specify either a hexadecimal or octal value. Hexadecimal sequences start with \x and are followed by two digits—00 to ff—to represent 256 characters. For example, the á character can be represented in a string literal with the hexadecimal sequence \xe1 since e1 is the hexadecimal equivalent of 11100001:

```
$translation =
    "von Paulus Esterh\xe1zy und Markus Hoff-Holtmannus";
```

Escape sequence can only be used in string literals—PHP does not allow us to represent the variable $gesprächsnotiz as $gespr\xe4chsnotiz.

Like PHP's Zend engine, browsers need to know the character encoding of a page before the page can be correctly displayed. In this book we assume the default ISO-8859-1 character encoding, and accordingly we instruct browsers to use this encoding by including the mark-up as follows:

```
<meta http-equiv="Content-Type" content="text/html; charset=iso-8859-1">
```

Other ISO-8859-x character encoding standards allow Cyrillic, Arabic, Greek, and Hebrew characters to be encoded, and a full description of these encoding standards can be found at *http://en.wikipedia.org/wiki/ISO_8859*.

PHP can be configured to support UTF-8; an 8-bit encoding method that can represent Unicode characters. The Unicode Standard describes a universal character encoding that defines over 49,000 characters from the world's scripts. Unicode characters can also be encoded using UTF-16, a 16-bit encoding, however PHP does not support 16-bit characters. More information about the Unicode standard can be found at *http://www.unicode.org*.

Variables

Variables in PHP are identified by a dollar sign followed by the variable name. Variables don't need to be declared before you use them; normally you just assign them a value to create them. The following code fragment shows a variable $var assigned the integer 15. Therefore, $var is defined as being of type integer.

```
$var = 15;
```

Variables in PHP are simple: when they are used, the type is implicitly defined—or redefined—and the variable implicitly declared.

Variable names are case-sensitive in PHP, so $Variable, $variable, $VAriable, and $VARIABLE are all different variables.

> One of the most common sources of bugs in PHP is failing to detect that more than one variable has accidentally been created. The flexibility of PHP is a great feature but is also dangerous. We discuss in Chapter 14 how to set the error reporting of PHP so that it detects this type of error.

Types

Data exists in different *types* so that appropriate operations can be performed on it. For instance, numeric values can be manipulated with arithmetic operators such as addition and subtraction; whereas strings of characters can be manipulated by operations such as converting to uppercase. In this section, we introduce the basic types; their importance will become clear as we use data in more and more complex operations.

PHP has four scalar types—boolean, float, integer, and string—and two compound types, array and object. PHP also supports *null*—a special type that is used when a variable doesn't have a value.

Variables of a scalar type contain a single value. Variables of a compound type—array or object—are made up of multiple scalar values or other compound values.

Arrays are discussed in detail in the next chapter, and objects are discussed in Chapter 4. Other aspects of variables—including global variables and scope—are discussed later in this chapter.

Boolean variables are as simple as they get: they can be assigned either true or false. Here are two example assignments of a Boolean variable:

```
$variable = false;
$test = true;
```

An *integer* is a whole number, while a *float* is a number that has an exponent and mantissa. The number 123.01 is a float, and so is 123.0, while the number 123 is an integer. Consider the following two examples:

```
// This is an integer
$var1 = 6;

// This is a float
$var2 = 6.0;
```

A float can also be represented using an exponential notation:

```
// This is a float that equals 1120
$var3 = 1.12e3;

// This is a float that equals 0.02
$var4 = 2e-2
```

You've already seen examples of strings earlier in the chapter. Here are two more example string variables:

```
$variable = "This is a string";
$test = 'This is also a string';
```

Along with the value, the type of a variable can change over the lifetime of the variable. Consider an example:

```
$var = 15;
$var = "Sarah the Cat";
```

This fragment is acceptable in PHP. The type of `$var` changes from integer to string as the variable is reassigned. Letting PHP change the type of a variable as the context changes is very flexible and a little dangerous. Later in *Working with Types*, we show ways to avoid problems that can arise with loosely typed variables.

Constants

Constants associate a name with a scalar value. For example, the Boolean values `true` and `false` are constants associated with the values 1 and 0, respectively. It's also common to declare constants in a script. Consider this example constant declaration:

```
define("PI", 3.14159);

// This outputs 3.14159
print PI;
```

Constants aren't preceded by a $ character. They can't be changed once they have been defined and they can be accessed anywhere in a script (regardless of where they are declared).

Constants are useful because they allow parameters internal to the script to be grouped. When one parameter changes—for example, if you define a new maximum number of lines per web page—you can alter this constant parameter in only one place and not throughout the code.

PHP has a large number of built-in constants that a script can use. For example, the library of mathematical functions already include a definition of M_PI to hold the constant pi:

```
// This outputs 3.14159265358979323846
print M_PI;
```

By convention, constant names use uppercase characters, and predefined constants are often named to indicate the associated library. For example the constants defined for the mathematical functions library all start with M_. We introduce predefined constants as needed throughout this book.

Expressions, Operators, and Variable Assignment

We've already described simple examples of assignment, in which a variable is assigned the value of an integer, string, or value of some other data type. The value on the right side of the equal sign is actually the simplest example of an *expression*.

An expression is anything that can be reduced to a single value, for example the sum 1 + 2 is an expression with an integer value of 3. Expressions can be complex combinations of operators and values, just as in mathematics. Examples of expressions (the first involving integers, the second involving integers and one floating point number) are:

```
6 + 3 - 2
( 255.0 / 2 ) + 1
```

The basic syntax for expressions in PHP is taken from the C language and is familiar to someone who has worked in almost any high-level programming language. Here are some examples:

```
// Assign a value to a variable
$var = 1;

// Sum integers to produce an integer
$var = 4 + 7;

// Subtraction, multiplication, and division might have
// a result that is a float or an integer, depending on
// the initial value of $var
$var = (($var - 5) * 2) / 3;

// These all add 1 to $var
$var = $var + 1;
```

```
$var += 1;
$var++;

// And these all subtract 1 from $var
$var = $var - 1;
$var -= 1;
$var--;

// Double a value
$var = $var * 2;
$var *= 2;

// Halve a value
$var = $var / 2;
$var /= 2;

// These work with float types too
$var = 123.45 * 28.2;
```

There are many mathematical functions available in the math library of PHP for more complex tasks. We introduce some of these in the next chapter.

String expressions can be created using the dot-operator (.) to concatenate two strings:

```
// Assign a string value to a variable
$var = "test string";

// Concatenate two strings using the
// dot operator to produce "test string"
$var = "test" . " string";

// Add a string to the end of another
// to produce "test string"
$var = "test";
$var = $var . " string";

// Here is a shortcut to add a string to
// the end of another
$var .= " test";
```

The following are all equivalent. The syntax you use is a matter of taste.

```
echo "test string";
echo "test " . "string";
echo "test ", "string";
```

The first contains a single string. The second contains an expression combining two strings, while the third contains two arguments to the echo command.

The values returned from functions and many statements can be used as expressions including a variable assignment. In the following example, the assignment ($x = 42) is used as an integer expression with the value of 42:

```
// assign both $y and $x the value 42
$y = ($x = 42);
```

The parentheses are not needed in the example above; however, they highlight the fact that $x = 42 is an expression.

PHP automatically converts types when combining values in an expression. For example, the expression 4 + 7.0 contains an integer and a float; in this case, PHP considers the integer as a floating-point number, and the result is of type float. The type conversions are largely straightforward; however, there are some traps, which are discussed later in this chapter.

Operator precedence

The term *precedence* in mathematics and programming refers to the decision concerning which operator is evaluated first. For instance, in the following expression, by convention, the multiplication operator is evaluated first, leading to a value of 32:

```
2 + 5 * 6
```

PHP defines the precedence of operators in an expression similar to how it is done in other languages. Multiplication and division occur before subtraction and addition, and so on. However, reliance on evaluation order leads to unreadable, confusing code. Rather than memorize the rules, we recommend you construct unambiguous expressions with parentheses, because parentheses have the highest precedence in evaluation.

For example, in the following fragment $variable is assigned a value of 32 because of the precedence of multiplication over addition:

```
$variable = 2 + 5 * 6;
```

But the result is much clearer if parentheses are used:

```
$variable = 2 + (5 * 6);
```

Conditions and Branches

Conditionals add control to scripts and permit choices. Different statements are executed depending on whether expressions are true or false. There are two branching statements in PHP: if, with the optional else clause, and switch, usually with two or more case clauses.

if...else Statement

The if statement conditionally controls execution. The basic format of an if statement is to test whether a condition is true and, if so, to execute one or more statements.

The following if statement executes the print statement and outputs the string when the conditional expression, $var is greater than 5, is true:

```
if ($var > 5)
    print "The variable is greater than 5";
```

The expressions used in the examples in this section compare integers. They can be used to compare strings but usually not with the expected results. If strings need to be compared, use the PHP string library function *strcmp()*. It's discussed in more detail in Chapter 3.

Multiple statements can be executed as a block by encapsulating the statements within braces. If the expression evaluates as true, the statements within the braces are executed. If the expression isn't true, none of the statements are executed. Consider an example in which three statements are executed if the condition is true:

```
if ($var > 5)
{
    print "The variable is greater than 5.";

    // So, now let's set it to 5
    $var = 5;
    print "In fact, now it is equal to 5.";
}
```

Without the braces, an if statement executes only the single, immediately following statement when the conditional expression evaluates to true.

The if statement can have an optional else clause to execute a statement or block of statements if the expression evaluates as false. Consider an example:

```
if ($var > 5)
    print "Variable greater than 5";
else
    print "Variable less than or equal to 5";
```

It's also common for the else clause to execute a block of statements in braces, as in this example:

```
if ($var < 5)
{
    print "Variable is less than 5";
    print "----------------------";
}
else
{
    print "Variable is equal to or larger than 5";
    print "-----------------------------------";
}
```

Consecutive conditional tests can lead to examples such as:

```
if ($var < 5)
    print "Value is very small";
else
    if ($var < 10)
        print "Value is small";
    else
        if ($var < 20)
```

```
        print "Value is normal";
    else
        if ($var < 30)
            print "Value is big";
        else
            print "Value is very big";
```

The indentation in the preceding example highlights the nested nature of the multiple tests. If consecutive, cascading tests are needed, the elseif statement can be used. The choice of which method to use is a matter of personal preference. This example has the same functionality as the previous example:

```
if ($var < 5)
    print "Value is very small";
elseif ($var < 10)
    print "Value is small";
elseif ($var < 20)
    print "Value is normal";
elseif ($var < 30)
    print "Value is big";
else
    print "Value is very big";
```

switch Statement

The switch statement can be used as an alternative to if to select an option from a list of choices. The following example executes different code for different integer values, or cases of the variable $menu. A case clause is provided for values 1, 2, 3, and 4, with a default: case provided for all other values:

```
switch ($menu)
{
    case 1:
        print "You picked one";
        break;
    case 2:
        print "You picked two";
        break;
    case 3:
        print "You picked three";
        break;
    case 4:
        print "You picked four";
        break;
    default:
        print "You picked another option";
}
```

This example can be implemented with if and elseif, but the switch method is usually more compact, readable, and easier to type. The use of break statements is important: they prevent execution of statements that follow in the switch statement and force execution to jump to the statement that follows the closing brace.

If break statements are omitted from a switch statement, you can get an unexpected result. For example, without the break statements, if the user chooses option 3, the script outputs:

```
You picked three. You picked four. You picked another option
```

These results are often a source of difficult-to-detect bugs; however, by intentionally omitting the break statement, you can group cases together as shown in the following switch statement:

```
$score = "Distinction";

switch ($score)
{
    case "High Distinction":
    case "Distinction":
        print "Good student";
        break;

    case "Credit":
    case "Pass":
        print "Average student";
        break;

    default:
        print "Poor student";
}
```

While not mandatory, the default: case is useful when default processing is performed on all but selected special cases, or to handle unexpected values when expected values have corresponding cases.

Conditional Expressions

Now we'll look at what can go inside the parentheses of an if statement, and other control statements. The most common conditional comparison is to test the equality or inequality of two expressions. Equality is checked with the double-equal operator, ==; if the value on the left-hand side is equal to the value on the right-hand side, then the expression evaluates to true. The expression ($var == 3) in the following example evaluates to true:

```
$var = 3;

if ($var == 3)
    print "Equals 3";
```

Inequality is tested with the not-equals operator, !=. Both evaluate to a Boolean result of true or false.

If the equality operator == and the assignment operator = are unfamiliar, beware: they are easy to inadvertently interchange. This is a very common bug and hard to detect.

The value of the conditional expression ($var = 1) evaluates as true, because the expression takes its value from the value on the right hand side of the assignment operator; in this case 1. Here is an example of a common mistake, which overwrites the original value of the variable and always prints the statement:

```
if ($var = 1)
    print "Variable equals 1.";
```

The error of incorrectly replacing an assignment with == is a far less common mistake. However, it's also difficult to detect because an incorrectly written assignment of $var == 1; is quietly evaluated as true or false with no effect on $var.

Expressions can be combined with parentheses and with the Boolean operators && (and) and || (or). For example, the following expression returns true and prints the message if $var is equal to 3 or $var2 is equal to 7:

```
if (($var == 3) || ($var2 == 7))
    print "Equals 3 or 7";
```

The following expression returns true and prints the message if $var equals 2 and $var2 equals 6:

```
if (($var == 2) && ($var2 == 6))
    print "The variables are equal to 2 and 6";
```

Interestingly, if the first part of the expression ($var == 2) evaluates as false, PHP doesn't evaluate the second part of the expression ($var2 == 6), because the overall expression can never be true; both conditions must be true for an && (and) operation to be true. Similarly, in the previous example, if ($var == 3), then there's no need to check if ($var2 == 7).

This *short-circuit* evaluation property has implications for design; to speed code, write the expression most likely to evaluate as false as the left-most expression, and ensure that computationally expensive operations are as right-most as possible.

Never assume that expressions combined with the Boolean operators && and || are evaluated. PHP uses short-circuit evaluation when determining the result of a Boolean expression.

Conditional expressions can be negated with the Boolean not operator !. The following example shows how an expression that tests if $var is equal to 2 or 6 is negated:

```
if (($var == 2) || ($var == 6))
    print "The variable var is equal to 2 or 6";

if (!(($var == 2) || ($var == 6)))
    print "The variable var is not equal to 2 or 6";
```

Unlike the && and || operators, ! works on a single value as the following example highlights:

```
// Set a Boolean variable
$found = false;

// The following message is printed
if (!$found)
    print "Expression is true";
```

More complex expressions can be formed through combinations of the Boolean operators and the liberal use of parentheses. For example, the following expression evaluates as true and prints the message if one of the following is true: $var equals 6 and $var2 equals 7, or $var equals 4 and $var2 equals 1.

```
if ((($var == 6) && ($var2 == 7)) || (($var == 4) && ($var2 == 1)))
    print "Expression is true";
```

As in assignment expressions, parentheses ensure that evaluation occurs in the required order.

Loops

Loops add control to scripts so that statements can be repeatedly executed as long as a conditional expression remains true. There are four loop statements in PHP: while, do...while, for, and foreach. The first three are general-purpose loop constructs, while the foreach is used exclusively with arrays and is discussed in the next chapter.

while

The while loop is the simplest looping structure but sometimes the least compact to use. The while loop repeats one or more statements—the loop body—as long as a condition remains true. The condition is checked first, then the loop body is executed. So, the loop never executes if the condition isn't initially true. Just as with the if statement, more than one statement can be placed in braces to form the loop body.

The following fragment illustrates the while statement by printing out the integers from 1 to 10 separated by a space character:

```
$counter = 1;
while ($counter < 11)
{
    print $counter . " ";
    $counter++;
}
```

do...while

The difference between while and do...while is the point at which the condition is checked. In do...while, the condition is checked *after* the loop body is executed. As long as the condition remains true, the loop body is repeated.

You can emulate the functionality of the previous while example as follows:

```
$counter = 1;
do
{
    print $counter . " ";
    $counter++;
} while ($counter < 11);
```

The contrast between while and do...while can be seen in the following example:

```
$counter = 100;
do
{
    print $counter . " ";
    $counter++;
} while ($counter < 11);
```

This example outputs 100, because the body of the loop is executed once before the condition is evaluated as false.

The do...while loop is the least frequently used loop construct, probably because executing a loop body once when a condition is false is an unusual requirement.

for

The for loop is the most complicated of the loop constructs, but it also leads to the most compact code.

Consider this fragment that implements the example used to illustrate while and do...while:

```
for($counter=1; $counter<11; $counter++)
{
    print $counter;
    print " ";
}
```

The for loop statement has three parts separated by semicolons, and all parts are optional:

Initial statements
  Statements that are executed once, before the loop body is executed.

Loop conditions
  The conditional expression that is evaluated before each execution of the loop body. If the conditional expression evaluates as false, the loop body is not executed.

End-loop statements
  Statements that are executed each time after the loop body is executed.

The previous code fragment has the same output as our while and do...while loop count-to-10 examples. $counter=1 is an initial statement that is executed only once, before the loop body is executed. The loop condition is $counter<11, and this is checked each time before the loop body is executed; when the condition is no longer true (when $counter reaches 11) the loop is terminated. The end-loop statement $counter++ is executed each time after the loop body statements.

Our example is a typical for loop. The initial statement sets up a counter, the loop condition checks the counter, and the end-loop statement increments the counter. Most for loops used in PHP scripts have this format.

Conditions can be as complex as required, as in an if statement. Moreover, several initial and end-loop statements can be separated by commas. This allows for complexity:

```
for($x=0,$y=0; $x<10&&$y<$z; $x++,$y+=2)
```

However, complex for loops can lead to confusing code.

Changing Loop Behavior

To break out of a loop early—before the loop condition becomes false—the break statement is useful. This example illustrates the idea:

```
for($x=0; $x<100; $x++)
{
    if ($x > $y)
        break;
    print $x;
}
```

If $x reaches 100, the loop terminates normally. However, if $x is (or becomes) greater than $y, the loop is terminated early, and program execution continues after the closing brace of the loop body. The break statement can be used with all loop types.

To start again from the top of the loop without completing all the statements in the loop body, use the continue statement. Consider this example:

```
$x = 1;

while($x<100)
{
    print $x;
    $x++;
    if ($x > $y)
        continue;
    print $y;
}
```

The example prints and increments $x each time the loop body is executed. If $x is greater than $y, the sequence starts again with the print $x; statement (and $x keeps the value that was assigned to it during the loop). Otherwise, $y is printed and the loop begins again normally. Like the break statement, continue can be used with any loop type.

The use of break and continue statements to change loop behavior makes code harder to understand and should be avoided.

Functions

A *function* is another concept that programming derived from mathematics. Some programming functions are direct implementations of common mathematical functions, such as sines and other trigonometric functions. (Naturally, these are not used much in PHP.) But you are sure to use functions related to strings, dates, and other everyday objects in your code. PHP has a large number of useful functions built in, and you can define your own functions as we describe later in this chapter.

Functions are called in PHP scripts and can often be used as expressions. For instance, the following example uses the *strtoupper()* function to change a string to uppercase:

```
$var = "A string";

print strtoupper($var); // prints "A STRING"
```

A function is followed by parentheses, which can contain zero or more parameters. This function accepts just one parameter. It can be summarized as follows:

string strtoupper(string subject)

The previous statement is called a *prototype* and is very useful for introducing functions. Prototypes are used throughout PHP documentation, and the following chapters of this book, when a function is described. The first word indicates what is returned by the function: in this case, its output is a string. The name of the function follows, and then a list of parameters within parentheses. Each parameter is described by a type and a parameter name—*strtoupper()* is defined with a single *string* parameter named *subject*. Names allow us to distinguish multiple parameters when we describe the function.

Prototypes use brackets to indicate that function parameters that are optional. Consider the following prototype for the *date()* function:

string date(string format [, integer timestamp])

The *date()* function returns the current date and time as a string where the format is specified by the parameter *format*. The optional integer parameter *timestamp* allows non-current dates and times to be formatted. We discuss the *date()* function and timestamps in the next chapter.

When there is more that one optional parameter, then the parameters are shown in nested brackets:

string x(string p1 [, integer p2 [, integer p3]])

The fictional function *x()* must be called with at least *p1*, but optionally *p2* and *p3*. The nesting of brackets indicates that parameter *p3* can't be included without *p2*.

Some functions allow an unspecified number of parameters; these are indicated with three periods:

string y(string p1 , ...)

Working with Types

PHP is a loosely typed language, allowing variables and function parameters to be set to any type of data. Similarly, functions can return different data types in different circumstances.

In the last section, we introduced the function prototype as a way of describing the type of parameters that functions are designed to work with and the types of data that are returned. Since PHP is loosely typed, PHP can't enforce these types as strongly typed languages do. To illustrate this, the PHP library function *strtoupper()* is designed to operate on strings, but can be called with an integer parameter:

```
$var = 42;

print strtoupper($var); // prints the string "42"
```

When functions are designed to work with different data types, prototypes describe parameters and return values as *mixed*. Other functions may not work as expected, or may not work at all, when the wrong type of data is used.

Type Conversion

PHP provides several mechanisms to allow variables of one type to be considered as another type. Variables can be explicitly converted to another type with the following functions:

string strval(mixed variable)
integer intval(mixed variable [, integer base])
float floatval(mixed variable)

The functions convert the *variable* into a string, integer, or float respectively. The *intval()* function also allows an optional *base* that determines how the *variable* is interpreted.

```
$year = 2003;

// Sets $yearString to the string value "2003"
```

```
$yearString = strval($year);

$var = "abc";

// sets $value to the integer 0
$value = intval($var);

// sets $count to the integer value 2748 - the
// integer value of "abc" as a hexadecimal number
$count = intval($var, 16);
```

Because the string "abc" doesn't look anything like an integer, the first call to the *intval()* function sets $value to zero.

PHP also supports type conversion with *type-casting* operators in much the same way as C, to allow the type of an expression to be changed. When you place the type name in parentheses in front of a variable, PHP converts the value to the desired type:

```
// cast to an integer: the following are equivalent
$int = (int) $var;
$int = (integer) $var;
$int = intval($var);

// cast to a Boolean
$bool = (bool) $var;
$bool = (boolean) $var;


// cast to a float
$float = (float) $var;
$float = floatval($var);

// cast to a string
$str = (string) $var;
$str = strval($var);

// cast to an array
$arr = (array) $var;

// cast to an object
$obj = (object) $var;
```

In the previous example, type casting, and calls to the *strval()*, *intval()*, and *floatval()* functions don't change the value or type of the variable $var. The *settype()* function actually modifies the variable that it is called with. For example:

```
boolean settype(mixed variable, string type)
```

settype() explicitly sets the type of *variable* to *type*, where *type* is one of array, boolean, float, integer, object, or string.

```
// cast to an integer: the following are equivalent
$var = 39;
```

```
// $var is now a string
settype($var, "string");
```

The rules for converting types are mostly common sense, but some conversions may not appear so straightforward. Table 2-1 shows how various values of $var are converted using the (int), (bool), (string), and (float) casting operators.

Table 2-1. Examples of type conversion in PHP

Value of $var	(int) $var	(bool) $var	(string) $var	(float) $var
null	0	false	""	0
true	1	true	"1"	1
false	0	false	""	0
0	0	false	"0"	0
3.8	3	true	"3.8"	3.8
"0"	0	false	"0"	0
"10"	10	true	"10"	10
"6 feet"	6	true	"6 feet"	6
"foo"	0	true	"foo"	0

Automatic Type Conversion

Automatic type conversion occurs when two differently typed variables are combined in an expression or when a variable is passed as an argument to a library function that expects a different type. When a variable of one type is used as if it were another type, PHP automatically converts the variable to a value of the required type. The same rules are used for automatic type conversion as demonstrated previously in Table 2-1.

Some simple examples show what happens when strings are added to integers and floats, and when strings and integers are concatenated:

```
// $var is set as an integer = 115
$var = "100" + 15;

// $var is set as a float = 115.0
$var = "100" + 15.0;

// $var is set as a string = "39 Steps"
$var = 39 . " Steps";
```

Not all type conversions are so obvious and can be the cause of hard-to-find bugs:

```
// $var is set as an integer = 39
$var = 39 + " Steps";


// $var is an integer = 42
$var = "3 blind mice" + 39;
```

```
// $var is a float, but what does it mean?
$var = "test" * 4 + 3.14159;
```

Automatic type conversion can change the type of a variable. Consider the following example:

```
$var = "1";    // $var is a string == "1"
$var += 2;     // $var is now an integer == 3
$var /= 2;     // $var is now a float == 1.5
$var *= 2;     // $var is still a float == 3
```

 Care must be taken when interpreting non-Boolean values as Boolean. Many library functions in PHP return values of different types in different circumstances. For example, many functions return the Boolean value false if a valid result could not be determined. If the function is successful, they return the valid integer, string, or compound type. However, a valid return value of 0, 0.0, "0", an empty string, null, or an empty array is also equal to the Boolean value false and can be misinterpreted as failure.

The solution is to test the type of the variable using the functions described in the next section.

Examining Variable Type and Content

Because PHP is flexible with types, it provides the following functions that can check a variable's type:

> *boolean is_int(mixed variable)*
> *boolean is_float(mixed variable)*
> *boolean is_bool(mixed variable)*
> *boolean is_string(mixed variable)*
> *boolean is_array(mixed variable)*
> *boolean is_object(mixed variable)*

All the functions return a Boolean value of true or false depending on whether the type of *variable* matches the variable type that forms the name of the function. For example, *is_float()* evaluates to true in the following code:

```
$test = 13.0;

// prints "Variable is a float"
if (is_float($test))
    print "Variable is a float";
```

Is-identical and is-not-identical operators

While the PHP equals operator == tests the values of two variables, it doesn't test the variables types. Consider the comparisons of string and integer variables:

```
$stringVar = "10 reasons to test variable type";
$integerVar = 10;
```

```
// Prints "Variables have the same value"
if ($stringVar == $integerVar)
    print "Variables have the same value";
```

Because of PHP's automatic type conversion, $stringVar == $integerVar evaluates to true. PHP provides the is-identical operator === that tests not only values, but types. In the fragment below, the expression $stringVar === $integerVar evaluates to false:

```
$stringVar = "10 reasons to test variable type";
$integerVar = 10;

// Does not print anything
if ($stringVar === $integerVar)
    print "Variables have the same value and type";
```

PHP also provides the is-not-identical operator, !==, that returns true if the value or type of two expressions are different.

Debugging with gettype(), print_r(), and var_dump( )

PHP provides the *gettype()*, *print_r()*, and *var_dump()* functions, which print the type and value of an *expression* in a human-readable form:

string gettype(mixed expression)
print_r(mixed expression)
var_dump(mixed expression [, mixed expression ...])

These functions are useful for debugging a script, especially when dealing with arrays or objects. To test the value and type of $variable at some point in the script, the following code can be used:

```
$variable = "3 Blind mice" + 39;
var_dump($variable);
```

This prints:

```
int(42)
```

While the *var_dump()* function allows multiple variables to be tested in one call, and provides information about the size of the variable contents, *print_r()* provides a more concise representation of arrays and objects, and will prove useful later when we start to use those variables.

The *gettype()* function simply returns the type name for an expression:

```
$variable = "3 Blind mice" + 39;

// prints: "integer"
print(gettype($variable));
```

The name that *gettype()* returns should only be used for information and not to programmatically test the type of a variable as the output is not guaranteed to remain stable with future PHP releases. To programmatically test a variable type, you should use the *is_int()*, *is_float()*, *is_bool()*, *is_string()*, *is_array()*, or *is_object()* functions described earlier.

The *gettype()*, *print_r()*, and *var_dump()* functions can be used on variables and expressions of any type, and we use them throughout the book to help illustrate the results of our examples.

Testing, setting, and unsetting variables

During the running of a PHP script, a variable may be in an unset state or may not yet be defined. PHP provides the *isset()* function and the *empty()* language construct to test the state of variables:

> *boolean isset(mixed var)*
> *boolean empty(mixed var)*

isset() tests if a variable has been set with a non-null value, while *empty()* tests if a variable is equal to *false*. The two are illustrated by the following code:

```
$var = 0;

// prints: "Variable is Set"
if (isset($var)) print "Variable is Set";

// prints: "Variable is Empty"
if (empty($var)) print "Variable is Empty";

$var = "test";

// prints: "Variable is Set"
if (isset($var)) print "Variable is Set";

// Doesn't print
if (empty($var)) print "Variable is Empty";
```

A variable can be explicitly destroyed using *unset()*:

> *unset(mixed var [, mixed var [, ...]])*

After the call to unset in the following example, $var is no longer defined:

```
$var = "foo";

// Later in the script
unset($var);

// Does not print
if (isset($var)) print "Variable is Set";
```

Table 2-2 show the return values for isset($var) and empty($var)when the variable $var is tested. Some of the results may be unexpected: when $var is set to "0," *empty()* returns true.

Table 2-2. Expression values

State of the variable $var	isset($var)	empty($var)
unset $var;	false	true
$var = null;	false	true
$var = 0;	true	true
$var = true;	true	false
$var = false;	true	true
$var = "0";	true	true
$var = "";	true	true
$var = "foo";	true	false
$var = array();	true	true

A variable is always set when it is assigned a value—with the exception of a null assignment—and *isset()* returns true. The *empty()* function tests the Boolean value of the variable and returns true if the variable is false. The statement

```
$result = empty($var);
```

is equivalent to

```
$result = not (boolean) $var;
```

However, PHP issues a warning when a cast operator is used on an unset variable, whereas *empty()* doesn't.

User-Defined Functions

User-defined functions provide a way to group together related statements into a cohesive block. For reusable code, a function saves duplicating statements and makes maintenance of the code easier. Consider an example of a simple user-developed function as shown in Example 2-3.

Example 2-3. A user-defined function to output bold text

```
<!DOCTYPE HTML PUBLIC "-//W3C//DTD HTML 4.01 Transitional//EN"
                    "http://www.w3.org/TR/html401/loose.dtd">
<html>
<head>
  <meta http-equiv="Content-Type" content="text/html; charset=iso-8859-1">
  <title>Simple Function Call</title>
</head>
<body bgcolor="#ffffff">
<?php
```

Example 2-3. A user-defined function to output bold text (continued)

```php
function bold($string)
{
    print "<b>" . $string . "</b>";
}

// First example function call (with a static string)
print "this is not bold ";
bold("this is bold ");
print "this is again not bold ";

// Second example function call (with a variable)
$myString = "this is bold";
bold($myString);
?>
</body></html>
```

The script defines the function *bold()*, which takes one parameter, $string, and prints that string prefixed by a bold <b> tag and suffixed with a </b> tag. The parameter $string is a variable that is available in the body of the function, and the value of $string is set when the function is called. As shown in the example, the function can be called with a string literal expression or a variable as the parameter.

Functions can also return values. For example, consider the following code fragment that declares and uses a function *heading()*, which returns a string using the return statement:

```php
function heading($text, $headingLevel)
{
    switch ($headingLevel)
    {
    case 1:
        $result = "<h1>$text</h1>";
        break;

    case 2:
        $result = "<h2>$text</h2>";
        break;

    case 3:
        $result = "<h3>$text</h3>";
        break;

    default:
        $result = "<p><b>$text</b></p>";
    }
    return($result);
}

$test = "User-defined Functions";
print heading($test, 2);
```

The function takes two parameters: the text of a heading and a heading level. Based on the value of $headingLevel, the function builds the HTML suitable to display the heading. The example outputs the string:

```
<h2>User-defined Functions</h2>
```

The variable that is returned by a return statement can optionally be placed in parentheses: the statements return($result) and return $result are identical.

Parameter Types and Return Types

The parameter and return types of a function aren't declared when the function is defined. PHP allows parameters of any type to be passed to the function, and as with variables, the return type is determined when a result is actually returned. Consider a simple function that divides two numbers:

```
function divide($a, $b)
{
    return ($a/$b);
}
```

The value returned from the function *divide()* is the value of the expression ($a/$b). The type that is returned depends on the parameters passed to *divide()*. For example:

```
$c = divide(4, 2);     // assigns an integer value = 2
$c = divide(3, 2);     // assigns a float value = 1.5
$c = divide(4.0, 2.0); // assigns a float value = 2.0
```

If the types of parameters passed to the function are critical, they should be tested as shown earlier in "Type Conversion."

The return statement causes the execution of the function to end. To illustrate this, consider an improved *divide()* function definition that tests the parameter $b to avoid divide-by-zero errors:

```
function divide($a, $b)
{
    if ($b == 0)
        return false;

    return ($a/$b);
}
```

If $b is 0, then the function returns false and the division of $a/$b is never executed.

The return statement can also be used to exit from functions that don't return values. Consider the following definition of *bold()* that simply prints the parameter $string without any bold mark-up when passed non-string values:

```
function bold($string)
{
    if (! is_string($string))
    {
        print $string;
        return;
```

```
    }
    print "<b>" . $string . "</b>";
}
```

Variable Scope

Variables used inside a function are different from those used outside a function. The variables used inside the function are limited to use within the function. This is called the *scope* of the variable. There are exceptions to this rule, which are discussed later in this section. Consider an example that illustrates variable scope:

```
function doublevalue($var)
{
    $temp = $var * 2;
}

$variable = 5;
doublevalue($variable);
print "\$temp is: $temp";
```

This example outputs the string:

```
$temp is:
```

with no value for $temp. The scope of the variable $temp is local to the function *doublevalue()* and is discarded when the function returns.

The PHP script engine doesn't complain about an undeclared variable being used. It just assumes the variable is empty. However, this use of an undefined variable can be detected by configuring the error-reporting settings. Error reporting is discussed in Chapter 14.

The easiest way to use a value that is local to a function elsewhere in a script is to return the value from the function with the return statement. The calling script can simply assign the returned value to a local variable. The following example does this:

```
function doublevalue($var)
{
    $returnVar = $var * 2;
    return($returnVar);
}

$variable = 5;
$temp = doublevalue($variable);
print "\$temp is: $temp";
```

The example prints:

```
$temp is: 10
```

You could have still used the variable name $temp inside the function *doublevalue()*. However, the $temp inside the function is a different variable from the $temp outside the function. The general rule is that variables used exclusively within functions are local to the function, regardless of whether an identically named variable is used else-where. There are three exceptions to this general rule: variables passed by reference, variables declared `global` in the function, and superglobals that contain user and environment values and are automatically created by PHP at runtime. Global variables are discussed in the next section, and superglobals are discussed in Chapter 6.

Global variables

If you want to use the same variable everywhere in your code, including within functions, you can do so with the `global` statement. The `global` statement declares a variable within a function as being the same as the variable that is used outside of the function. Consider this example:

```
function doublevalue()
{
    global $temp;
    $temp = $temp * 2;
}

$temp = 5;
doublevalue();
print "\$temp is: $temp";
```

Because `$temp` is declared inside the function as `global`, the variable `$temp` used in *doublevalue()* is a global variable that can be accessed outside the function. Because the variable `$temp` can be seen outside the function, the script prints:

```
$temp is: 10
```

A word of caution: avoid overuse of `global` as it makes for confusing code.

 The global variable declaration can be a trap for experienced programmers. In some other languages, global variables are usually declared global outside the functions and then used in the functions.

In PHP, it's the opposite: to use a global variable inside a function, declare the variable as global inside the function.

Allowing a function to modify global variables solves the problem that a `return` statement can only pass back one value. An alternative to using `global` is to return an array of values—this approach becomes clear when we discuss arrays in Chapter 3. A better approach is to pass parameters by reference instead of by value, a practice described later.

Static variables

Variables can also be declared within a function as static. The static variable is available only in the scope of the function, but the value is not lost between function calls. Consider simple function *count()* that declares a static counter variable `$count`:

```
function count()
{
```

```
        static $count = 0;
        $count++;
        return $count;
}

// prints 1
print count( );

// prints 2
print count( );
```

The first time the function *count()* is called, the static variable $count is set to zero, and incremented. The value of $count is maintained for subsequent calls.

Passing Variables to Functions

By default, variables are passed to functions by value, not by reference. Consider an example:

```
function doublevalue($var)
{
    $var = $var * 2;
}

$variable = 5;
doublevalue($variable);
print "\$variable is: $variable";
```

This produces the output:

```
$variable is: 5
```

The parameter $variable that is passed to the function *doublevalue()* isn't changed by the function. What actually happens is that the value 5 is passed to the function, doubled to be 10, and the result lost forever! The value is passed to the function, not the variable itself.

Passing parameters by reference

An alternative to returning a result or using a global variable is to pass a *reference* to a variable as a parameter to the function. This means that any changes to the variable within the function affect the original variable. Consider this example:

```
function doublevalue(&$var)
{
    $var = $var * 2;
}

$variable = 5;
doublevalue($variable);
print "\$variable is: $variable";
```

This prints:

```
$variable is: 10
```

The only difference between this example and the previous one is that the parameter $var to the function *doublevalue()* is prefixed with an ampersand character: &$var. The effect is a bit too hard to understand unless one learns low-level computer languages, but it means that the parameter doesn't contain the value of the variable—instead, it points to where the variable is stored in memory. The result is that changes to $var in the function affect the original variable $variable outside the function.

If a parameter is defined as a reference, you can't pass the function a literal expression as that parameter because the function expects to modify a variable. PHP reports an error when the following is executed:

```
function doublevalue(&$var)
{
    $var = $var * 2;
}

// The following line causes an error
doublevalue(5);
```

Assigning by reference

Referencing with the ampersand can also be used when assigning variables, which allows the memory holding a value to be accessed from more than one variable. This example illustrates the idea:

```
$x = 10;
$y = &$x;
$y++;
print $x;
print $y;
```

This fragment prints:

```
1111
```

Because $y is a reference to $x, any change to $y affects $x. In effect, they are the same variable. The reference $y can be removed with:

```
unset($y);
```

This has no effect on $x or its value.

Assigning variables with a reference to another variable can also be done with the reference assignment operator =& with exactly the same outcome as shown in the previous example. The following fragment sets up three variables—$x, $y, and $z—that all point to the same value:

```
$x = 10;

// Use the reference assignment operator =& to assign a reference to $x
$y =& $x;
```

```
// Use the assignment operator = to copy a reference to $x
$z = &$x;

$x = 100;

// Prints "x = 100,  y = 100,  z = 100"
print "x = {$x},  y = {$y},  z = {$z}";
```

Default parameter values

PHP allows functions to be defined with default values for parameters. A default value is simply supplied in the parameter list using the = sign. Consider the *heading()* function described earlier; here we modify the function definition to include a default value:

```
function heading($text, $headingLevel = 2)
{
    switch ($headingLevel)
    {
    case 1:
        $result = "<h1>$text</h1>";
        break;

    case 2:
        $result = "<h2>$text</h2>";
        break;

    case 3:
        $result = "<h3>$text</h3>";
        break;


    default:
        $result = "<p><b>$text</b></p>";
    }

    return($result);
}

$test = "User-defined Functions";
print heading($test);
```

When calls are made to the *heading()* function, the second argument can be omitted, and the default value 2 is assigned to the $headingLevel variable.

Reusing Functions with Include and Require Files

It's valuable to be able to reuse functions in many scripts. PHP provides the include and require statements that allow you to reuse PHP scripts containing statements, function definitions, and even static HTML.

If you decide to reuse the *bold()* function from Example 2-3 in more than one script, you can store it in a separate *include file*. For example, you can create a file called *functions.inc* and put the *bold()* function in the file:

```php
<?php
function bold($string)
{
    print "<b>" . $string . "</b>";
}
?>
```

 Any PHP code in an include file must be surrounded by the PHP start and end script tags. The PHP script engine treats the contents of include files as HTML unless script tags are used.

You can then use include to provide access to the *bold()* function:

```html
<!DOCTYPE HTML PUBLIC "-//W3C//DTD HTML 4.01 Transitional//EN"
                      "http://www.w3.org/TR/html401/loose.dtd">
<html>
<head>
  <meta http-equiv="Content-Type" content="text/html; charset=iso-8859-1">
  <title>Simple Function Call</title>
</head>
<body bgcolor="#ffffff">
<?php
include "functions.inc";

// First example function call (with a string expression)
print "this is not bold ";
bold("this is bold ");
print "this is again not bold ";

// Second example function call (with a variable)
$myString = "this is bold";
bold($myString);
?>
</body></html>
```

Include files can also be used to incorporate resources such as static HTML or a set of variable initializations. The following example could be written to the file *release.inc* and included in all the scripts of an application:

```php
<!-- Beta Release Only -->
<?php
    $showDebug = true;
?>
```

Both include and require read external include files, the only difference is in the behavior when a file can't be included: include provides a warning whereas require terminates the script with a fatal error.

When you are including a file that contains user-defined functions, or other mandatory content, you should use the require directive. We use the require directive in all of our code.

The include and require statements can be treated in the same way as other statements. For example, you can conditionally include different files using the following code fragment:

```
if ($netscape == true)
{
    require "netscape.inc";
}
else
{
    require "other.inc";
}
```

The file is included only if the include statement is executed in the script. The braces used in this example are necessary: if they are omitted, the example doesn't behave as expected.

Scripts can include more than one include file, and include files can themselves include other files. Writing scripts that use include or require can lead to an include file being included and evaluated twice. To avoid problems with variable reassignments and function redefinitions, PHP provides the include_once or require_once constructs statements that ensure that the contents of the file are included only once.

Managing include files

As you develop reusable code, you should consider how you will arrange your include files. By default, when a file is included using the include or require statements, PHP searches for the file in the same directory as the script being executed. You can include files in other directories by specifying a file path in the include or require statements. The following example shows how relative and absolute file paths can be used:

```
// a relative file path
require "../inc/myFunctions.php";

// an absolute file path
require "/library/database/db.inc";
```

The paths can be specified with forward slashes for both Unix and Microsoft Windows environments, allowing scripts to be moved from one environment to another. However, using paths can make it difficult to change the directory structure of your application.

A more sophisticated, and flexible alternative to accessing include files is to set the include_path parameter defined in the *php.ini* configuration file. One or more directories can be specified in the include_path parameter, and when set, PHP will search for include files relative to those directories. The following extract from the *php.ini* file shows how to set the include_path parameter:

```
;;;;;;;;;;;;;;;;;;;;;;;;;;;;;
; Paths and Directories ;
;;;;;;;;;;;;;;;;;;;;;;;;;;;;

; UNIX: "/path1:/path2"
;include_path = ".:/php/includes:/usr/local/php/projectx"
;
; Windows: "\path1;\path2"
include_path = ".;c:\php\includes;d:\php\projectx"
```

Path specifications for this parameter are system specific. Unix paths use the forward slash and are separated with the colon (:) character, while Microsoft Windows paths use the backslash and are separated by semi colons (;).

The *php.ini* configuration file defines many parameters that are used to define aspects of PHP's behavior. Whenever you change *php.ini*, you need to restart your Apache web server so that the changes are re-read; instructions for restarting are in Appendix A.

If you set the include_path parameter, include and require directives need only specify a path relative to a directory listed in the include_path. For example, if the include_path is set to point at */usr/local/php/projectx*, and you have an include file *security.inc* that's stored in */usr/local/php/projectx/security*, you only need to add:

```
include "security/security.inc";
```

to your script file. The PHP engine will check the directory */usr/local/php/projectx*, and locate the subdirectory *security* and its include file. Include files that are placed in directories outside of the web server's document root are protected from access via the web server. In Chapter 6 we describe how to protect include files that are under the web server root directory.

For a large project, you might place the project-specific code into one directory, while keeping reusable code in another; this is the approach we use in our case study, *Hugh and Dave's Online Wines*, as we describe in Chapter 15.

A Working Example

In this section, we use some of the techniques described so far to develop a simple, complete PHP script. The script doesn't process input from the user, so we leave some of the best features of PHP as a web scripting language for discussion in later chapters.

Our example is a script that produces a web page containing the times tables. Our aim is to output the 1–12 times tables. The first table is shown in Figure 2-2 as rendered by a Mozilla browser.

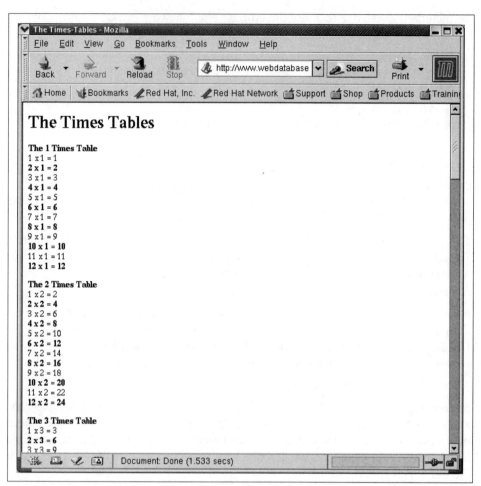

Figure 2-2. The output of the times-tables script rendered in a Mozilla browser

The completed PHP script and HTML to produce the times tables are shown in Example 2-4. The first ten lines are the HTML markup that produces the `<head>` components and the `<h1>The Times Tables</h1>` heading at the top of the web page. Similarly, the last two lines are HTML that finishes the document: `</body>` and `</html>`.

Between the two HTML fragments that start and end the document is a PHP script to produce the times-table content and its associated HTML. The script begins with the PHP open tag `<?php` and finishes with the close tag `?>`.

Example 2-4. A script to produce the times tables

```
<!DOCTYPE HTML PUBLIC "-//W3C//DTD HTML 4.01 Transitional//EN"
                    "http://www.w3.org/TR/html401/loose.dtd">
<html>
<head>
```

Example 2-4. A script to produce the times tables (continued)

```
  <meta http-equiv="Content-Type" content="text/html; charset=iso-8859-1">
  <title>The Times-Tables</title>
</head>
<body bgcolor="#ffffff">
<h1>The Times Tables</h1>
<?php

// Go through each table
for($table=1; $table<13; $table++)
{
    print "<p><b>The " . $table . " Times Table</b>\n";

    // Produce 12 lines for each table
    for($counter=1; $counter<13; $counter++)
    {
        $answer = $table * $counter;

        // Is this an even-number counter?
        if ($counter % 2 == 0)
            // Yes, so print this line in bold
            print "<br><b>$counter x $table = " .
                "$answer</b>";

        else
            // No, so print this in normal face
            print "<br>$counter x $table = $answer";
    }
}

?>
</body>
</html>
```

The script is designed to process each times table and, for each table, to produce a heading and 12 lines. To do this, the script consists of two nested loops: an outer and inner for loop.

The outer for loop uses the integer variable $table, incrementing it by 1 each time the loop body is executed until $table is greater than 12. The body of the outer loop prints the heading and executes the inner loop that actually produces the body of each times table.

The inner loop uses the integer variable $counter to generate the lines of the times tables. Inside the loop body, the $answer to the current line is calculated by multiplying the current value of $table by the current value of $counter.

Every second line of the tables and the times-table headings are encapsulated in the bold tag <b> and bold end tag </b>, which produces alternating bold lines in the resulting HTML output. After calculating the $answer, an if statement follows that decides whether the line should be output in bold tags. The expression the `if` statement tests uses the modulo operator `%` to test if $counter is an odd or even number.

The modulo operation divides the variable $counter by 2 and returns the remainder. So, for example, if $counter is 6, the returned value is 0, because 6 divided by 2 is exactly 3 with no remainder. If $counter is 11, the returned value is 1, because 11 divided by 2 is 5 with a remainder of 1. If $counter is even, the conditional expression:

```
($counter % 2 == 0)
```

is true, and bold tags are printed.

Example 2-4 is complete but not especially interesting. Regardless of how many times the script is executed, the result is the same web page. In practice, you might consider running the script once, capturing the output, and saving it to a static HTML file. If you save the output as HTML, the user can retrieve the same page, with less web-server load and a faster response time.

In later chapters, we develop scripts with output that can change from run to run, and can't be represented in a static file. In Chapter 6, we show scripts that interact with the MySQL database management system; the result is dynamic pages that change if the underlying data in the database is updated. We also show scripts that interact with the system environment and with user input from fill-in forms.

CHAPTER 3

Arrays, Strings, and Advanced Data Manipulation in PHP

In the previous chapter, we introduced the basics of the PHP language. In this chapter we show you some important techniques you'll need to manipulate data in PHP. This includes ways of dealing with arrays, strings, dates, and numerical data. The topics in this chapter cover:

- Arrays and array library functions
- Strings and string library functions
- Regular expressions
- Date and time functions
- Integer and float functions

We don't attempt to cover every function and library supported by PHP. However, we provide brief descriptions of them in Appendix E. In later chapters, we discuss selected specialized library functions that support the topics and techniques presented here.

Arrays

Programmers continually have to deal with collections of data items. For instance, when you query a database for products, you may get a collection with multiple results. In PHP, as with many programming languages, you can handle these results through an *array*. An array can be considered a name that refers to many related items.

Arrays in PHP are sophisticated and more flexible than in many other high-level languages. A PHP *array* is an ordered set of variables, in which each variable—called an *element*—has an associated *key*. PHP allows elements to be accessed using either string or integer keys—PHP automatically assigns integer key values if keys are not specified when arrays are constructed.

Arrays can hold scalar values (integers, Booleans, strings, or floats) or compound values (objects and even other arrays). The same array can even hold elements of different types. In this section, we show how arrays are constructed and introduce several useful array functions from the PHP library.

Creating Arrays

PHP provides the *array()* language construct that creates arrays. The following examples show how arrays of integers and strings can be constructed and assigned to variables for later use:

```
$numbers = array(5, 4, 3, 2, 1);
$words = array("Web", "Database", "Applications");

// Print the third element from the array of integers: 3
print $numbers[2];

// Print the first element from the array of strings: "Web"
print $words[0];
```

By creating arrays this way, PHP assigns integer keys, or *indexes* to each element. By default, the index for the first element in an array is 0—this may seem odd but think of the index as an offset from the starting position in an array. The values contained in an array can be retrieved and modified using the bracket [ ] syntax. You can also create an array by assigning elements to a new, unset variable. The following code fragment illustrates the bracket syntax with an array of strings:

```
$newArray[0] = "Potatoes";
$newArray[1] = "Carrots";
$newArray[2] = "Spinach";

// Replace the third element
$newArray[2] = "Tomatoes";
```

In this example, PHP automatically treats $newArray as an array without a call to *array()*.

An empty array can be created by assigning to a variable the return value of *array()*. Values can then be added using the bracket syntax. PHP automatically assigns the next numeric index as the key (the largest integer key value plus one) when a key isn't supplied. The result of the following fragment is an array containing three items.

```
$shopping = array();

$shopping[] = "Milk";
$shopping[] = "Coffee";
$shopping[] = "Sugar";
```

It's also easy to print individual element values themselves:

```
print $shopping[0];    // prints "Milk"
print $shopping[1];    // prints "Coffee"
print $shopping[2];    // prints "Sugar"
```

When printing array elements in double-quoted strings, you need to use the braces syntax introduced in Chapter 2, for example:

```
// prints "The first item in my list is Milk"
print "The first item in my list is {$shopping[0]}";
```

You can also print out the entire contents of an array using the *print_r()* function that we introduced in Chapter 2. Passing the variable $shopping from the previous example to *print_r()*:

```
print_r($shopping);
```

prints the entire array showing each element and associated index:

```
Array
(
    [0] => Milk
    [1] => Coffee
    [2] => Sugar
)
```

To include *print_r()* output as part of a web page, you should use <pre> tags to preserve the formatting, otherwise the output is rendered on one line because one or more consecutive white space characters is treated as a single space in HTML. Generally you should avoid the use of the <pre> tag in your HTML output, however preserving the *print_r()* format makes debugging much easier. Here's how you can use the <pre> tags:

```
<pre>
<?php  print_r($shopping);  ?>
</pre>
```

While the *print_r()* function is really only intended for debugging purposes, and the use of <pre> elements in HTML is discouraged, we use the *print_r()* function extensively in this chapter to help illustrate our examples.

Associative arrays

An associative array uses string keys to access values stored in the array. An associative array can be constructed with *array()* by associating each key to a value using the => operator as shown in the following example:

```
$array = array("first"=>1, "second"=>2, "third"=>3);

// Print out the second element: prints "2"
print $array["second"];
```

The same array of integers can also be created with the bracket syntax:

```
$array["first"] = 1;
$array["second"] = 2;
$array["third"] = 3;
```

The => operator can also be used to create numerically indexed arrays that start at any index value. Often it's convenient to start an array at index 1, as shown in the following example:

```
$numbers = array(1=>"one", "two", "three", "four");
```

Arrays can also be created where each numeric key is specified, such as:

```
$oddNumbers = array(1=>"one", 3=>"three", 5=>"five");
```

All arrays in PHP are associative with elements accessed either by a string key or an integer key. You can create arrays that use both integer and string keys, however such arrays add complexity to an application and should be avoided. Associative arrays are common in other languages and are sometimes called hash arrays or hash tables—a reference to how the array is implemented.

Removing elements from an array

An element can be removed from an array, or an entire array can be deleted, by calling *unset()*. However, removing an element doesn't reassign the indexes as the following example shows:

```
$favorites = array("PHP", "Ace", "COBOL", "Java", "C++");

// remove COBOL from the array
unset($favorites[2]);
print_r($favorites);
```

Initially, each element is assigned a numeric key starting from zero, and after removing an element, the script prints:

```
Array ( [0] => PHP [1] => Ace [3] => Java [4] => C++ )
```

There is no longer an element defined for index 2. This example illustrates the associative nature of all PHP arrays: after a value is added to an array, the associated key remains unchanged unlike a true index that would adjust when an array changes.

To destroy a whole array, call *unset()* on the array variable:

```
// destroy the whole array
unset($favorites);
```

Array order

Arrays preserve the order of the elements that they contain, and new elements are appended to the end of an existing array. The following fragment creates an array specifying the integer indexes 1, 3, and 5; then adds values with the index values 2, 4, and 6.

```
$numbers = array(1=>"one", 3=>"three", 5=>"five");

$numbers[2] = "two";
$numbers[4] = "four";
```

```
$numbers[6] = "six";

print_r($numbers);
```

The resulting order is shown when the array contents are viewed with *print_r()*:

```
Array
(
    [1] => one
    [3] => three
    [5] => five
    [2] => two
    [4] => four
    [6] => six
)
```

Heterogeneous arrays

The values that can be stored in a single PHP array don't have to be of the same type; PHP arrays can contain *heterogeneous* values—that is any mix of integer, string, Boolean, float, object, and even array variables. The following example shows the heterogeneous array $mixedBag:

```
$mixedBag = array("cat", 42, 8.5, false);

var_dump($mixedBag);
```

The function *var_dump()* displays the types and values of each element (with some whitespace added for clarity):

```
array(4)
{
    [0] => string(3) "cat"
    [1] => int(42)
    [2] => float(8.5)
    [3] => bool(false)
}
```

Multidimensional arrays

Often data can't be represented in a simple array of scalar values—integers, strings, Booleans, and floats. Some data can only be represented when arrays hold other arrays of values. Consider representing the results from the twelve times table we showed in the previous chapter. We could create an array for each table from one to twelve:

```
$one = array(1, 2, 3, 4, 5, 6, 7, 8, 9, 10, 11, 12);
$two = array(2, 4, 6, 8, 10, 12, 14, 16, 18, 20, 22, 24);
$three = array(3, 6, 9, 12, 15, 18, 21, 24, 27, 30, 33, 36);
// etc..
```

or we can create a multidimensional array like this:

```
$table = array(
    1 => array(1 => 1, 2, 3, 4, 5, 6, 7, 8, 9, 10, 11, 12),
    2 => array(1 => 2, 4, 6, 8, 10, 12, 14, 16, 18, 20, 22, 24),
```

```
        3 => array(1 => 3, 6, 9, 12, 15, 18, 21, 24, 27, 30, 33, 36),
    ...
    );
```

The variable `$table` is a two-dimensional array: each element—accessed by the integer 1, 2, 3, and so on—is an array that holds the results of a multiplication. Values can be accessed using [] operators for each dimension. We have explicitly set the index for the first element in each row, and for each row, allowed the terms used in a multiplication to be used as keys. For example, the following prints the result of 3 times 8:

```
    // Prints 24
    print $table[3][8];
```

Example 3-1 shows how more complex multidimensional arrays can be constructed.

Example 3-1. Examples of multidimensional arrays in PHP

```
<!DOCTYPE HTML PUBLIC "-//W3C//DTD HTML 4.01 Transitional//EN"
                    "http://www.w3.org/TR/html401/loose.dtd">
<html>
<head>
  <meta http-equiv="Content-Type" content="text/html; charset=iso-8859-1">
  <title>Multi-dimensional arrays</title>
</head>
<body bgcolor="#ffffff">
<h2>A two dimensional array</h2>
<?php

  // A two dimensional array using integer indexes
  $planets = array(array("Mercury", 0.39, 0.38),
                   array("Venus",   0.72, 0.95),
                   array("Earth",   1.0,  1.0),
                   array("Mars",    1.52, 0.53) );

  // prints "Earth"
  print $planets[2][0]
?>

<h2>More sophisticated multi-dimensional array</h2>
<?php

  // More sophisticated multi-dimensional array
  $planets2 = array(
    "Mercury"=> array("dist"=>0.39, "dia"=>0.38),
    "Venus"  => array("dist"=>0.72, "dia"=>0.95),
    "Earth"  => array("dist"=>1.0,  "dia"=>1.0,
                      "moons"=>array("Moon")),
    "Mars"   => array("dist"=>1.52, "dia"=>0.53,
                      "moons"=>array("Phobos", "Deimos"))
    );

  // prints "Moon"
```

Example 3-1. Examples of multidimensional arrays in PHP (continued)

```
  print $planets2["Earth"]["moons"][0];
?>
</body>
</html>
```

The first array constructed in Example 3-1 is two-dimensional and is accessed using integer indexes. The array `$planets` contains four elements, each of which is an array that contains three values: the planet's name, its distance from the Sun relative to the Earth's distance, and the planet's diameter relative to the Earth.

The second array in Example 3-1 is a little more sophisticated: the array `$planets2` uses associative keys to identify an array that holds information about a planet. Each planet has an array of values that are associatively indexed by the name of the property that is stored. For those planets that have moons, an extra property is added that holds an array of the moon names.

To include an element from a multi-dimensional array in a double-quoted string, you need to use the braces syntax introduced in Chapter 2. When using braces, you don't need to escape the double-quotes that surround the array key; for example:

```
// prints "The Moon is a balloon"
print "The {$planets2["Earth"]["moons"][0]} is a balloon";
```

Many data structures (such as property lists, stacks, queues, and trees) can be created using PHP arrays. We limit our usage of arrays to simple structures; the examination of more complex data structures is outside the scope of this book.

Using foreach Loops with Arrays

The easiest way to traverse or iterate through an array is using the foreach statement. The foreach statement has two forms:

```
foreach(array_expression as $value)
{
    // body of loop
}

foreach(array_expression as $key => $value)
{
    // body of loop
}
```

Both step through an *array expression*, executing the statements contained in the body of the loop for each element in the array. The first form assigns the value from the element to a variable identified with the as keyword. The second form assigns both the key and the value to a pair of variables. Variables assigned with an element value and key, are available in the body of the loop.

The following example shows the first form in which the array expression is the variable $lengths, and each value is assigned to the variable $cm:

```
// Construct an array of integers
$lengths = array(0, 107, 202, 400, 475);

// Convert an array of centimeter lengths to inches
foreach($lengths as $cm)
{
    $inch = $cm / 2.54;
    print "{$cm} centimeters = {$inch} inches\n";
}
```

The example iterates through the array in the same order it was created:

```
0 centimeters = 0 inches
107 centimeters = 42.125984251969 inches
202 centimeters = 79.527559055118 inches
400 centimeters = 157.48031496063 inches
475 centimeters = 193.87755102041 inches
```

The first form of the foreach statement iterates through the values of an associative array, but keys are not retrieved. The second form assigns both the key and the value to variables identified as $key => $value. The next example shows how the key is assigned to $animal, and the value is assigned to $sound to generate verses of "Old MacDonald":

```
// Old MacDonald
$sounds = array("cow"=>"moo", "dog"=>"woof",
                "pig"=>"oink", "duck"=>"quack");

foreach ($sounds as $animal => $sound)
{
    print "<p>Old MacDonald had a farm EIEIO";
    print "<br>And on that farm he had a {$animal} EIEIO";
    print "<br>With a {$sound}-{$sound} here";
    print "<br>And a {$sound}-{$sound} there";
    print "<br>Here a {$sound}, there a {$sound}";
    print "<br>Everywhere a {$sound}-{$sound}";
    print "<p>Old MacDonald had a farm EIEIO";
}
```

This prints a verse for each $animal/$sound pair in the $sounds array; here are the first two verses:

```
Old MacDonald had a farm EIEIO
And on that farm he had a cow EIEIO
With a moo-moo here
And a moo-moo there
Here a moo, there a moo
Everywhere a moo-moo
Old MacDonald had a farm EIEIO

Old MacDonald had a farm EIEIO
And on that farm he had a dog EIEIO
```

```
With a woof-woof here
And a woof-woof there
Here a woof, there a woof
Everywhere a woof-woof
Old MacDonald had a farm EIEIO
```

When the second form of the foreach statement is used with an array with integer keys, the key is assigned the integer index.

Basic Array Functions

In this section, we introduce selected basic PHP array library functions.

Counting elements in arrays

The *count()* function returns the number of elements in the array *var*:

integer count(mixed var)

Using it, the following example prints 7:

```
$days = array("Mon", "Tue", "Wed", "Thu", "Fri", "Sat", "Sun");

print count($days);  // 7
```

The *count()* function works on any variable type and returns 0 when either an empty array or an unset variable is examined. If you want to be sure that *count()* is called on an array variable, the *is_array()* function should be called first.

The *array_count_values()* function counts the instances of each value in an input array, returning a new associative array of the resultant counts:

array array_count_values(array input)

The following example illustrates how the function works:

```
$pets = array("Beth"=>"Dog", "Arabella"=>"Rabbit", "Meg"=>"Cat",
              "Louise"=>"Chicken", "Ben"=>"Dog", "Neda"=>"Cat");

$petFrequency = array_count_values($pets);

// prints 2
print $petFrequency["Dog"];

// prints:
// Array ( [Dog] => 2 [Rabbit] => 1 [Cat] => 2 [Chicken] => 1 )
print_r($petFrequency);
```

Functions that create arrays

PHP provides two functions that create new arrays with pre-filled values:

array array_fill(integer start, integer count, mixed value)
array range(mixed low, mixed high [, integer step])

The function *array_fill()* returns a new array of *count* elements, their keys starting at index *start*, all set to the same *value*. The function *range()* returns a new array filled with a sequence of elements starting with the value *low* to the value *high*. The optional *step* value—introduced in PHP 5—determines the increments between elements in the new array. The following examples show how these two functions work:

```
// Sets $unity to:
//    Array ( [2] => one [3] => one [4] => one [5] => one [6] => one )
$unity = array_fill(2, 5, "one");

// sets $teens to:
//    Array ( [0] => 13 [1] => 14 [2] => 15 [3] => 16
//            [4] => 17 [5] => 18 [6] => 19 )
$teens = range(13, 19);

// sets $letters to:
//    Array ( [0] => A [1] => B [2] => C [3] => D [4] => E [5] => F )
$letters = range("A", "F");

// This only works in PHP5
// sets $oddNumbers to
//    Array ( [0] => 1 [1] => 3 [2] => 5 [3] => 7 [4] => 9 )
$oddNumbers = range(1, 10, 2);

// This only works in PHP5
// sets $fifthLetters to
//    Array ( [0] => a [1] => f [2] => k [3] => p [4] => u [5] => z )
$fifthLetters = range("a", "z", 5);
```

Exploding and imploding strings

PHP provides the *explode()*, *implode()*, and *join()* functions, which convert strings to arrays and back to strings:

array explode(string separator, string subject [, integer limit])
string implode(string glue, array pieces)
string join(string glue, array pieces)

The *explode()* function returns an array of strings created by breaking the *subject* string at each occurrence of the *separator* string. The optional integer *limit* determines the maximum number of elements in the resulting array; when the *limit* is met, the last element in the array is the remaining unbroken *subject* string. The *implode()* function returns a string created by joining each element in the array *pieces*, inserting the string *glue* between each piece. *join()* is an alias to *implode()* and operates exactly the same way. The following example shows both the *implode()* and *explode()* functions:

```
$words = explode(" ", "Now is the time");

// Prints: Array ( [0] => Now [1] => is [2] => the [3] => time )
print_r($words);

$animalsSeen = array("kangaroo", "wombat", "dingo", "echidna");
```

```
// prints:
// Animals I've seen: kangaroo, wombat, dingo, echidna
print "Animals I've seen: " . implode(", ", $animalsSeen);
```

In the example, *explode()* creates a new array by breaking the phrase "Now is the time" at each space. The resulting elements do not incorporate the separating spaces—they get thrown away. The *implode()* function turns the array into a string; the glue results in a comma-separated animal names. It is common to use the *implode()* function when you want to print the contents of an array in a message.

Later in "Regular Expressions" we describe the functions *split()* and *spliti()* as alternatives to the *explode()*. While these functions use regular expressions to define the separator and allow more complex behavior, the *explode()* function is more efficient and should be used for simple tasks.

Finding the maximum and minimum values in an array

The maximum and minimum values can be found from an array *numbers* with *max()* and *min()*, respectively:

> *number max(array numbers)*
> *number min(array numbers)*

If an array of integers is examined, the returned result is an integer as in the following example:

```
$var = array(10, 5, 37, 42, 1, -56);
print max($var);  // prints 42
print min($var);  // prints -56
```

If an array of floats is examined, *min()* and *max()* return a float.

Both *min()* and *max()* can also be called with a list of integer or float arguments:

> *number max(number arg1, number arg2, number arg3, ...)*
> *number min(number arg1, number arg2, number arg3, ...)*

In this case, they return the maximum or minimum value in the list. Neither *max()* or *min()* complain when they're passed strings or arrays of strings, but the results may not always be as expected and the string functions we discuss later should be used instead.

Finding values in arrays with in_array() and array_search( )

The *in_array()* function returns true if an array *haystack* contains a specific value *needle*:

> *boolean in_array(mixed needle, array haystack [, boolean strict])*

The following example searches the array of integers $smallPrimes for the integer 19:

```
$smallPrimes = array(2, 3, 5, 7, 11, 13, 17, 19, 23, 29);

$var = 19;
```

```
if (in_array($var, $smallPrimes))
    print "{$var} is a small prime number"; // Always printed
```

A third, optional argument can be passed that enforces a strict type check when comparing each element with the *needle*. In the following example, *in_array()* with two parameters would return true as automatic type conversion turns the string into an integer. However, with strict type checking, the string "19 Bridge Rd, Richmond" doesn't match the integer 19 held in the array and so the function returns false:

```
$smallPrimes = array(2, 3, 5, 7, 11, 13, 17, 19, 23, 29);

$var = "19 Bridge Rd, Richmond";

// Strict type checking -- message not printed
if (in_array($var, $smallPrimes, true))
    print "{$var} is a small prime number";

// No type checking -- message is printed
if (in_array($var, $smallPrimes))
    print "{$var} is a small prime number";
```

The *array_search()* function (introduced with PHP 4.0.5) works the same way as the *in_array()* function, except the key of the matching value *needle* is returned rather than the Boolean value true:

> *mixed array_search(mixed needle, array haystack [, boolean strict])*

The following fragment shows how *array_search()* works:

```
$measure = array("inch"=>1, "foot"=>12, "yard"=>36);

// prints "foot"
print array_search(12, $measure);

$units = array("inch", "centimeter", "chain", "furlong");

// prints 2
print array_search("chain", $units);
```

If the value isn't found, *array_search()* returns false. The third, optional parameter *strict* directs *array_search()* to compare both value and type when searching for a match.

A problem can exist when the first element is found, because the return value is 0 and is hard to distinguish from false.

 Care must be taken with functions, such as *array_search()*, that return a result on success, or the Boolean value false to indicate when a result can't be determined. If the return value is used as a Boolean—in an expression or as a Boolean parameter to a function—a valid result may be automatically converted to false. If such a function returns 0, 0.0, an empty string, or an empty array, PHP's automatic type conversion converts the result to false when a Boolean value is required.

The correct way to test the result of functions that return mixed values is to use the is-identical operator ===, as shown in the following example:

```
$units = array("inch", "centimeter", "chain", "furlong");

$index = array_search("inch", $units);

if ($index === false)
    print "Unknown unit: inch";
else
    // OK to use $index
    print "Index = {$index}"; // Prints Index = 0
```

Keys and values

You can check the existence of an element before using it with the *array_key_exists()* function. If there is an element in the *source* array associated with the *key*, then the function returns true:

> *boolean array_key_exists(mixed key, array source)*

The following example searches the array $pets for a particular $owner and either prints the corresponding pet $pets[$owner], or reports that the $owner was not found as a key in the source array:

```
$pets = array("Beth"=>"Dog", "Arabella"=>"Rabbit", "Meg"=>"Cat",
              "Louise"=>"Chicken", "Ben"=>"Dog", "Neda"=>"Cat");

$owner = "Eddie";

if (array_key_exists($owner, $pets))
    print "{$owner} has a {$pets[$owner]} as a pet";
else
{
    print "{$owner} doesn't have a pet.\n";
    print "Pet owners are: " . implode(array_keys($pets), ", ");
}
```

A list of known pet owners is printed by calling the *array_keys()* function and gluing the result together using the *implode()* function discussed earlier in the chapter. The preceding example prints the message:

```
Eddie doesn't have a pet.
Pet owners are: Beth, Arabella, Meg, Louise, Ben, Neda
```

The *array_keys()* function can also be used to find the keys for a particular value:

> *array array_keys(array input [, mixed search_value])*

When the function is called with an optional *search_value*, only keys associated with that value are returned:

```
$pets = array("Beth"=>"Dog", "Arabella"=>"Rabbit", "Meg"=>"Cat",
              "Louise"=>"Chicken", "Ben"=>"Dog", "Neda"=>"Cat");

$dogOwners = array_keys($pets, "Dog");
```

```
// Prints: Array ( [0] => Beth [1] => Ben )
print_r($dogOwners);
```

Sometimes it's useful to consider the values of an associative array without the keys. PHP provides the *array_values()* function that creates a new array with the values from the input array and adds a numeric index:

> *array array_values(array input)*

For example, the $pets array in the following fragment is transformed into a numerically-indexed list of pet types:

```
$pets = array("Beth"=>"Dog", "Arabella"=>"Rabbit", "Meg"=>"Cat",
              "Louise"=>"Chicken", "Ben"=>"Dog", "Neda"=>"Cat");

// Array ( [0] => Dog [1] => Rabbit [2] => Cat [3] => Chicken
//         [4] => Dog [5] => Cat )
$petTypes = array_values($pets);
```

The following fragment generates a list of unique values from the array $pets by passing the array returned by *array_values()* directly into the function *array_unique()*. The *implode()* function is called to create a simple message:

```
$pets = array("Beth"=>"Dog", "Arabella"=>"Rabbit", "Meg"=>"Cat",
              "Louise"=>"Chicken", "Ben"=>"Dog", "Neda"=>"Cat");

$uniquePetTypes = array_unique(array_values($pets));

// Prints
// Pets seen : Dog, Rabbit, Cat, Chicken
print "Pets seen : " . implode(", ", $uniquePetTypes);
```

Joining two or more arrays

Arrays can be merged using the + operator. However, values with the same index or key are overwritten. In contrast, the *array_merge()* function provides a method of appending two or more arrays together without overwriting values:

> *array array_merge(array array1, array array2 [, array ...])*

The behavior of both the + operator and the *array_merge()* function is illustrated in this example:

```
$clothing = array("silk", "satin", "cotton", "rags");
$dwelling = array("house", "tree", "palace");
$cointoss = array("heads", "tails");

$added = $cointoss + $dwelling + $clothing;

// prints:
// Array ( [0] => heads [1] => tails [2] => palace [3] => rags )
print_r($added);

$merged = array_merge($cointoss, $dwelling, $clothing);
```

```
// prints:
// Array ( [0] => heads [1] => tails [2] => house [3] => tree
//         [4] => palace [5] => silk [6] => satin [7] => cotton
//         [8] => rags )
print_r($merged);
```

The result of the array addition in the previous example deserves some explanation:

```
$added = $cointoss + $dwelling + $clothing;
```

PHP calculates the addition from right to left: first the $clothing array is overwritten by the $dwelling array, then the result of that addition is overwritten by the $cointoss array.

Reordering elements with array_reverse( )

The *array_reverse()* function returns a new array by reversing the elements from a *source* array:

> *array array_reverse(array source [, bool preserve_keys])*

The following example shows how to reverse an indexed array of strings:

```
$count = array("zero", "one", "two", "three", "four");
$countdown = array_reverse($count);
```

Setting the optional *preserve_keys* argument to true reverses the order but preserves the association between the index and the elements. For a numerically indexed array, this means that the order of the elements is reversed, but the indexes that access the elements don't change. The following example shows what happens:

```
$count = array("zero", "one", "two", "three", "four");
$countdown = array_reverse($count, true);
print_r($countdown);
```

This prints:

```
Array ( [4] => four [3] => three [2] => two [1] => one [0] => zero )
```

Sorting Arrays

In this section, we show you how to sort arrays. Unlike the *array_reverse()* function discussed in the previous section (which returns a copy of the source array), the sorting functions rearrange the elements of the source array itself—the source array parameter is passed as a reference, not a value. Because of this behavior, the sort functions must be passed a variable and not an expression.

Sorting with sort() and rsort( )

The simplest array-sorting functions are *sort()* and *rsort()*, which rearrange the elements of the *subject* array in ascending and descending order, respectively:

> *sort(array subject [, integer sort_flag])*
> *rsort(array subject [, integer sort_flag])*

Both functions sort the *subject* array based on the values of each element. The following example shows the *sort()* function applied to an array of integers:

```
$numbers = array(24, 19, 3, 16, 56, 8, 171);
sort($numbers);

foreach($numbers as $n)
    print $n ." ";
```

The output of the example prints the elements sorted by value:

```
3 8 16 19 24 56 171
```

The result of the *sort()* function is further illustrated with the output of print_r($numbers):

```
Array
(
    [0] => 3
    [1] => 8
    [2] => 16
    [3] => 19
    [4] => 24
    [5] => 56
    [6] => 171
)
```

The following example shows the *rsort()* function on the same array:

```
$numbers = array(24, 19, 3, 16, 56, 8, 171);
rsort($numbers);
print_r($numbers);
```

The output of the example shows the elements sorted in reverse order by value:

```
Array
(
    [0] => 171
    [1] => 56
    [2] => 24
    [3] => 19
    [4] => 16
    [5] => 8
    [6] => 3
)
```

By default, PHP sorts strings in alphabetical order and numeric values in numeric order. An optional parameter, *sort_flag*, can be passed to force either string or numeric sorting behavior. In the following example, the PHP constant SORT_STRING sorts the numbers as if they were strings:

```
$numbers = array(24, 19, 3, 16, 56, 8, 171);
sort($numbers, SORT_STRING);
print_r($numbers);
```

The output of the example shows the result:

```
Array
(
    [0] => 16
    [1] => 171
    [2] => 19
    [3] => 24
    [4] => 3
    [5] => 56
    [6] => 8
)
```

Many of the array sorting functions accept a *sort_flag* parameter. Other sort flags are SORT_REGULAR to compare items using the default approach and SORT_NUMERIC that forces items to be compared numerically. When an array that contains both strings and numeric values is sorted with the SORT_REGULAR flag, string values are sorted alphabetically and appear first, and numeric values are sorted numerically. Consider the result of sorting the following array $mixed:

```
$mixed= array(24, "dog", 19, 3, 56, 8, 171, "Bruce", "cat", "Nemo");

sort($mixed, SORT_REGULAR);
print_r($mixed);
```

The sorted elements in the $mixed array are printed with *print_r()*:

```
Array
(
    [0] => Bruce
    [1] => Nemo
    [2] => cat
    [3] => dog
    [4] => 3
    [5] => 8
    [6] => 19
    [7] => 24
    [8] => 56
    [9] => 171
)
```

sort() and *rsort()* can be used on associative arrays, but the keys are lost. The resulting array contains only the values in the sorted order. Consider the following example:

```
$map =  array("o"=>"kk", "e"=>"zz", "z"=>"hh", "a"=>"rr");

sort($map);
print_r($map);
```

The *print_r()* output shows the modified array without the key values:

```
Array
(
    [0] => hh
    [1] => kk
    [2] => rr
    [3] => zz
)
```

Sorting associative arrays

It's often desirable to keep the key/value associations when sorting associative arrays. To maintain the key/value association the *asort()* and *arsort()* functions are used:

asort(array subject [, integer sort_flag])
arsort(array subject [, integer sort_flag])

Like *sort()* and *rsort()*, these functions rearrange the elements in the *subject* array from lowest to highest and highest to lowest, respectively. The sort order reflects the element values in the array, not the keys. The following example shows a simple array sorted by *asort()*:

```
$map = array("o"=>"kk", "e"=>"zz", "z"=>"hh", "a"=>"rr");

asort($map);
print_r($map);
```

The *print_r()* function outputs the structure of the sorted array:

```
Array
(
    [z] => hh
    [o] => kk
    [a] => rr
    [e] => zz
)
```

When *asort()* and *arsort()* are used on non-associative arrays, the order of the elements is arranged in sorted order, but the indexes that access the elements don't change. The indexes are treated as association keys in the resulting array. The following example shows what is happening:

```
$numbers = array(24, 19, 3, 16, 56, 8, 171);
asort($numbers);
print_r($numbers);
```

This outputs:

```
Array
(
    [2] => 3
    [5] => 8
    [3] => 16
    [1] => 19
    [0] => 24
    [4] => 56
    [6] => 171
)
```

Sorting on keys

Rather than sort on element values, the *ksort()* and *krsort()* functions rearrange elements in an array by sorting on the keys or the indexes:

```
integer ksort(array subject [, integer sort_flag])
integer krsort(array subject [, integer sort_flag])
```

ksort() sorts the elements in the *subject* array from lowest key to highest key, and *krsort()* sorts in the reverse order. The following example demonstrates the *ksort()* function:

```
$map = array("o"=>"kk", "e"=>"zz", "z"=>"hh", "a"=>"rr");

ksort($map);
print_r($map);
```

The sorted array $map is now:

```
Array
(
    [a] => rr
    [e] => zz
    [o] => kk
    [z] => hh
)
```

Sorting with user-defined element comparison

The sorting functions described so far in this section sort elements in alphabetic or numeric order. To sort elements based on user-defined criteria, PHP provides three functions:

```
usort(array subject, string compare_function)
uasort(array subject, string compare_function)
uksort(array subject, string compare_function)
```

usort() sorts the *subject* array based on the value of each element and applies a new, numeric index, *uasort()* preserves the key/value associations as described earlier for the *asort()* function, and *uksort()* rearranges the elements based on the key of each element. When these functions sort the *subject* array, the user-defined *compare* function is called to determine if one element is greater than, lesser than, or equal to another. The compare function can be written to implement any sort order, but the function must conform to the prototype:

```
integer my_compare_function(mixed a, mixed b)
```

We discuss how to write functions in Chapter 2. Your compare function must take two parameters, *a* and *b*, and return a negative number if *a* is less than *b*, a positive number if *a* is greater than *b*, and 0 if *a* and *b* are equal. The method that the function uses to determine that one value is less than, greater than, or equal to another depends on the requirements of the sorting. The following example shows how *usort()* sorts an array of strings based on the length of each string:

```
// Compare two string values based on the length
function cmp_length($a, $b)
{
```

```
    if (strlen($a) < strlen($b))
        return -1;

    if (strlen($a) > strlen($b))
        return 1;

    // If we've reached this point,
    // string lengths must be equal
    return 0;
}


$animals = array("cow", "ox", "hippopotamus", "platypus");

usort($animals, "cmp_length");

print_r($animals);
```

The array $animals is printed:

```
Array
(
    [0] => ox
    [1] => cow
    [2] => platypus
    [3] => hippopotamus
)
```

In this example, *cmp_length()* is defined as the compare function, but it isn't called directly by the script. The name of the function, "cmp_length", is passed as an argument to *usort()*, and *usort()* uses *cmp_length()* as part of the sorting algorithm. User-defined functions used in this way are referred to as *callback functions*.

Strings

A *string* of characters is probably the most commonly used data type when developing scripts, and PHP provides a large library of string functions to help transform, manipulate, and otherwise manage strings. We introduced the basics of PHP strings in Chapter 2. In this section, we show you many of the useful PHP string functions.

Length of a String

The length property of a string is determined with the *strlen()* function, which returns the number of eight-bit characters in the *subject* string:

   integer strlen(string subject)

We used *strlen()* earlier in the chapter to compare string lengths. Consider another simple example that prints the length of a 16-character string:

```
print strlen("This is a String");  // prints 16
```

Printing and Formatting Strings

In the previous chapter, we presented the basic method for outputting text with echo and print. Earlier in this chapter, we showed you the functions *print_r()* and *var_dump()*, which can determine the contents of variables during debugging. PHP provides several other functions that allow more complex and controlled formatting of strings, and we discuss them in this section.

Creating formatted output with sprintf() and printf( )

Sometimes, more complex output is required than can be produced with echo or print. For example, a floating-point value such as 3.14159 might need to be truncated to 3.14 in the output. For complex formatting, the *sprintf()* or *printf()* functions are useful:

> *string sprintf (string format [, mixed args...])*
> *integer printf (string format [, mixed args...])*

The operation of these functions is modeled on the identical C programming language functions, and both expect a *format* string with optional conversion specifications, followed by variables or values as arguments to match any formatting conversions. The difference between *sprintf()* and *printf()* is that the output of *printf()* goes directly to the output buffer that PHP uses to build a HTTP response, whereas the output of *sprintf()* is returned as a string.

Consider an example *printf()* statement:

```
$variable = 3.14159;

// prints "Result: 3.14"
printf("Result: %.2f\n", $variable);
```

The format string Result: %.2f\n is the first parameter to the *printf()* statement. Strings such as Result: are output the same as with echo or print. The %.2f component is a conversion specification that describes how the value of $variable is to be formatted. Conversion specifications always start with the % character and end with a type specifier; and can include width and precision components in between. The example above includes a precision specification .2 that prints two decimal places.

A specifier %5.3f means that the minimum width of the number before the decimal point should be five (by default, the output is padded on the left with space characters and right-aligned), and three digits should occur after the decimal point (by default, the output on the right of the decimal point is padded on the right with zeros).

Table 3-1 shows all the types supported by *sprintf()* and *printf()*. While width specifiers can be used with all types—we show examples in Example 3-2—decimal precision can only be used with floating point numbers.

Table 3-1. Conversion types used in sprintf() and printf()

Type	Description
%%	A literal percent character
%b	An integer formatted as a binary number
%c	An integer formatted as an ASCII character
%d	An integer formatted as a signed decimal number
%u	An integer formatted as an unsigned decimal number
%o	An integer formatted as an octal number
%x or %X	An integer formatted as a hexadecimal number using lowercase letters or uppercase letters
%f	A float formatted with specified decimal places
%s	A string

Both *sprintf()* and *printf()* allow the formatting of multiple parameters: each conversion specification in the *format* string formatting the corresponding parameter. Example 3-2 illustrates the use of *printf()* and *sprintf()*, including how multiple parameters are formatted.

Example 3-2. Using printf to output formatted data

```
<!DOCTYPE HTML PUBLIC "-//W3C//DTD HTML 4.01 Transitional//EN"
                      "http://www.w3.org/TR/html401/loose.dtd">
<html>
<head>
  <meta http-equiv="Content-Type" content="text/html; charset=iso-8859-1">
  <title>Examples of using printf()</title>
</head>
<body bgcolor="#ffffff">
<h1>Examples of using printf()</h1>
<pre>
<?php
    // Outputs "pi equals 3.14159"
    printf("pi equals %f\n", 3.14159);

    // Outputs "3.14"
    printf("%.2f\n", 3.14159);

    // Outputs "      3.14"
    printf("%10.2f\n", 3.14159);

    // Outputs "3.1415900000"
    printf("%.10f\n", 3.14159);

    // Outputs "halfofthe"
    printf("%.9s\n", "halfofthestring");

    // Outputs "1111011 123 123.000000 test"
    printf("%b %d %f %s\n", 123, 123, 123, "test");
```

Example 3-2. Using printf to output formatted data (continued)

```
    // Outputs "Over 55.71% of statistics are made up."
    printf("Over %.2f%% of statistics are made up.\n", 55.719);

    // sprintf() works just the same except the
    // output is returned as a string
    $c = 245;
    $message = sprintf("%c = %x (Hex) %o (Octal)", $c, $c, $c);

    // prints "õ = f5 (Hex) 365 (Octal)"
    print($message);?>
</pre>
</body>
</html>
```

Padding strings

A simple method to space strings is to use the *str_pad()* function:

> *string str_pad(string input, int length [, string padding [, int pad_type]])*

Characters are added to the input *string* so that the resulting string has *length* characters. The following example shows the simplest form of *str_pad()* that adds spaces to the end of the input string:

```
    // prints "PHP" followed by three spaces
    print str_pad("PHP", 6);
```

An optional string argument *padding* can be supplied that is used instead of the space character. By default, *padding* is added to the end of the string. By setting the optional argument *pad_type* to STR_PAD_LEFT or to STR_PAD_BOTH, the padding is added to the beginning of the string or to both ends. The following example shows how *str_pad()* can create a justified index:

```
    $players =
        array("DUNCAN, king of Scotland"=>"Larry",
              "MALCOLM, son of the king"=>"Curly",
              "MACBETH"=>"Moe",
              "MACDUFF"=>"Rafael");

    print "<pre>";

    // Print a heading
    print str_pad("Dramatis Personae", 50, " ", STR_PAD_BOTH) . "\n";

    // Print an index line for each entry
    foreach($players as $role => $actor)
        print str_pad($role, 30, ".")
            . str_pad($actor, 20, ".", STR_PAD_LEFT)
            . "\n";

    print "</pre>";
```

A foreach loop is used to create a line of the index: the loop assigns the key and value of the $players array to $role and $actor. The example prints:

```
                 Dramatis Personae
DUNCAN, king of Scotland.....................Larry
MALCOLM, son of the king....................Curly
MACBETH.......................................Moe
MACDUFF....................................Rafael
```

We have included the <pre> tags so a web browser doesn't ignore the spaces used to pad out the heading, and that a non-proportional font is used for the text; without the <pre> tags in this example, things don't line up.

Changing case

The following PHP functions return a copy of the *subject* string with changes in the case of the characters:

string strtolower(string subject)
string strtoupper(string subject)
string ucfirst(string subject)
string ucwords(string subject)

The following fragment shows how each operates:

```
print strtolower("PHP and MySQL"); // php and mysql
print strtoupper("PHP and MySQL"); // PHP AND MYSQL
print ucfirst("now is the time");  // Now is the time
print ucwords("now is the time");  // Now Is The Time
```

Trimming whitespace

PHP provides three functions that trim leading or trailing whitespace characters from strings:

string ltrim(string subject [, string character_list])
string rtrim(string subject [, string character_list])
string trim(string subject [, string character_list])

The three functions return a copy of the *subject* string: *trim()* removes both leading and trailing whitespace characters, *ltrim()* removes leading whitespace characters, and *rtrim()* removes trailing whitespace characters. The following example shows the effect of each:

```
$var = trim(" Tiger Land \n");   // "Tiger Land"
$var = ltrim(" Tiger Land \n");  // "Tiger Land \n"
$var = rtrim(" Tiger Land \n");  // " Tiger Land"
```

By default these functions trim space, tab (\t), newline (\n), carriage return (\r), NULL (\x00), and the vertical tab (\x0b) characters. The optional *character_list* parameter allows you to specify the characters to trim. A range of characters can be specified using two periods (..) as shown in the following example:

```
$var = trim("16 MAY 2004", "0..9 ");    // Trims digits and spaces
print $var;                             // prints "MAY"
```

Comparing Strings

PHP provides the string comparison functions *strcmp()* and *strncmp()* that compare two strings in alphabetical order, *str1* and *str2*:

> *integer strcmp(string str1, string str2)*
>
> *integer strncmp(string str1, string str2, integer length)*

While the equality operator == can compare two strings, the result isn't always as expected for strings with binary content or multi-byte encoding: *strcmp()* and *strncmp()* provide binary safe string comparison. Both *strcmp()* and *strncmp()* take two strings as parameters, *str1* and *str2*, and return 0 if the strings are identical, 1 if *str1* is than *str2*, and -1 if *str1* is greater that *str2*. The function *strncmp()* takes a third argument *length* that restricts the comparison to *length* characters. String comparisons are often used as a conditional expression in an if statement like this:

```
$a = "aardvark";
$z = "zebra";

// Test if $a and $z are not different (i.e. the same)
if (!strcmp($a, $z))
    print "a and z are the same";
```

When *strcmp()* compares two different strings, the function returns either -1 or 1 which is treated as true in a conditional expression. These examples show the results of various comparisons:

```
print strcmp("aardvark", "zebra");        // -1
print strcmp("zebra", "aardvark");        //  1
print strcmp("mouse", "mouse");           //  0
print strcmp("mouse", "Mouse");           //  1
print strncmp("aardvark", "aardwolf", 4); //  0
print strncmp("aardvark", "aardwolf", 5); // -1
```

The functions *strcasecmp()* and *strncasecmp()* are case-insensitive versions of *strcmp()* and *strncmp()*. For example:

```
print strcasecmp("mouse", "Mouse");       //  0
```

The functions *strcmp()*, *strncmp()*, *strcasecmp()*, or *strncasecmp()* can be used as the callback function when sorting arrays with *usort()*. See "Sorting Arrays" earlier in this chapter for a discussion on *usort()*.

Finding and Extracting Substrings

PHP provides several simple and efficient functions that can identify and extract specific substrings of a string. As is common with string libraries in other languages, PHP string functions reference characters using an index that starts at zero for the first character, one for the next character and so on.

Extracting a substring from a string

The *substr()* function returns a substring from a *source* string:

> *string substr(string source, integer start [, integer length])*

When called with two arguments, *substr()* returns the characters from the *source* string starting from position *start* (counting from zero) to the end of the string. With the optional *length* argument, a maximum of *length* characters are returned. The following examples show how *substr()* works:

```php
$var = "abcdefgh";

print substr($var, 2);      // "cdefgh"
print substr($var, 2, 3);   // "cde"
print substr($var, 4, 10);  // "efgh"
```

If a negative *start* position is passed as a parameter, the starting point of the returned string is counted from the end of the *source* string. If the *length* is negative, the returned string ends *length* characters from the end of the *source* string. The following examples show how negative indexes can be used:

```php
$var = "abcdefgh";

print substr($var, -1);     // "h"
print substr($var, -3);     // "fgh"
print substr($var, -5, 2);  // "de"
print substr($var, -5, -2); // "def"
```

Finding the position of a substring

The *strpos()* function returns the index of the first occurring substring *needle* in the string *haystack*:

> *integer strpos(string haystack, string needle [, integer offset])*

When called with two arguments, the search for the substring *needle* is from the start of the string *haystack* at position zero. When called with three arguments, the search occurs from the index *offset* into the *haystack*. The following examples show how *strpos()* works:

```php
$var = "To be or not to be";

print strpos($var, "T");    // 0
print strpos($var, "be");   // 3

// Start searching from the 5th character in $var
print strpos($var, "be", 4); // 16
```

The *strrpos()* function returns the index of the last occurrence of the single character *needle* in the string *haystack*:

> *integer strrpos(string haystack, string needle)*

Prior to PHP 5, *strrpos()* uses the first character of needle to search. The following example shows how *strrpos()* works:

```
$var = "and by a sleep to say we end the heart-ache";

// Prints 18 using PHP 4.3 matching the "s" in "say"
// Prints 9 using PHP 5 matching the whole string "sleep"
print strrpos($var, "sleep");

// Prints 22 using PHP 4.3 matching the "w" of "we"
// The function returns false using PHP 5 as "wally"
//    is not found
print strrpos($var, "wally");
```

If the substring *needle* isn't found by *strpos()* or *strrpos()*, both functions return false. The is-identical operator ===, or the is-not-identical operator !== should be used when testing the returned value from these functions. This is because if the substring *needle* is found at the start of the string *haystack*, the index returned is zero and is interpreted as false if used as a Boolean value.

Example 3-3 shows how *strpos()* can be repeatedly called to find parts of a structured sequence like an Internet domain name.

Example 3-3. Using strpos() and substr()

```
<!DOCTYPE HTML PUBLIC "-//W3C//DTD HTML 4.01 Transitional//EN"
                    "http://www.w3.org/TR/html401/loose.dtd">
<html>
<head>
  <meta http-equiv="Content-Type" content="text/html; charset=iso-8859-1">
  <title>Hello, world</title>
</head>
<body bgcolor="#ffffff">
<?php

    $domain = "orbit.mds.rmit.edu.au";

    $a = 0;
    while (($b = strpos($domain, ".", $a)) !== false)
    {
        print substr($domain, $a, $b-$a) . "\n";
        $a = $b + 1;
    }

    // print the piece to the right of the last found "."
    print substr($domain, $a);

?>
</body>
</html>
```

A while loop is used to repeatedly find the period character (.) in the string $domain. The body of the loop is executed if the value returned by *strpos()* is not false—we also assign the return result to $b in the same call. This is possible because an assignment can be used as an expression. In Example 3-3, the value of the assignment

```
($b = strpos($domain, ".", $a))
```

is the same as the value returned from calling *strpos()* alone

```
strpos($domain, ".", $a)
```

Each time *strpos()* is called, we pass the variable $a as the starting point in $domain for the search. For the first call, $a is set to zero and the first period in the string is found. The body of the while loop uses *substr()* to print the characters from $a up to the period character that's been found—the first time through the loop *substr()* prints $b characters from the string $domain starting from position zero. The starting point for the next search is calculated by setting $a to the location of the next character after the period found at position $b. The loop is then repeated if another period is found. When no more period characters are found, the final print statement uses *substr()* to print the remaining characters from the string $domain.

```
// print the piece to the right of the last found "."
print substr($domain, $a);
```

The output of Example 3-3 is:

```
orbit
mds
rmit
edu
au
```

Extracting a found portion of a string

The *strstr()* and *stristr()* functions search for the substring *needle* in the string *haystack* and return the portion of *haystack* from the first occurrence of *needle* to the end of *haystack*:

> *string strstr(string haystack, string needle)*
> *string stristr(string haystack, string needle)*

The *strstr()* search is case-sensitive, and the *stristr()* search isn't. If the *needle* isn't found in the *haystack* string, both *strstr()* and *stristr()* return false. The following examples show how the functions work:

```
$var = "To be or not to be";

print strstr($var, "to");    // "to be"
print stristr($var, "to");   // "To be or not to be"
print stristr($var, "oz");   // false
```

The *strrchr()* function returns the portion of *haystack* by searching for the single character *needle*; however, *strrchr()* returns the portion from the last occurrence of *needle*:

> *string strrchr(string haystack, string needle)*

Unlike *strstr()* and *stristr()*, *strrchr()* searches for a single character, and only the first character of the *needle* string is used. The following examples show how *strrchr()* works:

```
$var = "To be or not to be";

// Prints: "not to be"
print strrchr($var, "n");

// Prints "o be": Only searches for "o" which
// is found at position 14
print strrchr($var, "or");
```

Replacing Characters and Substrings

PHP provides several simple functions that can replace specific substrings or characters in a string with other strings or characters. These functions don't change the input string, instead they return a copy of the input modified by the require changes. In the next section, we discuss regular expressions, which are powerful tools for finding and replacing complex patterns of characters. However, the functions described in this section are faster than regular expressions and usually a better choice for simple tasks.

Replacing substrings

The *substr_replace()* function returns a copy of the *source* string with the characters from the position *start* to the end of the string replaced with the *replace* string:

string substr_replace(string source, string replace, int start [, int length])

If the optional *length* is supplied, only *length* characters are replaced. The following examples show how *substr_replace()* works:

```
$var = "abcdefghij";

// prints "abcDEF";
print substr_replace($var, "DEF", 3);

// prints "abcDEFghij";
print substr_replace($var, "DEF", 3, 3);

// prints "abcDEFdefghij";
print substr_replace($var, "DEF", 3, 0);
```

The last example shows how a string can be inserted by setting the length to zero.

The *str_replace()* function returns a string created by replacing occurrences of the string *search* in *subject* with the string *replace*:

mixed str_replace(mixed search, mixed replace, mixed subject)

In the following example, the *subject* string, "old-age for the old", is printed with both occurrences of old replaced with new:

```
$var = "old-age for the old.";

print str_replace("old", "new", $var);
```

The result is:

```
new-age for the new.
```

Since PHP 4.0.5, *str_replace()* allows an array of search strings and a corresponding array of replacement strings to be passed as parameters. The following example shows how the fields in a very short form letter can be populated:

```
// A short form-letter for an overdue account
$letter = "Dear #title #name, you owe us $#amount.";

// Set-up an array of three search strings that will be
// replaced in the form-letter
$fields = array("#title", "#name", "#amount");

// Set-up an array of debtors. Each element is an array that
// holds the replacement values for the form-letter
$debtors = array(
    array("Mr", "Cartwright", "146.00"),
    array("Ms", "Yates", "1,662.00"),
    array("Dr", "Smith", "84.75"));

foreach($debtors as $debtor)
    print str_replace($fields, $debtor, $letter) . "\n";
```

The $fields array contains a list of strings that are to be replaced. These strings don't need to follow any particular format; we have chosen to prefix each field name with the # character to clearly identify the fields in the letter. The body of the foreach loop calls *str_replace()* to replace the corresponding fields in $letter with the values for each debtor. The output of this script is as follows:

```
Dear Mr Cartwright, you owe us $146.00.
Dear Ms Yates, you owe us $1,662.00.
Dear Dr Smith, you owe us $84.75.
```

If the array of replacement strings is shorter than the array of search strings, the unmatched search strings are replaced with empty strings.

Translating characters and substrings

The *strtr()* function translates characters or substrings in a *subject* string:

string strtr(string subject, string from, string to)
string strtr(string subject, array map)

When called with three arguments, *strtr()* translates the characters in the *subject* string that match those in the *from* string with the corresponding characters in the *to*

---

string. When called with two arguments, you must use an associative array called a *map*. Occurrences of the *map* keys in *subject* are replaced with the corresponding *map* values.

The following example uses *strtr()* to replace all lowercase vowels with the corresponding umlauted character:

```
$mischief = strtr("command.com", "aeiou", "äëïöü");
print $mischief;  // prints cömmänd.cöm
```

When an associative array is passed as a translation map, *strtr()* replaces substrings rather than characters. The following example shows how *strtr()* can expand acronyms:

```
// Create an unintelligible email
$geekMail = "BTW, IMHO (IOW) you're wrong!";

// Short list of acronyms used in e-mail
$glossary = array("BTW"=>"by the way",
                  "IMHO"=>"in my humble opinion",
                  "IOW"=>"in other words",
                  "OTOH"=>"on the other hand");

// Maybe now I can understand
// Prints: by the way, in my humble opinion (in other words) you're wrong!
print strtr($geekMail, $glossary);
```

Regular Expressions

In this section, we show how *regular expressions* can achieve more sophisticated pattern matching to find, extract, and replace complex substrings within a string. While regular expressions provide capabilities beyond those described in the last section, complex pattern matching isn't as efficient as simple string comparisons. The functions described in the previous section are more efficient than those that use regular expressions and should be used if complex pattern searches aren't required.

This section begins with a brief description of the POSIX regular expression syntax. This isn't a complete description of all of the capabilities, but we do provide enough details to create quite powerful regular expressions. The second half of the section describes the functions that use POSIX regular expressions. Examples of regular expressions can also be found in Chapter 9.

Regular Expression Syntax

A regular expression follows a strict syntax to describe patterns of characters. PHP has two sets of functions that use regular expressions: one set supports the Perl Compatible Regular Expression (PCRE) syntax, and the other supports the POSIX extended regular expression syntax. In this book, we use the POSIX functions.

To demonstrate the syntax of regular expressions, we introduce the function *ereg()*:

> *boolean ereg(string pattern, string subject [, array var])*

ereg() returns true if the regular expression *pattern* is found in the *subject* string. We discuss how the *ereg()* function can extract values into the optional array variable *var* later in this section.

The following trivial example shows how *ereg()* is called to find the literal pattern cat in the subject string "raining cats and dogs":

```
// prints "Found 'cat'"
if (ereg("cat", "raining cats and dogs"))
    print "Found 'cat'";
```

The regular expression cat matches the *subject* string, and the fragment prints "Found 'cat'".

Characters and wildcards

To represent any character in a pattern, a period is used as a wildcard. The pattern c.. matches any three-letter string that begins with a lowercase c; for example, cat, cow, cop, and so on. To express a pattern that actually matches a period, use the backslash character \. For example, .com matches both .com and xcom but \.com matches only .com.

The use of the backslash in a regular expression can cause confusion. To include a backslash in a double-quoted string, you need to escape the meaning of the backslash with a backslash. The following example shows how the regular expression pattern "\.com" is represented:

```
// Sets $found to true
$found = ereg("\\.com", "www.ora.com");
```

It's better to avoid the confusion and use single quotes when passing a string as a regular expression:

```
$found = ereg('\.com', "www.ora.com");
```

Character lists

Rather than using a wildcard that matches any character, a list of characters enclosed in brackets can be specified within a pattern. For example, to match a three-character string that starts with a "p", ends with a "p", and contains a vowel as the middle letter, you can use the following expression:

```
ereg("p[aeiou]p", $var)
```

This returns true for any string that contains "pap", "pep", "pip", "pop", or "pup". The character list in the regular expression "p[aeiou]p" matches with exactly one character, so strings like "paep" don't match. A range of characters can also be specified; for example, "[0-9]" specifies the numbers 0 through 9:

```
// Matches "A1", "A2", "A3", "B1", ...
$found = ereg("[ABC][123]", "A1 Quality");  // true

// Matches "00" to "39"
$found = ereg("[0-3][0-9]", "27"); //true
$found = ereg("[0-3][0-9]", "42"); //false
```

A list can specify characters that aren't matches using the not operator ^ as the first
character in the brackets. The pattern "[^123]" matches any character other than 1,
2, or 3. The following examples show regular expressions that make use of the not
operator in lists:

```
// true for "pap", "pbp", "pcp", etc. but not "php"
$found = ereg("p[^h]p", "pap"); //true

// true if $var does not contain alphanumeric characters
$found = ereg("[^0-9a-zA-Z]", "123abc"); // false
```

The ^ character can be used without meaning by placing it in a position other than
the start of the characters enclosed in the brackets. For example, "[0–9^]" matches
the characters 0 to 9 and the ^ character. Similarly, the – character can be matched
by placing it at the start or the end of the list; for example, "[–123]" matches the
characters -, 1, 2, or 3. The characters ^ and – have different meanings outside the [ ]
character lists.

Anchors

A regular expression can specify that a pattern occurs at the start or end of a subject
string using *anchors*. The ^ anchors a pattern to the start, and the $ character anchors
a pattern to the end of a string. (Don't confuse this use of ^ with its completely different use in character lists in the previous section.) For example, the expression:

```
ereg("^php", $var)
```

matches strings that start with "php" but not others. The following code shows the
operation of both:

```
$var = "to be or not to be";

$match = ereg('^to', $var); // true
$match = ereg('be$', $var); // true
$match = ereg('^or', $var); // false
```

The following illustrates the difference between the use of ^ as an anchor and the use
of ^ in a character list:

```
$var = "123467";

// match strings that start with a digit
$match = ereg("^[0-9]", $var); // true

// match strings that contain any character other than a digit
$match = ereg("[^0-9]", $var); // false
```

Both start and end anchors can be used in a single regular expression to match a whole string. The following example illustrates this:

```
// Must match "Yes" exactly
$match = ereg('^Yes$', "Yes");      // true
$match = ereg('^Yes$', "Yes sir"); // false
```

Optional and repeating characters

When a character in a regular expression is followed by a ? operator, the pattern matches zero or one times. In other words, ? marks something that is optional. A character followed by + matches one or more times. And a character followed by * matches zero or more times. Let's look at concrete examples of these powerful operators.

The ? operator allows zero or one occurrence of a character, so the expression:

```
ereg("pe?p", $var)
```

matches either "pep" or "pp", but not the string "peep". The * operator allows zero or many occurrences of the "o" in the expression:

```
ereg("po*p", $var)
```

and matches "pp", "pop", "poop", "pooop", and so on. Finally, the + operator allows one to many occurrences of "b" in the expression:

```
ereg("ab+a", $var)
```

so while strings such as "aba", "abba", and "abbba" match, "aa" doesn't.

The operators ?, *, and + can also be used with a wildcard or a list of characters. The following examples show you how:

```
$var = "www.rmit.edu.au";

// True for strings that start with "www" and end with "au"
$matches = ereg('^www.*au$', $var); // true


$hexString = "x01ff";

// True for strings that start with 'x' followed by at least
// one hexadecimal digit
$matches = ereg('x[0-9a-fA-F]+$', $hexString); // true
```

The first example matches any string that starts with "www" and ends with "au"; the pattern ".*" matches a sequence of any characters, including an empty string. The second example matches any sequence that starts with the character "x" followed by one or more characters from the list [0-9a-fA-F].

A fixed number of occurrences can be specified in braces. For example, the pattern "[0-7]{3}" matches three-character numbers that contain the digits 0 through 7:

```
$valid = ereg("[0-7]{3}", "075"); // true
$valid = ereg("[0-7]{3}", "75");  // false
```

The braces syntax also allows the minimum and maximum occurrences of a pattern to be specified as demonstrated in the following examples:

```
$val = "58273";

// true if $val contains numerals from start to end
// and is between 4 and 6 characters in length
$valid = ereg('^[0-9]{4,6}$', $val); // true

$val = "5827003";
$valid = ereg('^[0-9]{4,6}$', $val); // false

// Without the anchors at the start and end, the
// matching pattern "582768" is found
$val = "582768986456245003";

$valid = ereg("[0-9]{4,6}", $val);    // true
```

Groups

Subpatterns in a regular expression can be grouped by placing parentheses around them. This allows the optional and repeating operators to be applied to groups rather than just a single character. For example, the expression:

```
ereg("(123)+", $var)
```

matches "123", "123123", "123123123", and so on. Grouping characters allows complex patterns to be expressed, as in the following example that matches an alphabetic-only URL:

```
// A simple, incomplete, HTTP URL regular expression
// that doesn't allow numbers
$pattern = '^(http://)?[a-zA-Z]+(\.[a-zA-z]+)+$';

$found = ereg($pattern, "www.ora.com"); // true
```

Figure 3-1 shows the parts of this complex regular expression and how they're interpreted. The regular expression assigned to $pattern includes both the start and end anchors, ^ and $, so the whole *subject* string, "www.ora.com" must match the pattern. The start of the pattern is the optional group of characters "http://", as specified by "(http://)?". This doesn't match any of the subject string in the example but doesn't rule out a match, because the "http://" pattern is optional. Next the "[a-zA-Z]+" pattern specifies one or more alpha characters, and this matches "www" from the *subject* string. The next pattern is the group "(\.[a-zA-z]+)". This pattern must start with a period (the wildcard meaning of . is escaped with the backslash) followed by one or more alphabetic characters. The pattern in this group is followed by the + operator, so the pattern must occur at least once in the subject and can repeat many times. In the example, the first occurrence is ".ora" and the second occurrence is ".com".

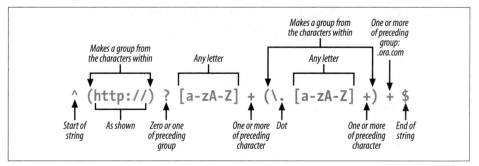

Figure 3-1. Regular expression with groups

Groups can also define subpatterns when *ereg()* extracts values into an array. We discuss the use of *ereg()* to extract values later in this section.

Alternative patterns

Alternatives in a pattern are specified with the | operator; for example, the pattern "cat|bat|rat" matches "cat", "bat", or "rat". The | operator has the lowest precedence of the regular expression operators, treating the largest surrounding expressions as alternative patterns. To match "cat", "bat", or "rat" another way, the following expression can be used:

```
$var = "bat";
$found = ereg("(c|b|r)at", $var);  // true
```

Another example shows alternative endings to a pattern:

```
// match some URL damains
$pattern = '(com$|net$|gov$|edu$)';

$found = ereg($pattern, "http://www.ora.com"); // true
$found = ereg($pattern, "http://www.rmit.edu.au"); // false
```

Escaping special characters

We've already discussed the need to escape the special meaning of characters used as operators in a regular expression. However, when to escape the meaning depends on how the character is used. Escaping the special meaning of a character is done with the backslash character as with the expression "2\+3, which matches the string "2+3". If the + isn't escaped, the pattern matches one or many occurrences of the character 2 followed by the character 3. Another way to write this expression is to express the + in the list of characters as "2[+]3". Because + doesn't have the same meaning in a list, it doesn't need to be escaped in that context. Using character lists in this way can improve readability. The following examples show how escaping is used and avoided:

```
// need to escape '(' and ')'
$phone = "(03) 9429 5555";
$found = ereg("^\([0-9]{2,3}\)", $phone); // true
```

```
// No need to escape (*.+?)| within brackets
$special = "Special Characters are (, ), *, +, ?, |";
$found = ereg("[(*.+?)|]", $special); // true

// The backslash always needs to be quoted
$backSlash = 'The backslash \ character';
$found = ereg('^[a-zA-Z \\]*$', $backSlash); //true

// Don't need to escape the dot within brackets
$domain = "www.ora.com";
$found = ereg("[.]com", $domain); //true
```

Another complication arises due to the fact that a regular expression is passed as a string to the regular expression functions. Strings in PHP can also use the backslash character to escape quotes and to encode tabs, newlines, and so on. Consider the following example, which matches a backslash character:

```
// single-quoted string containing a backslash
$backSlash = '\ backslash';

// Evaluates to true
$found = ereg("^\\\\ backslash", $backSlash);
```

The regular expression looks quite odd: to match a backslash, the regular expression function needs to escape the meaning of backslash, but because we are using a double-quoted string, each of the two backslashes needs to be escaped.

Metacharacters

Metacharacters can also be used in regular expressions. For example, the tab character is represented as \t and the carriage-return character as \n. There are also shortcuts: \d means any digit, and \s means any whitespace. The following example returns true because the tab character, \t, is contained in the $source string:

```
$source = "fast\tfood";

$result = ereg('\s', $source); // true
```

Special metacharacters in the form [:...:] can be used in character lists to match other character classes. For example, the character class specifications [:alnum:] can be used to check for alphanumeric strings:

```
$str = "abc123";

// Evaluates to true
$result = ereg('^[[:alnum:]]+$', $str);

$str = "abc\xf623";

// Evaluates to false because of the \xf6 character
$result = ereg('^[[:alnum:]]+$', $str);
```

Be careful to use special metacharacter specifications only within a character list. Outside this context, the regular expression evaluator treats the sequence as a list specification:

```
$str = "abc123";

// Oops, left out the enclosing [] pair, Evaluates to false
$result = ereg('^[:alnum:]+$', $str);
```

Table 3-2 shows the POSIX character class specifications supported by PHP.

Table 3-2. POSIX character classes

Pattern	Matches
[:alnum:]	Letters and digits
[:alpha:]	Letters
[:blank:]	The Space and Tab characters
[:cntrl:]	Control characters—those with an ASCII code less than 32
[:digit:]	Digits. Equivalent to \d
[:graph:]	Characters represented with a visible character
[:lower:]	Lowercase letters
[:print:]	Characters represented with a visible character, and the space and tab characters
[:space:]	Whitespace characters. Equivalent to \s
[:upper:]	Uppercase letters
[:xdigit:]	Hexadecimal digits

The behavior of these character class specifications depends on your locale settings. By default, the classes are interpreted for the English language, however other interpretations can be achieved by calling *setlocale()* as discussed in Chapter 9.

Regular Expression Functions

PHP has several functions that use POSIX regular expressions to find and extract substrings, replace substrings, and split a string into an array. The functions to perform these tasks come in pairs: a case-sensitive version and a case-insensitive version.

Finding and extracting values

The *ereg()* function, and the case-insensitive version *eregi()*, are defined as:

> *boolean ereg(string pattern, string subject [, array var])*
> *boolean eregi(string pattern, string subject [, array var])*

Both functions return true if the regular expression *pattern* is found in the *subject* string. An optional array variable *var* can be passed as the third argument; it is populated with the portions of *subject* that are matched by up to nine grouped subexpressions in *pattern*. Subexpressions consist of characters enclosed in parentheses. Both functions return false if the *pattern* isn't found in the *subject*.

To extract values from a string into an array, patterns can be arranged in groups contained by parentheses in the regular expression. The following example shows how the year, month, and day components of a date can be extracted into an array:

```
$parts = array();
$value = "2007-04-12";
$pattern = '^([0-9]{4})-([0-9]{2})-([0-9]{2})$';

ereg($pattern, $value, $parts);

// Array ( [0] => 2007-04-12  [1] => 2007  [2] => 04  [3] => 12 )
print_r($parts);
```

The expression:

```
'^([0-9]{4})-([0-9]{2})-([0-9]{2})$'
```

matches dates in the format YYYY-MM-DD. After calling *ereg()*, $parts[0] is assigned the portion of the string that matches the whole regular expression, in this case the whole string 2007-04-12. The portion of the date that matches each group in the expression is assigned to the following array elements: $parts[1] contains the year matched by ([0-9]{4}), $parts[2] contains the month matched by ([0-9]{2}), and $parts[3] contains the day matched by ([0-9]{2}).

Replacing substrings

The following functions create new strings by replacing substrings:

> *string ereg_replace(string pattern, string replacement, string source)*
> *string eregi_replace(string pattern, string replacement, string source)*

They create a new string by replacing substrings of the *source* string that match the regular expression *pattern* with a *replacement* string. These functions are similar to the *str_replace()* function described earlier in "Replacing Characters and Substrings," except that the replaced substrings are identified using a regular expression. Consider the examples:

```
$source = "The quick red fox jumps";

// prints "The quick brown fox jumps"
print ereg_replace("red", "brown", $source);

$source = "The quick brown fox jumps
        over    the    lazy    dog";

// replace all whitespace sequences with a single space
// prints "The quick brown fox jumps over the lazy dog";
print ereg_replace("[[:space:]]+", " ", $source);
```

You can also use include patterns matched by subexpressions in the replacement string. The following example replaces all occurrences of uppercase letters with the matched letter surrounded by <b> and </b> tags:

```
$source = "The quick red fox jumps over the lazy Dog.";

// prints "<b>T</b>he quick brown fox jumps over the lazy <b>D</b>og"
print ereg_replace("([A-Z])", '<b>\1</b>', $source);
```

The grouped subexpression is referenced in the replacement string with the \1 sequence. Multiple subexpressions can be referenced with \2, \3, and so on. The following example uses three subexpressions to rearrange a data from YYYY-MM-DD format to DD/MM/YYYY format:

```
$value = "2004-08-24";
$pattern = '^([0-9]{4})-([0-9]{2})-([0-9]{2})$';

// prints "24/08/2004"
print ereg_replace($pattern, '\3/\2/\1', $value);
```

Splitting a string into an array

The following two functions split strings:

array split(string pattern, string source [, integer limit])
array spliti(string pattern, string source [, integer limit])

They split the *source* string into an array, breaking the string where the matching *pattern* is found. These functions perform a similar task to the *explode()* function described earlier and as with *explode()*, a *limit* can be specified to determine the maximum number of elements in the array.

The following simple example shows how *split()* can break a sentence into an array of "words" by recognizing any sequence of non-alphabetic characters as separators:

```
$sentence = "I wonder why he does\nBuzz, buzz, buzz";
$words = split("[^a-zA-Z]+", $sentence);

print_r($words);
```

The $words array now contains each word as an element:

```
Array
(
    [0] => I
    [1] => wonder
    [2] => why
    [3] => he
    [4] => does
    [5] => Buzz
    [6] => buzz
    [7] => buzz
)
```

When complex patterns aren't needed to break a string into an array, the *explode()* function is a better, faster choice.

Dates and Times

There are several PHP library functions that work with dates and times. Most either generate a Unix timestamp or format a Unix timestamp in a human-readable form. Validation using dates, and working with the flexible PEAR Date package, is discussed in Chapter 9. In this section, we introduce timestamps and PHP library functions that work with Dates and Times.

Generating a Timestamp

A Unix timestamp consists of the number of seconds since the arbitrarily chosen time 1 January 1970 00:00:00 Greenwich Mean Time. Most systems represent a timestamp using a signed 32-bit integer, allowing a range of dates from December 13, 1901 through January 19, 2038. While timestamps are convenient to work with, care must be taken when manipulating timestamps to avoid integer overflow errors. While PHP automatically converts integers that overflow to floats, these values aren't valid timestamps.

 In the Microsoft Windows environment, the timestamp functions don't support negative timestamps and can be used only with dates between January 1, 1970 and January 19, 2038.

Current time

PHP provides several functions that generate a Unix timestamp. The simplest:

integer time()

returns the timestamp for the current date and time, as shown in this fragment:

```
// prints the current timestamp: e.g., 1064699133
print time();
```

Creating timestamps with mktime( ) and gmmktime( )

To create a timestamp for a past or future date in the range December 13, 1901 through January 19, 2038, the *mktime()* and *gmmktime()* functions are defined:

int mktime(int hour, int minute, int second, int month, int day, int year [, int is_dst])
int gmmktime(int hour, int minute, int second, int month, int day, int year [, int is_dst])

Both create a timestamp from the parameters supplied; the parameters supplied to *gmmktime()* represent a GMT date and time, while the parameters supplied to *mktime()* represent the local time. This example creates a timestamp for 9:30 A.M. on June 18, 1998:

```
$aDate = mktime(9, 30, 0, 6, 18, 1998);
```

Both functions correctly handle parameter values that you might consider out-of-range. For example, the following call passes 14 for the month value, 29 for the day, and 2004 for the year, creating a time stamp for 1 March 2005:

```
// Creates a time stamp for 1 March 2005
$aDate = mktime(0, 0, 0, 14, 29, 2004);
```

Setting the month to 14 and the year to 2004 overflows to February in 2005 and setting the day to 29 overflows to the first of March. This characteristic allows scripts to add a quantum of time without range checking. The following example shows how 30 days can be added to a date and time:

```
$paymentPeriod = 30;  // Days

// generates a timestamp for 26 June 2002 by
// adding 30 days to 27 May 2002
$paymentDue = mktime(0, 0, 0, 5, 27 + $paymentPeriod, 2002);

// A different approach adds the appropriate number
// of seconds to the timestamp for 27 May 2002
$paymentDue = mktime(0, 0, 0, 5, 27, 2002)
                + ($paymentPeriod * 24 * 3600);
```

If the components of a date are outside the range of dates the function is defined for, -1 is returned. Both functions allow the supplied date to be interpreted as daylight savings time by setting the flag *is_dst* to 1.

The order of the arguments to these functions is unusual and easily confused. While the *mktime()* and *gmmktime()* functions are similar to the Unix *mktime()* function, the arguments aren't in the same order.

String to timestamp

The *strtotime()* function generates a timestamp by parsing a human-readable date and time (between December 13, 1901 and January 19, 2038) from the string *time*:

integer strtotime(string time)

The function interprets several standard representations of a date, as shown here:

```
// Absolute dates and times
$var = strtotime("25 December 2002");
$var = strtotime("14/5/1955");
$var = strtotime("Fri, 7 Sep 2001 10:28:07 -1000");

// The current time: equivalent to time()
$var = strtotime("now");
```

```
// Relative to now
print strtotime("+1 day"); // tomorrow
print strtotime("-2 weeks"); // two weeks ago
print strtotime("+2 hours 2 seconds"); // in two hours and two seconds
```

Care should be taken when using *strtotime()* with user-supplied dates. It's better to limit the use of *strtotime()* to cases when the string to be parsed is under the control of the script. For example, it's used here to check a minimum age using a relative date:

```
// date of birth: timestamp for 16 August, 1982
$dob = mktime(0, 0, 0, 8, 16, 1982);

// Now check that the individual is over 18
if ($dob < strtotime("-18 years"))
    print "Legal to drive in the state of Victoria"; // prints
```

Subsecond times

A Unix timestamp represents a date and time accurate to the second, but many applications require times to be represented to the subsecond. PHP provides the function:

string microtime()

The *microtime()* function returns a string that contains both a Unix timestamp in seconds and a microsecond component. The returned string begins with the microsecond component, followed by the integer timestamp:

```
// prints the time now in the format "microsec sec"
// Example: 0.55512200 1064700291
print microtime();
```

One common use of the function *microtime()* is to generate an integer seed for a random-number generator:

```
// Generate a seed.
$seed = (float)microtime() * 1000000;

// prints (for example) 555206
print $seed;
```

Because the microsecond component appears at the start of the string returned from *microtime()*, the returned value can be converted to a float with the (float) cast operator. Multiplying the float result by 1,000,000 ensures that you create a suitably varying integer.

The following fragment shows how you can use both the microsecond and second components to create a floating point representation of the time:

```
$parts = explode(" ", microtime());
$f = (float)$parts[0] + (int)$parts[1];

// prints (for example) 1064700291.56
print $f;
```

Formatting a Date

While the Unix timestamp is useful in a program, it isn't a convenient display format. The *date()* and *gmdate()* functions return a human-readable formatted date and time:

> *string date(string format [, integer timestamp])*
> *string gmdate(string format [, integer timestamp])*

The format of the returned string is determined by the *format* argument. Passing in the optional *timestamp* argument can format a predetermined date. Otherwise, both functions format the current time. The format string uses the formatting characters listed in Table 3-3 to display various components or characteristics of the timestamp. To include characters without having the function interpret them as formatting characters, escape them with a preceding backslash character. The following examples show various combinations:

```
// Set up a timestamp for 08:15am 24 Aug 1974
$var = mktime(8, 15, 25, 8, 24, 1974);

// "24/08/1974"
print date('d/m/Y', $var);

// "08/24/74"
print date('m/d/y', $var);

// prints "Born on Saturday 24th of August"
print date('\B\o\r\n \o\n l jS \of F', $var);
```

Table 3-3. Formatting characters used by the date() function

Formatting character	Meaning
a, A	"am" or "pm"; "AM" or "PM"
S	Two-character English ordinal suffix: "st", "nd", "rd", "th"
d, j	Day of the month: with leading zeros e.g., "01"; without e.g., "1"
D, l	Day of the week: abbreviated e.g., "Mon"; in full e.g., "Monday"
M, F	Month: abbreviated e.g., "Jan"; in full e.g., "January"
m, n	Month as decimal: with leading zeros: "01"–"12"; without: "1"–"12"
h, g	Hour 12-hour format: with leading zeros e.g., "09"; without e.g., "9"
H, G	Hour 24-hour format: with leading zeros e.g., "01"; without e.g., "1"
i	Minutes:"00" to "59"
s	Seconds: "00" to "59"
Y, y	Year: with century e.g., "2004"; without century e.g., "04"
r	RFC-2822 formatted date: e.g., "Tue, 29 Jan 2002 09:15:33 +1000" (added in PHP 4.0.4)
w	Day of the week as number: "0" (Sunday) to "6" (Saturday)

Table 3-3. Formatting characters used by the date() function (continued)

Formatting character	Meaning
t	Days in the month: "28" to "31"
z	Days in the year: "0" to "365"
B	Swatch Internet time
L	Leap year: "0" for normal year; "1" for leap year
I	Daylight savings time: "0" for standard time; "1" for daylight savings
O	Difference to Greenwich Mean Time in hours: "+0200"
T	Time zone setting of this machine
Z	Time zone offset in seconds: "-43200" to "43200"
U	Seconds since the epoch: 00:00:00 1/1/1970

PHP also provides the equivalent functions:

> *string strftime(string format [, integer timestamp])*
> *string gmstrftime(string format [, integer timestamp])*

The *format* string uses the same % sequence formatting character sequences as the C library function *strftime()*. For example:

```
// Prints "24/08/1974 08:15:25"
print strftime("%d/%m/%Y %H:%M:%S", mktime(8, 15, 25, 8, 24, 1974));

// Prints "08/24/1974"
print strftime("%D", mktime(8, 15, 25, 8, 24, 1974));
```

The result of some % sequences used by *strftime()* and *gmstrftime()* depends on the locale settings. The following sets the locale so the printed date used the Estonian language and conventions:

```
setlocale (LC_TIME, 'es');

// prints "laupäev 24 august 1974"
print strftime ("%A %d %B %Y", mktime(8, 15, 25, 8, 24, 1974));
```

Formatting sequences supported by *strftime()* and *gmstrftime()* are shown in Table 3-4. Some of these % sequences are not supported under Windows as noted.

Table 3-4. Formatting characters used by the strftime() and gmstrftme() functions

Formatting sequence	Meaning
%a, %A	Day of the week dependant on locale settings: abbreviated e.g., "Mon"; in full e.g., "Monday".
%b, %B	Month: abbreviated e.g., "Jan"; in full e.g., "January"
%c, %x, %X	Default Date and Time format for the local settings: with time e.g., "01/27/04 22:06:03"; without time e.g., "01/27/04"; without the date e.g., "06:03"
%C	Century e.g., "04" for 2004 (does not work with Windows)
%d	Day of month padded with leading zero e.g., "01"

Table 3-4. Formatting characters used by the strftime() and gmstrftme() functions (continued)

Formatting sequence	Meaning
%D	Same as "%m/%d/%y" (does not work with Windows)
%e	Day of month padded with leading space e.g., "1" (does not work with Windows)
%H, %I	Hour: 24-hour format with leading zero e.g., "15"; 12-hour format with leading zero e.g., "03"
%j	Day of the year: "001" to "366"
%m	Month with leading zero e.g., "01"
%M	Minute with leading zero e.g., "01"
%p	"AM" or "PM". Value dependant on locale settings
%r	Time in am/pm notation (does not work with Windows)
%R	Time in 24 hour notation (does not work with Windows)
%S	Seconds with leading zero
%T	Same as "%H:%M:%S" (does not work with Windows)
%u, %w	Day of the week as a decimal: 1-7 with "1" = Monday, "2" = Tuesday, etc..; 0-6 with "0" = Sunday, "1" = Monday, etc.. %u (does not work with Windows)
%U	Week number in a year where the first week starts with the first Sunday in the year
%V	Week number in a year where the first week is the week, with at least four days, starting on a Monday, in the current year. This is the ISO 8601:1988 definition of the week number (does not work with Windows)
%W	Week number in a year where the first week starts with the first Monday in the year
%y, %Y	Year: without the century e.g., "04" for 2004; with the century e.g., "2004"
%Z	Time zone information e.g., "AUS Eastern Standard Time"
%%	Literal % character

Validating a Date

The function *checkdate()* returns true if a given *month*, *day*, and *year* form a valid Gregorian date:

> *boolean checkdate(integer month, integer day, integer year)*

This function isn't based on a timestamp and so can accept any dates in the years 1 to 32767. It automatically accounts for leap years.

```
// Works for a wide range of dates
$valid = checkdate(1, 1, 1066); // true
$valid = checkdate(1, 1, 2929); // true

// Correctly identify bad dates
$valid = checkdate(13, 1, 1996); // false
$valid = checkdate(4, 31, 2001); // false
```

```
// Correctly handles leap years
$valid = checkdate(2, 29, 1996); // true
$valid = checkdate(2, 29, 2001); // false
```

Integers and Floats

As we discussed in Chapter 2, PHP supports both integer and floating-point numbers. PHP stores integers as a 32-bit signed word, providing a range of integers from -2147483647 to +2147483647. PHP automatically converts numbers that *overflow* out of this range to floats. You can see this behavior by adding one to the largest integer value:

```
// Largest positive integer (for a 32 bit signed integer)
$variable =  2147483647;

// prints int(2147483647)
var_dump($variable);

$variable++;

// prints float(2147483648)
var_dump($variable);
```

Floating-point numbers can store a wide range of values, both very large and very small, by storing a mantissa and an exponent. However a floating-point number can't precisely represent all numbers—for example, the fraction 2/3—and some precision can be lost.

Integers can be represented in a decimal, hexadecimal, or octal notation:

```
$var = 42;       // a positive integer
$var = -186;     // a negative integer
$var = 0654;     // 428 expressed as an octal number
$var = 0xf7;     // 247 expressed as a hexadecimal number
```

Floating-point numbers can represented in a decimal or exponential notation:

```
$var = 42.0;     // a positive float
$var = -186.123; // a negative float
$var = 1.2e65;   // a very big number
$var = 10e-75;   // a very small number
```

Apart from the basic operators +, -, /, *, and %, PHP provides the usual array of mathematical library functions. In this section, we present some of the library functions that are used with integer and float numbers.

Absolute Value

The absolute value of an integer or a float can be found with the *abs()* function:

integer abs(integer number)
float abs(float number)

The following examples show the result of *abs()* on integers and floats:

```
print abs(-1);         // prints 1
print abs(1);          // prints 1
print abs(-145.89);    // prints 145.89
print abs(145.89);     // prints 145.89
```

Ceiling and Floor

The *ceil()* and *floor()* functions return the integer value above and below a fractional *value*, respectively:

float ceil(float value)
float floor(float value)

The return type is a float because an integer may not be able to represent the result when a large value is passed as an argument. Consider the following examples:

```
print ceil(27.3);   // prints 28
print floor(27.3);  // prints 27
```

Rounding

The *round()* function uses 4/5 rounding rules to round up or down a *value* to a given *precision*:

float round(float value [, integer precision])

By default, rounding is to zero decimal places, but the precision can be specified with the optional *precision* argument. The 4/5 rounding rules determine if a number is rounded up or down based on the digits that are lost due to the rounding *precision*. For example, 10.4 rounds down to 10, and 10.5 rounds up to 11. Specifying a negative precision rounds a value to a magnitude greater than zero, for example a precision of -3 rounds a value to the nearest thousand. The following examples show rounding at various precisions:

```
print round(10.4);          // prints 10
print round(10.5);          // prints 11
print round(2.40964, 3);    // prints 2.410
print round(567234.56, -3); // prints 567000
print round(567234.56, -4); // prints 570000
```

Number Systems

PHP provides the following functions that convert numbers between integer decimal and the commonly used number systems, binary, octal, and hexadecimal:

string decbin(integer number)
integer bindec (string binarystring)
string dechex(integer number)
integer hexdec(string hexstring)

string decoct(integer number)
integer octdec(string octalstring)

The decimal numbers are always treated as integers, and the numbers in the other systems are treated as strings. Here are some examples:

```
print decbin(45);        // prints "101101"
print bindec("1001011"); // prints 75
print dechex(45);        // prints "2D"
print hexdec("5a7b");    // prints 23163
print decoct(45);        // prints "55"
print octdec("777");     // prints 511
```

It is possible to represent binary, octal, and hexadecimal numbers that are bigger than can be held in a 32-bit integer. The results of such conversions automatically overflow to a float value. For example:

```
// $a is an integer assigned the largest possible value
$a = hexdec("7fffffff");

// $a is a float
$a = hexdec("80000000");
```

Basic Trigonometry Functions

PHP supports the basic set of trigonometry functions listed in Table 3-5.

Table 3-5. Trigonometry functions supported by PHP

Function	Description
`float sin(float arg)`	Sine of *arg* in radians
`float cos(float arg)`	Cosine of *arg* in radians
`float tan(float arg)`	Tangent of *arg* in radians
`float asin(float arg)`	Arc sine of *arg* in radians
`float acos(float arg)`	Arc cosine of *arg* in radians
`float atan(float arg)`	Arc tangent of *arg* in radians
`float atan2(float y, float x)`	Arc tangent of *x/y* where the sign of both arguments determines the quadrant of the result
`float pi( )`	Returns the value 3.1415926535898
`float deg2rad(float arg)`	Converts *arg* degrees to radians
`float rad2deg(float arg)`	Converts *arg* radians to degrees

Powers and Logs

The PHP mathematical library includes the exponential and logarithmic functions listed in Table 3-6.

Table 3-6. Exponential and logarithmic functions

Function	Description
float exp(float arg)	e to the power of *arg*
float pow(float base, number exp)	Exponential expression *base* to the power of *exp*
float sqrt(float arg)	Square root of *arg*
float log(float arg [, float base])	Natural logarithm of *arg*, unless a base is specified, in which case the function returns log(arg)/ log(base)
float log10(float arg)	Base-10 logarithm of *arg*

Testing Number Results

Many of the functions described in this section can return values that are undefined, or are too big or small to hold in a floating point number. PHP provides three functions that can be used to test numeric results before they cause problems later in a script:

boolean is_nan(float val)
boolean is_infinite(float val)
boolean is_finite(float val)

The function *is_nan()* tests the expression *val* and returns true if *val* is not a number. For example, the square root of a negative number is not a real number. *is_finite()* returns true if the number *val* can be represented as a valid float, and *is_infinite()* returns true if *val* can't. Here are some examples:

```
// square root of a negative number
$a = -1;
$result = sqrt($a);

print $result;    // prints -1.#IND

// Test if not a number
if (is_nan($result))
    print "Result not defined"; // prints
else
    print "Square root of {$a} = {$result}";
```

Random Number Generation

PHP provides the function *rand()*, which returns values from a generated sequence of *pseudo-random* numbers. The sequence generated by *rand()* is pseudo random because the algorithm used appears to have random behavior but isn't truly random. The function *rand()* can be called in one of two ways:

integer rand()
integer rand(integer min, integer max)

When called with no arguments, *rand()* returns a random number between 0 and the value returned by *getrandmax()*. When *rand()* is called with two arguments, the *min* and *max* values, the returned number is a random number between *min* and *max*. Consider an example:

```
// Generate some random numbers
print rand();        // between 0 and getmaxrand()
print rand(1, 6);  // between 1 and 6 (inclusive)
```

Prior to PHP 4.2.0, you needed to seed the random number generator with a call to *srand()* before the first use of *rand()*, otherwise the function returns the same numbers each time a script is called. Since 4.2.0, the call to *srand()* is not required, however you can reliably reproduce a random sequence by calling *srand()* with the same argument at the start of the script. The following example reliably prints the same sequence of numbers each time it is called:

```
srand(123456);

// Prints six random numbers
for ($i=0; $i<6; $i++)
    print rand() . "    ";
```

CHAPTER 4

Introduction to Object-Oriented Programming with PHP 5

Object-oriented programming is a several-decades-old concept that has spread to almost every aspect of modern programming languages and practices. The reason is clear as soon as you start to use a convenience such as the powerful PHP-related packages. We introduce PEAR packages in Chapter 7; many operate by defining objects, providing a wealth of useful features in a simple form. You should understand the basics of object-oriented programming in order to make use of packages and an error-recovery feature called exceptions. You may also find object-oriented programming a useful practice in your own code. We'll give you an introduction in this chapter, and present some advanced features in Chapter 14.

While many of the concepts and techniques presented in this chapter work in PHP 4, support is greatly enhanced in PHP 5. In this chapter we describe what you can and can't do in each version of PHP.

Classes and Objects

The basic idea of object-oriented programming is to bind data and functions in convenient containers called *objects*. For instance, in Chapter 7 we'll show you how to standardize the look of your own web pages through an object called a template. Your PHP code can refer to this object through a variable; we'll assume here you've decided to call the variable $template. All the complex implementation of templates is hidden: you just load in the proper package and issue a PHP statement such as:

```
$template = new HTML_Template_IT("./templates");
```

As the statement suggests, you've just created a new object. The object is called $template and is built by the *HTML_Template_IT* package—a package whose code you don't need to know anything about. Once you have a template object, you can access the functionality provided by the *HTML_Template_IT* package.

After various manipulations of the $template object, you can insert the results into your web page through the PHP statement:

```
$template->show();
```

The syntax of this statement is worth examining. As the parentheses indicate, *show()* is a function. However the -> operator associates *show()* with the object variable $template. When the function *show()* is called, it uses the data that is held by the $template object to calculate a result: put another way, *show()* is called *on* the $template object.

The functions that you can call depend on the support provided by the package—the *show()* function is provided by the *HTML_Template_IT* package and can be called on *HTML_Template_IT* objects such as $template. In traditional object-oriented parlance, *show()* is called a *method* or *member function* of the *HTML_Template_IT* object.

HTML_Template_IT is called a *class* because you can use it to create many similar template objects. Each time you issue a new statement you are said to create an *instance* of the class. Thus, the $template object is an instance of the *HTML_Template_IT* class.

We've shown how to use objects created by other packages. However, to understand objects better, it's time to define a class of our own. Example 4-1 shows a simple class invented for the purposes of this chapter that's called *UnitCounter*. The *UnitCounter* class provides two trivial features: we can use a *UnitCounter* object to keep a count of things, and to calculate the total weight of the things we have counted. Later in this chapter, and in Chapter 14 we use the *UnitCounter* class, together with other classes, to develop a simple freight-cost calculator.

Example 4-1 shows how the class *UnitCounter* is defined using the class keyword. The *UnitCounter* class defines two *member variables* $units and $weightPerUnit, and two functions *add()* and *totalWeight()*. Collectively, the variables and the functions are *members* of the class *UnitCounter*.

Example 4-1. Definition of the user-defined class UnitCounter

```php
<?php

// Definition of the class UnitCounter
//
class UnitCounter
{
    // Member variables
    var $units = 0;
    var $weightPerUnit = 1.0;


    // Add $n to the total number of units, default $n to 1
    function add($n = 1)
    {
        $this->units = $this->units + $n;
    }

    // Member function that calculates the total weight
```

Example 4-1. Definition of the user-defined class UnitCounter (continued)

```
    function totalWeight( )
    {
        return $this->units * $this->weightPerUnit;
    }
}

?>
```

The class definition defines how data and functionality are actually bound together—member variables and functions take their meaning from the class of which they're a part. The class definition shown in Example 4-1 does not actually run any code or produce any output. Instead a class definition creates a new data type that can be used in a PHP script. In practice, you might save the class definition in an include file, and include that file into any script that makes use of the class.

To use the member variables and functions defined in a class, an *instance* of the class or *object* needs to be created. Like other data types such as integers, strings, or arrays, objects can be assigned to variables. However, unlike other types, objects are created using the new operator. An object of class *UnitCounter* can be created and assigned to a variable as follows:

```
    // Create a new UnitCounter object
    $bottles = new UnitCounter;
```

Unlike variable names, class names in PHP are not case sensitive. While we start all our class names with an uppercase letter, *UnitCounter*, *unitcounter*, and *UNITCOUNTER* all refer to the same class.

Once a new *UnitCounter* object is created and assigned to the $bottles variable, the member variables and functions can be used. Members of the object, both variables and functions, are accessed using the -> operator. The $units member variable can be accessed as $bottles->units and used like any other variable:

```
    // set the counter to 2 dozen bottles
    $bottles->units = 24;

    // prints "There are 24 units"
    print "There are {$bottles->units} units";
```

To include the value of an object's member variables in a double-quoted string literal, the braces syntax is used. String literals and the braces syntax are discussed in Chapter 2.

The *add( )* member function can be called to operate on the $bottles variable by calling *$bottles->add( )*. The following fragment increases the value of $bottles->units by 3:

```
    // Add three bottles
    $bottles->add(3);
```

```
// prints "There are 27 units"
print "There are {$bottles->units} units";
```

Many objects of the same class can be created. For example, you can use the following fragment to create two *UnitCounter* objects and assign them to two variables:

```
// Create two UnitCounter objects
$books = new UnitCounter;
$cds = new UnitCounter;

// Add some units
$books->add(7);
$cds->add(10);

// prints "7 books and 10 CDs"
print "{$books->units} books and {$cds->units} CDs";
```

Both the $books and $cd variables reference *UnitCounter* objects, but each object is independent of the other.

Member Variables

Member variables are available in PHP4 and PHP5.

Member variables are declared as part of a class definition using the var keyword. Member variables can also be defined with the private and protected keywords as we describe later in the chapter. Member variables hold the data that is stored in an object.

The initial value assigned to a member variable can be defined in the class definition. The *UnitCounter* class defined in Example 4-1 sets initial values for both member variables:

```
var $units = 0;
var $weightPerUnit = 1.0;
```

The var keyword is required to indicate that $units and $weightPerUnit are class member variables. When a new *UnitCounter* object is created, the initial values of $units and $weightPerUnit are set to 0 and 1.0 respectively. If a default value is not provided in the class definition, then the member variable is not set to any value.

You don't have to explicitly declare member variables as we have in Example 4-1. However, we recommend that you always declare them and set an initial value because it makes the initial state of the variables obvious to users of your code.

Member Functions

Member functions are available in PHP4 and PHP5.

Member functions are defined as part of the class definition—the *UnitCounter* class defined in Example 4-1 includes two member functions *add()* and *totalWeight()*.

Both these functions access the member variables of the object with the special variable $this. The variable $this is special because PHP uses it as a placeholder until a real object is created. When a member function is run, the value of $this is substituted with the actual object that the function is called on. Consider the implementation of the *add()* member function of *UnitCounter* from Example 4-1:

```
// Add $n to the total number of units, default $n to 1 if
// no parameters are passed to add( )
function add($n = 1)
{
    $this->units = $this->units + $n;
}
```

The function adds the value of the parameter $n to the member variable $this->units. If no parameter is passed, $n defaults to 1. When the *add()* function is called on the $bottles object in the following example,

```
// Create a new UnitCounter object
$bottles = new UnitCounter;

// Call the add( ) function
$bottles->add(3);
```

the placeholder $this in the *add()* function acts as the object $bottles.

The *totalWeight()* member function also accesses member variables with the $this placeholder: the function returns the total weight by multiplying the value of the member variables $this->units and $this->weightPerUnit.

```
// Create a new UnitCounter object
$bricks = new UnitCounter;

$bricks->add(15);

// Prints 15 - 15 units at 1 Kg each
print $bricks->totalWeight( );
```

PHP5 allows the result of a member function to be included into a string literal using the braces syntax. The following fragment shows how, and shows an alternative that can be used with PHP4:

```
// This line only works for PHP5
print "total weight = {$bottles->totalWeight( )} kg";

// This works for both PHP4 and PHP5
print "total weight = " . $bottles->totalWeight( ) . " kg";
```

Using include Files for Class Definitions

By placing the definition in Example 4-1 into a file—for example *UnitCounter.inc*—you can include or require the *UnitCounter* class in other scripts. Example 4-2 uses the require directive to include the *UnitCounter* class definition.

Example 4-2. Using the UnitCounter class

```
<!DOCTYPE HTML PUBLIC "-//W3C//DTD HTML 4.01 Transitional//EN"
                      "http://www.w3.org/TR/html401/loose.dtd">
<html>
<head>
  <meta http-equiv="Content-Type" content="text/html; charset=iso-8859-1">
  <title>Using UnitCounter</title>
</head>
<body>
<?php
    require "UnitCounter.inc";

    // Create a new UnitCounter object
    $bottles = new UnitCounter;

    // set the counter to 2 dozen bottles
    $bottles->units = 24;

    // Add a single bottle
    $bottles->add( );

    // Add three more
    $bottles->add(3);

    // Show the total units and weight
    print "There are {$bottles->units} units, ";
    print "total weight = " . $bottles->totalWeight( ) . " kg";

    // Change the default weight per unit and show the new total weight
    $bottles-> weightPerUnit = 1.2;
    print "<br>Correct total weight = " . $bottles->totalWeight( ) . " kg";

?>
</body>
</html>
```

We introduce the include and require directives in Chapter 2, and further examples are given in Chapter 6 and Chapter 16 where we develop practical libraries for our case study, *Hugh and Dave's Online Wines*.

Constructors

Two different methods of defining constructors are available in PHP5, and one method is available in PHP4.

As discussed previously, when an object is created from the *UnitCounter* class defined in Example 4-1, PHP will initialize the member variables $units and $weightPerUnit to 0 and 1.0 respectively. If you needed to set the weight per unit to another value, you can set the value directly after creating the object. For example:

```
    // Create a new UnitCounter object
    $bottles = new UnitCounter;
```

```
// Set the true weight of a bottle
$bottles->weightPerUnit = 1.2;
```

However, a better solution is to define a *constructor function* that correctly sets up the initial state of a new object before it is used. If a constructor is defined, you don't have to do anything in your code because PHP automatically calls it when a new object is created.

PHP5 allows you to declare a constructor method by including the member function *_construct()* in the class definition—the function name *_construct()* is reserved for this purpose (the characters preceding the word *construct* are two consecutive underscores). Example 4-3 shows a modified *UnitCounter* class with a constructor that automatically sets the weight per unit.

Example 4-3. Defining a constructor for the class UnitCounter

```php
<?php

class UnitCounter
{
    var $units;
    var $weightPerUnit;

    function add($n = 1)
    {
        $this->units = $this->units + $n;
    }

    function totalWeight()
    {
        return $this->units * $this->weightPerUnit;
    }

    // Constructor function that initializes the member variables
    function __construct($unitWeight = 1.0)
    {
        $this->weightPerUnit = $unitWeight;
        $this->units = 0;
    }
}

?>
```

The class definition works the same as the definition shown in Example 4-1. However, the initial values for $units and $weightPerUnit are no longer defined with the variable declaration instead they are set in the *_construct()* member function. A new *UnitCounter* object that uses the class defined in Example 4-3 is created as follows:

```
// Create a UnitCounter where each unit is 1.2 kg -- the
// weight of a full wine bottle.
$bottles = new UnitCounter(1.2);
```

When the object is created, PHP automatically calls the __construct()_ with the parameters supplied after the class name. So, in this example, 1.2 is passed as a value to the __construct()_ method and the $bottles->weightPerUnit variable is set to 1.2. _UnitCounter_ objects can still be created without passing a value to the constructor as the parameter variable $unitWeight defaults to 1.0.

You can also define a constructor method by including a function with the same name as the class. This is the only way constructors can be defined in PHP 4, but it can also be used as an alternative in PHP5. For example, using this technique, the __construct()_ function in Example 4-3 could be replaced with:

```
function UnitCounter($weightPerUnit = 1)
{
    $this->weightPerUnit = $weightPerUnit;
    $this->units = 0;
}
```

Using the __construct()_ function makes managing large projects easier, because it allows classes to be moved, renamed, and reused in a class hierarchy without changing the internals of the class definition. We discuss class hierarchies in Chapter 14.

Destructors

Destructors are available in PHP5.

If it exists, a constructor function is called when an object is created. Similarly, if it exists, a _destructor function_ is called when an object is destroyed. Like other PHP variables, objects are destroyed when they go out of scope or when explicitly destroyed with a call to the _unset()_ function. We discuss variable scope in Chapter 2.

A destructor function is defined by including the function __destruct()_ in the class definition (again, the prefix before the keyword _destruct_ is two consecutive underscore characters, and __destruct()_ is a reserved function name). __destruct()_ can't be defined to take any parameters (unlike the __construct()_ function). However, the __destruct()_ function does have access to the member variables of the object that is being destroyed—PHP calls __destruct()_ just before the member variables are destroyed.

Destructor functions are useful when you want to perform some housekeeping tasks when a process has ended. For example, you might want to gracefully close down a connection to a DBMS or save user preferences to a file. Destructors can also be used as a debugging tool when developing object-oriented applications. For example, by adding the following __destruct()_ function to the _UnitCounter_ defined in Example 4-3, you can track when objects are destroyed:

```
// Destructor function called just before a UnitCounter object
// is destroyed
function __destruct()
{
```

```
        print "UnitCounter out of scope. Units: {$this->units}";
    }
```

We give another example of __*destruct()* later in the chapter in "Static Member Variables."

Private Members Variables

Private member variables are available in PHP5.

When using the *UnitCounter* class defined previously in Example 4-3, a script can use the member variables $units and $weightPerUnit directly, the *UnitCounter* class doesn't implement any safeguards that prevent inconsistent values being assigned. For example, consider the following fragment that erroneously sets the number of units to a fractional value and the weight per unit to a negative number:

```
// Construct a new UnitCounter object
$b = new UnitCounter;

// Set some values
$b->units = 7.3;
$b->weightPerUnit = -5.5;

$b->add(10);

// Show the total units and weight
print "There are {$b->units} units, ";
print "total weight = {$b->totalWeight()} kg";
```

This prints:

```
There are 7.3 units, total weight = -40.15 kg
```

In PHP5, a better solution is to define member variables as *private* and provide member functions that control how the variables are used. Example 4-4 shows both the $units and $weightPerUnit member variables defined as private.

Example 4-4. Private member variables

```
<?php
class UnitCounter
{
    private $units = 0;
    private $weightPerUnit = 1.0;

    function numberOfUnits()
    {
        return $this->units;
    }

    function add($n = 1)
    {
        if (is_int($n) && $n > 0)
            $this->units = $this->units + $n;
```

Example 4-4. Private member variables (continued)

```
    }

    function totalWeight( )
    {
        return $this->units * $this->weightPerUnit;
    }

    function __construct($unitWeight)
    {
        $this->weightPerUnit = abs((float)$unitWeight);
        $this->units = 0;
    }
}
?>
```

When a *UnitCounter* object is created using the class defined in Example 4-4, the $units and $weightPerUnit member variables can only be accessed by code defined in the class. Attempts to access the private member variables cause an error:

```
// Construct a UnitCounter object as defined in Example 4-4
$b = new UnitCounter(1.1);

// These lines cause an error
$b->units = 7.3;
$b->weightPerUnit = -5.5;
```

The member function *numberOfUnits()* provides access to the value of $units, and the member function *add()* has been improved so only positive integers can be added to the count value. We have also improved the *__construct()* function to ensure that $weightPerUnit is only set with a positive value.

Providing member functions that control how member variables are used is good object-oriented practice. However, without making member variables private, there is little point in providing such safeguards, because users can directly access and modify the member variable values.

Private Member Functions

Private member functions are available in PHP5.

Member functions can also be defined as private to hide the implementation of a class. This allows the implementation of a class to be modified, or replaced without any effect on the scripts that use the class. Example 4-5 demonstrates how the class *FreightCalculator* hides the internal methods used by the publicly-accessible member function *totalFreight()*. The method calculates a freight cost using two private functions *perCaseTotal()* and *perKgTotal()*.

Example 4-5. Private member functions

```php
class FreightCalculator
{
    private $numberOfCases;
    private $totalWeight;

    function totalFreight()
    {
        return $this->perCaseTotal() + $this->perKgTotal();
    }

    private function perCaseTotal()
    {
        return $this->numberOfCases * 1.00;
    }

    private function perKgTotal()
    {
        return $this->totalWeight * 0.10;
    }

    function __construct($numberOfCases, $totalWeight)
    {
        $this->numberOfCases = $numberOfCases;
        $this->totalWeight = $totalWeight;
    }
}
```

Like private member variables, private functions can only be accessed from within the class that defines them. The following example causes an error:

```php
// Construct a FreightCalculator object as defined in Example 4-5
$f = new FreightCalculator(10, 150);

// These lines cause an error
print $f->perCaseTotal();
print $f->perKgTotal();

// This is OK -- prints "25"
print $f->totalFreight();
```

Static Member Variables

Static member variables are available in PHP5.

PHP allows member variables and functions to be declared as *static* using the static keyword. As we have shown in our examples so far, normal member variables are independent from object to object. In contrast, static member variables are shared across all instances of a class. This allows you to share values between several instances of a class without declaring a global variable that's accessible throughout your application.

Example 4-6 defines the class *Donation* that records a donor name and donation amount in the private member variables $name and $amount. The class keeps track of the total amount donated, and the total number of donations using two static variables $totalDonated and $numberOfDonors. The values of these two variables are accessible to all instances of the class, and each instance can update and read the values. Static member variables are accessed using a *class reference* rather than the -> operator. In Example 4-6, the static variables $totalDonated and $numberOfDonors are prefixed by the class reference Donation:: when they are used.

Example 4-6. Static member variables

```php
<?php
class Donation
{
    private $name;
    private $amount;

    static $totalDonated = 0;
    static $numberOfDonors = 0;

    function info( )
    {
        $share = 100 * $this->amount / Donation::$totalDonated;
        return "{$this->name} donated {$this->amount} ({$share}%)";
    }

    function __construct($nameOfDonor, $donation)
    {
        $this->name = $nameOfDonor;
        $this->amount = $donation;

        Donation::$totalDonated = Donation::$totalDonated + $donation;
        Donation::$numberOfDonors++;
    }

    function __destruct( )
    {
        Donation::$totalDonated = Donation::$totalDonated - $donation;
        Donation::$numberOfDonors--;
    }

}
?>
<!DOCTYPE HTML PUBLIC "-//W3C//DTD HTML 4.01 Transitional//EN"
                    "http://www.w3.org/TR/html401/loose.dtd">
<html>
<head>
  <meta http-equiv="Content-Type" content="text/html; charset=iso-8859-1">
  <title>Using Donation</title>
</head>
<body>
<pre>
```

Example 4-6. Static member variables (continued)

```php
<?php
    $donors = array(
        new Donation("Nicholas", 85.00),
        new Donation("Matt", 50.00),
        new Donation("Emily", 90.00),
        new Donation("Sally", 65.00));

    foreach ($donors as $donor)
        print $donor->info() . "\n";

    $total = Donation::$totalDonated;
    $count = Donation::$numberOfDonors;
    print "Total Donations  = {$total}\n";
    print "Number of Donors = {$count}\n";

?>
</pre>
</body>
</html>
```

The static variables $totalDonated and $numberOfDonors are updated in the __construct() function: the $donation amount is added to the value of $totalDonated, and $numberOfDonors is incremented. We have also provided a __destruct() function that decreases the value of $totalDonated and $numberOfDonors when a *Donation* object is destroyed.

After the class *Donation* is defined, Example 4-6 creates an array of donation objects, then prints the total donated and the total number of donations:

```php
$total = Donation::$totalDonated;
$count = Donation::$numberOfDonors;
print "Total Donations  = {$total}\n";
print "Number of Donors = {$count}\n";
```

The previous fragment demonstrates that static variables can be accessed from outside the class definition with the Donation:: class reference prefix. You don't access static member variable with the -> operator (which is used with instances of a class) because they are not associated with any particular object.

A foreach loop is used to print information about each donation by calling the member function *info()* for each *Donation* object. The *info()* member function returns a string that contains the donor name, amount, and the percentage of the total that the donor has contributed. The percentage is calculated by dividing the value stored for the instance in $this->amount by the static total value Donation::$totalDonated.

The output of Example 4-6 is as follows:

```
Nicholas donated 85 (29.3103448276%)
Matt donated 50 (17.2413793103%)
Emily donated 90 (31.0344827586%)
Sally donated 65 (22.4137931034%)
```

```
Total Donations  = 290
Number of Donors = 4
```

Unlike other member variables, you don't need to create an object to use static member variables. As long as the script has access to the class definition, static variables are available using the class reference as shown in the following fragment:

```
// provide access to the Donation class definition
require "example.4-6.php";

// Now set the static total
Donation::$totalDonated = 124;
Donation::$numberOfDonors = 5;
```

Static Member Functions

Static member functions are available in PHP5.

Static member functions are declared using the static keyword, and like static member variables, aren't accessed via objects but operate for the whole class and are accessed using a class reference. We can modify Example 4-6 to provide access to the static member variables using static member functions:

```
private static $totalDonated = 0;
private static $numberOfDonors = 0;

static function total()
{
    return Donation::$totalDonated;
}

static function numberOfDonors()
{
    return Donation::$numberOfDonors;
}
```

Code that uses the modified *Donation* class can then access the $totalDonated and $numberOfDonors values by calling the static functions *Donation::total()* and *Donation::numberOfDonors()* respectively.

Static functions can only operate on static member variables and can't operate on objects, and therefore the function body can't refer to the placeholder variable $this.

Like static member variables, you can access static functions without actually creating an object instance. Indeed we could have implemented the static member variables defined in Example 4-6, and the static member functions *total()* and *numberOfDonors()* described earlier using global variables and normal user-defined functions. Defining member variables and functions as static provides a way of grouping related functionality together in class definitions, promoting a modular approach to code development.

Cloning Objects

Objects can optionally be cloned in PHP5, and are always cloned in PHP4. We explain how this works in this section.

Cloning in PHP5

When a new object is created, PHP5 returns a reference to the object rather than the object itself. A variable assigned with an object is actually a reference to the object. This is a significant change from PHP4 where objects are assigned directly to variables. Copying an object variable in PHP5 simply creates a second reference to the same object. This behavior can be seen in the following fragment of code that creates a new *UnitCounter* object, as defined earlier in Example 4-1:

```
// Create a UnitCounter object
$a = new UnitCounter();

$a->add(5);
$b = $a;
$b->add(5);

// prints "Number of units = 10";
print "Number of units = {$a->units}";
```

The _ _*clone()* method is available if you want to create an independent copy of an object. PHP5 provides a default _ _*clone()* function that creates a new, identical object by copying each member variable. Consider the following fragment:

```
// Create a UnitCounter object
$a = new UnitCounter();

$a->add(5);
$b = $a->_ _clone();
$b->add(5);

// prints "Number of units = 5"
print "Number of units = {$a->units}";

// prints "Number of units = 10"
print "Number of units = {$b->units}";
```

The code creates an object $a, and adds five units to it using $a->add(5) to give a total of 5 units in object $a. Then, $a is cloned and the result is assigned to a new object $b. Five units are then added to the new object $b, to give a total of 10 units in $b. Printing out the number of units for the original object $a outputs 5, and printing the number of units for $b outputs 10.

You can control how an object is copied by including a custom _ _*clone()* function in a class definition. If you wanted cloned *UnitCounter* objects to maintain the $weightPerUnit value, but to reset the $units value to zero, you can include the following function in the class definition:

```
function __clone()
{
    $this->weightPerUnit = $that->weightPerUnit;
    $this->units = 0;
}
```

The original, source object is referred to in the *__clone()* function using the special place-holder variable $that, and the variable $this is used to reference the new, cloned object.

Cloning in PHP4

Rather than use references by default, new objects created with PHP4 can be assigned directly to variables. When an object variable is copied, PHP4 automatically clones the object. For example, consider the following PHP4 fragment:

```
// Create a UnitCounter object
$a = new UnitCounter();

$a->add(5);
$b = $a;
$b->add(5);

// prints "Number of units = 5"
print "Number of units = {$a->units}";

// prints "Number of units = 10"
print "Number of units = {$b->units}";
```

The variable $b is a clone or copy of $a, and so modifying $b does not affect $a.

If you don't want to clone an object, use the reference assignment =& to copy a reference. The following shows how $b is assigned as a reference to *UnitCounter* object assigned to $a:

```
// Create a UnitCounter object
$a = new UnitCounter();

$a->add(5);
$b =& $a;
$b->add(5);

// prints "Number of units = 10"
print "Number of units = {$a->units}";

// prints "Number of units = 10"
print "Number of units = {$b->units}";
```

We discuss variable references and the reference assignment operator =& in Chapter 2.

Inheritance

Inheritance is available in PHP4 and PHP5.

One of the powerful concepts in object-oriented programming is inheritance. *Inheritance* allows a new class to be defined by extending the capabilities of an existing *base class* or *parent class*. PHP allows a new class to be created by extending an existing class with the extends keyword.

Example 4-7 shows how the *UnitCounter* class from Example 4-4 is extended to create the new class *CaseCounter*. The aim of the extended class is to track the number of cases or boxes that are needed to hold the units accumulated by the counter. For example, if bottles of wines are the units, then a case might hold 12 bottles.

Example 4-7. Defining the CaseCounter class by extending UnitCounter

```php
<?php

// Access to the UnitCounter class definition
require "example.4-1.php";

class CaseCounter extends UnitCounter
{
    var $unitsPerCase;

    function addCase( )
    {
        $this->add($this->unitsPerCase);
    }

    function caseCount( )
    {
        return ceil($this->units/$this->unitsPerCase);
    }

    function CaseCounter($caseCapacity)
    {
        $this->unitsPerCase = $caseCapacity;
    }
}

?>
```

Before we discuss the implementation of the *CaseCounter*, we should examine the relationship with the *UnitCounter* class. Figure 4-1 illustrates this relationship in a simple *class diagram*. There are several different notations for representing class diagrams; we show the inheritance relationship by joining two classes with an annotated line with a solid arrowhead.

The new *CaseCounter* class provides features related to counting cases worth of units—for example, bottles of wine—while the *UnitCounter* base class provides the

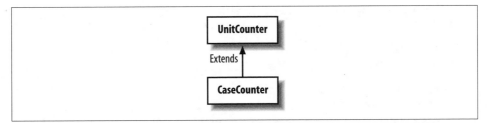

Figure 4-1. Class diagram showing UnitCounter and CaseCounter

counting and total weight capabilities. To create a *CaseCounter* object, the number of units that are stored in a case needs to be specified. This value is passed to the constructor when new *CaseCounter* object is created,

```
// Create a CaseCounter that holds 12 bottles in a case
$order = new CaseCounter(12);
```

the value is then recorded in the member variable $unitsPerCase.

The *addCase()* member function uses the $unitsPerCase member variable to add a case of units to the counter:

```
function addCase( )
{
  // The add( ) function is defined in the
  // base class UnitCounter
  $this->add($this->unitsPerCase);
}
```

The units are added by calling the base *UnitCounter* member function *add()*. Unless they are declared as private, member variables and functions defined in the base class can be called in derived classes using the -> operator and the special placeholder variable $this.

The *caseCount()* member function calculates the number of cases needed to contain the total number of units. For example, if there are 50 bottles of wine, and a case can hold 12 bottles, then 5 cases are needed to hold the wine. The number of cases is therefore calculated by dividing the total number of units—stored in the member variable $unit defined in the *UnitCounter* class—by the member variable $unitsPerCase. The result of the division is rounded up to the next whole case with the *ceil()* function. The *ceil()* function is described in Chapter 3.

When a new *CaseCounter* object is created and used, all of the publicly accessible member variables and functions of the base class are also available. This means that you can use a *CaseCounter* object as if it were a *UnitCounter* but it also has the extra features of the *CaseCounter* class. Consider an example:

```
// Create a CaseCounter that holds 12 bottles in a case
$order = new CaseCounter(12);

// Add seven bottles using the UnitCounter defined function
$order->add(7);
```

```
// Add a case using the CaseCounter defined function
$order->addCase( );

// Print the total number of Units : 19
print $order->units;

// Print the number of cases: 2
print $order->caseCount( );
```

Unlike some other object-oriented languages, PHP only allows a single base class to be specified when defining new classes. Allowing inheritance from multiple base classes can lead to unnecessarily complex code and, in practice, isn't very useful. In Chapter 14, we explore advanced techniques that eliminate the need for multiple inheritance.

Calling Parent Constructors

The ability to call parent constructors is available in PHP5.

CaseCounter objects use three member variables: two are defined in the *UnitCounter* class, and the third is defined in *CaseCounter*. When a *CaseCounter* object is created, PHP calls the _ _construct( ) function defined in *CaseCounter* and sets the value of the member variable $unitsPerCase with the value passed as a parameter. In the following fragment, the value passed to the _ _construct( ) function is 12:

```
// Create a CaseCounter that holds 12 bottles in a case
$order = new CaseCounter(12);
```

PHP only calls the _ _construct( ) function defined in *CaseCounter*; the constructor of the parent class *UnitCounter* is not automatically called. Therefore, objects created from the *CaseCounter* class defined in Example 4-7 always have the weight defined as 1 kg, the value that's set in the member variable of the parent class. The *CaseCounter* class shown in Example 4-8 solves this problem by defining a _ _construct( ) function that calls the *UnitCounter* _ _construct( ) function using the parent:: reference.

Example 4-8. Calling parent constructor function

```
<?php

// Access to the UnitCounter class definition
include "example.4-4.php";

class CaseCounter extends UnitCounter
{
    private $unitsPerCase;

    function addCase( )
    {
        $this->add($this->unitsPerCase);
    }
```

Example 4-8. Calling parent constructor function (continued)

```
    function caseCount( )
    {
        return ceil($this->numberOfUnits( )/$this->unitsPerCase);
    }

    function __construct($caseCapacity, $unitWeight)
    {
        parent::__construct($unitWeight);
        $this->unitsPerCase = $caseCapacity;
    }
}

?>
```

As Example 4-8 is written to use features provided by PHP5, we extend the more sophisticated *UnitCounter* class defined in Example 4-4. Also, the member variable $unitsPerCase is now defined to be private and we use the PHP5 __construct() function. The constructor function of the improved *CaseCounter* shown in Example 4-8 takes a second parameter, $unitWeight which is passed to the __construct() function defined in the *UnitCounter* class.

Redefined Functions

Both PHP4 and PHP5 allow functions to be redefined, and the parent:: and class reference operators are available in PHP5.

Functions defined in a base class can be redefined in a *descendant* class. When objects of the descendant class are created, the redefined functions take precedence over those defined in the base class. We have already seen the __construct() function of the base *UnitCounter* class redefined in the *CaseCounter* class in Example 4-8.

Consider the *Shape* and *Polygon* classes defined in the following code fragment:

```
    class Shape
    {
        function info( )
        {
            return "Shape.";
        }
    }

    class Polygon extends Shape
    {
        function info( )
        {
            return "Polygon.";
        }
    }
```

The class *Shape* is the base class to *Polygon*, making *Polygon* a descendant of *Shape*. Both classes define the function *info()*. So, following the rule of redefined functions, when an object of class *Polygon* is created, the *info()* function defined in the *Polygon* class takes precedence. This is shown in the following example:

```
$a = new Shape;
$b = new Polygon;

// prints "Shape."
print $a->info( );

// prints "Polygon."
print $b->info( );
```

With PHP 5, we can use the parent:: reference to access the *info()* function from the parent class. For example, we can modify the *Polygon* class definition of *info()* as follows:

```
class Polygon extends Shape
{
    function info( )
    {
        return parent::info( ) . "Polygon.";
    }
}

$b = new Polygon;

// prints "Shape.Polygon."
print $b->info( );
```

This approach can be used in descendant classes, proving a way of accumulating the result of ancestor functionality. Consider a *Triangle* class that extends the *Polygon* class:

```
class Triangle extends Polygon
{
    function info( )
    {
        return parent::info( ) . "Triangle.";
    }
}

$t = new Triangle;

// prints "Shape.Polygon.Triangle."
print $t->info( );
```

The parent:: reference operator only allows access to the immediate parent class. PHP allows access to any known ancestor class using a *class reference* operator—we introduced the class reference earlier in our discussion of static member variables and functions in "Classes and Objects." We can rewrite the *Triangle* class to call the ancestor version of the *info()* functions directly:

```
class Triangle extends Polygon
{
    function info()
    {
        return Shape::info() . Polygon::info() . "Triangle.";
    }
}

$t = new Triangle;

// prints "Shape.Polygon.Triangle."
print $t->info();
```

Using the class access operators makes code less portable. For example, you would need to modify the implementation of the *Triangle* class if you decided that *Triangle* would extend *Shape* directly. Using the parent:: reference operator allows you to rearrange class hierarchies more easily.

Protected Member Variables and Functions

Protected members are available in PHP5.

Member variables and functions can be defined using the protected keyword. This offers a compromise between being public and private: it allows access to member variables and functions defined in a class from within descendant classes, but it prevents access to the member variables and functions from code outside of the class hierarchy. So, for example, a child class can access a parent class's protected functions, but the parent class protected functions can't be accessed from an unrelated class or from within a script that uses the class.

In Example 4-5, we introduced the *FreightCalculator* class to work out freight costs based on the number of cases and the total weight of a shipment. The *FreightCalculator* class defined in Example 4-5 calculates the per case and per kilogram costs using the two private functions *perCaseTotal()* and *perKgTotal()*.

In Example 4-9, we rewrite the *FreightCalculator* class to define these functions as *protected*. This allows a new class *AirFreightCalculator* to extend *FreightCalculator* and redefine the functions to apply different rates per kilogram and case count.

Example 4-9. An air freight calculator

```
class FreightCalculator
{

    protected $numberOfCases;
    protected $totalWeight;

    function totalFreight()
    {
        return $this->perCaseTotal() + $this->perKgTotal();
    }
}
```

Example 4-9. An air freight calculator (continued)

```
    protected function perCaseTotal( )
    {
        return $this->numberOfCases * 1.00;
    }

    protected function perKgTotal( )
    {
        return $this->totalWeight * 0.10;
    }

    function __construct($numberOfCases, $totalWeight)
    {
        $this->numberOfCases = $numberOfCases;
        $this->totalWeight = $totalWeight;
    }
}


class AirFreightCalculator extends FreightCalculator
{

    protected function perCaseTotal( )
    {
        // $15 + $1 per case
        return 15 + $this->numberOfCases * 1.00;
    }

    protected function perKgTotal( )
    {
        // $0.40 per kilogram
        return $this->totalWeight * 0.40;
    }
}
```

Because the *AirFreightCalculator* implementation of *perCaseTotal()* and *perKgTotal()* requires access to the *FreightCalculator* member variables $totalWeight and $numberOfCases, these have also been declared as protected.

Final Functions

Declaring final functions is available in PHP5.

The *AirFreightCalculator* class defined in Example 4-9 doesn't redefine the *totalFreight()* member function because the definition in *FreightCalculator* correctly calculates the total. Descendant classes can be prevented from redefining member functions in base classes by declaring them as *final*. Declaring the *totalFreight()* member function with the final keyword prevents accidental redefinition in a descendant class:

```
    final function totalFreight( )
    {
```

```
        return $this->perCaseTotal() + $this->perKgTotal();
}
```

Throwing and Catching Exceptions

PHP 5 has introduced an exception model that allows objects to be *thrown* and *caught* using the throw and try...catch statements.

The throw and try...catch statements provide a way of jumping to error handling code in exceptional circumstances: rather than terminating a script with a fatal error, exceptions are *thrown*, and can be *caught* and processed. The throw statement is always used in conjunction with the try...catch statement, and the following fragment shows the basic structure:

```
$total = 100;
$n = 5;

$result;

try
{
    // Check the value of $n before we use it
    if ($n == 0)
        throw new Exception("Can't set n to zero.");

    // Calculate an average
    $result = $total / $n;
}
catch (Exception $x)
{
    print "There was an error: {$x->getMessage()};
}
```

The block of statements contained in the braces that follow the try keyword are executed normally as part of the script; the braces are required, even for a single statement. If a throw statement is called in the try block, then the statements contained in the braces that follow the catch keyword are executed. The throw statement *throws* an object and the catch block of code *catches* the thrown object, assigning it to the variable specified.

The catch statement specifies the type of object that is caught by placing the class name before the variable: the following fragment catches *Exception* objects and assigns them to the variable $x:

```
catch (Exception $x)
{
    print "There was an error: {$x->getMessage()};
}
```

Specifying the type of object that is caught in the catch block is an example of a *class type hint*. We discuss *class type hints* in Chapter 14.

The Exception Class

While objects of any class can be thrown, PHP5 predefines the *Exception* class that has useful features suitable for exception reporting.

Exception objects are constructed with a message and an optional integer error code. The message and error code are retrieved using the *getMessage()* and *getCode()* member functions. The line number and filename of the script that creates an *Exception* object is also recorded and retrieved with the *getLine()* and *getFile()* member functions. These functions are used in Example 4-10 to define the *formatException()* function that returns a simple error message for a given *Exception* object $e.

Example 4-10. Simple try-catch

```php
<?php

function formatException(Exception $e)
{
    return "Error {$e->getCode()}: {$e->getMessage()}
        (line: {$e->getline()} of {$e->getfile()})";
}


function average($total, $n)
{
    if ($n == 0)
        throw new Exception("Number of items = 0", 1001);

    return $total / $n;
}


// Script that uses the average() function
try
{
    $a = average(100, 0);
    print "Average = {$a}";
}
catch (Exception $error)
{
    print formatException($error);
}

?>
```

Example 4-10 shows how a try...catch statement is used to catch exceptions thrown by the function *average()*. The *Exception* object is created—with a message and error code—and thrown from the *average()* function if the value of $n is zero. Example 4-10 calls the *average()* function inside a try block. If *average()* throws an exception, it is caught by the catch block and the *formatException()* function is called to format the caught *Exception* object $error. When Example 4-10 is run the call to *average()* causes an *Exception* object to be thrown, and the following is output:

```
Error 1001: Number of items = 0
        (line: 13 of c:\htdocs\book\example.4-10.php)
```

If you called the *average()* as shown in Example 4-10 without a try...catch statement, any exceptions thrown wouldn't be caught and PHP 5 terminates the script with a fatal "Uncaught exception" error.

The throw and try...catch statements provide an alterative to calling the PHP *exit()* or *die()* functions that terminate a script. Using throw and try...catch statements allow you to develop applications that can handle exceptional circumstances in a controlled manner. However, exceptions are quite different from the errors and warnings that PHP generates when things go wrong. Unfortunately, a try...catch statement can't be used to catch fatal errors such as divide by zero. (You can suppress errors with the @ operator; we explain how in Chapter 6.) In Example 4-10, the code that implements the *average()* function tests the value of $n before using it in a division to avoid the fatal "Divide by Zero" error.

We discuss the management of PHP errors and warnings in Chapter 12.

CHAPTER 5

SQL and MySQL

In this chapter, we introduce the SQL database query language and the MySQL™*
database management system. Using our case study *winestore* database as a worked
example, we show you how to use SQL to define, manipulate, and query databases.
At the end of this chapter, you'll have the database skills to build a database tier for
your web database applications.

In this chapter, we cover the following topics:

- A short introduction to relational databases
- A quick start guide to the example *winestore* database and its entity-relationship
  model
- The MySQL command interpreter and the basic features of MySQL
- Using SQL to create and drop databases and tables
- Using SQL to insert, delete, and update data
- Querying with SQL, illustrated through examples and a case study

We assume that you have already installed MySQL and loaded the sample *winestore*
database. If not, the guides in Appendixes A through C will help you.

The techniques that we discuss are used to interact with MySQL after a database has
been designed and expressed as SQL statements. An introduction to relational modeling and design can be found in Appendix E. Managing and using the MySQL database server, and more advanced SQL features, are discussed in Chapter 15.
Chapter 8 covers issues that arise when multiple users are writing to web databases.

---

* MySQL is a trademark of MySQL AB.

Database Basics

The field of databases has its own terminology. Terms such as database, table, attribute, row, primary key, and relational model have specific meanings and are used throughout this chapter. In this section, we present an example of a simple database to introduce the basic components of relational databases, and we list and define selected terms used in the chapter. We then show you our *winestore* database that we use throughout our examples in this chapter, and as the basis of our sample application in Chapters 16 through 20. More detail on the database can be found in Appendix E.

Introducing Relational Databases

A simple example relational database is shown in Figure 5-1. This database stores data about wineries and the wine regions they are located in. A relational database is organized into *tables*, and there are two tables in this example: a *winery* table that stores information about wineries, and a *region* table that has information about wine regions. Tables collect together information that is about one object.

Winery Table

Winery ID	Winery name	Address	Region ID
1	Moss Brothers	Smith Rd.	3
2	Hardy Brothers	Jones St.	1
3	Penfolds	Arthurton Rd.	1
4	Lindemans	Smith Ave.	2
5	Orlando	Jones St.	1

Region Table

Region ID	Region name	State
1	Barossa Valley	South Australia
2	Yarra Valley	Victoria
3	Margaret River	Western Australia

Figure 5-1. An example relational database containing two related tables

Databases are managed by a *database management system* (DBMS) or *database server*. A database server supports a database language to create and delete databases and to manage and search data. The database language used by almost all database servers is *SQL*, a set of statements that define and manipulate data. After creating a database, the most common SQL statements used are INSERT, UPDATE, DELETE, and SELECT, which add, change, remove, and search data in a database, respectively.

In this book, we use the MySQL database server to manage databases. MySQL runs as a server (daemon) process or service, like Apache or IIS, and supports several different clients including a command-line interpreter (that we use in this chapter) and a PHP function library (that we use throughout later chapters). One MySQL server can manage multiple databases for you for multiple applications, and each can store different data organized in different ways.

A database table may have multiple *attributes*, each of which has a name. For example, the *winery* table in Figure 5-1 has four attributes, winery ID, winery name, address, and region ID. A table contains the data as *rows*, and a row contains values for each attribute that together represent one related object. (Attributes are also known as *fields* or *columns*, while rows are also known as *records*. We use attribute and row throughout this book.)

Consider an example. The *winery* table has five rows, one for each winery, and each row has a value for each attribute. For example, in the first winery row, the attribute winery ID has a value of 1, the winery name attribute has a value of Moss Brothers, the attribute address has a value of Smith Rd., and the region ID attribute has a value of 3. There is a row for region 3 in the *region* table and it corresponds to Margaret River in Western Australia. Together this data forms the information about an object, the Moss Brothers Winery in Western Australia.

In our example, the relationship between wineries and regions is maintained by assigning a region ID to each winery row. The region ID value for each region is unique, and this allows you to unambiguously discover which region each winery is located in. Managing relationships using unique values is fundamental to relational databases. Indeed, good database design requires that you can make the right choice of which objects are represented as tables and which relationships exist between the tables. We discuss good database design in Appendix E.

In our example of the relationship between wineries and regions, there's a one-to-many mapping between regions and wineries: more than one winery can be situated in a region (three wineries in the example are situated in the Barossa Valley) but a winery can be situated in only one region. It's also possible to have two other types of relationship between tables: a one-to-one relationship where, for example, each bottle of wine has one label design, and a many-to-many relationship where, for example, many wines are delivered by many couriers. As we show you later, unique values or *primary keys* allow these relationships to be managed and they're essential to relational databases.

Attributes have *data types*. For example, in the *winery* table, the winery ID is an integer, the winery name and address are strings, and the region ID is an integer. Data types are assigned when a database is designed.

Tables usually have a *primary key*, which is formed by one or more values that uniquely identify each row in a table. The primary key of the *winery* table is the winery ID, and the primary key of the *region* table is the region ID. The values of these attributes aren't usually meaningful to the user, they're just unique ordinal numbers that are used to uniquely identify a row of data and to maintain relationships.

Figure 5-2 shows our example database modeled using *entity-relationship (ER) modeling*. An ER model is a standard method for visualizing a database and for understanding the relationships between the tables. It's particularly useful for more complex databases where relationships of different types exist and you need to understand how to keep these up-to-date and use them in querying. As we show you later, our *winestore* database needs a moderately complex ER model.

In the ER model in Figure 5-2, the *winery* and *region* tables or *entities* are shown as rectangles. An entity is often a real-world object and each one has *attributes*, where those that are part of the primary key are shown underlined. The relationship between the tables is shown as a diamond that connects the two tables, and in this example the relationship is annotated with an M at the *winery*-end of the relationship. The M indicates that there are potentially many winery rows associated with each region. Because the relationship isn't annotated at the other end, this means that there is only one region associated with each winery. We discuss ER modeling in more detail in Appendix E.

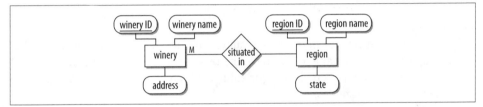

Figure 5-2. An example relational model of the winery database

Database Terminology

Database
> A repository to store data. For example, a database might store all of the data associated with finance in a large company, information about your CD and DVD collection, or the records of an online store.

Table
> A part of a database that stores data related to an object, thing, or activity. For example, a table might store data about customers. A table has columns, fields, or attributes. The data is stored as rows or records.

Attributes
> The columns in a table. All rows in a table have the same attributes. For example, a *customer* table might have the attributes name, address, and city. Each attribute has a data type such as string, integer, or date.

Rows
> The data entries stored in a table. Rows contain values for each attribute. For example, a row in a *customer* table might contain the values "Matthew Richardson," "Punt Road," and "Richmond." Rows are also known as records.

Relational model

A formal model that uses database, tables, and attributes to store data and manages the relationship between tables.

(Relational) database management system (DBMS)

A software application that manages data in a database and is based on the relational model. Also known as a database server.

SQL

A standard query language that interacts with a database server. SQL is a set of statements to manage databases, tables, and data. Despite popular belief, SQL does not stand for Structured Query Language and isn't pronounced Sequel: it's pronounced as the three-letter acronym S-Q-L and it doesn't stand for anything.

Constraints

Restrictions or limitations on tables and attributes. A database typically has many constraints: for example, a wine can be produced only by one winery, an order can't exist if it isn't associated with a customer, and having a name attribute is mandatory for a customer.

Primary key

One or more attributes that contain values that uniquely identify each row. For example, a *customer* table might have the primary key named cust ID. The cust ID attribute is then assigned a unique value for each customer. A primary key is a constraint of most tables.

Index

A data structure used for fast access to rows in a table. An index is usually built for the primary key of each table and can then be used to quickly find a particular row. Indexes are also defined and built for other attributes when those attributes are frequently used in queries.

Entity-relationship (ER) modeling

A technique used to describe the real-world data in terms of entities, attributes, and relationships. This is discussed in Appendix E.

Normalized database

A correctly designed database that is created from an ER model. There are different types or levels of normalization, and a *third-normal form* database is generally regarded as being an acceptably designed relational database. We discuss normalization in Appendix E.

The Winestore Database

This section is a summary of the entity-relationship model of the *winestore* database. It's included for easy reference, and you'll find it useful to have at hand as you work through this chapter.

The winestore entity-relationship model

Figure 5-3 shows the complete entity-relationship model for our example *winestore* database; this model is derived from the system requirements listed in Chapter 16, and is derived following the process described in Appendix E. Appendix E also includes a description of the meaning of each shape and line type used in the figure.

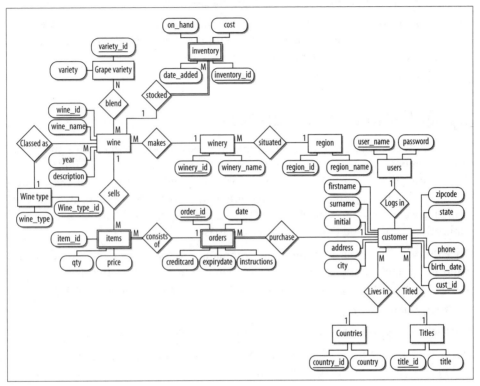

Figure 5-3. The winestore ER model

The *winestore* model can be summarized as follows:

- A *customer* at the online winestore purchases wines by placing one or more *orders*.
- Each *customer* has exactly one set of *user* details.
- Each customer has a title (such as "Mr" or "Dr") and lives in a country.
- Each *order* contains one or more *items*.
- Each *item* is a specific quantity of *wine* at a specific price.
- A *wine* is of a type such as "Red," "White," or "Sparkling."
- A *wine* has a vintage year; if the same wine has two or more vintages from different years, these are treated as two or more distinct wines.

- Each *wine* is made by one *winery*.

- Each *winery* is located in one *region*.

- Each *wine* has one or more *grape_variety* entries. For example, a wine of wine_name "Archibald" might be made of the *grape_variety* entries "Sauvignon" and "Cabernet." The order of the entries is important. For example, a "Cabernet Sauvignon" is different from a "Sauvignon Cabernet."

- Each *inventory* for a *wine* represents the on-hand stock of a wine. If a wine is available at two prices, there are two inventories. Similarly, if the stock arrived at the warehouse at two different times, there are two inventories.

- Each *wine* may have one or more *inventories*.

MySQL Command Interpreter

The MySQL command interpreter is commonly used to create databases and tables in web database applications and to test queries. Throughout the remainder of this chapter we discuss the SQL statements for managing a database. All these statements can be directly entered into the command interpreter and executed. In later chapters, we'll show how to include SQL statements in PHP scripts so that web applications can get and change data in a database.

Once the MySQL server is running, the command interpreter can be used. The command interpreter can be run using the following command from the shell in a Unix or Mac OS X system, assuming you've created a user hugh with a password shhh:

```
% /usr/local/bin/mysql -uhugh -pshhh
```

The shell prompt is represented here as a percentage character, %.

On a Microsoft Windows platform, you can access the command interpreter by clicking on the Start menu, then the Run option, and typing into the dialog box:

```
"C:\Program Files\EasyPHP1-7\mysql\bin\mysql.exe" -uhugh -pshhh
```

Then, press the Enter key or click OK.

(For both Unix and Microsoft Windows environments, we're assuming you've installed MySQL in the default directory location using our instructions in Appendixes A through C.)

Running the command interpreter displays the output:

```
Welcome to the MySQL monitor.  Commands end with ; or \g.
Your MySQL connection id is 3 to server version: 4.0.15-log

Type 'help;' or '\h' for help. Type '\c' to clear the buffer.

mysql>
```

The command interpreter displays a mysql> prompt and, after executing any command or statement, it redisplays the prompt. For example, you might issue the statement:

```
mysql> SELECT NOW();
```

This statement reports the time and date in the following output:

```
+---------------------+
| NOW( )              |
+---------------------+
| 2004-03-01 13:48:07 |
+---------------------+
1 row in set (0.00 sec)

mysql>
```

After running a statement, the interpreter redisplays the mysql> prompt. We discuss the SELECT statement later in this chapter.

As with all other SQL statements, the SELECT statement ends in a semicolon. Almost all SQL command interpreters permit any amount of whitespace (spaces, tabs, or carriage returns) in SQL statements, and they check syntax and execute statements only after encountering a semicolon that is followed by a press of the Enter key.

We have used uppercase for the SQL statements throughout this book so that it's clear what's an SQL statement and what isn't. However, any mix of upper- and lowercase is equivalent in SQL keywords. Be careful, though: other parts of SQL statements such as database and table names are case sensitive. You also need to be careful with values: for example, Smith, SMITH, and smith are all different.

On startup, the command interpreter encourages the use of the help command. Typing help produces a list of commands that are native to the MySQL interpreter and that aren't part of SQL. All non-SQL commands can be entered without the terminating semicolon, but the semicolon can be included without causing an error.

The MySQL command interpreter provides a lot of flexibility and many shortcuts:

- To quit the interpreter, type **quit**.
- The up- and down-arrow keys allow you to browse previously entered commands and statements. On most platforms, the history of commands and statements is kept when you quit the interpreter. When you run it again, you can once again scroll up using the up arrow and execute commands and statements that were entered in the previous session.
- The interpreter has command completion. If you type the first few characters of a string that has previously been entered and press the Tab key, the interpreter automatically completes the command. For example, if wines is typed and the Tab key pressed, the command interpreter outputs winestore, assuming the word winestore has been previously used.

- If there's more than one option that begins with the characters entered, or you wish the strings that match the characters to be displayed, press the Tab key twice to show all matches. You can then enter additional characters to remove any ambiguity and press the Tab key again for command completion.

- If you're a Unix user, you can use a text editor to create SQL statements by entering the command edit in the interpreter. This invokes the editor defined by the EDITOR shell environment variable. After you exit the editor, the MySQL command interpreter reads, parses, and runs the file created in the editor.

- You can run single commands and SQL statements without waiting for a MySQL command prompt. This is particularly useful for adding SQL statements to startup scripts. For example, to run SELECT now( ) from a Unix shell, enter the following command:

```
% /usr/local/mysql/bin/mysql -uhugh -pshhh -e "SELECT now( );"
```

- You can create MySQL statements in a file using a text editor, and then load and run them. For example, if you have statements stored in the file *statements.sql*, type the following into the command interpreter to load and run the statements:

```
mysql> source statements.sql
```

You can also include a directory path before the filename. This feature is discussed in more detail in Chapter 15.

- Sometimes, you'll find you've mistyped a statement, forgotten a semicolon, or forgotten a quote character. In most cases, to solve the problem you can type a semicolon and press Enter: this causes MySQL to report an error and you can then start again. If you're missing a matching quote character, type it in, then a semicolon, and then press Enter. If you're in a real mess, type Control-C (by holding the Ctrl key and pressing C): this aborts the command interpreter completely.

Managing Databases and Tables

In this section, we use the MySQL command interpreter to create databases and tables using the *winestore* database as a case study. We also show you the statements that remove databases and tables.

A discussion of advanced features is in Chapter 15. We show you how to manage indexes and alter tables after they've been created, and delete and update data using queries and multiple tables. We also show you how the details of how to store multiple statements in a file and execute them; this is how we created our winestore script that you used in the installation steps in Appendixes A through C.

Creating Databases

The CREATE DATABASE statement creates a new, empty database without any tables or data. The following statement creates a database called *winestore*:

```
mysql> CREATE DATABASE winestore;
```

A database name can be 64 characters in length at most and can contain any character except the forward slash, backward slash, or period characters.

Database and table names are used as the disk file names that store the data. Therefore, if your operating system has case-sensitive filenames, MySQL is case-sensitive to database and table names; in general, Unix platforms are case sensitive and Microsoft Windows platforms aren't. Attribute names are not case sensitive on all platforms. Aliases (which are discussed in Chapter 15) are partially case sensitive: table aliases follow the same rule as table names (and so are case sensitive on some platforms), while attribute aliases are case insensitive.

For the rest of this chapter, we omit the `mysql>` prompt from the command examples. To work with a database, the command interpreter requires the user to be using a database before SQL statements can be issued. Database servers have different methods for using a database and these aren't part of the SQL standard. In the MySQL interpreter, you issue the command:

```
use winestore;
```

Creating Tables

After issuing the use `winestore` command, you then usually enter statements to create the tables in the database. Let's look one table from the *winestore* database, the *customer* table. The statement that creates this table is shown in Example 5-1.

Example 5-1. Creating the customer table with SQL

```
CREATE TABLE customer (
  cust_id int(5) NOT NULL,
  surname varchar(50),
  firstname varchar(50),
  initial char(1),
  title_id int(3),
  address varchar(50),
  city varchar(50),
  state varchar(20),
  zipcode varchar(10),
  country_id int(4),
  phone varchar(15),
  birth_date char(10),
  PRIMARY KEY (cust_id)
) type=MyISAM;
```

The CREATE TABLE statement has three parts:

- Following the CREATE TABLE statement is a table name, which in this case is customer.
- Following an opening bracket is a list of attribute names, types and lengths, and modifiers. These are comma separated.

- After this is a list of other information about the structure and use of the table. In this example, a `PRIMARY KEY` is defined and the table type is set to `MyISAM`.
- Like all SQL statements, this one ends with a semi-colon.

We explain most of these in detail later in this section. Tables types are discussed in Chapter 15.

The `CREATE TABLE` statement for the *customer* table is derived from the entity-relationship model in Figure 5-3, and the process of converting this model to `CREATE TABLE` statements is described in Appendix E. The complete list of tables in the *winestore* database and a brief description of each and its relationships is shown in Table 5-1.

Table 5-1. The tables in the winestore database

Table	Description
countries	Lookup table containing country names. Related to customer.
customer	Customer details, including address, contact details, and date of birth. Related to countries, orders, titles, and users.
grape_variety	Lookup table containing grape variety names. Related to wine_variety.
inventory	Stock records that show much wine is available and its price. Related to wine.
items	The wines in an order and their quantity and price. Related to wine and orders.
orders	Orders placed by customer, which contain items. Related to customer and items.
region	Wine growing districts that contain wineries. Related to winery.
titles	Lookup table containing titles (such as Mr. or Miss). Related to customer.
users	Email addresses (which are also used as user names) and encrypted passwords for each customer. Related to customer.
wine	Details about the wines. Related to items, inventory, wine_type, wine_variety, and winery.
wine_type	Lookup table containing wine categories (such as red or white). Related to wine.
wine_variety	The link between a wine and its grape varieties. Related to wine and grape_variety.
winery	Winery details. Related to wine and region.

If you followed our installation instructions in Appendixes A through C, you've already downloaded the installation script that contains the statements to create all of the *winestore* database tables and this has been loaded into your MySQL installation (along with example data). To view the `CREATE TABLE` statements for the other tables in database, you can use the `SHOW CREATE TABLE` command in the command interpreter. For example, to see the statement used to create the *wine* table, type:

```
SHOW CREATE TABLE wine;
```

This statement is discussed in more detail in Chapter 15. You can also view the `CREATE TABLE` statements by opening the installation file *winestore.data* in a text editor; this is a good way to view all of the statements at once.

Tables and attributes

A table name can be 64 characters in length at most and may contain any character except a forward slash or a period. As you've seen, the name is usually the name of an entity created in the ER model. Attribute names may be up to 64 characters in length and can contain any character.

There are many possible data types for attributes, and details of selected commonly-used types are shown in Table 5-2. A complete list is provided in Section 6.2 of the MySQL manual. The MySQL manual is found at *http://www.mysql.com/documentation*. You can also download a copy from the same location and open it as a local file using your web browser; we recommend this approach, as it allows you fast access to the manual.

Table 5-2. Common SQL data types for attributes

Data type	Comments
int(*length*)	Integer with a maximum *length*; used for IDs, age, counters, etc.
decimal(*width*[,*decimal_digits*])	A number with a *width* including an optional number of *decimal_digits* after the decimal point; used for currency, measurements, etc.
datetime	Stores a date and time in the format YYYY-MM-DD HH:MM:SS.
time	Stores a time in the format HH:MM:SS.
date	Stores a date in the format YYYY-MM-DD.
timestamp	Stores the date and time in the format YYYYMMDDHHMMSS.
	The first-occurring timestamp attribute in a row has a special property: it is set to the current date and time when the row that contains it is created and it updates each time the row that contains it is modified. You can also update it to the current date and time by setting the attribute to NULL.
	Any other timestamp attributes in a row do not have this special property, but they can be updated to the current date and time by assigning NULL.
varchar(*length*)	An unpadded, variable-length text string with a specified maximum *length*.
char(*length*)	A padded, fixed-length text string of size *length*.
blob	An attribute that stores up to 64 KB of data.

For situations where the data stored is always much smaller or larger than the usual maximum possible value, most attribute types can be defined as tiny, small, medium, and big. For example, int can be specified as tinyint, smallint, mediumint, and bigint that are for signed integers in the ranges -128 to 127, -32768 to 32767, -8388608 to 8388607, and -9223372036854775808 to 9223372036854775807 respectively. The normal-size int has the range -2147483648 to 2147483647. We recommend choosing the smallest type that is suitable for a task: this saves space, and makes data retrieval and updates faster.

You'll find more detail of attribute types in Section 6.4 of the MySQL manual.

Modifiers

Modifiers may be applied to attributes. The most common modifier is NOT NULL, which means that a row can't exist without this attribute having a value. For example:

```
cust_id int(5) NOT NULL,
```

Another common modifier is DEFAULT, which sets the data to the value that follows when no data is supplied. For example, suppose you want to set the state attribute to the value Unknown when it isn't provided. You can do this using:

```
state varchar(20) DEFAULT "Unknown",
```

DEFAULT and NOT NULL can be used in combination: if a value isn't supplied for an attribute, NULL can be avoided by using the DEFAULT value; we return to this later in the section "Inserting, Updating, and Deleting Data."

All numeric attributes have optional zerofill and unsigned modifiers. The former left-pads a value with zeros up to the size of the attribute type. The latter allows only positive values to be stored and roughly doubles the maximum positive value that can be stored.

Finally, the useful auto_increment modifier is described in the section "Inserting, Updating, and Deleting Data."

Keys

A primary key is one or more attributes that uniquely identify a row in a table. As we discussed previously, primary keys are essential to maintaining relationships between tables in the database, and every table should have one. In the *customer* table in Example 5-1, the primary key is the cust_id attribute: each customer has a unique cust_id, and these are assigned sequentially as customers are added to the table.

You don't always have to create an extra attribute that serves the purpose of being the primary key. For example, in our *users* table we could choose the user_name attribute as the primary key, because each customer must have a unique email address. In our *customer* table, we could also have defined the primary key to be the combination of the surname plus the firstname plus the initial plus the zipcode (in the hope that's enough information to uniquely identify a customer!). As this example illustrates, if you don't already have an attribute that unique, it's easier to add an extra attribute that's purpose is to be the primary key. Determining primary keys from an ER model is discussed in detail in Appendix E.

The final component of the CREATE TABLE statement includes a specification of the keys. In Example 5-1, we specify that the unique identifier is the cust_id attribute by adding the statement PRIMARY KEY (cust_id). The PRIMARY KEY constraint has two restrictions: the attribute must be defined as NOT NULL, and any value inserted must be unique.

You can add other non-primary keys to a table. As we show you in Chapter 15, extra keys can make querying and updating of data in the database much faster. Each additional key definition creates an additional index that permits fast access to the data using the attributes defined in the key. As an example, suppose you want to access the customer data by a surname and firstname combination. In this case, you can add a KEY definition to the end of the CREATE TABLE statement:

```
    PRIMARY KEY (cust_id),
    KEY names (surname,firstname)
) type=MyISAM;
```

Each new KEY is given a unique label that you choose, in this case we've chosen the label names.

In many cases, without yet knowing what kinds of queries will be made on the database, it is difficult to determine what keys you should specify. MySQL permits at least 16 indexes to be created on any table (this depends on the table type), but unnecessary indexes should be avoided. Each index takes additional storage space, and it must be updated by the database server as the data stored in the table is inserted, deleted, and modified. In addition, indexes on multiple attributes can only be used to speed up certain queries. We discuss how to use indexes and index tuning in Chapter 15.

Deleting Databases and Tables

The DROP statement is used to remove tables and databases. Removing a table or database also deletes the data contained in it. For example, to remove the *customer* table and its data, use:

```
    DROP TABLE customer;
```

To remove the complete *winestore* database (including all tables, indexes, and data), use:

```
    DROP DATABASE winestore;
```

Take care with DROP—the command interpreter won't ask you if you're sure. However, we show you how to prevent accidental deletion (and prevent other database users from deleting databases, tables, and data) in Chapter 15.

Both DROP TABLE and DROP DATABASE support an optional IF EXISTS keyword which can be used to prevent an error being reported if the database or table doesn't exist. For example, to drop the *winestore* database and avoid an error if it's already been dropped (or was never created), use:

```
    DROP DATABASE IF EXISTS winestore;
```

We've used this feature at the beginning of the *winestore.data* file that contains the SQL statements for loading the *winestore* database. The first three lines remove the database if it exists, create a new database, and use the new database:

```
    DROP DATABASE IF EXISTS winestore;
    CREATE DATABASE winestore;
    USE winestore;
```

You can therefore reload the file by following our instructions in Appendixes A through C, and it'll create and load a new *winestore* database every time.

Inserting, Updating, and Deleting Data

There are four major statements for working with data in SQL: SELECT, INSERT, DELETE, and UPDATE. We describe the latter three statements in this section. SELECT is covered it in its own section later in this chapter.

Inserting Data

Having created a database and the accompanying tables and indexes, the next step is to insert data into the tables. Inserting a row can follow two different approaches. We show both approaches by inserting the same data for a new customer, Lucy Williams.

Consider an example of the first approach using the *customer* table:

```
INSERT INTO customer VALUES (1,'Williams','Lucy','E',3,
'272 Station St','Carlton North','VIC','3054',12,'(613)83008460',
'2002-07-02');
```

The statement creates a new row in the *customer* table, then the first value 1 is inserted into the first attribute, cust_id. The second value 'Williams' is inserted into the second attribute surname, 'Lucy' into firstname, and so on.

The number of values inserted is the same as the number of attributes in the table (and an error is generated if the number of values doesn't match the number of attributes). If you don't want to supply data for an attribute, you can include NULL instead of a value (as long as the attribute isn't defined as NOT NULL and NULL is valid for that data type). For example, to create a partial customer row, you could use:

```
INSERT INTO customer VALUES (1,'Williams','Lucy',NULL,3,
NULL,NULL,NULL,NULL,12,NULL,NULL);
```

To create an INSERT statement using this first format, you need to know the ordering of the attributes in the table. You can discover the table structure by typing **SHOW COLUMNS FROM customer** into the MySQL command interpreter or by reviewing the CREATE TABLE statement used to create the table. The SHOW statement is described in detail in Chapter 15.

If you want to insert more than one row, you can write more than one INSERT statement. Alternatively, you can write one INSERT statement and separate each row with a comma. Consider an example that uses the latter approach and inserts the details for two customers:

```
INSERT INTO customer VALUES (1,'Williams','Lucy','E',3,
'272 Station St','Carlton North','VIC','3054',12,'(613)83008460',
'2002-07-02'), (2,'Williams','Selina','J',4,'12 Hotham St',
'Collingwood','VIC','3066',12,'(613)99255432','1980-06-03');
```

This approach is the fastest way to insert data into MySQL.

Data can also be inserted using a second approach. Consider this example:

```
INSERT INTO customer SET cust_id = 1, surname = 'Williams',
    firstname = 'Lucy', initial='E', title_id=3,
    address='272 Station St', city='Carlton North',
    state='VIC', zipcode='3054', country_id=12,
    phone='(613)83008460', birth_date='2002-07-10';
```

In this approach, the attribute name is listed, followed by the assignment operator (=) and then the value to be assigned. This approach doesn't require the same number of values as attributes, and it also allows arbitrary ordering of the attributes. This can save you lots of typing when a row has many attributes but is sparsely populated with values. For example, to create a partial customer row, you could use:

```
INSERT INTO customer SET cust_id = 653, surname = 'Williams',
    firstname = 'Lucy', title_id = 3, country_id = 12;
```

The first approach can actually be varied to function in a similar way to the second by including parenthesized attribute names before the VALUES keyword. For example, you can create an incomplete *customer* row with:

```
INSERT INTO customer (cust_id, surname, city)
    VALUES (1, 'Williams','North Carlton');
```

When inserting data, non-numeric attributes must be enclosed in either single or double quotes. If a string contains single quotation marks, the string can be enclosed in double quotation marks. For example, consider the string "Steve O'Dwyer". Likewise, strings containing double quotation marks can be enclosed in single quotation marks. An alternative approach is to escape the quotation character by using a backslash character; for example, as in the string 'Steve O\'Dwyer'. Numeric values can also be enclosed in quotes but they aren't mandatory.

There are other ways to insert data in addition to those discussed here. For example, a popular variation is to insert data from another table using a query or to insert data from a formatted text file. These two approaches and other variants are discussed in Chapter 15.

Defaults

If you don't include the value for an attribute, it is set to the DEFAULT value if it's supplied in the table definition or to NULL otherwise (if it is valid for the attribute to be NULL). If an attribute is defined as being NOT NULL and does not have a DEFAULT value, the value that's set depends on the attribute type; for example, integer attributes are set to 0 (which causes an auto_increment attribute to be populated with a new identifier, as discussed next) and strings to the empty string. However, rather than worry about what happens, we recommend that you define a DEFAULT value for any attribute that you don't always want to list in an INSERT statement. Even if you want NULL to be inserted when nothing is provided, you can define it as the DEFAULT.

Inserting NULL into a TIMESTAMP (or any date or time type) attribute stores the current date and time. Inserting 0 into a TIMESTAMP attribute doesn't have the same effect as inserting NULL, because 0 is a valid date and time combination.

Auto-increment

MySQL provides a non-standard SQL auto_increment modifier that makes management of primary keys easy; most other database servers provide a similar non-standard feature. The goal of using auto_increment is to make sure that each row in your table has a unique primary key so that you can refer to it in other tables; as discussed previously, this is a common requirement in databases.

The following is a simple table definition that uses the auto_increment feature to create a unique value for the primary key:

```
CREATE TABLE names (
  id smallint(4) NOT NULL auto_increment,
  name varchar(20),
  PRIMARY KEY (id)
);
```

You can insert data into this table by setting only the name attribute:

```
INSERT INTO names SET name = "Bob";
```

In this example, the id is set to the next available identifier because the default value of an integer attribute is 0 and this invokes the auto_increment feature.

In general, when you insert NULL (or zero) as the next value for an attribute with the auto_increment modifier, the value that is stored is the maximum value + 1. For example, if there are already 10 rows in the *names* table with id values of 1 to 10, inserting a row with NULL as the id (or not providing an id and invoking the default behavior) creates a row with an id value of 11.

The auto_increment modifier is a useful feature when you want to insert data with a unique primary key, but don't want to have to read the data first to determine the next available value to use. As we show you later in Chapter 8, this also helps avoid concurrency problems (and, therefore, the need for locking) when several users are using the same database. The disadvantage is that it's a proprietary MySQL feature. However, we also show you how to develop a generic approach to managing identifiers in Chapter 9 and we also show you how it's done with PHP's PEAR DB.

Only one attribute in a table can have the auto_increment modifier.

The result of an auto_increment modifier can be checked with the MySQL-specific function *last_insert_id( )*. For the previous example, you can check which id was created with the statement:

```
SELECT last_insert_id( );
```

This statement reports:

```
+------------------+
| last_insert_id() |
+------------------+
|               11 |
+------------------+
1 row in set (0.04 sec)
```

You can see that the new row has id=11. To check an identifier value, the function should be called immediately after inserting the new row.

Deleting Data

The DELETE statement removes data from tables. For example, the following deletes all data in the *customer* table but doesn't remove the table:

```
DELETE FROM customer;
```

A DELETE statement with a WHERE clause can remove specific rows; WHERE clauses are frequently used in querying, and they are explained later in the section "Querying with SQL SELECT." Consider a simple example:

```
DELETE FROM customer WHERE cust_id = 1;
```

This deletes the customer with a cust_id value of 1. Consider another example:

```
DELETE FROM customer WHERE surname = 'Smith';
```

This removes all rows for customers with a surname value of Smith.

Updating Data

Data can be updated using a similar syntax to the INSERT statement. Consider an example:

```
UPDATE customer SET state = upper(state);
```

This replaces the string values of all state attributes with the same string in upper-case. The function *upper( )* is one of many MySQL functions discussed in Chapter 15.

You can update more than one attribute in a statement. For example, to set both the state and city to uppercase, use:

```
UPDATE customer SET state = upper(state), city = upper(city);
```

The UPDATE statement is also often used with the WHERE clause. For example:

```
UPDATE customer SET surname = 'Smith' WHERE cust_id = 7;
```

This updates the surname attribute of customer #7. Consider a second example:

```
UPDATE customer SET zipcode = '3001' WHERE city = 'Melbourne';
```

This updates the zipcode of all rows with a city value Melbourne.

After an UPDATE is completed, MySQL returns the number of rows that were changed. If MySQL finds that a value doesn't need to be changed (because it's already set to the value you want to change it to), it isn't updated and isn't included in the count that's returned.

Querying with SQL SELECT

The SELECT statement is used to query and retrieve one or more rows from a database. We introduce it in this section, and then show you the WHERE clause for selecting data that matches a condition. The section concludes with an introduction to the more advanced features of SELECT statements and a short case study.

Basic Querying

Consider an example SELECT statement:

```
SELECT surname, firstname FROM customer;
```

This outputs the values of the attributes surname and firstname from all rows in the *customer* table. Assuming we previously inserted four rows when we created the *winestore* database, the output from the MySQL command interpreter is:

```
+-----------+-----------+
| surname   | firstname |
+-----------+-----------+
| Marzalla  | Dimitria  |
| LaTrobe   | Anthony   |
| Fong      | Nicholas  |
| Stribling | James     |
+-----------+-----------+
4 rows in set (0.04 sec)
```

Any attributes of a table may be listed in a SELECT statement by separating them with a comma. If all attributes are required, the shortcut of an asterisk character (*) can be used. Consider the statement:

```
SELECT * FROM region;
```

This outputs all the data from the table *region*:

```
+-----------+---------------------+
| region_id | region_name         |
+-----------+---------------------+
|         1 | All                 |
|         2 | Goulburn Valley     |
|         3 | Rutherglen          |
|         4 | Coonawarra          |
|         5 | Upper Hunter Valley |
|         6 | Lower Hunter Valley |
|         7 | Barossa Valley      |
|         8 | Riverland           |
|         9 | Margaret River      |
|        10 | Swan Valley         |
+-----------+---------------------+
10 rows in set (0.01 sec)
```

SELECT statements can also output data that isn't from a database. Consider the following example:

```
SELECT curtime();
```

This example runs a function that displays the current time:

```
+-----------+
| curtime() |
+-----------+
| 08:41:50  |
+-----------+
1 row in set (0.02 sec)
```

The SELECT statement can even be used as a simple calculator, using the MySQL mathematical functions described in Chapter 15:

```
SELECT pi()*(4*4);
```

This outputs:

```
+------------+
| pi()*(4*4) |
+------------+
|  50.265482 |
+------------+
1 row in set (0.01 sec)
```

WHERE Clauses

A WHERE clause is used as part of most SELECT queries to limit the rows that are retrieved to those that match a condition.

Consider this grape-growing *region* table containing the details of ten regions:

```
mysql> SELECT * from region;
+-----------+---------------------+
| region_id | region_name         |
+-----------+---------------------+
|         1 | All                 |
|         2 | Goulburn Valley     |
|         3 | Rutherglen          |
|         4 | Coonawarra          |
|         5 | Upper Hunter Valley |
|         6 | Lower Hunter Valley |
|         7 | Barossa Valley      |
|         8 | Riverland           |
|         9 | Margaret River      |
|        10 | Swan Valley         |
+-----------+---------------------+
10 rows in set (0.09 sec)
```

To show only the first three regions, you can type:

```
SELECT * FROM region WHERE region_id <= 3;
```

This outputs all attributes for the first three rows:

```
+-----------+-----------------+
| region_id | region_name     |
+-----------+-----------------+
|         1 | All             |
|         2 | Goulburn Valley |
|         3 | Rutherglen      |
+-----------+-----------------+
3 rows in set (0.03 sec)
```

You can combine the attribute and row restrictions and select only the region_name attribute for the first three regions:

```
mysql> SELECT region_name FROM region WHERE region_id <= 3;
+-----------------+
| region_name     |
+-----------------+
| All             |
| Goulburn Valley |
| Rutherglen      |
+-----------------+
3 rows in set (0.01 sec)
```

The SQL Boolean operators AND and OR have the same function as the PHP && and || operators introduced in Chapter 2. These can be used to develop more complex WHERE clauses (and these can be combined with the MySQL functions described in Chapter 15). Consider an example query:

```
SELECT * FROM customer WHERE surname='Marzalla' AND firstname='Dimitria';
```

This retrieves rows that match both criteria, that is, those customers with a surname Marzalla and a firstname Dimitria. In this example, you need to be careful to type the strings 'Marzalla' and 'Dimitria' using the correct case because string values are case sensitive.

Consider a more complex example:

```
SELECT cust_id FROM customer
  WHERE (surname='Marzalla' AND firstname LIKE 'M%') OR
    birth_date='1980-07-14';
```

This finds rows with either the surname Marzalla and a firstname beginning with M, or customers who were born on 14 July 1980; the LIKE operator is discussed in more detail in Chapter 15. The OR operator isn't exclusive, so a row can contain a birth date of 14 July 1980, a surname of Marzalla, and a firstname beginning with M. This query, when run on the *winestore* database, returns:

```
+---------+
| cust_id |
+---------+
|     440 |
|     493 |
+---------+
2 rows in set (0.01 sec)
```

SELECT queries are often sophisticated and a long WHERE clause may include many AND and OR operators. More complex examples of queries are shown later in this chapter. As discussed previously, the WHERE clause is also a common component of UPDATE and DELETE statements.

Sorting and Grouping Output

Listing attributes in the SELECT statement and using WHERE allows you to decide what rows and columns in a table are returned from a query. However, you might also want to sort the data after it's returned, or you might want to group it together beforehand so that you can count the number of rows with different values, find a minimum or maximum value, or sum a numeric field. This section shows you how to pre- and post-process your data.

ORDER BY

The ORDER BY clause sorts the data after the query has been evaluated. Consider an example:

```
SELECT surname, firstname FROM customer
    WHERE city = 'Portsea' and firstname = 'James' ORDER by surname;
```

This query finds all customers who live in Portsea and who have the first name James. It then presents the results sorted alphabetically by ascending surname:

```
+-----------+-----------+
| surname   | firstname |
+-----------+-----------+
| Leramonth | James     |
| Mockridge | James     |
| Ritterman | James     |
+-----------+-----------+
3 rows in set (0.00 sec)
```

Sorting can be on multiple attributes. For example:

```
SELECT surname, firstname, initial FROM customer
    WHERE city = 'Coonawarra' OR city = 'Longwood'
    ORDER BY surname, firstname, initial;
```

This presents a list of customers who live in Coonawarra or Longwood, sorted first by ascending surname, then (for those customers with the same surname) by firstname, and (for those customers with the same surname and first name), by initial. The output for the winestore *customer* table is:

```
+------------+-----------+---------+
| surname    | firstname | initial |
+------------+-----------+---------+
| Archibald  | Belinda   | Q       |
| Chester    | Marie     | S       |
| Dalion     | Marie     | C       |
| Eggelston  | Martin    | E       |
```

```
| Florenini  | Melinda  | O |   |
| Holdenson  | Jasmine  | F |   |
| Mellaseca  | Craig    | Y |   |
| Mockridge  | Dimitria | I |   |
| Morfooney  | Chris    | K |   |
| Nancarral  | Samantha | W |   |
| Oaton      | Joel     | V |   |
| Oaton      | Rochelle | F |   |
| Patton     | Joel     | Z |   |
| Patton     | Penelope | E |   |
| Patton     | Samantha |   |   |
| Rosenthal  | Chris    | A |   |
| Tonkin     | Michelle | Z |   |
| Tonnibrook | Belinda  | T |   |
+------------+----------+---------+
18 rows in set (0.00 sec)
```

By default, the ORDER BY clause sorts in ascending order, or ASC. To sort in reverse or descending order, DESC can be used. Consider an example:

```
SELECT * FROM customer WHERE city='Melbourne' ORDER BY surname DESC;
```

GROUP BY

The GROUP BY clause is different from ORDER BY because it doesn't sort the data for output. Instead, it sorts the data early in the query process, for the purpose of grouping or *aggregation*. Grouping data using a sort is the easiest way to discover properties such as maximums, minimums, averages, and counts of values.

Consider an example:

```
SELECT city, COUNT(*) FROM customer GROUP BY city;
```

This query first sorts the rows in the *customer* table by city and groups the rows with matching values together. The output of the query consists of two columns. The first is a sorted list of unique cities. The second shows, for each city, the COUNT of the number of customers who live in that city. The number of rows that are output is equal to the number of different city values in the *customer* table, and the effect of COUNT(*) is to count the number of rows per group.

Here are the first few lines output by the query:

```
+--------------+----------+
| city         | COUNT(*) |
+--------------+----------+
| Alexandra    |       14 |
| Armidale     |        7 |
| Athlone      |        9 |
| Bauple       |        6 |
| Belmont      |       11 |
| Bentley      |       10 |
| Berala       |        9 |
| Broadmeadows |       11 |
```

So, for example, there are 14 customers who live in Alexandra, that is, 14 rows in the *customer* table are grouped together because they have a city value of Alexandra.

The GROUP BY clause can find different properties of the aggregated rows. Here's an example:

```
SELECT city, MIN(birth_date) FROM customer GROUP BY city;
```

This query first groups the rows by city and then shows the oldest customer in each city. The first few rows of the output are as follows:

```
+---------------+-----------------+
| city          | MIN(birth_date) |
+---------------+-----------------+
| Alexandra     | 1938-04-01      |
| Armidale      | 1943-04-04      |
| Athlone       | 1943-04-04      |
| Bauple        | 1922-11-26      |
```

 The GROUP BY clause should be used only when the query is designed to find a characteristic of a group of rows, not the details of individual rows.

There are several functions that can be used in aggregation with the GROUP BY clause. Five particularly useful functions are:

AVG()
Finds the average value of a numeric attribute in a set

MIN()
Finds a minimum value of a string or numeric attribute in a set

MAX()
Finds a maximum value of a string or numeric attribute in a set

SUM()
Finds the sum total of a numeric attribute

COUNT()
Counts the number of rows in a set

The SQL standard places a constraint on the GROUP BY clause that MySQL doesn't enforce. In the standard, all attributes that are selected (those that are listed immediately after the SELECT statement) must appear in the GROUP BY clause. Most examples in this chapter don't meet this unnecessary constraint.

HAVING

The HAVING clause permits conditional aggregation of data into groups. For example, consider the following query:

```
SELECT city, count(*), min(birth_date) FROM customer
  GROUP BY city HAVING count(*) > 10;
```

The query groups rows by `city`, but only for cities that have more than 10 resident customers. For those groups, the city, count of customers, and earliest birth date of a customer in that city is output. Cities with less than 10 customers are omitted from the result set. The first few rows of the output are as follows:

```
+---------------+----------+-----------------+
| city          | count(*) | min(birth_date) |
+---------------+----------+-----------------+
| Alexandra     |       14 | 1938-04-01      |
| Belmont       |       11 | 1938-04-01      |
| Broadmeadows  |       11 | 1955-10-13      |
| Doveton       |       13 | 1943-04-04      |
| Eleker        |       11 | 1938-04-01      |
| Gray          |       12 | 1943-04-04      |
```

The HAVING clause must contain an attribute or expression (such as a function or an alias) from the SELECT clause; in this example, count(*) is listed after the SELECT and is used in the HAVING condition.

The HAVING clause should be used exclusively with the GROUP BY clause. It is slow and should never be used instead of a WHERE clause. For example, don't do this:

```
SELECT cust_id, surname FROM customer HAVING surname = "Leramonth";
```

Do this instead:

```
SELECT cust_id FROM customer WHERE surname = "Leramonth";
```

Combining clauses

You can combine ORDER BY, GROUP BY, HAVING, and WHERE. When all four are used, they must appear in the order WHERE, then GROUP BY, then HAVING, and then ORDER BY. This is intuitive because the WHERE clause picks the rows from the table, then GROUP BY organizes the rows into sets, then HAVING picks the sets that match a condition, and then the data is sorted by the ORDER BY condition just before it's output.

Consider an example. Suppose we want to find the number of customers with the same name who live in each city in the state of Victoria, where the same name is defined as the same first name and surname. For example, this might determine that there are five John Smiths who live in Inverloch and three Tuong Nguyens in Carlton. Here's the query:

```
SELECT city, surname, firstname, count(*) FROM customer
  WHERE state = 'VIC'
  GROUP BY surname, firstname, city HAVING count(*) > 2
  ORDER BY city;
```

The query first uses the WHERE clause to pick the rows of customers that live in the state of Victoria. The rows are then grouped together into sets, where the grouping condition is that the customer surname and firstname are the same. Then, only those sets that have more than one customer with the same name are kept by the HAVING clause; this gets rid of unique names. Last, the ORDER BY clause sorts the customers by their city, and the city, first name, surname, and count of the number of customers is output. Here is the output from the winestore *customer* table:

```
+--------------+-----------+-----------+----------+
| city         | surname   | firstname | count(*) |
+--------------+-----------+-----------+----------+
| Broadmeadows | Mellaseca | Anthony   |        2 |
| Eleker       | Leramonth | Harry     |        2 |
| Kalimna      | Galti     | Nicholas  |        2 |
| Lucknow      | Mellili   | Derryn    |        2 |
| McLaren      | Chester   | Betty     |        2 |
+--------------+-----------+-----------+----------+
5 rows in set (0.00 sec)
```

The output shows, for example, that there are two Betty Chesters who live in McLaren city in the state of Victoria.

The GROUP BY clause sorts before it groups the rows into sets. Therefore, you don't need to use ORDER BY if you want the data to be output in the sort order used by the GROUP BY. For example, you don't need to do this:

```
SELECT * FROM customer GROUP BY surname ORDER BY surname;
```

If you leave out the ORDER BY clause, you'll get the same output:

```
SELECT * FROM customer GROUP BY surname;
```

However, in practice, it doesn't really matter: the MySQL query optimizer will ignore the ORDER BY clause if it's unnecessary. We discuss the query optimizer in Chapter 15.

DISTINCT

Suppose we want to find out which different cities our customers live in. The following query shows the cities for all of the customers:

```
SELECT city FROM customer;
```

The problem is that a city name appears more than once if more than one customer lives in that city. What we really want is a list of unique cities that the customers live in.

The DISTINCT clause presents only one example of each identical row from a query. We can use it to find out the unique cities the customers live in:

```
SELECT DISTINCT city FROM customer;
```

This shows one example of each different city in the *customer* table.

This example has exactly the same result as:

```
SELECT city FROM customer GROUP BY city;
```

The DISTINCT clause is often slow to run, much like the GROUP BY and HAVING clauses. We discuss how indexes and query optimization can speed queries in Chapter 15.

Limiting Output in MySQL

The LIMIT operator is MySQL-specific and is used to control the size of the output. For example, the following query returns only the first five rows from the *customer* table:

```
SELECT * FROM customer LIMIT 5;
```

This saves query evaluation time and reduces the size of the result set that's buffered in memory by MySQL. It's particularly useful in a web database application where one page of results is presented from a large table.

You can also specify which row to begin at, and then how many rows you want:

```
SELECT * FROM customer LIMIT 100,5;
```

This returns the 100th to 104th rows from the *customer* table.

Row numbering begins at row zero. For example, if you want the first five rows of the *customer* table, use:

```
SELECT * FROM customer LIMIT 0,5;
```

The following statement produces five rows beginning with row two:

```
SELECT * FROM customer LIMIT 1,5;
```

Be careful: forgetting to count from zero is a common mistake.

If you want all rows after a particular row, the second parameter can be set to -1:

```
SELECT * FROM customer LIMIT 600,-1;
```

For the winestore *customer* table, this returns 50 rows with cust_id values of 601 to 650.

The LIMIT operator is included at the end of an SQL statement, after the optional WHERE, GROUP BY, HAVING, and ORDER BY clauses.

Join Queries

You'll often want to output data that's based on relationships between two or more tables. For example, in the *winestore* database, you might want to know which customers have placed orders, which customers live in Australia, or how many bottles of wine Lucy Williams has bought. These are examples of *join queries*, queries that match rows between tables based (usually) on primary key values. In SQL, a *join query* matches rows from two or more tables based on a condition in a WHERE clause and outputs only those rows that meet the condition.

As part of the process of converting the winestore entity-relationship model to SQL statements, we've included the attributes required in any practical join condition. To understand which tables can be joined in the *winestore* database, and how the joins are processed, it's helpful to have a copy of the ER model at hand as you work your way through this section.

Beware of the Cartesian Product

Suppose you want to find out the names of the wineries in the *winestore* database and, for each winery, the name of the region that it's located in. To do this, you examine the ER model and discover that the *region* and *winery* tables are related, and that they both contain attributes that you need in the answer to your query. Specifically, you need to retrieve the winery_name attribute from the *winery* table and the region_name attribute from the *region* table, and you need to join the two tables together to find the result.

Consider this query, which we might intuitively, but wrongly, use to find all the wineries in a region:

```
SELECT winery_name, region_name FROM winery, region;
```

This query produces (in part) the following results:

```
+-------------------------------+-------------+
| winery_name                   | region_name |
+-------------------------------+-------------+
| Durham and Sons Premium Wines | Coonawarra  |
| Durham Brook Group            | Coonawarra  |
| Durham Creek                  | Coonawarra  |
| Durham Estates                | Coonawarra  |
| Durham Hill Vineyard          | Coonawarra  |
```

The impression here is that, for example, Durham Creek winery is located in the Coonawarra region. This might not be the case. Why? First, you can use the techniques covered so far in this chapter to check which region the Durham Creek winery is located in:

```
SELECT region_id FROM winery WHERE winery_name='Durham Creek';
```

The result is:

```
+-----------+
| region_id |
+-----------+
|         9 |
+-----------+
1 row in set (0.01 sec)
```

Now, you can query the *region* table to find the name of the region using:

```
mysql> SELECT region_name FROM region WHERE region_id=9;
+---------------+
| region_name   |
+---------------+
| Margaret River |
+---------------+
1 row in set (0.00 sec)
```

So, Durham Creek winery isn't in Coonawarra at all!

What happened in the first attempt at a join query? The technical answer is that you just evaluated a *Cartesian product:* you produced as output all the possible combinations of wineries and regions, most of which don't make any sense. These odd results can be seen if you add an ORDER BY clause to the original query:

```
SELECT winery_name, region_name FROM winery, region
   ORDER BY winery_name, region_name;
```

Recall that the ORDER BY clause sorts the results after the query has been evaluated and that it has no effect on which rows are returned from the query. Here is the first part of the output:

```
+--------------------------------+---------------------+
| winery_name                    | region_name         |
+--------------------------------+---------------------+
| Anderson and Sons Premium Wines | All                |
| Anderson and Sons Premium Wines | Barossa Valley     |
| Anderson and Sons Premium Wines | Coonawarra         |
| Anderson and Sons Premium Wines | Goulburn Valley    |
| Anderson and Sons Premium Wines | Lower Hunter Valley |
| Anderson and Sons Premium Wines | Margaret River     |
| Anderson and Sons Premium Wines | Riverland          |
| Anderson and Sons Premium Wines | Rutherglen         |
| Anderson and Sons Premium Wines | Swan Valley        |
| Anderson and Sons Premium Wines | Upper Hunter Valley |
```

The query produces all possible combinations of the 10 region names and 300 wineries in the sample database! In fact, the number of rows output is the total number of rows in the first table multiplied by the total rows in the second table. In this case, the output is 10 x 300 = 3,000 rows.

Elementary Natural Joins

A cartesian product isn't the join we want. Instead, we want to limit the results to only the sensible rows, where the winery is actually located in the region. To do this, you need to understand how the relationship between the *region* and *winery* tables is maintained. If you examine the ER model, you'll see that many wineries are located in a region.

In the database tables, the relationship between the *winery* and *region* tables is maintained using the primary key of the *region* table, the attribute region_id that's also an attribute in the *winery* table. To understand this, consider the first three rows from the *winery* table:

```
mysql> SELECT * FROM winery LIMIT 3;
+-----------+-------------------------+-----------+
| winery_id | winery_name             | region_id |
+-----------+-------------------------+-----------+
|         1 | Hanshaw Estates Winery  |         2 |
|         2 | De Morton and Sons Wines |        5 |
|         3 | Jones's Premium Wines   |         3 |
+-----------+-------------------------+-----------+
3 rows in set (0.04 sec)
```

The first winery has a `region_id` of 2, the second a `region_id` of 5, and the third a `region_id` of 3. Consider now the first five rows of the *region* table:

```
mysql> SELECT * FROM region LIMIT 5;
+-----------+----------------------+
| region_id | region_name          |
+-----------+----------------------+
|         1 | All                  |
|         2 | Goulburn Valley      |
|         3 | Rutherglen           |
|         4 | Coonawarra           |
|         5 | Upper Hunter Valley  |
+-----------+----------------------+
5 rows in set (0.04 sec)
```

If you match up each winery's `region_id` value with a region's `region_id` value, you can determine the relationship and answer the query. For example, you can now see that the first winery (Hanshaw Estates Winery) is located in region 2, the Goulburn Valley.

From a querying perspective, we want to output `winery_name` and `region_name` values where the `region_id` in the *winery* table matches the corresponding `region_id` in the *region* table. This is a *natural join*.

You can perform a natural join on the *winery* and *region* tables using:

```
SELECT winery_name, region_name FROM winery NATURAL JOIN region
  ORDER BY winery_name;
```

The query produces (in part) the following sensible results:

```
+--------------------------------+----------------------+
| winery_name                    | region_name          |
+--------------------------------+----------------------+
| Anderson and Sons Premium Wines | Coonawarra          |
| Anderson and Sons Wines        | Coonawarra           |
| Anderson Brothers Group        | Rutherglen           |
| Anderson Creek Group           | Riverland            |
| Anderson Daze Group            | Rutherglen           |
| Anderson Daze Vineyard         | Margaret River       |
| Anderson Daze Wines            | Barossa Valley       |
| Anderson Ridge Wines           | Lower Hunter Valley  |
```

A natural join query relies on the DBMS matching attributes with the same name across the two tables. In this example, MySQL discovers that there's a region_id attribute in the *winery* and *region* tables, and it only outputs combinations where the region_id in both tables is the same.

You can write a join query that explicitly specifies which attributes should be matched to produce the correct result. The following query uses a WHERE clause to produce identical results to our previous example:

```
SELECT winery_name, region_name FROM winery, region
  WHERE winery.region_id = region.region_id
  ORDER BY winery_name;
```

We recommend writing out your joins so that they include the join condition in the WHERE clause. This is safer and clearer than relying on the NATURAL JOIN operator to discover common attribute names across tables and allowing the DBMS to figure out how the join is done.

Several features are shown in this second example:

- The FROM clause contains the two table names *winery* and *region, and so retrieves rows from both tables.*

- Attributes in the WHERE clause are specified using both the table name and attribute name, separated by a period. This is useful because the same attribute name is often used in different tables, and the query can't figure out which table is meant unless you include it. When an attribute name occurs in only one table, you can omit the table name.

- In this example, region_id in the *region* table and region_id in the *winery* table have to be specified unambiguously as region.region_id and winery.region_id. In contrast, winery_name and region_name don't need the table name because they occur only in the *winery* and *region* tables respectively.

  The use of both the table and attribute name can also be used for clarity in queries, even if it isn't required. So, for example, you could write winery.winery_name in the example query. It can also be used in all parts of the query, not just the WHERE clause.

- The WHERE clause includes a join clause that matches rows between the multiple tables. In this example, the output is reduced to those rows where wineries and regions have matching region_id attributes, resulting in a list of all wineries and which region they are located in. This is the key to joining two or more tables to produce sensible results.

Examples

A join can be used to find lots of useful information from the *winestore* database. Suppose we want to find the names of wineries and the wines they make. Again, after examining the ER model, you'll see that you need to join together the related *wine* and *winery* tables to get the required names. Here's the query you'd need to write to get the correct result:

```
SELECT winery_name, wine_name FROM winery, wine
   WHERE wine.winery_id = winery.winery_id;
```

This query joins the *winery* and *wine* tables by matching the winery_id attributes. The result is the names and wineries of the 1,048 wines stocked at the winestore.

You can extend this query to produce a list of wines made by a specific winery or group of wineries. For example, to find all wines made by wineries with a name beginning with Borg, use:

```
SELECT winery_name, wine_name FROM winery, wine
  WHERE wine.winery_id = winery.winery_id
  AND winery.winery_name LIKE 'Borg%';
```

The LIKE clause is discussed in detail in Chapter 15.

Here are two more example join queries:

- To find the name of the region that the Ryan Ridge Winery is situated in:

```
SELECT region_name FROM region, winery
  WHERE winery.region_id=region.region_id
  AND winery_name='Ryan Ridge Winery';
```

- To find which wineries make Tonnibrook wines:

```
SELECT winery_name FROM winery, wine
  WHERE wine.winery_id=winery.winery_id
  AND wine_name='Tonnibrook';
```

Using DISTINCT in joins

The next example uses the DISTINCT operator to find wines that cost less than $10:

```
SELECT DISTINCT wine.wine_id FROM wine, inventory
  WHERE wine.wine_id=inventory.wine_id AND cost<10;
```

Wines can have more than one inventory row, and the DISTINCT operator shows each wine_id once by removing any duplicates.

Here are two examples that use DISTINCT to show only one matching answer:

- To find which countries the customers live in:

```
SELECT DISTINCT country FROM customer, countries
  WHERE customer.country_id = countries.country_id;
```

- To find which customers have ordered wines:

```
SELECT DISTINCT surname,firstname FROM customer,orders
  WHERE customer.cust_id = orders.cust_id
  ORDER BY surname,firstname;
```

Joins with More than Two Tables

Queries can join more than two tables. Suppose you want to find the details of the wine purchases made by a customer, including the customer's details, the dates they made an order, and the quantity and price of the items purchased. You examine the ER model, and see that the *customer* table that contains the customer information is related to the *orders* table that contains the date, and the *orders* table is related to the *items* table that contains the quantities and prices. So, to get the information you need, you have to join all three tables together.

By examining the database structure or the CREATE TABLE statements, you can see that the cust_id attribute can be used to join together the *customer* and the *orders* table. Joining the *orders* table and *items* table is a little trickier: the primary key of the *orders* table isn't just the order_id, it's both the cust_id and the order_id. So, for example there are many rows with an order_id of 1, but what makes a row unique is the combination of the cust_id for a customer and the order_id. These two attributes together are used to join the *orders* and *items* tables.

Suppose now that we want run this query for customer #2. Here's the query you'd use:

```
SELECT * FROM customer, orders, items
  WHERE customer.cust_id = orders.cust_id AND
  orders.order_id = items.order_id AND
  orders.cust_id = items.cust_id AND customer.cust_id = 2;
```

The WHERE clause contains the join condition between the three tables, *customer*, *orders*, and *items*, and the rows selected are those in which the cust_id is the same for all three tables, the cust_id is 2, and the order_id is the same in the *orders* and *items* tables. The example illustrates how frequently the Boolean operators AND and OR are used.

If you remove the cust_id=2 clause, the query outputs all items from all orders by all customers. This is a large result set, but still a sensible one that is much smaller than the cartesian product!

Here are two more examples that join three tables:

- To find which wines are made in the Margaret River region:

```
SELECT wine_id FROM wine, winery, region
  WHERE wine.winery_id=winery.winery_id AND
  winery.region_id=region.region_id AND
  region.region_name='Margaret River';
```

- To find which region contains the winery that makes wine #28:

```
SELECT region_name FROM wine, winery, region
  WHERE wine.winery_id=winery.winery_id AND
  winery.region_id=region.region_id AND
  wine.wine_id=28;
```

Extending to four or more tables generalizes the approach further. To find the details of customers who have purchased wines from the Ryan Estates Group winery, use:

```
SELECT DISTINCT customer.cust_id, surname, firstname
  FROM customer, winery, wine, items
  WHERE customer.cust_id=items.cust_id AND
    items.wine_id=wine.wine_id AND
    wine.winery_id=winery.winery_id AND
    winery.winery_name='Ryan Estates Group'
  ORDER BY surname, firstname;
```

This query is the most complex so far and has four parts. The easiest way to understand a query is usually to start at the end of the WHERE clause and work toward the SELECT clause:

1. The WHERE clause restricts the *winery* rows to the Ryan Estates Group (which, in this case, only matches one winery).

2. The resultant *winery* row is joined with the *wine* table to find all wines made by the Ryan Estates Group.

3. The wines made by Ryan Estates Group are joined with the *items* that have been purchased by joining to the *items* table.

4. The purchased wines are then joined with the *customer* rows to find the purchasers. You can leave out the *orders* table, because the *items* table contains a cust_id for the join; if you need the order number or credit card number (or another *orders* attribute), the *orders* table needs to be included in the query.

5. The result is the details of customers who have purchased Ryan Estates Group wines. The DISTINCT clause is used to show each customer only once. ORDER BY sorts the customer rows into telephone directory order.

Designing a query like this is a step-by-step process. We began by testing a query to find the winery_id of wineries with the name Ryan Estates Group. Then, after testing the query and checking the result, we progressively added additional tables to the FROM clause and the join conditions. Finally, we added the ORDER BY clause.

The next example uses three tables. It queries the complex many-to-many relationship that exists between the *wines* and *grape_variety* tables via the *wine_variety* table. A wine can have one or more grape varieties and these are listed in a specific order (e.g., Cabernet, then Sauvignon). From the other perspective, a grape variety such as Cabernet can be in hundreds of different wines. The many-to-many relationship is managed by creating an intermediate table between *grape_variety* and *wine* called *wine_variety*. The id attribute value stored in that table represents the order in which the grape varieties should appear for the wine. You can find a longer discussion of how these tables were designed and how they're used in Appendix E.

Here is the example query that joins the three tables to find what grape varieties are in wine #1004:

```
SELECT variety FROM grape_variety, wine_variety, wine
  WHERE wine.wine_id=wine_variety.wine_id AND
  wine_variety.variety_id=grape_variety.variety_id AND
  wine.wine_id=1004
  ORDER BY wine_variety.id;
```

The result of the query is:

```
+-----------+
| variety   |
+-----------+
| Cabernet  |
| Sauvignon |
+-----------+
2 rows in set (0.00 sec)
```

The join condition is the same as any three-table query. The only significant difference is the `ORDER BY` clause that presents the results in `id` order (the first listed variety was stored with ID=1, the second ID=2, and so on).

Case Study: Adding a New Wine

In this section, we show you an example that combines some of the statements we've discussed in this chapter, and shows you the basics of writing data to databases.

In this example, let's insert a new wine into the database using the MySQL command-line interpreter. Let's suppose that 24 bottles of a new wine, a Curry Cabernet Merlot 1996 made by Rowley Brook Winery, have arrived, and you wish to add a row to the database for the new wine. This new wine costs $14.95 per bottle.

The addition has several steps, the first of which is to find out the next available `wine_id`. You need to do this because we're not using the MySQL-proprietary auto_ increment feature in the *winestore* database. Here's the query:

```
SELECT max(wine_id) FROM wine;
```

This reports:

```
+--------------+
| max(wine_id) |
+--------------+
|         1048 |
+--------------+
1 row in set (0.00 sec)
```

Now, we can use an `INSERT INTO` statement to create the basic row for the wine in the *wine* table:

```
INSERT INTO wine SET wine_id=1049, wine_name='Curry Hill', year=1996,
    description='A beautiful mature wine. Ideal with red meat.';
```

This creates a new row and sets the basic attributes. The `wine_id` is set to the 1048 + 1 = 1049. The remaining attributes (the `wine_type` identifier, the `winery_id` identifier, and the varieties in the *wine_variety* table) require further querying and then subsequent updates.

The second step is to set the `winery_id` for the new wine. We need to search for the Rowley Brook Winery winery to identify the `winery_id`:

```
SELECT winery_id FROM winery WHERE winery_name='Rowley Brook Winery';
```

The result returned is:

```
+-----------+
| winery_id |
+-----------+
|       298 |
+-----------+
1 row in set (0.00 sec)
```

We can now update the new wine row to set the winery_id=298:

```
UPDATE wine SET winery_id = 298 WHERE wine_id = 1049;
```

The third step is similar to the second, and is to set the wine_type identifier in the *wine* table. You can discover the *wine_type_id* for a Red wine using:

```
SELECT wine_type_id FROM wine_type WHERE wine_type = "Red";
```

This reports that:

```
+--------------+
| wine_type_id |
+--------------+
|            6 |
+--------------+
1 row in set (0.01 sec)
```

Now, you can set the identifier in the *wine* table:

```
UPDATE wine SET wine_type = 6 WHERE wine_id = 1049;
```

The fourth step is to set the variety information for the new wine. We need the variety_id values for Cabernet and Merlot. These can be found with a simple query:

```
SELECT * FROM grape_variety;
```

In part, the following results are produced:

```
+------------+------------+
| variety_id | variety    |
+------------+------------+
|          1 | Riesling   |
|          2 | Chardonnay |
|          3 | Sauvignon  |
|          4 | Blanc      |
|          5 | Semillon   |
|          6 | Pinot      |
|          7 | Gris       |
|          8 | Verdelho   |
|          9 | Grenache   |
|         10 | Noir       |
|         11 | Cabernet   |
|         12 | Shiraz     |
|         13 | Merlot     |
```

Cabernet has variety_id=11 and Merlot variety_id=13. We can now insert two rows into the *wine_variety* table. Because Cabernet is the first variety, set its ID=1, and ID=2 for Merlot:

```
INSERT INTO wine_variety SET wine_id=1049, variety_id=11, id=1;
INSERT INTO wine_variety SET wine_id=1049, variety_id=13, id=2;
```

The final step is to insert the first *inventory* row into the *inventory* table for this wine. There are 24 bottles, with a per-bottle cost of $14.95:

```
INSERT INTO inventory SET wine_id=1049, inventory_id=1, on_hand=24,
  cost=14.95, date_added="04/03/01";
```

We've finished inserting the wine into the database. Now, to conclude, let's retrieve the details of the wine to make sure everything is as it should be. We'll retrieve the wine name, its year, the winery, the varieties, the wine type, and its cost. Here's the query:

```
SELECT year, wine_name, winery_name, variety, wine_type.wine_type, cost
  FROM wine, winery, wine_variety, grape_variety, wine_type, inventory
  WHERE wine.wine_id = 1049 AND
  wine.wine_id = wine_variety.wine_id AND
  wine_variety.variety_id = grape_variety.variety_id AND
  wine.wine_type = wine_type.wine_type_id AND
  wine.winery_id = winery.winery_id AND
  wine.wine_id = inventory.wine_id
  ORDER BY wine_variety.id;
```

The WHERE clause looks complicated, but it just joins together all of the tables in the FROM clause by matching up the identifier attributes and specifies we want for wine #1049. Here's the output:

```
+------+-----------+---------------------+----------+-----------+-------+
| year | wine_name | winery_name         | variety  | wine_type | cost  |
+------+-----------+---------------------+----------+-----------+-------+
| 1996 | Curry Hill | Rowley Brook Winery | Cabernet | Red      | 14.95 |
| 1996 | Curry Hill | Rowley Brook Winery | Merlot   | Red      | 14.95 |
+------+-----------+---------------------+----------+-----------+-------+
2 rows in set (0.01 sec)
```

Two rows are returned because there are two varieties for this wine in the *wine_variety* table.

We've now covered as much complex querying in SQL as we need for you to develop most web database applications. You'll find a discussion of advanced features you can use in Chapter 15. Beginning in the next chapter, we show you how to include SQL statements in PHP scripts to automate querying and build web database applications.

CHAPTER 6

Querying Web Databases

This chapter is the first of eight that introduce practical web database application development. In the first section, we introduce the basics of connecting to the MySQL server with PHP. We detail the key MySQL functions used to connect, query databases, and retrieve result sets, and we present the five-step process for dynamically serving data from a database. In the second section, we show you how to drive the queries by user input from an HTML form and by clicking on hypertext links.

The first section of this chapter introduces you to the following techniques:

- Using the five-step web database querying approach to develop database-driven queries
- Using the MySQL library functions for querying databases
- Handling MySQL server errors during development
- Using include and require files to modularize database code

After we've covered the basics, the second section introduces you to using user data in the querying process. We show you the following techniques:

- Passing data from a web browser to a web server
- Accessing user data in scripts
- Securing an application
- Querying databases with user data

The final section is a MySQL function reference that explains each library function in detail.

The focus of this chapter is database server and user interaction, not presentation in the browser. Presentation is a subject of Chapter 7. Extended examples of querying that use the techniques of Chapters 6 and 7 can be found in Chapters 16 to 20.

Querying a MySQL Database Using PHP

In PHP, library functions are provided for executing SQL statements, as well as for managing result sets returned from queries, error handling, and controlling how data is passed from the database server to the PHP engine. We overview these functions here and show how they can be combined to access the MySQL server.

At the time of writing, PHP4.3 and MySQL 4.0 were the stable releases. The MySQL library functions that are discussed here work with those versions. The PHP5 MySQL library functions also work with MySQL 4.0.

However, the MySQL functions discussed here do not work with the alpha release of MySQL 4.1. Instead, a new improved library is being developed for MySQL 4.1, and it is intended to be part of PHP5 in addition to the regular library. An introduction to this library is included as Appendix H.

Opening and Using a Database Connection

In this section, we introduce the basic PHP scripting techniques to query a MySQL server and produce HTML for display in a web browser.

Connecting to and querying a MySQL server with PHP is a five-step process. Example 6-1 shows a script that connects to the MySQL server, uses the *winestore* database, issues a query to select all the records from the *wine* table, and reports the results as pre-formatted HTML text. The example illustrates four of the key functions for connecting to and querying a MySQL database with PHP. Each function is prefixed with the string *mysql_*.

Example 6-1. Connecting to a MySQL database with PHP

```
<!DOCTYPE HTML PUBLIC
                "-//W3C//DTD HTML 4.01 Transitional//EN"
                "http://www.w3.org/TR/html401/loose.dtd">
<html>
<head>
  <meta http-equiv="Content-Type" content="text/html; charset=iso-8859-1">
  <title>Wines</title>
</head>
<body>
<pre>
<?php
   // (1) Open the database connection
   $connection = mysql_connect("localhost","fred","shhh");

   // (2) Select the winestore database
   mysql_select_db("winestore", $connection);
```

Example 6-1. Connecting to a MySQL database with PHP (continued)

```
   // (3) Run the query on the winestore through the connection
   $result = mysql_query ("SELECT * FROM
                          wine", $connection);

   // (4) While there are still rows in the result set, fetch the current
   // row into the array $row
   while ($row = mysql_fetch_array($result, MYSQL_NUM))
   {
      // (5) Print out each element in $row, that is, print the values of
      // the attributes
       foreach ($row as $attribute)
          print "{$attribute} ";

      // Print a carriage return to neaten the output
      print "\n";
   }
?>
</pre>
</body>
</html>
```

The five steps of querying a database are numbered in the comments in Example 6-1, and they are as follows:

1. Connect to the server with the MySQL function *mysql_connect( )*. We use three parameters here: the hostname of the database server, a username, and a password. Let's assume here that MySQL is installed on the same server as the scripting engine and, therefore, localhost is the hostname. If the servers are on different machines, you can replace localhost with the domain name of the machine that hosts the database server.

   The function *mysql_connect( )* returns a *connection resource* that is used later to work with the server. Many server functions return resources that you pass to further calls. In most cases, the variable type and value of the resource isn't important: the resource is simply stored after it's created and used as required. In Step 3, running a query also returns a resource that's used to access results.

   To test this example—and all other examples in this book that connect to the MySQL server—replace the username *fred* and the password *shhh* with those you selected when MySQL was installed following the instructions in Appendixes A through C. This should be the same username and password you used throughout Chapter 5.

2. Select the database. Once you connect, you can select a database to use through the connection with the *mysql_select_db( )* function. In this example, we select the *winestore* database.

3. Run the query on the *winestore* database using *mysql_query( )*. The function takes two parameters: the SQL query itself and the server connection resource to use. The connection resource is the value returned from connecting in the first step. The function *mysql_query( )* returns a *result set resource*, a value that can retrieve the result set from the query in the next step.

4. Retrieve a row of results. The function *mysql_fetch_array( )* retrieves one row of the result set, taking the result set resource from the third step as the first parameter. Each row is stored in an array $row, and the attribute values in the array are extracted in Step 5. The second parameter is a PHP constant that tells the function to return a numerically accessed array; we explain how array indexing affects query processing later in this section.

   A while loop is used to retrieve rows of database results and, each time the loop executes, the variable $row is overwritten with a new row of database results. When there are no more rows to fetch, the function *mysql_fetch_array( )* returns false and the loop ends.

5. Process the attribute values. For each retrieved row, a foreach loop is used with a print statement to display each of the attribute values in the current row. For the *wine* table, there are six attributes in each row: wine_id, wine_name, wine_type, year, winery_id, and description.

   The script prints each row on a line, separating each attribute value with a single space character. Each line is terminated with a carriage return using print "\n" and Steps 4 and 5 are repeated.

The first ten wine rows produced by the script in Example 6-1 are shown in Example 6-2. The results are shown marked up as HTML.

Example 6-2. Marked-up HTML output from the code shown in Example 6-1

```
<!DOCTYPE HTML PUBLIC
                "-//W3C//DTD HTML 4.01 Transitional//EN"
                "http://www.w3.org/TR/html401/loose.dtd">
<html>
<head>
  <meta http-equiv="Content-Type" content="text/html; charset=iso-8859-1">
  <title>Wines</title>
</head>
<body><pre>
1 Archibald Sparkling 1997 1
2 Pattendon Fortified 1975 1
3 Lombardi Sweet 1985 2
4 Tonkin Sparkling 1984 2
5 Titshall White 1986 2
6 Serrong Red 1995 2
7 Mettaxus White 1996 2
8 Titshall Sweet 1987 3
```

Example 6-2. Marked-up HTML output from the code shown in Example 6-1 (continued)

```
9 Serrong Fortified 1981 3
10 Chester White 1999 3
...
</pre>
</body>
</html>
```

PHP does programmatically what you have done by hand in Chapter 5 with the MySQL command line interpreter. The function *mysql_connect( )* performs the equivalent function to running the interpreter. The *mysql_select_db( )* function provides the use database command, and *mysql_query( )* permits an SQL statement to be executed. The *mysql_fetch_array( )* function manually retrieves a result set that's automatically output by the interpreter.

The basic principles and practice of using MySQL with PHP are shown in the four functions we've used. These key functions and all others are described in detail in "MySQL Function Reference."

Using mysql_fetch_array( )

In our first example, we accessed attributes in order using the foreach loop statement. In many cases, you'll also want to access the attributes in another way, and this is usually best achieved by using the attribute names themselves. It's much easier to remember that you want to show the user the vintage year, the wine's name, the varieties, and the price, than to remember you want to show attributes four, two, six, and one from the SELECT statement. It's also a much better programming methodology because your code will be independent of the structure of the SQL statement and it'll be more readable. What's more, it's faster to access only the values you need.

Consider a fragment of PHP that displays information about wineries:

```php
$result = mysql_query("SELECT winery_name, phone, fax FROM winery");

while($row = mysql_fetch_array($result))
{
    print "The {$row["winery_name"]} winery's fax is {$row["fax"]}".
    print "Their phone is {$row["phone"]}.\n";
}
```

The array *$row* contains one row of the results, and each of the attributes of the *winery* table is accessible using its attribute name as the associative key. We've used the curly brace style discussed in Chapter 2 to output variables within a double-quoted string: you can see its usefulness here!

There are four tricks to using *mysql_fetch_array( )*:

- Table names aren't used to access values in the array. Even though an attribute might be referenced as `customer.name` in the `SELECT` statement, it must be referenced as `$row["name"]` in the associative array.

- Because table names are not used to access an array, if two attributes from different tables are used in the query and have the same name, only the last-listed attribute in the SQL statement can be accessed associatively. This is a good reason to design databases so that attribute names are unique across tables, or to use *attribute aliases*. We discuss aliases later in "MySQL Function Reference," and you'll find a discussion from a MySQL perspective in Chapter 15.

- Aggregates fetched with *mysql_fetch_array( )* are associatively referenced using their function name. So, for example, `SUM(cost)` is referenced as `$row["SUM(cost)"]`.

- In versions of PHP prior to 4.0.5, `NULL` values are ignored when creating the returned array. This changes the numbering of the array elements for numeric access. Even if you're using a recent version of PHP, this is a good reason to avoid `NULL` values by declaring a `DEFAULT` value for each attribute.

Error Handling of MySQL Database Functions

Database functions can fail. There are several possible classes of failure, ranging from critical—the server is inaccessible or a fixed parameter is incorrect—to recoverable, such as a password being entered incorrectly by the user. In this section, we show you how to detect and handle these errors during code development. Chapter 12 discusses how to develop a professional error handler that you can use when your application is deployed.

PHP has two error-handling functions, *mysql_error( )* and *mysql_errno( )*, for detecting and reporting errors. Example 6-3 shows the script illustrated earlier in Example 6-1 with additional error handling: it does exactly the same thing, but we've added error handling. In addition, we've deliberately included an error so that you can see what happens when one occurs: the keyword `SELECT` is misspelled as `SELEC`. The error handler is a function, *showerror( )*, that prints a phrase in the format:

```
Error 1064 : You have an error in your SQL syntax near
   'SELEC * FROM wine' at line 1
```

(Error messages often change between MySQL versions, so the error message might be worded differently when you run the example on your system.)

The error message shows both the numeric output of *mysql_errorno( )* and the string output of *mysql_error( )*. The *die( )* function outputs the message and then gracefully ends the script. Ending the script is often useful—it prevents the PHP engine from outputting several warnings as consecutive database functions fail; for example, if a connection can't be established, the PHP engine will issue a warning, and this will be followed by warnings as each subsequent database function is attempted and fails.

You should be aware of three consequences of an error, and how each affects your processing.

First, a function that fails to carry out what you requested normally returns false. We'll show you how to check for a false value routinely so you can catch errors before the program goes too far. However, some unexpected outcomes, such as a query that returns no results, don't count as errors.

Second, after you establish a connection, any function that returns false also sets an error code. You can retrieve the code through *mysql_errno()* and an associated string through *mysql_error()*. The *mysql_connect( )* and *mysql_pconnect( )* functions don't set either the error number or error string on failure and so must be handled manually. This custom handling can be implemented using the *die( )* function call and an appropriate text message, as in Example 6-3.

Third, you may issues queries that return no results. If no data is returned, a subsequent call to *mysql_num_rows()* will report no rows in the result set. Alternatively, a call to *mysql_affected_rows()* will report that no rows were modified. These functions are discussed later in this chapter.

Example 6-3. Querying a database with error handling

```
<!DOCTYPE HTML PUBLIC
                "-//W3C//DTD HTML 4.01 Transitional//EN"
                "http://www.w3.org/TR/html401/loose.dtd">
<html>
<head>
  <meta http-equiv="Content-Type" content="text/html; charset=iso-8859-1">
  <title>Wines</title>
</head>
<body><pre>
<?php

    function showerror( )
    {
       die("Error " . mysql_errno() . " : " . mysql_error( ));
    }

    // (1) Open the database connection
    if (!($connection = @ mysql_connect("localhost","fred","shhh")))
       die("Could not connect");

    // (2) Select the winestore database
    if (!(@ mysql_select_db("winestore", $connection)))
       showerror( );

    // (3) Run the query on the winestore through the connection
    // NOTE : 'SELECT' is deliberately misspelt to cause an error
    if (!($result = @ mysql_query ("SELEC * FROM wine", $connection)))
       showerror( );

    // (4) While there are still rows in the result set,
    // fetch the current row into the array $row
```

Example 6-3. Querying a database with error handling (continued)

```
    while ($row = @ mysql_fetch_array($result, MYSQL_NUM))
    {
      // (5) Print out each element in $row, that is, print the values of
      // the attributes
       foreach ($row as $attribute)
          print "{$attribute} ";

       // Print a carriage return to neaten the output
       print "\n";
    }
?>
</pre>
</body>
</html>
```

MySQL functions should be used with the @ operator that suppresses default output of error messages by the PHP script engine. Omitting the @ operator produces messages that contain both the custom error message and the default error message produced by PHP. Consider an example where the string localhost is misspelled, and the @ operator is omitted:

```
    if (!($connection = mysql_connect("localhos",
                                      "fred",:"shhh") ))
        die("Could not connect");
```

This fragment outputs the following error message that includes first the PHP error and second the custom error message:

```
    Warning: mysql_connect( ) [function.mysql-connect]:
      Unknown MySQL Server Host 'localhos' (2) in bug.php on line 42

    Could not connect.
```

The error handling approach we've described here works well when you're developing and testing an application. However, when your application is finished and in production, it isn't a good approach: the error messages that are output interrupt the look and feel of the application, and stopping the processing with the *die()* function is likely to result in non-compliant HTML. We show you how to build a production error handler in Chapter 12.

Working with Table Structures

Example 6-4 is a script that uses the *mysql_fetch_field()* function to discover information about attributes in a table; *field* is another way of saying attribute, and you'll also find some database users call it a *column*. The script emulates most of the behavior of the SHOW COLUMNS or DESCRIBE commands discussed in Chapter 15. The code uses the same five-step query process discussed earlier, with the exception that *mysql_fetch_field()* is used in place of *mysql_fetch_array()*. Sample output for the table *wine* is shown in Example 6-5.

Example 6-4. Using mysql_fetch_field() to describe the structure of a table

```
<!DOCTYPE HTML PUBLIC
                 "-//W3C//DTD HTML 4.01 Transitional//EN"
                 "http://www.w3.org/TR/html401/loose.dtd">
<html>
<head>
  <meta http-equiv="Content-Type" content="text/html; charset=iso-8859-1">
  <title>Wine Table Structure</title>
</head>
<body><pre>
<?php
   // Open a connection to the server and USE the winestore
   $connection = mysql_connect("localhost","fred","shhh");
   mysql_select_db("winestore", $connection);

   // Run a query on the wine table in the winestore database to retrieve
   // one row
   $result = mysql_query ("SELECT * FROM wine LIMIT 1", $connection);

   // Output a header, with headers spaced by padding
   print str_pad("Field", 20) .
         str_pad("Type", 14) .
         str_pad("Null", 6) .
         str_pad("Key", 5) .
         str_pad("Extra", 12) . "\n";

   // How many attributes are there?
   $x = mysql_num_fields($result);

   // for each of the attributes in the result set
   for($y=0;$y<$x;$y++)
   {
      // Get the meta-data for the attribute
      $info = mysql_fetch_field ($result);

      // Print the attribute name
      print str_pad($info->name, 20);

      // Print the data type
      print str_pad($info->type, 6);

      // Print the field length in parentheses e.g.(2)
      print str_pad("({$info->max_length})", 8);

      // Print out YES if attribute can be NULL
      if ($info->not_null != 1)
          print " YES ";
      else
          print "      ";

      // Print out selected index information
      if ($info->primary_key == 1)
          print " PRI ";
      elseif ($info->multiple_key == 1)
```

Example 6-4. Using mysql_fetch_field() to describe the structure of a table (continued)

```
        print " MUL ";
      elseif ($info->unique_key == 1)
        print " UNI ";

      // If zero-filled, print this
      if ($info->zerofill)
        print " Zero filled";

      // Start a new line
      print "\n";
   }
?>
</pre>
</body>
</html>
```

Example 6-5. HTML output of the DESCRIBE WINE emulation script in Example 6-4

```
<!DOCTYPE HTML PUBLIC
                "-//W3C//DTD HTML 4.01 Transitional//EN"
                "http://www.w3.org/TR/html401/loose.dtd">
<html>
<head>
  <meta http-equiv="Content-Type" content="text/html; charset=iso-8859-1">
  <title>Wine Table Structure</title>
</head>
<body><pre>
Field             Type          Null Key  Extra
wine_id           int  (1)           PRI
wine_name         string(9)          MUL
type              string(9)
year              int  (4)
winery_id         int  (1)           MUL
description       blob (0)      YES
</pre>
</body>
</html>
```

Formatting Results

So far we've shown you the basic techniques for connecting to and querying a MySQL server using PHP. In this section, we extend this to produce results with embedded HTML that have better structure and presentation. We extend this further in Chapter 7, where we show you how to separate HTML from PHP code using templates.

Let's consider an example that presents results in an HTML table environment. Example 6-6 shows a script to query the *winestore* database and present the details of wines. Previously, in Example 6-1 and Example 6-3, the details of wines were displayed by wrapping the output in HTML <pre> tags. The script in Example 6-6 uses

---

the function *displayWines( )* to present the results as an HTML table. The main body of the script has a similar structure to previous examples, with the exceptions that the query is stored in a variable, and the username, password, and the *showerror( )* function are stored in separate files and included in the script with the require directive. We introduced the require directive in Chapter 2 and discuss it in more detail later in this section.

The *displayWines( )* function first outputs a <table> tag, followed by a table row <tr> tag with six <th> header tags and descriptions matching the six attributes of the *wine* table. We could have output these using *mysql_fetch_field( )* to return the attribute names rather than hard-coding the heading names. However, in most cases, the headers are hard-coded because attribute names aren't meaningful to users. Also, as we discuss later, giving users details about your database design can contribute to a security problem.

Example 6-6. Producing simple table output with MySQL

```
<!DOCTYPE HTML PUBLIC
                "-//W3C//DTD HTML 4.01 Transitional//EN"
                "http://www.w3.org/TR/html401/loose.dtd">
<html>
<head>
  <meta http-equiv="Content-Type" content="text/html; charset=iso-8859-1">
  <title>Wines</title>
</head>
<body>
<?php
  require 'db.inc';

  // Show the wines in an HTML <table>
  function displayWines($result)
  {

    print "<h1>Our Wines</h1>\n";

    // Start a table, with column headers
    print "\n<table>\n<tr>\n" .
        "\n\t<th>Wine ID</th>" .
        "\n\t<th>Wine Name</th>" .
        "\n\t<th>Type</th>" .
        "\n\t<th>Year</th>" .
        "\n\t<th>Winery ID</th>" .
        "\n\t<th>Description</th>" .
        "\n</tr>";

    // Until there are no rows in the result set, fetch a row into
    // the $row array and ...
    while ($row = @ mysql_fetch_row($result))
    {
      // ... start a TABLE row ...
      print "\n<tr>";
```

Example 6-6. Producing simple table output with MySQL (continued)

```
        // ... and print out each of the attributes in that row as a
        // separate TD (Table Data).
        foreach($row as $data)
            print "\n\t<td> {$data} </td>";

        // Finish the row
        print "\n</tr>";
    }

    // Then, finish the table
    print "\n</table>\n";
}

$query = "SELECT * FROM wine";

// Connect to the MySQL server
if (!($connection = @ mysql_connect($hostname, $username, $password)))
    die("Cannot connect");

if (!(mysql_select_db($databaseName, $connection)))
    showerror( );

// Run the query on the connection
if (!($result = @ mysql_query ($query, $connection)))
    showerror( );

// Display the results
displayWines($result);
?>
</body>
</html>
```

After producing the HTML <table> open tag, the *displayWines( )* function retrieves the rows in the result set, showing each row as a separate table row using the <tr> tag. Each attribute value for each wine, where the attributes match the headings, is displayed within the row as table data using the <td> tag. Carriage returns and tab characters are used to lay out the HTML for readability; this has no effect on the presentation of the document by a web browser, but it makes the HTML much more readable if the user views the HTML source. It also makes debugging your HTML easier.

The results of using a table environment instead of <pre> tags are more structured and more visually pleasing. The output in the Mozilla browser is shown in Figure 6-1, along with a window showing part of the HTML source generated by the script.

The downside of the approach we've shown is that the HTML is embedded in the script, making it difficult to work with the presentation and the code separately. In our simple example, this isn't a huge problem. In a larger application such as our online winestore, it makes changing the overall look and feel of the application difficult, and it can also make the code harder to modify. In Chapter 7, we show you how to solve this problem using templates.

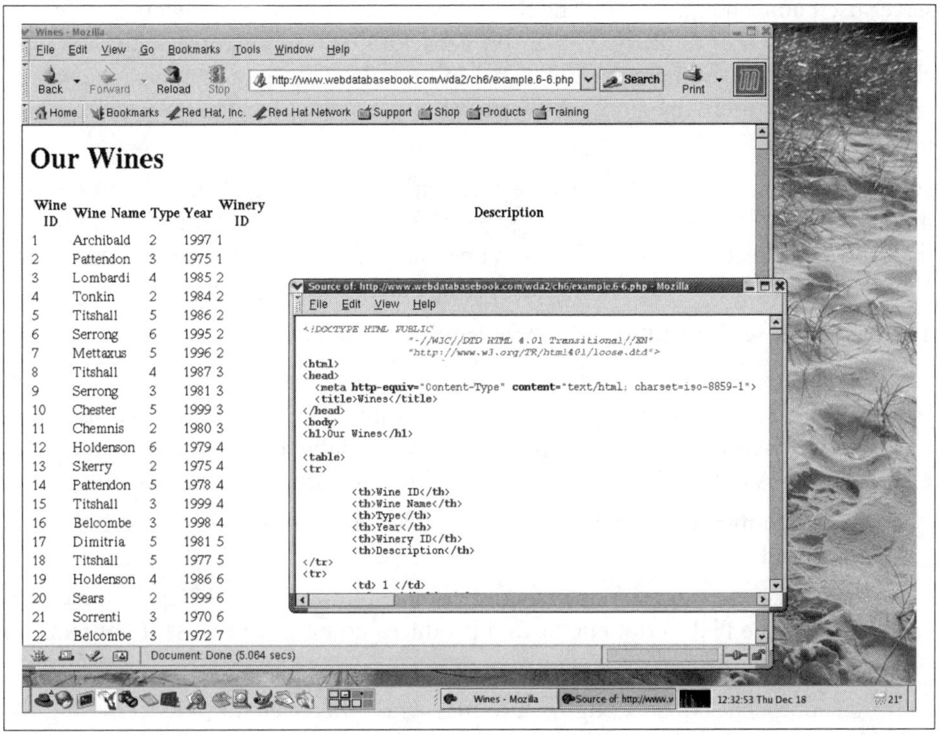

Figure 6-1. Presenting wines from the winestore in an HTML table environment

Using Require Files in Practice

Example 6-7 shows the file included with the require directive in Example 6-6. As discussed in Chapter 2, the require directive allows common functions, variables, and constants in other files to be accessible from within the body of a script without directly adding the functions to the code.

Example 6-7. The db.inc require file

```php
<?php
   $hostName = "localhost";
   $databaseName = "winestore";
   $username = "fred";
   $password = "shhh";

   function showerror()
   {
      die("Error " . mysql_errno() . " : " . mysql_error());
   }
?>
```

A require file is usually referenced by all code developed for an application and, in this case, allows easy adjustment of the database server name, database name, and server username and password. The flexibility to adjust these parameters in a central location allows testing of the system on a backup or remote copy of the data, by changing the database name or hostname in one file. This approach also allows the use of different username and password combinations with different privileges, for testing purposes.

We have chosen to name our include files with the *.inc* extension. This presents a minor security problem. If the user requests the file, the source of the file is shown in the browser. This may expose the username and password for the server, the source code, the database structure, and other details that should be secure.

There are three ways to address this problem:

1. You can store the require files outside the document tree of the Apache web server installation. For example, store the require files in the directory */usr/local/ include/php* on a Unix system or in *C:\winnt\php* or *C:\windows\php* on a Microsoft Windows system and use the complete path in the include directive.

2. You can configure Apache so that files with the extension *.inc* are forbidden to be retrieved.

3. You can use the extension *.php* instead of *.inc*. In this case, the require file is processed by the PHP script engine and produces no output because it contains no main body.

All three approaches to securing require files work effectively in practice. Using the extension *.php* for require files is the simplest solution but has the disadvantage that require files can't be easily distinguished from other files; however, this is the best approach if you're in a shared hosting environment and can't change Apache's configuration.

In the online winestore, we have configured Apache to disallow retrieval of files with the extension *.inc*. We did this by adding the following lines to Apache's *httpd.conf* file, and restarting the web server:

```
<Files ~ "\.inc$">
  Order allow,deny
  Deny from all
</Files>
```

Case Study: Producing a Select List

To conclude this section, we present a longer case study of dynamically producing values for an HTML select input type in a form. The example shows you how the PHP MySQL functions can be put to use to develop one of the components of an application. You'll find this a useful tool when you want the user to choose an item from a list of values stored in the database.

Consider an example where we want our users to be able to choose one of the wine regions from a drop-down list so that we can display the wineries in the area. For the wine regions, the select input might have the following structure:

```
<select name="regionName">
  <option value="All">All</option>
  <option value="Barossa Valley">Barossa Valley</option>
  <option value="Coonawarra">Coonawarra</option>
  <option value="Goulburn Valley">Goulburn Valley</option>
  <option value="Lower Hunter Valley">Lower Hunter Valley</option>
  <option value="Margaret River">Margaret River</option>
  <option value="Riverland">Riverland</option>
  <option value="Rutherglen">Rutherglen</option>
  <option value="Swan Valley">Swan Valley</option>
  <option value="Upper Hunter Valley">Upper Hunter Valley</option>
</select>
```

With only a small number of wine regions, it's tempting to develop a static HTML page with an embedded list of region names. However, this is poor design. If the *region* database table changes because you add, delete, or change a region_name value, you have to remember to update the HTML page. Moreover, a spelling mistake or an extra space when creating the HTML page renders a select option useless, because it no longer matches the values in the database when used in a query. A better approach is to dynamically query the database and produce a select element using the region_name values stored in the *region* table.

Let's consider dynamically producing HTML. First, the set of different values of the region_name attribute in the *region* table need to be retrieved. Then, the values need to be formatted as HTML option elements and presented as an HTML form to the user. When the user chooses a region and submits the form, a query needs to be run that uses the region name the user selected as one of the query parameters to match against data in the database and to produce a result set. Because the values chosen by the user in the form are compared against database values, it makes sense that the list values should originate from the database. We show you how to incorporate user data in a query in the next section.

In this section, we develop a component that can be reused to produce select lists in different modules of a web database application. An example fragment that uses this new component is shown in Example 6-8. The *selectDistinct()* function that produces the drop-down list isn't shown and we show you it in the next section.

Example 6-8. Producing an HTML form that contains a database-driven select list

```
<!DOCTYPE HTML PUBLIC
            "-//W3C//DTD HTML 4.01 Transitional//EN"
            "http://www.w3.org/TR/html401/loose.dtd">
<html>
<head>
  <meta http-equiv="Content-Type" content="text/html; charset=iso-8859-1">
  <title>Wines</title>
```

Example 6-8. Producing an HTML form that contains a database-driven select list (continued)

```
</head>
<body>
<form action="example.6-14.php" method="GET">
<?php
  require "db.inc";

  // selectDistinct( ) function shown in Example 6-9 goes here
  require "example.6-9.php";

  // Connect to the server
  if (!($connection = @ mysql_connect($hostName, $username, $password)))
     showerror( );

  if (!mysql_select_db($databaseName, $connection))
     showerror( );

  print "\nRegion: ";

  // Produce the select list
  // Parameters:
  // 1: Database connection
  // 2. Table that contains values
  // 3. Attribute that contains values
  // 4. <SELECT> element name
  // 5. Optional <OPTION SELECTED>
  selectDistinct($connection, "region", "region_name", "regionName",
               "All");
?>
<br>
<input type="submit" value="Show Wines">
</form>
</body>
</html>
```

The component itself is discussed later but is encapsulated in the function *selectDistinct()*, which takes the following parameters:

- A database connection handle, in this case, a connection opened with *mysql_connect()* and stored in $connection. The database that contains the values that are used in the list must have been selected on the connection using a call to *mysql_select_db()*.

- The database table from which to produce the list. In this case, the table *region* contains the region name data.

- The database table attribute with the values to be used as the text for each option shown to the user in the list. In this example, it's region_name from the *region* table.

- The name of the HTML <select> tag. We use regionName, but this can be anything and isn't dependent on the underlying database.

- An optional default value to output as the selected option in the list; this option is shown as selected when the user accesses the page. All is used as a default here.

The output of the function for the parameters used in Example 6-8 is shown in Figure 6-2.

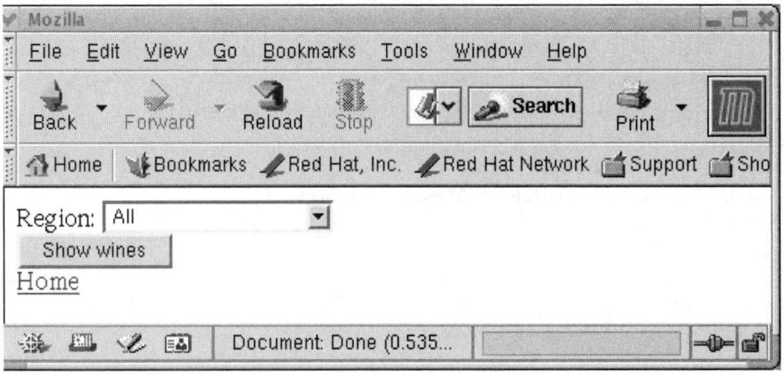

Figure 6-2. The selectDistinct( ) function in action

The remainder of the script fragment in Example 6-8 produces the other required tags in the HTML document.

Implementing the selectDistinct( ) function

This section details the implementation of the general-purpose *selectDistinct( )* function. The function produces a select list, with an optional selected item, using attribute values retrieved from a database table. The body of the function is shown in Example 6-9.

Example 6-9. The body of the selectDistinct( ) function for producing select lists

```php
<?php
  function selectDistinct ($connection, $tableName, $attributeName,
                            $pulldownName, $defaultValue)
  {
    $defaultWithinResultSet = FALSE;

    // Query to find distinct values of $attributeName in $tableName
    $distinctQuery = "SELECT DISTINCT {$attributeName} FROM
                      {$tableName}";

    // Run the distinctQuery on the databaseName
    if (!($resultId = @ mysql_query ($distinctQuery, $connection)))
       showerror( );

    // Start the select widget
    print "\n<select name=\"{$pulldownName}\">";
```

Example 6-9. The body of the selectDistinct() function for producing select lists (continued)

```
      // Retrieve each row from the query
      while ($row = @ mysql_fetch_array($resultId))
      {
        // Get the value for the attribute to be displayed
        $result = $row[$attributeName];

        // Check if a defaultValue is set and, if so, is it the
        // current database value?
        if (isset($defaultValue) && $result == $defaultValue)
          // Yes, show as selected
          print "\n\t<option selected value=\"{$result}\">{$result}";
        else
          // No, just show as an option
          print "\n\t<option value=\"{$result}\">{$result}";
        print "</option>";
      }
      print "\n</select>";
  } // end of function
?>
```

The implementation of *selectDistinct()* is useful for most cases in which a select list needs to be produced. The first section of the code queries the table $tableName passed as a parameter and produces a select element with the name attribute $pulldownName.

The second part of the function retrieves the database results row by row using a while loop. Inside the while loop, the value of the attribute to be displayed is saved in $result and then an option element is printed using that value. If a $defaultValue is passed through as a parameter and the current value in $result is equal to the default, the code produces the option as the selected option. If there's no default value or the current value doesn't match the default value, the current value is output without the selected attribute.

General-purpose, database-independent or table-independent code is a useful addition to a web database application. Similar functions to *selectDistinct( )* can be developed to produce radio buttons, checkboxes, multiple-select lists, or even complete form pages based on a database table. As we discussed in the previous section, the code can be improved with the use of templates that we show you in Chapter 7, and you'll find a template version of the code in this section on our book's web site *http://www.webdatabasebook.com/*.

Processing User Input

In this section, we build on the querying techniques discussed so far in this chapter. We focus on *user-driven querying*, in which the user provides data that controls the query process. To input parameters into the querying process, the user usually selects or types data into an HTML form environment, or clicks on links that request scripts.

We show you user-driven querying by introducing how to:

- Pass data from a web browser to a web server.
- Access user data in scripts.
- Secure interactive query systems.
- Query databases with user data.
- Process data using *one-component querying*, where the user clicks on a link that runs a query but leaves the user on the same page. This querying process is often used to add items to a shopping cart.

Passing Data from the Browser to the Server

Three techniques can be used to pass data that drives the querying process in a web database application:

- Data entry through HTML form environments. For example, form environments can capture textual input, and input is made by selecting radio buttons, selecting one or more items from a drop-down menu, clicking on buttons, or through other data entry widgets.
- Typing in a URL. For example, a user may open a URL using the Open Page option in the File menu of the Mozilla web browser, and typing in a URL such as *http://www.webdatabasebook.com/example.6-10.php?regionName=Riverland.*
- Embedded hypertext links that can be clicked to retrieve a PHP script resource and provide parameters to the script.

Of these, using an HTML form and clicking on hypertext links are the two most common techniques for providing user input for querying in web database applications.

User data or *parameters* are passed from a web browser to a web server using HTTP; Chapter 1 contains an introduction to HTTP and more details can be found in Appendix D. Using HTTP, data is passed with one of two methods, GET or POST. In the GET method, data is passed as part of the requested URL; the GET method gets a resource with the parameters modifying how the resource is retrieved. In the POST method, the data is encoded separately from the URL and forms part of the body of the HTTP request; the POST method is used when data is to be posted or stored on the server, and when large amounts of data is being transferred.

The HTML form environment can specify either the GET or POST method, while an embedded link or a manually entered URL with parameters always uses the GET method. In any case, the browser looks after encoding the parameters and transferring them to the server.

Passing Data with the HTML Form Environment

The first technique that captures data passed from a browser to a server is the HTML form environment.

Users enter data into an HTML form that is then encoded by the browser as part of an HTTP request. Example 6-10 is an HTML document that contains a form in which to enter the name of a wine region.

Example 6-10. An HTML form for entry of a regionName

```
<!DOCTYPE HTML PUBLIC
                "-//W3C//DTD HTML 4.01 Transitional//EN"
                "http://www.w3.org/TR/html401/loose.dtd">
<html>
<head>
  <meta http-equiv="Content-Type" content="text/html; charset=iso-8859-1">
  <title>Explore Wines in a Region</title>
</head>
<body bgcolor="white">
  <form action="example.6-11.php" method="GET">
    <br>Enter a region to browse :
    <input type="text" name="regionName" value="All">
      (type All to see all regions)
    <br><input type="submit" value="Show wines">
  </form>
  <br><a href="index.html">Home</a>
</body>
</html>
```

The page, rendered with a Mozilla browser, is shown in Figure 6-3.

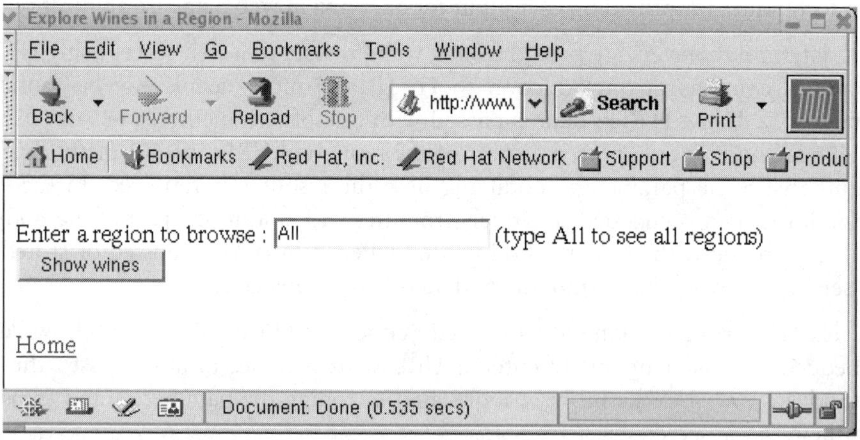

Figure 6-3. A simple page to capture user input

When the user presses the button labeled *Show Wines*, the data entered in the form is encoded in an HTTP request for the resource *example.6-11.php*. The resource to be

---

requested is specified in the action attribute of the form tag, as is the method used for the HTTP request:

```
<form action="example.6-11.php" method="GET">
```

In this form, there is only one input widget with the attribute type="text" and name="regionName". When the GET method is used, the name of this attribute and its value result are appended to the URL as query string parameters. If the user types **Riverland** into the text widget and then clicks on Show Wines, the following URL is requested:

```
http://localhost/example.6-11.php?regionName=Riverland
```

The resource that's requested is *example.6-11.php* and it's separated from the parameters by a question mark character ?.

The script *example.6-11.php* is shown in Example 6-11. Before this script is processed by the PHP scripting engine, variables associated with any parameters to the resource are initialized and assigned values. In this example, the array $_GET is initialized and contains an element with the key regionName. The value of $_GET["regionName"] is then automatically initialized by the PHP engine to Riverland. This variable and its value are then accessible from within the script, making the data passed by the user available in PHP.

Example 6-11. Printing a parameter value passed to the script with an HTTP request

```
<!DOCTYPE HTML PUBLIC
              "-//W3C//DTD HTML 4.01 Transitional//EN"
              "http://www.w3.org/TR/html401/loose.dtd">
<html>
<head>
  <meta http-equiv="Content-Type" content="text/html; charset=iso-8859-1">
  <title>Parameter</title>
</head>
<body>
<?php
  require 'db.inc';

  print "regionName is {$_GET["regionName"]}\n";
?>
</body>
</html>
```

Therefore, after submitting the form, the script in Example 6-11 outputs as a response an HTML document containing the phrase:

```
regionName is Riverland
```

The HTTP POST method can be used in a form instead of the GET method by changing the method="GET" attribute of the form tag to method="POST"; the merits of POST versus GET are discussed in more detail in Appendix D. This change of method has no effect on automatic variable initialization in PHP scripts, except that the data is stored in the array $_POST instead. You can change a script to process attributes that are passed with a POST request by changing all references to $_GET to $_POST.

 All form fields are automatically stored in either the PHP array $_GET or $_POST for direct use in scripts.

This is one of the best features of PHP, making it far simpler to write web-enabled scripts in PHP than in other languages. However, it introduces a security risk discussed later in the section "Security and User Data."

Passing Data with URLs

The second technique that passes data from a web browser to a web server is manual entry of a URL in a web browser.

Consider an example user request with a parameter. In this example, the user types the following URL directly into the location bar of a Mozilla browser:

```
http://localhost/example.6-11.php?regionName=Yarra+Valley
```

The URL specifies that the resource to be retrieved is *example.6-11.php* with a query string parameter of regionName=Yarra+Valley appended to the resource name. The user then presses the Enter key to issue an HTTP request for the resource and to use the GET method that passes the parameter to the resource. The query string parameter consists of two parts: a parameter name regionName and a value for that parameter of Yarra+Valley.

As with the form example in the previous section, an HTML document is created with the value of the query string parameter printed as part of the output:

```
regionName is Yarra Valley
```

The plus (+) character that was used instead of a space (since spaces aren't allowed in URLs) has been decoded back to a space character by the PHP scripting engine. A list of characters that must be encoded in URLs and an explanation of how encoding works can be found in Appendix D.

More than one parameter can be passed with an HTTP GET request by separating each parameter with the ampersand character; the browser performs this automatically when a form is used. For example, to pass two parameters regionName and type with the values Yarra and Red, respectively, the following URL can be created:

```
http://localhost/test.php?regionName=Yarra&type=Red
```

The values of these parameters can then be printed in the script *test.php* using the fragment:

```
print $_GET["regionName"];
print $_GET["type"];
```

Passing Data with Embedded Links

The third technique that passes data from a web browser to a web server is embedding links in an HTML document. It's conceptually similar to manually entering a URL.

Example 6-12 shows how embedded links in an HTML document are created in almost the same way as a URL is typed into a web browser.

Example 6-12. An HTML document with three links that pass two different parameters

```
<!DOCTYPE HTML PUBLIC
                "-//W3C//DTD HTML 4.01 Transitional//EN"
                "http://www.w3.org/TR/html401/loose.dtd">
<html>
<head>
  <meta http-equiv="Content-Type" content="text/html; charset=iso-8859-1">
  <title>Explore Wines</title>
</head>
<body bgcolor="#ffffff">
Explore all our
<a href="example.6-13.php?regionName=All&amp;wineType=All"> wines</a>
<br>Explore our
<a href="example.6-13.php?regionName=All&amp;wineType=Red"> red wines</a>
<br>Explore our
<a href="example.6-13.php?regionName=Riverland&amp;wineType=Red"> premium
 reds from the Riverland</a>
<br>
<a href="index.html">Home</a></body>
</html>
```

The script is rendered in a Mozilla browser in Figure 6-4.

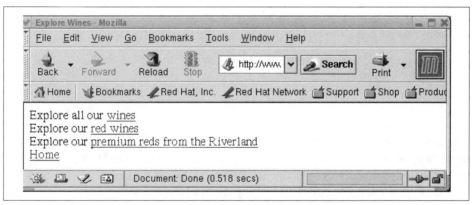

Figure 6-4. The HTML document shown in Example 6-12 rendered in a Mozilla browser

The script contains three links that can request the resource *example.6-13.php* and pass different parameters to the resource. For example, the first link in the HTML document is:

```
Explore all our
<a href="example.6-13.php?regionName=All&amp;wineType=All"> wines</a>
```

Clicking on this link creates an HTTP request for the URL:

```
http://localhost/example.6-13.php?regionName=All&wineType=All
```

The result of the request is that the script in Example 6-13 is run. The script doesn't query the database—we show you how to do that in the next section. Instead, the following simple HTML document is created:

```
<!DOCTYPE HTML PUBLIC
                "-//W3C//DTD HTML 4.01 Transitional//EN"
                "http://www.w3.org/TR/html401/loose.dtd">
<html>
<head>
  <meta http-equiv="Content-Type" content="text/html; charset=iso-8859-1">
  <title>Parameters</title>
</head>
<body>
regionName is All
<br>wineType is All
</body>
</html>
```

Example 6-13. A simple script to print out HTTP attributes and values

```
<!DOCTYPE HTML PUBLIC
                "-//W3C//DTD HTML 4.01 Transitional//EN"
                "http://www.w3.org/TR/html401/loose.dtd">
<html>
<head>
  <meta http-equiv="Content-Type" content="text/html; charset=iso-8859-1">
  <title>Parameters</title>
</head>
<body>
<?php
  require 'db.inc';

  print "regionName is {$_GET["regionName"]}\n";
  print "<br>wineType is {$_GET["wineType"]}\n";
?>
</body>
</html>
```

The ampersand characters in the URLs in the HTML document are replaced with & because the ampersand character has a special meaning in HTML and should not be included directly in a document. When the link is clicked, the encoded & is translated by the browser to & in forming the HTTP request.

More on Accessing User Data

As we discuss in this section, in PHP 4.2 or later, user data that is passed from the browser to the server using the GET or POST methods can be found in the PHP arrays $_GET and $_POST. Similarly:

- Cookie variables can be found in the array $_COOKIE.

- Environment variables can be found in the array $_ENV.

- Session variables can be found in the array $_SESSION.

- Server variables can be found in the array $_SERVER.

Cookies and sessions are discussed in Chapter 10.

The arrays that hold the external data are *superglobals*. This makes them a little different from the global variables that are discussed in Chapter 2. Superglobals are accessible anywhere within a script, even in functions, without declaring them using the global keyword. For example, the following code prints out the value of the variable input that was passed using the GET method:

```
function printout()
{
    print $_GET["input"];
}
```

The variable $_GET shouldn't be declared as global in the function.

Before PHP 4.2

Prior to PHP 4.2, variables were, by default, initialized differently. This behavior was controlled by the option register_globals=true in the *php.ini* configuration file; this option used to be set to true, but it is now set to false by default. The effect of this setting being on is that a PHP variable is automatically initialized for every external variable or parameter that is set. For example, if the user passes parameters with a URL:

```
http://localhost/example.4-11.php?regionName=Yarra+Valley
```

then a variable $regionName is automatically initialized and set to Yarra Valley when the script engine starts.

This feature is useful, and allows you to forget about the different arrays that contain external data. However, the problem is that it is a security risk if you're not careful: a user can override an internal parameter such as a path by passing a variable of the same name from the browser. The degree of risk depends on the configuration of the initialization process and how you go about validating the data. However, in this edition of the book, we follow the post-PHP 4.2 approach of accessing variables through their arrays. We recommend you leave the register_globals feature turned off.

If you are using a version of PHP prior to PHP 4.2 and you decide to turn off the register_globals feature, you'll find the arrays that contain the variables are different to PHP 4.2 and later. GET variables are found in $HTTP_GET_VARS, POST variables in $HTTP_POST_VARS, session variables in $HTTP_SESSION_VARS, environment variables in $HTTP_ENV_VARS, and server variables in $HTTP_SERVER_VARS. For backwards compatibility, you can still use these variable names in newer versions of PHP.

Processing Form Data

In this section, we discuss selected peculiarities of the HTML form environment and what is actually submitted from a form in an HTTP request.

The MULTIPLE attribute

As you've seen so far, simple form elements, such as the input element, allow only one value to be associated with them. For example, the tag `<input name="surname">` may have an associated value of Smith, and a URL using the GET method, this association is represented as surname=Smith.

The `<select multiple>` tag allows users to select zero or more items from a list. When the selected values are sent through using the GET or POST methods, each selected item has the same variable name but a different value. For example, consider what happens when the user selects options b and c from the following:

```
<select multiple name="choice">
<option value="a">a</option>
<option value="b">b</option>
<option value="c">c</option>
<option value="d">d</option>
</select>
```

When the user clicks Submit, the following URL is requested with the GET method:

```
http://localhost/click.php?choice=b&choice=c
```

From a PHP perspective, this means that the variable $_GET["choice"] is overwritten as the request is decoded, and $_GET["choice"] has the last value that was selected. In this example, print $_GET["choice"] outputs c.

The most elegant and simple solution to the multiple choice problem is to use a PHP array feature. This works as follows. First, you modify the form and replace the name of the select multiple element with an array-like structure, name="choice[]". In the previous example, the select multiple element is renamed as choice[]:

```
<select multiple name="choice[]">
<option value="a">a</option>
<option value="b">b</option>
<option value="c">c</option>
<option value="d">d</option>
</select>
```

Then, the PHP engine treats the variable as an array and adds the multiple values to the array $_GET["choice"], and the elements can be accessed as, for example, $_GET["choice"][0] and $_GET["choice"][1].

If the user selects options b and c, the following PHP fragment prints out all selected values, in this case both b and c:

```
foreach($_GET["choice"] as $value)
  print $value;
```

The bracket array notation in a form can cause some problems with client-side scripts (such as those written in JavaScript, which is discussed in Chapter 9) and such form elements should be referenced wrapped in single quotes in a JavaScript script.

Interestingly, the names of <textarea> and <input> tags can also be suffixed with brackets to put values into an array, should the need arise.

Other form issues

Checkbox elements in a form have the following format:

```
<input type="checkbox" name="showgraphics">
```

A checkbox has two states, on and off, and is usually rendered as a small clickable square in a graphical web browser. Assuming the form action requests the script *click.php* and the checkbox in the example is clicked, the following URL is requested:

```
http://localhost/click.php?showgraphics=on
```

However, if the checkbox isn't clicked, the URL requested is as follows:

```
http://localhost/click.php
```

The important difference is that a checkbox is never submitted with a value of off. If the checkbox isn't clicked, no variable or value is submitted to the server. Therefore, in a PHP script, a checkbox should be tested with the following fragment:

```
if ($_GET["showgraphics"] == "on")
    echo "Checkbox is on";
else
    echo "Checkbox is off";
```

Sometimes, if a checkbox is the only widget in a form and it isn't clicked, it isn't possible to determine whether the form has been submitted or has never been displayed. An easy solution is to add a name attribute to the submit input element. For example:

```
<form method="GET" action="click.php">
<input type="checkbox" name="showgraphics">
<input type="submit" name="submit" value="Submit Query">
</form>
```

If this form is submitted with the checkbox in the off state, the following URL is requested:

```
http://localhost/click.php?submit=Submit+Query
```

The variable $_GET["submit"] is now set when the form is submitted, even when the checkbox is in the off state. You can use this to identify when the checkbox is off using a PHP fragment such as the following:

```
// Was the form submitted but the checkbox not clicked?
if (isset($_GET["submit"]) && !isset($_GET["showgraphics"]))
  print "Checkbox wasn't clicked";
```

Multiple select elements have the same property as checkboxes: if no item in the list is selected, no variable or value is submitted to the server.

Security and User Data

This section introduces simple techniques that preprocess user data to solve many common security holes in web database applications. User data that has not been preprocessed or cleaned is often known as *tainted* data, a term originating from the Perl scripting language. Rectifying this through the processing we describe *untaints* user data. You should untaint user data before using it in your application.

 Using the techniques described here doesn't completely secure a system. Remember that securing a web database application is important, and that the advice offered here isn't a complete solution. A discussion of other security issues is presented in Chapter 11.

Data that is passed from a web browser to a web server should be secured using the steps described here. For this purpose, we have authored the *shellclean()* and *mysqlclean()* functions to ensure that the data passed to a script is of the correct length and that special characters aren't misused to attack the system. To understand why the functions are needed, we describe example attacks throughout this section. The functions are part of the require file *db.inc* that is used in all example scripts in Chapters 6 through 13.

Consider the following script. It uses the PHP *exec()* library function to run a program on the web server. The *exec()* function takes two parameters, the program to run and an array that is subsequently populated with any output of the program. In this example, the script uses *exec()* to run the unix *cal* program and to pass the user-entered parameter $_GET["userString"] to the program. The information in the parameter userString can be provided by using an HTML form with a text input widget, by manually creating a URL, or by embedding a link in an HTML document.

```php
<?php
  /* DO NOT INSTALL THIS SCRIPT ON A WEB SERVER */
?>
<!DOCTYPE HTML PUBLIC
             "-//W3C//DTD HTML 4.01 Transitional//EN"
             "http://www.w3.org/TR/html401/loose.dtd">
<html>
<head>
  <meta http-equiv="Content-Type" content="text/html; charset=iso-8859-1">
    <title>Calendar</title>
  </head>
<body>
<pre>
<?php
    // Run "cal" with the parameter $userString
    // Store the results in the array $result
```

```
    exec("/usr/bin/cal {$_GET["userString"]}", $result);

    // Print out each line of the calendar
    foreach($result as $element)
        echo "$element\n";
?>
</pre>
</body>
</html>
```

Never use *exec()* or other commands to run programs from a web
script or to query a database without untainting the user data. Do not
install the calendar example on a web server.

The Unix *cal* program is a useful utility that produces monthly or yearly calendars
for any date. For example, to produce a calendar for the whole of 2003, a user could
request the URL:

    http://localhost/cal.php?userString=2003

This runs the command */usr/bin/cal 2003* and outputs the complete 2003 calendar,
as shown in Figure 6-5.

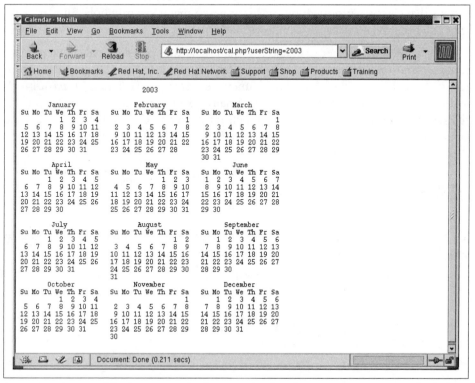

Figure 6-5. Output of the dangerous calendar example when the user requests a 2003 calendar

To produce a calendar for February 2007, the user requests:

```
http://localhost/cal.php?userString=2+2007
```

Requesting the URL without any parameters produces the calendar for the current month:

```
http://localhost/cal.php
```

While this script might seem useful and innocuous, this script is a major security hole and should never be installed on a web server.

Consider how the script can be misused. If a user wants to enter two or more commands on a single line, he can do so by separating the commands with a semicolon character. For example, to see who is logged in and then to list the files in the current directory, he can type the following commands at a Unix shell:

```
% who ; ls
```

Now consider what happens if he exploits this feature by requesting this URL:

```
http://localhost/cal.php?userString=2004;cat+/etc/passwd
```

The script produces a 2004 calendar, followed by the system password file, as shown in Figure 6-6! The script allows a creative user to do things the web server process can do. The identity of the owner of the web server process affects the severity of the actions that can be performed, but this is at best a major security hole. Similar problems can occur on a Microsoft Windows machine.

Semicolons, colons, greater-than and less-than signs, and other special characters can cause a script or a query to provide undesirable functions. This is especially a problem if the script uses the PHP library functions *system( )*, *shell_exec( )*, *passthru( )*, and *exec( )*, because these functions potentially give hackers access to programs on the server. Even if a form makes it difficult for a user to enter undesirable data, he can manually create his own request by entering a URL and authoring a query string.

 Never trust anything you don't have control of, which is anything not in the middle or database tiers.

To improve security and prevent special-character attacks, user data that is passed to programs should be processed with the *shellclean( )* function:

```
function shellclean($array, $index, $maxlength)
{
  if (isset($array["{$index}"]))
  {
    $input = substr($array["{$index}"], 0, $maxlength);
    $input = EscapeShellArg($input);
    return ($input);
  }
  return NULL;
}
```

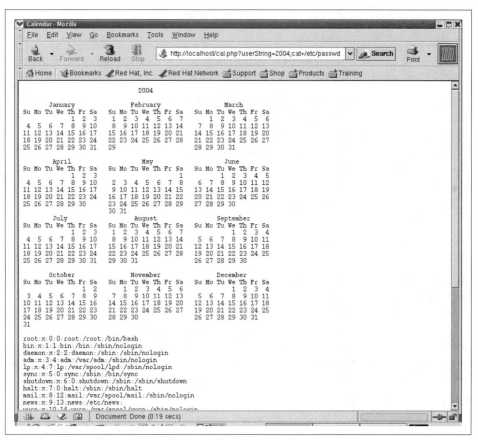

Figure 6-6. Output when the user requests a 2004 calendar and the system password file

The function expects an array (usually $_GET or $_POST) as the first parameter, and a name of a user variable as an index into the array as the second parameter. The third parameter specifies the maximum allowed length of the variable.

The first line of *shellclean()* checks if there's an element in $array with the name $index. If so, the second line uses the *substr( )* function to reduce the variable $input to a maximum length of $maxlength by taking a substring beginning at the first character. For the calendar example you might use a maximum length of seven. The third line calls the library function *EscapeShellArg()*, which encloses the string argument $input in single quotation marks. This has the same effect on a shell command as it does in PHP: it causes all characters except the single quotation to be treated as strings of symbols with no function. This makes special characters harmless when they're passed as parameters to programs.

For many purposes, the *shellclean( )* steps are sufficient to ensure data is safe. As an example, if a parameter userString is passed with the GET method and has a value of:

```
2001;cat /etc/passwd
```

then a call of:

```
shellclean($_GET, "userString", 7)
```

produces the harmless single-quoted string '2001;cat'. This string has no detrimental effect and provides the user with no hidden data.

Our philosophy for processing data is to allow all input except the subset of strings that may cause problems. A stricter approach is to deny all strings except the subset of strings that are allowed for a particular field. For example, in our calendar example, we might only allow strings that consist entirely of numbers and at most one space that match a template of allowed strings. We could do this with a regular expression such as:

```
if (ereg("^(([0-9]{1,2}[ ][0-9]{4})|([0-9]{4}))$", $_GET["userString"]))
  // Parameter is OK
```

We show you field validation techniques, including using regular expressions, in Chapter 9.

SQL querying also has problems. For example, a user can guess the structure of database tables and how a query is formed from user input. A user might guess that a query uses an AND clause and that a particular form text widget provides one of the values to the query. The user might then add additional AND and OR clauses to the query by entering a partial SQL query in the text widget. While such tricks may expose data that should remain hidden from the user, problems compound if the user inserts or deletes data with the techniques discussed in Chapter 8.

To deal with attacks that change your SQL statements, you can use the *shellclean()* function to enclose the user string in single quotations. This works reasonably well, but a better special-purpose approach is to make use of the *mysql_real_escape_string()* function that we discuss later in this chapter. This function inserts a backslash character before each special character, taking into consideration the character set being used on the current connection. We use this function together with *substr()* in our *mysqlclean()* function that we include in the *db.inc* file:

```
function mysqlclean($array, $index, $maxlength, $connection)
{
  if (isset($array["{$index}"]))
  {
    $input = substr($array["{$index}"], 0, $maxlength);
    $input = mysql_real_escape_string($input, $connection);
    return ($input);
  }
  return NULL;
}
```

As with running shell programs, many of the problems of SQL attacks can also be solved with careful server-side validation, and we return to this in Chapter 9.

Querying with User Input

To introduce querying with user input, we begin by explaining a script that retrieves the wines made in a wine region that is specified by a user. This script, shown in Example 6-14, is a companion to the HTML form from Example 6-10. (If you've installed our examples using the instructions in Appendixes A through C, you'll find a modified version of Example 6-10 in the file *example.6-14b.php*. Load the file *example.6-14b.php* in your browser to test Example 6-14.)

Example 6-14. A script to display all wineries in a region

```
<!DOCTYPE HTML PUBLIC
                "-//W3C//DTD HTML 4.01 Transitional//EN"
                "http://www.w3.org/TR/html401/loose.dtd">
<html>
<head>
  <meta http-equiv="Content-Type" content="text/html; charset=iso-8859-1">
  <title>Exploring Wines in a Region</title>
</head>

<body bgcolor="white">
<?php

  require 'db.inc';

  // Show all wines in a region in a <table>
  function displayWinesList($connection,
                            $query,
                            $regionName)
  {
     // Run the query on the server
     if (!($result = @ mysql_query ($query, $connection)))
        showerror();

     // Find out how many rows are available
     $rowsFound = @ mysql_num_rows($result);

     // If the query has results ...
     if ($rowsFound > 0)
     {
        // ... print out a header
        print "Wines of $regionName<br>";

        // and start a <table>.
        print "\n<table>\n<tr>" .
              "\n\t<th>Wine ID</th>" .
              "\n\t<th>Wine Name</th>" .
              "\n\t<th>Year</th>" .
              "\n\t<th>Winery</th>" .
              "\n\t<th>Description</th>\n</tr>";

        // Fetch each of the query rows
```

Example 6-14. A script to display all wineries in a region (continued)

```
        while ($row = @ mysql_fetch_array($result))
        {
            // Print one row of results
            print "\n<tr>\n\t<td>{$row["wine_id"]}</td>" .
                "\n\t<td>{$row["wine_name"]}</td>" .
                "\n\t<td>{$row["year"]}</td>" .
                "\n\t<td>{$row["winery_name"]}</td>" .
                "\n\t<td>{$row["description"]}</td>\n</tr>";
        } // end while loop body

        // Finish the <table>
        print "\n</table>";
    } // end if $rowsFound body

    // Report how many rows were found
    print "{$rowsFound} records found matching your criteria<br>";
} // end of function

// Connect to the MySQL server
if (!($connection = @ mysql_connect($hostName, $username, $password)))
    die("Could not connect");

// Secure the user parameter $regionName
$regionName = mysqlclean($_GET, "regionName", 30, $connection);

if (!mysql_select_db($databaseName, $connection))
    showerror();

// Start a query ...
$query = "SELECT wine_id, wine_name, description, year, winery_name
        FROM   winery, region, wine
        WHERE  winery.region_id = region.region_id
        AND    wine.winery_id = winery.winery_id";

    // ... then, if the user has specified a region, add the regionName
    // as an AND clause ...
    if (isset($regionName) && $regionName != "All")
        $query .= " AND region_name = \"{$regionName}\"";

    // ... and then complete the query.
    $query .= " ORDER BY wine_name";

    // run the query and show the results
    displayWinesList($connection, $query, $regionName);
?>
</body>
</html>
```

The script in Example 6-14 uses the querying techniques discussed so far in this chapter. However, this example differs from the previous ones in several ways:

- It expects input of a wine region to be provided through a form input element with the name regionName.

- The automatically initialized variable $_GET["regionName"] is untainted with the *mysqlclean()* function we discussed in the previous section and then stored in $regionName.
- The value of the variable $regionName is used in querying.

The script builds an SQL query to find wine and winery information for the region entered by the user through the form in Example 6-10. If the user enters a regionName into the form, an additional AND clause is added to the query that restricts the r.region_name to be equal to the user-supplied region name. For example, if the user enters Margaret River, the clause:

```
AND r.region_name = "Margaret River"
```

is added to the query.

If the $regionName is All, no restriction on region is made, and the query retrieves wines for all regions.

The function *displayWinesList()* is called to run the query. It produces a table with headings, processes the result set and produces table rows, and finishes the table with a message indicating how many rows are present in the table. This is similar functionality to that discussed earlier in this chapter.

Other than the processing of the user parameter and the handling of the All regions option, no new functionality is introduced in allowing the user to drive the query process in this example.

One-Component Querying

Many applications allow the user to click on a link that redisplays the same resource but incorporates a change, such as adding a shopping item chosen by the user. This is *one-component* querying, in which the query input component and the results are displayed on the same page. In this section, we discuss how one-component querying is used and the principles of adding one-component queries to an application.

Figure 6-7 illustrates the principle of one-component querying. Let's assume the user is viewing the page *browse.php* in which we refer to this as the *calling* page. When the user selects a link on the calling page, an HTTP request for a PHP script *addcart.php* is sent to the server. At the server, the script *addcart.php* is interpreted by the PHP script engine and, after carrying out the database actions in the script, no output is produced. Instead (and this is the key to one-component querying) an HTTP Location: header is sent as a response to the web browser, and this header causes the browser to request the original calling page, *browse.php*. The result is that the calling page is redisplayed, and the user has the impression that she remained on the query input component page.

A good example of an application of one-component querying is adding items to a shopping cart. One excellent way to support this in our winestore would be to

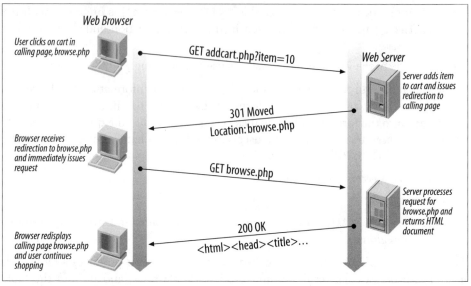

Figure 6-7. The principle of one-component querying

author a script that adds the wine to the user's cart and then redirects the user back to continue shopping. The cart is updated after a click, and the user can continue purchasing wines. We use this technique in Chapter 17.

Example 6-15 shows a one-component script that is requested by a calling page. In practice, the script adds items to a user's shopping cart. However, for simplicity the database queries are not included here.

Example 6-15. Implementing one-component querying

```php
<?php
    require 'db.inc';

    // Database activity occurs here -- process $_GET["input"]

    // This is the key to one-component querying:
    // Redirect the browser back to the calling page, using
    // the HTTP response header "Location:" and the PHP server
    // variable $_SERVER["HTTP_REFERER"]
    header("Location: {$_SERVER["HTTP_REFERER"]}");
    exit;
?>
```

The key to Example 6-15 is the final two lines of a successful execution of the script:

```php
    header("Location: {$_SERVER["HTTP_REFERER"]}");
    exit;
```

The *header()* function sends an additional HTTP response header. In one-component querying, the response includes the Location header that redirects a browser to another

URL, in this case the URL of the calling page. The URL of the calling page is automatically initialized into the PHP web server environment variable $_SERVER["HTTP_REFERER"]. The exit statement causes the script to abort after sending the header so any further statements in the script won't be executed.

 We've used the superglobal array element $_SERVER["HTTP_REFERER"] in conjunction with the *header()* function to redirect to the calling page. This doesn't work on all Microsoft Windows environments. To fix this problem, you need to replace $_SERVER["HTTP_REFERER"] with a script file name. For example, in Example 6-15, replace it with *example.6-16.php*.

Example 6-16 shows an example calling page for the script in Example 6-15. By clicking on the links in the page, the user can submit different values for the input variable to the one-component script for processing. In practice, the links themselves might be generated using an SQL query.

Example 6-16. An example calling page for one component querying.

```
<!DOCTYPE HTML PUBLIC
            "-//W3C//DTD HTML 4.01 Transitional//EN"
            "http://www.w3.org/TR/html401/loose.dtd">
<html>
<head>
  <meta http-equiv="Content-Type" content="text/html; charset=iso-8859-1">
  <title>One Component Test Page</title>
</head>
<body>
<br><a href="example.6-15.php?input=item1">Add Item 1</a>
<br><a href="example.6-15.php?input=item2">Add Item 2</a>
<br><a href="example.6-15.php?input=item3">Add Item 3</a>
<br><a href="example.6-15.php?input=item4">Add Item 4</a>
<br><a href="example.6-15.php?input=item5">Add Item 5</a>
</body>
</html>
```

 The *header()* command can be issued only before data is sent. In one-component querying, the script that carries out the database actions shouldn't produce any output, so this usually isn't a problem. A call to the *header()* function should also be followed by an exit statement if no further processing of statements after the *header()* function call is desired. We discuss the symptoms of *header()* function problems and how to solve them in Chapter 12.

One-component querying is useful in situations where only the query screen is required, or the results page and the query page are the same resource. For example, in the winestore, one-component querying is used to update quantities in the shopping cart when the user alters the quantities of wine. In general, one-component querying works well for simple update operations; these are the subject of Chapter 8.

MySQL Function Reference

This section lists PHP functions for interacting with a MySQL server. We've divided them into those that are frequently used and those that are less frequently used. We've also included a list of the functions we don't use, and the reasons why you should avoid them. We recommend that at a minimum you read the information about the five main functions we've used in this chapter: *mysql_connect( )*, *mysql_select_db( )*, *mysql_query( )*, *mysql_fetch_array( )*, and *mysql_error( )*.

Web database applications can be developed with only a few functions. However, in many cases, additional functionality is required. For example, you may want to choose performance-conscious alternatives and it's often useful to retrieve only a part of the data without processing the complete dataset. Functions for all of these tasks are described in this section. Writing data to a database and the functions *mysql_affected_rows( )* and *mysql_insert_id( )* are discussed in more detail in Chapter 8.

Frequently Used Functions

int mysql_affected_rows([resource connection])
> Returns the number of rows affected by the last UPDATE, DELETE, or INSERT SQL statement, and -1 if the last query failed. The function takes as an optional parameter a server connection resource handle. If no parameter is passed, the most recently opened connection is assumed.
>
> This function doesn't work for SELECT statements; *mysql_num_rows( )* should be used instead.
>
> For example, if a customer is deleted with the SQL statement:
>
> ```
> DELETE FROM customer WHERE CUST_ID=1
> ```
> then *mysql_affected_rows( )* returns a value of 1 if that customer has been successfully deleted.
>
> The function may report that zero rows were affected, even if a statement works successfully, because it is possible that an operation may not modify the database. For example, the statement:
>
> ```
> UPDATE customer SET zipcode='3053' WHERE city = 'Carlton'
> ```
> always executes but *mysql_affected_rows( )* returns 0 if there are no customers who live in Carlton or if the Zip Code of the customers who live in Carlton is already 3053.
>
> If all rows in a table are deleted using a DELETE statement without a WHERE clause, *mysql_affected_rows( )* reports 0 rows were affected.
>
> Examples using *mysql_affected_rows( )* are in Chapter 8.

resource mysql_connect([string hostname[, string username [, string password [, bool new_connection [, int flags]]]]])

Establishes a connection to the MySQL server. The function returns a connection resource handle on success that can be used to access databases through subsequent commands. Returns false on failure.

The command has five optional parameters. In practice, the first three parameters *hostname*, *username*, and *password* are almost always used. The first permits both a *hostname* and an optional port number; the default port for MySQL is 3306 (ports are discussed in more detail in Appendix D). The value localhost is usually supplied as the *hostname* when the server runs on the same machine as the PHP scripting engine.

This function should be called once in a script, assuming you don't close the connection (see *mysql_close( )*) and you don't want a connection with different parameters. Indeed, subsequent calls to the function in the same script with the same parameters don't return a new connection: they return the same connection resource returned from the first successful call to the function. The exception is if the fourth parameter *new_connection* is supplied and set to true: if this is the case, a new connection is always opened. This parameter was added in PHP 4.2.

The fifth parameter *flags* was added in PHP 4.3, and doesn't work reliably at the time of writing. We don't discuss it here.

The *mysql_pconnect()* function is a performance-conscious alternative to *mysql_connect()*, and it's discussed later in this section.

int mysql_errno([resource connection])

Returns the MySQL error number of the last error on the *connection* resource, or zero if no error occurred. If no connection is provided, the most recently opened connection is assumed. Any successful MySQL-related function call resets the value of this function to zero, with the exception of *mysql_error()* and *mysql_errno()*, which do not change the value.

string mysql_error(resource connection)

Returns a descriptive string of the last error on the *connection* resource or an empty string if no error occurred. An optional *connection* can be supplied; otherwise the most-recently opened connection is assumed. Any successful MySQL-related function call resets the text to the empty string, with the exception of *mysql_error()* and *mysql_errno()*, which do not change this value.

array mysql_fetch_array(resource result_set [, int result_type])

Fetches the result set data one row at a time. The first parameter is a result resource *result_set* that was returned from a *mysql_query( )* function call. The results are returned as an array. The function returns false when no more rows are available.

The second parameter, *result_type*, controls whether the returned array can be accessed associatively by attribute name (MYSQL_ASSOC), numerically (MYSQL_NUM), or using both styles (MYSQL_BOTH). The default is MYSQL_BOTH, and changing the parameter won't improve the speed of your code.

The default second parameter to *mysql_fetch_array()* of MYSQL_BOTH works well, except when you plan to print out elements of a row with the foreach loop statement. Because the elements are referenced both numerically and associatively, each element prints out twice. If you plan to use foreach, set the second parameter to MYSQL_ASSOC for associative access or MYSQL_NUM for numeric access, and you'll get only one copy of the data in the array.

When associative access is used, values can be referenced in the array by their table attribute names. Consider an example query on the *wine* table using the *mysql_query()* function:

```
$result = mysql_query("SELECT * FROM wine", $connection)
```

A row can then be retrieved into the array $row using:

```
$row = mysql_fetch_array($result)
```

After retrieving the row, elements of the array $row can be accessed by their attribute names in the *wine* table. For example, print $row["wine_name"] prints the value of the wine_name attribute from the retrieved row. In this example, because the default second parameter is MYSQL_BOTH, you can still access attributes by their element numbers. For example, print $row[1] also works.

If more than one attribute has the same name in a SELECT clause, only the last-listed attribute is available via the associative array, and the other attributes with identical names must be accessed using another approach. The easiest technique is to avoid the problem altogether by making attribute names unique within the database. Another approach is to use numeric access instead, but this leads to hard to maintain, unreadable code. Yet another approach you can use is *attribute aliases*. Attribute aliases allow you rename an attribute to another name, and this name can be used instead throughout the query and in your PHP code; attribute aliases use the SQL AS clause and are discussed in Chapter 15.

Let's assume you're stuck with a query that has duplicate attribute names. Consider the following PHP fragment that deals with dates in the *orders* and *items* tables:

```
$result = mysql_query("SELECT orders.date AS odate, items.date AS idate,
                FROM items, orders WHERE items.order_id = orders.order_id
                AND items.cust_id = orders.cust_id", $connection);

$row = mysql_fetch_array($result);

print "Order: {$row["cust_id"]}-{$row["order_id"]} ";
print "Created: {$row["odate"]} Item added: {$row["idate"]}\n";
```

In this example, the orders.date attribute is renamed to odate and items.date is renamed to idate. The new names can then be used to access the row values in the $row array that's returned from *mysql_fetch_array()*. If you use attribute aliases, the alias must be used to access the data; access with the original attribute name won't work.

You can also use attribute aliases to alias functions in queries, and with *mysql_fetch_array()* this leads to easier to write and read code when accessing the result data. For example, the following fragment shows how the count of customers of the winestore can be aliased and used:

```
$result = mysql_query("SELECT count(cust_id) AS custcount FROM customer",
$connection);

$row = mysql_fetch_array($result);

print "There are {$row["custcount"]} customers";
```

int mysql_insert_id([resource connection])

Returns the AUTO_INCREMENT identifier value associated with the most recently executed SQL INSERT statement. The function returns 0 if the most recent query doesn't use AUTO_INCREMENT. The last connection opened is assumed if the *connection* resource is omitted. This function is discussed in more detail in Chapter 8.

This function should be called immediately after the insertion of a row and the result saved in a variable, because the function works for a connection and not on a per-query basis. Subsequent queries through the same connection make it impossible to retrieve previous key values using this function.

The *mysql_insert_id( )* function doesn't work with the MySQL BIGINT attribute type. If you use BIGINT for an AUTO_INCREMENT attribute, use the MySQL function *LAST_INSERT_ID()* (that's discussed in Chapter 15) in an SQL SELECT statement to discover the value instead.

Consider an example where the AUTO_INCREMENT feature is used on the cust_id attribute of the *customer* table. The function can be used to find out which cust_id primary key value was assigned after a NULL or 0 was inserted into the attribute during an INSERT INTO customer operation.

int mysql_num_rows(resource result_set)

This function returns the number of rows associated with the *result_set* query result resource handle. Queries that modify a database should use *mysql_affected_rows( )*.

The function *mysql_num_rows( )* works only for SELECT queries, and it doesn't work with *mysql_unbuffered_query( )* until all rows have been retrieved from the result set. Unbuffered querying is discussed later in this section.

If the number of rows in a table is required but not the data itself, it is usually more efficient to run an SQL query of the form SELECT count(*) FROM table and retrieve the result, rather than running SELECT * FROM table and then using *mysql_num_rows( )* to determine the number of rows in the table.

resource mysql_pconnect([string host[:port] [, string user [, string password [, int flags]]]])

This function is a performance-oriented alternative to *mysql_connect( )* that reuses open connections to the MySQL server. The p in *mysql_pconnect( )* stands for *persistent*, meaning that a connection to the server stays open after a script terminates.

This function opens a connection and returns the same results as its non-persistent sibling *mysql_connect( )*. It has the same first three optional parameters as *mysql_connect( )*, and since PHP 4.3, it has a fourth optional parameter that is the same as the fifth parameter of *mysql_connect( )*. This function, unlike it's non-persistent sibling *mysql_connect( )*, doesn't offer an argument that lets you force open a new connection.

Open connections are maintained as a pool that is available to PHP. When a call to *mysql_pconnect( )* is made, a pooled connection is used in preference to creating a new connection. Using pooled connections saves the costs of opening and closing connections. Whether persistency is faster in practice depends on the server configuration and the application. However, in general, for web database applications with many users running on a server with plenty of main memory, persistency is likely to improve performance.

A connection opened with *mysql_pconnect( )* can't be closed with *mysql_close( )*. It stays open until unused for a period of time. The timeout is a MySQL server parameter, not a PHP parameter, and is set by default to 28800 seconds! It can (and should) be adjusted with a command-line option to the MySQL server script *mysqld_safe* or by changing the MySQL configuration file. For example, to start your MySQL with the timeout set to a more realistic 10 seconds on the command line, on a Unix system use:

```
% /usr/local/mysql/bin/mysqld_safe --set-variable interactive_timeout=10
```

To set the parameter permanently in your global MySQL configuration file, add the following line under the [mysql] heading:

```
set-variable= interactive_timeout = 10
```

If you followed the installation instructions in Appendixes A through C, you'll find the file as */etc/my.cnf* on a Unix system or *C:\winnt\my.ini* under Windows 2000/2003/NT and *C:\windows\my.ini* under Windows XP.

string mysql_real_escape_string (string query [, resource connection])

Escapes a *query* string so that it can be used as a parameter to *mysql_query( )* or *mysql_unbuffered_query( )*. The function returns a copy of the input string that has any special characters escaped so that is safe to use in an SQL query. This is useful when querying with user data, or when loading data from an external source; we discuss processing user data later in this chapter.

To carry out the escaping, the function checks the character set associated with the optional *connection*. If no *connection* is provided, the most recently opened connection is assumed. As an example, for the ASCII character set, this function escapes single quote, double quote, NULL, carriage return, line feed, and SUB (substitute) characters by inserting a backslash character before them.

This function is available since PHP 4.3. If you're using an older version, use *mysql_escape_string( )* which does not support the second parameter (and, therefore, does not take into account the character set of the connection).

resource mysql_query(string SQL [, resource connection [,int mode]])

Runs an SQL statement. The second argument is a *connection* resource returned from a call to *mysql_connect( )*. On success, the function never returns a false value. For SELECT, SHOW, EXPLAIN, or DESCRIBE queries, the function returns a query result resource that can be used to fetch data. For other SQL queries, the function returns true on success. The function returns false on failure.

The query string passed to *mysql_query( )* doesn't need to be terminated with a semicolon.

If the second parameter to *mysql_query( )* is omitted, PHP tries to use any open connection to the MySQL server starting with the most-recently opened. If no connections are open, a call to *mysql_connect( )* with no parameters is issued. In practice, the second parameter should be supplied.

The third parameter defaults to MYSQL_STORE_RESULT, and we recommend not changing it. Use the *mysql_unbuffered_query( )* function that's discussed later in this section if you don't want query results to be stored.

bool mysql_select_db (string database [, resource connection])

Uses the specified *database* on a *connection*. If the second parameter is omitted, the last connection opened is assumed, or an attempt is made to open a connection with *mysql_connect( )* and no parameters. We caution against omitting the *connection* parameter. The function returns true on success and false on failure.

resource mysql_unbuffered_query(string query [, resource connection [, int mode]])

This function starts a query, but returns immediately without retrieving and buffering the whole result set. The parameters and return values are the same as *mysql_query( )*.

This function is useful for queries that return large result sets or that are slow to execute, as it allows the script to continue with the processing or formatting of data while the query runs. Another advantage is that no resources are required to store a large result set. In contrast, by default, the function *mysql_query( )* doesn't return until the query is complete and the results have been buffered.

The third parameter defaults to MYSQL_USE_RESULT, and we recommend not changing it. Use the *mysql_query( )* function that's discussed earlier in this section if you want query results to be buffered.

There are four important issues associated with the function:

- The number of rows produced by the query can't be checked with *mysql_num_rows( )* until the total number of rows are known after the query finishes.

- Specific rows can't be retrieved with *mysql_data_seek( )* because data is retrieved sequentially, and it's not possible to seek to a row until it has been retrieved.

- You must completely process each query on a connection before you run another query. This means you have to retrieve all of the query results using, for example, a while loop, even if you don't need them. A workaround is to use two server connections to run two queries at the same time, or to better design your queries so that they only retrieve the data you really need.

- A script won't finish until its server connections are no longer active. This behavior confuses new users: the function call will return immediately, but the script won't end and free its resources until all of its queries finish running.

- The function is otherwise identical to *mysql_query( )*. It is available in PHP 4.0.6 or later.

Other Functions

string mysql_client_encoding([resource connection])
Returns the name of the character set in use on the *connection*. If a connection isn't provided, the most recently opened connection is assumed. Available since PHP 4.3.0.

bool mysql_close([resource connection])
Closes a MySQL connection that was opened with *mysql_connect( )*. The *connection* parameter is optional. If it is omitted, the most recently opened connection is closed. Returns true on success and false on failure.

The primary use of this function is to save resources when you don't want a connection to stay open while a script runs. Most programs do not need to call this function because they use the connection until shortly before they terminate, and their termination automatically cleans up open connections.

This function has no effect on persistent connections opened with *mysql_pconnect( )*.

bool mysql_data_seek(resource result, int row)
This function lets you retrieve only selected results from a query, which is useful to reduce processing in an application. For example, executing the function for a *result* with a *row* parameter of 10, and then issuing a *mysql_fetch_array( )* retrieves the eleventh row of the result set; rows are numbered from zero.

The parameter *result* is a result resource returned from *mysql_query( )*. The function returns true on success and false on failure. A common source of failure is that there are no rows in the result set associated with the *result* resource. A prior call to *mysql_num_rows( )* can be used to determine if results were returned from the query.

 The *mysql_data_seek( )* function cannot be used with *mysql_unbuffered_query( )*.

object mysql_fetch_field(resource result [, int attribute_number])
Returns the metadata for each attribute associated with a *result* resource returned from a query function call. An optional *attribute_number* can be specified to retrieve the metadata associated with a specific attribute. However, repeated calls process the attributes one by one.

The properties of the object returned by the function are:

name
> The attribute name

table
> The name of the table to which the attribute belongs.

max_length
> The maximum length of the attribute.

not_null
> Set to 1 if the attribute cannot be NULL.

primary_key
> Set to 1 if the attribute forms part of a primary key.

unique_key
> Set to 1 if the attribute is a unique key.

multiple_key
> Set to 1 if the attribute is a non-unique key.

numeric
> Set to 1 if the attribute is a numeric type.

blob
> Set to 1 if the attribute is a BLOB type.

type
> The type of the attribute.

unsigned
> Set to 1 if the attribute is an unsigned numeric type.

zerofill
> Set to 1 if the numeric column is zero-filled.

def
> The default value of the attribute (if specified).

array mysql_fetch_lengths(qresource query)

Returns an array of attribute lengths associated with the most-recently retrieved row of data. The argument to the function is a *query* result resource that has been used to retrieve at least one row. The elements of the returned array correspond to the length of the values in the array returned from the most-recent call to *mysql_fetch_array()* or *mysql_fetch_object()*. It returns false on error.

This function returns the length of a value within the query results, not the maximum length of an attribute as defined in the database table. Use the function *mysql_fetch_field()* to retrieve the maximum allowed length of an attribute.

object mysql_fetch_object(resource result)

This function is an alternative for returning results from a query. It returns an instance of an object that contains one row of results associated with the result resource, permitting access to values in an object by their table attribute names. It returns false when no more rows are available.

For example, after a query to SELECT * from wine, a row can be retrieved into the object $object using:

```
$object = mysql_fetch_object($result)
```

The attributes can then be accessed in $object by their attribute names. For example:

```
print $object->wine_name
```

prints the value of the wine_name attribute from the retrieved row.

It's hard work to use objects returned from *mysql_fetch_object( )* to access aggregate functions, and sometimes you'll get into trouble with attribute names and corresponding variable name limitations. Also, attributes can't be accessed numerically. However, attribute aliases (which are discussed in Chapter 15) can help in most cases.

In our applications, we exclusively use *mysql_fetch_array( )* instead.

bool mysql_free_result(resource result)

This function frees the resources associated with a query *result* resource. Resources are cleaned-up when a script finishes, so this function is only needed if a script repeatedly queries the server or if several large result sets are buffered. The function returns true on success and false on failure.

string mysql_get_client_info()

Returns a string that describes the MySQL client library used by PHP. Available since PHP 4.0.5.

string mysql_get_host_info([resource connection])

Returns a string that describes a MySQL server connection. The string contains the type of connection (TCP or Unix socket) and the host name. An optional *connection* resource handle may be provided as the parameter; otherwise the most recently opened connection is assumed. Available since PHP 4.0.5.

int mysql_get_proto_info([resource connection])

Returns an integer that is the protocol version used in a MySQL server connection. An optional *connection* resource handle may be provided as the parameter; otherwise the most recently opened connection is assumed. Available since PHP 4.0.5.

string mysql_get_server_info([resource connection])

Returns as a string the version of the MySQL server. An optional *connection* resource handle may be provided as the parameter, otherwise the most recently opened connection is assumed. Available since PHP 4.0.5.

string mysql_info([resource connection])

Returns a descriptive string such as *Records: 20 Duplicates: 0 Warnings: 0* that describes the results of the last INSERT, LOAD DATA INFILE, ALTER TABLE or UPDATE query; the ALTER TABLE and LOAD DATA INFILE statements are discussed in Chapter 15. The string is the same as returned in the MySQL command interpreter after running the query. This is useful to display to database administrators, or can be parsed and used in application logic when *mysql_affected_rows( )* doesn't serve the purpose. Available since PHP 4.3.0.

resource mysql_list_processes([resource connection])

Returns a resource that can be used with *mysql_fetch_array( )* to retrieve information about active processes running on the database server. An optional *connection* can be provided or the most recently opened connection is assumed. The data that is returned has the following array keys: Id (process ID), User, Host, db (currently selected database), Command (the currently running command in the process), Time (elapsed run time), State, and Info. Available since PHP 4.3.0.

int mysql_num_fields(resource result_set)

Returns the number of attributes associated with a result set handle *result_set*. The result set handle is returned from a prior call to *mysql_query( )*.

In practice, you probably don't need to use this function. If you use *mysql_fetch_array( )*, the *count( )* function gives you the same result.

bool mysql_ping([resource connection])

Checks whether a connection is working. Returns true on success, and false on failure. If a *connection* isn't provided, the most recently opened connection is assumed. When the connection isn't working, an automatic attempt is made to reestablish the connection.

The function's primary use is checking if a remote connection is still working during a lengthy operation, and trying to recover if it isn't. Most of the time, in simple PHP scripts, you'll be able to detect errors with the MySQL error functions that are discussed in the next section. Available since PHP 4.3.0.

int mysql_thread_id([resource connection])

Returns the current thread or process identifier. An optional *connection* can be provided, or the last opened connection is assumed. It returns false on failure, although it very rarely fails. Even if a connection is not open, a sensible value is returned—the function will fail only if the MySQL server isn't running. Available since PHP 4.3.0.

Functions to Avoid

Several MySQL functions don't need to be used:

- The functions of *mysql_fetch_field( )* are also available in the non-object-based alternatives *mysql_fetch_length( )*, *mysql_field_flags( )*, *mysql_field_name( )*, *mysql_field_len( )*, *mysql_field_table( )*, and *mysql_field_type( )*; as these functions are almost a complete subset of *mysql_fetch_field( )*, we don't describe them here and we don't use them in our applications.

- The function *mysql_result( )* is a slower alternative to fetching and processing a row with *mysql_fetch_array( )* and shouldn't be used in practice.

- *mysql_fetch_assoc( )* and *mysql_fetch_row( )* retrieve one row of results from a query. Each provides half the functionality of *mysql_fetch_array( )*. Because *mysql_fetch_array( )* provides both sets of functionality—or can provide the same functionality by passing through MYSQL_ASSOC or MYSQL_NUM as the second parameter—it can be used instead.

- *mysql_field_seek( )* can seek to a specific field for a subsequent call to *mysql_fetch_field( )*, but this is redundant because the field number can be supplied directly to *mysql_fetch_field( )* as the optional second parameter.

- *mysql_db_query( )* was popular in PHP 3, and combines the functionality of *mysql_select_db( )* and *mysql_query( )*. This function has been deprecated in recent releases of PHP because it is slower than selecting the database once with *mysql_select_db( )*, and then issuing queries.

- *mysql_change_user( )* is used to change the username associated with an open connection. This function is broken in PHP 4.

- *mysql_escape_string( )* is a deprecated version of *mysql_real_escape_string( )* that ignores the current character set for a MySQL connection.

- *mysql_drop_db( )* has been deprecated because it's easy to issue a MySQL DROP DATABASE statement instead.

- *mysql_create_db( )* performs the same function as a MySQL CREATE DATABASE statement.

- *mysql_db_name( )* and *mysql_list_dbs( )* perform the same function as a MySQL SHOW DATABASES, and then using *mysql_fetch_array( )* to retrieve the database names.

- *mysql_tablename( )* and *mysql_list_tables( )* perform the same function as a MySQL SHOW TABLES, and then using *mysql_fetch_array( )* to retrieve the table names.

- *mysql_stat( )* performs a subset of the functions of the MySQL SHOW STATUS command.

CHAPTER 7

PEAR

PEAR is the *PHP Extension and Application Repository* and is pronounced the same as the fruit. It provides standard, structured, maintained packages of code for common tasks such as data validation, accessing database servers, payment processing, using web services, processing images, and reading and writing files. Installing, updating, and using the PEAR packages is easy, and core components are now installed with the standard PHP installation. In this chapter, we explain how to build robust, maintainable middle-tier software using PEAR.

One of the original design features of PHP was its flexibility for adding scripts to HTML documents. For simple applications, this is an excellent feature. For complex applications, it leads to difficult-to-maintain code and inflexible HTML. We show you how to solve separating scripts from HTML using PEAR's Integrated Templates. We also show you how make your PHP code independent of the database server you choose with PEAR's DB layer. With these two techniques, you'll be able to develop maintainable code that's independent of the client and database tiers.

In addition to database access and templates, we also explain how to install PEAR packages and introduce 40 popular PEAR packages. Our case study application, *Hugh and Dave's Online Wines*, is built with several of these PEAR packages, as well as PEAR DB and Integrated Templates. It's discussed in detail in Chapters 16 through 20.

Overview

PEAR is a web-based repository for common application components and PHP extensions. Version 1.0 was released as an integrated part of PHP 4.3.0 for Unix systems, and in PHP 4.3.2 for Microsoft Windows. The current release of PEAR includes packages for:

- Working with HTML and HTTP
- Manipulating and validating user data

- Sending, receiving, and processing email
- Credit card payment processing
- Using web services including SOAP
- Encryption
- Reading and writing files including compressed archives
- Graphing and image processing
- Using XML

Each package is a separate product, with its own development team, but each uses PEAR foundation classes and almost all adhere to the PEAR coding standards. Similarly to PHP, the complete source code of the packages is available, and it's often useful as a supplement to the sparse and sometimes dated online documentation.

The package installation process is easy: packages are installed by typing a command at the shell prompt in Unix-style systems or by running a batch utility in Microsoft Windows. This is possible because all packages are registered and stored in the central *http://pear.php.net* repository that also provides account and version management to the developers. In addition, the packages are arranged so that if they depend on each other, you'll be alerted if you're missing a package during the installation process. We discuss installation in the section "Optional Packages."

Our focus in this chapter is describing how you can install and use packages, and how to work with the *Integrated Templates* and *PEAR DB* packages. We also briefly discuss other packages, and some are discussed further in Chapter 9 where we discuss data validation.

PEAR has other components that we don't discuss in detail here:

- A PHP coding standard primarily for the developers of packages.
- *PECL* (pronounced *pickle*), a repository of C programming language extensions that have traditionally been distributed with PHP.
- *Gtk packages* for use with the PHP-GTK project that provides tools for developing window-based applications. See *http://gtk.php.net.*

Core Components

PEAR's core components are general-purpose, reliable packages that work with most web servers, database servers, browsers, and operating systems. If you're using PHP 4.3 or later on a Unix system, the PEAR core components and the PEAR installer for adding other packages are already installed and ready for use. For Microsoft Windows, the integration occurred in PHP 4.3.2.

The list of core components can change but at the time of writing it includes:

PEAR base and error handling classes

These are the foundations of other PEAR packages, and you don't need a detailed understanding of them unless you plan to develop your own package. We discuss error handling in our introduction to PEAR DB in the next section.

PEAR Console command-line parsing

Used for non-web scripts.

PEAR DB

Database server abstraction. Discussed in detail in the next section.

HTTP methods

Used to format HTTP-compliant dates, negotiate language, and compress data for fast transfer.

PEAR Mail

Used for mail sending, including platform independence, MIME attachments, and correct email address validation.

PEAR System

Platform-independent commands for making and removing directories and files, concatenating files, and finding the full path of a program.

What's Installed?

Now, let's check the core components distributed with your PHP installation.

Unix systems—PHP 4.3.0 and later

For the instructions in this section to work, you must have followed our installation instructions in Appendixes A to C. You also need an active Internet connection.

To check the list of components installed, you need to login as the root user; to do this, type **su** at a shell prompt and provide the root user password.

If you're working with Mac OS X, type at a shell prompt:

```
% cd /usr/local/bin
```

Then, on all systems, type the following at a shell prompt:

```
% pear list
```

You'll see a list in the following format:

```
Installed packages:
===================
+------------------+---------+--------+
| Package          | Version | State  |
| Archive_Tar      | 0.9     | stable |
| Console_Getopt   | 1.0     | stable |
| DB               | 1.3     | stable |
| HTTP             | 1.2     | stable |
| Mail             | 1.0.1   | stable |
```

```
| Net_SMTP      | 1.0   | stable |
| Net_Socket    | 1.0.1 | stable |
| PEAR          | 1.0b3 | stable |
| XML_Parser    | 1.0   | stable |
| XML_RPC       | 1.0.4 | stable |
```

You may find that the versions you have are different. This isn't a problem.

Microsoft Windows—PHP 4.3.2 and later

For the instructions in this section to work, you must have followed our installation instructions in Appendixes A to C. You also need an active Internet connection.

Start by launching a command window. You can do this by running the file *command.com* or running a DOS prompt window (if it's listed in your Accessories group under Programs in your Start Menu).

To run *command.com*, click on the Start Menu, then the Run option. Now, type **command.com** and press Enter.

In your command window, change directory to the pear install directory. If you've followed our install instructions in Appendixes A to C, type:

```
C:\> cd c:\Progra~1\EasyPH~1\php\pear
```

Then, type the following:

```
C:\> pear.bat list
```

A list of installed packages is shown in the following format:

```
INSTALLED PACKAGES:
====================
PACKAGE         VERSION  STATE
Archive_Tar     0.9      stable
Console_Getopt  1.0      stable
DB              1.3      stable
HTTP            1.2      stable
Mail            1.0.1    stable
Net_SMTP        1.0      stable
Net_Socket      1.0.1    stable
PEAR            1.0b3    stable
XML_Parser      1.0      stable
XML_RPC         1.0.4    stable
```

You may find that the versions you have are different. This isn't a problem.

If you want to close the command window, type **exit**. However, you'll need this window later in this chapter, so keeping it open is fine.

Using PEAR DB

In most PHP applications, one of the server-specific database libraries is used to access the database server. In Chapter 6, we showed you how to access the MySQL

---

sever using the MySQL library functions. In this section, we show you how to develop reasonably server-independent scripts using PEAR's DB component. We also use the PEAR DB class throughout our online winestore in Chapters 16 through 20.

Should I use PEAR DB?

If you want server-independent function calls, PEAR's DB component is ideal because the code usually doesn't change when you change the underlying database server. However, there are sometimes needs for small changes, such as catering for different function return values or rewriting code because a database server doesn't support a feature. For example, only some of the underlying servers support the *tableInfo()* method for returning metadata about table attributes.

If you don't use PEAR DB, changing database servers can be time-consuming. If you switch between similar libraries—such as the MySQL and PostgreSQL libraries—then updating the code usually doesn't require too much work: it's largely a case of changing the *mysql_* prefix to a *pgsql_* prefix, and perhaps tackling complex querying in a different way. However, if you change to a less-similar library—such as one of the Oracle libraries or ODBC—then more work is required even for the simple tasks.

PEAR DB will almost give you function library independence, but it won't give you complete database server independence. SQL isn't the same between any two servers: as we discussed in Chapter 1, combinations of the features of SQL-89, SQL-92, and SQL-99 are often implemented, and many servers have proprietary statements for tasks. For example, MySQL supports entry-level SQL-92, but uses proprietary clauses such as LIMIT and AUTO_INCREMENT, and attribute types such as LONGINT and TIMESTAMP. Even if you use PEAR DB, it's almost impossible (and probably not sensible) to avoid using proprietary SQL.

For many developers, it isn't clear whether database abstraction offers an advantage: many developers don't bother writing server-independent code because their SQL is tied to the database server. In fact, if you're sure you'll be using one database server for the lifetime of an application, we recommend using the proprietary library so that you can take advantage of the specialized functions designed for the database server.

In most of the applications we've developed, we've used the MySQL library functions outlined in Chapter 6. However, to illustrate how to use PEAR DB and to give you code that will work with minimal modification for other database servers, we've used it to develop our online winestore in Chapters 16 through 20.

Getting started

In this section, we assume you've read Chapter 6 and are familiar with the basic querying processes and the core MySQL library functions. Also, you'll need to be familiar with the basic object-oriented PHP features discussed in Chapter 4.

Example 7-1 shows how to connect, query, and retrieve results using PEAR DB. The example is an extended version of Example 6-1 that includes error handling.

Example 7-1. Using PEAR DB to query the winestore database

```
<!DOCTYPE HTML PUBLIC
                "-//W3C//DTD HTML 4.01 Transitional//EN"
                "http://www.w3.org/TR/html401/loose.dtd">
<html>
<head>
  <meta http-equiv="Content-Type" content="text/html; charset=iso-8859-1">
  <title>Wines</title>
</head>
<body><pre>
<?php
   require_once "DB.php";
   require "db.inc";

   $dsn = "mysql://{$username}:{$password}@{$hostName}/{$databaseName}";

   // Open a connection to the DBMS
   $connection = DB::connect($dsn);

   if (DB::isError($connection))
      die($connection->getMessage());

   // (Run the query on the winestore through the connection
   $result = $connection->query("SELECT * FROM wine");

   if (DB::isError($result))
      die ($result->getMessage());

   // While there are still rows in the result set, fetch the current
   // row into the array $row
   while ($row = $result->fetchRow(DB_FETCHMODE_ASSOC))
   {
     // Print out each element in $row, that is, print the values of
     // the attributes
     foreach ($row as $attribute)
        print "{$attribute} ";

     print "\n";
   }
?>
</pre>
</body>
</html>
```

As discussed previously, there's no need to download or install any extra components to use the PEAR core components. The PEAR DB class is used within a script by requiring it:

```
require_once "DB.php";
```

If you find that your PHP engine can't find *DB.php*, it's likely that your include_path directive in your *php.ini* configuration file doesn't include the PEAR directory. Check the installation instructions for your platform in Appendixes A to C.

Connecting to a database server uses a URL-style string. In the example, this string consists of the familiar $username, $password, $hostName, and $databaseName from the *db.inc* require file:

```
$dsn = "mysql://{$username}:{$password}@{$hostName}/{$databaseName}";
```

For the defaults in the *db.inc* file, this gives the string:

```
mysql://fred:shhh@localhost/winestore
```

We store the string in a variable with the acronym $dsn to signify this is the *data source name*. The prefix mysql:// indicates the MySQL server, and the string fred: shhh@localhost specifies the username, password, and host parameters that are used with the *mysql_connect()* and *mysql_pconnect()* functions. Rather than use the separate *mysql_select_db()* function to use the database, it's specified following a forward slash character.

The connection itself is established with the method *DB::connect()*:

```
$connection = DB::connect($dsn);
```

The notation *DB::* means that the method *connect()* is a member of the class DB. Error handling is discussed in the next section.

The *DB::query()* method works similarly to *mysql_query()*, taking the SQL query as a parameter and returning a result resource that can be used to retrieve data from a SELECT query:

```
$result = $connection->query("SELECT * FROM wine");
```

The result rows are retrieved using the *DB::fetchRow()* method:

```
while ($row = $result->fetchRow(DB_FETCHMODE_ASSOC))
```

The method behaves similarly to *mysql_fetch_array()*. The parameter DB_FETCHMODE_ ASSOC specifies that the return array has associatively-accessible elements that are named with the database attribute names or attribute aliases; however, this isn't important in this example because we use foreach to iteratively process all elements of the array.

Handling errors in PEAR DB

The error status of any database server method can be tested using *DB::isError()*. Unlike in the MySQL library, this method can be used regardless of whether a connection has been established yet or not. If an error occurs, the *getMessage()* method can be used to retrieve a descriptive string as in the following example:

```
// Open a connection to the DBMS
$connection = DB::connect($dsn);

if (DB::isError($connection))
  die($connection->getMessage());
```

The *getMessage()* method is part of the core PEAR error class. The method works similarly for testing errors from queries:

```
$result = $connection->query("SELECT * FROM wine");

if (DB::isError($result))
    die ($result->getMessage( ));
```

Note that the method can be used with many types of objects: for connections, we use the $connection object and for results we use $result.

If a method or parameter is unsupported by the underlying database server, you'll find that the following error is reported:

```
DB_error: database not capable
```

Essential functions for accessing MySQL with PEAR DB

Methods for interacting with database servers using PEAR DB are the subject of this section. We've included the essential methods, and omitted those that are less-frequently used, redundant, or aren't used with MySQL. More detail on all methods can be found in the PEAR manual at *http://pear.php.net/manual/en/package.database. php#package.database.db*.

For most PEAR DB methods, we've noted which native MySQL functions are used in the library to implement the functionality that's described. Chapter 6 presents the detail of the underlying MySQL functions, and you'll find that the limitations and advantages of those functions affects PEAR DB too. We recommend reading the MySQL function notes in conjunction with the PEAR DB descriptions.

mixed DB::affectedRows( )
> Returns the number of rows that were affected by the previous database-modifying query. Returns a DB_ERROR object on failure. (The return type *mixed* indicates that the type of the value returned by the method isn't always one type.)

> For MySQL, the underlying function is *mysql_affected_rows( )*. However, unlike *mysql_affected_rows( )* a workaround ensures *affectedRows( )* provides the correct value when all rows are deleted from a table. *DB_Result::numRows( )* should be used for queries that do not modify the database.

> This method, and database modifications in general, are discussed in Chapter 8.

mixed DB::connect(string dsn [, bool persistent])
> Connect to a DBMS using the parameters specified in the data source name *dsn*. If *persistent* is true and the DBMS supports persistent connections, a persistent connection is used, otherwise the default of false returns a non-persistent connection. The function returns a database connection object on success or a DB_ error object on failure.

> The data source name *dsn* is specified in the following format or one of its simplifications:

```
dbms://username:password@protocol+host:port/database
```

where the following is applicable:

dbms

> The type of DBMS to connect to. The options that are supported in release 1.17 are dbase (dBase file support), fbase (FrontBase), ibase (InterBase), ifx (Informix), mssql (Microsoft SQL server), msql (mSQL), mysql (MySQL 3.x), mysql4 (MySQL 4.x), oci8 (Oracle OCI8), odbc (ODBC), pgsql (PostgreSQL), and sybase (Sybase).

username

> The username to connect with.

password

> The password associated with the username.

protocol

> Communication protocol such as tcp or unix. Often omitted.

host

> The hostname of the DBMS server. Often localhost for the local machine.

port

> The port to connect to on the host.

database

> The name of the database to use on the connection.

Several simplifications of the *dsn* are possible and are described in the manual. By far the most common format uses the default protocol and port:

```
dbms://username:password@host/database
```

For MySQL, *mysql_connect()* is used if the second parameter is false or omitted, and *mysql_pconnect()* is used when it's true.

mixed DB::createSequence(string name)

> Creates a new sequence *name*. Returns the result of the query that creates the sequence, or a DB_ERROR object on failure. See *DB::nextId()* for an introduction to sequences. An example of using sequences in presented in Chapter 8.

mixed DB::dropSequence(string name)

> Deletes a sequence *name*. Returns the result of the query that deletes the sequence, or a DB_ERROR object on failure. See *DB::nextId()* for an introduction to sequences. An example of using sequences in presented in Chapter 8.

mixed DB_Result::fetchRow([int mode [, int row]])

> Retrieve a row of results using an optional *mode* and an optional *row*. By default, the rows are returned into a numerically-accessed array. The function returns the row on success and NULL when there is no more data to fetch. On error, it returns a DB_ERROR object.

> The *mode* can be one of DB_FETCHMODE_ORDERED (a numerically accessed array, which is the default when no parameter is supplied), DB_FETCHMODE_ASSOC (an associatively accessed array), or DB_FETCHMODE_OBJECT (an object with attribute names as properties). An optional *row* to retrieve can be specified after the *mode*.

For MySQL, the current release uses *mysql_fetch_array( )* to provide the functionality of DB_FETCHMODE_ASSOC and DB_FETCHMODE_OBJECT, and its numeric-only sibling *mysql_fetch_row( )* for numeric access. The function *mysql_data_seek( )* is used to retrieve specific rows.

bool DB::isError(DB_error object)

Reports true when the parameter *object* is of type DB_error, and false otherwise. It is often used with the return values of *DB::connect( )* and *DB::query( )* as the parameter. The error is usually output using *getMessage( )* as shown in the previous section.

mixed DB::nextId(string name [, bool create])

Returns the next unique identifier value associated with the string *name* or a DB_ ERROR object on failure. The identifier that is returned is usually used as input into an INSERT statement to create a new row with a unique primary key value. If the sequence *name* does not exist, it is automatically created if *create* is set to true (which is the default). Sequences can be manually created with *DB:: createSequence( )* and deleted with *DB::dropSequence( )*.

In the PHP MySQL library, the *mysql_insert_id( )* function returns the unique value associated with an INSERT operation after the operation has occurred. In contrast, the *DB::nextId( )* method reports a table-independent value prior to the INSERT operation occurring. Database modifications are discussed further in Chapter 8, and an example of using *DB::nextId( )* is presented there.

int DB_Result::numRows( )

Returns the number of rows associated with a query result object, or a DB_ERROR object on failure. *DB::affectedRows( )* should be used for queries that modify the database.

In MySQL, the function *mysql_num_rows( )* provides the underlying functionality.

mixed DB::query (string query [, array parameters])

Executes an SQL *query*. An optional array of *parameters* can be provided to prepare a query; we discuss query preparation in Appendix F.

For MySQL, the function returns a MySQL result resource for SELECT queries on success, the constant DB_OK for other successful queries, and a DB_ERROR object on failure.

string DB::quote(string query)

Escapes a *query* string so that it can be used a parameter to *DB::query( )*. It returns a copy of the input string that has any special characters escaped. For a MySQL connection, the function uses *mysql_real_escape_string( )* in PHP 4.3 or later, and *mysql_escape_string( )* otherwise.

mixed DB_Result::tableInfo(DB_Result result [, int mode])

Returns an array of metadata about the attributes of the `result` set using an optional `mode`. Returns a DB_ERROR object on failure. The function works for MySQL, MS-SQL, FrontBase, and PostgreSQL.

With no second parameter, the array that is returned is two-dimensional. The first dimension is the attribute number, and the second has the following associative keys:

name
> The name of the attribute.

type
> The attribute type.

len
> The attribute maximum length.

flags
> A string containing a list of attribute flags. For example, in MySQL the flags can include not_null, primary_key, auto_increment, and timestamp.

table
> The name of the table associated with the attribute.

You can pass a second parameter, DB_TABLEINFO_ORDER, which makes one additional element available. This element can be retrieved through the associative key order. Its second dimension is filled with the names of the attributes and the values are set to the attribute numbers. This allows you to determine the attribute number using the attribute name, so that the metadata can be accessed in two steps by attribute name. For example, to access the attribute length metadata for the attribute wine_name:

```
$array = $result->tableInfo($result, DB_TABLEINFO_ORDER);

// What's the attribute number of wine_name?
$number = $array["order"]["wine_name"];

// Print out the length of the wine_name
print "Attribute length: {$array[$number]["len"]}";
```

Another second parameter is available, but it is unnecessary if you use attribute aliases in your queries to avoid duplicate attribute names as discussed in Chapter 6.

The function is similar in concept to *mysql_fetch_field( )* but it returns an array instead of an object. It is implemented for MySQL using the non-object based siblings of *mysql_fetch_field( )* (which are listed in Chapter 6 as functions we don't recommend you use).

Packages

In this section, we discuss the optional packages that are available with PEAR, how to find out about them, how to find new ones, and how to install the ones you need. However, our focus is the optional *HTML Integrated Template (IT) package*, which is used to separate HTML presentation from PHP code. We show you how to use templates in an application, present working examples, and detail the key functions from the package and its extended child *ITX templates*. A longer template case study is presented in Chapter 16.

After our discussion of the IT package, we list the other packages that are available, and point to where selected packages are used in other chapters of this book.

Installing, Upgrading, and Understanding Packages

This section describes how to install and upgrade PEAR packages, and how to find out more information about them. For Unix platforms, including Mac OS X, the instructions are valid for PHP 4.3.0 or later versions. For Microsoft Windows, PEAR installation and upgrade is available after PHP 4.3.2.

Finding out about packages

At the time of writing, the PEAR documentation available at *http://pear.php.net/manual/en/* was incomplete. However, you'll find some useful information there, particularly about the core components and a handful of the popular optional packages.

To go beyond the limited documentation, the first step is to access the package browser at *http://pear.php.net/packages.php* or search for a known package directly at *http://pear.php.net/package-search.php*. You can also access the same information using the PEAR installer, as described later in this section. This process provides you with concise information that sums up a package, and often a link to the project's homepage that may contain more details and code examples.

To begin to use a package, the best approach is to install it, review the source code of the package, and read any relevant postings to the *php.pear.general* newsgroup which is accessible at *http://news.php.net/*. To review the source code, you can follow two approaches: first, visit the source at *http://cvs.php.net/cvs.php/pear/*; or, second, view it on your system after the install process using the approach described later in this section. This process can sometimes be laborious but it's worth remembering that many of these packages are new, emerging, and supported to different degrees by their development teams. Reading source code is definitely worthwhile.

Using the PEAR installer

You need an Internet connection to complete this section.

As we discussed previously, a list of the packages installed with your PHP installation can be obtained at a shell prompt in a Unix system (when you're logged in as root) using:

```
% pear list
```

On a Microsoft Windows platform, you do this in a command window with:

```
C:\> pear.bat list
```

In the remainder of this section, we only list the Unix commands and show a Unix shell prompt. To use the command in Microsoft Windows, replace *pear* with **pear.bat**.

To find out about one of the packages installed on your system, you can ask for details or visit the package browser at *http://pear.php.net/packages.php*. For example, to find out more about the *HTML_Template_IT* package type:

```
% pear info HTML_Template_IT
```

In response, you'll get a page of information that describes the package, its current release, licensing requirements, and its release state. The release state is one of *Stable*, *Beta*, *Alpha*, or *Devel(opment)*. The majority of packages are *Stable*, with the remaining majority in *Beta* testing. Use non-stable packages with caution.

If your computer has an Internet connection, you can check whether your packages can be upgraded to later releases by typing:

```
% pear list-upgrades
```

This requests information from the *pear.php.net* server. In response, the pear installer will report information such as:

```
Available Upgrades (stable):
=============================
+-------------+---------+--------+
| Package     | Version | Size   |
| Archive_Tar | 1.0     | 12.4kB |
| Mail        | 1.0.2   | 12.1kB |
| Net_SMTP    | 1.1.2   | 5.2kB  |
| PEAR        | 1.0.1   | 75kB   |
| XML_Parser  | 1.0.1   | 4.9kB  |
```

You can obtain the same information by browsing the packages at the PEAR web site *http://pear.php.net/*.

All information is for stable releases of packages, which can be safely installed and used. You can choose to upgrade a specific package or upgrade all out-of-date packages. For example, to upgrade only the PEAR base class:

```
% pear upgrade PEAR
```

The PEAR installer retrieves the package and responds with:

```
downloading PEAR-1.0.1.tar ...
...done: 395,776 bytes
upgrade ok: PEAR 1.0.1
```

Sometimes, the upgrade process can fail but helpful information is provided as to why. For example, an upgrade of the *Net_SMTP* package often fails for PHP 4.3.2:

```
% pear upgrade Net_SMTP
downloading Net_SMTP-1.1.2.tar ...
...done: 29,184 bytes
requires package `Auth_SASL'
Net_SMTP: dependencies failed
```

In order to proceed, the *Auth_SASL* package is needed first. This can be achieved with:

```
% pear install Auth_SASL
```

You can then try again to install the *Net_SMTP* package using *pear upgrade*.

As discussed in the previous section, viewing source code is an excellent method to understand how a package works. After you've installed a package, you'll find it below the directory */usr/local/lib/php/* on most Unix systems, in */usr/local/php/lib/php* under Mac OS X, or in *C:\Program Files\EasyPHP1-7\php\pear\pear* on a Microsoft Windows system if you've followed our PHP installation instructions in Appendixes A to C. The majority of the core packages are in the directory itself, while the optional packages are stored in subdirectories that are named according to the package category. For example, the IT templates that are discussed in the next section are found in the *HTML* subdirectory. Other popular package categories are listed later in the section "Optional Packages."

The PEAR installer isn't always reliable or well-configured on every system. If you have problems installing or upgrading packages, you can download packages from the PEAR web site and put them in the PEAR directories manually. This is also a useful trick for getting PEAR packages working without root or administrator user access: download the packages you need, uncompress them, put them in a directory that you've created, and then include the package file in your PHP script.

Using HTML Templates

Separating code from HTML can be difficult in PHP. As we discussed in Chapter 1 and have shown so far in this book, one of the best features of PHP is that scripts can be embedded anywhere in HTML documents. However, this can lead to maintenance problems: if you want to redesign the presentation of the web site, you may need to rewrite code or, at the very least, understand how PHP and HTML are interleaved in the application. This also makes it difficult to maintain code when it is interleaved with presentational components.

A good solution for medium- to large-scale web database applications is to use *templates* to separate markup and code. In this section, we illustrate how PEAR *Integrated Templates* (IT) can be used in PHP applications through simple examples, and also show you an example with *Extended Integrated Templates (ITX)*.

There are many other good templating environments, including a few others in PEAR itself. Outside of PEAR, the *Smarty PHP template engine* is popular and flexible, and available from *http://www.phpinsider.com/php/code/Smarty*.

To use the IT and ITX packages, you need to install the package *HTML_Template_IT*. To do this, you can follow the general instructions in the previous section or the detailed instructions for Linux, Mac OS X, and Microsoft Windows platforms in Appendices A to C.

Working with blocks and placeholders

In our first example, we show you how to develop the basic components needed in most templated PHP code: an HTML template and its accompanying PHP script. Our aim in this example is to display a list of customers in an HTML table environment. The customer data is stored in a *customer* table in MySQL that was created with the following statement:

```
CREATE TABLE customer (
  cust_id int(5) NOT NULL,
  surname varchar(50),
  firstname varchar(50),
  initial char(1),
  title_id int(3),
  address varchar(50),
  city varchar(50),
  state varchar(20),
  zipcode varchar(10),
  country_id int(4),
  phone varchar(15),
  birth_date char(10),
  PRIMARY KEY (cust_id)
) type=MyISAM;
```

Example 7-2 is the template that acts as a placeholder to show selected customer information. In our example, the template is saved in the file *example.7-2.tpl* and stored in a *templates* directory below our main *htdocs* directory that contains the PHP scripts.

Perhaps the most surprising thing about a template is that it is usually well-formed HTML 4.01. Indeed, when it's viewed in a Mozilla browser as shown in Figure 7-1, it has the features of a customer listing but with only one row and with placeholders in curly braces shown instead of the customer details. We always use uppercase characters for our placeholders so that they stand out in the template and in the code, but this isn't required.

Placeholder and block names can consist of alphabetic and numeric characters, as well as underscores and hyphens. Spaces and other characters aren't allowed.

For blocks, a single space must precede and follow the keywords BEGIN and END, and a single space must follow the block name.

The other difference between a typical HTML page and a template is that the template contains comments that include the tags BEGIN and END. These comment tags are in pairs that have matching labels that define a *block*. In this example, there's one block that has the label CUSTOMER.

Blocks represent units of information that are optional or can repeat. In Example 7-2, the CUSTOMER block surrounds a prototype data row that is output once for each customer in the database. In our PHP script, we control the presentation by assigning each row of data from the database to the block, and then parsing and outputting the completed row as HTML to the browser.

Example 7-2. A template for displaying customer details

```
<!DOCTYPE HTML PUBLIC
               "-//W3C//DTD HTML 4.01 Transitional//EN"
               "http://www.w3.org/TR/html401/loose.dtd">
<html>
<head>
  <meta http-equiv="Content-Type" content="text/html; charset=iso-8859-1">
  <title>Customer Details</title>
<body>
<table>
<tr><th>Name<th>Address<th>City<th>State<th>Zipcode
<!-- BEGIN CUSTOMER -->
<tr><td>{FIRSTNAME} {SURNAME}<td>{ADDRESS}
    <td>{CITY}<td>{STATE}<td>{ZIPCODE}
<!-- END CUSTOMER -->
</table>
</body>
</html>
```

The template, as viewed in a Mozilla browser, is shown in Figure 7-1 (to view it, we renamed the *.tpl* file with an *.html* extension).

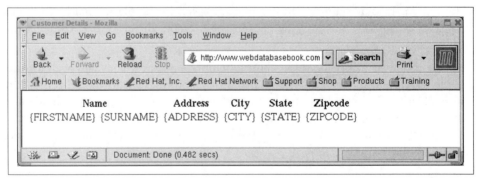

Figure 7-1. The customer template from Example 7-2 viewed in a Mozilla browser.

The script that populates the template with the customer data is shown in Example 7-3. To access the DBMS, no new functionality is included: the script uses the query process explained in Chapter 6 to connect, query, and extract results. What is new is the use of templates: the script itself doesn't output data using print but instead assigns data to elements of the customer template.

Example 7-3. A PHP script that populates the customer template in Example 7-2

```php
<?php
  require_once "HTML/Template/IT.php";
  include "db.inc";

  // Connect to the MySQL server
  if (!($connection = @ mysql_connect($hostname, $username, $password)))
    die("Cannot connect");

  if (!(mysql_select_db($databaseName, $connection)))
    showerror();

  // Run the query on the connection
  if (!($result = @ mysql_query ("SELECT * FROM customer LIMIT 50",
                                 $connection)))
    showerror();

  // Create a new template, and specify that the template files are
  // in the subdirectory "templates"
  $template = new HTML_Template_IT("./templates");

  // Load the customer template file
  $template->loadTemplatefile("example.7-2.tpl", true, true);

  while ($row = mysql_fetch_array($result))
  {
    // Work with the customer block
    $template->setCurrentBlock("CUSTOMER");

    // Assign the row data to the template placeholders
    $template->setVariable("FIRSTNAME", $row["firstname"]);
    $template->setVariable("SURNAME", $row["surname"]);
    $template->setVariable("ADDRESS", $row["address"]);
    $template->setVariable("CITY", $row["city"]);
    $template->setVariable("STATE", $row["state"]);
    $template->setVariable("ZIPCODE", $row["zipcode"]);

    // Parse the current block
    $template->parseCurrentBlock();
  }

  // Output the web page
  $template->show();
?>
```

The code fragment:

```php
    require_once "HTML/Template/IT.php";
```

loads PEAR's Integrated Template class into the script. After this, we create a new IT template $template, and specify that the templates we're using are found in the *templates* subdirectory:

```
$template = new HTML_Template_IT("./templates");
```

(The period and forward slash in ./templates means the *templates* directory is a subdirectory of the directory that contains the PHP script.)

After that, we load in our template file from Example 7-2:

```
$template->loadTemplatefile("example.7-2.tpl", true, true);
```

The two additional parameters are discussed later in this section.

Having set up our template, we can now use it with the data from our query. This is a three-step process:

1. Select the block to work with; in this example, there's only the CUSTOMER block.
2. Assign data to the placeholders within the block.
3. Parse the block.

This process is repeated each time we want to output a block (which, in this case, is a row of customer data). By default, if you don't use a block, it's assumed you don't want to output it and it isn't included in the HTML output.

In our script, the repeating three-step process is encapsulated in the following code fragment:

```
// Work with the customer block
$template->setCurrentBlock("CUSTOMER");

// Assign the row data to the template placeholders
$template->setVariable("FIRSTNAME", $row["firstname"]);
$template->setVariable("SURNAME", $row["surname"]);
$template->setVariable("ADDRESS", $row["address"]);
$template->setVariable("CITY", $row["city"]);
$template->setVariable("STATE", $row["state"]);
$template->setVariable("ZIPCODE", $row["zipcode"]);

// Parse the current block
$template->parseCurrentBlock();
```

The parameter to *HTML_Template_IT::setCurrentBlock( )* is the name of the block you want to work with in the template file. The parameters to *HTML_Template_IT:: setVariable( )* are a placeholder name within the block, and the data to assign to the placeholder. The method *HTML_Template_IT::parseCurrentBlock()* processes the currently selected block.

The script repeats the three-step process until there's no more data to process from the query. After that, the entire web page is output by the statement:

```
$template->show( );
```

The result of running the script and using the template is shown in Figure 7-2.

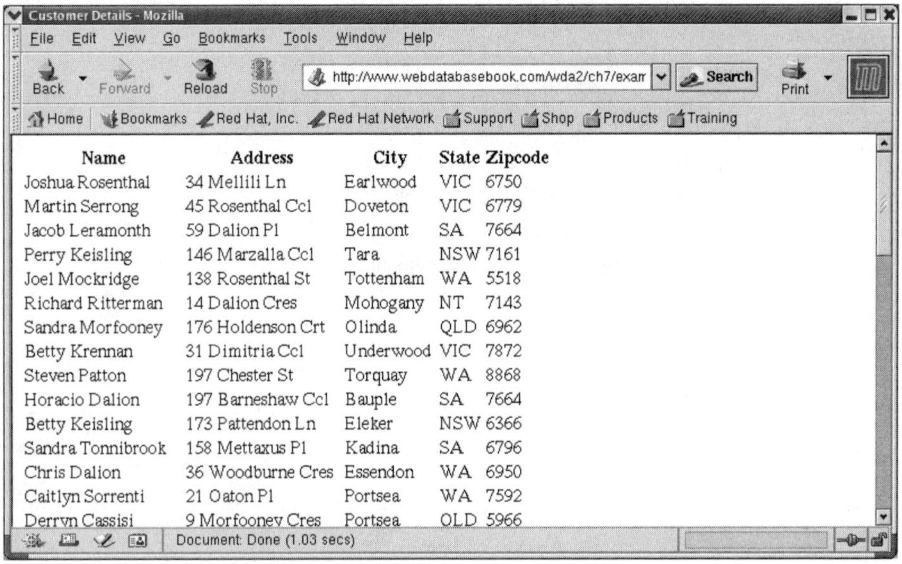

Figure 7-2. The output of running Example 7-3 shown in a Mozilla web browser

Nested blocks

Example 7-4 shows a more complex template example. This template is designed to display information about wine regions and, for each region, a list of the wineries that are situated there.

We use two database tables in our example, *winery* and *region*. These are created with the following statements:

```
CREATE TABLE winery (
  winery_id int(4) NOT NULL,
  winery_name varchar(100) NOT NULL,
  region_id int(4) NOT NULL,
  PRIMARY KEY (winery_id),
);

CREATE TABLE region (
  region_id int(4) NOT NULL,
  region_name varchar(100) NOT NULL,
  PRIMARY KEY (region_id),
);
```

There's a one-to-many relationship between the tables: each *winery* row has a region_id attribute that stores the identifier of a row in the *region* table.

The blocks in the template in Example 7-4 are nested. The REGION block spans most of the HTML listing and contains within it a WINERY block. The nesting matches the table relationship: there can be many region blocks, and many winery blocks within each region.

Example 7-4. A template with nested blocks for showing regions and wineries

```
<!DOCTYPE HTML PUBLIC
                "-//W3C//DTD HTML 4.01 Transitional//EN"
                "http://www.w3.org/TR/html401/loose.dtd">
<html>
<head>
  <meta http-equiv="Content-Type" content="text/html; charset=iso-8859-1">
  <title>Regions and Wineries</title>
<body>
<ul>
<!-- BEGIN REGION -->
<li>Region: {REGIONNAME}
<ul>
<!-- BEGIN WINERY -->
<li>{WINERYNAME}.
<!-- END WINERY -->
</ul>
<!-- END REGION -->
</ul>
</body>
</html>
```

Sample output from Example 7-4 is shown in Figure 7-3.

Example 7-5 shows the PHP script that works with the template. The logic of the script flows similarly to the template. The three-step process of selecting a block, assigning data to placeholders, and parsing is repeated for each region in the database. Nested inside that looping process, the same three steps occur for the wineries within each region.

One simple rule needs to be followed when a nested template is used: the innermost block must be parsed first, followed by the second innermost block, and so on until the outermost block has been parsed. In our example, this means that each repeating WINERY block must be parsed before the REGION block it belongs in. After all blocks that need to be populated have been parsed, the web page is output using *HTML_Template_IT::show( )*.

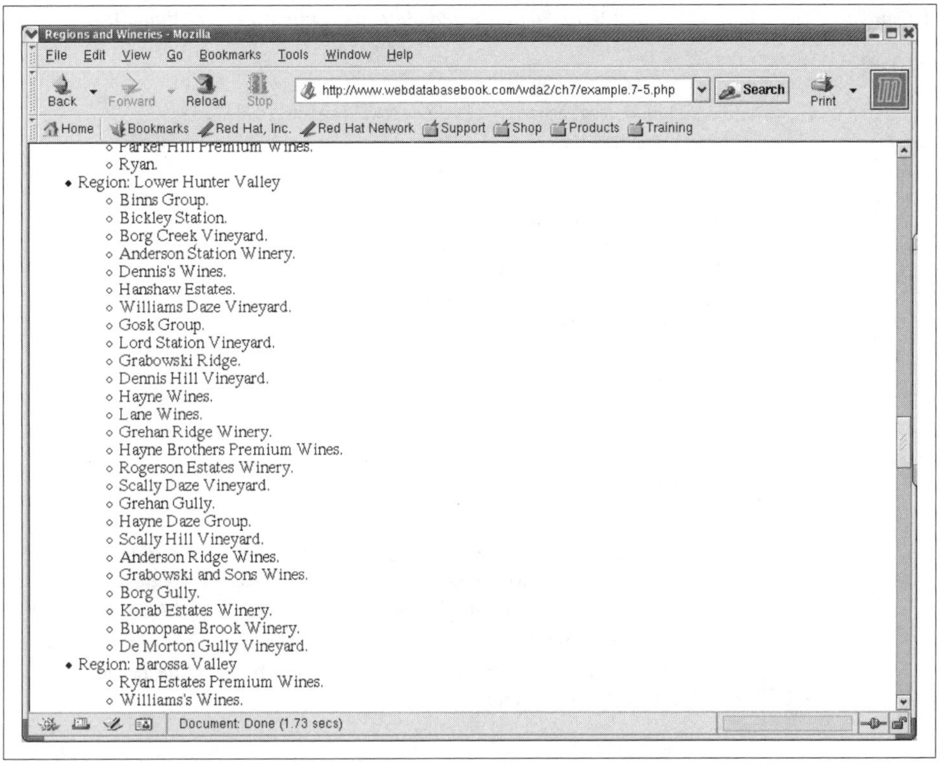

Figure 7-3. The output of running Example 7-4 shown in a Mozilla web browser

Example 7-5. The PHP script that works with the template in Example 7-4

```php
<?php
require_once "HTML/Template/IT.php";
require "db.inc";

if (!($connection = @ mysql_connect($hostname, $username, $password)))
   die("Cannot connect");

if (!(mysql_select_db($databaseName, $connection)))
   showerror();

if (!($regionresult = @ mysql_query ("SELECT * FROM region LIMIT 10",
                                   $connection)))
   showerror();

$template = new HTML_Template_IT("./templates");
$template->loadTemplatefile("example.7-4.tpl", true, true);

while ($regionrow = mysql_fetch_array($regionresult))
{
   $template->setCurrentBlock("REGION");
   $template->setVariable("REGIONNAME", $regionrow["region_name"]);
```

Example 7-5. The PHP script that works with the template in Example 7-4 (continued)

```
    if (!($wineryresult =
        @ mysql_query ("SELECT * FROM winery
                        WHERE region_id = {$regionrow["region_id"]}",
                        $connection)))
        showerror( );

    while ($wineryrow = mysql_fetch_array($wineryresult))
    {
        $template->setCurrentBlock("WINERY");
        $template->setVariable("WINERYNAME", $wineryrow["winery_name"]);
        $template->parseCurrentBlock( );
    }
    $template->setCurrentBlock("REGION");
    $template->parseCurrentBlock( );
  }
  $template->show( );
?>
```

> Make sure you remember to use *HTML_Template_IT::setCurrentBlock( )*
> to select the block before you call either *HTML_Template_IT::*
> *setVariable( )* or *HTML_Template_IT::parseCurrentBlock( )*. Failing to do
> so can cause unpredictable results and difficult-to-detect errors.
>
> Also, be careful that you don't have two blocks with the same name.
> Unpredictable results are likely.

Preserving and removing blocks

In our previous example, we used the following fragment to load a template file:

```
$template->loadTemplatefile("example.7-4.tpl", true, true);
```

The second and third parameters specify sensible default behavior for working with unused placeholders and blocks. The second parameter specifies that if a block isn't used in a template, it shouldn't be output. This is useful if you have an optional block that that's sometimes used, as we discuss in the next section. The third parameter behaves similarly for placeholders: when set to true, placeholders that haven't had data assigned to them are removed during parsing.

If you have chosen to remove empty blocks but need to preserve a block at runtime, this is possible using the *HTML_Template_IT::touchBlock( )* method. Touching means a block is marked as needing to be output, even if nothing has been assigned to its placeholders. For example, to preserve a DETAILS block you can use:

```
$template->touchBlock("DETAILS");
```

This is a useful feature in two situations: first, when you want to output a block but don't want to assign data to its placeholders; or, second, if a block has no placeholders and you want it to be shown. We show you an example in the next section.

More on nesting and optional blocks

Blocks aren't always nested: if data isn't related, it shouldn't be nested. For example, if we wanted to output information about the ten most popular wineries and the ten best customers, we might use the following template:

```
<!DOCTYPE HTML PUBLIC
                "-//W3C//DTD HTML 4.01 Transitional//EN"
                "http://www.w3.org/TR/html401/loose.dtd">
<html>
<head>
  <meta http-equiv="Content-Type" content="text/html; charset=iso-8859-1">
  <title>Details</title>
<body>
<h1>Our best customers</h1>
<!-- BEGIN CUSTOMER -->
Name: {FIRSTNAME SURNAME}
<!-- END CUSTOMER -->
<h1>Our most popular wineries</h1>
<!-- BEGIN WINERY -->
Name: {WINERYNAME}
<!-- END WINERY -->
</body>
</html>
```

In this structure, we can choose to repeat the CUSTOMER block zero or more times, and to independently repeat the WINERY block zero or more times. There is no relationship between the two blocks, and it doesn't matter whether you work with the customers or wineries first. Unrelated, unnested blocks can be assigned and parsed in any order. However, regardless of how you process and assign the data, all CUSTOMER blocks will always appear before all WINERY blocks because that's how the template is structured.

In the previous example, if you don't assign any data to the CUSTOMER block, the heading *Our best customers* will still be output because it isn't part of a block that you can control in your code. Moving the heading inside the CUSTOMER block doesn't solve the problem because the heading would then be repeated for each customer. One solution is to add another unnested block to the template so that the heading is optional:

```
<!DOCTYPE HTML PUBLIC
                "-//W3C//DTD HTML 4.01 Transitional//EN"
                "http://www.w3.org/TR/html401/loose.dtd">
<html>
<head>
  <meta http-equiv="Content-Type" content="text/html; charset=iso-8859-1">
  <title>Details</title>
<body>
<!-- BEGIN CUSTOMERHEADING -->
<h1>Our best customers</h1>
<!-- END CUSTOMERHEADING -->
<!-- BEGIN CUSTOMER -->
Name: {FIRSTNAME SURNAME}
```

```
<!-- END CUSTOMER -->
<h1>Our most popular wineries</h1>
<!-- BEGIN WINERY -->
Name: {WINERYNAME}
<!-- END WINERY -->
</body>
</html>
```

You can then use program logic to choose whether to output a CUSTOMERHEADING or not, depending on whether there are any CUSTOMER blocks being used. Note, however, that the CUSTOMERHEADING block doesn't contain any placeholders, and so with the default behavior you'll need to call *$template->touchBlock("CUSTOMERHEADING")* so that it's displayed in the output.

Our previous example can be improved. To avoid having to use program logic and the *HTML_Template_IT::touchBlock( )* method, you can restructure the template so that it's nested:

```
<!DOCTYPE HTML PUBLIC
                 "-//W3C//DTD HTML 4.01 Transitional//EN"
                 "http://www.w3.org/TR/html401/loose.dtd">
<html>
<head>
  <meta http-equiv="Content-Type" content="text/html; charset=iso-8859-1">
  <title>Details</title>
<body>
<!-- BEGIN CUSTOMERHEADING -->
<h1>Our best customers</h1>
<!-- BEGIN CUSTOMER -->
Name: {FIRSTNAME SURNAME}
<!-- END CUSTOMER -->
<!-- END CUSTOMERHEADING -->
<h1>Our most popular wineries</h1>
<!-- BEGIN WINERY -->
Name: {WINERYNAME}
<!-- END WINERY -->
</body>
</html>
```

This works better because the CUSTOMERHEADING block contains the CUSTOMER block. With nesting, if the CUSTOMER block is used, there's no need to use *HTML_Template_ IT::touchBlock( )* on CUSTOMERHEADING. Similarly, if nothing is assigned to a CUSTOMER block, CUSTOMERHEADING hasn't been touched and won't be output. This is another example of our basic relationship rule: if data is related, use nesting; if it isn't, don't.

So far, we've dealt with related and unrelated blocks that appear in a fixed order. Sometimes, however, you may want to display data in an arbitrary order that you want to be flexible at runtime. To do this, you can create a block that contains several nested blocks at the same level. For example, if we wanted to output several red, green, or blue messages in any order on a page, we could use the following template:

```
<!DOCTYPE HTML PUBLIC
                 "-//W3C//DTD HTML 4.01 Transitional//EN"
                 "http://www.w3.org/TR/html401/loose.dtd">
```

```
<html>
<head>
  <meta http-equiv="Content-Type" content="text/html; charset=iso-8859-1">
  <title>Color lines</title>
<body>
<!-- BEGIN COLORLINES -->
<!-- BEGIN RED -->
<font color="red">{MESSAGE}</font>
<!-- END RED -->
<!-- BEGIN GREEN -->
<font color="green">{MESSAGE}</font>
<!-- END GREEN -->
<!-- BEGIN BLUE -->
<font color="blue">{MESSAGE}</font>
<!-- END BLUE -->
<!-- END COLORLINES -->
</body>
</html>
```

So, to output a blue line, you select the BLUE block, assign the data to MESSAGE place-holder, parse the BLUE block, and then select and parse the COLORLINES block. To output another color, you repeat the same process for that different colored block. Using this technique, the COLORLINES block repeats, but with each repeat you can choose a different inner block. In Chapters 10 and 16, we explain a template for displaying form widgets that uses this technique.

Extended Integrated Templates (ITX)

Optional blocks allow most of the flexibility you'll need to develop template applications. However, sometimes you may need to dynamically create a template at runtime. Usually, this is done by using a main template file, and then adding template fragments in the PHP script. A popular use of this technique is to store a standard header and footer for an application in a main template file, and then to dynamically add the page body at runtime. This is what we do in our sample application in Chapters 16 through 20.

The *Extended Integrated Template (ITX)* class extends IT templates, adding the functionality to dynamically construct templates at runtime. The following is an example main template file stored in the file *about_today.tpl*:

```
<!DOCTYPE HTML PUBLIC
              "-//W3C//DTD HTML 4.01 Transitional//EN"
              "http://www.w3.org/TR/html401/loose.dtd">
<html>
<head>
  <meta http-equiv="Content-Type" content="text/html; charset=iso-8859-1">
  <title>About Today</title>
</head>
<body>
{MESSAGE}
</body>
</html>
```

The placeholder MESSAGE is the position at which our choice of template fragment is inserted. In this example, our script will insert a different template depending on the day of the week. If today is a weekday, the following template fragment stored in the file *weekday.tpl* is inserted:

```
Oh no. It's {DAY}, which is a weekday.
```

If today is on a weekend, this fragment stored in the file *weekend.tpl* is inserted:

```
Good news. It's {DAY}, which is on the weekend.
```

All of the template files are stored in the same directory.

The script that works with the templates is as follows:

```php
<?php
  require_once "HTML/Template/ITX.php";

  $template = new HTML_Template_ITX('.');
  $template->loadTemplatefile("about_today.tpl", true, true);

  $daynumber = date("w");

  // Is it a weekday?
  if ($daynumber != 0 && $daynumber != 6)
    // Include the weekday template fragment
    $template->addBlockfile("MESSAGE", "NEWMESSAGE", "weekday.tpl");
  else
    // Include the weekend template fragment
    $template->addBlockfile("MESSAGE", "NEWMESSAGE", "weekend.tpl");

  $template->setCurrentBlock("NEWMESSAGE");
  $template->setVariable("DAY", date("l"));
  $template->parseCurrentBlock();
  $template->show();
?>
```

Rather than work with *IT.php* library, this script uses the *ITX.php* file. The ITX templates provide several new methods, the most useful of which is *HTML_Template_ ITX::addBlockFile( )*. This method takes three parameters: the placeholder to replace, the name of the block to replace it with, and the template fragment file that forms the body of the block.

In our example, depending on the day of week determined with the *date( )* function, a choice is made as to whether to replace the MESSAGE placeholder with the fragment *weekday.tpl* or the fragment *weekend.tpl*; the *date( )* function is discussed in Chapter 3. After the replacement, the script proceeds in the same way as previous examples by selecting our new block, assigning values to placeholders, parsing, and outputting the results. The template fragments do not include the name of the new block, this is supplied as the second parameter to *HTML_Template_ITX:: addBlockFile( )*.

As we've shown you, the *HTML_Template_ITX::addBlockFile( )* inserts a file into a template at a location defined by a placeholder and then redefines the replaced section as a block. Blocks can also be replaced at runtime by other blocks using the *HTML_Template_ITX::replaceBlockFile( )* method that's explained in the next section.

Essential IT and ITX functions

void `HTML_Template_IT::HTML_Template_IT ([string root])`
> This is the constructor for the *HTML_Template_IT* class. It is called to create a new template and takes an optional *root* directory as a parameter. If the *root* directory is provided, the template file that is loaded with *HTML_Template_IT:: loadTemplateFile( )* is assumed to be based in this directory. (The return type of *void* means that the method does not return a value.)

Boolean HTML_Template_ITX::addBlock(string `placeholder,` `string block,` `string` `template`)
> Replaces a `placeholder` in the current template with a `block` that is stored in the `template` file. The `template` file should not contain the block `BEGIN` and `END` tags: these are created by the method and associated with the block name.

array HTML_Template_ITX::blockExists(string `block`)
> Returns `true` if the `block` exists and `false` otherwise.

array HTML_Template_ITX::BlockvariableExists(string `placeholder`)
> Returns `true` if the `placeholder` exists and `false` otherwise.

string HTML_Template_IT::get([string `block`])
> Returns a `block` after all placeholders have been replaced. If a parameter isn't supplied, the entire template is returned. In most applications, the template is output using *HTML_Template_IT::show( )* rather than returned with this method. However, this method can be used, for example, to produce template-based emails (as used in Chapter 19) or textual reports.

array HTML_Template_ITX::getBlockList( )
> Returns a list of template block names in a one-dimensional array.

array HTML_Template_ITX::getBlockVariables(string `block`)
> Returns a list of `block` placeholder names in a one-dimensional array.

Boolean HTML_Template_IT::loadTemplatefile(string `file [,` `Boolean removeVars [,` `Boolean removeBlocks]]`)
> Reads a template `file` from disk. The directory is a concatenation of any root directory supplied to the constructor plus the `file` provided. If `removeVars` is `true`, unassigned placeholders are deleted from the output. If `removeBlocks` is set to `true`, unused blocks are removed except if the block has been accessed with *HTML_Template_IT::touchBlock( )*. Both optional parameters are set to `true` by default. Returns `true` on success and `false` on failure.

void HTML_Template_IT::parse ([string block])

> Process a *block* by replacing all placeholders with their assigned values. If no parameter is supplied, the entire template is parsed. Child blocks should be parsed before their parents, that is, blocks should be processed from most- to least-nested.

void HTML_Template_IT::parseCurrentBlock ()

> Process the current block selected with *HTML_Template_IT::setCurrentBlock()* by replacing all placeholders with their assigned values. Child blocks should be parsed before their parents, that is, blocks should be processed from most- to least-nested.

string HTML_Template_ITX::placeholderExists(string placeholder [, string block])

> Returns the name of the first block that contains the *placeholder* in the template or in an optional *block*. If no block contains the placeholder, the empty string is returned.

Boolean HTML_Template_ITX::replaceBlock(string block, string file [, Boolean preserve])

> Replaces a *block* in the current template with a block of the same name that is stored in a *file*. The *file* should not contain the block BEGIN and END tags: these are created by the method. The existing assignments to placeholders can be preserved if the optional parameter *preserve* is set to true; by default it is false. Returns true on success and false on failure.

Boolean HTML_Template_IT::setCurrentBlock ([string block])

> Makes a *block* the currently selected block. If no parameter is provided, no block is set but instead any placeholders that are outside of blocks are made current; all of our examples use only placeholders inside blocks, but several examples without blocks are in later chapters. Returns true on success and false on failure.
>
> A call to this method should be made prior to assigning variables to placeholders with *HTML_IT_Template::setVariable()*.

void HTML_Template_IT::setVariable(string placeholder, string variable)

> Assign a *variable* to the *placeholder* in the currently selected block. Blocks are selected with *HTML_Template_IT::setCurrentBlock()*.
>
> The function has an alternate, array parameter that isn't useful for the majority of applications, and we ignore it here.

void HTML_Template_IT::show([string block])

> Outputs a *block* after all replacements have been made. Without the parameter, the complete template is output. In our examples, the parameter is not provided and this is the final step in working with the template.

Boolean HTML_Template_IT::touchBlock(string block)
> Preserves an empty *block* in the output when no data has been assigned to its placeholders. This works even if the third parameter to *HTML_Template_IT:: loadTemplateFile( )* is set to true. Returns true on success and false on failure.

Optional Packages

Of the 154 PEAR packages at the time of writing, this section lists the 40 most popular as determined by download frequency at *http://pear.php.net/package-stats.php*. As discussed at the beginning of this section, the complete list is available by requesting the package installer to provide the information or by browsing packages in the repository. Selected packages are used in other sections of the book, and we've noted this next to those packages.

Authentication

There are six packages available, and two are popular.

- *Auth* is a session-based authentication class that supports all PEAR DB DBMSs, as well as authentication for text files, LDAP servers, POP3 servers, IMAP servers, vpopmail accounts, RADIUS, and SOAP. Our authentication in Chapter 11 supports similar features.

- *Auth_HTTP* provides methods for HTTP authentication. We discuss HTTP authentication in Chapter 11.

Benchmarking

There's only one package, and it's in the top 40.

- *Benchmark* is a framework for benchmarking the performance of PHP functions and scripts. Its similar in style to the popular GNU C programming tool *gprof*.

Caching

Two packages are available, and one is popular.

- *Cache* stores the results of previous function calls, script executions, and other activities so that they can be used in the future. Caching often speeds-up program execution if results or scripts are re-used frequently, and your web site is under high load.

Console

Five packages are available. The popular one is the core component *Console_Getopt* for retrieving command-line arguments from non-web scripts.

Database

There are fourteen packages, of which four are popular.

- *DB* is a core component described in its own section in this chapter.
- *DB_DataObject* is an SQL builder and object interface to database tables.
- *DB_Pager* retrieves data in chunks after a query using PEAR DB. The aim is to allow you to retrieve and display data for subsequent display in pages.
- *MDB* is a merging of PEAR DB and Metabase; Metabase is an alternative to PEAR DB. The MDB package provides a superset of the functionality of PEAR DB.

Date

There is one package that's popular.

- *Date* is classes for manipulating and working with dates and time zones without timestamps, and without year range restrictions. We use Date in Chapter 9.

Filesystem

There are six packages, of which two are popular.

- *Archive_Tar* supports creating, listing, extracting, and adding to tar (Unix archive) files, a common format of zip-like archives on Unix-style systems. This is a core component of PEAR that's used by the installer.
- *File* provides methods to read and write files, and to deal with paths. It also provides an interface for working with comma-separated value (CSV) files.

HTML

There are fifteen packages, including five popular ones.

- *HTML_QuickForm* for creating, processing, and validating HTML form environments. We develop our own framework for creating template-based forms in Chapter 16.
- *HTML_Table* for developing, manipulating, and reusing HTML <table> environments.
- *HTML_Template_IT* is a templating environment described in its own section in this chapter. It includes the extended template package ITX.
- *HTML_TreeMenu* creates attractive menus for display using JavaScript at the client. We discuss developing simple menus using JavaScript in Chapter 9.
- *Pager* is a class for viewing data in pages with previous and next buttons. We develop our own approach to this in Chapter 17.

HTTP

There are six packages and three are popular.

- *HTTP* is a core component discussed at the beginning of this chapter.

- *HTTP_Request* is designed for easy formatting of HTTP requests, including all methods, basic authentication, proxy authentication, and redirection. We discuss HTTP in Appendix D, HTTP authentication in Chapter 11, and redirection in Chapter 6.

- *HTTP_Upload* allows easy management of files uploaded from browsers to web servers using form environments.

Internationalization

There's one popular package for internationalization.

- *I18N* is designed to help you localize applications by determining browser language, currency, date and time, and numbers.

Logging

There is one package, and it's popular.

- *Log* is a logging system that can log data to many different targets including PEAR DB, files, and email.

Mail

There are six packages, and two are popular.

- *Mail* is described in the core components section at the beginning of this chapter. It's used in Chapter 19.

- *Mail_Mime* provides classes to encode and decode Mime-encoded attachments.

Networking

There are twenty-nine packages, of which four are popular: we use the *Net_DNS* package (which isn't discussed here) in Chapter 9.

- *Net_POP3* is a class for accessing POP3 mail servers.

- *Net_Socket* is a core component for working with network sockets and is described at the beginning of this chapter.

- *Net_URL* provides easy parsing of URLs, allowing components to be extracted without difficult string processing

- *Net_UserAgent_Detect* determines the web browser, version, and platform from the HTTP headers.

PEAR

There are three packages and two are popular.

- *PEAR* is a set of core classes described at the beginning of this chapter.
- *PEAR_Frontend_Web* is a web interface to the PEAR package manager. We describe the command-line version in this chapter, but it's likely that this package will become popular for configuration on all platforms when it leaves the beta-testing phase.

PHP

There are nine packages and three are popular.

- *apd* is a profiler and debugger that helps in optimizing code.
- *bcompiler* allows you to protect your code by compiling it rather than distributing PHP source.
- *PHPDoc* generates documentation from source code.

XML

There are eleven packages, of which three are popular.

- *XML_Parser* is designed to parse XML.
- *XML_RPC* is a core package that implements XML-RPC.
- *XML_Tree* represents XML data as a tree structure.

Web services

There are three packages, of which one is popular.

- *SOAP* is a client and server package for implementing Simple Object Access Protocol (SOAP) protocols and services. SOAP is an emerging standard, and a good introduction to SOAP is available at *http://www.w3.org/TR/SOAP/*.

Writing to Web Databases

Many web database applications are not only information resources for users but also tools for storing new information. For example, in an online store, users and administrators write data to the database in several situations: they can purchase products by creating an order, they can become members, they can manage a shopping cart, and the administrator can manage the stock.

Writing data in web database applications requires different techniques from reading data. Issues of transactions and concurrency become important, and we introduce these issues and the principles of dealing with them in this chapter. The introduction is practical: we focus on the basic management techniques of locking and unlocking tables, and show you how to safely implement simple database writes in MySQL when there is more than one user simultaneously accessing a database. Most importantly, we identify when special approaches are required, and when these can be safely omitted from a web database application.

At the conclusion of this chapter, you will have covered the skills to build a simple but complete web database application.

Database Inserts, Updates, and Deletes

Simple database modifications are much the same as queries. We begin this section with a simple case study similar to the querying examples we presented in the previous two chapters. However, inserting, updating, and deleting data does require some additional care. After this first example, we show you why it suffers from the *reload problem* and discuss a solution. After that, we return to further, richer examples of writing to a database and discuss more complex problems and solutions.

For this case study, we won't use the winestore database because it doesn't make use of MySQL's auto_increment feature that we want to use in this section. Instead, let's assume you need to maintain a list of names (surnames and first names) of people and their phone numbers, and that you want to write a script to add new data to the database. To begin, let's create a new *telephone* database and a *phonebook* table to store the details. Start the MySQL command interpreter and login as the root user. Then, type the following SQL statements into the command interpreter:

```
mysql> CREATE DATABASE telephone;
Query OK, 1 row affected (0.01 sec)

mysql> use telephone
Database changed
mysql> CREATE TABLE phonebook (
    -> phonebook_id int(6) NOT NULL auto_increment,
    -> surname CHAR(50) NOT NULL,
    -> firstname CHAR(50) NOT NULL,
    -> phone CHAR(20) NOT NULL,
    -> PRIMARY KEY (phonebook_id)
    -> ) type=MyISAM;
Query OK, 0 rows affected (0.00 sec)
```

We've created a phonebook_id attribute that is the primary key to uniquely identify each row in the table and we've used the auto_increment modifier with it. As we discussed in Chapter 5, inserting NULL into an auto_increment PRIMARY KEY attribute allocates the next available key value, and we use this feature in our script.

We also need a new user who can access the new database. To set one up with the right privileges, you can use the same approach used in Appendixes A through C to configure MySQL. In the MySQL command interpreter, type:

```
mysql> GRANT SELECT, INSERT, UPDATE, DELETE, LOCK TABLES ON telephone.* TO
    -> fred@127.0.0.1 IDENTIFIED BY 'shhh';
Query OK, 0 rows affected (0.00 sec)
```

Replace fred and shhh with the username and password you want to use (and do the same later in all of the PHP scripts in this chapter).

Now we need an HTML form that allows users to provide the details to create a new row in the *phonebook* table. Example 8-1 shows such a form that's laid out for presentation using a table element. It collects three values into three input elements with the names surname, firstname, and phone, and it uses the GET method to pass values to the script *example.8-2.php*.

Example 8-1. An HTML form to capture the name of a new region

```
<!DOCTYPE HTML PUBLIC
                "-//W3C//DTD HTML 4.01 Transitional//EN"
                "http://www.w3.org/TR/html401/loose.dtd">
<html>
<head>
  <meta http-equiv="Content-Type" content="text/html; charset=iso-8859-1">
  <title>Add a Phonebook Entry</title>
</head>
<body>
<h1>Add a Phonebook Entry</h1>
<form method="GET" action="example.8-2.php">
```

```
<table>
<tr>
  <td>Surname:
  <td><input type="text" name="surname" size=50>
</tr>
<tr>
  <td>First name:
  <td><input type="text" name="firstname" size=50>
</tr>
<tr>
  <td>Phone number:
  <td><input type="text" name="phone" size=20>
</tr>
</table>
<br><input type="submit">
</form>
</body>
</html>
```

Example 8-2 shows the script that adds the new data to the *phonebook* table. It works as follows: if a surname, first name, and phone number are supplied by the user, an INSERT SQL statement is prepared to insert the new row; the *mysqlclean()* function (and the *db.inc* include file where it's stored) are discussed in Chapter 6. As described in Chapter 5, inserting NULL results in the auto_increment modifier allocating the next available key value. If any of the values are missing, it redirects back to the form using the *header()* function that's discussed in Chapter 6.

Example 8-2. A script to insert a new phonebook entry

```php
<?php
require "db.inc";
require_once "HTML/Template/ITX.php";

// Test for user input
if (!empty($_GET["surname"]) &&
    !empty($_GET["firstname"]) &&
    !empty($_GET["phone"]))
{
  if (!($connection = @ mysql_connect("localhost", "fred", "shhh")))
    die("Could not connect to database");

  $surname = mysqlclean($_GET, "surname", 50, $connection);
  $firstname = mysqlclean($_GET, "firstname", 50, $connection);
  $phone = mysqlclean($_GET, "phone", 20, $connection);

  if (!mysql_select_db("telephone", $connection))
    showerror();

  // Insert the new phonebook entry
  $query = "INSERT INTO phonebook VALUES
          (NULL, '{$surname}', '{$firstname}', '{$phone}')";
```

Example 8-2. A script to insert a new phonebook entry (continued)

```
  if (!(@mysql_query ($query, $connection)))
    showerror();

  $template = new HTML_Template_ITX("./templates");
  $template->loadTemplatefile("example.8-3.tpl", true, true);
  $template->setCurrentBlock();
  $template->setVariable("SURNAME", $surname);
  $template->setVariable("FIRSTNAME", $firstname);
  $template->setVariable("PHONE", $phone);
  $template->parseCurrentBlock();

  $template->show();
} // if empty()
else
  // Missing data: Go back to the <form>
  header("Location: example.8-1.html");
?>
```

If the query is successful, then a template that shows the results is loaded and displayed (this is discussed next). If an error occurs, error handling using the methods
described in Chapter 6 is used.

We use a PEAR IT template file in Example 8-2. The template file is stored as
example.8-3.tpl and shown in Example 8-3. This template has three placeholders to
show the details of the new row. The PEAR template package is explained in
Chapter 7.

Example 8-3. The template file used in Example 8-2

```
<!DOCTYPE HTML PUBLIC
                "-//W3C//DTD HTML 4.01 Transitional//EN"
                "http://www.w3.org/TR/html401/loose.dtd">
<html>
<head>
  <meta http-equiv="Content-Type" content="text/html; charset=iso-8859-1">
  <title>Added a Phonebook Entry</title>
</head>
<body>
<h1>Added a Phonebook Entry</h1>
<table>
<tr>
  <td>Surname:
  <td>{SURNAME}
</tr>
<tr>
  <td>First name:
  <td>{FIRSTNAME}
</tr>
<tr>
  <td>Phone number:
```

Example 8-3. The template file used in Example 8-2 (continued)

```
  <td>{PHONE}
</tr>
</table>
</body>
</html>
```

Most write operations can use a format similar to that of Example 8-2. In particular, where database changes are reasonably infrequent and can be performed in one step, most of the more complex issues we describe later in "Issues in Writing Data to Databases" can be ignored. However, as noted earlier, Example 8-2 does have one undesirable side effect that is common in web database applications. The problem isn't really related to modifying the database but rather to the statelessness of the HTTP protocol. We discuss this side effect, the reload problem, and an effective solution in the next section.

Reloading Data and Relocation Techniques

Simple updates using the approach shown in Example 8-2 are susceptible to a common problem of the stateless HTTP protocol that we call the *reload problem*. Consider what happens when a user successfully enters a new phonebook entry, and clicks the Submit button. The code in Example 8-2 is executed, a new row is inserted in the *phonebook* table, and a success message is displayed. So far, everything is going according to plan.

Consider now what happens if the user reloads the success message page with the Reload or Refresh button in the browser. The variables and values are resubmitted to the same script, and another identical row (except for the phonebook_id value, which is automatically incremented) is added to the *phonebook* table. There is no way in this example that the first click of the Submit button to add the first row can be distinguished from a second action that sends the same variables and values to the script. A representation of the reload problem is shown in Figure 8-1.

The reload problem occurs in many situations. Actions that re-request a document from the server include pressing the Reload or Refresh buttons, printing, saving the URL in the browser and returning to the page using a bookmark or favorite, using the Back or Forward buttons, pressing the Enter key in the URL Location entry box, and resizing the browser window.

The reload problem isn't always a significant problem. For example, if you use the SQL UPDATE statement to update phonebook details, and the values are amended with the same correct values repeatedly, there is no data duplication. Similarly, if a row is deleted and the user repeats the operation, the row can't be deleted twice. However, while some UPDATE and DELETE operations are less susceptible to the reload

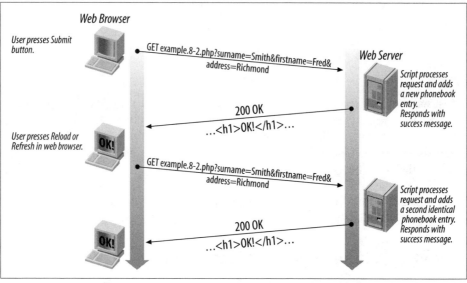

Figure 8-1. The reload problem

problem, a well-designed system avoids the problem altogether. Avoidance prevents user confusion and unnecessary DBMS activity. We discuss a solution in a moment.

The HTTP POST method is a little less susceptible to the reload problem than the GET method. If a user again retrieves the script after the first database change, the browser should ask the user is they're sure they want to repeat the action. Most of the time, this will prevent the problem because the user will click Cancel. However, if the user does click OK, the database operation will be repeated and cause the reload problem.

A solution to the reload problem is shown in Figure 8-2. It is based on the HTTP Location: header, the same header used for one-component querying in Chapter 6.

The reload solution works as follows:

1. The user submits the form with the variables and values for a database write operation (an SQL INSERT, UPDATE, or DELETE).

2. The SQL write operation is attempted.

3. Whether or not the modification is successful, an HTTP Location: header is sent to the browser to redirect the browser to a new, receipt page.

   HTTP GET encoded variables and values are usually included with the Location: header to indicate whether the action was successful. Additionally, text to display might be sent as part of the redirection URL.

4. An informative receipt page is displayed to the user, including a success or failure message, and other appropriate text. The script that displays the message doesn't perform any database writes.

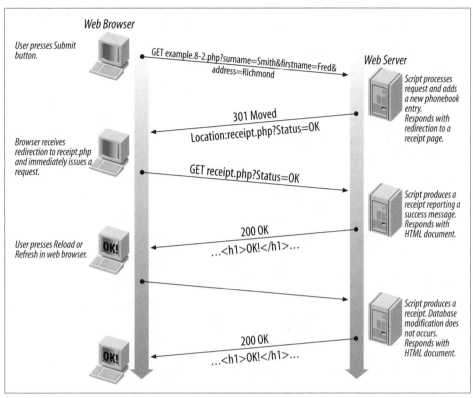

Figure 8-2. Solving the reload problem with a redirection to a receipt page

The HTTP redirection solves the reload problem. If the user reloads the receipt page, he sees the receipt again, and no database write operations occur. Moreover, because the receipt page receives information about the write operation encoded in the URL, the receipt page URL can be saved and reloaded in the future without any undesirable effect.

Solving the reload problem in practice

A modified version of Example 8-2 with the redirect functionality is shown in Example 8-4. The code that works with the database is identical to that of Example 8-2. A template is no longer used in the script because it doesn't produce any output and, regardless of whether the database insert succeeds or fails, the *header()* function is called. This redirects the browser to the script shown in Example 8-5 by sending a Location: example.8-5.php HTTP header.

The difference between the success and failure cases is what is appended to the URL as a query string. When it works, status=T and the value of the phonebook_id attribute are sent. A value of status=F is sent on failure. On success, the value for phonebook_id (which is created using the auto_increment feature) is found by calling *mysql_insert_id()*; the function is described in Chapter 6.

Example 8-4. A modified insertion script that solves the reload problem

```php
<?php
require "db.inc";

// Test for user input
if (!empty($_GET["surname"]) &&
    !empty($_GET["firstname"]) &&
    !empty($_GET["phone"]))
{
  if (!($connection = @ mysql_connect("localhost", "fred", "shhh")))
     die("Could not connect to database");

  $surname = mysqlclean($_GET, "surname", 50, $connection);
  $firstname = mysqlclean($_GET, "firstname", 50, $connection);
  $phone = mysqlclean($_GET, "phone", 20, $connection);

  if (!mysql_select_db("telephone", $connection))
     showerror();

  // Insert the new phonebook entry
  $query = "INSERT INTO phonebook VALUES
           (NULL, '{$surname}', '{$firstname}', '{$phone}')";

  if (@mysql_query ($query, $connection))
  {
    header("Location: example.8-5.php?status=T&" .
           "phonebook_id=". mysql_insert_id($connection));
    exit;
  }
} // if empty()

header("Location: example.8-5.php?status=F");
?>
```

The script in Example 8-5 produces the receipt page. Its accompanying template is shown in Example 8-6. When requested with a parameter status=T, the script queries the database and displays the details of the newly inserted phonebook entry. The entry is identified by the value of the query string variable phonebook_id. On failure, where status=F, the script displays a database failure message. If the script is unexpectedly called without a status parameter, an error message is displayed.

Example 8-5. The phonebook receipt script

```php
<?php
require "db.inc";
require_once "HTML/Template/ITX.php";

if (!($connection = @ mysql_connect("localhost", "fred", "shhh")))
```

Example 8-5. The phonebook receipt script (continued)

```
    die("Could not connect to database");

$status = mysqlclean($_GET, "status", 1, $connection);

$template = new HTML_Template_ITX("./templates");
$template->loadTemplatefile("example.8-6.tpl", true, true);

switch ($status)
{
  case "T":
    $phonebook_id = mysqlclean($_GET, "phonebook_id", 5, $connection);

    if (!empty($phonebook_id))
    {
      if (!mysql_select_db("telephone", $connection))
        showerror();

      $query = "SELECT * FROM phonebook WHERE
                phonebook_id = {$phonebook_id}";

      if (!($result = @mysql_query ($query, $connection)))
        showerror();

      $row = @ mysql_fetch_array($result);

      $template->setCurrentBlock("success");
      $template->setVariable("SURNAME", $row["surname"]);
      $template->setVariable("FIRSTNAME", $row["firstname"]);
      $template->setVariable("PHONE", $row["phone"]);
      $template->parseCurrentBlock();
      break;
    }

  case "F":
    $template->setCurrentBlock("failure");
    $template->setVariable("MESSAGE", "A database error occurred.");
    $template->parseCurrentBlock();
    break;

  default:
    $template->setCurrentBlock("failure");
    $template->setVariable("MESSAGE", "You arrived here unexpectedly.");
    $template->parseCurrentBlock();
    break;
}

$template->show();
?>
```

Example 8-6. The redirection receipt template

```
<!DOCTYPE HTML PUBLIC
                "-//W3C//DTD HTML 4.01 Transitional//EN"
                "http://www.w3.org/TR/html401/loose.dtd">
<html>
<head>
  <meta http-equiv="Content-Type" content="text/html; charset=iso-8859-1">
  <title>Phonebook Entry Receipt</title>
</head>
<body>
<!-- BEGIN success -->
<h1>Added a Phonebook Entry</h1>
<table>
<tr>
  <td>Surname:
  <td>{SURNAME}
</tr>
<tr>
  <td>First name:
  <td>{FIRSTNAME}
</tr>
<tr>
  <td>Phone number:
  <td>{PHONE}
</tr>
</table>
<!-- END success -->
<!-- BEGIN failure -->
<h1>{MESSAGE}</h1>
<!-- END failure -->
</body>
</html>
```

Inserting, Updating, and Deleting Data

In this section, we complete our discussion of the basics of modifying data by individually considering inserting, updating, and deleting data. We illustrate the principles of each technique in PHP through introductory case study examples; longer examples are presented in Chapters 16 through 20.

Inserting data

We have already illustrated a worked example of inserting data. In this section, we discuss the principles of insertion and expand our example to use a template to create a form. Inserting data is a three-step process:

1. Data is entered by the user into a form.
2. The data is validated and, if it passes the tests, written into the database using an SQL INSERT statement. A key value is usually created during this process. If the

validation fails, then error information is displayed and the third step doesn't occur.

3. The user is shown a receipt page, which is generally used to display the inserted data using the key value passed from the second step. If the insert operation fails, an error message is displayed.

Stage one of the insertion process is data entry. Example 8-7 shows a script that creates an HTML form for capturing data to be inserted into the *phonebook* table we created in the previous section. The form allows details to be entered into text input controls and is shown rendered in a Mozilla browser in Figure 8-3. A more sophisticated form using the same techniques is used to gather customer details for our online winestore in Chapter 17.

The script makes extensive use of the template shown in Example 8-8. The template has three configurable components:

- Placeholders for a MESSAGE that gives the user instructions on how to fill out the form and for a SUBMITVALUE on the submit button widget. For the customer insertion in Example 8-7 the message asks the user to *Please fill in the details below to add an entry.* and the button says *Add Now!*.

- A hiddeninput block for creating hidden form input widgets. We don't use this for insertion, and we discuss it later when we introduce updates.

- A mandatoryinput block for creating mandatory text input widgets. The block has placeholders for the text that the user sees and for the input's name, its size, and its initial value.

The template isn't complicated and just uses the techniques we discussed in Chapter 6. It allows you to create text inputs as you need by repeatedly selecting the mandatoryinput block, assigning values to it, and parsing it. This makes the template very useful: it allows us to dynamically create different forms at runtime, and it can easily be adapted for other applications. We extend this template in Chapter 17 to support optional inputs, select inputs, and other components.

Example 8-7. A script to collect phonebook data

```php
<?php
require 'db.inc';
require_once "HTML/Template/ITX.php";

$template = new HTML_Template_ITX("./templates");
$template->loadTemplatefile("example.8-8.tpl", true, true);

$template->setVariable("MESSAGE",
                    "Please fill in the details below to add an entry");
$template->setVariable("SUBMITVALUE", "Add Now!");

$template->setCurrentBlock("mandatoryinput");
$template->setVariable("MINPUTTEXT", "First name");
```

Example 8-7. A script to collect phonebook data (continued)

```
$template->setVariable("MINPUTNAME", "firstname");
$template->setVariable("MINPUTVALUE", "");
$template->setVariable("MINPUTSIZE", 50);
$template->parseCurrentBlock("mandatoryinput");

$template->setCurrentBlock("mandatoryinput");
$template->setVariable("MINPUTTEXT", "Surname");
$template->setVariable("MINPUTNAME", "surname");
$template->setVariable("MINPUTVALUE", "");
$template->setVariable("MINPUTSIZE", 50);
$template->parseCurrentBlock("mandatoryinput");

$template->setCurrentBlock("mandatoryinput");
$template->setVariable("MINPUTTEXT", "Phone");
$template->setVariable("MINPUTNAME", "phone");
$template->setVariable("MINPUTVALUE", "");
$template->setVariable("MINPUTSIZE", 20);
$template->parseCurrentBlock("mandatoryinput");

$template->parseCurrentBlock( );
$template->show( );
?>
```

Example 8-8. The PEAR IT template that collects phonebook data

```
<!DOCTYPE HTML PUBLIC
            "-//W3C//DTD HTML 4.01 Transitional//EN"
            "http://www.w3.org/TR/html401/loose.dtd">
<html>
<head>
  <meta http-equiv="Content-Type" content="text/html; charset=iso-8859-1">
  <title>Phonebook Details</title>
</head>
<body bgcolor="white">
<form method="post" action="example.8-9.php">
<h1>Phonebook Details</h1>
<h2>{MESSAGE}.
    Fields shown in <font color="red">red</font> are mandatory.</h2>
<table>
<!-- BEGIN hiddeninput -->
<tr>
 <td><input type="hidden" name="{HINPUTNAME}" value="{HINPUTVALUE}"></td>
</tr>
<!-- END hiddeninput -->
<!-- BEGIN mandatoryinput -->
<tr>
  <td><font color="red">{MINPUTTEXT}:</font></td>
  <td>
  <input type="text" name="{MINPUTNAME}" value="{MINPUTVALUE}"
        size={MINPUTSIZE}>
  </td>
</tr>
<!-- END mandatoryinput -->
```

Example 8-8. The PEAR IT template that collects phonebook data (continued)

```
<tr>
   <td><input type="submit" value="{SUBMITVALUE}"></td>
</tr>
</table>
</form>
</body>
</html>
```

Figure 8-3 shows the forms created in Examples 8-7 and 8-8.

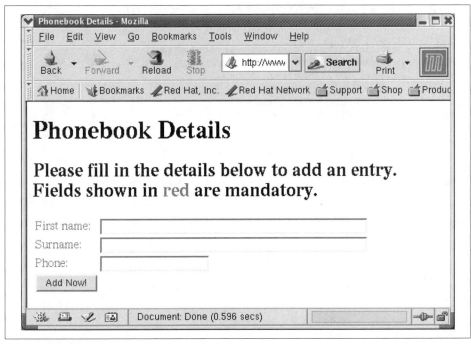

Figure 8-3. The phonebook entry form from Examples 8-7 and 8-8 rendered in a Mozilla browser

The second phase of insertion is data validation, followed by the database operation itself. Example 8-9 shows the PHP script to validate and insert a new phonebook entry. The script has a simple structure, with naive validation that tests only whether values have been supplied for the fields. If an error occurs, the function *formerror()* is called that flags the error by setting the $errors variable and populates an error template placeholder with a message.

Example 8-9. A validation example that tests for mandatory fields and then stores data in the customer table

```
<?php
require 'db.inc';
require_once "HTML/Template/ITX.php";
```

Example 8-9. A validation example that tests for mandatory fields and then stores data in the customer table (continued)

```
function formerror(&$template, $message, &$errors)
{
  $errors = true;
  $template->setCurrentBlock("error");
  $template->setVariable("ERROR", $message);
  $template->parseCurrentBlock("error");
}

if (!($connection = @ mysql_connect("localhost", "fred", "shhh")))
   die("Could not connect to database");

$firstname = mysqlclean($_POST, "firstname", 50, $connection);
$surname = mysqlclean($_POST, "surname", 50, $connection);
$phone = mysqlclean($_POST, "phone", 20, $connection);

$template = new HTML_Template_ITX("./templates");
$template->loadTemplatefile("example.8-10.tpl", true, true);

$errors = false;

if (empty($firstname))
  formerror($template, "The first name field cannot be blank.", $errors);

if (empty($surname))
  formerror($template, "The surname field cannot be blank.", $errors);

if (empty($phone))
  formerror($template, "The phone field cannot be blank", $errors);

// Now the script has finished the validation, show any errors
if ($errors)
{
  $template->show( );
  exit;
}

// If we made it here, then the data is valid
if (!mysql_select_db("telephone", $connection))
  showerror( );

// Insert the new phonebook entry
$query = "INSERT INTO phonebook VALUES
          (NULL, '{$surname}', '{$firstname}', '{$phone}')";

if (!(@ mysql_query ($query, $connection)))
   showerror( );

// Find out the phonebook_id of the new entry
$phonebook_id = mysql_insert_id( );
```

Example 8-9. A validation example that tests for mandatory fields and then stores data in the customer table (continued)

```
// Show the phonebook receipt
header("Location: example.8-5.php?status=T&phonebook_id={$phonebook_id}");
?>
```

After all validation is complete, all errors are displayed using the template in Example 8-10. After the error messages are output to the browser, an embedded link is shown to allow the user to return to the form in Example 8-8. Unfortunately, if the user does click on this link (instead of pressing the Back button) she is returned to an empty form. A solution to this problem is presented in Chapter 10.

Example 8-10. The error display template

```
<!DOCTYPE HTML PUBLIC
            "-//W3C//DTD HTML 4.01 Transitional//EN"
            "http://www.w3.org/TR/html401/loose.dtd">
<html>
<head>
  <meta http-equiv="Content-Type" content="text/html; charset=iso-8859-1">
  <title>Phonebook Details Error</title>
</head>
<body bgcolor="white">
<h1>Phonebook Data Errors</h1>
<!-- BEGIN error -->
<br><font color="font">{ERROR}</font>
<!-- END error -->
<br>
<a href="example.8-7.php">Return to the form</a>
</body>
</html>
```

If the validation succeeds, the second phase of the insertion process continues. The INSERT query is executed and NULL is inserted as the phonebook_id attribute to use the auto_increment feature. Using auto_increment avoids the problems discussed later in section "Issues in Writing Data to Databases."

If the query succeeds, the third phase of the insertion process occurs when the script redirects to a receipt page that reports the results. As part of the redirection, the new phonebook_id is passed to the receipt as a URL query string parameter and the status of the operation is set to T (for True). The receipt script then queries the database and displays the phonebook details that match the phonebook_id. For this step, we reuse the receipt script shown in Example 8-5 and its template in Example 8-6.

Updating data

Updating data is usually a more complex process than inserting it. A four-step process that extends the insertion process is used in most web database applications:

1. Using a key value, matching data is read from the database.

2. The data is presented to the user in a form for modification.

3. Once the user submits the form, the data is validated and, if that succeeds, the database is updated using an SQL UPDATE statement. The key value from the first step is used in the WHERE clause.

4. The user is redirected to a receipt page. If the update was successful, the page displays the modified data. If the update fails, an error message is displayed.

The first step of this process is usually user-driven: the user provides information that identifies the data to be updated. The information to identify the data (for example, a primary key value such as a phonebook_id) might be gathered in one of several ways:

- It may be entered into a form by the user. For example, the user may be asked to type in or select from a list the phonebook identifier of the entry he wishes to modify.

- It may be determined from another user-driven query. For example, the user might provide a phone number through a form, and a SELECT query can then retrieve the unique identifier of the entry from the database (assuming the phone number is unique).

- It may be formatted into an embedded link by a script. For example, a list of phonebook entries might be produced, where each entry in the list is a hypertext link that has the unique phonebook_id identifier encoded as a query string.

These methods of gathering data from the user are discussed in Chapter 6. Let's assume here that a primary key is provided through one of these techniques, and the value of the primary key has been encoded in an HTTP request that can be processed by the update script. The first phase is then completed by retrieving the data that matches the primary key value provided by the user.

Phase two is to present the data to the user. To achieve this, a form is usually created that contains the values of each attribute that can be modified. In some cases, some attributes may not be presented to the user. For example, the primary key is usually hidden because you don't want the user to change it.

In addition to presenting the data to the user, a method is required to store the primary key value associated with the data, because it is needed in phases three and four. There are several approaches to maintaining this key across the update process, and one simple approach is presented in the next section. Better solutions are the subject of Chapter 10.

Phase two is complete when the user submits the form containing the modified data. Phase three validates the data and updates the database, and phase four shows a receipt; these phases use the same techniques as inserting new data.

Case study: updates in practice

Example 8-11 shows a modified version of Example 8-7 that supports database updates and uses a copy of the template shown in Example 8-8 (that's modified so it requests *example.8-12.php*). The script implements the first two phases of the update process described in the previous section. We discuss the third and fourth phases later in this section.

Example 8-11. Updating and adding new phonebook details

```php
<?php
require 'db.inc';
require_once "HTML/Template/ITX.php";

if (!($connection = @ mysql_connect("localhost", "fred", "shhh")))
    die("Could not connect to database");

$phonebook_id = mysqlclean($_GET, "phonebook_id", 5, $connection);

// Has a phonebook_id been provided?
if (empty($phonebook_id))
    die("You must provide a phonebook_id in the URL.");

$template = new HTML_Template_ITX("./templates");
$template->loadTemplatefile("example.8-8b.tpl", true, true);

// Retrieve details for editing
if (!mysql_select_db("telephone", $connection))
    showerror();

$query = "SELECT * FROM phonebook WHERE phonebook_id = {$phonebook_id}";

if (!($result = @ mysql_query($query, $connection)))
    showerror();

$row = mysql_fetch_array($result);

$template->setVariable("MESSAGE",
                       "Please amend the details below");
$template->setVariable("SUBMITVALUE", "Update Details");

$template->setCurrentBlock("hiddeninput");
$template->setVariable("HINPUTNAME", "phonebook_id");
$template->setVariable("HINPUTVALUE", $row["phonebook_id"]);
$template->parseCurrentBlock("hiddeninput");

$template->setCurrentBlock("mandatoryinput");
$template->setVariable("MINPUTTEXT", "First name");
$template->setVariable("MINPUTNAME", "firstname");
$template->setVariable("MINPUTVALUE", $row["firstname"]);
$template->setVariable("MINPUTSIZE", 50);
$template->parseCurrentBlock("mandatoryinput");

$template->setCurrentBlock("mandatoryinput");
$template->setVariable("MINPUTTEXT", "Surname");
$template->setVariable("MINPUTNAME", "surname");
$template->setVariable("MINPUTVALUE", $row["surname"]);
$template->setVariable("MINPUTSIZE", 50);
```

Example 8-11. Updating and adding new phonebook details (continued)

```
$template->parseCurrentBlock("mandatoryinput");

$template->setCurrentBlock("mandatoryinput");
$template->setVariable("MINPUTTEXT", "Phone");
$template->setVariable("MINPUTNAME", "phone");
$template->setVariable("MINPUTVALUE", $row["phone"]);
$template->setVariable("MINPUTSIZE", 20);
$template->parseCurrentBlock("mandatoryinput");

$template->parseCurrentBlock( );
$template->show( );
?>
```

Phase one of the update process works as follows. The script in Example 8-11 processes a phonebook_id passed through with an HTTP request. If it is set, the script queries the database for the matching phonebook row and stores it in the variable $row. If it isn't set, the script reports an error and stops. Because there's only one row of results that match the unique primary key value, we don't need a loop to retrieve the data.

The second phase, displaying the retrieved data for modification by the user, is achieved by initializing template placeholders with the results of the query. For example, when a surname is retrieved for an entry, the placeholder MINPUTVALUE is initialized using:

```
$template->setVariable("MINPUTVALUE", $row["surname"]);
```

This allows the user to edit the database surname in the surname text input widget.

The second phase of the process also embeds the value of $phonebook_id in the form as a hidden input element that the user can't see or edit. The $phonebook_id is embedded so it is passed to the next script and used to construct the SQL query to perform the update operation. We use the hiddeninput placeholder for this purpose and initialize it using the following fragment:

```
$template->setCurrentBlock("hiddeninput");
$template->setVariable("HINPUTNAME", "phonebook_id");
$template->setVariable("HINPUTVALUE", $row["phonebook_id"]);
$template->parseCurrentBlock("hiddeninput");
```

There are other ways this value can be passed throughout the update process; these techniques are the subject of Chapter 10.

Example 8-12 implements the third phase. The process is the same as inserting new data, with the exception of the SQL query that uses the phonebook_id from the form to identify the row to be updated. As previously, after the database operation, the browser is redirected to a receipt page to avoid the reload problem. However, the update process is now susceptible to other problems that are described in "Issues in Writing Data to Databases."

Example 8-12. Updating existing and inserting new phonebook rows

```php
<?php
require 'db.inc';
require_once "HTML/Template/ITX.php";

function formerror(&$template, $message, &$errors)
{
  $errors = true;
  $template->setCurrentBlock("error");
  $template->setVariable("ERROR", $message);
  $template->parseCurrentBlock("error");
}

if (!($connection = @ mysql_connect("localhost", "fred", "shhh")))
    die("Could not connect to database");

$phonebook_id = mysqlclean($_POST, "phonebook_id", 5, $connection);
$firstname = mysqlclean($_POST, "firstname", 50, $connection);
$surname = mysqlclean($_POST, "surname", 50, $connection);
$phone = mysqlclean($_POST, "phone", 20, $connection);

$template = new HTML_Template_ITX("./templates");
$template->loadTemplatefile("example.8-10.tpl", true, true);

$errors = false;

if (empty($firstname))
  formerror($template, "The first name field cannot be blank.", $errors);

if (empty($surname))
  formerror($template, "The surname field cannot be blank.", $errors);

if (empty($phone))
  formerror($template, "The phone field cannot be blank", $errors);

// Now the script has finished the validation, show any errors
if ($errors)
{
  $template->show( );
  exit;
}

// If we made it here, then the data is valid
if (!mysql_select_db("telephone", $connection))
  showerror( );

// Update the phonebook entry
$query = "UPDATE phonebook SET surname = '{$surname}',
        firstname = '{$firstname}',
        phone = '{$phone}'
        WHERE phonebook_id = {$phonebook_id}";

if (!(@ mysql_query ($query, $connection)))
    showerror( );
```

Example 8-12. Updating existing and inserting new phonebook rows (continued)

```
// Show the phonebook receipt
header("Location: example.8-5.php?status=T&phonebook_id={$phonebook_id}");
?>
```

Deleting data

Deletion is a straightforward two-step process:

1. Using a key value, data is removed with an SQL DELETE statement.
2. On success, the user is redirected to a receipt page that displays a confirmation message. On failure, an error is reported.

As with updates, the first phase requires a key value be provided, and any technique used for capturing keys in updates can be used.

Deleting rows using a primary key value is very similar to the update process. First, a phonebook_id key value is pre-processed using *mysqlclean()*, validated, and assigned to $phonebook_id. Then, the following fragment uses a query to delete the customer identified by the value of $phonebook_id:

```
// We have a phonebook_id. Set up a delete query
$query = "DELETE FROM phonebook WHERE phonebook_id = {$phonebook_id}";

if ( (@ mysql_query ($query, $connection)) &&
     @ mysql_affected_rows( ) == 1)
  // Query succeeded and one row was deleted
  header("Location: delete_receipt.php?status=T");
else
  // Query failed or one row wasn't deleted
  header("Location: delete_receipt.php?status=F");
```

The function *mysql_affected_rows()* reports how many rows were modified by the query and, if everything is successful, this should be 1; the function is described in Chapter 6. The delete receipt lets the user know that the operation succeeded or failed.

Issues in Writing Data to Databases

In this section, we discuss issues that emerge in web database applications when multiple users access an application. Typically, a few users are inserting, updating, or deleting data, while most are running queries. This environment requires careful code design: without it, data can unexpectedly or unreliably change. This may lead to database inconsistencies and confused users.

Some of the problems we describe in this section can be solved with restrictive system requirements, knowledge of how the DBMS behaves, and careful script development. Others solutions require an understanding of database theory. We discuss both types of solution in the next section.

Transactions and Concurrency

Problems can occur when users read and write to a web database at the same time, that is, *concurrently*. The management of groups of SQL statements that read and write, or *transactions*, is one important area of the theory and practice of relational databases. Here are four of the more common problems of concurrent read and write transactions:

Lost update problem

User A reads from the database, recording a value. User B reads the same value, then updates the value immediately. User A then updates the value, overwriting the update written by User B.

Consider an example. Imagine that a winestore manager wants to order one dozen more bottles of a popular wine, but only if there are less than two dozen bottles currently in stock. The manager runs a query to sum the total stock for that wine from the inventory. The result is that there are fifteen bottles left, so the manager decides to place an order. However, he heads off to fill his coffee cup first, leaving the system displaying the query result.

A second stock manager arrives at her desk with the same intention: to order more of this popular wine if there are less than two dozen bottles. The result of the query is the same: fifteen bottles. The second manager orders a dozen bottles, and updates the inventory to 27, knowing the bottles will arrive in the afternoon. The problem occurs when the first manager returns: he doesn't rerun the query and he too orders 12 bottles and updates the inventory to 27. Now the system has record of 27 bottles, but 24 will arrive in the afternoon to take the actual stock total to 39!

Dirty read problem

User A reads a value from the database, changes the value, and writes it back to the database. User B then reads the value, changes the value, and writes it back to the database. User A then decides not to confirm the changes for some reason and undoes the changes he made. The problem is that User B has read and used the changed value, resulting in a dirty read problem.

Consider an example. A manager decides to add a 3% surcharge to a particular wine inventory, so she reads and updates the cost of that wine. Another manager decides to apply a 10% discount to all wines made by a particular winery, which happens to include the wine just surcharged. After all this, the first manager realizes she has made a mistake: the wrong wine was updated! Unfortunately, the second manager has already used this incorrect value as input into his update, and the change can't be undone correctly.

Incorrect summary problem

> User A updates values while User B reads and summarizes the same values. Values summarized may be read before or after each individual update, resulting in unpredictable results.

> Consider an example in the online winestore where a manager wants to produce a management stock report. The report details wine sales, winery sales, wine region sales, and total sales. The reporting process has four steps: first, the sales of each wine are tallied; second, the total sales of wines for each winery are tallied; third, the total sales of wines for each region are tallied; and, last, the overall total sales of wines is determined. The report uses four queries and takes a few minutes to run.

> Now, imagine that during this process, a customer purchases a bottle of Paradise Pinot Noir wine from the Paradise Enough winery. Specifically, let's imagine this happens after the total sales of the Paradise Pinot Noir wine are tallied but before the Paradise Enough winery sales are tallied. The result is that the tally of the Pinot Noir's sales doesn't include this purchase, but the tally of Paradise Enough winery sales does. The result is an inconsistency: adding together all of the wine sales won't give the same value that's reported for the winery.

Unrepeatable read problem

> A value is read in by User A, updated by User B, and subsequently reread by User A for verification. Despite not modifying the value, User A encounters two different values, that is, the read operation is unrepeatable.

> Consider an example. Imagine a user of an online winestore wants to buy the last bottle of an expensive, rare wine that's in stock. He browses the database and finds the wine. There is only bottle left, and he quickly adds this to his shopping cart; in our implementation, this creates new rows in two tables in the database. Now, he decides to finalize the purchase and is presented with a summary of the shopping cart.

> However, while the user fumbles about finding his password to log in, another user enters the system. She quickly locates the same wine, sees that there is only one bottle left, adds it to her shopping cart, logs in to the system, and purchases the wine. When our first user finally logs in to finalize the order, all the details look fine, but the wine has actually been sold. Our database operation to deduct from the inventory reports an error because the stock value is already zero (the value has changed during the transaction), and we end up reporting the error to our original (now very unhappy and confused!) user.

Fortunately, most of these problems can be solved through *locking* or careful design of scripts that carry out database transactions. However, you might choose not to solve some problems because they restrict the system requirements or add unnecessary complexity. We discuss locking in the next section.

Locking to Achieve Concurrency in MySQL

It has been shown that a simple scheme called *locking* (actually, it's correctly known as *two-phase locking*) solves the four transaction problems identified in the last section.

When and how to lock tables

Locking is needed only when multiple steps must be performed together, and when two or more operations can be going on at the same time. If scripts are being implemented that write to the database but aren't multi-step operations susceptible to the problems described in the previous section, locks aren't needed.

Specifically, the following situations do not require a lock:

- Simple queries that insert rows, delete rows, or update rows, and that don't use results of a previous SELECT or data entered by the user as input. For example, updating a customer's details, adding a new phonebook entry, or unconditionally deleting a row do not require a lock.

- Single-user applications or applications where only one user can alter the data do not require locks regardless of what queries are used.

The following situations do require locks:

- Multi-user applications require locks, but only if either of the next two points are true.

- A script first reads a value from a database and later writes that value to the database. For example, to create a row without using MySQL proprietary features, you first need to find the highest value used for the primary key using a SELECT and then INSERT a new row with the next available key value.

- A script first writes a value to a database and later reads that value from the database. For example, to update and display an inventory, you might first add an extra quantity with an UPDATE and then read it back with a SELECT to check the total and show it to the user.

Locking may not be required for all parts of a web database application: parts of the application can still be safely used without violating any locking conditions.

With its default settings, each MySQL table has two associated lock variables. If a user sets or *holds* a lock variable for a particular table, no other user can perform particular actions on that table. There are two kinds of locks for each table: read locks, when a user is only reading from a table, and write locks, when a user is both reading and writing to a table.

Having locks in a DBMS leads to four rules of use:

- If a user wants to write to a table, and she is performing a transaction susceptible to a concurrency problem, she must obtain a write lock on that table.

- If a user only wants to read from a table, and she is performing a transaction susceptible to a concurrency problem, she must obtain a read lock on that table.

- If a user requires a lock, she must lock all tables used in the transaction in a single LOCK statement.

- A user must release all locks when a database transaction is complete using the UNLOCK statement.

When a user holds a write lock on a table, no other users can read or write to that table. When a user holds a read lock on a table, other users can also read or hold a read lock, but no user can hold a write lock on that table, or write to that table.

 SELECT, UPDATE, INSERT, or DELETE operations that don't use LOCK TABLES are held up if locks are held in other transactions that would logically prevent their operation. For example, if a user holds a write lock on a table, no other user can issue a SELECT, UPDATE, INSERT, DELETE, or LOCK operation on that table.

The following segment of an interaction with the MySQL command interpreter illustrates the use of locks in a summarization task that requires locking:

```
mysql> LOCK TABLES items READ, temp_report WRITE;

mysql> SELECT sum(price) FROM items WHERE cust_id=1;
+-------------+
| sum(price)  |
+-------------+
|      438.65 |
+-------------+
1 row in set (0.04 sec)

mysql> UPDATE temp_report SET purchases=438.65
       WHERE cust_id=1;
mysql> UNLOCK TABLES;
```

In this example, a temporary table called *temp_report* is updated with the result of a SELECT operation on an *items* table. If locks aren't used, the *items* table can be modified by another user, possibly altering the summary value of $438.65 used as input to the UPDATE operation. There are two locks obtained for this transaction: first, a read lock on *items* because we don't need to change *items* but we don't want another user to make a change to it; and, second, a write lock on *temp_report* because we want to change the table, and we don't want other users to read or write to the report while we make changes. The UNLOCK TABLES operation releases all locks held; locks can't be progressively released.

MySQL doesn't permit us to lock only one of the two tables used in the transaction above. The following rules apply to locks:

- If a lock is held, all other tables that are to be used must also be locked. Failing to do so results in a MySQL error.

- If aliases are used in queries, the alias must be locked. For example, in the following query:

  ```
  SELECT * from customer c where c.custid=1
  ```

  the alias must be locked with one of:

  ```
  LOCK TABLES customer c READ
  ```

  or:

  ```
  LOCK TABLES customer c WRITE
  ```

  If different aliases for the same table are used, each different alias must be locked. Aliases are discussed in Chapter 15.

In many cases, locking can be avoided through careful query design:

- Use MySQL's auto_increment feature to create new primary key values. Alternatively, use PEAR DB's *DB::nextId( )* method that we discuss later in this chapter.

- Use *mysql_insert_id( )* (as opposed to using the *max()* function in a SELECT query) to find the value of a newly-created primary key. Again, PEAR DB's *DB:: nextId( )* method can be alternatively used.

- Use advanced features of SQL to combine two queries into one; these features are discussed in Chapter 15. For example, you can use a single nested query to discover the total value in our previous example and then use that to create a new row in the temporary report.

- Perform updates that are relative. For example, UPDATE customer SET discount = discount*1.1.

The LOCK TABLES and UNLOCK TABLES statements in MySQL

The LOCK TABLES statement is used to lock the listed tables in either READ or WRITE mode. As discussed earlier, all tables that are accessed in the transaction must be locked in either READ or WRITE mode, and must be listed in a single LOCK TABLES statement.

A script that issues a LOCK TABLES statement is suspended until all locks listed are successfully obtained. There is no time limit in waiting for locks. If the lock is held by another user or an operation is running on the table already, a request is placed at the back of either the *write-* or *read-lock queue* for the table, depending on the lock required. The write-lock queue has priority over the read-lock queue, so a user who wants a write lock obtains it when it becomes available, regardless of how long another user has been waiting in the read-lock queue.

MySQL gives priority to database modifications over read queries. This can lead to a problem called *starvation*, where a transaction never completes because it can't obtain its required read locks. However, most web database applications read from databases much more than they write, and locks are required in only a few situations, so starvation is very uncommon in practice.

If low-priority writing is essential to an application, a LOW_PRIORITY option can be prefixed before the WRITE clause. If a transaction is queued for a LOW_PRIORITY WRITE, it receives the lock only when the read lock queue is empty and no other users are reading from the table. Again, consideration of possible starvation is important.

Locks can't be progressively obtained through several LOCK TABLES statements. Indeed, issuing a second LOCK TABLES is the same as issuing an UNLOCK TABLES to release all locks and then issuing the second LOCK TABLES. There are good reasons for this strict rule, related to a locking problem called *deadlock*, which we don't discuss here. However, MySQL is deadlock-free because it enforces the risk-free use of the LOCK TABLES and UNLOCK TABLES statements.

If an unlocked table needs to be accessed or locking must be avoided for a particular table, a second server connection can be opened and used.

MySQL has a feature called INSERT DELAYED for insertion that is described in the MySQL manual.

Don't use locking with INSERT DELAYED for insert operations. The INSERT DELAYED process is carried out by the MySQL server at a later time and the locks held by the user can't be used by the server.

Locking for performance

Locking is primarily designed to ensure that concurrent transactions can execute safely. However, locking is also a useful performance tool to optimize the performance of important transactions.

Consider, for example, a situation where we urgently require a complex report that uses a slow query. With other users running queries and using system resources, this query may run even slower. A solution is to use LOCK TABLES with the WRITE option to stop other users running queries or database updates, and to have exclusive access to the database for the query duration. This permits better optimization of the query processing by the server, dedication of all the system resources to the query, and faster disk access.

The downside of locking for performance is the reduction in concurrent access to the database. Users may be inconvenienced by slow responses or timeouts from the web database application. Locking for performance should be used sparingly.

Locking Tables in Web Database Applications

Example 8-13 shows a PHP script that requires locking to ensure that the value returned from the SELECT query can't change before the INSERT operation. The script adds a row to the *phonebook* table and does exactly same thing as Example 8-9.

However, it doesn't use the MySQL proprietary `auto_increment` modifier and so it needs to read the maximum primary key value that's in use and then write a new row based on that value.

Without the `auto_increment` modifier and with no locking, it's possible that two rows could be created with the same `phonebook_id`. This can happen if two or more users run the script at the same time and get the same result from the `SELECT` query. Both users would then attempt to `INSERT` a new row with the same primary key value and, if this happens, MySQL will report an error because the primary key value must be unique. Locking solves the problem because it stops users running the queries in the script at the same time.

Example 8-13. Creating a phonebook entry using locking

```php
<?php
require 'db.inc';
require_once "HTML/Template/ITX.php";

function formerror(&$template, $message, &$errors)
{
  $errors = true;
  $template->setCurrentBlock("error");
  $template->setVariable("ERROR", $message);
  $template->parseCurrentBlock("error");
}

if (!($connection = @ mysql_connect("localhost", "fred", "shhh")))
    die("Could not connect to database");

$firstname = mysqlclean($_POST, "firstname", 50, $connection);
$surname = mysqlclean($_POST, "surname", 50, $connection);
$phone = mysqlclean($_POST, "phone", 20, $connection);

$template = new HTML_Template_ITX("./templates");
$template->loadTemplatefile("example.8-10.tpl", true, true);

$errors = false;

if (empty($firstname))
  formerror($template, "The first name field cannot be blank.", $errors);

if (empty($surname))
  formerror($template, "The surname field cannot be blank.", $errors);

if (empty($phone))
  formerror($template, "The phone field cannot be blank", $errors);

// Now the script has finished the validation, show any errors
if ($errors)
{
  $template->show();
  exit;
```

Example 8-13. Creating a phonebook entry using locking (continued)

```
}

// If we made it here, then the data is valid
if (!mysql_select_db("telephone", $connection))
  showerror();

// Lock the table
$query = "LOCK TABLES phonebook WRITE";
if (!(@ mysql_query ($query, $connection)))
  showerror();

// Find the maximum phonebook_id value that's in use
$query = "SELECT max(phonebook_id) FROM phonebook";
if (!($result = @ mysql_query ($query, $connection)))
  showerror();

$row = @ mysql_fetch_array($result);

// Set the new value for the primary key
$phonebook_id = $row["max(phonebook_id)"] + 1;

// Insert the new phonebook entry
$query = "INSERT INTO phonebook VALUES
         ({$phonebook_id}, '{$surname}', '{$firstname}', '{$phone}')";
if (!(@ mysql_query ($query, $connection)))
  showerror();

// Unlock the table
$query = "UNLOCK TABLES";
if (!(@ mysql_query ($query, $connection)))
  showerror();

// Show the phonebook receipt
header("Location: example.8-5.php?status=T&phonebook_id={$phonebook_id}");
?>
```

The locking of the *phonebook* table is performed before the SELECT query, and the UNLOCK TABLES statement is issued after the INSERT. As you can see, the lock and unlock statements are executed just like any other query using *mysql_query()*.

Locking methods that don't work in web database applications

There are several locking paradigms that don't work in a web database application because of the statelessness of HTTP. Each approach fails because there is either no guarantee or no possibility that the locked tables will be unlocked. If tables are locked indefinitely, other transactions can't proceed, and the DBMS will most likely need to be shut down and restarted.

Be careful with locking in web database applications. Remember the basic rule that all locks should be unlocked by the same script during the same execution of the script.

All web scripts that require locking should have the sequence 1) lock, 2) query, 3) update, delete, or insert, and 4) unlock. There must be no user interaction or intervening calls to other scripts that require input.

The following must be avoided in web database applications:

- Failing to issue an UNLOCK TABLES on a locked persistent database connection (such as one that opened with *mysql_pconnect( )*). The locks aren't released when the script terminates.

  It isn't necessary to issue an UNLOCK TABLES if a nonpersistent connection is used (such as one opened with *mysql_connect( )*). Locks are automatically released when the script finishes and the connection closes. However, it is good practice to include the UNLOCK TABLES statement.

- Locking one or more tables during the first execution of a script, leaving them locked, and then querying or updating during a second or subsequent execution of the script. Remember that each database connection in a script is independent and is treated as a different user by MySQL.

- Retrieving a value such as the next available primary key value, presenting this to the user, waiting for the user to enter further details, and then adding a row to the database with that identifier. Remember that another user may add a row while the first user is entering the required details, and locks should never be carried across several scripts or different executions of the same script.

Locking with an auxiliary table

Locking limits concurrency in your web database application. If tables are locked, then other users won't be able to run the same script at the same time and other scripts may also not be able to proceed. For example, suppose you write lock the *phonebook* table we've used in our examples throughout this chapter. With the table locked, any other query on the *phonebook* table in any script won't proceed until you unlock the table; this means, for example, while you insert one row, no other users can search for a phone number. Sometimes, you want to avoid this and this section shows you how.

One technique you can use to minimize locking of your frequently used tables is to add an additional table to the database. This additional table stores and manages the next available primary key values for all other tables in the database. The additional table is then locked, queried, updated, and unlocked each time a new primary key value is needed; the main tables in the database are then never locked when data is inserted. In the remainder of this section, we show you how to do this using the

MySQL function library; the next section shows you how to do the same thing using PEAR DB.

Let's consider an example. Suppose you want to add new rows to the *phonebook* table without locking it and without using the proprietary MySQL auto_increment modifier. You first create an additional table in the *telephone* database using the following CREATE TABLE statement:

```
CREATE TABLE identifiers (phonebook_id int(5));
```

As we show you next, this table only contains one row and therefore there's no need to declare or use a primary key.

The new *identifiers* table stores one row that contains the next available value of the phonebook_id primary key attribute from the *phonebook* table. To set this up, you add the row to the table and set the phonebook_id attribute to the next available value. Let's suppose your *phonebook* table is empty, and so the next primary key value for phonebook_id is 1. Here's the INSERT statement you use to set up the table:

```
INSERT INTO identifiers VALUES (1);
```

Now you can use the *identifiers* table to read and write a primary key value for the *phonebook* table. Having done this, you use the primary key value to create a new row without locking the *phonebook* table. Here's how you do it using the MySQL command interpreter:

```
mysql> LOCK TABLES identifiers WRITE;
Query OK, 0 rows affected (0.00 sec)

mysql> SELECT phonebook_id FROM identifiers;
+--------------+
| phonebook_id |
+--------------+
|            1 |
+--------------+
1 row in set (0.00 sec)

mysql> UPDATE identifiers SET phonebook_id = phonebook_id + 1;
Query OK, 1 row affected (0.00 sec)
Rows matched: 1  Changed: 1  Warnings: 0

mysql> UNLOCK TABLES;
Query OK, 0 rows affected (0.00 sec)

mysql> INSERT INTO phonebook VALUES (1, "Williams",
        "Lucy", "61388763452");
Query OK, 1 row affected (0.01 sec)
```

The locking, querying, modifying, and unlocking process proceeds similarly to our example in the previous section, except that it doesn't use the *phonebook* table. Instead, the new row is inserted into the *phonebook* table without a lock using the value discovered with the SELECT query from the *identifiers* table, thereby maximizing concurrency (but requiring three SQL queries instead of two). Example 8-14 shows a rewritten version of Example 8-13 that uses this approach.

Example 8-14. Maintaining the phonebook table using an external identifiers table

```php
<?php
require 'db.inc';
require_once "HTML/Template/ITX.php";

function formerror(&$template, $message, &$errors)
{
  $errors = true;
  $template->setCurrentBlock("error");
  $template->setVariable("ERROR", $message);
  $template->parseCurrentBlock("error");
}

if (!($connection = @ mysql_connect("localhost", "fred", "shhh")))
   die("Could not connect to database");

$firstname = mysqlclean($_POST, "firstname", 50, $connection);
$surname = mysqlclean($_POST, "surname", 50, $connection);
$phone = mysqlclean($_POST, "phone", 20, $connection);

$template = new HTML_Template_ITX("./templates");
$template->loadTemplatefile("example.8-10.tpl", true, true);

$errors = false;

if (empty($firstname))
  formerror($template, "The first name field cannot be blank.", $errors);

if (empty($surname))
  formerror($template, "The surname field cannot be blank.", $errors);

if (empty($phone))
  formerror($template, "The phone field cannot be blank", $errors);

// Now the script has finished the validation, show any errors
if ($errors)
{
  $template->show();
  exit;
}

// If we made it here, then the data is valid
if (!mysql_select_db("telephone", $connection))
  showerror();

// Lock the identifiers table
$query = "LOCK TABLES identifiers WRITE";
if (!(@ mysql_query ($query, $connection)))
   showerror();
```

```php
// Find the maximum phonebook_id value that's in use
$query = "SELECT phonebook_id FROM identifiers";
if (!($result = @ mysql_query ($query, $connection)))
   showerror();

$row = @ mysql_fetch_array($result);

$phonebook_id = $row["phonebook_id"];

// Update the phonebook_id identifier
$query = "UPDATE identifiers SET phonebook_id = phonebook_id + 1";
if (!($result = @ mysql_query ($query, $connection)))
   showerror();

// Unlock the table
$query = "UNLOCK TABLES";
if (!(@ mysql_query ($query, $connection)))
   showerror();

// Insert the new phonebook entry
$query = "INSERT INTO phonebook VALUES
          ({$phonebook_id}, '{$surname}', '{$firstname}', '{$phone}')";
if (!(@ mysql_query ($query, $connection)))
   showerror();

// Show the phonebook receipt
header("Location: example.8-5.php?status=T&phonebook_id={$phonebook_id}");
?>
```

To extend this scheme for a database containing several tables, there are two possible approaches: first, add an additional attribute (or more than one attribute if the primary key isn't on only one attribute) to the *identifiers* table for each additional table; or, second, add an additional identifier table for each additional table. The first approach is the simplest (and the one we recommend) but it does have the potential disadvantage that concurrency could be limited by excessive locking of the *identifiers* table if too many tables are maintained by using it. The second approach maximizes concurrency but is probably only necessary for high-throughput applications.

Managing identifiers with PEAR DB

In the previous section, we showed you how to maintain identifiers using an additional table. PEAR DB allows you to do the same thing using its *DB::nextId()* method and this is useful if you want to write database independent code. We show you how to use it in this section. The PEAR DB sequence methods are also briefly described in Chapter 7.

A sequence is a value associated with a name and it's typically used to create primary key values. A sequence is always initialized to 1, and increments each time you access it with *DB::nextId()*. For example, suppose you want to maintain the primary key value for the phonebook_id from the *phonebook* table that we've used in our examples in this chapter. To do this, you can use the *DB::nextID()* method as shown in Example 8-15:

```
// Get a new primary key value for phonebook_id
$phonebook_id = $connection->nextId("phonebook_id");
```

When this is called for the first time, *DB::nextId()* creates a new sequence named phonebook_id, assigns it the value 1, and returns the value. When you call it for the second time, it returns 2, and so on. It performs exactly the same function as our *identifiers* table approach in Example 8-14.

Example 8-15. Using PEAR DB to maintain primary key values

```
<?php
require "db.inc";
require_once "HTML/Template/ITX.php";
require_once "DB.php";

function formerror(&$template, $message, &$errors)
{
  $errors = true;
  $template->setCurrentBlock("error");
  $template->setVariable("ERROR", $message);
  $template->parseCurrentBlock("error");
}

$dsn = "mysql://fred:shhh@localhost/telephone";

$connection = DB::connect($dsn, false);
if (DB::isError($connection))
  die($connection->getMessage());

$firstname = mysqlclean($_POST["firstname"], 50, $connection);
$surname = mysqlclean($_POST["surname"], 50, $connection);
$phone = mysqlclean($_POST["phone"], 20, $connection);

$template = new HTML_Template_ITX("./templates");
$template->loadTemplatefile("example.8-10.tpl", true, true);

$errors = false;

if (empty($firstname))
  formerror($template, "The first name field cannot be blank.", $errors);

if (empty($surname))
  formerror($template, "The surname field cannot be blank.", $errors);

if (empty($phone))
  formerror($template, "The phone field cannot be blank", $errors);

// Now the script has finished the validation, show any errors
```

Example 8-15. Using PEAR DB to maintain primary key values (continued)

```
if ($errors)
{
  $template->show( );
  exit;
}

// Get a new primary key value for phonebook_id
$phonebook_id = $connection->nextId("phonebook_id");
if (DB::isError($connection))
   die($connection->getMessage( ));

// Insert the new phonebook entry
$query = "INSERT INTO phonebook VALUES
          ({$phonebook_id}, {$surname}, {$firstname}, {$phone})";
$result = $connection->query($query);
if (DB::isError($result))
   die($result->getMessage( ));

// Show the phonebook receipt
header("Location: example.8-5.php?status=T&phonebook_id={$phonebook_id}");
?>
```

Behind the scenes, PEAR DB maintains a sequence in a table of the same name. When you create a sequence, it creates a table and an attribute and initializes the attribute to 1. When you call *DB::nextId()*, it adds 1 and returns the value. PEAR DB correctly looks after safe concurrent access.

If you call *DB::nextID()* without its optional second parameter or with the second parameter set to true, a sequence with the name supplied as the first parameter is created if it doesn't exist. You can also manually create a sequence using *DB::createSequence()* and you can remove it using *DB::dropSequence()*.

CHAPTER 9

Validation with PHP and JavaScript

Validation is essential to web database applications. In this chapter, we begin by discussing the types of validation that can be implemented in a web database application, and then show you how to validate data at the server using PHP and at the client using JavaScript.

This chapter extends our discussion of validation in PHP. We have already introduced basic security validation and empty field checks in Chapter 6. We continue here by introducing the principles of validation and the practice of validating form variables and values with PHP. We show you how to validate strings, numbers, dates, times, and Internet addresses, and how some of these tasks can be simplified using PEAR packages.

This chapter also introduces client-side JavaScript. We compare it to PHP and show you the basic techniques used in most common applications. We then describe how simple validation can be performed at the client to save network costs and improve responsiveness of an application to the user. We also introduce other simple tasks that can be effectively accomplished with JavaScript.

This chapter is about user data and helping users to meet system requirements. Parse errors, database server failures, debugging code, and other PHP and database server problems are the subject of Chapter 12.

Validation and Error Reporting Principles

There is nothing worse for a user than annoying, overly persistent, inaccurate, or uninformative validation. For example, error messages that describe an error but don't specify which field contains the error are difficult to correct. However, there is no recipe for balancing validation with system requirements: what is pleasing or mandated by requirements in one application might be annoying or useless in another. In this section, we consider practical validation models for web database applications.

Validation is actually two processes: finding errors and presenting error messages. Finding errors can be *interactive*, where data is checked as it's entered, or *post-validation*, where the data is checked after entry. Presenting errors can be *field-by-field*—where a new error message is presented to the user for each error found—or it can be *batched*, where all errors are presented as a single message. There are other dimensions to validation and error processing, such as the *degree of error* that is tolerated and the *experience level* of the user. However, considering only the basic processes, the choice of when to error-check and when to notify the user, leads to four common approaches:

Interactive validation with field-by-field errors
> The data in each field is validated when the user exits or changes the field. If there is an error, the user is alerted to that error and may be required to fix the error before proceeding.

Interactive validation with batched errors
> The data in all fields is validated when the user leaves one field. If there are one or more errors, the user is alerted to these, and can't proceed beyond the current page without fixing all errors.

Post-validation with field-by-field errors
> The user first enters all data with no validation. The data is then checked and errors are reported for each field, one by one. The user fixes each error in turn and resubmits the data for revalidation.

Post-validation with batched errors
> The user first enters all data with no validation. The data is then checked, and all errors in the data are reported in one message to the user. The user then fixes all errors and resubmits the data for revalidation.

In Chapter 8—without discussing the details—we covered several simple post-validation techniques to check whether mandatory form data was entered before inserting or updating data in the database. In addition, we used a batch reporting method, where errors were reported as a list by constructing an error page using a template.

In the examples in this chapter, we discuss additional validation techniques to inspect both mandatory and optional fields. We use these techniques to create a batch error report in Chapter 10. Examples of complete validation code for a customer details form are listed in Chapter 17.

Models That Don't Work

Interactive models are difficult to implement in the web environment. Server-side scripts are impractical for this task, because an HTTP request and response is required to validate each field that's entered. This is usually unacceptable, because the user is required to submit the data after entering each field. The result is that response times are likely to be slow and the server load high.

Client-side scripts can implement an interactive model. However, validation on the client side should not be the only method of validation because the user can passively or actively bypass the client-side processes. We discuss the partially interactive solution of including client-side scripts with an HTML form later in this chapter.

Models That Do Work

Post-validation models are practical in web database applications. Both client- and server-side scripts can validate all form data during the submission process.

In many applications, reasonably comprehensive validation is performed on the client side when the user clicks the form submit button. Client-side validation reduces server and network load, because the user's browser ensures the data is valid prior to the HTTP request. Client-side validation is also usually faster for the user.

If client-side validation succeeds, data is submitted to the server and the same (or often more comprehensive) validation is performed. Duplicating client validation on the server is essential because of the unreliability of client-side scripts and lack of control over the client environment.

The post-validation model can be combined with either field-by-field or batch error reporting. For server-side validation, the batch model is preferable to a field-by-field implementation, as the latter approach has more overhead and is usually slower because each form error requires an additional HTTP request and response.

For client-side post-validation, either error-reporting model can be used. The advantage of the field-by-field model is that it leads the user through the process of correcting the data and the cursor can be directed to the field containing the error, making error correction easier. The disadvantage is that several errors require several error messages, and this can be frustrating for the user. The advantage of the batch approach is that all errors are presented in one message but the disadvantage is that the cursor can't easily be directed to the field requiring correction and its sometimes unclear to the user how to correct the data.

Server-side validation is essential to secure a web database and to ensure that system and DBMS constraints are met.

Client-side validation may be implemented in addition to server-side validation, but all client-side functionality should be duplicated at the server side. Never trust the user or the client browser.

The choice of which reporting model to use depends on the size and complexity of the form and on the system requirements.

Server-Side Validation with PHP

In this section, we introduce validation on the server using PHP. We show you how to validate numbers including currencies and credit cards, strings including email addresses and Zip Codes, and dates and times. We also show you how to check for mandatory fields, field lengths, and data types. Many of the PHP functions we use— including the regular expression and string functions—are discussed in detail in Chapter 3.

We illustrate many of our examples in this section with a case study of validating customer details. The techniques described here are typical of those that validate a form after the user has submitted data to the server. We show how to extend and integrate this approach further in Chapter 10 so that the batch errors are reported as part of a customer form, and we show a completed customer entry form and validation in Chapter 17.

Mandatory Data

Testing whether mandatory fields have been entered is straightforward, and we have implemented this in our examples in Chapter 8. For example, to test if the user's surname has been entered, the following approach is used:

```
/// Validate the Surname
if (empty($surname))
  formerror($template, "The surname field cannot be blank.", $errors);
```

The *formerror( )* function outputs the error message as a batch error using a template and is discussed in detail in Chapter 8. For simplicity and compactness in the remainder of our examples in this chapter, we omit the *formerror()* function from code fragments and simply output the error messages using print.

Validating Strings

In this section, we discuss nonnumeric validation. We begin with the basics of validating strings, and then discuss the specifics of email addresses, URLs, and Zip or post codes.

Basic techniques

It's likely that most of the data entered by users will be strings and require validation. Indeed, checking that strings contain legal characters, are of the correct length, or have the correct format is the most common validation task. Strings are popular for two reasons: first, all data from a form that is stored in the superglobals $_GET and $_POST is of the type string; and, second, some nonstring data such as a date of birth or a phone number is likely to be stored as a string in a database table because it may contain brackets, dashes, and slashes. However, despite dates and phone numbers being sometimes stored as strings, we discuss their validation in the section "Validating numbers."

The simplest test of a string is to check if it meets a minimum or maximum length requirement. For example:

```
if (strlen($password) < 4 || strlen($password) > 8)
  print "Password must contain between 4 and 8 characters";
```

Length validation can also be performed using a regular expression, as we show in later examples in this section. Our *mysqlclean( )* and *shellclean( )* functions also include an implicit maximum length validation. As discussed in Chapter 6, these functions should be used as a first step in validation that helps to secure an application.

Common tests for legal characters include checking if strings are uppercase, lowercase, alphabetic, or are drawn from a defined character set (such as, for example, alphabetic strings that may include hyphens or apostrophes). In PHP, the *is_string( )* function can be used to check if a variable is a string type. However, this is of limited use in validation because a string can contain any character including (or even exclusively) digits or special characters. It's more useful to test what characters are in the string or detect characters that shouldn't be there.

Regular expressions offer three shortcuts for use in basic tests that are discussed in Chapter 3. To test if a string is alphabetic, use:

```
if (!ereg("^[[:alpha:]]+$", $string))
  print "String must contain only alphabetic characters.";
```

To test if a string is uppercase or lowercase, use:

```
if (ereg("^[[:upper:]]+$", $string))
  print "String contains only uppercase characters.",;
```

```
if (ereg("^[[:lower:]]+$", $string))
  print "String contains only lowercase characters";
```

The expressions work for the English character sets, and also work for French if you set your locale at the beginning of the script using, for example, *setlocale('LC_ALL', 'fr')*. In the future, it should work for all localities and, therefore, these techniques are useful for internationalizing your application.

If you're working with only the English language a simpler alphabetic test works:

```
if (!eregi("^[a-z]*$", $string))
  print "String must contain only alphabetic characters.";
```

For other character sets (or if you want detailed control over English validation), a handcrafted expression works well. For example, the following works as an alphabetic test for Spanish:

```
if (!eregi("^[a-zñ]*$", $string))
  print "La cadena debe contener solamente caracteres alfabeticos";
```

Sometimes it's easier to check what characters shouldn't be there. For example, at our university, student email accounts must begin with an S:

```
if (!ereg("^S", $text))
  print "Student accounts must begin with S.";
```

However, for this simple example, a regular expression will run slower than using a string library function. Instead, a better approach is to use *substr( )*:

```
if (substr($text, 0 , 1) != "S")
    print "Student accounts must begin with S.";
```

In general, you should use string functions for low complexity tasks.

For our customer case study, we might allow the firstname and surname of the customer to contain only alphabetic characters, hyphens, and apostrophes; white space, numbers, and other special characters aren't allowed. For the firstname we use:

```
elseif (!eregi("^[a-z'-]*$", $firstName))
    print "The first name can contain only alphabetic " .
        "characters or - or '";
```

Length validation and character checks are often combined. For example, the customer's middle initial might be limited to exactly one alphabetic character:

```
if (!empty($initial) && !eregi("^[a-z]$", $initial))
    print "The initial field must be empty or one character in length.";
```

The if statement contains two clauses: a check as to whether the field contains data and, if that's true, a check of the contents of the field using *eregi( )*. As discussed in Chapter 2, the second clause is checked only if the first clause is true when an AND (&&) expression is evaluated. If the variable is empty, the *eregi( )* expression isn't evaluated.

The expression ^[a-z]$ is the same as ^[a-z]{1}$. To check if a string is exactly four alphabetic characters in length use ^[a-z]{4}$. To check if it's between two and four characters use ^[a-z]{2,4}$.

Validating Zip and postcodes

Zip or postcodes are numeric in most countries but are typically stored as strings because spaces, letters, and special characters are sometimes allowed. In our customer case study, we might validate Zip Codes using a simple regular expression:

```
// Validate Zipcode
if (!ereg("^([0-9]{4,5})$", $zipcode))
    print "The zipcode must be 4 or 5 digits in length.";
```

This permits a Zip Code of either four or five digits in length; this works for both U.S. Zip Codes, and Australia's and several other countries' postcodes, but it's unsuitable for many other countries. For example, postcodes from the United Kingdom include letters and a space and have a complex structure.

For complete validation, we could adapt our Zip or postcode validation to match the country that the user has entered. Example 9-1 shows a validation function that adapts for many Zip and postcodes. The final five case statements check postcodes that must include spaces, dashes, and letters.

Example 9-1. A code fragment to validate many popular Zip and postcodes

```php
function checkcountry($country, $zipcode)
{
  switch ($country)
  {
    case "Austria":
    case "Australia":
    case "Belgium":
    case "Denmark":
    case "Norway":
    case "Portugal":
    case "Switzerland":
      if (!ereg("^[0-9]{4}$", $zipcode))
      {
        print "The postcode/zipcode must be 4 digits in length";
        return false;
      }
      break;
    case "Finland":
    case "France":
    case "Germany":
    case "Italy":
    case "Spain":
    case "USA":
      if (!ereg("^[0-9]{5}$", $zipcode))
      {
        print "The postcode/zipcode must be 5 digits in length";
        return false;
      }
      break;
    case "Greece":
      if (!ereg("^[0-9]{3}[ ][0-9]{2}$", $zipcode))
      {
        print "The postcode must have 3 digits, a space,
              and then 2 digits";
        return false;
      }
      break;
    case "Netherlands":
      if (!ereg("^[0-9]{4}[ ][A-Z]{2}$", $zipcode))
      {
        print "The postcode must have 4 digits, a space, and then 2
              letters";
        return false;
      }
      break;
    case "Poland":
      if (!ereg("^[0-9]{2}-[0-9]{3}$", $zipcode))
      {
        print "The postcode must have 2 digits, a dash,
              and then 3 digits";
        return false;
      }
      break;
```

Example 9-1. A code fragment to validate many popular Zip and postcodes (continued)

```
    case "Sweden":
      if (!ereg("^[0-9]{3}[ ][0-9]{2}$", $zipcode))
      {
        print "The postcode must have 3 digits, a space,
               and then 2 digits";
        return false;
      }
      break;
    case "United Kingdom":
      if (!ereg("^(([A-Z][0-9]{1,2})|([A-Z]{2}[0-9]{1,2})|" .
                "([A-Z]{2}[0-9][A-Z])|([A-Z][0-9][A-Z])|" .
                "([A-Z]{3}))[ ][0-9][A-Z]{2}$", $zipcode))
      {
        print "The postcode must begin with a string of the format
               A9, A99, AA9, AA99, AA9A, A9A, or AAA,
               and then be followed by a space and a string
               of the form 9AA.
               A is any letter and 9 is any number.";
      return false;
      }
      break;
    default:
      // No validation
  }
  return true;
}
```

Another common validation check with Zip Codes is to check that they match the city or state using a database table, but we don't consider this approach here.

Validating email addresses

Email addresses are another common string that requires field organization checking. There is a standard maintained by the Internet Engineering Task Force (IETF) called RFC-2822 that defines what a valid email address can be, and it's much more complex than might be expected. For example, an address such as the following is valid:

```
    " <test> "@webdatabasebook.com
```

In our customer case study, we might use a regular expression and network functions to validate an email address. A function for this purpose is shown in Example 9-2.

Example 9-2. A function to validate an email address

```
function checkemail($email)
{
  // Check syntax
  $validEmailExpr =  "^[0-9a-z~!#$%&_-]([.]?[0-9a-z~!#$%&_-])*" .
                     "@[0-9a-z~!#$%&_-]([.]?[0-9a-z~!#$%&_-])*$";
```

Example 9-2. A function to validate an email address (continued)

```
  // Validate the email
  if (empty($email))
  {
    print "The email field cannot be blank";
    return false;
  }
  elseif (!eregi($validEmailExpr, $email))
  {
    print "The email must be in the name@domain format.";
    return false;
  }
  elseif (strlen($email) > 30)
  {
    print "The email address can be no longer than 30 characters.";
    return false;
  }
  elseif (function_exists("getmxrr") && function_exists("gethostbyname"))
  {
    // Extract the domain of the email address
    $maildomain = substr(strstr($email, '@'), 1);

    if (!(getmxrr($maildomain, $temp) ||
          gethostbyname($maildomain) != $maildomain))
    {
      print "The domain does not exist.";
      return false;
    }
  }
  return true;
}
```

If any email test fails, an error message is output, and no further checks of the email value are made. A valid email passes all tests.

The first check tests to make sure that an email address has been entered. If it's omitted, an error is generated. It then uses a regular expression to check if the email address matches a template. It isn't RFC-2822-compliant but works reasonably for most email addresses:

- It uses *eregi()*, so either upper- or lowercase are matched by the use of a-z.
- It expects the string to begin with a character from the set 0-9, a-z, and ~!#$%&_-. There has to be at least one character from this set at the beginning of the email address for it to be valid.
- After the first character matches, there is an optional bracketed expression: ([.]?[0-9a-z~!#$%&_-])*

  This expression is optional because it's suffixed with the * operator. However, if it does match, it matches any number of the characters specified. There can only be one consecutive full-stop if a full-stop occurs, as determined by the expression [.]?. The expression, for example, matches the string fred.williams but not fred..williams.

- After the initial part of the email address, the character @ is expected. The @ has to occur after the first word for the string to be valid; our regular expression rejects an email address such as fred that has only the initial or local component.

- Our validation expects there to be another word of at least one character after the @ symbol, and this can be followed by any combination of the permitted characters. Strings of permitted characters can be separated by a single full-stop.

The function is imperfect. It allows several illegal email addresses and doesn't allow many that are legal but unusual.

The third step is to check the length of the email address. If it exceeds 30 characters, an error is generated.

The fourth and final step is to check whether the domain of the email address actually exists. The fragment only works on platforms that support the network library functions *getmxrr( )* and *gethostbyname( )*:

```
elseif (function_exists("getmxrr") && function_exists("gethostbyname"))
{
  // Extract the domain of the email address
  $maildomain = substr(strstr($email, '@'), 1);

  if (!(getmxrr($maildomain, $temp) ||
        gethostbyname($maildomain) != $maildomain))
  {
    print "The domain does not exist.";
    return false;
  }
}
```

The function *getmxrr( )* queries an Internet domain name server (DNS) to check if there is a record of the email domain as a mail exchanger (MX). If the domain isn't an 'MX', the domain is checked with *gethostbyname( )* to see if it has an 'A' record; the relevant standard RFC-974 states that when a domain does not have an 'MX', it should be interpreted as having one equal to the host name. If both tests fail, the domain of the email address isn't valid and we reject the email address.

For platforms (such as Microsoft Windows) that don't have the *getmxrr( )* and *gethostbyname( )* functions, the PEAR Net_DNS package can be used instead. It must be installed using the PEAR installer. The DNS lookup package must then be included into the source code using:

```
require_once "Net/DNS.php";
```

Installation of packages is discussed in Chapter 7.

The following fragment is a function *checkMailDomain( )* that uses PEAR Net_DNS to check if the domain parameter $domain has a record of the type matching the parameter $type:

```
// Call with $type of MX, then A to check if an email address
// domain is valid
```

```
function checkMailDomain($domain, $type)
{
  // Create a DNS resolver, and look up an $type record for $domain
  $resolver = new Net_DNS_Resolver();
  $answer = $resolver->search($domain, $type);

  // Is there an answer record?
  if (isset($answer->answer))
    // Iterate through the answers
    foreach($answer->answer as $ans)
      // If it's a $type answer, return true
      if ($ans->type == $type)
        return true;

  return false;
}
```

The function returns true if the DNS server responds with an answer that includes a record of the type that's been requested; it returns false otherwise.

The following code fragment can then be used to validate an email address:

```
// Extract the domain of the email address
$maildomain = substr(strstr($email, '@'), 1);

if (!(checkMailDomain($maildomain, "MX") ||
      checkMailDomain($maildomain, "A")))
  {
    print "The domain does not exist.";
    return false;
  }
```

As in the previous example that uses *getmxrr()* and *gethostbyname()*, we check if there is a record of the email domain as a mail exchanger (MX). If the domain isn't an 'MX', the domain is checked to see if it has an 'A' record. If both tests fail, the domain of the email address isn't valid and we reject the email address.

Validating URLs

Home pages, links, and other URLs are sometimes entered by users. In PHP, validating these is straightforward because the library function *parse_url( )* can do most of the work for you.

The *parse_url( )* function takes one parameter, a URL string, and returns an associative array that contains the components of the URL. For example:

```
$bits =
  parse_url("http://www.webdatabasebook.com/test.php?status=F#message");
foreach($bits as $var => $val)
  echo "{$var} is {$val}\n";
```

produces the output:

```
scheme is http
host is www.webdatabasebook.com
```

```
path is /test.php
query is status=F
fragment is message
```

The *parse_url( )* function can be used in validation as follows:

```
$bits = parse_url($url);

if ($bits["scheme"] != "http")
  print "URL must begin with http://.";
elseif (empty($bits["host"]))
  print "URL must include a host name.";
elseif (function_exists('checkdnsrr') && !checkdnsrr($bits["host"], 'A'))
  print "Host does not exist.";
```

You might also add `elseif` clauses to check for specific path, query, or fragment components. In addition, you could modify the test of the scheme to check for other valid URL types, including *ftp://*, *https://*, or *file://*.

Unfortunately, at the time of writing, *parse_url( )* is slightly broken in PHP 4.3; it works fine in earlier and later versions of PHP. The bug is that if no path is present in the URL, all following components (such as a query or fragment) are incorrectly appended to the host element. To fix this, you can include the following fragment after the call to *parse_url( )*:

```
// Fix the hostname (if needed) in PHP 4.3
if (strpos($bits["host"], '?'))
  $bits["host"] = substr($bits["host"], 0, strpos($bits["host"], '?'));
if (strpos($bits["host"], '#'))
  $bits["host"] = substr($bits["host"], 0, strpos($bits["host"], '#'));
```

For non-Unix environments, you can check the host domain exists by using the PEAR-based approach described in the previous section.

Validating numbers

Checking that values are numeric, are within a range, or have the correct format is a common validation task. For our case study customer example, there might be several semi-numeric fields such as fax and telephone numbers, the customer's salary, or a credit card number. Zip and post codes aren't always numeric, and are discussed in the Section "Validating Strings."

The two most common checks for numbers are whether they are in fact numeric and whether they're within a required range. In PHP, the *is_numeric( )* function can be used to check if a variable contains only digits or if it matches one of the legal number formats. For example, to check if a salary is numeric, you can use:

```
if (!is_numeric($salary))
  print "Salary must be numeric";
```

The *is_numeric( )* function doesn't always behave in the way you expect. Leading and trailing spaces, carriage returns, commas, and spaces after minus signs can result in a false return value. Leading and trailing spaces can be removed with the *trim( )* function, while allowing specialized formats may instead require the use of a regular expression.

The legal number formats to *is_numeric( )* include integers such as 87000, scientific notation such as 12e4, floating point numbers such as 3.14159 (or 3,14159 if your locale is set to France), hexadecimal notation such as 0xff, and negative numbers such as -1.

Before checking variables initialized from form data, they should be converted to a numeric type using the functions *intval( )* or *floatval( )* that convert a string to a number. A test such as if ($_GET["year"] < 1902) may not work as expected, because $_GET["year"] is a string and 1902 is an integer. The test if (intval($_GET["year"]) < 1902) works reliably. Both functions are discussed in Chapter 3.

Consider an example. Suppose that a whole-dollar salary is provided from a form through the POST method and is stored as $_POST["salary"]. To check if it's a valid number, use the following steps:

```
if (!is_numeric($salary))
    print "Salary must be numeric";
else
    // remove spaces and convert to an integer
    $salary = intval($_POST["salary"]);
```

After type conversion to numbers, form data can be validated to check whether it meets range requirements using the basic comparison operators. For example, to check that an age is in a sensible range, you could use:

```
if ($age < 5 || $age > 105)
    print "Age must be in the range 5 to 105";
```

Another common type of numeric validation is checking currencies. Generally, these have one of two common formats: only a currency amount (for example, 10 dollars, 10 cents, or 25 Yen), or a currency amount and a unit amount (for example, $10.15). Currencies should be checked to see if they match the required format, and then (if needed) to see if they're within a range. For example, to check if a currency amount is in whole dollars and between four and six digits in length, you could use:

```
if (!ereg("^[0-9]{4,6}", $salary))
    print "Salary must be in whole dollars";
```

To check if a value is in the currency and unit format, you could use:

```
if (!ereg("^[0-9]{1,3}[.][0-9]{2}$", $price))
    print "Item price must be between US$0.00 and US$999.99, " .
        "and must include the cent amount.";
```

It's important for an internationalized web database application to inform the user what currencies are allowed.

Simple variations of the currency validation techniques can be used to check the format of floating point numbers. For example, if a maximum of five decimal places are allowed for a length value, use:

```
if (!ereg("^[0-9]*([.][0-9]{1,5})?$", strval($length)))
    print "Length can have a maximum of five decimal places";
```

The expression ^[0-9]* allows any number of digits at the beginning of the number and before the optional decimal place. The ? in the expression ([.][0-9]{1,5})?$ implements an optional mantissa by allowing either zero or one copies of a string that matches the bracketed expression that precedes the ?. The bracketed expression itself requires a decimal point (represented by [.]), and then between one and five digits (represented by [0-9]{1,5}). The end of the number is expected after the optional mantissa. To allow positive or negative values to be specified, you could add [+-]? immediately after the ^ at the beginning of the expression.

It doesn't always make sense to range check numeric data. For example, phone and fax numbers aren't usually added, subtracted, or tested against ranges. In our customer example, we might validate a phone number using a regular expression that checks it has a reasonable structure:

```
// Phone is optional, but if it is entered it must have
// correct format
$validPhoneExpr = "^([0-9]{2,3}[ ]*)?[0-9]{4}[ ]*[0-9]{4}$";

if (!empty($phone) && !ereg($validPhoneExpr, $phone))
    print "The phone number must be 8 digits in length, " .
        "with an optional 2 or 3 digit area code";
```

This is an AND (&&) expression, so the *ereg( )* function is only evaluated if the $phone variable is not empty.

The first expression ^([0-9]{2,3}[ ]*)? matches either zero or one occurrence of the bracketed expression at the beginning of the value. Inside the brackets, the expression that is matched is two or three digits and any number of optional space characters (represented as [ ]*). For example, a string 03 matches, as does 835. The second part of the expression [0-9]{4}[ ]*[0-9]{4}$ matches exactly four digits, followed by any number of optional spaces, followed by another four digits, and then the end of the string is expected. For example, the strings 1234 1234 and 12341234 both match the expression.

Validating credit cards

The last numeric type we consider in this section is credit card numbers. There are two steps to validating a credit card that's entered for payment of goods or services: first, we need to check the credit card number and its expiration date are valid; and, second, we need to verify that the payment will be honored by the bank or other credit card provider. If the user's entering their credit card as part of the account creation process, the second step isn't usually needed until they make a payment.

In this section, we show you how to validate a credit card number. Expiration dates can be validated using the date checking functions discussed later in this section.

Checking that payment will be honored by the credit card provider is outside the scope of this book. However, many credit card payment validation network libraries are available for this purpose: PEAR contains a few, several are available as PHP libraries as listed in Appendix G, and open source solutions have been developed and are readily available on the Web. All credit checking facilities require a paid subscription to a validation service.

Example 9-3 shows a function *checkcard( )* that validates credit card numbers. The function works as follows. First, it checks the card number contains only digits and spaces, and after the check it removes the spaces using *ereg_replace( )* leaving only the card number. Second, it extracts the first four digits and checks which of the different credit cards it matches and uses this to determine the correct length of the number; we discuss this further next. Third, it rejects cards that aren't supported or where the length doesn't match the correct length for the card. Last, the credit card is validated using the *Luhn* algorithm, which we return to in a moment.

Example 9-3. A function to validate credit card numbers

```php
function checkcard($cc, $ccType)
{
  if (!ereg("^[0-9 ]*$", $cc))
  {
    print "Card number must contain only digits and spaces.";
    return (false);
  }

  // Remove spaces
  $cc = ereg_replace('[ ]', '', $cc);

  // Check first four digits
  $firstFour = intval(substr($cc, 0, 4));
  $type = "";
  $length = 0;

  if ($firstFour >= 8000 && $firstFour <= 8999)
  {
    // Try: 8000 0000 0000 1001
    $type = "SurchargeCard";
    $length = 16;
  }
  elseif ($firstFour >= 9100 && $firstFour <= 9599)
  {
    // Try: 9100 0000 0001 7
    $type = "AustralianExpress";
    $length = 13;
  }

  if (empty($type) || strcmp($type, $ccType) != 0)
  {
```

Example 9-3. A function to validate credit card numbers (continued)

```
    print "Please check your card details.";
    return (false);
  }

  if (strlen($cc) != $length)
  {
    print "Card number must contain {$length} digits.";
    return (false);
  }

  $check = 0;

 // Add up every 2nd digit, beginning at the right end
  for($x=$length-1;$x>=0;$x-=2)
    $check += intval(substr($cc, $x, 1));

  // Add up every 2nd digit doubled, beginning at the right end - 1.
  // Subtract 9 where doubled value is greater than 10
  for($x=$length-2;$x>=0;$x-=2)
  {
    $double = intval(substr($cc, $x, 1)) * 2;
    if ($double >= 10)
      $check += $double - 9;
    else
      $check += $double;
  }

  // Is $check not a multiple of 10?
  if ($check % 10 != 0)
  {
    print "Credit card invalid. Please check number.";
    return (false);
  }
  return (true);
}
```

Table 9-1 shows the prefixes of the four most popular credit cards and the card number length for those cards. For example, *MasterCard* cards always begin with four digits in the range 5100 to 5599, and are sixteen digits in length. The function in Example 9-2 supports two fictional cards: *SurchargeCard* that begins with numbers in the range 8000 to 8999 and has 16 digits, and *AustralianExpress* with prefixes from 9100 to 9599 and 13 digits in length. Example valid card numbers for these fictional cards are included as comments in the code. You can find sample numbers for all popular cards at *http://www.verisign.com/support/payflow/link/pfltestprocess.html*.

Table 9-1. Popular credit card prefixes and lengths

Card name	Four-digit prefix	Length
American Express	3400-3499, 3700-3799	15
Diners Club	3000-3059, 3600-3699, 3800-3889	14

Table 9-1. Popular credit card prefixes and lengths (continued)

Card name	Four-digit prefix	Length
MasterCard	5100-5599	16
Visa	4000-4999	13 or 16

Credit card validation is performed with the Luhn algorithm. This works as follows:

1. Sum up every second digit in the credit card number, beginning with the last digit and proceeding right-to-left.

2. Sum up the double of every second digit in the credit card number, beginning with the second to the last digit and proceeding right-to-left. If the double of the digit is greater than 10, subtract 9 from the value before adding it to the sum.

3. Determine if the sum of the two steps is a multiple of 10. If it is, the credit card number is valid. If not, the number is rejected.

Consider an example credit card of ten digits in length: 1234000014. In the first step, we add every second digit from the right, beginning with the last. So, 4+0+0+4+2=10. Then, in the second step, we add the double of each digit beginning with the second last (subtracting 9 if any doubling is over 10) and then add the sum to the total from the first step. So, 2+0+0+6+2=10, and adding to 10 from the first step gives 20. Since 20 is exactly divisible by 10, the card has a valid number.

Validating Dates and Times

Dates of birth, expiry dates, order dates, and other dates are commonly entered by users. Most dates require specialized checks to see if the date is valid and if it's in a required date range. Times are less complicated, but specialized checks are still useful.

Dates

Dates can be given in several different formats and using many different calendars. We only discuss the Gregorian calendar here.

In the U.S., months are listed before days, but the majority of the rest of the world uses the opposite approach. Years can be provided as two or four digits, although we recommend avoiding two digit years for the obvious confusion caused when 99 comes before 00. This leads to four formats: DDMMYY, DDMMYYYY, MMDDYY, and MMDDYYYY, where Y is a year digit, M is month digit, and D is a day digit.

In all date formats, a forward slash, a hyphen, or (rarely) a colon can be used to separate the groups, leading to twelve formats in total. For sorting, a thirteenth (convenient) format is YYYYMMDD without the separators. Dates can also be specified using month names, leading to strings such as 11-Aug-1969 and 11 August 1969.

Date values have complex validation requirements, and are difficult to manipulate. Months have different numbers of days, some years are leap years, and some annual holidays fall on different days in different years. Adding and subtracting dates, working out the date of tomorrow or next week, and finding the first Sunday of the month aren't straightforward. A particularly non-straightforward task is finding when the Christian religion's Easter holiday falls in a year, as explained at the Astronomical Society of South Australia web site, *http://www.assa.org.au/edm.html*.

Consider an example from our customer case study. Let's suppose the user is required to provide a date of birth in the format common to most of the world, DD/ MM/YYYY. We then need to validate this date of birth to check that it has been entered and to check its format, its validity, and whether it's within a range. The range of valid dates in the example begins with the user being alive—for simplicity, we assume alive users are born after 1902—and ends with the user being at least 18 years of age.

Date-of-birth checking is implemented with the code in Example 9-4.

Example 9-4. Date-of-birth validation

```
function checkdob($birth_date)
{
  if (empty($birth_date))
  {
    print "The date of birth field cannot be blank.";
    return false;
  }
  // Check the format and explode into $parts
  elseif (!ereg("^([0-9]{2})/([0-9]{2})/([0-9]{4})$",
         $birth_date, $parts))
  {
    print "The date of birth is not a valid date in the
           format DD/MM/YYYY";
    return false;
  }
  elseif (!checkdate($parts[2],$parts[1],$parts[3]))
  {
    print "The date of birth is invalid. Please check that the month is
           between 1 and 12, and the day is valid for that month.";
    return false;
  }
  elseif (intval($parts[3]) < 1902 ||
         intval($parts[3]) > intval(date("Y")))
  {
    print "You must be alive to use this service.";
    return false;
  }
  else
  {
    $dob = mktime(0, 0, 0, $parts[2], $parts[1], $parts[3]);

    // Check whether the user is 18 years old.
    if ((float)$dob > (float)strtotime("-18years"))
    {
```

Example 9-4. Date-of-birth validation (continued)

```
        print "You must be 18+ years of age to use this service";
        return false;
    }
  }
  return true;
}
```

If any date test fails, an error is reported, and no further checks of the date are made. A valid date passes all the tests.

The first check tests if a date has been entered. The second check uses a regular expression to check whether the date consists of numbers and if it matches the template 99/99/9999 (where 9 means a number):

```
elseif (!ereg("^([0-9]{2})/([0-9]{2})/([0-9]{4})$", $birth_date, $parts))
{
  print "The date of birth is not a valid date in the format DD/MM/YYYY";
  return false;
}
```

You can adapt this check to match any of the other thirteen basic formats we outlined at the beginning of this section.

Whatever the result of this formatting check, the expression also explodes the date into the array $parts so that the component that matches the first bracketed expression ([0-9]{2}) is found in $parts[1], the second bracketed expression in $parts[2], and the third bracketed expression in $parts[3]. Using this approach, the day of the month is accessible as $parts[1], the month as $parts[2], and the year as $parts[3]. The *ereg( )* function also stores the string matching the complete expression in $parts[0].

The third check uses the exploded data stored in the array $parts and the function *checkdate( )* to test if the date is a valid calendar date. For example, the date 31/02/1970 would fail this test. The fourth check tests if the year is in the range 1902 to the current year. The function *date("Y")* returns the current year as a string.

The fifth and final check tests if the user is 18 years of age or older, and uses the approach described in Chapter 3. It finds the difference between the date of birth and the current date using library functions, and checks that this difference is more than 18 years. We use the *mktime( )* function to convert the date of birth to a large numeric Unix timestamp value, and the *strtotime( )* function to discover the timestamp of exactly 18 years ago. Both are cast to a large floating number to ensure reliable comparison, and if the user is born in the past 18 years, an error is produced.

The *mktime( )* function works for years between 1901 and 2038 on Unix systems, and only from 1970 to 2038 for variants of Microsoft Windows. The PEAR Date package doesn't suffer from year limitations, and we discuss how to use it later in this section.

Times

Times are easier to work with than dates, but they also come in several valid formats. These include the 24-hour clock format 9999, the 12-hour clock formats 99:99am or 99:99pm (or with a period instead of a colon), and formats that include seconds and hundredths of seconds. In each format, different ranges of values are allowed.

Consider an example where a user is required to enter a date in the 12-hour format using a colon as the separator. With this format, 12:42p.m. and 1:01a.m. are valid times. You can validate this format using the following regular expression:

```
if (!eregi("^(1[0-2]|0[1-9]):([0-5][0-9])(am|pm)$", $time))
    print "Time must be a valid 12-hour clock time in the format
            HH:MMam or HH:MMpm.";
```

The first part of the expression ^(1[0-2]|0[1-9]) requires that the time begins with a number in range 10 to 12, or 01 to 09. After the colon, the second part of the expression requires the minute value to be in the range 00 to 59 as specified by the expression ([0-5][0-9]). Either AM or PM (in either upper- or lowercase) must then follow to conclude the time string.

For 24-hour times, a simple variant works:

```
if (!eregi("^([0-1][0-9]|2[0-3])([0-5][0-9])$", $time))
    print "Time must be a valid 24-hour clock time in the format HHMM.";
```

Working out differences between times is reasonably straightforward, after the time has been parsed into its components! For example, to check if a 12-hour clock arrival time is before a 12-hour clock departure time, use the following fragment:

```
// Explode departure time into the array $depBits
if (!eregi("^(1[0-2]|[1-9]):([0-5][0-9])(am|pm)$", $depTime, $depBits))
    print "Departure time must be a valid 12-hour clock time
            in the format HH:MMam or HH:MMpm.";

// Explode arrival time into the array $arrBits
if (!eregi("^(1[0-2]|[1-9]):([0-5][0-9])(am|pm)$", $arrTime, $arrBits))
    print "Arrival time must be a valid 12-hour clock time
            in the format HH:MMam or HH:MMpm.";

if (($depBits[3] == "pm" && $arrBits[3] == "am")) ||
    ($depBits[1] > $arrBits[1] && $depBits[3] == $arrBits[3]) ||
    ($depBits[2] >= $arrBits[2] && $depBits[1] == $arrBits[1]
      && $depBits[3] == $arrBits[3]))
    print "Arrival time must be after departure time.";
```

The two *ereg( )* expressions validate the format of a time using the approach we described previously. Similarly to our date validation, both expressions also explode the times into the arrays $arrBits and $depBits. The arrays contain the hour as elements $arrBits[1] and $depBits[1], the minutes as $arrBits[2] and $depBits[2], and the AM or PM suffix as $arrBits[3] and $depBits[3].

To determine if the arrival time is earlier than the departure time, there are three tests: first, if the arrival time is AM, the departure time can't be PM; second, if both times are AM or both times are PM the arrival hour can't be earlier than the departure hour; and, last, if both times are AM or both times are PM, and the departure hour is the arrival hour the arrival minutes can't be less than or equal to the departure minutes. With 24-hour times, only one test is needed; this is perhaps a good reason to use them in preference to 12-hour times in your applications.

For this type of validation, you could also convert a time to an integer value and then compare values. For example, you could convert two times to Unix timestamps and then compare these to determine if the arrival time is earlier than the departure time. However, as discussed in the previous section, the PHP date and time functions don't behave the same on all platforms, and so this approach isn't always portable between operating systems. For this reason, using logic as in our previous example or using a reliable package, such as the PEAR Date package discussed in the next section, is preferable.

Using the PEAR Date package

The PEAR Date package introduced in Chapter 7 is not limited in year ranges and provides a wide range of date validation and manipulation tools. It must be installed using the PEAR installer (as discussed in Chapter 7) and then the date calculation package must be included into the source code using:

```
require_once "Date/Calc.php";
```

An object can then be created using:

```
$date = new Date_Calc();
```

Using the PEAR Date package, we can rewrite our date of birth checking in Example 9-4. Our third date of birth check can be rewritten to use the method *isValidDate( )* as follows:

```
elseif (!$date->isValidDate($parts[1], $parts[2], $parts[3]))
{
  print "The date of birth is invalid. Please check that the month
         is between 1 and 12, and the day is valid for that month.";
  return false;
}
```

The fourth check can be modified slightly to use the *isFutureDate( )* method to check if the user has been born:

```
elseif (intval($parts[3]) < 1902 ||
        $date->isFutureDate($parts[1], $parts[2], $parts[3]))
{
  print "You must be alive to use this service.";
  return false;
}
```

The fifth check can make use of the *compareDates( )* method to avoid the use of *strtotime( )* and *mktime( )* and solve the year limitation problem. The method compares two dates each specified as a day, month, and year. In our check, we test the difference between the date of birth and eighteen years earlier than today:

```
else
{
  // Check whether the user is 18 years old.
  if ($date->compareDates($parts[1], $parts[2], $parts[3],
      intval(date("d")), intval(date("m")), intval(date("Y"))-18) > 0)
  {
    print "You must be 18+ years of age to use this service.";
    return false;
  }
}
```

The *compareDates( )* method returns 0 if the two dates are equal, -1 if the first date is less than the second, and 1 if the first date is greater than the second.

We've used three of the methods from the PEAR Date package. The package also has useful methods for determining if a year is a leap year, discovering the date of the beginning or end of the previous or next month, finding the date of the beginning or end of the previous or next week, finding the previous or next day or weekday, returning the number of days or weeks in a month, finding out the day of the week, converting dates to days, and returning formatted date strings.

Like many other PEAR packages, this one contains almost no documentation or examples. However, the methods are readable code and easy to use, and most are simple and reliable applications of the date functions that are discussed in Chapter 3. If you followed our PHP installation instructions in Appendixes A through C and our PEAR installation instructions in Chapter 7, you'll find *Date.php* in */usr/local/lib/php/*. The Date package also includes code in the file *TimeZone.php* for working with and finding the date and time in different time zones. If you're working with dates, PEAR Date is worth investigation and avoids most of the limitations of the PHP library functions.

Logic, the date function, and MySQL

There are other approaches to working with dates that don't use PEAR Date or Unix timestamps. Logic and the *date( )* function can be combined to check and compare days, months, and years, similarly to our approach to testing times. For example, to check if a user is over 18, you can use this fragment after exploding the date into the array $parts:

```
// Were they born more than 19 years ago?
if (!((intval($parts[3]) < (intval(date("Y")) - 19))) ||

// No, so were they born exactly 18 years ago, and
// has the month they were born in passed?
(intval($parts[3]) == (intval(date("Y")) - 18) &&
(intval($parts[2]) < intval(date("m")))) ||
```

```
// No, so were they born exactly 18 years ago in this
// month, and was the day today or earlier in the month?
(intval($parts[3]) == (intval(date("Y")) - 18) &&
(intval($parts[2]) ==  intval(date("m"))) &&
(intval($parts[1]) <= intval(date("d"))))))
   print "You must be 18+ years of age to use this service.";
```

You can also use the MySQL functions described in Chapter 15 through an SQL query as a simple calculator. However, the MySQL approach, which involves communication with the database, adds a lot more overhead and therefore is often less desirable than using PHP. However, if one or more dates are extracted from a database, MySQL date and time functions are a useful alternative for pre-processing prior to working with dates in PHP.

JavaScript and Client-Side Validation

In this section, we introduce the JavaScript scripting language as a client-side method for validation and other simple tasks. JavaScript isn't a full-fledged programming language like PHP: it can't connect to databases, it offers only limited interaction with certain system resources, and it can't do most tasks a web database application requires. However, JavaScript is good for interacting with a form and for controlling the display of data to the user.

Client-side validation with JavaScript is optional but has benefits, including faster response to the user than server-side validation, a reduction in web server load, and a reduction in network traffic. Also, unlike server-side validation, it can be implemented as interactive validation where errors are checked as they occur and field-by-field reporting where error messages are shown individually. However, validation in the client tier is unreliable: the user can bypass the validation through design, error, or misconfiguration of their web browser. For that reason, client-side validation should be used only to improve speed, reduce load, and add features, and never to replace server-side validation.

The client-side scripting language we use here is best known as JavaScript. However, in June 1998, the European Computer Manufacturers Association (ECMA) agreed to be responsible for the standard implementations of the scripting language by Microsoft, Netscape, and Sun. Accordingly, the real name of the language is now ECMA-Script, based on the standard ECMA-262. The most recent version of ECMA-262 is the third edition, dated December 1999. Netscape still use the name JavaScript, and JavaScript 1.5 is fully compatible with ECMA-262 Version 3.

The standard is available from *http://www.ecma-international.org/publications/standards/ECMA-262.htm*

Besides validation, there are many other common uses of JavaScript in web database applications including:

- Simple interaction with form data. For example, JavaScript is often used to calculate values and display these in an input widget.
- Enhancing user interactions by adding dynamic elements to a web page. Common features include pull-down menus, mouseover changes to the presentation (*rollovers*), and dialog boxes.
- Customizing the browser and using information from the browser to enhance presentation.

Most of these techniques are oriented around events. An *event* is an action that can be trapped through JavaScript code, such as a mouse passing over an object, a window opening, or a user clicking on a button.

The next section introduces JavaScript through a simple example. After that, we show you the basics of JavaScript by contrasting and comparing it with PHP, and then we show you several more examples including a case study. However, this section isn't comprehensive and isn't aimed as a replacement for many of the excellent resources that are available; selected resources are listed in Appendix G.

Introducing JavaScript

Consider the short JavaScript validation example in Example 9-5.

Example 9-5. A simple JavaScript example to check if a form field is empty

```
<!DOCTYPE HTML PUBLIC
                "-//W3C//DTD HTML 4.01 Transitional//EN"
                "http://www.w3.org/TR/html401/loose.dtd">
<html>
<head>
  <meta http-equiv="Content-Type" content="text/html; charset=iso-8859-1">
  <title>Simple JavaScript Example</title>
<script type="text/javascript">
<!-- Hide the script from old browsers
function containsblanks(s)
{
  for(var i = 0; i < s.value.length; i++)
  {
    var c = s.value.charAt(i);
    if ((c == ' ') || (c == '\n') || (c == '\t'))
    {
      alert('The field must not contain whitespace');
      return false;
    }
  }
  return true;
}
// end hiding -->
```

Example 9-5. A simple JavaScript example to check if a form field is empty (continued)

```
</script>
</head>
<body>
<h1>Username Form</h1>
<form onSubmit="return(containsblanks(document.userform.username));"
                method="POST" name="userform" action="test.php">
<input type="text" name="username" size=10>
<input type="submit">
</form>
</body>
</html>
```

This example is designed to check if an optional username field contains whitespace and, if so, to show a dialog box containing an error message to the user. The dialog box is shown in Figure 9-1. The example contains a mixture of HTML and JavaScript, and almost all the JavaScript is encapsulated between the <script> and </script> tags in the <head> tag of the document.

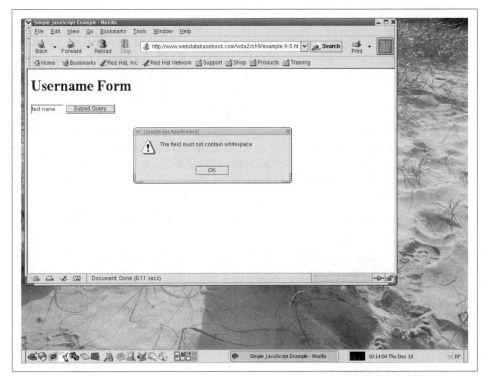

Figure 9-1. The dialog box produced when whitespace is entered in the username field

The JavaScript function *containsBlanks( )* is called when the user submits the form. The function call is part of the form element:

```
<form onSubmit="return(containsblanks(document.userform.username));"
  method="post" name="userform" action="test.php">
```

When the submission event occurs (when the user presses the Submit button or presses the Enter key while the cursor is in the text widget) the onSubmit event is triggered. In this case, the result is that the function *containsblanks( )* is called with one parameter, document.userform.username. The object document refers to the document loaded in the browser window, the userform is the name of the form itself, and username is the name of the input widget within the form. The function call itself is wrapped in a *return( )* expression. The overall result of executing *containsblanks( )* is that if the function returns false, the form isn't submitted to the server; if the function returns true, the HTTP request proceeds as usual.

The function *containsblanks( )* works as follows:

- A for loop iterates through the characters entered by the user. The expression s.value.length refers to the length of the string value entered by the user into the username widget. The length property is one of the predefined properties of the value attribute of the <input> widget.

- Each character in the string entered by the user is assigned to a character variable c using the expression s.value.charAt(i) to return the characters in the value entered by the user. The value attribute of the widget has an associated method *charAt( )* that returns the value of the character at the position passed as a parameter. For example, if the user enters **test** in the widget, s.value. charAt(0) returns t, and s.value.charAt(1) returns e.

- The if statement checks whether the current character is a space, a tab character, or a carriage return. If so, the *alert( )* method is called with an error string as a parameter. The *alert( )* method presents a dialog box in the browser that shows the error message and has an OK button, as shown in Figure 9-1. When the user clicks OK, the function returns false, and the submission process stops.

  If the string doesn't contain any whitespace, the function *containsblanks( )* returns true, and the form submits as usual.

HTML comment tags are included inside the <script> tags and surround the JavaScript script. This is good practice, because if JavaScript is disabled or the user has an old browser that knows nothing about scripts, the comments hide the script from a potentially confused browser. An old browser happily displays the HTML page as usual. In addition, an old browser or one that has JavaScript turned off will ignore the onSubmit event handler in the form element.

JavaScript and PHP

The syntax of JavaScript is similar to PHP and to other languages such as C and Java. Table 9-2 compares some of the basic features of PHP and JavaScript that we used in Example 9-5 and others that are used later in this chapter. The key differences are that JavaScript variables aren't prefixed with a dollar sign, local variables must be declared in JavaScript, different open and close script tags are used, and string concatenation in JavaScript uses a plus sign and PHP uses a period. Other than that, the languages are very similar when used for basic tasks.

Table 9-2. The language basics in PHP and JavaScript

Language component	PHP	JavaScript
Open and close script tags	`<?php ?>`	`<script type="text/javascript"> </script>` or `<% %>`
Block statement	`{ }`	`{ }`
Multi-line comment	`/* hello */`	`/* hello */`
Single-line comment	`// hello`	`// hello`
Constant declaration	`define("z", 1);`	`const a = 1;`
Variable declaration	Not required	Required for local variables, var a = 0;
Variable assignment	`$a = 0;`	`a = 0;`
Assignment shortcut style	`$a += 5;`	`a += 5;`
Variable typing	At runtime	At runtime
Statement terminator	`;`	; or the end-of-line
Equality value testing	Double-equals, ==	Double-equals, ==
Equality type and value testing	Triple-equals, ===	Triple equals, ===
Inequality testing	`!=`	`!=`
Strings	`"string" 'string'`	`"string" 'string'`
String constants	`\n and \t`	`\n and \t`
String concatenation	`$a = $b . $c;`	`$a = $b + $c;`
Boolean values	`true false`	`true false`
Logical AND	`&&`	`&&`
Logical OR	`||`	`||`
Logical NOT	`!`	`!`

Generating output

In PHP, output to the browser is generated using the `print` or `printf` statements, or by using a template and template methods as discussed in Chapter 7. In JavaScript, there are several different ways output can be produced including writing output to the browser window as a document is created, creating dialog boxes, updating values in form widgets, and creating new windows.

To write output to a window, the *writeln()* method can be used:

```
<script type="text/javascript">
  document.writeln("Hello, world.");
</script>
```

The document object refers to the document that is displayed in the browser window, and *writeln()* is a method associated with that document. You can write to a document only as it's created, you can't use this method to write text to the document after it's been rendered in the browser. The basic objects and methods are discussed later in this section.

In Example 9-5, a dialog box with an OK button is created with the *alert()* method. For example, you can pop up a dialog box when the user clicks on a button:

```
<form action="test.php">
<input type="button" value="Pop a box" onclick="alert('Pop!');">
</form>
```

The onclick attribute causes the box to appear when the user clicks on the button.

It's also possible to create dialog boxes using the *confirm( )* method that displays both an OK and Cancel button:

```
<script type="text/javascript">
if (confirm("Are you sure?"))
  alert("Great!");
else
  alert("What a pity!");
</script>
```

The *confirm( )* method returns true when the user clicks Ok and false otherwise.

Another approach to producing output is to write to the browser window status line. However, this isn't a very effective mechanism: the status bar may be hidden or disabled, and it's easy to overlook messages displayed at the base of the window. Yet another approach is to create a new fully-featured non-dialog browser window, which we discuss later in this chapter. The final approach is to update values in input widgets, an approach we use later in our examples.

Loops and conditionals

Loops and conditionals are almost the same in both languages. As discussed in Chapter 2, PHP has the for, while, foreach, and do...while loops, and the if and switch conditionals. JavaScript has the for, while, do...while, and for...in loops, and the if and switch statements. The continue and break statements are available in both languages.

The for, while, and do...while loops are the same in PHP and JavaScript, with the exception that in JavaScript it's possible to declare a variable in a for loop with the var statement; an example is shown in Example 9-5. JavaScript also has the for...in statement which allows you to iterate through properties of objects, while PHP has the foreach statement for iterating through elements in arrays. An example with the for...in statement is presented later in this section.

Functions

Functions are similar in PHP and JavaScript. Consider the following JavaScript example:

```
function bold(string)
{
    document.writeln("<b>" + string + "</b>\n");
}
```

When called with the function call *bold("this is bold")*, the function prints the string `<b>this is bold</b>` as part of the document. Similarly to PHP, functions are declared with the statement function, parameters are listed in brackets and separated by commas, and the function body is surrounded by curly braces. Functions can optionally return values using the return statement, which behaves identically in PHP and JavaScript.

Variables that are declared within a function are local to that function. Local variables must be declared using the var statement as in the following example:

```
function count()
{
    var x=1;
    while (x<6)
    {
        document.writeln(x + " ");
        x++;
    }
}
```

Variables that are used or declared outside functions are global variables. Declaring globals with var is optional: as in PHP, they can be declared implicitly by assigning values to them. However, unlike PHP, global variables in JavaScript are accessible everywhere in the current document; global variables are not declared in functions using the global keyword.

Debugging JavaScript

JavaScript has two types of errors that report messages: *load-time* and *run-time* errors. Load-time errors are sometimes reported by the user agent before it runs the JavaScript, and you'll be shown a warning box that details the error, its line number, and the code fragment itself. Run-time errors occur when a code fragment is running and, again, a warning box is sometimes displayed with the line number of the code that caused the error.

The inconsistent nature of error reporting can be annoying: often, you'll get no messages at all but the script won't run. However, in many browsers (including Mozilla and Netscape), you can get more detailed error information by typing **javascript:** in the Location box and pressing Enter. The JavaScript console that pops up lists all errors that have occurred since the browser began running. You can remove old messages by clicking on the Clear button that's shown at the top of the console window;

periodically doing this is a good way to avoid confusion about which errors are applicable to what.

Errors can also be annoying because they are often platform- or browser-dependent and change from one release to the next. Complex JavaScript adds a thicker client to a web database application, and this may reveal differences between browser applications, browser versions, and different platforms.

If complex JavaScript is required or desired, make sure it's tested on all the popular platforms with the popular browser products and versions. However, we recommend that JavaScript be kept simple: complex tasks should be left to PHP scripts, and you should ensure that user interfaces function correctly even if JavaScript is faulty or disabled.

Objects

Objects associated with the browser, windows, and the document are accessible in JavaScript. For example, in Example 9-5, the form object and its child (an input text widget) are accessed and used. Historically, the definition of these objects (and the events, properties, and methods described in the next sections) was part of the JavaScript standard and they were loosely known as the *Navigator objects*. This has now changed, and the objects are defined as part of the Document Object Model (DOM).

In this section, we informally describe the objects and properties that are accessible from within JavaScript, and avoid the details of DOM. However, the complete specification is accessible at *http://www.w3.org/TR/2003/REC-DOM-Level-2-HTML-20030109/*.

The window object is the top of the DOM hierarchy, and it contains the toolbars and menus of the browser, as well as the document and its sub-components. The hierarchy of the objects that descend from window is shown in Figure 9-2.

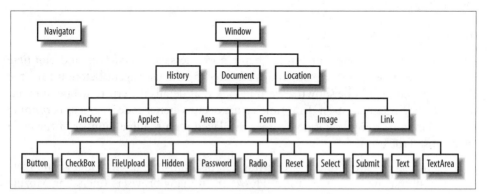

Figure 9-2. The hierarchy of window objects in the DOM

In JavaScript code, the document object can be referenced using the same notation as in PHP's object-oriented model using window.document, or just document for short (because there is only one window when you're not using frames, which we don't in this book).

Each of the objects in the hierarchy has *properties* and *methods*, and creates *events*. Properties are characteristics that describe the appearance of the object, while the methods are its behaviors. Events are actions that the object can act on such as mouse clicks or key presses. Events are discussed in the next section, and methods and properties in the following section. However, selected events, methods, and properties are used in examples here.

Consider a document that contains a form that has a text input widget and a submit button:

```
<form name="custform" method="GET" action="cust.php">
Surname: <input type="text" name="surname">
<br><input type="submit" name="submit">
</form>
```

The text widget is accessible using the names associated with the objects in the hierarchy. In this example, the form widget has the attribute name="custform", and the input widget has the attribute name="surname". You can therefore reference the text widget's value as document.custform.surname.value. The value is a property of the text input widget and it contains the data the user has entered, or it can be assigned a value to modify the data that's shown in the widget.

The value could be output when an onchange event is triggered in the widget itself:

```
<input type="text" name="surname"
   onchange="alert('You entered ' + document.custform.surname.value);">
```

The browser automatically generates an onchange event when the text in the widget changes; we explain events more later.

Alternatively, you could output the value when the submission process itself occurs:

```
<form name="custform" method="GET" action="cust.php"
   onsubmit="alert('You entered ' + document.custform.surname.value);">
```

Another way to access the properties of an object is to access the DOM element array. For example, the value of the text input widget in the custform can be referenced as:

```
document.forms[0].elements[0].value
```

The notation forms[0] means the first form in the document, and elements[0] means the first element of that form. You can iterate through all properties in an object using the for...in statement that we introduced previously. For example, to show the names of all elements in the form, use:

```
for (o in document.custform)
   string += o + ' ';
alert("Here are the elements: " + string);
```

The loop assigns each element in document.custform in turn to the variable o, and then o is appended to string. If you include this fragment in a document containing the custform, you may be surprised that it outputs not just the surname widget and the submit button, but more than 50 properties. Some of these are discussed in the next section.

Some browsers are fussier than others. For example, Microsoft's Internet Explorer complains when you reference an object before it's defined. This means that you can't reference a form earlier in your HTML source than where the form is actually declared. You'll find that these kinds of issues make developing complex or portable code difficult. As we've already discussed, we recommend you use JavaScript for simple tasks and leave the complex ones to PHP on the server side.

In JavaScript, there are also several other pre-defined objects. These include core objects such as Array, RegExp, Date, and Math that are discussed in detail in the *Core JavaScript Guide* available from *http://devedge.netscape.com/library/manuals/*.

Events

Events are triggered by both the user agent (usually a web browser), and the user working with the document and browser. These events are useful triggers for JavaScript actions. For example, a function might be called as a page loads, when the user presses the submit button, when a form field changes, or when the mouse passes over a document element. Examples using many of these events are included in later examples in this chapter.

The key events that can be trapped and handled by JavaScript are as follows:

onblur
> When a user removes focus from form elements or a window. This occurs when the user presses the Tab key to move to the next widget, clicks on another widget or window, or carries out some other action that takes the focus away from the current window or widget.

onchange
> When a select, text, or textarea input loses focus and has been modified since it gained focus.

onclick
> When a pointing device (usually a left mouse button) clicks on an area, button, checkbox, hypertext link, radio button, reset, or submit.

onfocus
> When a user brings focus to form elements or a window, normally by clicking in it.

onload
> When a user agent finishes loading a window (or all frames in a frameset).

onmouseout
> When the pointing device moves out from an element, area, or hypertext link.

onmouseover

When the pointing device moves over an element, area, or hypertext link.

onreset

When a form is reset.

onsubmit

When a form is submitted.

onunload

When the user exits a page, that is, when the user agent unloads the document from the window. For example, this happens when a new page is loaded, a browser window or tab is closed, or the browser program ends.

We have omitted other events related to key presses and text selection, as well as other types of mouse clicks and movements. These are detailed in the HTML 4.01 documentation at *http://www.w3.org/TR/html4/interact/scripts.html.* and in the DOM documentation listed in the previous section.

Methods and properties

The window, document, form, and input element objects have properties and methods that are commonly accessed and used in validation tasks. This section lists selected methods and properties, and examples later in this chapter show many of these used in scripts. Images, tables, the document body, document styles, and frames also have their own methods and properties, but we don't discuss these here. The complete list of objects, methods, and properties can be found at *http://www.w3.org/TR/2003/REC-DOM-Level-2-HTML-20030109/ecma-script-binding.html.*

The navigator object is outside of the window hierarchy we showed in Figure 9-2 and the standards. However, it is useful because it describes the browser environment. Its properties include:

platform

The operating system.

userAgent

The same information as sent in the HTTP request that includes the user agent name and version.

The window object properties and methods include:

location.href

The URL in the location box.

name

The window's name. Can be used to retrieve or set the window name. For example, window.name = "Hello!" sets the title to Hello!.

locationbar.visible

Determines whether the location bar is visible. It can be set to true or false, making the location bar visible or hidden respectively.

`menubar.visible`

Determines whether the menu bar is visible. It can be set to `true` or `false`, making the menu bar visible or hidden respectively.

`personalbar.visible`

Determines whether the personal or directories bar is visible. It can be set to `true` or `false`, making the personal bar visible or hidden respectively.

`scrollbars.visible`

Determines whether the horizontal and vertical scroll bars are visible. It can be set to `true` or `false`, making the scroll bars visible or hidden respectively.

`statusbar.visible`

Determines whether the status bar is visible. It can be set to `true` or `false`, making the status bar visible or hidden respectively.

`toolbar.visible`

Determines whether the toolbar is visible. It can be set to `true` or `false`, making the toolbar visible or hidden respectively. It can be set or unset only before the window is opened.

`status`

The text displayed in the status bar at the base of window. This can be set to display a message to the user.

alert( )

Shows a dialog box with an OK button, and takes text as a parameter.

back( )

Causes the user agent to return to the previous resource in its history list. This has the same effect as pressing the Back button in the web browser.

close( )

Closes the current window.

confirm( )

Shows a dialog box with OK and Cancel buttons, and takes text as a parameter. Returns `true` when the user presses OK and `false` otherwise.

forward( )

Causes the user agent to go forward to the next resource in its history list. This has the same effect as pressing the Forward button in the web browser.

open( )

Opens a new window, taking a URL, name, and features as parameters.

print( )

Sends the contents of the window to a printer.

prompt( )

Shows a dialog box with an input widget and OK and Cancel buttons. Takes a text question to display, and optional default text to display in the input widget. Returns `true` when the user presses OK and `false` otherwise.

The document object properties and methods include:

lastModified
> The date the resource was last modified.

title
> The text contained in the `<title>` tag of the document.

URL
> The URL of the current document.

write( ) and writeln( )
> Writes text to the current document during its creation. The latter adds a carriage return character to the string.

The form objects in a document include the following properties and methods:

name
> The value of the name attribute.

action
> The value of the action attribute.

method
> The value of the method attribute (GET or POST).

submit( )
> Sends the form to the server.

reset( )
> Clears all user-entered input from the form. If the form was shown with pre-filled values, it is reset to those values. If the form was initially empty, it is reset to empty.

The form elements select, textarea, input, and button have common methods and properties that include:

type
> The type of input as defined by the type attribute in the form element.

value
> The value contained or selected in the form element.

value.length
> The length of the value contained or selected in the form element.

name
> The value of the name attribute in the form element.

focus( )
> Brings the focus to the form element (not used with button elements).

blur( )
> Removes the focus from the form element (not used with button elements).

select( )

> Selects (usually by highlighting) the text in an input or textarea element (not used with select or button elements).

value.charAt( )

> Returns the character in the value at the position of the integer parameter. For example, value.charAt(0) returns the first character in the value.

JavaScript Examples

The short examples in this section implement simple, common, and useful JavaScript web database application features that use the techniques we have discussed so far. These include:

- Checking if two passwords are the same
- Mouse rollovers, where an image is changed to highlight an option as the mouse cursor passes over it
- Calculating and updating form fields based on user changes to data
- Interacting with the web browser and windows to trigger events and manipulate presentation
- Detecting the browser application and version
- Drop-down menus that load a new URL into the current window

A password form validation function

Example 9-6 is an example of JavaScript validation that checks whether a password is the same when the user enters it twice. The validation is interactive: an onchange event is trapped for the two password widgets, formPassword1 and formPassword2, and the function *thesame( )* is called whenever the user changes the data in a widget and then leaves it. The error reporting is field-by-field.

Example 9-6. Using JavaScript for interactive validation of password fields

```
<!DOCTYPE HTML PUBLIC
            "-//W3C//DTD HTML 4.0 Transitional//EN"
            "http://www.w3.org/TR/html4/loose.dtd">
<html>
<head>
  <meta http-equiv="Content-Type" content="text/html; charset=iso-8859-1">
  <title>Password Validation</title>
<script type="text/javascript">
<!-- Hide the script
function thesame(value1, value2)
{
  if (((value1 != null) || (value1 != ""))
      && value2 != "" && value1 != value2)
  {
      alert("The passwords must be identical.");
      return (false);
```

```
  }
  return (true);
}
// end hiding -->
</script>
</head>

<body>
<h1>Username Form</h1>
<form method="post" action="test.php" name="userForm">
<br>Username: <input type="text" name="userName" size=10>
<br>Password:
  <input type="password" name="formPassword1" size=10
  onchange="thesame(document.userForm.formPassword1.value,
                    document.userForm.formPassword2.value);">
<br>Re-enter password:
  <input type="password" name="formPassword2" size=10
  onchange="thesame(document.userForm.formPassword2.value,
                    document.userForm.formPassword1.value);">
<br><input type="submit" value="SUBMIT">
</form>
</body>
</html>
```

The function *thesame( )* checks if the current widget contains data. If it does, and the other password widget also contains data, the data in the two widgets is compared. If the data in the widgets is different, an error message is shown to the user. It's necessary to test whether both widgets actually contain data in interactive validation; without this check, the function annoyingly displays an error before the user has the opportunity to enter data into both widgets.

Rollover presentation with mouseover events

Example 9-7 shows a basic implementation of the common rollover feature used in many web applications.

Example 9-7. mouseover example with JavaScript

```
<!DOCTYPE HTML PUBLIC
            "-//W3C//DTD HTML 4.01 Transitional//EN"
            "http://www.w3.org/TR/html401/loose.dtd">
<html>
<head>
  <meta http-equiv="Content-Type" content="text/html; charset=iso-8859-1">
  <title>MouseOver Example</title>
</head>

<body bgcolor="#ffffff">
<a href="add_to_cart.php" onmouseout="cart.src='cart_off.jpg'"
                          onmouseover="cart.src='cart_on.jpg'">
```

Example 9-7. mouseover example with JavaScript (continued)

```
<img src="cart_off.jpg" border=0 name="cart" alt="cart picture"></a>
</body>
</html>
```

When the page is first loaded, an un-highlighted image of a shopping cart is shown; the image is used in the front page of the winestore in Chapter 16. The image is loaded with the HTML fragment:

```
<img src="cart_off.jpg" border=0 name="cart">
```

The only difference to the usual approach of loading images is that the `<img>` tag has the attribute `name="cart"`.

If the mouse passes over the cart image, an `onmouseover` event is triggered, and the JavaScript action carried out is:

```
onmouseover="cart.src='cart_on.jpg'"
```

The event handler changes the value of the `src` attribute of the `<img>` tag with the `name="cart"`. The result is that a new highlighted image is loaded to replace the un-highlighted image. In the case of our winestore, a shopping cart with a blue foreground is shown.

When the mouse leaves the image region, the `onmouseout` event is generated and handled with the following JavaScript fragment:

```
onmouseout="cart.src='cart_off.jpg'"
```

This restores the original image. The impression to the user is that the cart element is highlighted as the user focuses on the element.

Rollovers are straightforward to develop and the approach we've shown you works in all graphical browsers. You can even use the same technique to highlight menu options, and to produce pop-up and pull-down menus.

Prefilling form data with JavaScript calculations

Another common use of JavaScript is to pre-fill a form with data from a calculation. Example 9-8 shows how data can be managed and updated in a shopping cart.

When the user changes the quantity of a wine he intends to purchase, an onchange event is generated. This change event is handled by the *update( )* function, which modifies the value attribute of the `total` widget, showing the new total cost to the user. The new value shown to the user is calculated by multiplying together the `quantity.value` and the `unit.value`. Of course, as in all web database applications, the values and mathematics should be rechecked at the server when the form is submitted to the server.

Example 9-8. Using JavaScript to dynamically update values of form widgets

```
<!DOCTYPE HTML PUBLIC
            "-//W3C//DTD HTML 4.01 Transitional//EN"
            "http://www.w3.org/TR/html401/loose.dtd">
<html>
<head>
  <meta http-equiv="Content-Type" content="text/html; charset=iso-8859-1">
  <title>Dynamic Form Update Example</title>
</head>

<body>
<h1>Your Shopping Cart</h1>
<form method="get" action="test.php">
<table border="0" width="100%" cellpadding="0" cellspacing="5">
<tr>
  <td>Quantity </td>
  <td>Wine</td>
  <td>Unit Price</td>
  <td>Total</td>
</tr>

<tr>
  <td><input type="text" name="quantity" value="1" size=3
      onchange="total.value = unit.value * quantity.value;">
  <td>1997 Anderson and Sons Wines Belcombe Grenache</td>
  <td>$<input type="text" value="17.29" name="unit" readonly></td>
  <td>$<input type="text" value="17.29" name="total"
        align="right" readonly></td>
</tr>
</table>
<input type="submit" value="Purchase Wines">
</form>
</body>
</html>
```

Interacting with the web browser

Example 9-9 shows four examples of handlers for buttons that use the methods defined for the window object. The method *window.close( )* closes the focused window, *window.print( )* shows the print dialog window, *window.back( )* goes back one page, and *window.open( )* opens a new browser window.

Example 9-9. Closing and opening windows with JavaScript, printing the current page, and adding a Back button to a form

```
<!DOCTYPE HTML PUBLIC
            "-//W3C//DTD HTML 4.01 Transitional//EN"
            "http://www.w3.org/TR/html401/loose.dtd">
<html>
<head>
  <meta http-equiv="Content-Type" content="text/html; charset=iso-8859-1">
  <title>Playing with the Browser and Windows</title>
</head>
```

Example 9-9. Closing and opening windows with JavaScript, printing the current page, and adding a Back button to a form (continued)

```
<body>
<h1>Playing with the Browser and Windows</h1>
<form action="example.9-6.php">
<input type="button" value="Close Window" onClick="window.close();">
<br><input type="button" value="Print Window" onClick="window.print( );">
<br><input type="button" value="Go Back" onclick="window.back();">
<br><input type="button" value="Visit the book site"
  onClick="window.open('http://www.webdatabasebook.com/','BookSite',
  'toolbar=yes,location=yes,menubar=yes,directories=yes,scrollbars=yes,
  resizable=yes');">
</form>
</body>
</html>
```

Only *window.open( )* is complex. The first parameter is the URL to request in the new window, the second is a title, and the third is a set of properties of the new window. Without the list of properties that are included, the default new window has no Location box, no toolbars, no scrollbars, and can't be resized.

Which browser is the user using?

As discussed previously, even simple JavaScript sometimes highlights annoying differences in the way browsers support standard features. Indeed, even different versions of the same browsers support different JavaScript features from the same version of the standard.

Example 9-10 shows how the browser application name and version can be detected with both JavaScript and PHP. If a JavaScript script requires customization for a particular product, if statements can carry out actions in different ways. Another common approach in JavaScript-intensive web database applications is to write two sites: one that uses Internet Explorer JavaScript (known as Jscript), and another that uses Netscape Navigator or Mozilla JavaScript. However, as we recommended earlier, complex JavaScript is often best avoided in favor of server-side scripts.

Example 9-10. Which browser is the user using?

```
<!DOCTYPE HTML PUBLIC
            "-//W3C//DTD HTML 4.01 Transitional//EN"
            "http://www.w3.org/TR/html401/loose.dtd">
<html>
<head>
  <title>Playing with the Browser and Windows</title>
  <meta http-equiv="Content-Type" content="text/html; charset=iso-8859-1">
</head>
<body>
<script type="text/javascript">
<!-- Hide the script from old browsers
  alert("You are using " + navigator.userAgent);
```

Example 9-10. Which browser is the user using? (continued)

```
// end the hiding -->
</script>

This page should pop up a box if you have a JavaScript-capable and enabled
browser.
<br>But, using PHP, we can tell you that you're using the
<?php print $_SERVER["HTTP_USER_AGENT"]; ?> browser.
</body>
</html>
```

Drop-down menus

A common use of JavaScript is to automatically load a new page when a user selects
a menu option from a drop-down list. Example 9-11 shows how to do this using a
select widget and its properties. The JavaScript in the body of the document is
straightforward: when the user changes their selection of menu item, an onchange
event is triggered, and the *loadNewPage( )* function is called.

Example 9-11. Drop-down menus that load a new URL

```
<!DOCTYPE HTML PUBLIC
               "-//W3C//DTD HTML 4.01 Transitional//EN"
               "http://www.w3.org/TR/html401/loose.dtd">
<html>
<head>
  <meta http-equiv="Content-Type" content="text/html; charset=iso-8859-1">
  <title>Menu Example</title>
<script type="text/javascript">
<!--
function loadNewPage( )
{
  var listItem = document.menuForm.newPage.selectedIndex;
  var newPage = document.menuForm.newPage.options[listItem].value;
  location.href = newPage;
}
//-->
</script>
<body>
Where do you want to go now?
<br><form method="GET" action="menus.html" name="menuForm">
<select name="newPage" onchange="loadNewPage( );">
<option value="menus.html">This page
<option value="http://www.webdatabasebook.com/">The book web site
<option value="http://www.oreilly.com/">O'Reilly and Associates
<option value="http://www.hughwilliams.com/">Hugh's homepage
<option value="http://www.mds.rmit.edu.au/~dave/">Dave's homepage
</select>
</form>
</body>
</html>
```

The form in Example 9-11 has a name attribute of menuForm and the select list has a name attribute of newPage. Therefore, the list is referenced as document.menuForm.newPage. The *loadNewPage( )* function references the list to load the new page in three steps:

1. The local variable listItem is assigned the ordinal number of the selected value from the list. To discover which item is selected, the selectedIndex property of the newPage <select> is inspected. For example, if the first item is selected then the value is 0.

2. The value of the selected item (which contains the new URL) is determined by accessing the options array property of the list and retrieving the value of the element listItem. This value is stored in the local variable newPage. For example, if the first item in the list is selected listItem is 0, the value is the URL *http://www.webdatabasebook.com/*, and newPage is set to that value.

3. To load the new URL in the current window, the location.href property is set to newPage. This causes the new document to load.

Case Study: A Generic JavaScript Validation Function

The example in this section shows how JavaScript can be used as a validation tool across multiple HTML pages or templates. An example of errors produced by applying the techniques described in this section to customer validation is shown in Figure 9-3. We show you the JavaScript code, the PEAR IT template, and the PHP code in this section.

The JavaScript validation script

The general-purpose *verify()* function for post-validation and field-by-field error reporting is shown in Example 9-12. The code is stored in the file *example.9-12.js* and is designed to be added to a template, such as the phonebook template developed in Chapter 8. Later in this section, we show you how to add it to a customer details template that has diverse validation needs.

By storing JavaScript code in its own file, it can be reused across multiple HTML pages or templates. To do this, instead of including code between the <script> and </script> tags, you add a src attribute to the <script> element that specifies the file that contains the JavaScript code. For example, to load the code in Example 9-12 into a document or template, you use:

```
<script type="text/javascript" src="example.9-12.js">
</script>
```

This approach saves cutting and pasting the code into more than one file, and avoids the need to update several pages when the script changes. It also has the additional advantage of reducing network traffic if the user has a web browser cache, because a copy of the script can be reused in multiple HTML pages without retrieving it again from the web server.

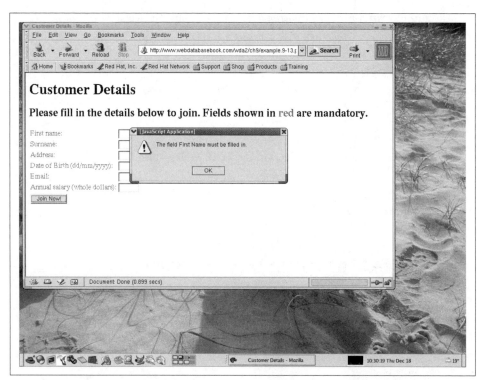

Figure 9-3. A dialog box showing an error produced by the JavaScript validation function

Example 9-12. A general-purpose JavaScript form validation function

```
// A utility function that returns true if a string contains only
// whitespace characters.
function isblank(e)
{
  if (e.value == null || e.value == "")
    return true;

  for(var i = 0; i < e.value.length; i++)
  {
    var c = e.value.charAt(i);
    if ((c != ' ') &&
        (c != '\n') &&
        (c != '\t'))
      return false;
  }
  return true;
}

// Checks if an optional field is blank
function checkblank(e)
{
  if (isblank(e))
  {
```

```
      alert("The field " + e.description + " must be filled in.");
      return false;
  }
  return true;
}

// Checks if a field is numeric.
// If the optional min property is set, it checks it is greater than
// its value
// If the optional max property is set, it checks it is less than
// its value
function checknumber(e)
{
  var v = parseFloat(e.value);

  if (isNaN(v))
  {
    alert("The field " + e.description + " must be a number");
    return false;
  }

  if ((e.minNumber != null) && (v < e.minNumber))
  {
    alert("The field " + e.description +
          " must be greater than or equal to " + e.minNumber);
    return false;
  }

  if (e.maxNumber != null && v > e.maxNumber)
  {
    alert("The field " + e.description +
          " must be less than or equal to " + e.maxNumber);
    return false;
  }

  return true;
}

// Checks if a field looks like a date in the 99/99/9999 format
function checkdate(e)
{
  var slashCount = 0;
  if (e.value.length != 10)
  {
    alert(" The field " + e.description +
          " must have the format 99/99/9999" +
          " and be 10 characters in length");
    return false;
  }

  for(var j = 0; j < e.value.length; j++)
  {
```

```
    var c = e.value.charAt(j);

    if ((c == '/'))
       slashCount++;

    if (c != '/' && (c < '0' || c > '9'))
    {
       alert(" The field " + e.description +
             " can contain only numbers and forward-slashes");
       return false;
    }
  }

  if (slashCount != 2)
  {
    alert(" The field " + e.description +
          " must have the format 99/99/9999");
    return false;
  }

  return true;
}

// Checks if a field contains any whitespace
function checkwhitespace(e)
{
  var seenAt = false;

  for(var j = 0; j < e.value.length; j++)
  {
    var c = e.value.charAt(j);

    if ((c == ' ') || (c == '\n') || (c == '\t'))
    {
      alert("The field " + e.description +
            " must not contain whitespace");
      return false;
    }
  }
  return true;
}

// Now check for fields that are supposed to be emails.
// Only checks that there's one @ symbol and no whitespace
function checkemail(e)
{
  var seenAt = false;

  for(var j = 0; j < e.value.length; j++)
  {
    var c = e.value.charAt(j);
```

Example 9-12. A general-purpose JavaScript form validation function (continued)

```
    if ((c == ' ') || (c == '\n') || (c == '\t'))
    {
      alert("The field " + e.description +
            " must not contain whitespace");
      return false;
    }

    if ((c == '@') && (seenAt == true))
    {
      alert("The field " + e.description + " must contain only one @");
      return false;
    }

    if ((c == '@'))
      seenAt = true;
  }

  if (seenAt == false)
  {
    alert("The field " + e.description + " must contain one @");
    return false;
  }
  return true;
}

// This is the function that performs <form> validation.
// It is invoked from the onSubmit( ) event handler.
// The handler should return whatever value this function
// returns.
function verify(f)
{
  // Loop through the elements of the form, looking for all
  // text and textarea elements. Report errors using a post validation,
  // field-by-field approach
  for(var i = 0; i < f.length; i++)
  {
    var e = f.elements[i];

    if (((e.type == "text") || (e.type == "textarea")))
    {
      // first check if the field is empty and shouldn't be
      if (!e.isOptional && !checkblank(e))
        return false;

      // Now check for fields that are supposed to be numeric.
      if (!isblank(e) && e.isNumeric && !checknumber(e))
        return false;

      // Now check for fields that are supposed to be dates
      if (!isblank(e) && e.isDate && !checkdate(e))
        return false;
```

```
        // Now check for fields that are supposed to be emails
        if (!isblank(e) && e.isEmail && !checkemail(e))
          return false;

        // Now check for fields that are supposed
        // not to have whitespace
        if (!isblank(e) && e.hasNospaces && !checkwhitespace(e))
          return false;
      } // if (type is text or textarea)
    } // for each character in field

  // There were no errors if we got this far
  return true;
}
```

Example 9-12 contains several functions and the main function is the last one in the file, *verify()*. The *verify()* function is called when a form is submitted, and it expects the form object to be passed to it as a parameter. The function iterates through the elements in the form and carries out validation checks on each field, depending on what properties you set for that field. If any check fails, the function returns false. If all checks succeed, the function returns true. We show you how to call the function and set the element properties later.

The first fragment of the *verify()* function is as follows:

```
function verify(f)
{
  // Loop through the elements of the form, looking for all
  // text and textarea elements. Report errors using a post validation,
  // field-by-field approach
  for(var i = 0; i < f.length; i++)
  {
      var e = f.elements[i];
```

A form object f is expected as a parameter. The for loop iterates through each element object in f. The first element is numbered 0 and the total elements in the form is stored in the property f.length. As discussed previously, the element objects are stored in the elements array and so, for example, f.elements[0] is the object representation of the first element in f. For compactness in the code, with each iteration of the loop, we assign the current element object to the local variable e.

The next fragment in *verify()* checks whether the current input element is of type text or textarea:

```
if (((e.type == "text") || (e.type == "textarea")))
{
```

We've only written validation functions for these types of element, and we leave it to you to extend this further to meet your needs.

The remainder of the *verify()* function tests different properties of the current element and calls functions to validate it. For example, the following fragment tests if the element contains a value (that is, it's not blank), if the isNumeric property is set, and if the value is not a number:

```
// Now check for fields that are supposed to be numeric.
if (!isblank(e) && e.isNumeric && !checknumber(e))
   return false;
```

The result of this check is that if the element isn't blank and is supposed to be numeric and isn't a number, the function returns false. In the same way as PHP's short-circuit evaluation discussed in Chapter 2, the second and subsequent tests in the if expression are only carried out if all preceding tests are true. The *isblank()* and *checknumber()* functions are validation functions in Example 9-12, and the isNumeric property is a user defined property that we discuss later.

There are several functions in Example 9-12 that each begin with the prefix *check*. In addition to testing if a mandatory field is blank and if a field is numeric, these check whether mandatory fields have data in them, dates are in a reasonable format, email addresses look plausible, and whether there's whitespace within a value. As an example, we discuss the *checkdate()* function next; we don't discuss the others in detail but they use the same ideas and validation steps.

The *checkdate()* functions perform very simple date format checking: it tests if a date has the format 99/99/9999 where 9 is a digit. More explicitly, it checks that the value is exactly 10 characters in length, contains only forward slashes and digits, and has only two forward slashes. It doesn't check the ordering of the characters, nor the validity of the date by the calendar. It's therefore a simple first step in validation: if the check succeeds, there's more chance it'll pass the more detailed server-side validation that occurs after the form is submitted. The *checkdate()* function returns true if validation succeeds and false otherwise.

The *checkdate()* function begins as follows:

```
// Checks if a field looks like a date in the 99/99/9999 format
function checkdate(e)
{
  var slashCount = 0;

  if (e.value.length != 10)
  {
    alert(" The field " + e.description +
          " must have the format 99/99/9999" +
          " and be 10 characters in length");
    return false;
  }
```

It expects a form element e as a parameter. The local variable slashCount is used later to count the number of forward slashes. The first test checks if the value is ten characters in length and, if not, it shows an error dialog and the function returns false.

The description property of the element is set before the *verify()* function is called and we show you this later.

The next fragment is as follows:

```
for(var j = 0; j < e.value.length; j++)
{
    var c = e.value.charAt(j);
```

The for loop iterates through each character of the value in the element; the first element is 0 and the last is determined from the property e.value.length. For compactness in the later code, we store the current character in the local variable c by retrieving is using the built-in *charAt()* method discussed previously.

The body of the loop has two straightforward steps. First, if the current character is a forward slash, we increment the counter:

```
if ((c == '/'))
    slashCount++;
```

Second, if the current character isn't a forward slash and isn't a digit we pop up an error dialog and the function returns false:

```
if (c != '/' && (c < '0' || c > '9'))
{
    alert(" The field " + e.description +
         " can contain only numbers and forward-slashes");
    return false;
}
}
```

If the execution of the function makes it to the next fragment only digits and forward slashes have been encountered in the value. Now, we check whether there were two forward slashes:

```
if (slashCount != 2)
{
    alert(" The field " + e.description +
         " must have the format 99/99/9999");
    return false;
}
return true;
}
```

If the check fails, we pop up an error dialog and return false. If all checks have succeeded the value looks like a date and the function returns true.

Using the JavaScript validation function

To use the *verify( )* function, you call it from the onsubmit handler of a form. For example, suppose you have authored the customer details input form that's shown in Figure 9-4.

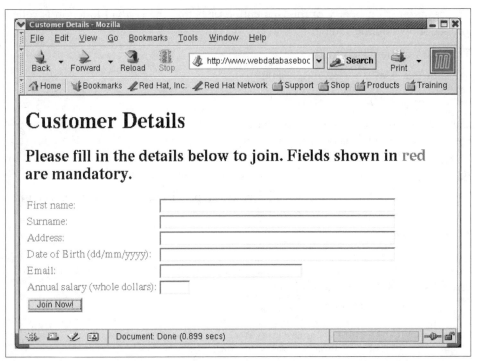

Figure 9-4. A customer form with JavaScript validation

The form requires users to provide a first name, surname, address, email address, date of birth, and salary. For this form, the onsubmit handler that's used is as follows:

```
<form action="test.php" method="post" name="custform"
onsubmit="document.custform.firstname.hasNospaces = true;
document.custform.firstname.description = 'First Name';
document.custform.surname.description = 'Surname';
document.custform.address.description = 'Address';
document.custform.email.description = 'Email';
document.custform.email.isEmail = true;
document.custform.dob.isDate = true;
document.custform.dob.description = 'Date of Birth (99/99/9999)';
document.custform.salary.description = 'Salary';
document.custform.salary.isNumeric = true;
document.custform.salary.minNumber = 1;
document.custform.salary.maxNumber = 1000000;
document.custform.salary.hasNospaces = true;
return verify(document.custform);">
```

This code fragment creates and sets properties for each form element. These are properties that we've created (and not part of JavaScript itself), and each is used by some part of our *verify()* function. For example, when validation fails, the validation functions show error messages that inform the user which field contains the error.

To pass this string to the validation function, we create a `description` property for all elements that are validated. For instance, the fragment:

```
document.custform.email.description = 'Email';
```

sets the `description` property of the email input element to `'Email'`. As shown in the previous section, this description is displayed in a dialog box when an error occurs.

To control validation, you set a property that triggers a validation function in the *verify()* function. For example, if you want an element to be validated using the *checkdate()* function we described previously, you set the `isDate` property to be true:

```
document.custform.dob.isDate = true;
```

The *verify()* function inspects this property and, because it's `true`, it calls the *checkdate()* function to validate the dob field.

The other properties we've set up can be used to trigger other types of validation. You can set are `isEmail` (for an email address), `hasNoSpaces` (if an element should not contain whitespace), `isNumeric` (for integers), `minNumber` (a minimum value for an `isNumeric` element), `maxNumber` (a maximum value for an `isNumeric` element), and `isOptional` (for an element that can be left blank).

The PHP and template components

To complete our JavaScript validation case study, Example 9-13 and Example 9-14 show the PHP script and template respectively that create the customer details form.

Example 9-13 is a variation of Example 8-7 (which displays the phonebook form) with three differences. The first is that it displays several more elements than the phonebook script. The second is that it sets a new SUBMITACTION placeholder in the template to the JavaScript code fragment discussed in the previous section. The final difference is that it also sets the name of the form into a new placeholder, FORMNAME.

Example 9-13. The PHP script to produce the customer details form

```php
<?php
require 'db.inc';
require_once "HTML/Template/ITX.php";

$template = new HTML_Template_ITX("./templates");
$template->loadTemplatefile("example.9-11.tpl", true, true);

$template->setVariable("MESSAGE",
                       "Please fill in the details below to join");
$template->setVariable("SUBMITVALUE", "Join Now!");
$template->setVariable("FORMNAME", "custform");
$template->setVariable("SUBMITACTION", "
  document.custform.firstname.hasNospaces = true;
  document.custform.firstname.description = 'First Name';
  document.custform.surname.description = 'Surname';
  document.custform.address.description = 'Address';
  document.custform.email.description = 'Email';
```

```
    document.custform.email.isEmail = true;
    document.custform.dob.isDate = true;
    document.custform.dob.description = 'Date of Birth (99/99/9999)';
    document.custform.salary.description = 'Salary';
    document.custform.salary.isNumeric = true;
    document.custform.salary.minNumber = 1;
    document.custform.salary.maxNumber = 1000000;
    document.custform.salary.hasNospaces = true;
    return verify(document.custform);");

$template->setCurrentBlock("mandatoryinput");
$template->setVariable("MINPUTTEXT", "First name");
$template->setVariable("MINPUTNAME", "firstname");
$template->setVariable("MINPUTVALUE", "");
$template->setVariable("MINPUTSIZE", 50);
$template->parseCurrentBlock("mandatoryinput");

$template->setCurrentBlock("mandatoryinput");
$template->setVariable("MINPUTTEXT", "Surname");
$template->setVariable("MINPUTNAME", "surname");
$template->setVariable("MINPUTVALUE", "");
$template->setVariable("MINPUTSIZE", 50);
$template->parseCurrentBlock("mandatoryinput");

$template->setCurrentBlock("mandatoryinput");
$template->setVariable("MINPUTTEXT", "Address");
$template->setVariable("MINPUTNAME", "address");
$template->setVariable("MINPUTVALUE", "");
$template->setVariable("MINPUTSIZE", 50);
$template->parseCurrentBlock("mandatoryinput");

$template->setCurrentBlock("mandatoryinput");
$template->setVariable("MINPUTTEXT", "Date of Birth (dd/mm/yyyy)");
$template->setVariable("MINPUTNAME", "dob");
$template->setVariable("MINPUTVALUE", "");
$template->setVariable("MINPUTSIZE", 50);
$template->parseCurrentBlock("mandatoryinput");

$template->setCurrentBlock("mandatoryinput");
$template->setVariable("MINPUTTEXT", "Email");
$template->setVariable("MINPUTNAME", "email");
$template->setVariable("MINPUTVALUE", "");
$template->setVariable("MINPUTSIZE", 30);
$template->parseCurrentBlock("mandatoryinput");

$template->setCurrentBlock("mandatoryinput");
$template->setVariable("MINPUTTEXT", "Annual salary (whole dollars)");
$template->setVariable("MINPUTNAME", "salary");
$template->setVariable("MINPUTVALUE", "");
$template->setVariable("MINPUTSIZE", 6);
$template->parseCurrentBlock("mandatoryinput");
```

Example 9-13. The PHP script to produce the customer details form (continued)

```
$template->parseCurrentBlock( );
$template->show( );
?>
```

Example 9-14 is almost identical to the template in Example 8-8.

Example 9-14. The template used to produce the customer form

```
<!DOCTYPE HTML PUBLIC
                "-//W3C//DTD HTML 4.01 Transitional//EN"
                "http://www.w3.org/TR/html401/loose.dtd">
<html>
<head>
  <script type="text/javascript" src="example.9-12.js">
  </script>
  <meta http-equiv="Content-Type" content="text/html; charset=iso-8859-1">
  <title>Customer Details</title>
</head>
<body bgcolor="white">
<form name="{FORMNAME}" method="post" action="test.php"
      onsubmit="{SUBMITACTION}">
<h1>Customer Details</h1>
<h2>{MESSAGE}.
    Fields shown in <font color="red">red</font> are mandatory.</h2>
<table>
<!-- BEGIN mandatoryinput -->
<tr>
  <td><font color="red">{MINPUTTEXT}:</font></td>
  <td>
  <input type="text" name="{MINPUTNAME}" value="{MINPUTVALUE}"
        size={MINPUTSIZE}>
  </td>
</tr>
<!-- END mandatoryinput -->
<tr>
   <td><input type="submit" value="{SUBMITVALUE}"></td>
</tr>
</table>
</form>
</body>
</html>
```

The differences are that the JavaScript code from Example 9-12 is included using the src attribute (as discussed at the beginning of this case study), and that the FORMNAME and SUBMITACTION placeholders have been added to the form element. The FORMNAME is the name of the form, and the SUBMITACTION supports the onsubmit function call.

CHAPTER 10
Sessions

A fundamental characteristic of the Web is the stateless interaction between browsers and web servers. As discussed in Chapter 1, HTTP is a stateless protocol. Each HTTP request sent to a web server is independent of any other request. The stateless nature of HTTP allows users to browse the Web by following hypertext links and visiting pages in any order. HTTP also allows applications to distribute or even replicate content across multiple servers to balance the load generated by a high number of requests.

This stateless nature suits applications that allow users to browse or search collections of documents. However, applications that require complex user interaction can't be implemented as a series of unrelated, stateless web pages. An often-cited example is a shopping cart in which items are added to the cart while searching or browsing an on-line store. The state of the shopping cart (the selected items) needs to be stored somewhere to be displayed when the user visits the order page.

Stateful web database applications can be built using *sessions*, and session management is the topic of this chapter. In this chapter, we:

- Discuss how sessions are managed in the stateless environment of the Web and introduce the three characteristics of server-side session management
- Show you how to use the PHP session management library, and discuss design strategies for session-based applications
- Use PHP session management to improve the phonebook entry form
- Provide a brief list of reasons for using, or avoiding, session management over the Web
- Provide details of the PHP session management API and configuration

There are two ways to build an application that keeps state: variables that hold the state can be stored in the browser and included with each request, or variables can be stored on the server. The focus of this chapter is storing variables on the server using PHP session management techniques. Storing variables on the client is usually a less attractive option: it requires additional network traffic, is insecure, and relies on the user's browser configuration.

Introducing Session Management

A *session* manages the interaction between a web browser and a web server. For example, a session allows an application to track the items in a shopping cart, the status of a customer account application process, whether or not a user is logged in, or the finalizing of an order. Sessions are essential to most web database applications.

A session has two components: *session variables* and a *session identifier (ID)*. The session variables are the state information that's related to a user's interaction with an application. For example, the session variables might store that the user's shopping cart contains five items, what those items are, their price, what items the user has viewed, and that the user is logged into the application. The session variables are stored at the web server or database server, and are located using the session ID.

When a session is started, the user's browser is given a session ID. This ID is then included with subsequent requests to the server. When a browser makes a request, the server uses the session ID to locate the corresponding session variables, and the variables are read or written as required. In practice, session variables are typically stored at the web server in a file (the PHP default) or at the database server in a table. Figure 10-1 shows how the session variables for Beth's session are identified and stored in the web server environment; the session ID distinguishes between Beth's session and other users of the system.

Using sessions, all of the variables that represent the state of an application don't need to be transmitted over the Web. The session ID is transmitted between the browser and server with each HTTP request and response, but the session data itself is stored at the server. The session ID is therefore like the ticket given at a cloakroom. The ticket is much easier to carry around and ensures that you get back your own hat and coat. Storing variables at the server also helps prevent accidental or intentional tampering with state information.

The session ID is usually transmitted as a *cookie*. A cookie is a named piece of text that is stored in a web browser, and is sent with HTTP requests, like data sent with the GET or POST methods. You can find out more about cookies from the interesting Cookie Central web site at *http://www.cookiecentral.com/faq/* or more formally in RFC 2109 at *http://ietf.org/rfc/rfc2109.txt?number=2109*.

When you manage session variables at the web server, they need to be stored for each browser session. But for how long should the session variables be stored? Because HTTP is stateless, there is no way to know when a user has finished with a session. Ideally, the user logs out of an application by requesting a logout script that explicitly ends the session. However, because a server can never be sure if a user is still there, the server needs to clean up old sessions that have not been used for a

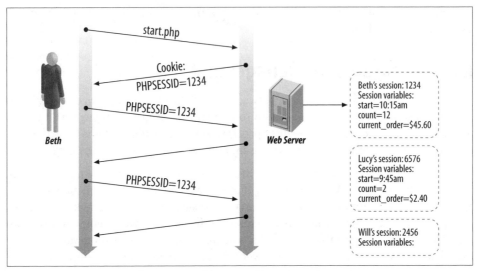

Figure 10-1. Session IDs and session variables

period of time. Unused sessions consume resources on the server and present a security risk. How long the timeout should be depends on the needs of the application, and we discuss this in more detail later in this chapter.

In summary, there are three characteristics of session management over the Web:

- Information or state must be *stored*. Information that must be maintained across multiple HTTP requests is stored in session variables.
- Each HTTP request must carry an *identifier* that allows the server to process the request with the correct session variables.
- Sessions need to have a *timeout*. Otherwise, if a user leaves the web site, there is no way the server can tell when the session should end.

PHP Session Management

Developing applications that use PHP sessions is straightforward. The three important features of session management—identifying sessions, storing session variables, and cleaning up old sessions—are mostly taken care of by the PHP session management library.

In this section, we show you how sessions are started and ended, and how session variables are used, and provide strategies for designing session-based applications.

The out-of-the-box configuration of PHP session management uses disk-based files to store session variables, and our discussion in this section assumes this default PHP 4.3 behavior. Using files as the session store is adequate for most applications in which the number of concurrent sessions is limited. A more scalable solution that uses a MySQL database as a session store is provided in Appendix F.

Starting a Session

The *session_start()* function is used to create a new session. A session is unique to the interaction between a browser and a web database application. If you use your browser to access several sites at once, you'll have several unrelated sessions. Similarly, if several users access your application each has their own session. However, if you access an application using two browsers (or two browser windows) at the same time, in most cases the browsers will share the same session; this can lead to unpredictable behavior—that's the reason why many web sites warn against it.

The first time a user requests a script that calls *session_start()*, PHP generates a new session ID and creates an empty file to store session variables. PHP also sends a cookie back to the browser that contains the session ID. However, because the cookie is sent as part of the HTTP headers in the response to the browser, you need to call *session_start( )* before any other output is generated, just as with other functions that set HTTP header fields (this is a common source of error and it's discussed in more detail in Chapter 12).

The session identifier generated by PHP is a random string of 32 hexadecimal digits, such as fcc17f071bca9bf7f85ca281094390b4. When a new session is started, PHP creates a session file, using the session identifier, prefixed with sess_, for the filename. For example, the filename associated with our example session ID on a Unix system is */tmp/sess_fcc17f071bca9bf7f85ca281094390b4*.

Using Session Variables

The *session_start( )* function is also used to find an existing session. If a call is made to *session_start( )*, and a session has previously been started, PHP attempts to find the session file and initialize the session variables. PHP does this automatically by looking for the session cookie in the browser request whenever you call *session_start()*. You don't need to do anything different when starting a new session or restoring an existing one. Even if the identified session file can't be found, *session_start( )* simply creates a new session file.

Once a script has called *session_start()*, PHP provides access to session variables through the superglobal associative array $_SESSION. When an existing session is found, PHP automatically reads the session variables from the session file into the array. PHP also automatically writes changes to the array back to the session file once the script ends. However, be careful: if your script doesn't call *session_start()*, the $_SESSION array behaves like any other variable and any values are lost when the script ends.

The script shown in Example 10-1 uses session variables to record the number of times a user requests the page and the time of the first visit. The script is used with the template shown in Example 10-2.

Example 10-1. A simple PHP script that uses a session

```php
<?php
  require_once "HTML/Template/ITX.php";

  // This call either creates a new session or finds an existing one.
  session_start();

  // Check if the value for "count" exists in the session store
  // If not, set a value for "count" and "start"
  if (!isset($_SESSION["count"]))
  {
    $_SESSION["count"] = 0;
    $_SESSION["start"] = time();
  }

  // Increment the count
  $_SESSION["count"]++;

  $template = new HTML_Template_ITX("./templates");
  $template->loadTemplatefile("example.10-2.tpl", true, true);

  $template->setVariable("SESSION", session_id());
  $template->setVariable("COUNT", $_SESSION["count"]);
  $template->setVariable("START", $_SESSION["start"]);
  $duration = time() - $_SESSION["start"];
  $template->setVariable("DURATION", $duration);

  $template->parseCurrentBlock();

  $template->show();
?>
```

Example 10-2. The session display template used with Example 10-1

```html
<!DOCTYPE HTML PUBLIC "-//W3C//DTD HTML 4.01 Transitional//EN"
                      "http://www.w3.org/TR/html401/loose.dtd">
<html>
<head>
  <meta http-equiv="Content-Type"
        content="text/html; charset=iso-8859-1">
  <title>Session State Test</title>
</head>
<body>
    <p>This page points at a session {SESSION}
    <br>count = {COUNT}
    <br>start = {START}
    <p>This session has lasted {DURATION} seconds.
</body>
</html>
```

Example 10-1 starts by initializing a session with a call to *session_start( )*. When the script is called for the first time, this creates a new session and initializes an empty $_ SESSION array. When the script is called for the second or subsequent time, the stored values from the previous time the script was run are restored into the $_SESSION array. Whenever the script ends, the current values in the $_SESSION array are written back to the session store.

After initializing a session, the script tests if the $_SESSION array contains a value for the element count as follows:

```
// Check if the value for "count" exists in the session store
// If not, set a value for "count" and "start"
if (!isset($_SESSION["count"]))
{
  $_SESSION["count"] = 0;
  $_SESSION["start"] = time();
}
```

If there's no value set, then this is the first time the script has been run and values for count and start are set up in the $_SESSION array. If count is set, then values have been read from the session store and these values are used instead.

The remainder of the script does the same thing whether or not this is the first time the script has been called. The value of count is incremented, and then the session ID (retrieved with the PHP library function *session_id()*), count, start time, and session duration (the start time subtracted from the current time) are displayed.

The overall effect of the script is that each time you call it, the count increases by one and the duration updates to the length of time since you first called the script. However, as we explain later, if you don't request the script for a while, your session may be automatically destroyed by PHP's garbage collection and the count will begin again from one.

Unsetting session variables

To unset a session variable, you use the *unset( )* function. To remove all the session variables, you can unset the whole $_SESSION array or re-assign a new array. Here are two examples:

```
// To remove the "count" session variable only
unset($_SESSION["count"]);

// To remove all the session variables without destroying the session
$_SESSION = array();
```

Session variable types

Session variables can be of any type supported by PHP. However, if objects are saved as session variables, you should include class definitions for those objects in all scripts that call *session_start()*, regardless of whether the scripts use the objects or not. This is needed so that PHP can correctly read and write objects from the *session store* (the file that stores the session variables).

To do this, you might store your class definition in an require file such as *my_class.inc* as shown in the following example:

```
require "my_class.inc";

// Find the session
start_session();

// later on in the script, store an object as a session variable
$_SESSION["some_object"] = new my_class();
```

Objects and classes are described in Chapter 4.

Serialization of session variables

PHP stores session variables in the session file by *serializing* the values. The serialized representation of a variable includes the name, the type, and the value as a stream of characters suitable for writing to a file. Here's an example of a file that was created when the script shown in Example 10-1 was run several times:

```
count|i:3;start|i:1049624957;
```

You don't need to worry how serialization occurs; PHP session management takes care of reading and writing session variables automatically.

Ending a Session

At some point in an application, sessions should be destroyed. For example, when a user logs out of an application, a call to the *session_destroy( )* function should be made to clean-up the session variables and remove the session file. Be aware that while a call to *session_destroy( )* removes the session file from the system, it doesn't remove the session cookie from the browser. In practice, it doesn't matter that the cookie is still there because PHP can transparently handle a session cookie being presented without a matching file on the server; in this case, it just creates a new session store with the name that matches the cookie value.

Example 10-3 shows how the *session_destroy( )* function is called. Note that a session must be initialized with a call to *session_start( )* before the *session_destroy( )* call can be made. In the example, after destroying the session, the script redirects to a receipt page, *logout.html*. This avoids the reload problem discussed in Chapter 8.

Example 10-3. Ending a session

```
<?php
  session_start();
  session_destroy();
  header("Location: logout.html");
?>
```

Designing Session-Based Applications

The PHP session management library provides a way of storing state but does not dictate how sessions are used in an application. When you design a session-based application, you therefore need to give thought to:

- How and when a session is started
- What data needs to be stored as session variables
- When a session is destroyed

Sessions can be used in a variety of ways, and in this section, we describe two distinctly different types of session-based applications and provide design strategies for both. The following section uses a case study to show a third application of sessions.

Session to track authenticated users

Applications that require a user to log in—such as online banking—often use sessions to manage the user interaction. Figure 10-2 shows a typical flow of pages in such an application, and interaction with PHP session management.

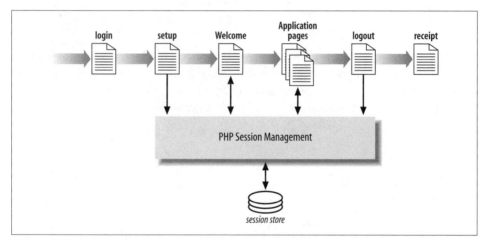

Figure 10-2. Typical session-based application

The login page collects the user credentials using an HTML form and passes these using the POST method to the setup script. The setup script is responsible for creating the new session with the first call to *session_start()* and for setting up the initial session variables. After the session is started, the setup script sends a Location header field, instructing the browser to relocate to the welcome page. Relocating to the welcome page prevents the setup script being re-run during the session, and avoids the reload problem we described in Chapter 8. The following fragment shows the sequence of code in the setup script:

```
// Process the POST variables
$username = $_POST["username"];
```

```
// Start the session
session_start();

// Setup the session variables
$_SESSION["name"] = $username;
$_SESSION["counter"] = 0;

// Relocate to the welcome page
header("Location: welcome.php");
```

The welcome page, and the other application pages, begin by calling *session_start()* to set up the $_SESSION superglobal array with the session variables. Each page of the application then interacts with the $_SESSION variables as required. For example, consider the following fragment:

```
// Find the session
session_start();

// Welcome the user to the application
print "Hi {$_SESSION["name"]}), Welcome to my Application";
// ...

// Update session variables
$_SESSION["counter"]++;
// ...
```

Finally, the session is destroyed when the user requests the logout page. As with all the other pages that interact with the session, the logout script must begin by calling *session_start()*. As discussed previously, a logout page should also redirect to a receipt page to avoid the reload problem. Here's an example logout script:

```
<?
// Find the session
session_start();

// Destroy the session
session_destroy();

// Redirect to a receipt page.
header("Location: logout.html");
?>
```

We develop a session-based user authentication framework that follows this pattern in Chapter 11.

Sessions to track anonymous users

Not all session-based applications follow the pattern presented in Figure 10-2, and not all require a user to log in. For example, consider an application that tracks the pages a user has visited. Multiple pages share information using session variables, however the user can enter the web site from any page. Each page in the application can potentially start the session, so each page should be written to test for the existence of the session variable.

The following fragment of code shows how a session variable $_SESSION["visited_pages"] is tested and set up prior to being used:

```
// Start or find the session
session_start();

// Test for the required session variables and add
// them to the session store if they don't exist
if (!isset($_SESSION["visited_pages"]))
  $_SESSION["visited_pages"] = array();

// Now use the session
// Add the name of this page to the end of the array
$_SESSION["visited_pages"][] = $_SERVER["PHP_SELF"];
```

If the variable isn't in the session store, it's initialized as a new array; if it is in the session store, it's restored automatically by the PHP session handler. After this first step, the name of the current page is added to the end of the array; the superglobal $_SERVER contains many elements that describe the server environment, including PHP_SELF which is the name of the current PHP script. This same fragment would be added to each script in the application. For compactness, you might put the fragment into a function in a require file.

The result of using this code is that, for every page the user visits, a new element is added to the array that contains the name of the page. If a user visits a page twice, a second element for that page is added. You could determine how many pages the user has visited by inspecting the size of the array with *count()*, or you could print out the list of pages as in the following fragment:

```
// Print out all of the pages the user has visited
foreach ($_SESSION["visited_pages"] as $page)
  print "Thanks for visiting the {$page} page<br>";
```

For applications that record sensitive information in session variables, you should offer a page that destroys the session. However, for a non-sensitive application, setting a short session timeout and letting the PHP session management garbage collection remove the session is adequate. We discuss garbage collection and how to change the default session timeout later in this chapter.

Case Study: Using Sessions in Validation

In this section, we use sessions to improve the user interaction with the phonebook details form developed in Chapter 8. The improvements focus on the interaction when the form is submitted and fields fail validation. We modify the scripts to:

- Display error messages interleaved with the phonebook's entry form widgets.
- Use session variables to pass back the submitted fields to the form generation script, saving the user the trouble of re-keying the data to correct the errors.

Improving the Phonebook Details Form

We designed several phonebook scripts in Chapter 8. In Example 8-7, the form generated by the script collects values to create a new entry. The script shown in Example 8-9 performs simple server-side validation of the form data, and inserts a row in the *phonebook* table if there are no errors. We improve these scripts in this section, but the techniques we show you can be easily adapted to the other phonebook scripts or to any form pages you've authored.

If validation fails, the script shown in Example 8-9 generates a page to display the errors to the user, and the user then follows a hypertext link back to the phonebook entry form to reenter the fields. The solution provided by Example 8-7 and Example 8-9 has three problems:

- The user is forced to reenter the entire phonebook entry form from scratch when an error is encountered during validation
- Example 8-9 displays all the errors in a stand-alone page with no connection to the form page, so the user cannot easily see the relation between errors and the original input fields.
- The error page generated by Example 8-9 isn't safe from the reload problem described in Chapter 8.

In this section we develop scripts that make use of session variables to solve these problems. Rather than displaying the error messages on a page generated by the validation script, we show you how to display the errors in red above the appropriate input fields on the data entry form, as shown in Figure 10-3 (the red text appears as a light gray in the figure).

Figure 10-4 shows how the improved form and the validate scripts interact with session management to communicate errors and submitted fields.

Because the validation script processes the fields collected in the phonebook form and generates any associated errors, we look at the changes required for that script first.

The Validation Script

We begin the improvements to the validation script with the changes required to support an error message session variable and then discuss how to record the values to pass back to the phonebook entry form generation code. We then show you the complete structure of the modified validation script.

Improving error messages

The validation script checks each variable submitted from the phonebook form to make sure data has been entered. The script shown in Example 8-9 builds up a template by adding blocks as errors are found. In the modified script we use in this case

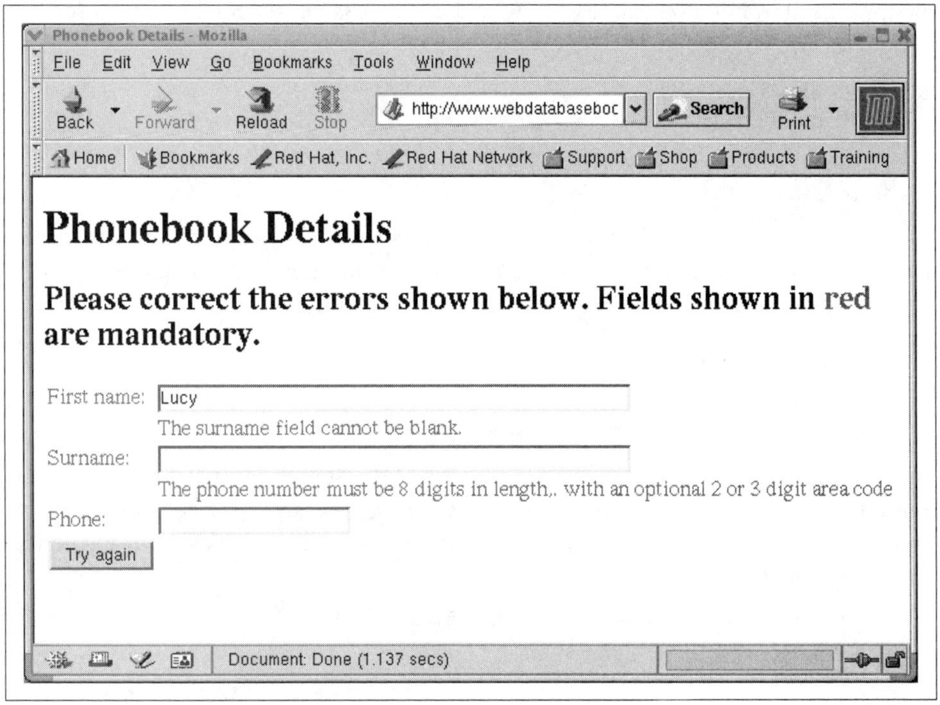

Phonebook Details

Please correct the errors shown below. Fields shown in red are mandatory.

First name: Lucy

The surname field cannot be blank.

Surname:

The phone number must be 8 digits in length,. with an optional 2 or 3 digit area code

Phone:

Try again

Figure 10-3. The phonebook entry form showing error messages

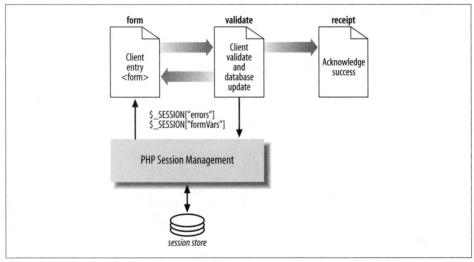

Figure 10-4. Phonebook entry form and validation

study, an associative array is registered instead to hold error messages associated with each field, providing greater flexibility when displaying the error messages.

First, we need to initialize the session with a call to *session_start()* and set up $errors to hold an array of errors:

```
// Initialize a session
session_start();

// Set-up an empty $errors array to hold errors
$errors = array();
```

The script then checks each variable and adds an error message to the associative array $errors if an error is encountered. The error message array is indexed by the name of the field being checked. For example, the validation of the surname is coded as:

```
// Validate the Surname
if (empty($surname))
    $errors["surname"] = "The surname field cannot be blank.";
```

Once all the fields have been validated, the size of the $errors array is tested to determine if any errors were encountered. If the size of the array is zero, we create or update the row as before, otherwise we carry out several steps as shown in the following fragment:

```
// Now the script has finished the validation, check if
// there were any errors
if (count($errors))
{
  // Set up a $lastformVars array to store the previously-entered data
  $lastformVars = array();
  $lastFormVars["surname"] = $surname;
  $lastFormVars["firstname"] = $firstname;
  $lastFormVars["phone"] = $phone;

  // Save the array as a session variable
  $_SESSION["lastFormVars"] = $lastFormVars;

  // Store the $errors array as a session variable
  $_SESSION["errors"] = $errors;

  //  Relocate to the phonebook form
  header("Location: example.10-5.php");
  exit;
}
```

The setup and use of the lastFormVars array is discussed in the next section. The remainder of the fragment saves the $errors array as a session variable and relocates to the phonebook entry form script.

In Example 8-9, the script itself displays any errors, and because the request contains variables in a POST method request, the error page suffers from the reload problem discussed in Chapter 8. The script has to display the errors immediately, in isolation, because without sessions there is no convenient way to save the errors and retrieve them again when displaying the form. In the validation script developed here, we relocate to the phonebook entry form (shown later in Example 10-5) and let it display the errors held in the session variable $_SESSION["errors"].

Saving last-entered values as a session variable

We now show you how to pass the field data from the validation script back to the phonebook entry form, so the user does not have to re-key data after an error occurs. The fields are passed back the session array variable lastFormVars.

The following code fragment saves each value entered into the form into a $lastFormVars array, indexed by the name of the variable. The $lastFormVars array is then saved as the session variable $_SESSION["lastFormVars"].

```
// Set up a $lastformVars array to store the previously-entered data
$lastformVars = array();
$lastFormVars["surname"] = $surname;
$lastFormVars["firstname"] = $firstname;
$lastFormVars["phone"] = $phone;

// Save the array as a session variable
$_SESSION["lastFormVars"] = $lastFormVars;
```

When the modified form is run, the most recent values entered from the session variable $_SESSION["lastFormVars"] are shown.

The final change needed is to destroy the session when the script successfully saves a row in the *phonebook* table:

```
// Destroy the session
session_destroy();
```

However, your application may make use of the session for other purposes and you may not want to destroy the session at this point. If this is the case then you should unset the variables used in these scripts.

```
// Clean up the lastFormVars from the session store
unset($_SESSION["lastFormVars"]);
```

The final validation script

Example 10-4 shows the final validation script derived from Example 8-9.

Example 10-4. The complete validation script derived from Example 8-9

```
<?php
require 'db.inc';

if (!($connection = @ mysql_pconnect("localhost", "fred", "shhh")))
   die("Could not connect to database");

$firstname = mysqlclean($_POST, "firstname", 50, $connection);
$surname = mysqlclean($_POST, "surname", 50, $connection);
$phone = mysqlclean($_POST, "phone", 20, $connection);
```

Example 10-4. The complete validation script derived from Example 8-9 (continued)

```
// Initialize a session
session_start();

// Set-up an empty $errors array to hold errors
$errors = array();

// Validate the Firstname
if (empty($firstname))
  $errors["firstname"] = "The firstname field cannot be blank.";

// Validate the Surname
if (empty($surname))
  $errors["surname"] = "The surname field cannot be blank.";

// Validate the Phone number. It must have the correct format
$validPhoneExpr = "^([0-9]{2,3}[ ]?)?[0-9]{4}[ ]?[0-9]{4}$";

if (empty($phone) || !ereg($validPhoneExpr, $phone))
  $errors["phone"] = "The phone number must be 8 digits in length,.
                      with an optional 2 or 3 digit area code";

// Now the script has finished the validation, check if
// there were any errors
if (count($errors))
{
  // Set up a $lastformVars array to store
  // the previously-entered data
  $lastformVars = array();
  $lastFormVars["surname"] = $surname;
  $lastFormVars["firstname"] = $firstname;
  $lastFormVars["phone"] = $phone;

  // Save the array as a session variable
  $_SESSION["lastFormVars"] = $lastFormVars;

  // Store the $errors array as a session variable
  $_SESSION["errors"] = $errors;

  //  Relocate to the phonebook form
  header("Location: example.10-5.php");
  exit;
}

// If we made it here, then the data is valid
if (!mysql_select_db("telephone", $connection))
  showerror();

// Insert the new phonebook entry
$query = "INSERT INTO phonebook VALUES
          (NULL, '{$surname}', '{$firstname}', '{$phone}')";

if (!(@ mysql_query ($query, $connection)))
```

Example 10-4. The complete validation script derived from Example 8-9 (continued)

```
    showerror();

// Find out the phonebook_id of the new entry
$phonebook_id = mysql_insert_id();

// Destroy the session
session_destroy();

// Show the phonebook receipt
header("Location: example.8-5.php?status=T&phonebook_id={$phonebook_id}");
?>
```

The Phonebook Entry Form Script

Now let's turn to the changes required for the script that generates the phonebook entry form shown in Example 8-7. In the last section, we set up two session variables: $_SESSION["errors"] to hold an associative array of error messages found by the validation script, and $_SESSION["lastFormVars"] to hold an associative array filled with the form values. Both session variables are read and incorporated into a new form in this section.

Displaying previously entered form values

In our update phonebook details form in Example 8-11, we read data from the *phonebook* table and display it in the input widgets so that the user can amend it. The form uses the array $row to populate the data entry fields from a *phonebook* row when editing an existing entry in the database. In this section, we adapt this approach to displaying previously-entered data that has failed validation.

Adapting the approach from Example 8-11 to our sessions-based script is straightforward. Consider the following fragment:

```
    $row = array();

    // Has previous data been entered?
    // If so, initialize $row from $_SESSION["lastFormVars"]
    if (isset($_SESSION["lastFormVars"]))
    {
      $row = $_SESSION["lastFormVars"];
      $template->setVariable("MESSAGE",
                             "Please correct the errors shown below");
      $template->setVariable("SUBMITVALUE", "Try again");
    }
```

If the $_SESSION["lastFormVars"] variable is set, $row is set to $_SESSION["lastFormVars"], and a message and submit button value set to inform the user that errors have occurred. Then, for each widget in the form, the script displays the value the user previously entered (or an empty widget if no previous value was supplied):

```
if (!empty($row))
    $template->setVariable("MINPUTVALUE", $row["firstname"]);
else
    $template->setVariable("MINPUTVALUE", "");
```

Displaying error messages

To display the error messages above the input widgets, we've modified our phone-book template; the phonebook template is discussed in more detail in Chapter 8. It now includes the following fragment:

```
<!-- BEGIN mandatoryinput -->
<tr>
<!-- BEGIN mandatoryerror -->
  <td>
  <td><font color="red">{MINPUTERROR}</font>
</tr>
<tr>
<!-- END mandatoryerror -->
  <td><font color="red">{MINPUTTEXT}:</font></td>
  <td>
  <input type="text" name="{MINPUTNAME}" value="{MINPUTVALUE}"
         size={MINPUTSIZE}>
  </td>
</tr>
<!-- END mandatoryinput -->
```

The mandatoryerror block is an optional block that's included before the input element and is used to show an error message in a red font using the placeholder MINPUTERROR. If no error occurs, we don't set MINPUTERROR and don't use the mandatoryerror block.

To decide whether to display an error message or not, we check the contents of the $_SESSION["errors"] array. If there's an entry for the input name in the associative array of error messages, we use the mandatoryerror block and display the message. Here's an example for the firstname element:

```
if (!empty($_SESSION["errors"]["firstname"]))
{
  $template->setCurrentBlock("mandatoryerror");
  $template->setVariable("MINPUTERROR", $_SESSION["errors"]["firstname"]);
  $template->parseCurrentBlock("mandatoryerror");
}
```

Figure 10-4 shows the final results: a form with error messages placed over the corresponding fields.

The final phonebook entry script

Example 10-5 shows the complete data entry script, derived from Example 8-7, that displays the previous form values and the error messages held in session variables. Example 10-6 shows the template.

Example 10-5. Phonebook entry form derived from Example 8-7

```php
<?php
require 'db.inc';
require_once "HTML/Template/ITX.php";

if (!($connection = @ mysql_connect("localhost", "fred", "shhh")))
   die("Could not connect to database");

session_start();

$template = new HTML_Template_ITX("./templates");
$template->loadTemplatefile("example.10-6.tpl", true, true);

$row = array();

// Has previous data been entered?
// If so, initialize $row from $_SESSION["lastFormVars"]
if (isset($_SESSION["lastFormVars"]))
{
  $row = $_SESSION["lastFormVars"];
  $template->setVariable("MESSAGE",
                         "Please correct the errors shown below");
  $template->setVariable("SUBMITVALUE", "Try again");
}
else
{
  // If they're not correcting an error show a
  // "fill in the details" message
  $template->setVariable("MESSAGE",
                     "Please fill in the details below to add an entry");
  $template->setVariable("SUBMITVALUE", "Add Now!");
}

$template->setCurrentBlock("mandatoryinput");
$template->setVariable("MINPUTTEXT", "First name");
$template->setVariable("MINPUTNAME", "firstname");
if (!empty($row))
  $template->setVariable("MINPUTVALUE", $row["firstname"]);
else
  $template->setVariable("MINPUTVALUE", "");
if (!empty($_SESSION["errors"]["firstname"]))
{
  $template->setCurrentBlock("mandatoryerror");
  $template->setVariable("MINPUTERROR", $_SESSION["errors"]["firstname"]);
  $template->parseCurrentBlock("mandatoryerror");
}
$template->setCurrentBlock("mandatoryinput");
$template->setVariable("MINPUTSIZE", 50);
$template->parseCurrentBlock("mandatoryinput");

$template->setCurrentBlock("mandatoryinput");
$template->setVariable("MINPUTTEXT", "Surname");
$template->setVariable("MINPUTNAME", "surname");
```

Example 10-5. Phonebook entry form derived from Example 8-7 (continued)

```
if (!empty($row))
  $template->setVariable("MINPUTVALUE", $row["surname"]);
else
  $template->setVariable("MINPUTVALUE", "");
if (!empty($_SESSION["errors"]["surname"]))
{
  $template->setCurrentBlock("mandatoryerror");
  $template->setVariable("MINPUTERROR", $_SESSION["errors"]["surname"]);
  $template->parseCurrentBlock("mandatoryerror");
}
$template->setCurrentBlock("mandatoryinput");
$template->setVariable("MINPUTSIZE", 50);
$template->parseCurrentBlock("mandatoryinput");

$template->setCurrentBlock("mandatoryinput");
$template->setVariable("MINPUTTEXT", "Phone");
$template->setVariable("MINPUTNAME", "phone");
if (!empty($row))
  $template->setVariable("MINPUTVALUE", $row["phone"]);
else
  $template->setVariable("MINPUTVALUE", "");
if (!empty($_SESSION["errors"]["phone"]))
{
  $template->setCurrentBlock("mandatoryerror");
  $template->setVariable("MINPUTERROR", $_SESSION["errors"]["phone"]);
  $template->parseCurrentBlock("mandatoryerror");
}
$template->setCurrentBlock("mandatoryinput");
$template->setVariable("MINPUTSIZE", 20);
$template->parseCurrentBlock("mandatoryinput");

$template->setCurrentBlock();
$template->parseCurrentBlock();
$template->show();
?>
```

Example 10-6. The template to display the phonebook form

```
<!DOCTYPE HTML PUBLIC
               "-//W3C//DTD HTML 4.01 Transitional//EN"
               "http://www.w3.org/TR/html401/loose.dtd">
<html>
<head>
  <meta http-equiv="Content-Type" content="text/html; charset=iso-8859-1">
  <title>Phonebook Details</title>
</head>
<body bgcolor="white">
<form method="post" action="example.10-4.php">
<h1>Phonebook Details</h1>
<h2>{MESSAGE}.
    Fields shown in <font color="red">red</font> are mandatory.</h2>
<table>
```

Example 10-6. The template to display the phonebook form (continued)

```
<!-- BEGIN mandatoryinput -->
<tr>
<!-- BEGIN mandatoryerror -->
  <td>
  <td><font color="red">{MINPUTERROR}</font>
</tr>
<tr>
<!-- END mandatoryerror -->
  <td><font color="red">{MINPUTTEXT}:</font></td>
  <td>
  <input type="text" name="{MINPUTNAME}" value="{MINPUTVALUE}"
         size={MINPUTSIZE}>
  </td>
</tr>
<!-- END mandatoryinput -->
<tr>
  <td><input type="submit" value="{SUBMITVALUE}"></td>
</tr>
</table>
</form>
</body>
</html>
```

When to Use Sessions

So far in this chapter we've described how to implement stateful applications using sessions, but we have not discussed when you should or should not use them. Sessions allow some kinds of applications to be developed that otherwise would be difficult to implement on the Web. However, because HTTP is a stateless protocol, building a stateful application can present problems and restrictions. Avoiding the need to maintain state information is often a desirable goal. In this section, we list some reasons sessions are used and some reasons to avoid them.

Reasons to Use Sessions

Sessions can be used in web database applications for several reasons. Many traditional database applications use sessions to help control user interaction, while other applications use sessions to reduce server processing.

Performance

In a stateless environment, an application may need to repeat a computationally expensive or slow operation. An example might be a financial calculation that requires many SQL statements and calls to mathematics libraries before displaying the results on several web pages. An application that uses a session variable to remember the result exposes the user, and the server, to the cost of the calculation only once.

Sequence of interaction

Often a web database application needs to present a series of screens in a controlled order. One style of application (known as a *wizard*) guides a user through what would otherwise be a complex task using a sequence of screens. Wizards are sometimes used for complex configurations, such as some software installations, and often alter the flow of screens based on user input.

Intermediate results

Many web database applications validate data before creating or updating a row in the database, preventing erroneous data from being saved. Sessions can keep the intermediate data, so that incomplete data can be corrected when errors are detected. Earlier in this chapter, we used sessions to improve the interaction between the phonebook entry form and its validation script. In the case study, the fields entered by the user are held in an array as a session variable until the validation is successful.

Another example where intermediate results can be used is when a database application collects and validates data for a single row over several fill-in forms. We show you an example in Chapter 19 for the ordering process of our online winestore.

Personalization

Sessions can be used to personalize a web site by tracking a user's preferences. For example, a user might specify a background color, layout preferences, or their interests. This information is then saved in the session store, and can be accessed by all scripts to personalize the application. In addition, the information might be saved in a database when the user logs out and restored later when they log in again.

Reasons to Avoid Sessions

The reasons to avoid sessions focus mainly on the stateless nature of HTTP. HTTP provides many features that enhance the performance and robustness of web browsing, and these are often limited by the requirements of a stateful application.

Need for centralized session store

In an application that uses sessions, each HTTP request needs to be processed in the context of the session variables to which that request belongs. The state information recorded as the result of one request needs to be available to subsequent requests. Most applications that implement sessions store session variables at the web server. Once a session is created, all subsequent requests must be processed on the web server that holds the session variables. This requirement prevents such applications from using HTTP to distribute requests across multiple servers and therefore can't easily scale horizontally to handle large numbers of requests.

One way for a web database application to allow multiple web servers is to store session variables in the database tier. This approach is described in Appendix F, where we provide a PHP and MySQL implementation of a database-tier session store.

Performance

When a server that offers session management processes a request, identifying and accessing session variables introduces unavoidable overhead. The session overhead results in longer processing times for requests, which affects the performance and capacity of a site. While sessions can improve application performance (for example, a session can keep the result of an expensive operation) the gains may be limited and outweighed by the extra processing required.

You can configure PHP session management to store session variables in memory, however as the amount of memory used by the web server grows, a system may need to move portions of memory to disk through an operation known as *swapping*. Swapping memory in and out of disk storage is slow and can severely degrade the performance of a server. Servers that use files—such as the default PHP session management—incur the cost of reading and writing a file on disk each time a session is accessed.

Timeouts

Sessions can also cause synchronization problems. Because HTTP is stateless, there is no way of knowing when a user has really finished with an application. Other network applications can catch the fact that a connection has been dropped and clean up the state that was held on behalf of that user, even if the user did not use a logout procedure (such as typing exit or clicking on a logout button).

In the Telnet application, a user makes a connection to a system over the Internet. However, unlike HTTP, the TCP/IP connection for Telnet is kept for the length of the session, and if the connection is lost—say, if the client's PC crashes or the power is lost—the user is logged out of the remote system. With a session over the Web, the server doesn't know about these events and has to make a decision as to how long to keep the session information. In the case of PHP session management, a garbage collection scheme is used; garbage collection is discussed in the next section.

Bookmark restrictions

Because HTTP is stateless, browsers allow users to save URLs as a list of bookmarks or favorite sites. The user can return to a web site at a later date by simply selecting a bookmarked URL. Web sites that provide weather forecasts, stock prices, and even search results from a web search engine are examples of the sites a user might want to bookmark. Consider the URL for a fictional site that provides stock prices:

```
http://www.someexchange.com/stockprice.php?code=TLS
```

The URL encodes a query that identifies a particular stock, and presumably, the script stockprice.php uses the query to display the current stock price of the company. The URL can be bookmarked because it contains all that is needed to generate the stock price page for the given company code.

Bookmarking can fail when sessions are used in the script that's bookmarked. For example, if a user bookmarks a session-based stock price page and comes back in a week, the session that stored the company details is unlikely to still exist, and the script fails to display the desired company's stock price.

When you develop an application, you need to be aware that users frequently bookmark pages that use sessions. To deal with this, you need to gracefully handle a user unexpectedly arriving at a page when their session has been destroyed. For example, you might check if a session variable is set and, if not, you might redirect the user to the log in page. We show you how to do this in Chapter 11.

Security

Sessions can provide a way for an intruder to break into a system. Sessions can be open to hijacking; an intruder can take over after a legitimate user has logged into an application. There is much debate about the security of session-based applications on the Web, and we discuss some issues of session security in Chapter 11.

PHP Session API and Configuration

This section describes the PHP Session Management API and Configuration parameters. We also discuss how to configure PHP to use sessions without cookies, and how PHP garbage collection removes old unused session files.

Functions for Accessing Sessions in PHP

In this section we list the key functions used to build session-based applications in PHP. By accessing session variables using the $_SESSION array, you can write complete session-based applications using just four functions:

Boolean session_start()

> Creates a new session, or finds an existing one. Checks for a session ID in the HTTP request—either as a cookie or a GET variable named PHPSESSID. If a session ID isn't included in the request, or an identified session isn't found, a new session is created. If a session ID is included in the request, and a session isn't found, a new session is created using the session ID encoded in the request. When an existing session is found, the session variables are read from the session store and initialized. Using PHP's default settings, a new session is created as a file in the */tmp* directory. This function always returns true.

string session_id([string id])

Can be used in two ways: to return the session ID of an initialized session or to set the value of a session ID before a session is created. When used to return the session ID, the function must be called without arguments after a session has been initialized. When used to set the value of the session ID, the function must be called with the *id* as the parameter before the session has been initialized.

Boolean session_destroy()

Removes the session from the PHP session management. With PHP's default settings, a call to this function removes the session file from the */tmp* directory. Returns true if the session is successfully destroyed and false otherwise.

void session_readonly()

Initializes an existing session in read-only mode. This allows session variables to be read without PHP placing a write lock on the session store. This can improve performance if you expect simultaneous requests on the session; such is the case when a browser loads a HTML frame set and makes a parallel request for the framed pages.

Functions used when register_globals is enabled

PHP provides several functions that register variables in your code as session variables. Once registered, the values of these variables are tracked and automatically updated in the session store. However, as we have already shown, session variables can be set and accessed using the global array $_SESSION, and these functions need not be used. Also these functions should not be used if register_globals is disabled. We include a description of these functions because you are likely to find them used in older code:

Boolean session_register(mixed name [, mixed ...])

Registers one or more variables in the session store. Each argument is the name of a variable, or an array of variable names. Once a variable is registered, it becomes available to any script that identifies that session. Registering variables with this function calls the *session_start()* code internally if a session has not been initialized. Returns true if registration is successful and false otherwise.

Boolean session_is_registered(string variable_name)

Returns true if the variable *variable_name* has been registered with the current session and false otherwise. Older code would use this function to test if a variable is registered to determine if a script has created a new session or initialized an existing one.

Boolean session_unregister(string variable_name)

Unregisters the variable *variable_name* from the initialized session. Like the *session_register()* function, the argument is the name of the variable, not the variable itself. Unlike the *session_register()* function, the session needs to be initialized before calling this function. Once a variable has been removed from a session with this call, it is no longer available to other scripts that initialize the session. However, the variable is still available to the rest of the script that calls *session_unregister( )*. Returns true when the variable is unregistered and false otherwise.

void session_unset( )

Unsets the values of all session variables. This function doesn't unregister the actual session variables. A call to *session_is_registered( )* still returns true for the session variables that have been unset.

Session Management Without Cookies

While cookies are used in a large number of web sites around the world—including popular sites such as Amazon and Google—you may need to build session-based applications that don't rely on them. This section shows how your application code can pass the session ID encoded in the URL and avoid the need to set a cookie. We also discuss turning off cookies altogether. To begin, we look at what happens when cookie support is turned off.

No cookie?

A simple experiment that illustrates what happens when a user disables cookies is to request the script shown in Example 10-1 from a browser that has cookie support turned off. When repeated requests are made, the counter doesn't increment, and the session duration remains at zero seconds. Because a cookie isn't sent from the browser, PHP never looks for an existing session, but creates a new session each time the script is run. Some users configure their browsers to not accept cookies, so session-based applications should include an alternative communication mechanism.

Requests that don't contain the cookie can identify an existing session by setting the value of the session ID as a variable in the URL with the name PHPSESSID. For example, an initial request can be made to Example 10-1 with the URL:

```
http://localhost/example.10-1.php
```

This creates a session and its associated file.

Subsequent requests can be made that include the PHPSESSID in the URL as shown (we've truncated the session ID to fit on the page):

```
http://localhost/example.10-1.php?PHPSESSID=be20081806199800da22e24...
```

The response shows the counter set to 2 and the correct session duration. Repeated requests to this URL behave as expected: the counter increments, and the calculated duration increases.

If you write session-based applications to use the URL to identify sessions, the application doesn't fail for users who disable cookies. Applications can test if $_COOKIE["PHPSESSID"] is set and then start encoding the session ID in URLs, or just not use cookies at all.

Some browsers, such as Netscape, Mozilla, and Internet Explorer, share cookies across all windows or tabs that are running for the same user on the same machine. Because the cookies are shared, users cannot log into a web database application more than once and have independent sessions. If the session ID is stored in the URL, then this problem is solved.

There are some security issues with having the session ID encoded in the URL: session IDs can be stored in log files and bookmarks, and sessions can be shared amongst users. For example, if a users wants to share a session with another user, he can log in to the site and email the session URL to a friend who then has access to the session.

Including the session ID in URLs

Scripts that generate embedded links to pages that use session variables need to include a GET attribute named PHPSESSID in the URL. This can be done using the basic PHP string support and calls to *session_id( )*. For example:

```php
<?php
// Initialize the session
session_start();

// Generate the embedded URL to link to
// a page that processes an order
$orderUrl = "/order.php?PHPSESSID=" . session_id();
?>

<a href="<?php print $orderUrl ?>">Create Order</a>
```

To aid the creation of URLs that link to session-based scripts, PHP sets the constant SID to the session ID in a name=id format suitable to use as a URL query string. If no session has been initialized, PHP sets the value of SID to be a blank string. If a session is initialized, it sets the SID to a string containing the session ID in the form:

```
PHPSESSID=be20081806199800da22e24081964000
```

By including the value of SID when URLs are constructed, the hypertext links correctly identify the session. A link that points to a script that expects a session ID can be encoded like this:

```php
<?php
// Initialize the session
session_start( );
?>

<a href="/order.php?<?php print SID;?>">Create Order</a>
```

URL rewriting

As an alternative to writing code to formulate the session ID into the URL, PHP includes a URL *rewrite* feature that automatically modifies URLs embedded in HTML.

To activate this feature you need to set the parameter session.use_trans_sid in the *php.ini* file to 1. To activate the URL rewrite feature prior to PHP 4.2, the PHP source also needs to be configured with the --enable-trans-id directive and then recompiled.

After URL rewrite is activated, PHP parses the HTML generated by scripts and automatically alters embedded URLs to include the PHPSESSID query string. PHP allows you to specify which URLs to be rewritten in the url_rewriter.tags parameter in the *php.ini* file.

The URL rewrite feature has the disadvantage that extra processing is required to parse every page generated by a PHP script, and modify embedded URLs.

Turning off cookies

PHP session management can be instructed not to set the PHPSESSID cookie by changing the session.use_cookies parameter to 0 in the *php.ini* file. The session configuration parameters in the *php.ini* file are described later in this section.

Garbage Collection

While it is good practice to build applications that provide a way to end a session—such as with a logout script that makes a call to *session_destroy( )*—there is no guarantee that a user will log out by requesting the appropriate PHP script. PHP session management has a built-in garbage collection mechanism that ensures unused session files are eventually cleaned up. This is important for two reasons: it prevents the directory from filling up with session files that can cause performance to degrade and, more importantly, it reduces the risk of someone guessing session IDs (more on this later) and hijacking an old unused session.

There are three parameters that control garbage collection: session.gc_maxlifetime, session.gc_probability, and session.gc_dividend, all defined in the *php.ini* file. A garbage collection process is run when a session is initialized, for example, when *session_start( )* is called. The garbage collection process examines each session, and any sessions that have not been accessed for a specified period of time are removed. This period is specified as seconds of inactivity in the gc_maxlifetime parameter; the default value is 1,440 seconds, which is 24 minutes. The file-based session management uses the last access time of the file to determine if a session is to be destroyed.

If you are running PHP on Microsoft Windows and storing session files on a FAT file system, the last access time is not recorded when session variables are read. If a session is actively being read, but not updated for a period of gc_maxlifetime seconds, garbage collection may remove the session incorrectly. You can write your own session handlers to define when garbage collection removes old sessions. Appendix F shows how to write your own session handlers.

The garbage collection process can become expensive to run, especially in sites with high numbers of users, because the last accessed time of every session file must be examined. The parameters gc_probability and gc_dividend set the percentage probability that the garbage collection process will check for timed-out sessions. If gc_probability is set to 1 and gc_dividend is set to 100—the default settings—garbage collection occurs with a probability of 1 in 100.* Setting gc_probability to 100 ensures that sessions are examined for garbage collection with every session initialization. Depending on the requirements, some figure between these two extremes balances the needs of the application and performance. Unless a site is receiving less than 1,000 hits per day, you should set the probability quite low. For example, an application that receives 1,000 hits in a 10-hour period with a probability set to 10%, runs the garbage collection function, on average, once every 6 minutes. Setting the probability of running the garbage collection too high adds unnecessary processing load on the server.

Prior to PHP 4.3 probability was simply the value of gc_probability as a percentage; a value of 12 represented a 12% probability. The gc_dividend parameter allows probabilities to be set below 1%, which is useful for heavily loaded sites.

Configuration Parameters

Several parameters can be manipulated to change the behavior of the PHP session management. These parameters are set in the *php.ini* file under the heading [Session].

session.save_handler
> This parameter specifies the method used by PHP to store and retrieve session variables. The default value is files, to indicate the use of session files as described in the previous sections. The other values that this parameter can have are: mm to store and retrieve variables from shared memory, and user to store and retrieve variables with user-defined handlers. In Appendix F we show you how to create your own handlers to store session variables in a MySQL database. We don't recommend using the mm shared memory approach, as locking isn't correctly implemented to avoid the transaction problems discussed in Chapter 8.

session.save_path
> This parameter specifies the directory in which session files are saved when the session.save_handler is set to files. The default value is the temporary directory, /tmp. On Unix systems, you may want to use a directory only accessible to the owner of the Apache process to prevent other users reading session files. For Microsoft Windows systems, you will need to change this to an appropriate path. The specified directory must exist.

---

* Perhaps the gc_maxlifetime parameter should have been called gc_minlifetime, because the value represents the minimum time garbage collection permits an inactive session to exist. Remember that garbage collection is performed only when a request that initializes a session is made, and then only with the probability set by gc_probability.

As of PHP 4.0.1, you can modify the save path to store session files in deeper level sub-directories. This can improving efficiency for operating systems that don't perform well with large numbers of session files in a single directory. We don't discuss this in detail.

session.use_cookies

This parameter determines if PHP sets a cookie to hold the session ID. Setting this parameter to 0 stops PHP from setting cookies and may be considered for the reasons discussed in the previous section. The default value is 1, meaning that a cookie stores the session ID.

session.only_use_cookies

When this parameter is set to 1 PHP is prevented from overwriting the session ID set from a cookie with the value from URL, thereby improving the security of an application. This parameter was introduced in PHP 4.3 and has a default value of 0, which is also the default behavior in earlier versions of PHP. However, if you use this parameter and cookies are not enabled in sessions or in a user's browser, then sessions will not be able to be used.

session.name

This parameter controls the name of the cookie, GET attribute, or POST attribute that is used to hold the session ID. The default is PHPSESSID, and there is no reason to change this setting unless there is a name collision with another variable.

session.auto_start

With the default value of 0 for this setting, PHP initializes a session only when a session call such as *session_start( )* or *session_register( )* is made. If this parameter is set to 1, sessions are automatically initialized if a session ID is found in the request. Allowing sessions to autostart adds unnecessary overhead if session values aren't required for all scripts.

session.cookie_lifetime

This parameter holds the life of a session cookie in seconds and is used by PHP when setting the expiration date and time of a cookie. The default value of 0 sets up a session cookie that lasts only while the browser program is running. When a user quits their browser, their session is destroyed (and the user is logged out of the application).

Setting this value to a number of seconds other than 0 sets up the cookie with an expiration date and time. The expiration date and time of the cookie is set as an absolute date and time, calculated by adding the cookie_lifetime value to the current date and time on the server machine.*

---

* The actual expiration of the cookie is performed by the browser, which compares the expiration date and time of the cookie with the client machine's date and time. If the date and time are incorrectly set on the client, a cookie might expire immediately or persist longer than expected.

`session.cookie_path`

This parameter sets the valid path for a cookie. The default value is /, which means that browsers include the session cookie in requests for resources in all paths for the cookie's domain. Setting this value to the path of the session-based scripts can reduce the number of requests that need to include the cookie. For example, setting the parameter to /winestore on a server hosting the *www. webdatabasebook.com* domain instructs the browser to include the session cookie only with requests that start with *http://www.webdatabasebook.com/ winestore/*.

`session.cookie_domain`

This parameter can override the domain for which the cookie is valid. The default is a blank string, meaning that the cookie is set with the domain of the machine running the web server, and the browser includes the cookie only in requests sent to that domain.

`session.cookie_secure`

This parameter sets the secure flag of a cookie, which prevents a browser from sending the session cookie over non-encrypted connections. When this setting is 1, the browser sends the session cookie only over a network connection that is protected using the Secure Sockets Layer, SSL. Setting this parameter to 1 only makes sense when you have configured your Web server to use SSL. We discuss SSL in the next chapter and show how to install and configure Apache with SSL for Unix platforms in Appendixes A-C. The default value of 0 allows a browser to send the session cookie over encrypted and non-encrypted services. This parameter was added in PHP 4.0.4.

`session.serialize_handler`

This parameter sets up the method by which variables are serialized, that is, how they are converted into a stream of bytes suitable for the chosen session store. The default value is php, which indicates use of the standard PHP serialization functions. An alternative is wddx, which uses the WDDX libraries that encode variables as XML; the library is described in Appendix G.

`session.gc_probability` *and* `session.gc_dividend`

The probability that the garbage collection process will be performed when a session is initialized is the value of gc_probability divided by the value of gc_ dividend. The default values of 1 and 100 result in a 1% chance of garbage collection each time the collector runs. See the discussion in the previous section for a full explanation of garbage collection.

`session.gc_maxlifetime`

This parameter sets the life of a session in number of seconds. The default value is 1440, or 24 minutes. Garbage collection destroys a session that has been inactive for this period. See the discussion in the previous section for a full explanation of garbage collection.

`session.referer_check`

This parameter can restrict the creation of sessions to requests that have the HTTP Referer header field set. This is a useful feature if access to an application is allowed only by following a hypertext link from a particular page, such as a welcome page. If the HTTP Referer header of a request that is external to the host doesn't contain the value of this parameter, PHP creates a session, but the session is marked as invalid and unusable. Subsequent requests will fail to initialize session variables from the session. The default value of a blank string applies no restriction.

`session.entropy_file`

PHP generates the session IDs from a random number seeded by the system date and time. Because the algorithm is known—it can be looked up in the PHP source code—it makes guessing session IDs a little easier. If this parameter is set to the name of a file, the first n bytes from that file (where n is specified by the `session.entropy_length` parameter) are used to seed the random number generator, making the ID less predictable. The default value is left blank, meaning the default seeding method is used. On Unix systems, an alternative is to use */dev/urandom*, a special Unix device that produces a pseudo-random number.

`session.entropy_length`

This parameter is the number of bytes to use when generating a session ID from the file specified by `session.entropy_file`. The default value of 0 is required when no entropy file is set.

`session.cache_limiter`

This parameter controls how clients and proxy servers cache responses. Web applications—and especially session-based web applications—can be adversely affected when pages are cached. The default value of nocache prevents caching in both clients and proxy servers. Setting this parameter to public allows caching in both clients and proxy servers, while the value of private allow caching in the client only. PHP 4.2 allows the value private_no_expire in this parameter, which avoids problems in some browsers when the Expire header field is used to control caching. See Appendix D for more details about HTTP caching.

`session.cache_expire`

This parameter is used when caching is allowed; it sets the expiration date and time of the response to be the current system time plus the parameter value in minutes. The default value is 180.

`session.bug_compat_42` *and* `session.bug_compat_warn`

Prior to PHP 4.2, session variables could be initialized in the global scope, even when register_globals was disabled. While this is considered a bug, PHP allows code written with this behavior to run with bug_compat_42 set to 1 and provides warnings with bug_compat_warn set to 1 (the default values). Setting these parameters to 0 turns off compatibility and warnings respectively. If you are writing new code, we recommend that bug_compat_42 is set to 0.

CHAPTER 11

Authentication and Security

Many web database applications require restrictions to control user access. Some applications deal with sensitive information such as bank account details, while others only provide information or services to paying customers. These applications need to authenticate and authorize user requests, typically by collecting a username and password that are checked against a list of valid users. As well as authenticating those who have access to a service, web applications often need to protect the data that is transmitted over the Internet from those who shouldn't see it.

In this chapter, we show you the techniques used to build web database applications that authenticate and authorize users and protect the data that is transmitted over the Web. The topics covered in this chapter include:

- How HTTP authentication works and how it can be used with Apache and PHP
- Writing PHP scripts to manage user authentication and authorization
- Authorizing access from an IP address or a range of IP addresses
- Writing PHP scripts that authenticate users against a table in a database
- The practical aspects of building session-based web database applications to authenticate users, including techniques that don't use HTTP authentication
- A case study example that develops an authentication framework, demonstrating many of the techniques presented in this chapter
- The features of the encryption services provided by the Secure Sockets Layer

HTTP Authentication

This section assumes an understanding of HTTP. If you're not familiar with it, you'll find an introduction in Appendix D.

The HTTP standard provides support to authenticate and authorize user access. When a browser sends an HTTP request for a resource that requires authentication, a server can challenge the request by sending a response with the status code of 401

Unauthorized. When it receives an unauthorized response, the browser presents a dialog box that collects a username and password; a dialog box presented by a Mozilla browser is shown in Figure 11-1. After the username and password have been entered, the browser then resends the original request with an extra header field that encodes the user credentials.

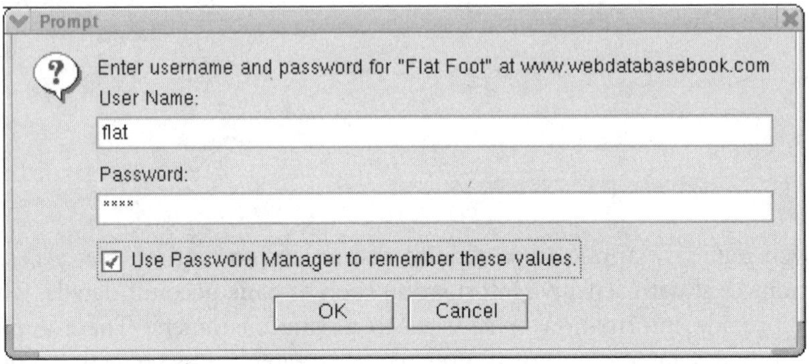

Figure 11-1. Mozilla requests a username and password

The HTTP header just collects the name and password; it doesn't authenticate a user or provide authorization to access a resource or service. The server must use the encoded username and password to decide if the user is authorized to receive the requested resource. For example, you might configure your Apache web server to require authentication by using a file that contains a list of usernames and encrypted passwords. In another application, you might use a table of usernames and passwords stored in a database and develop PHP code for the authentication process.

How HTTP Authentication Works

Figure 11-2 shows the interaction between a web browser and a web server when a request is challenged. The user requests a resource stored on the server that requires authentication and the server sends back a challenge response with the status code set to 401 Unauthorized. Included in this response is the header field WWW-Authenticate that contains parameters that instruct the browser on how to meet the challenge. The browser may then need to prompt for a username and password to meet the challenge. The browser then resends the request, including the Authorization header field that contains the credentials the server requires.

The following is an example of an HTTP response sent from an Apache server when a request is made for a resource that requires authentication:

```
HTTP/1.1 401 Authorization Required
Date: Thu, 2 Dec 2004 23:40:54 GMT
Server: Apache/2.0.48 (Unix) PHP/5.0.0
WWW-Authenticate: Basic realm="Marketing Secret"
```

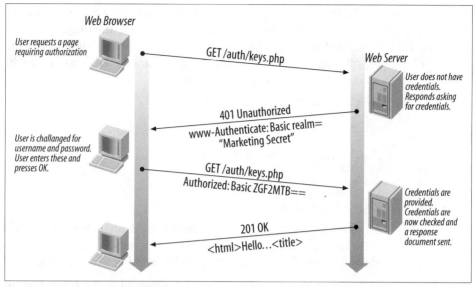

Figure 11-2. The sequence of HTTP requests and responses when an unauthorized page is requested

```
Connection: close
Content-Type: text/html; charset=iso-8859-1

<!DOCTYPE HTML PUBLIC "-//W3C//DTD HTML 4.01 Transitional//EN"
                      "http://www.w3.org/TR/html401/loose.dtd">
<html>
<head>
  <meta http-equiv="Content-Type" content="text/html; charset=iso-8859-1">
  <title>401 Authorization Required</title>
</head>
<body>
<h1>Authorization Required</h1>
This server could not verify that you
are authorized to access the document
requested. Either you supplied the wrong
credentials (e.g., bad password), or your
browser doesn't understand how to supply
the credentials required.
<p><hr>
</body>
</html>
```

The WWW-Authenticate header field contains the *challenge method*, instructing the browser how to collect and encode the user credentials. In the example, the method is set to Basic. The header also contains the name of the *realm* that the authentication applies to, in this case *Marketing Secret*. The realm is used by the browser as a key for a username and password pair, and it is also displayed when the credentials are collected.

Figure 11-1 shows the dialog displayed for the realm *Marketing Secret*. Once the browser has collected the credentials from the user, it resends the original request with an additional Authorization header field that contains the credentials. The following is an example of an HTTP request that contains credentials in the Authorization header field:

```
GET /auth/keys.php HTTP/1.1
Connection: Keep-Alive
User-Agent: Mozilla/4.51 [en] (WinNT; I)
Host: localhost
Accept: image/gif, image/jpeg, image/pjpeg, image/png, */*
Accept-Encoding: gzip
Accept-Language: en
Accept-Charset: iso-8859-1,*,utf-8
Authorization: Basic ZGF2ZTpwbGFOeXB1cw==
```

A browser can automatically respond to a challenge if credentials have previously been collected for the realm, and it will continue to include authorization credentials with requests until the browser program is terminated or another realm is entered.

The Basic encoding method sends the username and password in the Authorization header field after applying base-64 encoding. Base-64 encoding isn't designed to protect data and so isn't a form of encryption: it simply allows binary data to be transmitted over a network At best, it protects data from only casual inspection.

Some web servers, including Apache, support the Digest encoding method. The Digest method is more secure than the Basic method because the user's password isn't sent over the network. However, to use it, the browser must also include support. The major browsers that support digest authentication are Opera, Microsoft Internet Explorer, Amaya, Mozilla, and Netscape. Therefore, because digest authentication is not as widely implemented as basic authentication, you should use it only when you have control over your users' browser choice.

While the Basic encoding method provides no real security, the Secure Sockets Layer (SSL) protocol can protect the HTTP requests and responses sent between browsers and servers. This means that SSL also provides protection for the usernames and passwords sent with the Basic method. Therefore, for web database applications that transmit sensitive information, we recommend SSL be used. We discuss SSL later in this chapter.

Using Apache to Authenticate

The simplest method to restrict access to an application is to use your web server's built-in authentication support. The Apache web server can easily be configured to use HTTP authentication to protect the resources it serves. For example, Apache allows authentication to be set up on a directory-by-directory basis by adding parameters to the Directory setting in the *httpd.conf* configuration file.

The following example shows part of an *httpd.conf* file that protects the resources (such as HTML files, PHP scripts, images, and so on) stored in the */usr/local/apache/htdocs/auth* directory:

```
# Set up an authenticated directory
<Directory "/usr/local/apache/htdocs/auth">
  AuthType Basic
  AuthName "Secret Mens Business"
  AuthUserFile /usr/local/apache/allow.users
  require hugh, dave, jim
</Directory>
```

If you're using Microsoft Windows, you can replace */usr/local/apache/htdocs/auth* with a directory such as *C:\Program Files\EasyPHP1-7\www\auth*. On a Mac OS X platform, use a directory such as */Library/WebServer/Documents/auth*. In all cases, the *auth* directory must exist.

A user must pass the Apache authentication before access is given to resources—including PHP scripts—placed in an authenticated directory. The Apache server responds with a challenge to unauthorized requests for any resources in the protected directory. The AuthType is set to Basic to indicate the method used to authenticate the username and password collected from the browser, and the AuthName is set to the name of the realm. Apache authorizes users who are listed in the require setting by checking the username and password against those held in the file listed after the AuthUserFile directive. There are other parameters that aren't discussed here; you should refer to the Apache references listed in Appendix G for full configuration details.

If you don't have administrator or root access to your web server machine, you can still protect a directory (or selected resources in a directory). You do this by creating an *.htaccess* file in the directory you want to protect and include in it what resources are protected, who has access to them, and where to find the passwords. It's easy to use PHP to protect resources—as we discuss in the next section—we don't discuss this process in detail. You can find more information at *http://httpd.apache.org/docs-2.0/howto/htaccess.html*.

For many web database applications, Apache authentication provides a simple solution. However, when usernames and passwords need to be checked against a database, or when HTTP authentication can't meet the needs of the application, authentication can be managed by PHP instead. The next section describes how PHP can manage HTTP authentication directly without configuring Apache. Later, we also describe how to provide authentication without using HTTP.

HTTP Authentication with PHP

Writing PHP scripts to manage the authentication process allows for flexible authorization logic. For example, an application might apply restrictions based on group membership: a user in the finance department gets to see the reports from the budget database, while others can't. In another application, a user of a subscription-based service might supply a correct username and password, but be denied access when a fee is 14 days overdue. Or, access might be denied on Thursday evenings during Australian Eastern Standard Time when system maintenance is performed.

PHP scripts give you more control over the authentication process than Apache files or configuration. In this section, we show you how PHP scripts can use authentication credentials, and how to develop simple, flexible authentication scripts that use HTTP.

Accessing User Credentials

When PHP processes a request that contains user credentials encoded in the Authorized header field, access is provided to those credentials through the superglobal variable $_SERVER. The element $_SERVER["PHP_AUTH_USER"] holds the username that's supplied by the user, and $_SERVER["PHP_AUTH_PW"] holds the password.

The script shown in Example 11-1 reads the authentication superglobal variables and displays them in the body of the response. In practice, you wouldn't display them back to the user because it's insecure—we've just done this to illustrate how they can be accessed. Instead, you'd use the credentials to authenticate the user, and allow or deny access to the application. We explain how to do this in the next section.

For the PHP code in Example 11-1 to display the authentication credentials, the script needs to be requested after a user has been challenged for a username and password. For example, the challenge can be triggered by placing the script file in a directory configured by Apache to require authentication as discussed in the previous section. The use of the superglobal variables doesn't trigger authentication, it just provides access to the values the user has provided.

Example 11-1. PHP access to authentication

```
<!DOCTYPE HTML PUBLIC
                "-//W3C//DTD HTML 4.01 Transitional//EN"
                "http://www.w3.org/TR/html401/loose.dtd">
<html>
<head>
  <meta http-equiv="Content-Type" content="text/html; charset=iso-8859-1">
  <title>Authentication</title>
</head>
<body>
<?php
  if (isset($_SERVER["PHP_AUTH_USER"]))
    print "<h2>Hi there {$_SERVER["PHP_AUTH_USER"]}</h2>";
  else
    print "You need to be authenticated for this to work!";

  if (isset($_SERVER["PHP_AUTH_PW"]))
    print "<p>Thank you for your password {$_SERVER["PHP_AUTH_PW"]}!";
```

Example 11-1. PHP access to authentication (continued)

```
?>
</body>
</html>
```

With access to the authentication header field information, simple applications that rely on identifying the user can be developed. For example, an application that charges on a per-page view basis might use the $_SERVER["PHP_AUTH_USER"] variable when recording an access to a particular page. In this way, Apache can provide the authentication, and the application records the users' behavior.

While this simple approach to developing an application removes the need to write any PHP code to implement authentication, users and passwords need to be maintained in an Apache password file. In the next section, we describe how to manage HTTP authentication from within a PHP script, thus relieving Apache of authentication responsibilities and allowing more complex logic to be applied to request authorization.

Managing HTTP Authentication with PHP

PHP scripts can manage the HTTP authentication challenges. To do this, you check if the variables $_SERVER["PHP_AUTH_USER"] and $_SERVER["PHP_AUTH_PW"] are set. If they're not, the user hasn't been authenticated and you send a response containing the WWW-Authenticate header to the browser. If the variables are set, the user has answered the challenge, and you check them against the credentials stored in the script using any logic that's required. If the user's credentials match those stored in the script, the user is allowed to use the script; if not, the challenge is sent again to the browser.

In Example 11-2, the user credentials are passed to the function *authenticated( )*. This function uses the unsophisticated authentication scheme of checking that the password matches one that's hard-coded into the script and, if so, it allows the user to access the application. To test the script, you can use any username and the password kwAlIphIdE (the case is important). The template that's used with the example is shown in Example 11-3.

Example 11-2. A script that generates an unauthorized response

```php
<?php
require_once "HTML/Template/ITX.php";
require "db.inc";

function authenticated($username, $password)
{
  // If either the username or the password are
  // not set, the user is not authenticated
  if (!isset($username) || !isset($password))
    return false;
```

Example 11-2. A script that generates an unauthorized response (continued)

```
  // Is the password correct?
  // If so, the user is authenticated
  if ($password == "kwAlIphIdE")
    return true;
  else
    return false;
}

$template = new HTML_Template_ITX("./templates");
$template->loadTemplatefile("example.11-3.tpl", true, true);

$username = shellclean($_SERVER, "PHP_AUTH_USER", 20);
$password = shellclean($_SERVER, "PHP_AUTH_PW", 20);

if(!authenticated($username, $password))
{
  // No credentials found - send an unauthorized
  // challenge response
  header("WWW-Authenticate: Basic realm=\"Flat Foot\"");
  header("HTTP/1.1 401 Unauthorized");

  // Set up the body of the response that is
  // displayed if the user cancels the challenge
  $template->touchBlock("challenge");
  $template->show( );
  exit;
}
else
{
  // Welcome the user now they're authenticated
  $template->touchBlock("authenticated");
  $template->show( );
}
?>
```

Example 11-3. The template that's used with Example 11-2

```
<!DOCTYPE HTML PUBLIC
            "-//W3C//DTD HTML 4.01 Transitional//EN"
            "http://www.w3.org/TR/html401/loose.dtd">
<html>
<head>
  <meta http-equiv="Content-Type" content="text/html; charset=iso-8859-1">
  <title>Web Database Applications</title>
</head>
<body>
<!-- BEGIN challenge -->
  <h2>You need a username and password to access this service</h2>
  <p>If you have lost or forgotten your password, tough!
<!-- END challenge -->
<!-- BEGIN authenticated -->
  <h2>Welcome!</h2>
```

Example 11-3. The template that's used with Example 11-2 (continued)

```
<!-- END authenticated -->
</body>
</html>
```

The *authenticated()* function returns false if either the $username or $password hasn't been set, or if the password isn't equal to the string kwAlIphIdE. If the user credentials fail the test, the script responds with the header field WWW-Authenticate, and sets the encoding scheme to Basic and the realm name to Flat Foot. It also includes the status code 401 Unauthorized. The PHP manual suggests sending the WWW-Authenticate response line before the HTTP/1.1 401 Unauthorized response line to avoid problems with some versions of the Internet Explorer browser.

The first time a browser requests this page, the script sends the challenge response containing the 401 Unauthorized header field. If the user cancels the authentication challenge, usually by clicking the Cancel button in a dialog box that collects the credentials, the HTML encoded in the challenge response is displayed. When they provide the correct credentials (a username and the password kwAlIphIdE), a welcome message is displayed. If they don't provide the correct credentials and don't press Cancel, the authentication dialog is redisplayed until they do.

Limiting Access by IP Address

Sometimes it's useful to limit access to an application, or part of an application, to users who are on a particular network or using a particular machine. For example, access to administrative functions in an application could be restricted to a single machine, or the latest version of your application could be limited to only those users in the testing department. In PHP, implementing this type of restriction is straightforward: you can check the IP address of the machine from which a request was sent by inspecting the variable $_SERVER["REMOTE_ADDR"]. You can do the same thing in Apache, but we don't discuss that here. (In addition, IP addresses can also be used to help prevent session hijacking, a problem discussed later in this chapter.)

The script shown in Example 11-4 allows access for users who have machines on a particular network subnet. The script limits access to the main content of the script to requests sent from clients with a range of IP addresses that begins with 141.190.17. Because that is just the start of an address, we test just the first 10 characters. The template used with the example is shown in Example 11-5.

Example 11-4. PHP script that forbids access from browsers outside an IP subnet

```
<?php
require_once "HTML/Template/ITX.php";

$template = new HTML_Template_ITX("./templates");
$template->loadTemplatefile("example.11-5.tpl", true, true);
```

Example 11-4. PHP script that forbids access from browsers outside an IP subnet (continued)

```
if(strncmp("141.190.17", $_SERVER["REMOTE_ADDR"], 10) != 0)
{
  // Not allowed
  header("HTTP/1.1 403 Forbidden");
  $template->touchBlock("noaccess");
  $template->show( );
  exit;
}
else
{
  // Allowed
  $template->touchBlock("authenticated");
  $template->show( );
}
?>
```

Example 11-5. The template used with Example 11-4

```
<!DOCTYPE HTML PUBLIC
             "-//W3C//DTD HTML 4.01 Transitional//EN"
             "http://www.w3.org/TR/html401/loose.dtd">
<html>
<head>
  <meta http-equiv="Content-Type" content="text/html; charset=iso-8859-1">
  <title>Web Database Applications</title>
</head>
<body>
<!-- BEGIN noaccess -->
<h2>403 Forbidden</h2>
<p>You cannot access this page from outside the Marketing Department.
<!-- END noaccess -->
<!-- BEGIN authenticated -->
<h2>Marketing secrets!</h2>
<p>Need new development team - the old one says <i>No</i> far too often.
<!-- END authenticated -->
</body>
</html>
```

There are several HTTP status codes that are appropriate to use when denying access to a user. In the previous section, we used the response code of 401 Unauthorized to control HTTP authentication. However, the response status code of 403 Forbidden is more appropriate if an explanation as to why access has been denied is required and this is used in Example 11-4. The HTTP/1.1 standard describes 17 4xx status codes that have various meanings. The infamous 404 Not Found is returned by Apache if the requested resource doesn't exist, and a PHP script can return this code if the exact reason for the refusal needs to be hidden.

Authentication Using a Database

In this section, we show you how scripts can authenticate by querying a database table that contains usernames and passwords. Because users' credentials are sensitive information, we show how to protect passwords with encryption, and how the encrypted password is used in the authentication process.

Creating a database and table

To demonstrate the principles of using a database to manage authentication, we need a table that stores usernames and passwords, and we need a user who can access the database and the table. It's important to note that these are two different issues: the database table is used to store the usernames and passwords for the users of our application, while the MySQL database user is just used in our PHP scripts to read and write data to the database. We set up the database, table, and the MySQL account in this section.

In our examples in the remainder of the chapter, we use an *authentication* database that contains a *users* table. To create both, you need to log in as the MySQL root user and type the following into the MySQL command interpreter:

```
mysql> create database authentication;
Query OK, 1 row affected (0.05 sec)

mysql> use authentication;
Database changed
mysql> CREATE TABLE users (
    ->    user_name char(50) NOT NULL,
    ->    password char(32) NOT NULL,
    ->    PRIMARY KEY (user_name)
    -> ) type=MyISAM;
Query OK, 0 rows affected (0.02 sec)
```

The *users* table defines two attributes: user_name and password. The user_name must be unique and is defined as the primary key.

It's also necessary to have a MySQL user that has access to this database. You can create a user lucy with a password secret using the following statement, again entered into the MySQL command interpreter:

```
mysql> GRANT SELECT, INSERT, UPDATE, DELETE ON authentication.users TO
    -> lucy@127.0.0.1 IDENTIFIED BY 'secret';
Query OK, 0 rows affected (0.00 sec)
```

The syntax of this statement is discussed in Chapter 15. We use the user lucy in our scripts in the remainder of the chapter.

Protecting passwords

Storing user passwords as plain text represents a security risk because insiders, external hackers, and others may gain access to a database. Therefore, a common practice is to encrypt the password using a non-reversible, one-way encryption algorithm and store the encrypted version in the database. The encrypted version is then used in the authentication process. (One-way or asymmetric encryption is discussed later in this chapter.)

The process of protecting a password works as follows. First, a new username and password are collected from the user. Then, the password is encrypted and a new row is inserted into the *users* table that contains the plain text username and the encrypted password. Later, when the user returns and wants to log in to the application, they provide their username and password. The password provided by the user is encrypted, the row is retrieved from the *users* table that matches the provided username, and the encrypted version of the password supplied by the user is compared to the encrypted version stored in the table. If the username and encrypted passwords match, the credentials are correct and the user passes the authentication.

PHP provides two functions that can be used for one-way encryption of passwords. We define the functions next, and then show you examples that explain their behavior in more detail.

string crypt(string message [, string salt])
> On most platforms, this function returns an encrypted string that's calculated with a popular (if somewhat old) encryption algorithm known as *DES*. The plain text *message* to be encrypted is supplied as the first argument, with an optional second argument used to *salt* the DES encryption algorithm. By default, only the first eight characters of the *message* are encrypted, and the *salt* is a two-character string used by DES to make the encrypted string harder to crack. PHP generates a random salt if one isn't provided. The first two characters of the returned value is the salt used in the encryption process.
>
> As we show later, a salt is used to help prevent two passwords that are identical being encrypted to the same string. The salt and the password are both inputs to the encryption function and, therefore, when two passwords are the same but have different salts, the output is different. To encrypt another string to test if it's the same as the encrypted string, you need to know what salt was used so that you can re-use it. For this reason, the salt is returned as the first two characters of the encrypted string.
>
> This function is one-way: the returned value can't be decrypted back into the original string.
>
> Several PHP constants control the encryption process, and the default behavior is assumed in the description we've provided. However, on some platforms, the internals of the function actually use the MD5 approach discussed next or the salt can be longer. You should consult the PHP manual for more details.

string md5(string message)
> Returns a 32-character *message digest* calculated from the source *message* using the RSA Data Security, Inc. MD5 Message Digest Algorithm (*http://www.faqs.org/*

rfcs/rfc1321.html.). A digest is a 32-character fingerprint or signature of a message, and is not an encrypted representation of the message itself. The MD5 message digest is calculated by examining the whole message, and messages that differ by a single character produce very different digest results. Like the *crypt()* function, *md5()* is one-way.

It is impossible to generate the original message from a digest. The digest of the message is always 32 characters, and it's not an encrypted representation of the message. Instead, it's a string that's calculated from the message that is almost guaranteed to be unique to that message.

This function is widely supported on most platforms, and should be used in preference to *crypt()* for code that needs to be portable. Note that MD5 message digests and Apache's Digest authentication are unrelated concepts.

Example 11-6 shows how *crypt()* and *md5()* are used. The script generates the following output:

```
md5(aardvark7) = 94198c7f71931fdeb0a7f4b75a603586
crypt(aardvark7, 'aa') = aaE/1j3.0Ky/Y
crypt(aardvark7, 'bb') = bbptug8K4z6vA

md5(aardvark8) = 4a68f92613baa5202d523134e768db13
crypt(aardvark8, 'aa') = aaE/1j3.0Ky/Y
crypt(aardvark8, 'bb') = bbptug8K4z6vA
```

Example 11-6. Using crypt() and md5()

```
<!DOCTYPE HTML PUBLIC
                "-//W3C//DTD HTML 4.01 Transitional//EN"
                "http://www.w3.org/TR/html401/loose.dtd">
<html>
<head>
  <meta http-equiv="Content-Type" content="text/html; charset=iso-8859-1">
  <title>Passwords</title>
</head>
<body>
<?php
$passwords = array();
$passwords[] = "aardvark7";
$passwords[] = "aardvark8";

foreach($passwords as $password)
{
  print "\n<p> md5({$password}) = " . md5($password);
  print "\n<br> crypt({$password}, 'aa') = " . crypt($password, "aa");
  print "\n<br> crypt({$password}, 'bb') = " . crypt($password, "bb");
}
?>
</body>
</html>
```

Both functions have advantages and disadvantages:

- *md5()* works with strings of any length. It returns a fixed-length string of 32 characters that's different if the input strings are different. It differentiates between aardvark7 and aardvark8 in Example 11-6 as one would expect.

- *crypt()* uses only the first eight characters of a password and a salt to calculate the encrypted string and so, if the first eight characters and the salt are the same, the encrypted strings are the same. In Example 11-6, it does not differentiate between aardvark7 and aardvark8 when the salt is the same.

- The salt in *crypt()* adds a useful extra feature that isn't automatically supported by *md5()*: when the string is encrypted with a different salt string, it produces a different encrypted text even when two users have chosen the same password. In Example 11-6, the result of encrypting aardvark7 with the salts aa and bb is a very different string.

A common strategy is to use the first two characters of the username as the salt to *crypt()*. In general, this results in different encrypted strings even if the users choose the same password, because it's unlikely they'd also have the same first two characters in their username. If you want to salt the *md5()* input, you could pass both the username (or part of the username) and the password to the *md5()* function by concatenating the strings.

The *users* table has been defined to store the 32-character result of the *md5()* function. The following fragment of code shows how the password is protected using the *md5()* function and a new user is inserted into the *users* table.

```
function newUser($connection, $username, $password)
{
  // Create the digest of the password
  $stored_password = md5(trim($password));

  // Insert the user row
  $query = "INSERT INTO users SET password = '$stored_password',
                               user_name = '$username'";

  if (!$result = @ mysql_query ($query, $connection))
    showerror();
}
```

The function expects three parameters: a MySQL database connection that has the *authentication* database as the selected database, a plain text username, and a plain text password. In the next section, we show you how to authenticate a user by comparing a password that's provided by the user to the stored password. Later in this chapter, we show you how passwords are updated in the *users* table as part of a complete authentication framework.

Because both *crypt()* and *md5()* are one-way, after a password is stored, there is no way to read back the original value. This prevents desirable features such as reminding a user of his forgotten password. However, importantly, it prevents all but the most determined attempts to get access to the passwords.

Authenticating

When a script needs to authenticate a username and password collected from an authentication challenge, it needs to check the credentials against the database. To do this, the user-supplied password is encrypted, and then a query is executed to find a row in the *users* table that has a matching username and encrypted password. If a row is found, the user is valid.

Example 11-7 shows the *authenticateUser()* function that validates credentials. The function is called by passing in a handle to a connected MySQL server that has the *authentication* database selected and the username and password collected from the authentication challenge. The script begins by testing $username and $password, and if either variable is not set, the function returns false. The script then constructs a SELECT query to search the *users* table using $username and the digest of $password created using the *md5()* function. The query is executed and if a row is found, the $username and $password have been authenticated, and the function returns true.

Example 11-7. Authenticating a user against an encrypted password in the users table

```php
<?php

function authenticateUser($connection, $username, $password)
{
  // Test the username and password parameters
  if (!isset($username) || !isset($password))
    return false;

  // Create a digest of the password collected from
  // the challenge
  $password_digest = md5(trim($password));

  // Formulate the SQL find the user
  $query = "SELECT password FROM users WHERE user_name = '{$username}'
            AND password = '{$password_digest}'";

  if (!$result = @ mysql_query ($query, $connection))
    showerror();

  // exactly one row? then we have found the user
  if (mysql_num_rows($result) != 1)
    return false;
  else
    return true;
}
?>
```

The *authenticateUser()* function is likely to be used in many scripts, so it's useful to store it in a require file. For example, if the code is stored in the file *authentication. inc*, we could rewrite Example 11-4 to use the database authentication function by requiring the file. The rewritten version is shown in Example 11-8.

Example 11-8. A rewritten version of Example 11-4 that uses database authentication

```php
<?php
require "authentication.inc";
require "db.inc";
require_once "HTML/Template/ITX.php";

$template = new HTML_Template_ITX("./templates");
$template->loadTemplatefile("example.11-3.tpl", true, true);

if (!($connection = mysql_connect("localhost", "lucy", "secret")))
    die("Could not connect to database");

if (!mysql_selectdb("authentication", $connection))
    showerror();

$username = mysqlclean($_SERVER, "PHP_AUTH_USER", 50, $connection);
$password = mysqlclean($_SERVER, "PHP_AUTH_PW", 32, $connection);

if (!authenticateUser($connection, $username, $password))
{
  // No credentials found - send an unauthorized
  // challenge response
  header("WWW-Authenticate: Basic realm=\"Flat Foot\"");
  header("HTTP/1.1 401 Unauthorized");

  // Set up the body of the response that is
  // displayed if the user cancels the challenge
  $template->touchBlock("challenge");
  $template->show();
  exit;
}
else
{
  // Welcome the user now they're authenticated
  $template->touchBlock("authenticated");
  $template->show();
}
?>
```

Encrypting other data in a database

The PHP *crypt()* and *md5()* functions can be used only to store passwords, personal identification numbers (PINs), and so on. These functions are one-way: after the original password is encrypted and stored, you can't get it back (in fact, as discussed previously, an *md5()* return value is a signature or fingerprint and not an encrypted copy of the message). Therefore, these functions can't be used to store sensitive information that an application needs to retrieve. For example, you can't use them to store and retrieve credit card details or to encrypt a sensitive document.

To store sensitive information, you need two-way functions that use a secret key to encrypt and decrypt the data. One significant problem when using a key to encrypt and decrypt data is the need to securely manage the key. The issue of key management is beyond the scope of this book, however we discuss encryption briefly in the section "Protecting Data on the Web."

If you need to store data using two-way encryption, a good set of tools are in the mcrypt encryption library. PHP provides a set of functions that access it but, to use them, you must install the libmcrypt library and then compile PHP with the --with-mcrypt parameter; ready-to-use Microsoft Windows software is also available from the PHP web site. We don't discuss the mcrypt library in this book, but you can find more information at *http://www.php.net/manual/en/ref.mcrypt.php* and at *http://mcrypt.sourceforge.net/*.

MySQL also offers the reversible *encode()* and *decode()* functions described in Chapter 15.

Form-Based Authentication

So far in this chapter, we have presented authorization techniques based on HTTP. In this section, we describe how to build applications that don't rely on HTTP Authentication, but instead use HTML forms to collect user credentials and sessions to implement an authentication framework. We discuss why you might want to avoid HTTP authentication, and the types of applications that benefit from managing the authentication with forms.

Reasons to Use HTTP Authentication

Before you decide to build an application that manages its own authentication, you should consider the advantages of using HTTP Authentication:

- It is easy to use. Protecting an application can be as simple as configuring your web server or creating a file.
- The HTTP authentication process can be managed by PHP code when an application needs to take over the checking of user credentials. We described how to do this in the section "Managing HTTP Authentication with PHP" earlier in this chapter.
- Support to collect and remember user credentials is built into browsers.
- HTTP authentication works well with stateless applications.

Reasons to Avoid HTTP Authentication

Some applications, particularly session-based applications that track authenticated users, have requirements that are difficult to meet using HTTP authentication.

Browsers remember passwords
    Usernames and passwords entered into a browser authentication dialog box (such as that shown in Figure 11-1) are remembered until the browser program is terminated or a new set of credentials is collected. You can force a browser to for-

get credentials by deliberately responding with an unauthorized code even when a request contains authenticated credentials. The following fragment does this:

```
// Force the browser to forget with an unauthorized
// challenge response ...
header("WWW-Authenticate: Basic realm=\"Flat Foot\"");
header("HTTP/1.1 401 Unauthorized");
```

However if a user forgets to log out—and the page that sends the WWW-Authenticate header field is not requested—then an unattended browser becomes a security risk. By typing in a URL or simply using the Back button, another user can access the application unchallenged.

Limited to the browser authentication dialog

When an application uses HTTP authentication, the method for collecting user credentials is limited to the authentication dialog box provided by the browser. An online application might want to present the login page in a style that's consistent with the application, perhaps by using a template, or in another language.

HTTP does not support multiple realms

Some applications require multiple logins. For example, an application might be a corporate information system that requires all users to log in for basic access but then requires an additional username and password to access a restricted part of the site. HTTP doesn't allow for multiple Authorization header fields in the one request.

Authentication and Session-Based Applications

In Chapter 10, we presented session management as a technique for building stateful applications. For many applications that require authentication, a session is created when a user logs in, and tracks his interaction until he logs out or the session times out. We introduced this pattern in Chapter 10.

The basic pattern of session-based authentication is to authenticate a user's credentials once, and set up a session that records this authenticated status in session variables. Credentials are collected using a form and processed by the set-up script. Then, the authenticated status is recorded in the session; this contrasts with HTTP authentication, which sends the authenticated credentials with each request. If the session times out (or the user destroys the session), the authenticated status is destroyed; therefore, unlike authenticated HTTP credentials, the session ID cookie can't be used after the session has timed out and this makes the application more secure.

Collecting user credentials in a form and storing the authenticated state in a session has two disadvantages. First, the username and password aren't encrypted when passed from the browser to the web server. Therefore, in the PHP examples we present in the rest of this chapter, the username and password are transmitted as plain text; using the Secure Sockets Layer protocol, as discussed later in this chapter, solves this problem. Second, session hijacking is possible because the state of the session is used to control access to the application; session hijacking is discussed next.

Session hijacking

By using session variables to maintain authentication, an application can be open to hijacking. When a request is sent to a session-based application, the browser includes the session identifier, usually as a cookie, to access the authenticated session. Rather than snoop for usernames and passwords, a hacker can use a session ID to hijack an existing session.

Consider an online banking application in which a hacker waits for a real user to log in. The hacker then includes the session ID in a request, and transfers funds into his own account. If the session isn't encrypted, it's easy to read the session ID. We recommend that any application that transmits usernames, passwords, cookies that identify sessions, or personal details should be protected using encryption.

Even if the connection is encrypted, the session ID may still be vulnerable. If the session ID is stored in a cookie on the client, it is possible to trick the browser into sending the cookie unencrypted. This can happen if the cookie was set up by the server without the secure parameter that prevents cookie transmission over an insecure connection. How to set up PHP session management to secure cookies is discussed in Chapter 10.

Hijack attempts can also be less sophisticated. A hacker can hijack a session by randomly trying session IDs in the hope that an existing session can be found. On a busy site, many thousands of sessions might exist at any one time, increasing the chance of success for such an attack. One precaution is to reduce the number of idle sessions by setting a short maximum lifetime for dormant sessions, as discussed in Chapter 10.

Recording IP addresses to detect session hijack attempts

Earlier in this chapter, we showed how to access the IP address of the browser when processing a request. The script shown in Example 11-4 checks the IP address set in the $_SERVER["REMOTE_ADDR"] variable against a hard-coded string that limits access to users whose machines are on a particular subnet.

The IP address of the client can also be used to help prevent session hijacking. If the IP address set in the $_SERVER["REMOTE_ADDR"] variable is recorded as a session variable when a user initially connects to an application, subsequent requests can be checked and allowed only if they are sent from the same IP address. We show you how to do this in the next section.

 Using the IP address as recorded from the HTTP request has limitations. Network administrators often configure proxy servers to hide the originating IP address by replacing it with the address of the proxy server. All users who connect to an application via such a proxy server appear to be located on the one machine. Some large sites—such as that of a large university campus—might even have several proxy servers to balance load, so successive requests coming from a single user might appear to change address.

Session-Based Authentication Framework

The authentication framework developed in this section follows the pattern described in Chapter 10 and uses techniques developed earlier in the chapter. In this section we:

- Develop a login script that uses a form to collect user credentials
- Authenticate the user credentials against protected passwords stored in the *users* table
- Show how session variables are set up to support session authentication and hijacking detection
- Develop the *sessionAuthenticate()* function that protects each page that requires authentication
- Develop a logout function that destroys a session
- Develop scripts that allow a user to change his password

The scripts presented in this section have been kept as simple as possible to illustrate the concepts. They use the *authentication* database and *users* table described earlier in this chapter, and the MySQL database connection is established with the user lucy and the password secret. A more complex authentication framework that's based on the scripts described here is presented with the online winestore in Chapters 16 through 20.

Code overview

The basic pattern of session-based authentication is to authenticate a user's credentials once, and set up a session that records this authenticated status as session variables. Credentials are collected with the *login.html* page shown in Example 11-9, and processed by the *logincheck.php* script shown in Example 11-10.

Applications scripts—such as the *home.php* script shown in Example 11-12—start by checking the status of the authentication session variables before running any other code. This check is performed by the *sessionAuthenticate()* function. If this check fails, the user is redirected to the *logout.php* script shown in Example 11-14 that explicitly destroys the session. The *logout.php* script can also be called directly, and it's typically included as a link on most application pages such as *home.php*.

The functions that are reused in the framework are implemented in a require file *authentication.inc* shown in Example 11-11. The file contains the *authenticateUser()* function that compares user-supplied credentials to those in the database (the function is shown in Example 11-7) and the *sessionAuthenticate()* function.

The password change module is shown in Example 11-16 and Example 11-18. Example 11-16 lists the *password.php* script that displays a password change form to collect the current password and a new password, and Example 11-18 is the script *changepassword.php* that validates the user data and, if that succeeds, changes the password. On success or failure, the *changepassword.php* script redirects to the password change page and displays a message to inform the user.

Login page

Example 11-9 shows the *login.html* page with a form that collects a username and password. The login page does not contain any PHP code.

Example 11-9. Login page

```
<!DOCTYPE HTML PUBLIC "-//W3C//DTD HTML 4.01 Transitional//EN"
                      "http://www.w3.org/TR/html401/loose.dtd">
<html>
<head>
  <meta http-equiv="Content-Type" content="text/html; charset=iso-8859-1">
  <title>Login</title>
</head>
<body>
<h1>Application Login Page</h1>
<form method="POST" action="logincheck.php">
<table>
  <tr>
    <td>Enter your username:</td>
    <td><input type="text" size="10" name="loginUsername"></td>
  </tr>
  <tr>
    <td>Enter your password:</td>
    <td><input type="password" size="10" name="loginPassword"></td>
  </tr>
</table>
<p><input type="submit" value="Log in">
</form>
</body>
</html>
```

Proxy servers, web gateways, and web servers often log the URLs that are requested, so the page submits the form input fields using the POST method, rather than using the GET method that encodes field values in the URL. This prevents user credentials from appearing in log files.

Setup script

The *logincheck.php* script shown in Example 11-10 authenticates the user by processing the POST variables collected in the *login.html* page, and sets up the session variables that record the authenticated status. This script does not generate any output except a Location header to relocate to the home page of the application or the logout page if authentication fails.

Example 11-10. Setup script

```
<?php
require 'authentication.inc';
```

Example 11-10. Setup script (continued)

```php
require 'db.inc';

if (!$connection = @ mysql_connect("localhost", "lucy", "secret"))
  die("Cannot connect");

// Clean the data collected in the <form>
$loginUsername = mysqlclean($_POST, "loginUsername", 10, $connection);
$loginPassword = mysqlclean($_POST, "loginPassword", 10, $connection);

if (!mysql_selectdb("authentication", $connection))
  showerror();

session_start();

// Authenticate the user
if (authenticateUser($connection, $loginUsername, $loginPassword))
{
  // Register the loginUsername
  $_SESSION["loginUsername"] = $loginUsername;

  // Register the IP address that started this session
  $_SESSION["loginIP"] = $_SERVER["REMOTE_ADDR"];

  // Relocate back to the first page of the application
  header("Location: home.php");
  exit;
}
else
{
  // The authentication failed: setup a logout message
  $_SESSION["message"] =
    "Could not connect to the application as '{$loginUsername}'";

  // Relocate to the logout page
  header("Location: logout.php");
  exit;
}
?>
```

The username and password are read from the $_POST superglobal array and untainted. Then, the username and password are passed to the *authenticateUser()* function. If the *authenticateUser()* function returns true, the user has successfully been authenticated and the script sets up the $_SESSION["loginUsername"] and $_SESSION["loginIP"] session variables, and the Location header field is sent to relocate the browser to the *home.php* script. If the user credentials do not authenticate, the script sets up the message session variable and relocates to the *logout.php* script.

The authentication.inc require file

All pages that are protected by the authentication framework need to check the $_SESSION["loginUsername"] and $_SESSION["loginIP"] session variables to ensure that the user has successfully authenticated before running any other code. The *sessionAuthenticate()* function shown in Example 11-11 performs these checks and is included in the *authentication.inc* file.

Example 11-11. The sessionAuthenticate() and authenticateUser() functions

```php
<?php

function authenticateUser($connection, $username, $password)
{
  // Test the username and password parameters
  if (!isset($username) || !isset($password))
    return false;

  // Create a digest of the password collected from
  // the challenge
  $password_digest = md5(trim($password));

  // Formulate the SQL find the user
  $query = "SELECT password FROM users WHERE user_name = '{$username}'
            AND password = '{$password_digest}'";

  // Execute the query
  if (!$result = @ mysql_query ($query, $connection))
    showerror();

  // exactly one row? then we have found the user
  if (mysql_num_rows($result) != 1)
    return false;
  else
    return true;
}

// Connects to a session and checks that the user has
// authenticated and that the remote IP address matches
// the address used to create the session.
function sessionAuthenticate()
{
  // Check if the user hasn't logged in
  if (!isset($_SESSION["loginUsername"]))
  {
    // The request does not identify a session
    $_SESSION["message"] = "You are not authorized to access the URL
                          {$_SERVER["REQUEST_URI"]}";

    header("Location: logout.php");
    exit;
  }

  // Check if the request is from a different IP address to previously
  if (!isset($_SESSION["loginIP"]) ||
    ($_SESSION["loginIP"] != $_SERVER["REMOTE_ADDR"]))
  {
```

Example 11-11. The sessionAuthenticate() and authenticateUser() functions (continued)

```
      // The request did not originate from the machine
      // that was used to create the session.
      // THIS IS POSSIBLY A SESSION HIJACK ATTEMPT

      $_SESSION["message"] = "You are not authorized to access the URL
                              {$_SERVER["REQUEST_URI"]} from the address
                              {$_SERVER["REMOTE_ADDR"]}";

      header("Location: logout.php");
      exit;
    }
  }
}

?>
```

The *sessionAuthenticate()* function carries out two tests: first, if the session variable $_SESSION["loginUsername"] isn't set, the user isn't logged in; and, second, if session variable $_SESSION["loginIP"] isn't set or it doesn't have the same value as the IP address of the client that sent the current request, a possible hijack attempt has occurred. If either test fails, a $_SESSION["message"] variable is set with an appropriate message and the Location header field is used to relocate the browser to the logout script.

Example 11-11 also includes the *authenticateUser()* function that's reproduced from Example 11-7.

Application scripts and pages

Example 11-12 shows how the *home.php* script uses the *authentication.inc* file and the *sessionAuthenticate()* function. If the user requests this page before logging in, they're redirected to the *logout.php* page. If they have logged in, the *home.php* page is displayed.

Example 11-12. The home page of an application

```
<?php
require "authentication.inc";
require_once "HTML/Template/ITX.php";

session_start();

// Connect to an authenticated session or relocate to logout.php
session_authenticate();

$template = new HTML_Template_ITX("./templates");
$template->loadTemplatefile("home.tpl", true, true);

$template->setVariable("USERNAME", $_SESSION["loginUsername"]);
$template->parseCurrentBlock();
$template->show();
?>
```

The script uses the *home.tpl* template shown in Example 11-13 to display the $_
SESSION["loginUsername"] variable that shows who is logged on. This script also provides links to log out and to change the user's password.

Example 11-13. The home.tpl template that's used with Example 11-12

```
<!DOCTYPE HTML PUBLIC "-//W3C//DTD HTML 4.01 Transitional//EN"
                      "http://www.w3.org/TR/html401/loose.dtd">
<html>
<head>
  <meta http-equiv="Content-Type" content="text/html; charset=iso-8859-1">
  <title>Home</title>
</head>
<body>
  <h1>Welcome to the application</h1>
  You are logged on as {USERNAME}
  <p><a href="password.php">Change Password</a>
  <p><a href="logout.php">Logout</a>
</body>
</html>
```

Logout script

The *logout.php* script is shown in Example 11-14. It's either requested by another script (such as *logincheck.php*) when the user fails the authentication process, or a user can explicitly end a session by requesting it (for example, from the *home.php* page shown in the previous section).

Example 11-14. Logout script

```
<?php
  require_once "HTML/Template/ITX.php";
  session_start();

  $message = "";

  // An authenticated user has logged out -- be polite and thank them for
  // using your application.
  if (isset($_SESSION["loginUsername"]))
    $message .= "Thanks {$_SESSION["loginUsername"]} for
                 using the Application.";

  // Some script, possibly the setup script, may have set up a
  // logout message
  if (isset($_SESSION["message"]))
  {
    $message .= $_SESSION["message"];
    unset($_SESSION["message"]);
  }

  // Destroy the session.
  session_destroy();
```

Example 11-14. Logout script (continued)

```
  // Display the page (including the message)
  $template = new HTML_Template_ITX("./templates");
  $template->loadTemplatefile("logout.tpl", true, true);
  $template->setVariable("MESSAGE", $message);
  $template->parseCurrentBlock( );
  $template->show( );
?>
```

The *logout.php* script doesn't call the *sessionAuthenticate()* function to check that a user is authenticated, and so we don't need to include the *authentication.inc* file. Instead, the *logout.php* function calls *session_start()* and then tests if either of the session variables $_SESSION["loginUsername"] and $_SESSION["message"] are set. If either is set, they are used to create a message to show the user:

- The $_SESSION["message"] variable is created in the *logincheck.php* or *authentication.inc* scripts when user credentials fail to authenticate and it's used to explain why the process failed.

- The $_SESSION["loginUsername"] variable is used in *logout.php* to thank the user for using the application.

With the message complete, the script destroys the session by calling the *session_ destroy()* function. The logout page prints the $message variable using the template *logout.tpl* shown in Example 11-15, and this page provides a link back to the *login. html* page.

Example 11-15. The logout.tpl template file that's used with Example 11-14

```
<!DOCTYPE HTML PUBLIC "-//W3C//DTD HTML 4.01 Transitional//EN"
                      "http://www.w3.org/TR/html401/loose.dtd">
<html>
<head>
  <meta http-equiv="Content-Type" content="text/html; charset=iso-8859-1">
  <title>Logout</title>
</head>
<body>
  <h1>Application Logout Page</h1>
  {MESSAGE}
  <p>Click <a href="login.html">here</a> to log in.
</body>
</html>
```

Password management

The *password.php* script in Example 11-16 and the *changepassword.php* script in Example 11-18 allow a user to change their password. Both scripts start by requiring the *authentication.inc* file and calling the *sessionAuthenticate()* function, allowing access only when a user has successfully authenticated.

Example 11-16. The password.php password change form

```php
<?php
require "authentication.inc";
require_once "HTML/Template/ITX.php";

session_start();

// Connect to an authenticated session or relocate to logout.php
sessionAuthenticate();

$message = "";

// Check if there is a password error message
if (isset($_SESSION["passwordMessage"]))
{
  $message = $_SESSION["passwordMessage"];
  unset($_SESSION["passwordMessage"]);
}

// Display the page (including the message)
$template = new HTML_Template_ITX("./templates");
$template->loadTemplatefile("password.tpl", true, true);
$template->setVariable("USERNAME", $_SESSION["loginUsername"]);
$template->setVariable("MESSAGE", $message);
$template->parseCurrentBlock();
$template->show();
?>
```

The *password.php* script displays a form that collects the original password and the new password twice; the new password is collected twice to minimize the chances of a typing error rendering the new password unusable. The script uses the *password.tpl* template shown in Example 11-17. There are two template placeholders: USERNAME is used to display the name of the logged-in user, and MESSAGE is used to display a message that is stored in a session variable that is set by *changepassword.php*. Once a message has been recorded for display, it's unset in the session store so that it doesn't appear again.

Example 11-17. The password.tpl template used with Example 11-16

```html
<!DOCTYPE HTML PUBLIC "-//W3C//DTD HTML 4.01 Transitional//EN"
                      "http://www.w3.org/TR/html401/loose.dtd">
<html>
<head>
  <meta http-equiv="Content-Type" content="text/html; charset=iso-8859-1">
  <title>Password Change</title>
</head>
<body>
  <h1>Change Password for {USERNAME}</h1>
  {MESSAGE}
  <form method="POST" action="changepassword.php">
  <table>
    <tr>
```

Example 11-17. The password.tpl template used with Example 11-16 (continued)

```
      <td>Enter your existing password:</td>
      <td><input type="password" size="10" name="oldPassword"></td>
    </tr>
    <tr>
      <td>Enter your new password:</td>
      <td><input type="password" size="10" name="newPassword1"></td>
    </tr>
    <tr>
      <td>Re-enter your new password:</td>
      <td><input type="password" size="10" name="newPassword2"></td>
    </tr>
  </table>
  <p><input type="submit" value="Update Password">
  </form>
  <p><a href="home.php">Home</a>
  <p><a href="logout.php">Logout</a>
</body>
</html>
```

The data that's entered into the password form is processed by the *changepassword. php* script in Example 11-18.

Example 11-18. The changepassword.php script

```
<?php
require "authentication.inc";
require "db.inc";

session_start();

// Connect to an authenticated session or relocate to logout.php
sessionAuthenticate();

if (!$connection = @ mysql_connect("localhost", "lucy", "secret"))
  die("Cannot connect");

// Clean the data collected from the user
$oldPassword = mysqlclean($_POST, "oldPassword", 10, $connection);
$newPassword1 = mysqlclean($_POST, "newPassword1", 10, $connection);
$newPassword2 = mysqlclean($_POST, "newPassword2", 10, $connection);

if (!mysql_selectdb("authentication", $connection))
  showerror();

if (strcmp($newPassword1, $newPassword2) == 0 &&
  authenticateUser($connection, $_SESSION["loginUsername"], $oldPassword))
{
  // OK to update the user password

  // Create the digest of the password
  $digest = md5(trim($newPassword1));
```

Example 11-18. The changepassword.php script (continued)

```
  // Update the user row
  $update_query = "UPDATE users SET password = '{$digest}'
                   WHERE user_name = '{$_SESSION["loginUsername"]}'";

  if (!$result = @ mysql_query ($update_query, $connection))
    showerror();

  $_SESSION["passwordMessage"] =
    "Password changed for '{$_SESSION["loginUsername"]}'";
}
else
{
  $_SESSION["passwordMessage"] =
    "Could not change password for '{$_SESSION["loginUsername"]}'";
}

// Relocate to the password form
header("Location: password.php");
?>
```

The oldPassword, newPassword1, and newPassword2 fields are read from the $_POST superglobal array, and made safe with the *mysqlclean()* function. Then, if both the new password fields are identical, and the current password is valid for the currently logged in user, the update code runs. As discussed previously, collecting the new password twice helps prevent the introduction of typing errors, and calling the *authenticateUser()* function ensures that only the user herself can change the password.

Once the collected fields have been verified, the password can be updated in the database. The user's row is updated with the MD5 digest of the new password, and the $_SESSION["passwordMessage"] variable is set to indicate that the password has been changed. The message is displayed by the *password.php* script.

If the collected fields can't be verified—the two new passwords don't match or the current password isn't valid—the $_SESSION["passwordMessage"] variable is set to indicate that the password couldn't be changed.

The *changepassword.php* script doesn't display any output, but sets the Location header field to relocate the browser to the *password.php* page.

Protecting Data on the Web

The Web isn't a secure environment. The open nature of the networking and the web protocols TCP, IP, and HTTP has allowed the development of many tools that can listen in on data transmitted between web browsers and servers. It is possible to snoop on passing traffic and read the contents of HTTP requests and responses. With a little extra effort, a hacker can manipulate traffic and even masquerade as another user.

If an application transmits sensitive information over the Web, an encrypted connection should be provided between the web browser and server. For example, an encrypted connection is warranted when:

- Sensitive information is held on the server such as commercial-in-confidence documents or bank account balances.
- User credentials are used to gain access to sensitive services such as online banking or the administration of an application.
- Personal details are collected from the user, such as credit card numbers.
- Session IDs are used by the server to link HTTP requests to session variables, and the session needs to be secure from hijacking.

Even if none of these of reasons apply to your application, sometimes it's a good idea to use encryption anyway for a commercial application. Bad publicity from a security breach can be equally bad when private or public data is compromised.

In this section, we focus on encrypting data sent over the Web using the Secure Sockets Layer. We discuss the basic mechanics of SSL in this section. An installation and configuration guide for SSL and the Apache web server for Unix and Mac OS X platforms is part of Appendixes A through C. It's possible to set up a secure web server under Microsoft Windows, but we don't cover it in this book.

This section isn't designed to completely cover the topic of encryption. We limit our brief discussion to the features of SSL, and how SSL can protect web traffic. More details about cryptographic systems can be found in the references listed in Appendix G.

The Secure Sockets Layer Protocol

The data sent between web servers and browsers can be protected using the encryption services of the Secure Sockets Layer protocol, SSL. The SSL protocol addresses three goals:

Privacy or confidentiality
    The content of a message transmitted over the Internet is protected from observers.

Integrity
    The contents of a message received are correct and have not been tampered with.

Authentication
    Both the sender and receiver of a message can be sure of each other's identity.

SSL was originally developed by Netscape, and there are two versions: SSL v2.0 and SSL v3.0. We don't detail the differences here, but Version 3.0 supports more security features than 2.0. The SSL protocol isn't a standard as such, and the Internet Engineering Task Force (IETF) has proposed the Transport Layer Security 1.0 (TLS) protocol as an SSL v3.0 replacement; at the time of writing SSL v3.0 and TLS are almost the same. See *http://ietf.org/rfc/rfc2246.txt?number=2246* for more information on TLS.

SSL architecture

To understand how SSL works, you need to understand how browsers and web servers send and receive HTTP messages.

Browsers send HTTP requests by calling on the host systems' TCP/IP networking software, which does the work of sending and receiving data over the Internet. When a request is to be sent (for example, when a user clicks on a hypertext link) the browser formulates the HTTP request and uses the host's TCP/IP network service to send the request to the server. TCP/IP doesn't care that the message is HTTP; it is responsible only for getting the complete message to the destination. When a web server receives a message, data is read from its host's TCP/IP service and then interpreted as HTTP. We discuss the relationship between HTTP and TCP/IP in more detail in Appendix D.

As shown in Figure 11-3, the SSL protocol operates as a layer between the browser and the TCP/IP services provided by the host. A browser passes the HTTP message to the SSL layer to be encrypted before the message is passed to the host's TCP/IP service. The SSL layer, configured into the web server, decrypts the message from the TCP/IP service and then passes it to the web server. Once SSL is installed and the web server is configured correctly, the HTTP requests and responses are automatically encrypted. PHP scripting is not required to use the SSL services.

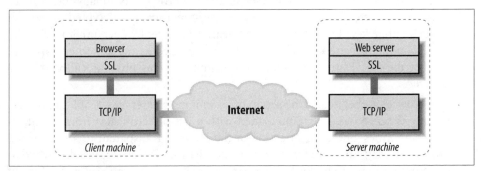

Figure 11-3. HTTP clients and servers, SSL, and the network layer that implements TCP/IP

Because SSL sits between HTTP and TCP/IP, secure web sites technically don't serve HTTP, at least not directly over TCP. URLs that locate resources on a secure server begin with *https://*, which means HTTP over SSL. The default port for an SSL service is 443, not port 80 as with HTTP; for example, when a browser connects to *https:// secure.example.com*, it makes a TCP/IP connection to port 443 on *secure.example. com*. Most browsers and web servers can support SSL, but keys and certificates need to be included in the configuration of the server (and possibly the browser, if client certification is required). In addition, web browsers need to be preconfigured with certificates from root CAs; fortunately, all browsers come with these. We discuss CAs and certificates later.

Cipher suites

To provide a service that addresses the goals of privacy, integrity, and authentication, SSL uses a combination of cryptographic techniques. These include message digests, digital certificates, and, of course, encryption. There are many different standard algorithms that implement these functions, and SSL can use different combinations to meet particular requirements (such as the legality of using a technique in a particular country!).

When an SSL connection is established, clients and servers negotiate the best combination of techniques—based on common capabilities—to ensure the highest level of protection. The combinations of techniques that can be negotiated are known as *cipher suites*.

SSL sessions

When a browser connects to a secure site, the SSL protocol performs the following four steps:

1. A cipher suite is negotiated. The browser and the server identify the major SSL version supported, and then the configured capabilities. The strongest cipher suit that can be supported by both systems is chosen.

2. A secret key is shared between the server and the browser. Normally the browser generates a secret key that is one-way (asymmetrically) encrypted using the server's public key. Only the server can learn the secret by decrypting it with the corresponding private key. The shared secret is used as the key to encrypt and decrypt the HTTP messages that are transmitted. This phase is called the *key exchange*.

3. The browser authenticates the server by examining the server's X.509 digital certificate. Often browsers are preloaded with a list of certificates from Certification Authorities, and authentication of the server is transparent to a user. If the browser doesn't know about the certificate, the user is warned, usually by a dialog box that pops up and asks whether the user wants to proceed in the face of failed authentication.

4. The server examines the browser's X.509 certificate to authenticate the client. This step is optional and requires that each client be set up with a signed digital certificate. Apache can be configured to use fields from the browser's X.509 certificate as if they were the username and password encoded into an HTTP Authorization header field. Client certificates aren't commonly used on the Web.

These four steps briefly summarize the network handshaking between the browser and server when SSL is used. Once the browser and server have completed these steps, the HTTP request can be encrypted by SSL and sent to the web server.

The SSL handshaking is slow, and if this was to occur with every HTTP request, the performance of a secure web site would be poor. To improve performance, SSL uses the concept of sessions to allow multiple requests to share the negotiated cipher suite, the shared secret key, and the certificates. An SSL session is managed by the SSL software and isn't the same as a PHP session.

Certificates and certification authorities

A signed *digital certificate* encodes information so that the integrity of the information and its signature can be tested. The information contained in a certificate used by SSL includes details about the organization and the organization's public key. The public key that is contained in a certificate is paired with a secret private key that is configured into the organization's web server; if you've followed our setup instructions for Unix or Mac OS X platforms in Appendixes A through C, you'll recall generating the pair of keys and adding the private key to the web server.

The browser uses the public key when an SSL session is established to encrypt a secret. The secret can be decrypted only using the private key configured into the organization's server. Encryption techniques that use a public and private key are known as *one-way* or *asymmetric*, and SSL uses asymmetric encryption to exchange a secret key. The secret key can then be used to encrypt the messages transmitted over the Internet.

You cannot, of course, trust an unknown server to be what it claims to be; you have to depend on a known authority to validate that the server is telling the truth and you have to trust that authority. That is the role of a *Certification Authority* (CA). Each signed certificate contains details about the CA. The CA digitally signs a certificate by adding its own organization details, an encrypted digest of the certificate (created using a technique such as MD5), and its own public key. With this information encoded, the complete signed certificate can be verified as being correct.

There are dozens, perhaps hundreds, of CAs. A browser (or the user confronted by a browser warning) can't be expected to recognize the digital signatures from all these authorities. The X.509 certificate standard solves this problem by allowing issuing CAs to have their signatures digitally signed by a more authoritative CA, who can in turn have its signature signed by yet another, more trusted CA. Eventually the chain of signatures ends with that of a root Certification Authority. As discussed previously, the certificates from the root CAs are usually pre-installed with browser software. In addition, most browsers allow users to add their own trusted certificates.

If you don't want to pay for a certificate or you need one for testing, free certificates can be created and used to configure a web server with SSL. We show how to create free self-signed certificates for Unix and Mac OS X platforms in Appendixes A through C, or you can obtain a free trial certificate for any platform from VeriSign at *http://www.verisign.com/*. However, self-signed or trial certificates are normally useful only in restricted environments such as corporate networks. They won't be trusted by users of secure applications on the Internet, and you'll probably need to pay to have yours signed before the application is actually deployed.

CHAPTER 12

Errors, Debugging, and Deployment

So far in this book, we've shown you the techniques to build the popular components of a web database application. This chapter shows you how to find bugs in those components and prepare your application for deployment by adding the finishing touches that will make it a professional web database application.

The first two sections introduce PHP errors, common causes of programming error, and how to find them. We show you examples of error types, and explain how error reporting can be configured for debugging while you're coding and adjusted later for deployment. We also discuss the common sources of error in PHP, their symptoms, and how to rectify them.

The second half of this chapter discusses application deployment. We show you how to add your own error handler that reports errors to the user in a framework that's managed by the application, sends errors to a log or the system administrator, and handles custom errors you can trigger from your code.

Chapters 16 through 20 present a complete, annotated online winestore web database application. The application is built using the techniques and components discussed in earlier chapters, and debugged using the approaches discussed in this chapter. It includes a full-featured custom error handler.

Errors

If you've written PHP code before you've read this chapter, you're already familiar with PHP errors. However, you've probably not thought much about the different error types and the situations in which they occur. This section discusses errors in detail, and shows you how to change the error reporting levels in PHP and make the most of debugging information during development.

PHP problems break down into four types or levels: errors, parse errors, warnings, and notices. They can occur in four different situations: internally within PHP itself (in the PHP core), during compilation when your script is first loaded, at run time when your script is being executed, or when explicitly triggered by you in your code.

While all this might seem complicated, the variety leads to more informed debugging, configurable error handling, and flexibility across all phases of the development of web database applications. In any case, to some extent it's unavoidable. A missing bracket is always discovered during compilation and aborts the run immediately, whereas division by zero or a failed connection to a database must wait till the script has run up to the point of the error.

Table 12-1 lists the problems and in what situations they occur; for simplicity, we refer to all of the possible problems and situation combinations as *errors*. The most serious of the error types are the ERROR and PARSE classes: both are fatal, that is, by default they stop script execution and report an error message. The WARNING class is also serious and still reports messages, but by default doesn't stop script execution. The least serious of the errors are in the NOTICE class, which by default don't report messages or stop the script. We discuss how to adjust the default behaviors later in this section.

Table 12-1. Errors in PHP

Constant	Description	Halts script?
E_ERROR	Fatal runtime error	Yes
E_WARNING	Non-fatal runtime error	No
E_PARSE	Compile-time parser error	Yes
E_NOTICE	Runtime notice	No
E_CORE_ERROR	Fatal PHP startup error	Yes
E_CORE_WARNING	Non-fatal PHP startup error	No
E_COMPILE_ERROR	Fatal compile-time error	Yes
E_COMPILE_WARNING	Non-fatal compile time error	No
E_USER_ERROR	Fatal programmer-generated error	Programmer-defined
E_USER_WARNING	Non-fatal programmer-generated error	Programmer-defined
U_USER_NOTICE	Programmer notice	Programmer-defined
E_ALL	All of the above	--

The ERROR class includes errors such as calling undefined functions, instantiating objects of a non-existent class, and issuing a statement when it isn't allowed (for example, a break or continue outside of a loop). The PARSE class includes syntax errors from missing semicolons, missing quotes and brackets, and statements with incorrect numbers of parameters. The WARNING class covers less serious problems—where a script may be able to continue successfully—such as the MySQL connection problems discussed in Chapter 6, divide by zero errors, passing the wrong number of parameters to a function, and including a file that doesn't exist. The NOTICE class errors are usually minor and informational and include, for example, warnings about using undefined variables.

The WARNING and ERROR class errors can be produced by the PHP core Zend engine, the compilation process, runtime processing, or deliberate triggering by the programmer. Notices can be produced by the latter two. While this sounds complicated to deal with, most of the time the only problems that your code needs to handle after it's deployed are the runtime E_WARNING errors; the E_USER_ERROR, E_USER_WARNING, and E_USER_NOTICE errors may also be handled in your code, and we discuss this later in the section "Custom Error Handlers." We've deliberately omitted E_PARSE, E_ERROR, and E_NOTICE from the list of errors your code needs to worry about: these are usually fixed by the programmer during development.

By default, error messages are displayed to the user agent (usually a web browser), along with whatever output has been produced up to the point the error occurred; the exception is E_NOTICE errors, which are ignored with the default settings. For example, consider the following script that contains an E_WARNING error that's detected at runtime:

```
<!DOCTYPE HTML PUBLIC
                "-//W3C//DTD HTML 4.01 Transitional//EN"
                "http://www.w3.org/TR/html401/loose.dtd">
<html>
<head>
  <meta http-equiv="Content-Type" content="text/html; charset=iso-8859-1">
  <title>Error</title>
<body>
<h1>Two times!</h1>
<?php
  function double($number)
  {
    return $number*2;
  }

  print "Two times ten is: " . double();
  print "<br>Two times five is: " . double(5);
?>
</body>
</html>
```

The function *double( )* is called without its parameter in the first print statement, and so a warning is produced as shown in the Mozilla browser in Figure 12-1. The PHP-generated warning occurs after the HTML <h1> text has been output, but before the output of the print statement that contains the error. Because it's a warning, the script continues, and both print statements produce output. The error itself is useful for debugging: it contains a description of what caused the error, and the source file and line number. We discuss the common sources of errors and how to find them later in this section.

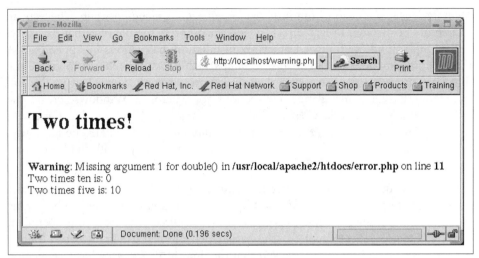

Figure 12-1. Script output that contains an E_WARNING error

When you use templates, you'll find that the errors are usually output before the output of the script. This is because template output is buffered until you call the *show( )* method, while error output is sent directly to the user agent. This can make debugging a little harder, but it does help prevent error messages from being confused amidst the script output.

The E_ERROR runtime errors stop script execution, so the script produces output only up to the point where the error occurred. In the case of templates, it's typical that no output except the error will be produced. Similarly, E_PARSE errors prevent any script output, as the problems are detected before runtime.

Accessing the PHP Manual

During development, the errors produced by PHP are useful tools for debugging your code. For example, suppose you attempt to establish a *mysql_connect( )* connection but misspell localhost. This produces the error:

```
Warning:  mysql_connect( ) [function.mysql-connect.html]:
  Unknown MySQL Server Host 'localhos' (1) in
  /usr/local/apache2/htdocs/examples/buggy.php on line 18
```

By default, because a library function is involved, PHP produces a link to the PHP manual function reference for *mysql_connect()*, which is shown surrounded by square braces. You can click on this link and visit the manual. However, as discussed in Chapter 6, if you prefix your function calls with @ then these error messages are suppressed.

To support development, it's useful to have a copy of the PHP manual in the document tree of your development environment. To do this, download a copy of the

Many Files HTML version from *http://www.php.net/download-docs.php*. Then create a directory below your htdocs directory and uncompress the file into that directory. For example, if you've followed our Unix installation instructions in Appendixes A through C, you could use *mkdir /usr/local/apache2/htdocs/php-manual* to create the directory, move the file there, and then uncompress it with *bunzip2*. If you've followed our EasyPHP installation instructions for Microsoft Windows, create the folder *C:\Program Files\EasyPHP1-7\www\php-manual* and put the file there. On Mac OS X, use */Library/WebServer/Documents/php-manual*. The PHP site has a useful FAQ entry for Microsoft Windows users who aren't familiar with the *bzip2* compressed file format: *http://au.php.net/manual/en/faq.misc.php#faq.misc.bz2*.

After downloading the file, you need to configure your PHP to link to your local manual. To do this, open your *php.ini* file in an editor and locate the line beginning docref_root =. Change the line to point to your new directory below your document root (for example, docref_root = /php-manual), ensure that the immediately following line reads docref_ext = .html, and that the line ;html_errors = has a semicolon at the beginning. Save the file, and restart your Apache web server using the instructions in Appendixes A through C.

Configuring Error Reporting

Errors provide useful information when you're debugging your application. However, when it's deployed, displaying PHP errors among the application output is messy, confusing for users, and uninformative for those who need to be alerted to rectify the problems. Most importantly, it's also a security problem: program internals are displayed as part of error messages and these shouldn't be displayed to end users.

Error reporting is configured in PHP in two common ways. First, by setting a global default in the *php.ini* file; and, second, by setting error reporting on a script-by-script basis. By default, in the *php.ini* file, you'll find that error reporting is globally set to:

```
error_reporting = E_ALL & ~E_NOTICE
```

This means that all error types are reported, except E_NOTICE errors; the & operator is the bitwise AND discussed in Chapter 2, and the ~ is the bitwise NOT used to negate E_NOTICE. The list of possible constants that can be used in shown in Table 12-1.

You can adjust this configuration to suit your requirements by modifying the global default for all scripts or by setting a specific value in a script that's used only in that script. For example, to change the global value to detect only the ERROR and PARSE classes, you can use:

```
error_reporting = E_COMPILE_ERROR|E_ERROR|E_CORE_ERROR|E_PARSE
```

By default, all warnings and notices are then ignored; the | operator is the bitwise OR. As before, after making any change to *php.ini*, you need to restart your Apache web server.

To set an error-reporting level for one script, you can use the *error_reporting( )* library function. For example, to detect all error types, you can add:

```
<?php
  error_reporting(E_ALL);
```

to the beginning of the script. The function also takes a constant from Table 12-1 as the parameter, and you can use the bitwise &, |, and ~ to combine the constant values. As we discussed in Chapter 6, you can also suppress error reporting for a specific function using the @ operator. For example, to prevent errors from a call to *mysql_connect( )*, you can use:

```
$connection = @ mysql_connect("localhost","fred","shhh");
```

We recommend that during development you turn on all error reporting using the global *php.ini* setting. Change it to:

```
error_reporting  =  E_ALL
```

However, we don't recommend this setting for deployment for the reasons we discussed previously. When you deploy your application, you can follow two approaches to handling errors: turn them off—a very optimistic approach!—or write a handler that tries to deal with them gracefully during the application's run. Turning them off is easy (set the *php.ini* setting error_reporting = 0) but it isn't recommended because it'll prevent any problems with your application being detected. Adding a professional error handler to your application is discussed later in "Custom Error Handlers."

Common Programming Errors

Now that we've discussed what errors PHP can produce, let's discuss how to fix them. In this section, we focus on situations where error messages aren't produced or are less useful in helping to find the bug. In particular, we focus on the common mistakes that even experienced programmers make.

A Page That Produces Partial or No Output

One of the most common problems in debugging PHP scripts is seeing:

- Nothing rendered by the web browser
- A pop-up dialog box stating that the "Document Contains No Data"
- A partial document when more is expected

Most of these problems are caused not by a bug in a script, but by a bug in the HTML produced by the script or template. For example, if </table>, </form>, or </frame> closing tags are omitted, a document may not be rendered in some browsers.

An HTML problem can often be identified by viewing the HTML page source using the web browser. For example, on a Linux platform running Mozilla or Netscape, the page source can be accessed with a right-mouse click anywhere over the document and by then selecting *View Page Source* from the pop-up menu.

For compound or hard-to-identify HTML bugs, the W3C validator at *http://validator.w3.org/* analyzes the correctness of the HTML and issues a report. It's an excellent assistant for debugging and final compliance checks before delivery of an application. You can enter the URL of your resource into the W3C validator, or you can upload the HTML output and have it checked. The former is easiest, but the latter is sometimes the only option if your page can't be retrieved from behind a firewall or because a PHP session or authentication is needed to access it.

If you want to upload a page to the validator, the easiest method is to use the *Save Page As...* menu option in your browser to save the document. Then, upload the saved file by clicking on *Browse* next to the *Local File* box at *http://validator.w3.org*. Remember when using the validator that you need to validate the script under all its different output conditions: for example, if your page can produce a form or display the results of a query in a table, you need to check both scenarios.

If an HTML problem still proves hard to find, and it doesn't use templates, consider adding calls to the *flush( )* function after print or printf statements. The *flush( )* function empties the output buffer maintained by the PHP engine, sending all currently buffered output to the web server; without *flush( )*, buffered output usually isn't sent to the browser when an error occurs and the script stops. The function has no effect on buffering at the web server or the web browser, but it does ensure that all data output by the script is available to the web server to be transmitted and rendered by a browser. Remember to remove the *flush( )* function calls after debugging, because unnecessary flushing may prevent efficient buffering of output by the PHP scripting engine. Buffering and its use in error reporting is discussed in more detail in "Custom Error Handlers."

A common problem that shouldn't be confused with those described here is not receiving a response from the web server and getting a "no response" error message. This problem is a symptom of the bugs described in the next section, and can be distinguished from the problems described here by observing the web browser. Most of the popular graphical browsers show they are waiting for a response by animating the logo in the top-right corner. For the HTML problems described here, the page loading process will be complete, the logo animation will have stopped, and the HTML page source can be viewed through the web browser menus.

Variable Problems

In this section, we discuss problems that cause a page never to arrive at the web browser, or complete pages to appear with missing output from variables. Many of these problems can be avoided if you follow our recommendation to report E_NOTICE errors during development.

Variable naming

If you haven't turned on E_NOTICE errors, making a mistake with a variable name sometimes inadvertently creates never-ending loops. The result of a never-ending loop is that one of two problems occurs: first, the web browser eventually times out and alerts the user that the web server isn't responding to an HTTP request; or, second, PHP complains that the maximum script execution time (usually 30 seconds) has been exceeded. Which error you see depends on your configuration: you'll see whichever timeout problem occurs first.

The following loop never ends, and no output is produced:

```
for($counter=0; $counter<10; $Counter++)
    myFunction( );
```

The variable $counter is never incremented because $Counter and $counter are different variables. Therefore, $counter is always less than 10. Common bugs result from subtle changes in variable names through changing case, omitting or including underscores, or simple typing errors.

Never-ending loops can also produce unexpected output. The following loop can render thousands of greetings in a web browser in a very short time:

```
for($counter=0; $Counter<10; $counter++)
    echo "<br>hello";
```

With error reporting set to detect E_ALL errors (or to a setting that include E_NOTICE), the error is detected. For example, the following fragment:

```
error_reporting(E_ALL);
for($counter=0; $Counter<10; $counter++)
    echo "<br>hello";
```

produces a never-ending number of notice messages stating:

```
Notice: Undefined variable: Counter in /usr/local/apache2/htdocs/count.php
 on line 3
```

The script keeps on running because it's only an E_NOTICE error. You can prevent the endless output of error messages from the same source file and line by changing your *php.ini* file to include the setting:

```
ignore_repeated_errors = On
```

As usual, you need to restart your Apache web server after the change. For the $Counter example, this will ensure one error message but it won't prevent endless greetings. However, this setting can also have the undesirable side-effect that the error will be reported exactly once: if you press reload or refresh, you'll never see the error again!

Missing output

If you still haven't turned on E_NOTICE errors, an uninitialized variable can leave you with no output but without an explicit error. This seems obvious, but it can be hard to identify if the problem is a subtle error. Consider this example of a change in case:

```
$testvariable = "hello";
echo "The value of test is $testVariable";
```

This produces the string:

```
The value of test is
```

If output appears but isn't as expected, an uninitialized variable is a possibility. The simplest approach to detecting the error is then to check for a bug by setting *error_reporting(E_ALL)* at the top of the script or in your *php.ini* as discussed in the last section.

A similar problem that can't be detected with PHP errors can also occur when single quotes are used instead of double quotes. As discussed in Chapter 2, the content of single-quoted strings is always output directly, and the string isn't interpreted like a double-quoted string is. For example, consider the fragment:

```
echo 'the value of test is $test';
```

This produces:

```
the value of test is $test
```

It doesn't output the value of the variable $test.

Less Common Problems

The two problem categories we have outlined so far are the most common mistakes programmers make in PHP. We outline three less common and less PHP-specific problems here.

Complaints about headers

Functions that output HTTP headers are discussed in Chapters 5, 10, and 11. Such functions include *header( )*, *setcookie( )*, and *session_start( )*. A common problem seen when using these is an error message such as:

```
Warning: Cannot modify header information - headers already sent by (output started
at /usr/local/apache2/htdocs/test.php:2) in /usr/local/apache2/htdocs/redirect.php on
line 3
```

Headers can be sent only before any HTML is output, and this includes any whitespace at the top of the file. So, for example, if there is a blank line or single space character before the script open tag <?php, HTML has been output (albeit not very interesting HTML) and any function that sends an HTTP header will fail. Fortunately, the error message gives you a hint where to look. In the above example, the

location that triggered the error is listed within parentheses, as a filename followed by the line number, which is 2.

It's possible to avoid header problems by altering how PHP buffers data using the output control library functions. We discuss these later in "Custom Error Handlers."

Missing semicolons, braces, and quotes

Omitting a semicolon at the end of a statement is usually easy to detect. The PHP interpreter continues to parse the script and, when it reaches a threshold of confusion or exceeds the maximum statement length, reports an error one or more lines later that indicates a semicolon has been missed. In most cases, this is easy to fix because the line missing the semicolon is identified in the error message.

However, in some cases, a missing semicolon can be as hard to identify as a missing closing brace or a missing quotation mark. The following erroneous code is missing a closing brace:

```
<?php
for($x=0; $x<100 ;$x++)
{
   for($y=0; $y<100; $y++) {
     echo "test1";
     for($z=0; $z<100; $z++)
       echo "test2";
}
?>
```

The error reported is:

```
Parse error: parse error, unexpected $ in
 /usr/local/apache2/htdocs/bug.php on line 9
```

Line 9 is the last line of the script, so the nature and cause of the problem aren't immediately clear. However, parse errors that aren't immediately obvious on the reported line in the error message are usually on the line above, or there may be a missing brace or quotation mark.

It takes only a minute or so to identify the missing brace in this example, but more complex functions can take much longer to fix. This highlights the importance of indentation in code and of avoiding the practice of placing opening braces at the ends of lines. Braces should always be placed on lines of their own and match up vertically with their partner. If you use an editor that has syntax highlighting, this also makes spotting bracket and quotation problems much easier.

Source shown in the browser

Missing open and close script tags can cause problems similar to missing quotation marks or braces, but are much easier to identify. If an open script tag is missing, it's obvious because code is displayed in the browser. A missing close tag usually causes a parse error, because the PHP script engine is confused when it tries to parse HTML and interpret it as PHP, or it unexpectedly reaches the end of the file.

If script source is always displayed and never run, it's likely that Apache is misconfigured. Specifically, it's likely that the AddType directive for processing PHP scripts was not added in the Apache installation process; for example, this seems to be the default in some recent Red Hat Linux distributions.

Another possible cause of scripts being displayed and not run is that the PHP scripts aren't saved in files ending with the *.php* suffix. This problem often occurs with legacy PHP3 code, because PHP3 scripts usually use the *.php3* suffix. The problem can be corrected by renaming the script files so they end in the *.php* suffix or by adding an additional AddType directive to the Apache *httpd.conf* file:

```
AddType application/x-httpd-php .php3
```

Custom Error Handlers

The errors produced by PHP are useful when developing scripts, but aren't sufficient for deployment in a web database application. Errors should inform users without confusing them, not expose secure internal information, report details to administrators, and have a look and feel consistent with the application. This section shows you how to add a professional error handler to your application, and also how to improve the internal PHP error handler to produce even more information during development.

If you're not keen to develop a custom handler (or don't want to use ours!), you'll find an excellent class that includes one at *http://www.phpclasses.org/browse.html/package/345*.

A Basic Custom Handler

To begin, we show you how to implement a simple custom handler. The *set_error_handler( )* function allows you to define a custom error handler that replaces the internal PHP handler for non-critical errors:

string set_error_handler(string error_handler)

> The function takes one parameter, a user-defined *error_handler* function that is called whenever an error occurs. On success, the function returns the previously defined error handler function name, which can be saved and restored later with another call to *set_error_handler( )*. The function returns false on failure.
>
> The custom error handler is not called for the following errors: E_ERROR, E_PARSE, E_CORE_ERROR, E_CORE_WARNING, E_COMPILE_ERROR, and E_COMPILE WARNING. For these, the PHP internal error handler is always used.

For example, to set up a new error handler that's defined in the function *customHandler( )*, you can register it with:

```
set_error_handler("customHandler");
```

The function name is passed as a quoted string, and doesn't include the brackets. After the new handler is defined, the error_reporting level in *php.ini* or defined in the script with *error_reporting( )* has no effect: all errors are either passed to the custom handler or, if they're critical, to the PHP internal default handler. We discuss this more later.

A custom error handler function must accept at least two parameters: an integer error number and a descriptive error string. Three additional optional parameters can be also be used: a string representing the filename of the script that caused the error; an integer line number indicating the line in that file where the error was noticed; and, an array of additional variable context information.

Our initial implementation of the *customHandler( )* function is shown in Example 12-1. It supports all five parameters, and uses them to construct an error string that displays more information than the default PHP internal handler. It handles only E_NOTICE and E_WARNING errors, and ignores all others.

After running the example, the handler outputs the following:

```
<hr><font color="red">
<b>Custom Error Handler -- Warning/Notice<b>
<br>An error has occurred on 38 line in the
  /usr/local/apache2/htdocs/example.12-1.php file.
<br>The error is a "Missing argument 1 for double( )" (error #2).
 <br>Here's some context information:<br>
<pre>
Array
(
    [number] =>
)
</pre></font>
<hr>
```

The useful additional information is the output of a call to the *print_r( )* that dumps the state of all variables in the current context. In this case, there's only one variable which doesn't have a value: that's not surprising, because the warning is generated because the parameter is missing!

The context information is extracted from the fifth, array parameter to the *customHandler()* function. It contains as elements all of the variables that are in the current scope when the error occurred. In our Example 12-1, only one variable was in scope within the function, $number. If the *customHandler()* function is called from outside of all functions (in the main body of the program), it shows the contents of all global variables including the superglobals $_GET, $_POST, and $_SESSION.

Example 12-1. A script with a custom error handler

```
<!DOCTYPE HTML PUBLIC
                "-//W3C//DTD HTML 4.01 Transitional//EN"
                "http://www.w3.org/TR/html401/loose.dtd">
<html>
<head>
  <meta http-equiv="Content-Type" content="text/html; charset=iso-8859-1">
  <title>Error</title>
<body>
<h1>Two times!</h1>
<?php
function customHandler($number, $string, $file, $line, $context)
{
  switch ($number)
  {
    case E_WARNING:
    case E_NOTICE:
      print "<hr><font color=\"red\">\n";
      print "<b>Custom Error Handler -- Warning/Notice<b>\n";
      print "<br>An error has occurred on {$line} line in
             the {$file} file.\n";
      print "<br>The error is a \"{$string}\" (error #{$number}).\n ";
      print "<br>Here's some context information:<br>\n<pre>\n";
      print_r($context);
      print "\n</pre></font>\n<hr>\n";
      break;
    default:
       // Do nothing
  }
}

function double($number)
{
  return $number*2;
}

set_error_handler("customHandler");

// Generates a warning for a missing parameter
print "Two times ten is: " . double();
?>
</body>
</html>
```

As we stated earlier, the *customHandler( )* function isn't called for the critical error types. For example, if we omit the semi-colon from the end of the first print statement:

```
print "Two times ten is: " . double()
```

then the parse error that's output is the PHP default:

```
Parse error: parse error, unexpected T_PRINT in
   /usr/local/apache2/htdocs/example.12-1.php on line 46
```

You can't change this behavior.* Custom handlers work only for the E_WARNING and E_NOTICE errors, and for the entire USER class. The techniques to generate USER class errors are discussed in the next section.

The custom handler we've shown here deliberately doesn't support USER class errors. If, for example, an E_USER_ERROR is generated, the handler is called, but nothing is output and the script doesn't stop. It's the responsibility of the programmer to deal with all error types, and to stop or continue the execution as appropriate. We develop a handler for all errors in the next section.

A Production Error Handler

The simple custom error handler in the previous section has several disadvantages:

- The handler offers only slightly more information than the PHP internal handler. Ideally, it should also include a backtrace, showing which function called the one containing the error, and so on back to the beginning of the script.

- It shows technical information to the user, which is both confusing and a security risk. It should explain to the user that there's a problem with their request, and then log or send the technical information to someone who can fix it.

- It can't handle programmer-generated errors. For example, in Chapter 6, we've used the *showerror( )* function to handle database server errors. These errors should be integrated with our custom handler.

- Our handler doesn't stop script execution, and doesn't leave the application in a known state. For example, if a session is open or the database is locked, the error handler doesn't clean these up.

In this section, we improve our custom handler to address these problems.

Including debugging information

Example 12-2 shows an improved error handler that reports more information about how and where the error occurred. For example, if an E_WARNING error is generated by the fragment:

```
// Generates a warning for a missing parameter
print "Two times ten is: " . double( );
```

then the handler outputs:

```
[PHP Error 20030616104153]E_WARNING on line 67 in bug.php.
[PHP Error 20030616104153]Error: "Missing argument 1 for double( )"
```

---

* This isn't strictly true. It isn't possible to change the behavior within your scripts or in the *php.ini* file. However, it is possible to force all output produced by your script through a function, and to catch them after they've been output; this has a significant performance penalty. See *http://www.webkreator.com/php/ configuration/handling-fatal-and-parse-errors.html* for detailed information.

```
    (error #2).
[PHP Error 20030616104153]Backtrace:
[PHP Error 20030616104153] 0: double (line 67 in bug.php)
[PHP Error 20030616104153] 1: double (line 75 in bug.php)
[PHP Error 20030616104153]Variables in double ( ):
[PHP Error 20030616104153] number is NULL
[PHP Error 20030616104153]Client IP: 192.168.1.1
```

The *backTrace( )* function uses the PHP library function *debug_backtrace( )* to show a call graph, that is, the hierarchy of functions that were called to reach the function containing the bug. In this example, call #1 was from the main part of the script (though this is shown as a call from *double( )*, which is the function name that was called—this is a bug in *debug_backtrace( )*) and call #0 was the *double( )* function that caused the error.

The *debug_backtrace( )* function stores more details than the function name, but they are in a multidimensional array. If you're interested in using the function directly, try adding the following to your code:

```
var_dump(debug_backtrace( ));
```

Our custom handler also includes the following fragment:

```
$prepend = "\n[PHP Error " . date("YmdHis") . "]";
$error = ereg_replace("\n", $prepend, $error);
```

This replaces the carriage return at the beginning of each error line with a fragment that includes the date and time. Later in this section, we write this information to an error log file.

Example 12-2. A custom handler with a backtrace

```php
<?php
function backTrace($context)
{
    // Get a backtrace of the function calls
    $trace = debug_backtrace( );

    $calls = "\nBacktrace:";

    // Start at 2 -- ignore this function (0) and the customHandler( ) (1)
    for($x=2; $x < count($trace); $x++)
    {
        $callNo = $x - 2;
        $calls .= "\n {$callNo}: {$trace[$x]["function"]} ";
        $calls .= "(line {$trace[$x]["line"]} in {$trace[$x]["file"]})";
    }

    $calls .= "\nVariables in {$trace[2]["function"]} ( ):";

    // Use the $context to get variable information for the function
    // with the error
    foreach($context as $name => $value)
    {
```

Example 12-2. A custom handler with a backtrace (continued)

```
    if (!empty($value))
      $calls .= "\n  {$name} is {$value}";
    else
      $calls .= "\n  {$name} is NULL";
  }
  return ($calls);
}

function customHandler($number, $string, $file, $line, $context)
{
  $error = "";

  switch ($number)
  {
    case E_WARNING:
      $error .= "\nE_WARNING on line {$line} in {$file}.\n";
      break;
    case E_NOTICE:
      $error .= "\nE_NOTICE on line {$line} in {$file}.\n";
      break;
    default:
      $error .= "UNHANDLED ERROR on line {$line} in {$file}.\n";
  }
  $error .= "Error: \"{$string}\" (error #{$number}).";
  $error .= backTrace($context);
  $error .= "\nClient IP: {$_SERVER["REMOTE_ADDR"]}";

  $prepend = "\n[PHP Error " . date("YmdHis") . "]";
  $error = ereg_replace("\n", $prepend, $error);

  // Output the error as pre-formatted text
  print "<pre>{$error}</pre>";
  // Log to a user-defined filename
  // error_log($error, 3, "/home/hugh/php_error_log");

}
```

Logging and notifying the user

Output of errors to the user agent (usually a web browser) is useful for debugging during development but shouldn't be used in a production application. Instead, you can use the PHP library *error_log( )* function to log to an email address or a file. Also, you should alert the user of actions they can take, without providing them with unnecessary technical information.

The *error_log( )* function has the following prototype:

int error_log (string message, int message_type [, string destination [, string extra_headers]])

> The string *message* is the error message to be logged. The *message_type* can be 0, 1, or 3. A setting of 0 sends the *message* to the PHP system's error logger, which is configured using the error_log directive in the *php.ini* file. A setting of 1 sends

an email to the *destination* email address with any additional email *extra_headers* that are provided. A setting of 3 appends the *message* to the file *destination*. A setting of 2 isn't available.

In practice, you should choose between logging to an email address or to a user-defined file; it's unlikely that the web server process will have permissions to write to the system error logger. To log to a file using our *customHandler( )* in Example 12-2, uncomment the statement:

```
error_log($error, 3, "/home/hugh/php_error_log");
```

This will log to whatever is set as the logging destination by the third parameter; in this example, we're writing into a file in the administrator's home directory. You could use the directory *C:\Windows\temp* on a Microsoft Windows platform. If you'd prefer that errors arrive in email, replace the *error_log( )* call with:

```
// Use a real email address!
error_log($error, 1, "hugh@asdfgh.com");
```

In practice, we recommend logging to a file and monitoring the file. Receiving emails might sound like a good idea, but in practice if the DBMS is unavailable or another serious problem occurs, you're likely to receive hundreds of emails in a short time.

When the application goes into production, we also recommend removing the print statement that outputs messages to the browser. Instead, you should add a generic message that alerts the user to a problem and asks them contact the system administrator. You might also follow these statements with a call to *die( )* to stop the program execution; remember, it's up to you whether you stop the program when an error occurs.

A better approach than adding print statements to show the error to the user is to create a template with the same look and feel as your application, and include the error messages there; we use this approach in our online winestore in later chapters. This approach also has the additional advantage that it prevents the problem we describe next.

An additional problem with printing errors without a template is that they can still appear anywhere in a partial page. This can lead to user confusion, produce non-compliant HTML, and look unattractive. If you use a template, you can choose whether to output the page or not: nothing is output until you call the *show( )* method. However, even without a template, it's possible to prevent this happening by using the PHP library output buffering library.

The output buffering approach works as shown in the simplified error handler in Example 12-3. The call to *ob_start( )* at the beginning of the script forces all output to be held in a buffer. When an error occurs, the *ob_end_clean( )* function in the *customHandler( )* function throws away whatever is in the buffer, and then outputs only the error message and stops the script. If no errors occur, the script runs as normal and the *ob_end_flush( )* function outputs the document by flushing the buffer. With this approach, partial pages can't occur.

Example 12-3. Using output buffering to prevent partial output pages

```php
<?php
  // start buffering
  ob_start();
?>
<!DOCTYPE HTML PUBLIC
                "-//W3C//DTD HTML 4.01 Transitional//EN"
                "http://www.w3.org/TR/html401/loose.dtd">
<html>
<head>
  <meta http-equiv="Content-Type" content="text/html; charset=iso-8859-1">
  <title>Error</title>
<body>
<?php
function customHandler($number, $string, $file, $line, $context)
{
  // Throw away the current buffer
  ob_end_clean();

  print "An error occurred!";
  die();
}

set_error_handler("customHandler");

// Generates an E_NOTICE
print $a;

// Output the buffer
ob_end_flush();

?>
</body>
</html>
```

Triggering your own errors

In Chapter 6, we triggered our own errors by calling the *showerror( )* function, which outputs MySQL error messages. We added our own calls to *die( )* to handle PEAR DB errors in Chapter 7. However, these approaches aren't consistent with using the custom error handler we've built in this chapter. Now that we have an error handler, it would be useful to be able to trigger its use through programmer-generated errors. This is where the USER class of errors and the PHP library function *trigger_error( )* are useful:

void trigger_error (string error_message [, int error_type])
> The function triggers a programmer-defined error using two parameters: an *error_message* and an optional *error_type* that's set to one of E_USER_ERROR, E_ USER_WARNING, or E_USER_NOTICE. The function calls the current error handler, and provides the same five parameters as other PHP error types.

Example 12-4 is a modified handler that processes errors generated by *trigger_error()*. In addition, it stops the script when WARNING or ERROR class errors occur.

Example 12-4. A custom error handler that supports programmer-generated errors

```
function customHandler($number, $string, $file, $line, $context)
{
  $error = "";

  switch ($number)
  {
    case E_USER_ERROR:
      $error .= "\nERROR on line {$line} in {$file}.\n";
      $stop = true;
      break;
    case E_WARNING:
    case E_USER_WARNING:
      $error .= "\nWARNING on line {$line} in {$file}.\n";
      $stop = true;
      break;
    case E_NOTICE:
    case E_USER_NOTICE:
      $error .= "\nNOTICE on line {$line} in {$file}.\n";
      $stop = false;
      break;
    default:
      $error .= "UNHANDLED ERROR on line {$line} in {$file}.\n";
      $stop = false;
  }
  $error .= "Error: \"{$string}\" (error #{$number}).";
  $error .= backTrace($context);
  $error .= "\nClient IP: {$_SERVER["REMOTE_ADDR"]}";

  $prepend = "\n[PHP Error " . date("YmdHis") . "]";
  $error = ereg_replace("\n", $prepend, $error);

  // Throw away the buffer
  ob_end_clean( );

  print "<pre>{$error}</pre>";
  // Log to a user-defined filename
  // error_log($error, 3, "/home/hugh/php_error_log");

  if ($stop == true)
    die( );
}
```

You can use this handler for several different purposes. For example, if a MySQL connection fails, you can report an error and halt the script:

```
    // Connect to the MySQL server
    if (!($connection = @ mysql_connect($hostname, $username, $password)))
      trigger_error("Could not connect to DBMS", E_USER_ERROR);
```

You can also send error codes and messages through to the handler that are reported as the error string:

```
if (!(mysql_select_db($databaseName, $connection)))
  trigger_error(mysql_errno() . " : " . mysql_error( ), E_USER_ERROR);
```

You could even use this to log security or other problems. For example, if the user fails to log in with the correct password, you could store a NOTICE:

```
if ($password != $storedPassword)
  trigger_error("Incorrect login attempt by {$username}", E_USER_NOTICE);
```

We use *trigger_error( )* extensively for error reporting in the online winestore in Chapters 16 through 20.

Cleaning up the application

An advantage of a custom error handler is that you can add additional features to gracefully stop the application when an error occurs. For example, you might delete session variables, close database connections, unlock a database table, and log out the user. What actions are carried out is dependent on the application requirements, and we don't discuss this in detail here. However, our online winestore error handler in Chapter 16 carries out selected cleanup actions based on the state of session variables, and leaves the application in a known state.

CHAPTER 13

Reporting

In many web database applications, you'll want to produce printable paper reports. For example, you might want to produce a stock report from an online store, a customer receipt, a printable version of an HTML page, or a fill-in form to be faxed. Unfortunately, this isn't easy: PHP doesn't have great built-in tools for reporting that are portable across all platforms. Because of this, reporting is one of the more difficult tasks in PHP.

This chapter shows you how to produce reports using PHP. We show you how to use R&OS Ltd.'s excellent pdf-php library to produce PDF (Adobe Portable Document Format) files that can be downloaded, saved, and printed by your users. PDF is now the most common format for providing reports on the Web, and the pdf-php library allows you to produce complex, configurable reports, and to include graphics and images. It's similar to a PEAR package, and we include a detailed discussion of almost all of its methods.

We don't discuss other reporting schemes for PHP, but we do discuss how to find out more about them in the next section.

Creating a Report

After you've decided you need to produce printable output, the next step is to decide what format to produce it and what tools to use to create it. As Andrew Tanenbaum said in his classic quote from the first edition of his book, *Computer Networks*, "The nice thing about standards is that you have so many to choose from; furthermore, if you do not like any of them, you can just wait for next year's model." He might have foreseen web reporting!

So, there are many things to think about in deciding on reporting tools and formats:

Middle-tier platform
> What platform is your middle-tier installed on? If it's Microsoft Windows, a choice for creating reports is Microsoft Word and a portable format to produce

is RTF (Rich Text Format). If it's a Unix environment, PostScript can be produced with several tools and is a well-supported format by Unix users. However, for almost all platforms, Adobe's PDF (Portable Document Format) has a wide range of tools and libraries for production.

Client platform

What platform do your users use? The answer is most likely to be mostly Microsoft Windows, and so a format that's friendly to those users is essential. Importantly, reporting tools are similar to browsers: you are unlikely to have control over the environment the user has, and the best approach is to choose a format that is likely to be used by the majority.

Richness of content

What features do you need? Are you producing reports that contain images, text, graphics, tables, forms, graphs, or a combination of those? Do you only need to produce a printable copy of the web page? The answers determine if you can use a simple library (or a template) for text and tables, or whether you need the full power of tools that can create pixels and lines.

Speed

How fast does reporting have to be? There are several easy-to-use tools that are slow to create a report file, and several hard-to-use tools that are fast. However, most tools allow you to save output in a file or database so that it can be delivered to many clients without recreating the report.

Price

Do you want to pay? Are you prepared to purchase tools for reporting, or do you want free or open source software?

Flexibility

Do you need to be flexible? Do you want to offer more than one format to minimize the chance that a user will need to install a third-party tool?

We discuss these issues in the remainder of this section.

Formats

There are many possible formats for reports, and this section discusses most of the popular choices for web reporting.

Portable Document Format (PDF)

Adobe's Portable Document Format (PDF) is a well-documented, well-understood and powerful format for reporting. It's now the dominant reporting format on the Web and we use it in this chapter because it meets most of our criteria in the previous section:

- It's ideal for reporting because it supports a wide range of fonts, colors, and graphics. Moreover, it doesn't matter what tools are used to create or view a report, it'll produce the same, high-quality output.

- It's portable. Adobe's free PDF viewer (known as Adobe Reader) is available for almost all platforms, including Mac OS X, Linux, Free BSD, Solaris, all Microsoft Windows variants, Pocket PC, and Palm. There are also Open Source viewers available such as xpdf and ghostview.

- It's full of features. It's simple to use, but it's also powerful: fonts can be embedded in a document, it can be combined with XML markup (which is discussed later in this section), embedded links can be included, forms are easy to integrate, and multimedia can be linked in. Adobe's distiller (a commercial product) is a powerful tool for creating PDFs, and it also allows you to create templates that you can later populate with data.

- It's used by very large organizations. For example, the U.S. government (including the IRS) delivers most of its documents to its users in PDF, as do newswire services such as Associated Press (AP). This means most of your users will already be familiar with the format.

- It's flexible for the Web. You can deliver one page from a large document and it can be rendered at the client without retrieving the rest of the document. (However, this requires some configuration that we don't discuss.)

- There's a wide variety of tools to produce it. We discuss this next.

You can read the PDF specification at *http://partners.adobe.com/asn/tech/pdf/ specifications.jsp*.

There are two major external libraries that can be used to create PDF with PHP: PDFlib (available from *http://www.pdflib.com/*) and ClibPDF (available from *http:// www.fastio.com/*). Both are function libraries that integrate into PHP, but both need to be downloaded, purchased (if you're doing commercial work), and configured, and then PHP needs to be recompiled to support them. The integration process is sometimes tricky, but good notes on the process can be found in the user-contributed comments in the online PHP manual. At the time of writing, PDFlib was more popular.

Both PDFlib and ClibPDF allow creation of low- and high-level report features. For example, you can create a text-only document using a few lines of code, or you can draw lines and shapes by moving a cursor with tens or hundreds of lines of code in a complex program. Both libraries also allow you to include external graphics in reports, and to use almost all of the features of PDF.

Because both function libraries are commercial products and require integration, we favor other, free solutions that are now becoming popular. Later in this chapter, we show you how to use the R&OS PDF class library. It's almost as powerful as PDFlib, and we show you how to use it create and format documents that contains tables, images, and reports.

There are also other, simpler libraries. For example, RustyPart's HTML_ToPDF is a simple tool to turn your HTML page into a PDF document for printing, and it makes use of freely available tools to carry out the process. You can find out more from *http://www.rustyparts.com/pdf.php*.

Rich Text Format (RTF)

Microsoft's Rich Text Format (RTF) is an interchange format for documents. Similarly to PDF, it's an open standard that's implemented in a wide range of tools on many platforms. For example, Microsoft Word can save and read documents in RTF format, as can tools such as the writers in OpenOffice, StarOffice, and most commercial word processors. However, much like HTML, there's no guarantee that an RTF document will look the same in a different word processor or on a different platform.

Reports in RTF are different from those in PDF. An RTF format document is designed to be opened, edited, and manipulated in the same way as any other word processor document. It's therefore a good format for reports that need to be edited or documents that need to be exchanged, but it's not a good format when you want to produce a report that's the same on all platforms. However, as a reporting format, it's preferable to Microsoft Word's proprietary .doc binary format.

You can find out more about the RTF specification from *http://msdn.microsoft.com/ library/default.asp?url=/library/en-us/dnrtfspec/html/rtfspec.asp*

PostScript

Adobe's PostScript format is a printer language. Most laser printers understand PostScript, and can convert a PostScript description into a high-quality printout. PostScript has within it tools to control whether printing is simplex or duplex, what paper to use, and even whether to staple. It's not designed for users in the same way as Adobe's PDF: for example, it doesn't support hypertext-style linking, embedding of sounds and movies, or pages being downloaded individually.

Despite its focus as a printer language, most Unix users are familiar with PostScript and happy with it as a report format. Tools such as GhostView (or GSView or ggv) are commonly installed on Unix platforms, and do a good job of rendering PostScript documents on a screen. Adobe's Reader and Mac OS X's Preview also display PostScript documents.

You can find out more about the PostScript language from *http://partners.adobe.com/ asn/tech/ps/index.jsp*.

HTML and XML

Perhaps the most obvious report type for a web database application is the web page itself.

This works as follows: using PHP code in an application you produce HTML, it's sent to the user, the user's browser renders the page, and (in most browsers) the user can then print the page directly. But despite its simplicity, this doesn't work well for most reporting: different browsers render pages differently, window width and depth doesn't usually align with paper width and depth, and there's no guarantee that colors, fonts, and images will transpose well into the printed environment. However, as discussed previously, there are some good tools available to convert HTML to PDF for printing.

So far in this section, we've described several different formats in which documents or reports are described using a language or markup. The Extensible Markup Language, XML, is another markup language designed to identify structure in text and it is a sibling of HTML (their parent is SGML). XML is conceptually simple, yet developers have found uses for it in a wide range of applications:

Storing content in large and dynamic web sites
Storing content marked-up with XML can make content re-use and management much easier.

Standardizing transporting data between applications
When applications are difficult to integrate, XML provides a common protocol that allows data to be shared.

To define new standards
Scalable Vector Graphics (SVG) and XSL-Flow Objects (XSL-FO) are both examples of standards that are represented with XML. It's also used in conjunction with PDF to, for example, markup forms within a document.

As a component for other technologies
The Simple Object Access Protocol (SOAP) provides a mechanism for manipulating objects over a wide area network—such as the Web—using XML to encode the object messages.

Much like RTF, XML is a possible choice for a reporting format (and for many other tasks): it's powerful and independent of presentation, platform, and operating system. PHP has excellent XML support, and this has been completely redeveloped in PHP5. However, a detailed discussion of XML is outside the scope of this book.

Email and plain text

Plain text without markup is a simple report format, as is a plain text email to a user. What's more, text is compact, easy to format, and fast to send by email or to a browser. However, you have even less control than with HTML over presentation or printing, and it's unlikely to be an effective way to layout information except for the shortest reports. Despite this, as we show in Chapter 19, email receipts are still a useful reporting tool to acknowledge actions in a web database application.

Producing PDF

In this section, we show you how to use R&OS Ltd's free PHP PDF creation library (we refer to this as *pdf-php* throughout this section). The library has two advantages over other approaches: it's free and it doesn't require any additional PHP configuration. What's more, it's powerful and you can do most things you need, including producing tables containing results from database queries and inserting images into a document.

You can find out more about pdf-php from *http://www.ros.co.nz/pdf* and you can download the source, documentation, and get involved in the project at *http://sourceforge.net/projects/pdf-php/*. Instructions for installing pdf-php are included in Appendixes A through C.

Hello, world

Example 13-1 shows a simple PHP example.

Example 13-1. A simple example that produces Hello, world on an A4 page

```php
<?php
  require "class.ezpdf.php";

  // Create a new PDF document
  $doc =& new Cezpdf( );

  // Add text to the document
  $doc->ezText("Hello, world");

  // Output the document
  $doc->ezStream( );
?>
```

This PHP example produces the PDF document shown in Figure 13-1.

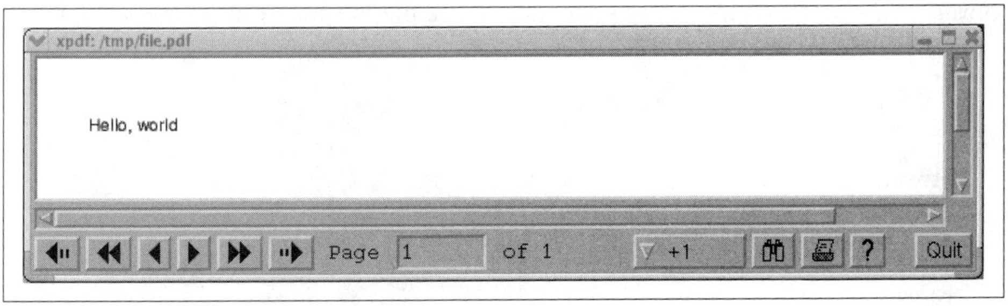

Figure 13-1. The PDF document produced by Example 13-1

The base class for producing PDF files is *class.pdf.php*, but we've used its extension *class.ezpdf.php* in our simple example. The extension has several useful utilities for document creation and it still includes all the methods of the base class, and so we recommend always using it instead.

In Example 13-1, it's assumed both class files are in the same directory as the example code (or in a directory set by the include_path directive in your *php.ini* file). In addition, it's assumed that the fonts are in a subdirectory of the example directory named *fonts*; the fonts are part of the pdf-php install package.

The constructor *Cezpdf()* creates a new PDF document with the default A4 paper size and the default portrait orientation. The =& operator creates an instance of a class, and returns a reference to the instance (and not the whole object itself). The =& operator is a faster, more memory efficient alternative to the = operator. It's discussed in Chapter 4.

The *ezText()* method adds text to the document at the current cursor position (which defaults to the top-left corner; there are, however, top and left margins of 30 points, where a point is 1/72 of an inch), with the current font (which defaults to Helvetica), and the current font size (which defaults to 12). The *ezStream()* method cleans up and then creates the PDF output and sends it to the browser; this is a similar approach to templates (as described in Chapter 7), where a document is first prepared and later output using a method.

In many browsers, when a PDF document arrives as part of an HTTP response, a window containing the PDF document will automatically appear. However, in some browsers, the arrival of a PDF document will cause a dialog box to pop up that asks whether to save or open the PDF file. If you choose open and have a PDF viewer correctly installed, you'll see the output. Now is a good time to get yourself a PDF viewer, as you'll need it throughout this chapter.

You might be wondering what the content of a PDF file looks like. The answer is that it's an ASCII text file that contains instructions on how to render and present the document content; however, it can be compressed, and so you might find it isn't always readable with a text editor. For a document containing graphics, the text can be a complicated list of instructions about lines and points. However, for simple text that's rendered using a font, it's basically human-readable text that you could conceivably edit. For example, here's the part of the file output from Example 13-1 that creates the Hello, world message:

```
7 0 obj
<<
/Length 55 >>
stream

BT 30.000 800.330 Td /F1 10.0 Tf  (Hello, world) Tj ET
endstream
endobj
```

A Full-Featured Document

Example 13-2 shows a more complex example that makes use of many of the features of the pdf-php library. The example prints the first two pages of Lewis Carroll's

Alice's Adventures in Wonderland in a two-column format, with a title on the first page and an image from the book.

Example 13-2. Formatting Alice's Adventures in Wonderland for printing

```php
<?php
  require "class.ezpdf.php";
  require "alice.inc";

  // Create a new PDF document
  $doc =& new Cezpdf( );

  // Use the Helvetica font for the headings
  $doc->selectFont("./fonts/Helvetica.afm");

  // Output the book heading and author
  $doc->ezText("<u>Alice's Adventures in Wonderland</u>", 24,
              array("justification"=>"center"));
  $doc->ezText("by Lewis Carroll", 20, array("justification"=>"center"));

  // Create a little bit of space
  $doc->ezSetDy(-10);

  // Output the chapter title
  $doc->ezText("Chapter 1: Down the Rabbit-Hole", 18,
              array("justification"=>"center"));

  // Number the pages
  $doc->ezStartPageNumbers(320, 15, 8,"",
     "{PAGENUM} of {TOTALPAGENUM} pages");

  // Create a little bit of space
  $doc->ezSetDy(-30);

  // Switch to two-column mode
  $doc->ezColumnsStart(array("num"=>2, "gap"=>15));

  // Use the Times-Roman font for the text
  $doc->selectFont("./fonts/Times-Roman.afm");

  // Include an image with a caption
  $doc->ezImage("rabbit.jpg", "", "", "none");
  $doc->ezText("<b>White Rabbit checking watch</b>",
              12,array("justification"=>"center"));

  // Create a little bit of space
  $doc->ezSetDy(-10);

  // Add chapter text to the document
  $doc->ezText($text,10,array("justification"=>"full"));

  // Output the document
  $doc->ezStream( );
?>
```

The first page is shown rendered by the xpdf viewer in Figure 13-2.

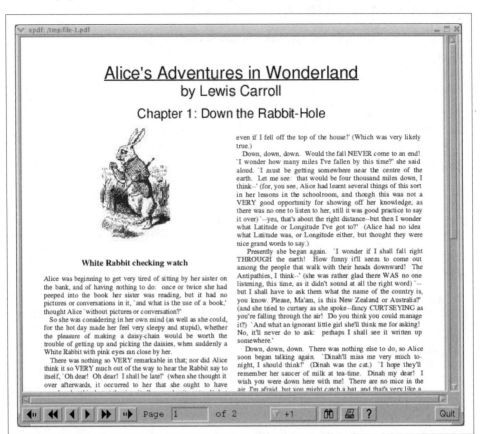

Figure 13-2. The output of Example 13-2 shown in the xpdf viewer

The following code fragment from Example 13-2 sets the font:

```
// Use the Helvetica font for the headings
$doc->selectFont("./fonts/Helvetica.afm");
```

We use Helvetica for the headings, and Times-Roman for the body of the document. The available fonts are in the subdirectory fonts in the pdf-php install package, and are passed to the *selectFont()* method using their path and the full file name. The font name must include the *.afm* extension, and only *.afm* format files are supported; however, there are free utilities, such as *t1utils* and *ttf2pt1*, that convert other font formats (such as *.ttf*) into *.afm* files.

This next fragment outputs the headings:

```
// Output the book heading and author
$doc->ezText("<u>Alice's Adventures in Wonderland</u>", 24,
             array("justification"=>"center"));
$doc->ezText("by Lewis Carroll", 20, array("justification"=>"center"));
```

The *ezText()* method has three parameters, but only the first is mandatory. The first parameter is the text to add to the document, and it can include simple HTML-like markup elements such as <u> for underline and <b> for bold. Text is output by the method, and followed with a carriage return in the same way as echo or print in PHP. The second parameter is the font size to use (the default is 12), and the third parameter is an array of options. In this example, we've set the justification parameter to center, but it can also be set to left, right, or full; we use full for the text. The complete list of options is described later in the section "PDF-PHP Reference"

The *ezSetDy()* method is used to create space between text and images. For example, the following fragment moves the cursor down the page by 10 points:

```
// Create a little bit of space
$doc->ezSetDy(-10);
```

A negative value is downwards, and a positive value is upwards. In PDF, the bottom-left-hand corner of a page is coordinate X=0, Y=0, and the top-right has the maximum X and Y values. For an A4 page, the top-right corner has a point value of X=595.28 and Y=841.89, and for US letter of X=612.00 and Y=792.00.

The class includes the useful *ezStartPageNumbers()* method for numbering pages. We use it as follows:

```
// Number the pages
$doc->ezStartPageNumbers(320, 15, 8, "",
   "{PAGENUM} of {TOTALPAGENUM} pages");
```

The first two parameters are the X and Y coordinates of where to put the page number text, and the third parameter is the font size to use; the first three parameters are mandatory. The optional fourth parameter can be set to left or right, and indicates whether to put the text to the left or right of the X coordinate; by default, the text is written to the left of the X coordinate. The optional fifth parameter specifies how to present the page numbering; by default, it is {PAGENUM} of {TOTALPAGENUM} but we've set it to {PAGENUM} of {TOTALPAGENUM} pages to get strings such as 1 of 2 pages. The optional sixth parameter is a page number and, if it is supplied, the current page is numbered beginning with the number.

We've presented the text of the book in a two column newspaper-like format. This is achieved by calling the *ezColumnsStart()* method as follows:

```
// Switch to two-column mode
$doc->ezColumnsStart(array("num"=>2, "gap"=>15));
```

The method takes one optional parameter. The parameter is an array that specifies the number of columns and the gap in points between the columns. If the parameter is omitted, the number of columns defaults to 2 and the gap to 10. The method *ezColumnsStop()* stops multi-column mode, but we don't use it here because we're working with only one chapter.

To include an image in the text, you can use the *ezImage()* method. We use it to include a picture of the white rabbit after the headings:

```
$doc->ezImage("rabbit.jpg", "", "", "none");
```

A great feature of this method is that it doesn't require any additional configuration: you don't need to install any graphics libraries (such as GD) and it'll work on all platforms without modification. The method takes six parameters. The first parameter is a mandatory image file path and name, and only JPEG and PNG format images are supported. All of the remaining parameters are optional. The second parameter is the amount of padding in points to place around the image, and it defaults to 5. The third parameter is the width of the image, and the default is the image's actual width. The fourth parameter is a resize value that controls how the image fits in a column, and we've used none so that the image isn't resized at all. The fifth parameter specifies justification, and can be set to left, right, or center with a default of center. The sixth parameter is a border to place around the image, and defaults to none. More details on all parameters are provided in the section "PDF-PHP Reference."

After we've finished with headings and images, the following fragment includes the text of the book into the PDF document:

```
$doc->ezText($text,10,array("justification"=>"full"));
```

The variable $text contains the text of the book. It is set in the *alice.inc* include file. Here are the first few lines of *alice.inc*:

```
<?php
$text = "Alice was beginning to get very tired of sitting by her sister on
the bank, and of having nothing to do:  once or twice she had peeped into
the book her sister was reading, but it had no pictures or conversations
in it, ... ";
```

Carriage returns and whitespace characters are preserved in the output. So, for example, a carriage return creates a new line in the PDF file; this is unlike HTML, where whitespace is ignored. The book text itself is sourced from the Project Gutenberg homepage at *http://gutenberg.net*.

A Database Example

Example 13-3 shows a script that produces a page containing one customer's details from a *customer* table. The *customer* table is discussed in Chapter 5 and created with the following CREATE TABLE statement:

```
CREATE TABLE customer (
  cust_id int(5) NOT NULL,
  surname varchar(50),
  firstname varchar(50),
  initial char(1),
  title_id int(3),
  address varchar(50),
  city varchar(50),
```

```
    state varchar(20),
    zipcode varchar(10),
    country_id int(4),
    phone varchar(15),
    birth_date char(10),
    PRIMARY KEY (cust_id)
  ) type=MyISAM;
```

The example also uses the *titles* lookup table that contains `title_id` values and titles (such as Mr. and Miss), and the *countries* lookup table that contains `country_id` values and country names. The output of Example 13-3 is shown in Figure 13-3.

Example 13-3. Producing customer information from the customer table

```php
<?php
  require "class.ezpdf.php";
  require "db.inc";

  $query = "SELECT * FROM customer, titles, countries
            WHERE customer.title_id = titles.title_id
            AND customer.country_id = countries.country_id
            AND cust_id = 1";

  if (!($connection = @ mysql_connect($hostName, $username, $password)))
    die("Could not connect to database");

  if (!(mysql_selectdb($databaseName, $connection)))
    showerror();

  if (!($result = @ mysql_query($query, $connection)))
    showerror();

  $row = mysql_fetch_array($result);

  // Construct the title and name
  $name = "{$row["title"]} {$row["firstname"]}";
  if (!empty($row["initial"]))
    $name .= " {$row["initial"]} ";
  $name .= "{$row["surname"]}";

  // Create a new PDF document
  $doc =& new Cezpdf();

  // Use the Helvetica font
  $doc->selectFont("./fonts/Helvetica.afm");

  // Create a heading
  $doc->ezText("<u>Customer Details for {$name}</u>",
               14, array("justification"=>"center"));

  // Create a little bit of space
  $doc->ezSetDy(-15);

  // Set up an array of customer information
```

Example 13-3. Producing customer information from the customer table (continued)

```
$table = array(
  array("Details"=>"Title and name",
        "Value"=>$name),
  array("Details"=>"Address",
        "Value"=>"{$row["address"]} {$row["city"]} {$row["zipcode"]}"),
  array("Details"=>"State and country",
        "Value"=>"{$row["state"]} {$row["country"]}"),
  array("Details"=>"Telephone",
        "Value"=>$row["phone"]),
  array("Details"=>"Date of birth",
        "Value"=>$row["birth_date"]));

$doc->ezTable($table);

// Output the document
$doc->ezStream();
?>
```

The database processing in Example 13-3 is similar to that of most examples in previous chapters. The script queries and retrieves the customer details for customer #1, including the customer's title and country. The results are stored in the array $row, and the array is then used as the source of data for the PDF document.

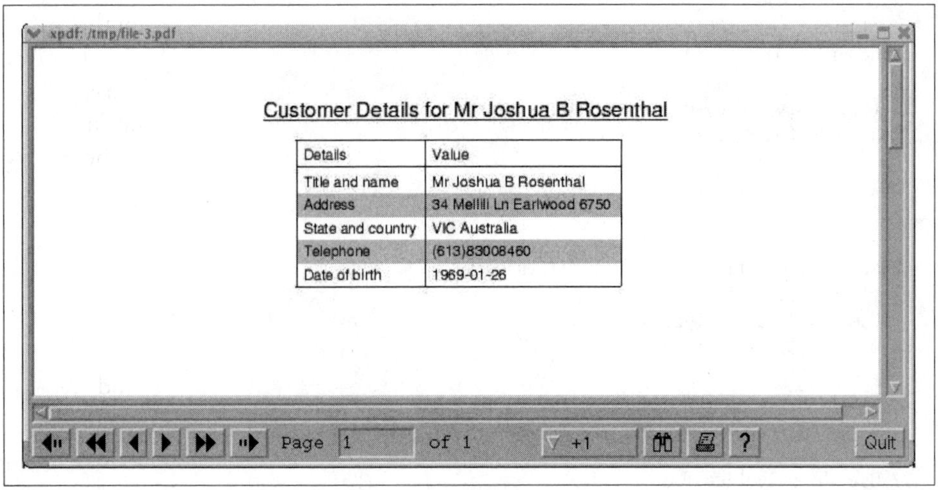

Figure 13-3. The customer details page output by Example 13-3

The use of the pdf-php library is also similar to that in our previous examples, with the exception that the customer details are shown in a table using the *ezTable()* method. The *ezTable()* method is a flexible tool that allows you to present data in different table styles and to configure the column headings, column widths, shading, borders, and alignment.

In this example, we only use the basic features of the *ezTable()* method. First, we've created an array that contains the data we want to display in the table:

```
// Set up an array of customer information
$table = array(
   array("Details"=>"Title and name",
         "Value"=>$name),
   array("Details"=>"Address",
         "Value"=>"{$row["address"]} {$row["city"]} {$row["zipcode"]}"),
   array("Details"=>"State and country",
         "Value"=>"{$row["state"]} {$row["country"]}"),
   array("Details"=>"Telephone",
         "Value"=>$row["phone"]),
   array("Details"=>"Date of birth",
         "Value"=>$row["birth_date"]));
```

The array contains five elements, each of which is itself an array. Each of these five inner arrays has two associatively-labeled elements: Details and Value. The Details element holds as a row label value such as Title and name, and the Value element holds the data that matches the label.

The PDF table itself is created with the fragment:

```
$doc->ezTable($table);
```

The method creates a table with the number of rows equal to the number of elements in the array (in our example, five rows). The number of columns in the table is equal to the number of elements in the inner arrays and, in our example, they each have two elements. By default, column headings are taken from the associative-access keys, and the data in the tables comes from the values. The default mode is to create a bordered table with shading in every second row, and to center the table in the output.

Creating a Report

Example 13-4 shows a script that produces a more complex purchase report. The report is a table that lists the customers in the winestore database, the number of orders they've placed, the number of bottles of wine they've bought, and the total dollar value of their purchases. We also show totals at the end of each page, and an overall total on the final page.

Example 13-4. A script to produce a customer purchasing report

```
<?php
  require "class.ezpdf.php";
  require "db.inc";

  // Do the querying to produce the customer report
  $query = "SELECT customer.cust_id, surname, firstname,
                   SUM(qty), SUM(price), MAX(order_id)
            FROM customer, items
```

```
            WHERE customer.cust_id = items.cust_id
            GROUP BY customer.cust_id";

  if (!($connection = @ mysql_connect($hostName, $username, $password)))
    die("Could not connect to database");

  if (!(mysql_selectdb($databaseName, $connection)))
    showerror();

  if (!($result = @ mysql_query($query, $connection)))
    showerror();

  // Now, create a new PDF document
  $doc =& new Cezpdf();

  // Use the Helvetica font
  $doc->selectFont("./fonts/Helvetica.afm");

  // Number the pages
  $doc->ezStartPageNumbers(320, 15, 8);

  // Set up running totals and an empty array for the output
  $counter = 0;
  $table = array();
  $totalOrders = 0;
  $totalBottles = 0;
  $totalAmount = 0;

  // Get the query rows, and put them in the table
  while ($row = mysql_fetch_array($result))
  {
    // Counts the total number of rows output
    $counter++;

    // Add current query row to the array of customer information
    $table[] = array(
          "Customer #"=>$row["cust_id"],
          "Name"=> "{$row["surname"]}, {$row["firstname"]}",
          "Orders Placed"=>$row["MAX(order_id)"],
          "Total Bottles"=>$row["SUM(qty)"],
          "Total Amount"=>"\${$row["SUM(price)"]}");

    // Update running totals
    $totalOrders += $row["MAX(order_id)"];
    $totalBottles += $row["SUM(qty)"];
    $totalAmount += $row["SUM(price)"];
  }

  // Today's date is used in the table heading
  $date = date("d M Y");

  // Right-justify the numeric columns
```

```
    $options = array("cols" =>
                array("Total Amount" =>
                    array("justification" => "right"),
                        "Total Bottles" =>
                    array("justification" => "right"),
                        "Orders Placed" =>
                    array("justification" => "right")));

    // Output the table with a heading
    $doc->ezTable($table, "", "Customer Order Report for {$date}",
                $options);

    $doc->ezSetDy(-10);

    // Show totals
    $doc->ezText("Total customers: {$counter}");
    $doc->ezText("Total orders: {$totalOrders}");
    $doc->ezText("Total bottles: {$totalBottles}");
    $doc->ezText("Total amount: \${$totalAmount}");

    // Output the document
    $doc->ezStream( );
?>
```

The first page of the output of Example 13-4 is shown in Figure 13-4 and the final page of the output in Figure 13-5.

The report makes use of two tables, the *customer* table shown in the previous section and an *items* table that's described in more detail in Chapter 5. The *items* table is created with the following statement:

```
    CREATE TABLE items (
        cust_id int(5) NOT NULL,
        order_id int(5) NOT NULL,
        item_id int(3) NOT NULL,
        wine_id int(4) NOT NULL,
        qty int(3),
        price decimal(5,2),
        PRIMARY KEY (cust_id,order_id,item_id)
    ) type=MyISAM;
```

We only use the order_id (which is used to count how many orders each customer has placed), qty (quantity of wine ordered in bottles), and price (per bottle price) attributes from the *items* table in this section.

We use the following query in our report:

```
    $query = "SELECT customer.cust_id, surname, firstname,
                SUM(qty), SUM(price), MAX(order_id)
            FROM customer, items
            WHERE customer.cust_id = items.cust_id
            GROUP BY customer.cust_id";
```

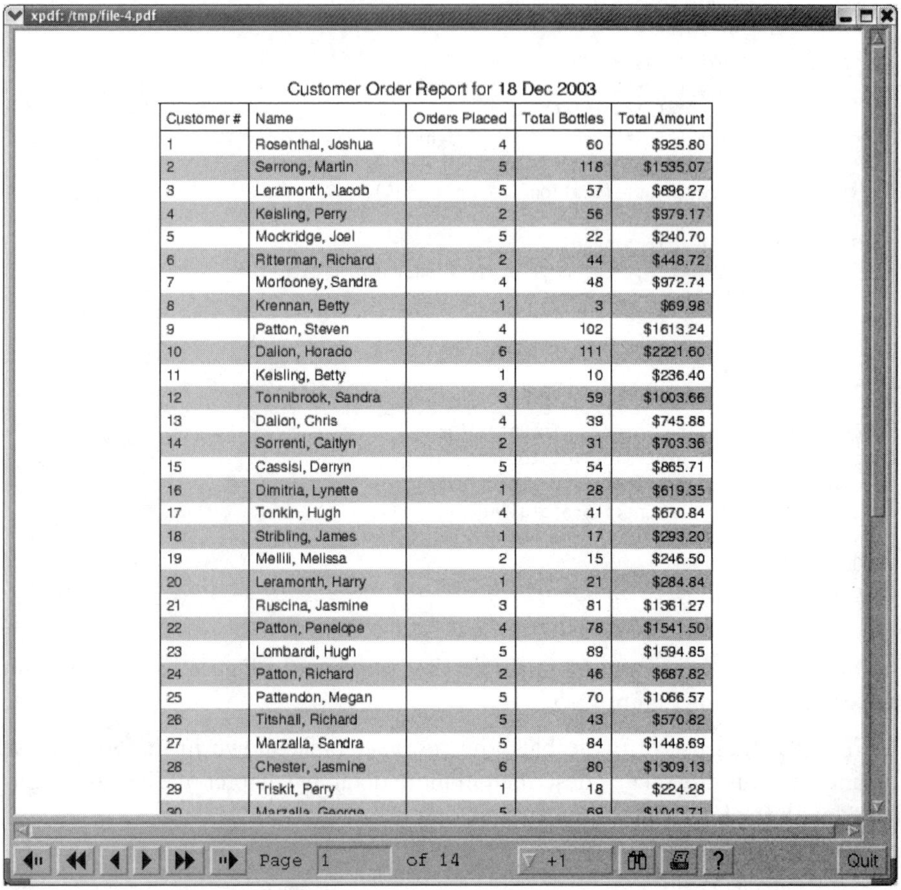

Customer Order Report for 18 Dec 2003

Customer #	Name	Orders Placed	Total Bottles	Total Amount
1	Rosenthal, Joshua	4	60	$925.80
2	Serrong, Martin	5	118	$1535.07
3	Leramonth, Jacob	5	57	$896.27
4	Keisling, Perry	2	56	$979.17
5	Mockridge, Joel	5	22	$240.70
6	Ritterman, Richard	2	44	$448.72
7	Morfooney, Sandra	4	48	$972.74
8	Krennan, Betty	1	3	$69.98
9	Patton, Steven	4	102	$1613.24
10	Dalion, Horacio	6	111	$2221.60
11	Keisling, Betty	1	10	$236.40
12	Tonnibrook, Sandra	3	59	$1003.66
13	Dalion, Chris	4	39	$745.88
14	Sorrenti, Caitlyn	2	31	$703.36
15	Cassisi, Derryn	5	54	$865.71
16	Dimitria, Lynette	1	28	$619.35
17	Tonkin, Hugh	4	41	$670.84
18	Stribling, James	1	17	$293.20
19	Mellili, Melissa	2	15	$246.50
20	Leramonth, Harry	1	21	$284.84
21	Ruscina, Jasmine	3	81	$1361.27
22	Patton, Penelope	4	78	$1541.50
23	Lombardi, Hugh	5	89	$1594.85
24	Patton, Richard	2	46	$687.82
25	Pattendon, Megan	5	70	$1066.57
26	Titshall, Richard	5	43	$570.82
27	Marzalla, Sandra	5	84	$1448.69
28	Chester, Jasmine	6	80	$1309.13
29	Triskit, Perry	1	18	$224.28
30	Marzalla, George	5	69	$1043.71

Page 1 of 14 ▽ +1 Quit

Figure 13-4. The first page of output from Example 13-4

The query groups each customer's items together by his unique cust_id, and we then discover the customer's name, cust_id, the sum of bottles sold using SUM(qty), the total value of the sales using SUM(price), and the number of orders placed using MAX(order_id). We run the query using the usual MySQL functions, and then retrieve each row of the results and add it to the PDF document as a table row.

We use the class constructor and the *SelectFont()*, *ezStartPageNumbers()*, *ezText()*, *ezSetDy()*, and *ezStream()* methods in the same way as in the previous three sections.

Data comes from multiple rows in our database query results and is displayed using the *ezTable()* method in this example. To create the table, we first initialize an empty array using:

```
$table = array( );
```

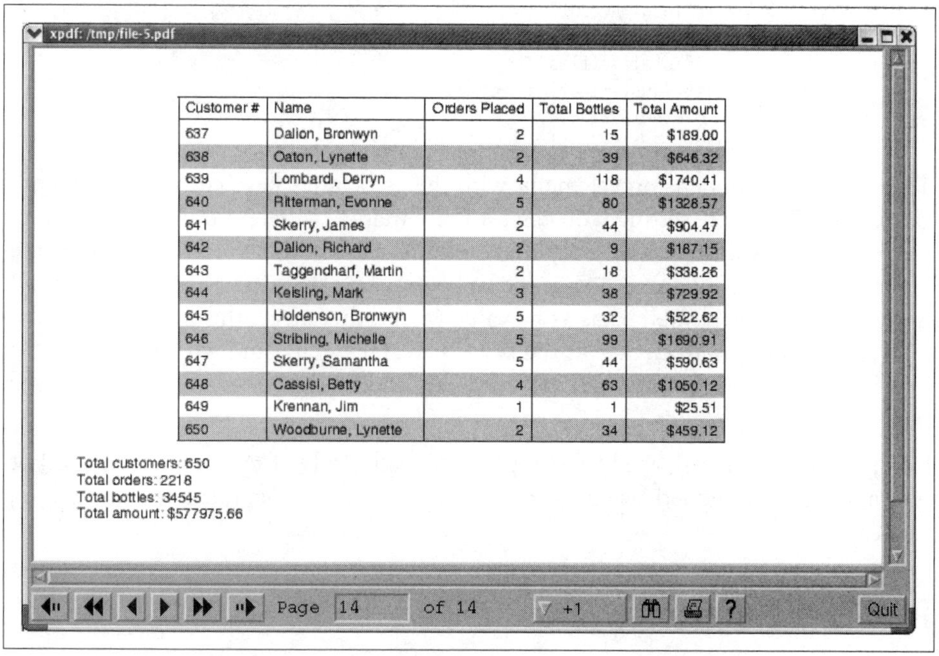

Customer #	Name	Orders Placed	Total Bottles	Total Amount
637	Dalion, Bronwyn	2	15	$189.00
638	Oaton, Lynette	2	39	$646.32
639	Lombardi, Derryn	4	118	$1740.41
640	Ritterman, Evonne	5	80	$1328.57
641	Skerry, James	2	44	$904.47
642	Dalion, Richard	2	9	$187.15
643	Taggendharf, Martin	2	18	$338.26
644	Keisling, Mark	3	38	$729.92
645	Holdenson, Bronwyn	5	32	$522.62
646	Stribling, Michelle	5	99	$1690.91
647	Skerry, Samantha	5	44	$590.63
648	Cassisi, Betty	4	63	$1050.12
649	Krennan, Jim	1	1	$25.51
650	Woodburne, Lynette	2	34	$459.12

Total customers: 650
Total orders: 2218
Total bottles: 34545
Total amount: $577975.66

Figure 13-5. The final page of output from Example 13-4

Then, for each row in the table, we add an element to that array that is itself an array that contains five elements:

```
// Add to the array of customer information
$table[] = array(
    "Customer #"=>$row["cust_id"],
    "Name"=> "{$row["surname"]}, {$row["firstname"]}",
    "Orders Placed"=>$row["MAX(order_id)"],
    "Total Bottles"=>$row["SUM(qty)"],
    "Total Amount"=>"\${$row["SUM(price)"]}");
```

The associative-access labels (Customer #, Name, Orders Placed, Total Bottles, and Total Amount) are used as the column headings for the table, and the customer data from the query is used to populate the rows.

The table itself is then output with the following fragment:

```
// Output the table
$doc->ezTable($table, "", "Customer Order Report for {$date}", $options);
```

We use the optional third parameter that adds a title to the table. This is output on the first page of output. The fourth optional parameter is also used in this example to right-justify the numeric columns (so that the differences in magnitude are obvious and so the decimal points line up). To do this, we create a nested array:

```
// Right-justify the numeric columns
$options = array("cols" =>
```

```
array("Total Amount" =>
   array("justification" => "right"),
      "Total Bottles" =>
   array("justification" => "right"),
      "Orders Placed" =>
   array("justification" => "right")));
```

The outer array contains one element, with the associative key 'cols', and this indicates the option we're setting (you can set more than 15 different options for a table). It contains as a value another array that contains as keys the names of the three columns we want to configure ('Total Amount', 'Total Bottles', and 'Orders Placed'). Each of these three elements has as its value yet another array, this time with the column setting we want to change as the key ('justification') and what we want to set it to ('right'). This complex options parameter is discussed in more detail in the section "PDF-PHP Reference."

Finally, with the pages of tables complete, overall totals of customers, orders, bottles, and sales are added using *ezText()* and the whole document is output using *ezStream()*.

PDF-PHP Reference

This section describes the methods that are available in the two classes that comprise the pdf-php library (version 009). The first section describes the EZPDF class extension that provides easy-to-use methods to create a PDF document, control basic formatting, and add text, tables, columns, and images. The second section lists the methods in the base class that can be used for more complex tasks, including drawing shapes and controlling fonts.

We recommend always using the EZPDF class in preference to the base class because it allows you to access all of the base class methods as well as all of the advanced features that simplify producing documents. For this reason, we've omitted PDF base class methods from our discussion that are a subset of the corresponding EZPDF methods. For example, we don't discuss the PDF base class constructor, because the EZPDF constructor has the same functionality and additional features. In addition, we've omitted discussion of using callback functions to add additional functionality; more details on this topic is in the final section of the pdf-php class manual.

EZPDF Class

void Cezpdf::Cezpdf([mixed paper[, string orientation]])
> This is the class constructor. Without parameters, it creates a new PDF document using A4 paper size with portrait orientation. It sets all margins on the page to 30 points (around 0.4 inches or just over 1 centimeter) and then defines the point at which the text starts to be the top-left corner of the margined page.

The first parameter defines an optional *paper* size and it can be either a string that represents a standard size (a full list is provided next), an array of two elements that contains the page width and depth in centimeters expressed as floats (for example, *array(21.0,29.7)* for an A4 page), or an array of four elements that defines the top-left and bottom-right positions on the page as two sets of (X,Y) coordinates, measured in points (for example, *array(0,0,595.28,841.89)* for an A4 page).

The second parameter defines the orientation. It can be set to `landscape`, otherwise portrait is assumed.

The complete list of possible paper sizes is `4A0`, `2A0`, `A0`, `A1`, `A2`, `A3`, `A4`, `A5`, `A6`, `A7`, `A8`, `A9`, `A10`, `B0`, `B1`, `B2`, `B3`, `B4`, `B5`, `B6`, `B7`, `B8`, `B9`, `B10`, `C0`, `C1`, `C2`, `C3`, `C4`, `C5`, `C6`, `C7`, `C8`, `C9`, `C10`, `RA0`, `RA1`, `RA2`, `RA3`, `RA4`, `SRA0`, `SRA1`, `SRA2`, `SRA3`, `SRA4`, `LETTER`, `LEGAL`, `EXECUTIVE`, or `FOLIO`.

void Cezpdf::ezColumnsStart([array options])

Switches output into multi-column mode. By default, the text that follows the method call is output in two columns per page, with a gap of 10 points between the columns. An *array* of options can be provided as a parameter containing either or both of the associative keys num and gap that define the number of columns and gap between the columns respectively. For example, *ezColumnsStart("num"=>3,"gap"=>5)* switches output to 3 columns per page with a gap of 5 points between each column.

void Cezpdf::ezColumnsStop()

Switches output back to one column per page mode and restores margins prior to the call to *ezColumnsStart()*. It is recommended that you start a new page by calling *ezNewPage()* immediately after a call to *ezColumnsStop()*.

void Cezpdf::ezImage(string image_file[, int padding [, int width [, string resize [, string justification [, array border]]]]])

Inserts an *image_file* of type JPEG or PNG into the document at the current position. The *image_file* parameter can include a path, and must include the full filename of the image. By default, the image is centered, and resized to the width of the current column (if in multi-column mode) or page (if not in multi-column mode) less a spacing of five points on each side of the image.

The optional *padding* parameter is used to alter the spacing on each side of the image from the default of 5 pixels.

The *width* and *resize* parameters are related as follows:

If resize is set to `none` and width is provided

The image is resized to a width of *width* pixels unless it is too wide for the current page or column.

If resize is set to `'none'` *and* `width` *is omitted*
> The image is not resized at all.

If resize is set to `'width'`
> The `width` parameter is ignored and the image is resized to fit the width of the current column or page (minus the padding).

If resize is set to `'full'`
> The `width` parameter is ignored and the image is resized to fit the width of the current column or page (minus the padding). Then, if the image doesn't fit vertically within the column or page, it is resized down proportionally until it does.

The `width` parameter defaults to the width of the image in pixels. The resize parameter defaults to `'full'`. As discussed, this causes the `'width'` parameter to be overridden.

The *justification* parameter defines where the image sits in the current column or page, and it can be set to `'center'`, `'left'`, or `'right'`. It has meaning only if the image is smaller in width than the column or page (that is, it has not been resized using the `width` or `resize` parameters so that it spans the whole column or page). The default is `'center'`.

The *border* array defines a border for the image. The array can have up to four associatively-indexed elements: `'width'` that defines the width of the border in pixels (the default is 1); `'cap'` that specifies the line cap type (the default is `'round'`, and the entry for *Cpdf::setLineStyle()* defines this in more detail); `'join'` that specifies the join type (the default is `'round'`, and the entry for *Cpdf:: setLineStyle()* defines this in more detail); and, `'color'` which defines the line color and itself has three elements that can be set to intensities of red, blue, and green respectively (the default is half intensity for all, and the options are discussed further in *Cpdf::setStrokeColor()*). The following array defines a *border* of two pixels in width with a bright red color:

```
$border = array("width" => 2, "color" => array(1.0, 0.0, 0.0));
```

void Cezpdf::ezInsertMode([int status *[, int* page *[, string* where*]]])*
> Controls whether new pages are inserted into a document rather than appended to the end. The default is a *status* value of 1, which turns on the insert mode that inserts pages into the document. A *status* value of 0 turns off insert mode and from then pages are added to the end.
>
> When *status* is set to 1, the optional *page* parameter defines the page number where new pages should be inserted (the default is 1) and the *where* parameter defines if the pages should be inserted `'before'` or `'after'` that page number (the default is `'before'`).

void Cezpdf::ezNewPage()

    Ends the current page and begins a new page. If you are using the EZPDF class, use this method in preference to the base class's *Cpdf::newpage()* (which is not discussed in this chapter).

string Cezpdf::ezOutput([int option])

    Returns the PDF document as a string. This allows you to save it to a file or store it in a database (if, for example, you're delivering the same file multiple times and want to save processing costs). The *option* parameter is set to 0 by default (no option), but it can also be set to 1 which prevents compression and thus allows the content to be viewed in a text editor for debugging purposes.

void Cezpdf::ezSetCmMargins(float top, float bottom, float left, float right)

    Sets the *top*, *bottom*, *left*, and *right* margins in centimeters.

void Cezpdf::ezSetDy(int points [, string force])

    Moves the drawing point by a relative vertical space *points* measured in points. A negative value is down the page, and a positive value is towards the top. If the drawing point moves below the bottom margin, a new page is started and the drawing point is set to the top margin.

    If the optional *force* parameter is set to 'makespace', the space created will always be *points* in size even if it spans multiple pages. This is designed to allow you to create a space that you later use for drawing.

void Cezpdf::ezSetMargins(float top, float bottom, float left, float right)

    Sets the *top*, *bottom*, *left*, and *right* margins in points.

void Cezpdf::ezSetY(int position)

    Moves the drawing point to the vertical point *position*, where the point 0 is the bottom of the page. If the new position is below the bottom margin, a new page is begun.

int Cezpdf::ezStartPageNumbers(float x, float y, int size [, string position [, string pattern [, int set_number]]])

    Starts page numbering on the current page and displays the page number at coordinates *x* and *y* with the requested font *size*. The bottom-left corner of the page is coordinate X=0, Y=0, and font used is the current font as set by *Cpdf::selectFont()*.

    The optional position can be set to 'left' or 'right' (the default is 'left') to indicate whether the text should be displayed to the left or right of coordinate *x*.

    The string *pattern* defines how the page numbering is displayed. Two placeholders can be used in specifying the numbering: {PAGENUM} and {TOTALPAGENUM}. and these represent the current page and total pages respectively. For examples, the *pattern* 'Total pages: {TOTALPAGENUM}. This page: {PAGENUM}' displays strings such as 'Total pages: 10. This page: 4'. The default display string is '{PAGENUM} of {TOTALPAGENUM}'.

The return value can be used to implement several concurrent numbering schemes in the same document and is used with the optional *set_number* parameter. It's unlikely you'll need this in practice, and we don't discuss it in detail here; more details and an example can be found in the pdf-php class manual.

void Cezpdf::ezStopPageNumbers([int stop_total *[, int* stop_when *[, int* set_number*]]])*

Stops numbering of pages. If *stop_total* is set to 0 (the default), the total number of pages that is reported stops as well; if it's set to 1, the reported total is the actual total number of pages. If the *stop_when* parameter is set to 0 (the default) numbering stops on the current page; if it's set to 1, numbering stops on the next page.

The *set_number* parameter is used to start and stop multiple numbering schemes within one document. It's unlikely you'll need this in practice, and we don't discuss it in detail here; more details and an example can be found in the pdf-php class manual.

void Cezpdf::ezStream([array options])

Outputs the PDF document to the web browser after finalizing EZPDF class processing.

The *options* array can be used to control three HTTP headers: first, you can set *options['Content-Disposition']* to a filename that the user's browser should respect in saving the file (the default is *file.pdf*); second, you can set *options['Accept-Ranges']* to 0 (off) or 1 (on) to indicate whether your server can handle retrieval of a range of bytes from the file (the default is 0); and, you can set *options['compress']* to 0 (off) or 1 (on) to compress the document content (the default is 1).

float Cezpdf::ezTable(array data *[, array* columns *[, string* title *[, array* options*]]])*

Creates a table that displays an array of *data*. The return value is the Y coordinate in points of the writing point on the page after the table has been output (where the bottom of the page is the point Y=0).

The *data* array should contain one or more elements that are arrays, where each such element is a row of data in the table. These row arrays should all have the same number of elements, and the elements should be in the same order in each row array (unless the optional *columns* parameter is supplied) and have the same associative labels. The following is an example of a *data* array with two rows and two columns:

```
$table = array(
    array("Col A" => "Row 1, Col A data", "Col B" => "Row 1, Col B data"),
    array("Col A" => "Row 2, Col A data", "Col B" => "Row 2, Col B data")
    );
```

By default, columns have headings set to the associative labels used in the row arrays; in the above example, the columns are headed 'Col A' and 'Col B'. In addition, by default, the table has a line border, alternate lines are shaded gray, and the table can wrap over multiple pages (with the column headings redisplaying on each page). Example 13-5 uses the $table array and default parameters to create a table and its output is shown in Figure 13-6.

Example 13-5. Producing a simple table with ezTable( )

```php
<?php
  require "class.ezpdf.php";
  $doc =& new Cezpdf( );
  $table = array(
    array("Col A" => "Row 1, Col A data", "Col B" => "Row 1, Col B data"),
    array("Col A" => "Row 2, Col A data", "Col B" => "Row 2, Col B data")
  );
  $doc->ezTable($table);
  $doc->ezStream( );
?>
```

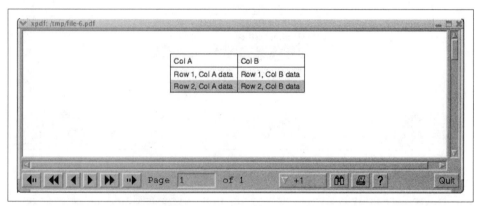

Figure 13-6. The output of Example 13-5

The *columns* parameter is an optional associative array that redefines headings for the columns and the display order of the columns. It can also be used to select only some columns from the *data* array. The associative keys of *columns* should be associative keys from the *data* array, and the associative values are the new names of the columns. The order in which elements are listed in *columns* defines the display order. For example, to replace the 'Col A' and 'Col B' headings in our previous example with 'Column A' and 'Column B' and reverse their display order, we could provide the following *columns* array:

```php
    $columns = array("Col B" => "Column B", "Col A" => "Column A")
```

The optional *title* parameter is a title to display at the beginning of the table. The script in Example 13-6 shows an extended version of Example 13-5 that renames the columns using the $columns array and includes a title. Its output is shown in Figure 13-7.

Example 13-6. Renaming columns and including a title with ezTable()

```php
<?php
  require "class.ezpdf.php";
  $doc =& new Cezpdf();
  $table = array(
    array("Col A" => "Row 1, Col A data", "Col B" => "Row 1, Col B data"),
    array("Col A" => "Row 2, Col A data", "Col B" => "Row 2, Col B data")
  );
  $columns = array("Col B" => "Column B", "Col A" => "Column A");

  $doc->ezTable($table, $columns, "The Table with Columns!");
  $doc->ezStream();
?>
```

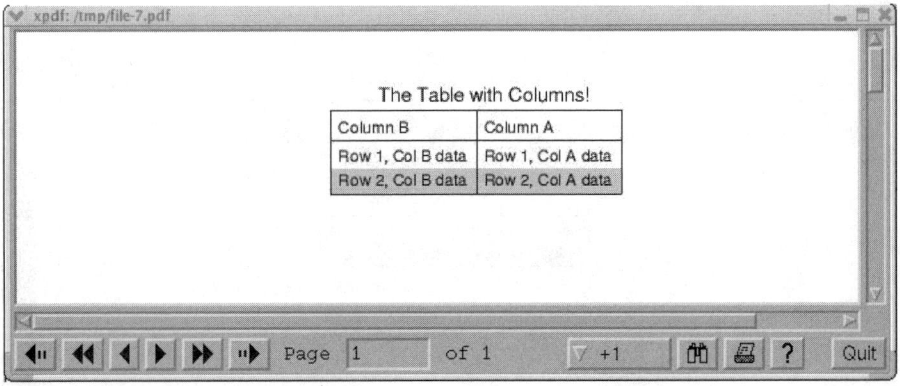

Figure 13-7. The output of Example 13-6

The *options* array is an associative array that can be used to define a wide range of table options. Valid options include:

options['colGap']

> The gap in points to use between the data and the column lines in the table. The default is 5.

options['cols']

> An array that contains the *column_name* associative keys from the *data* array (not the *columns* array!) and is used to set properties for each column. Each *column_name* element itself has two optional elements. First, justification defines the justification of *column_name* and is set to 'left', 'right', or 'center'; the default is 'left'. Second, width defines the column width in points and is set to a float value; text wraps within the cell when it exceeds the column width.

> For example, to set the width of 'Col A' to 100 points and its alignment to center, and the width of 'Col B' to 50 points and to right alignment, use the *options* parameter shown in Example 13-7. The output is shown in Figure 13-8.

Example 13-7. Defining column properties with an options array for ezTable()

```php
<?php
  require "class.ezpdf.php";
  $doc =& new Cezpdf();
  $table = array(
    array("Col A" => "Row 1, Col A data", "Col B" => "Row 1, Col B data"),
    array("Col A" => "Row 2, Col A data", "Col B" => "Row 2, Col B data")
  );
  $columns = array("Col B" => "Column B", "Col A" => "Column A");
  $options = array('cols' =>
    array('Col A' => array('width'=>100, 'justification' => 'center'),
          'Col B' => array('width'=>50, 'justification' => 'right')
        )
    );
  $doc->ezTable($table, $columns, "The Table with Columns!", $options);
  $doc->ezStream();
?>
```

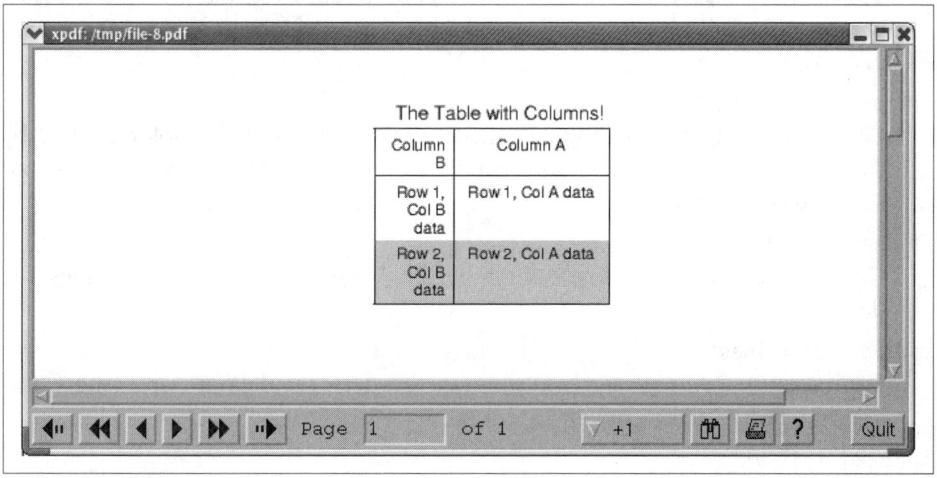

Figure 13-8. The output of Example 13-7

options['fontSize']

The font size to use in the body of the table. The default is 10.

options['innerLineThickness']

The width of lines inside the table body measured in points. It defaults to 1.

options['lineCol']

The color of the lines to use in the table specified as a three-element array of red, green, and blue values expressed as floats in the range 0 to 1. The default is black, that is, options['lineCol'] = array(0,0,0).

options['maxWidth']

Defines the maximum width of the table in points; cell widths are adjusted if necessary to stay within this width.

`options['outerLineThickness']`

> The width of lines bordering the table body measured in points. It defaults to 1.

`options['protectRows']`

> The number of rows from the first page to reproduce at the beginning of each subsequent page.

`options['rowGap']`

> The gap in points to use between the data and the row lines in the table. The default is 2.

`options['shadeCol']`

> An array of three float elements that represent the intensity of red, blue, and green to use when shading rows. The range is 0 to 1, and the default is `options['shadeCol'] = array(0.8, 0.8, 0.8)`.

`options['shadeCol2']`

> The same as `options['shadeCol']` except it is used for alternate rows when `options['shaded']` is set to 2. The default is `options['shadeCol'] = array(0.7, 0.7, 0.7)`.

`options['shaded']`

> Can be set to 0 (no shading), 1 (shade alternate rows in the color defined by shadeCol), or 2 (shade alternate rows in the colors defined by shadeCol and shadeCol2). The default is 1.

`options['showHeadings']`

> Can be set to 0 (do not show column headings) or 1 (show column headings, the default).

`options['showLines']`

> Can be set to 0 (no borders), 1 (show the borders, the default), or 2 (show borders and lines between rows).

`options['textcol']`

> The color of the text to use in the table specified as a three-element array of red, green, and blue values expressed as floats in the range 0 to 1. The default is black, that is, `options['textcol'] = array(0,0,0)`.

`options['titlefontSize']`

> The font size to use for the optional *title*. The default is 12.

`options['width']`

> Defines the width of the table in points and, if used, the cell widths will be adjusted to give this total width.

`options['xOrientation']`

> A string that defines the position of the table relative to `options['xPos']`. It can be set to `'left'`, `'right'`, or `'center'`.

`options['xPos']`

> Defines the horizontal alignment of the table on the page, and can be set to a string of `'left'`, `'right'`, or `'center'` (the default is `'center'`). It can alterna-

tively be set to a float value that is an X coordinate. It is used in conjunction with `options['xOrientation']`.

Bool Cezpdf::ezText(string text [, int size [, array options [, int overflow]]])

Writes *text* into a document including any carriage returns present in the string. By default, the font size is 12 or the last font size used if different; this can be overridden by providing the *size* parameter.

The *options* parameter is an array that can have one or more of seven associatively-accessed elements: `'left'` is a float that is a gap in points to leave from the left margin; `'right'` is a float that is a gap in points to leave from the right margin; `'aleft'` is a float that is a gap in points to leave from the left of the page (ignoring the left margin); `'aright'` is a float that is a gap in points to leave from the right of the page (ignoring the right margin); `'leading'` is a float that defines the height of the line and is independent of the font size (it used to create spacing); and, `'spacing'` is a float that defines the line spacing in word-processor style as 1.0 (single), 1.5, 2.0 (double), or any other desired value.

For example, to output a string in 14 point font size between the absolute X coordinate points 100 and 150 and using 1.5 spacing, you can use:

```
$pdf->ezText("This is a text string that is output between 100 and 150",
    14, array('aleft'=>100, 'aright'=>150, 'spacing'=>1.5));
```

Using both `'left'` and `'aleft'`, or `'right'` and `'aright'`, or `'leading'` and `'spacing'` does not make sense.

The *overflow* parameter is 0 by default. If it is set to 1, text is not actually output to the document. Instead, the method returns `true` if adding the *text* would cause a new page to be created and `false` if the *text* fits on the current page.

inline codes

There are three inline codes that can be used within the text passed as a parameter to the *ezText()* method. These are:

`<u>` *and* `</u>`

Produce underlined text. For example, *ezText("<u>hello</u>")* produces hello.

`<c:alink>` *and* `</c:alink>`

Create a link to a URL, marking text in the same way as the HTML `<a>` element. For example, *ezTest("<c:alink:http://www.webdatabasebook.com/> web database book website</c:alink>")* produces an underlined link web database book web site that when clicked will load the web site *http://www.webdatabasebook.com/* in a browser.

`<c:ilink>` *and* `</c:ilink>`

Link internally to a destination within a document. For example, *ezText("<c:ilink:page1>Jump to Page 1</c:ilink>")* produces an underlined link Jump to Page 1 that links to the destination marker page1. Adding a destination is described in *Cpdf::addDestination()* in the next section.

Base Class

void Cpdf::addDestination(string `label`, `string style` [, `float a` [, `float b, float c`]])

> Creates a destination `label` within a document (see also the inline codes defined at the conclusion of the previous section). Labels must be unique within a document.
>
> The `style` parameter defines what happens when the user visits the destination by clicking on an inline link. It can be set to several different values, and the value defines whether no additional parameters are needed, whether parameter *a* is supplied, or whether parameters *a*, *b*, and *c* are supplied. The options for `style` are as follows (for all options, the coordinate X=0, Y=0 is the bottom-left corner of the page):
>
> `'Fit'`
>> Opens the page containing the label resized to the PDF viewer. It has no additional parameters.
>
> `'FitB'`
>> Opens the page containing the label resized so that its bounding box fits the PDF viewer. It has no additional parameters.
>
> `'FitBH'`
>> Opens the page containing the label at the coordinate Y=*a* and horizontally fitted so that its bounding box fits the PDF viewer.
>
> `'FitBV'`
>> Opens the page containing the label at the coordinate X=*a* and vertically fitted so that its bounding box fits the PDF viewer.
>
> `'FitH'`
>> Opens the page containing the label at the coordinate Y=*a* and horizontally fitted to the PDF viewer.
>
> `'FitV'`
>> Opens the page containing the label at the coordinate X=*a* and vertically fitted to the PDF viewer.
>
> `'XYZ'`
>> Opens the page containing the label at coordinates X=*a*, Y=*b*, and with a zoom factor of *c*. For example, the following call sets a label myTable that when visited opens the page containing myTable at coordinates X=100 and Y=150 with a zoom factor of 2 (that is, the display is twice the normal size):
>>
>> ```
>> $doc->addDestination("myTable", "XYZ", 100, 150, 2);
>> ```

void Cpdf::addInfo(mixed `tag` [, `string value`])

> Adds information to the document. The *tag* parameter is either: first, the name of a tag, in which case the *value* parameter is used to supply the value; or, second, an associative array of tag name keys and value pairs (in which case, *value*

is not used). The valid tags are: `Title`, `Author`, `Subject`, `Keywords`, `Creator`, `Producer`, `CreationDate`, `ModDate`, and `Trapped`; the `Creator` and `CreationDate` are automatically set (to the class name and to today respectively) but may be over-ridden.

For example to set the author and title of a document, use:

```
$doc->addInfo(array("Author" => "Hugh W.", "Title" => "My document"));
```

void Cpdf::addInternalLink(string `label`, float `topX`, float `topY`, float `bottomX`, float `bottomY`)

Adds a clickable link within a document that points to a destination `label` that has been defined with *Cpdf::addDestination()*. The parameters `topX` and `topY` define the top-left corner of the clickable area. The parameters `bottomX` and `bottomY` define the bottom-right corner of the clickable area. All coordinates are point values represented as floats, and the point X=0 and Y=0 is the bottom left corner of the page.

This is an alternative to the simpler inline code `<c:ilink>` described in the previous section.

void Cpdf::addJpegFromFile(string `image_file`, float `X`, float `Y`, [, float `width` [, float `height`]])

Adds the JPEG image stored in the file `image_file` to the PDF document at coordinates `X` and `Y`. An optional image `width` and `height` may be provided. The coordinate X=0, Y=0 is the bottom left of the page, and all coordinates are point values. The method does not require the installation of any libraries.

This is a simpler alternative to *Cezpdf::ezImage()*.

void Cpdf::addLink(string `URL`, float `topX`, float `topY`, float `bottomX`, float `bottomY`)

Adds a clickable link within a document that points to a `URL`. The parameters `topX` and `topY` define the top left corner of the clickable area. The parameters `bottomX` and `bottomY` define the bottom right corner of the clickable area. All coordinates are point values represented as floats, and the point X=0 and Y=0 is the bottom-left corner of the page.

This is a simpler alternative to the inline code `<c:alink>` described in the previous section.

Cpdf::addObject(int `identifier` [, string `where`])

Adds an object referenced by `identifier` to the current page in the document. The identifier is a value returned from *Cpdf::openObject()* or another method that returns a page identifier. See *Cpdf::openObject()* for a discussion of objects.

The optional parameter `where` can be set to control where the object is added and can have the following values: `'add'` to add to the current page (the default value); `'all'` to add to all pages from the current page onwards; `'odd'` to add to all odd-numbered pages from the current page onwards; `'even'` to add to all even-numbered pages from the current page onwards; `'next'` to add to only the next page; `'nextodd'` to add to all odd-numbered pages from the next page onwards; or, 'nexteven' to add to all even-numbered pages from the next page onwards.

void Cpdf::addPngFromFile(string image_file, float X, float Y, [, float width [, float height]])

Adds the PNG image stored in the file *image_file* to the PDF document at coordinates *X* and *Y*. An optional image *width* and *height* may be provided. The coordinate X=0, Y=0 is the bottom left of the page, and all coordinates are point values. The method does not require the installation of any libraries.

This is a simpler alternative to *Cezpdf::ezImage( )*.

void Cpdf::addText(float X, float Y, int size, string text [, float angle [, float space_adjust]])

Adds *text* to the document beginning at coordinate *X* and *Y* in the font *size*. The coordinate X=0, Y=0 is the bottom left of the page, and coordinates are point values.

An optional *angle* in degrees can be provided (by default it is 0) and causes the text to be output at a counterclockwise angle relative to the bottom of the page. Unless you need an angle, use *Cezpdf::ezText( )* instead as it supports justification and line wrapping.

The *adjust* option adds space, measured in points, to whitespace such as space characters. This is used by the *Cezpdf::AddText( )* method for full justification. Negative values remove space.

The method supports basic HTML-like markup for the fonts that are distributed with the class (see *Cpdf::selectFont( )* for details). You can use <b> and </b> to begin and end bold text, and <i> and </i> to begin and end italics. You can output the < character using the entity reference <.

void Cpdf::closeObject( )

Closes the current object. All future writes then go to the document. See *Cpdf:: openObject( )* for a discussion of objects.

void Cpdf::curve(float X0, float Y0, float X1, float Y1, float X2, float Y2, float X3, float Y3)

Draws a Bezier curve between the points *X0, Y0* and *X3, Y3*, using the points *X1, Y1*, and *X2, Y2* to define the shape. The coordinate X=0, Y=0 is the bottom left of the page, and coordinates are point values.

void Cpdf::ellipse(float X, float Y, float radius1 [, float radius2 [, float angle [, int curves]]])

Draws an ellipse or circle centered at the point *X, Y* with a horizontal radius of *radius1* and an optional vertical radius of *radius2*; if *radius2* is omitted, a circle is drawn. The coordinate X=0, Y=0 is the bottom left of the page, and coordinates are point values.

An optional *angle* in degrees can be provided (by default it is 0) and this causes the ellipse to be output at a counterclockwise angle relative to the bottom of the page. The optional *curves* parameter is the number of Bezier curves to use to draw the ellipse; the default is 8, and this works well.

void Cpdf::filledRectangle(float X, float Y, float width, float height)

Draws a color-filled rectangle with the bottom-left corner defined by coordinates *X* and *Y* and with a *width* and *height*. The coordinate X=0, Y=0 is the bottom left of the page, and coordinates and dimensions are point values.

float Cpdf::getFontDecender(int size)

Returns the distance in negative points that the font descender (such as the lower part of a g, y, or q) goes below the baseline for the font *size*.

float Cpdf::getFontHeight(int size)

Returns the distance in points of the font height for the font *size* from the base of the font descender (such as the lower pixel of a g, y, or q) to the top of a capitalized character.

float Cpdf::getTextWidth(int size, string text)

Returns the length in points of the *text* for the font *size*.

void Cpdf::line(float X0, float Y0, float X1, float Y1)

Draws a line from point *X0, Y0* to *X1, Y1*. The coordinate X=0, Y=0 is the bottom left of the page, and coordinates are point values.

void Cpdf::openHere(string style [, float a [, float b, float c]])

Causes the document to begin at a specific page when it is opened; the page that is used is the current page in the document when the method is called. The *style* and other parameters are described in *Cpdf::addDestination()*.

int Cpdf::openObject()

Starts an object and returns an identifier representing the object; the return value must be saved in a variable for later use.

Having objects allows you to randomly access pages to add content. Using this, you can complete earlier pages in the document after writing later pages. For example, this is used internally by the page numbering schemes described in the previous section to add the total number of pages to each page.

When an object is started, all future writing to the PDF document goes to this object rather than to the document itself until another object is selected or the current object is closed. Several objects may be open at once, and you can select a different object to write to using *Cpdf::reopenObject()*. Objects are closed using *Cpdf::closeObject()* and after this all future writes will go to the document (until another object is selected or opened).

The *Cpdf::addObject()* method is used to add an object to the document, and this allows you to add the object to more than one page. You can call *Cpdf:: stopObject()* to stop the adding of an object to the document and this allows you to alter range of pages.

void Cpdf::partEllipse(float X, float Y, angle A1, angle A2, float radius1 [, float radius2 [, float angle [, int curves]]])

Draws a partial ellipse or circle centered at the point X, Y with a horizontal radius of *radius1* and an optional vertical radius of *radius2*; if *radius2* is omitted, a circle is drawn. The ellipse begins at a counterclockwise angle A1 relative to the bottom of the page and ends at angle A2.

The coordinate X=0, Y=0 is the bottom left of the page, and coordinates are point values.

An optional *angle* in degrees can be provided (by default it is 0) and this causes the ellipse to be output at that counterclockwise angle relative to the bottom of the page. The optional *curves* parameter is the number of Bezier curves to use to draw the ellipse; the default is 8, and this works well.

void Cpdf::polygon(array points, int count [, int fill])

Draws a polygon using *count* pairs of ordered coordinates from the array *points*. For example, if the array points is defined as *array(10,10,10,40,20,40,20,10)*, four lines are drawn to form a rectangle with its bottom-left corner at X=10, Y=10 and with a width of 10 and a height of 30. The optional *fill* parameter can be set to 0 (no fill, the default) or 1 (fill).

void Cpdf::rectangle(float X, float Y, float width, float height)

Draws an unfilled rectangle with the bottom left corner defined by coordinates X and Y and with a *width* and *height*. The coordinate X=0, Y=0 is the bottom left of the page, and coordinates and dimensions are point values.

void Cpdf::reopenObject(int identifier)

Reopens or selects the object associated with *identifier* that has previously been created with *Cpdf::addObject()*. The selected object will then be used for all future output until it is either closed or another object is selected. See "*Cpdf:: openObject()*" for a discussion of objects.

void Cpdf::selectFont(string font_file [, mixed encoding])

Selects the font found in the file *font_file*. The *font_file* can be a relative or absolute directory path, and must include the full filename of the fonts, which must end in *.afm*. Both PostScript Type 1 and TrueType fonts are supported.

The fonts Courier, Helvetica, php_Courier, php_Helvetica, php_Symbol, php_ Times, php_ZapfDingbats, Symbol, Times, Times-Roman, and ZapfDingbats are distributed with the base class in the subdirectory *fonts*. Without additional configuration (which we do not discuss here), only the fonts provided with the class can be used with the <b> and <i> HTML-like markup in *Cpdf::addText()*.

The *encoding* parameter is used to change the number-to-character mapping for a font. We do not discuss this here, but more details on this experimental setting can be found in the class manual.

void Cpdf::setColor(float red, float green, float blue [, int force])

> Sets the fill color to that defined by *red*, *green*, and *blue*. These parameters are values in the range 0.0 to 1.0, where a setting of 0.0 for all three is black and a setting of 1.0 for all three is white.
>
> When set to 1, the *force* option causes the color setting to be written into the PDF document even if it is the same as the current fill color setting; the default of 0 has the opposite behavior.

void Cpdf::setEncryption([string user_password [, string author_password [, array options]])

> Encrypts the document so that it cannot be printed, and so the user cannot use cut (or copy) and paste and cannot alter the document. This is the default behavior with no parameters.
>
> If a *user_password* is provided, the user must provide this before the document is displayed but they will still be unable to carry out the selected actions. If an *owner_password* is provided, the user must provide this before the document is displayed and they will then be able to use (edit and print) the document as usual.
>
> The optional *options* array allows you to define what actions the user can take on the document. For example, an array *array('print')* allows the user to print (if there is no password required, or after providing the *user_password*). The options are 'print', 'modify', 'copy', and 'add'.

void Cpdf::setLineStyle([int width [, string cap [, string join [, array dash [, int phase]]]]])

> Sets a new line drawing style for use with all drawing functions (for ellipses, lines, curves, polygons, and rectangles). Without any parameters, the method does nothing.
>
> The *width* defines the width in points, and the default is 1. The *cap* defines the end type of the line and can be set to 'butt', 'round', or 'square'; the default is 'butt'. The *join* defines how lines are joined and can be set to 'miter', 'round', or 'bevel'; the default is 'miter'.
>
> The *dash* parameter is used to define a dashed line and is an array that contains lengths of the dashes and gaps between them in points; the default is no dashing. For example, a *dash* parameter of *array(4,2,2,2)* defines that a dash of length 4 is followed by a gap of length 4, and then a dash of length 2 is followed by a gap of length 2, and then the sequence repeats. The *phase* parameter defines where in the dash array to start the processing of dashes; the default is at element 0.
>
> If you want to change one or more parameters but not others, you can leave out the other parameters that follow the parameter you want to change, or set the previous parameters to '' for a string or array parameter, and 0 for the *width*

parameter. For example, to change the cap type to 'butt' without changing the other parameters, use:

```
$doc->setLineStyle(0,'cap');
```

void Cpdf::setPreferences(mixed label [, string value])

Sets document viewing preferences. If `label` is a string, the `value` parameter for that label is required. If `label` is an array, it should contain associative key labels and values for each of those labels. To turn a label on, set the value to 1; to turn it off, set it to 0. The possible labels are `'HideToolbar'`, `'HideMenuBar'`, `'HideWindowUI'`, `'FitWindow'`, `'CenterWindow'`, `'NonFullScreenPageMode'`, and `'Direction'`.

For example, to hide the browser window user interface, use:

```
$doc->setPreferences(array('HideWindowUI' => 1));
```

It is up to the browser to obey these settings (xpdf, for example, ignores them).

Cpdf::setStrokeColor(float red, float green, float blue [, int force])

Sets the line (stroke) color to that defined by *red*, *green*, and *blue*. These parameters are values in the range 0.0 to 1.0, where a setting of 0.0 for all three is black and a setting of 1.0 for all three is white.

When set to 1, the *force* option causes the color setting to be written into the PDF document even if it is the same as the current line color setting; the default of 0 has the opposite behavior.

void Cpdf::stopObject(int identifier)

Stop an object from appearing from the next page onwards. This allows you to define an endpoint for the *Cpdf::addObject()* behavior during processing. Objects are discussed further in the entry for *Cpdf::openObject()*.

void Cpdf::transaction(string action)

Allows you to treat a block in a PDF document as an indivisible unit, in much the same way as the database transactions described in Chapter 15. The aim of this is to allow you try different layouts until you find one that fits desirably on the page or pages by, for example, varying table spacing or font sizes in *Cezpdf:: ezTable()*.

To mark the beginning of output that you want to treat as a unit, you start a transaction by providing 'start' as the *action*.

To complete a transaction, and write it to the current document or object, you provide 'commit' as the *action*. This ends the most-recent 'start'.

To go back to the start point and begin again, use the 'rewind' option. To give up completely, use the 'abort' option. These affect the most recent 'start'.

Commands may be nested; that is, you can have subtransactions.

CHAPTER 14

Advanced Features of Object-Oriented Programming in PHP 5

In Chapter 4, we introduced the basic concepts of object-oriented programming, showing how classes are defined and how objects are created and used with PHP. The techniques shown in Chapter 4 can be used to help build reusable, modular code, and are applicable when using object-oriented packages such as the PEAR packages we describe in Chapter 7. However, much of the power of object-oriented programming doesn't come from simply reusing code.

In this chapter, we show some more powerful techniques available with object-oriented programming, including:

- Class hierarchies
- Polymorphic behavior
- Class type hints
- Abstract classes and interfaces

Working with Class Hierarchies

In Chapter 4, we showed you how inheritance can be used as a powerful tool in object-oriented programming. Using the extends keyword, a class can inherit the capabilities from a parent class. As we explained in Chapter 4, PHP allows an inheritance from only one parent class, but a class can be extended to create any number of child classes.

Inheritance allows functionality to be built up from related classes. Each class provides specialized support that's specific to a class's purpose. It's common that functionality in an object-oriented application is provided by class hierarchies rather than single, unrelated classes.

Example 14-1 shows how a class hierarchy is formed to provide functionality that describes shapes.

Example 14-1. Shape classes

```php
<?php

class Shape
{
    var $color;
    var $sides;

    function color()
    {
        return $this->color;
    }

    function sides()
    {
        return $this->sides;
    }

    function __construct($color, $sides)
    {
        $this->color = $color;
        $this->sides = $sides;
    }
}

class Circle extends Shape
{

    function __construct($color)
    {
        parent::__construct($color, 1);
    }
}

class Polygon extends Shape
{
    var $angles;

    function angles()
    {
        return $this->angles;
    }

    function __construct($color, $sides)
    {
        parent::__construct($color, $sides);
        $this->angles = $sides;
    }
}

class Triangle extends Polygon
{
    function __construct($color)
```

Example 14-1. Shape classes (continued)

```
    {
        parent::__construct($color, 3);
    }
}

class Rectangle extends Polygon
{
    function __construct($color)
    {
        parent::__construct($color, 4);
    }
}

?>
```

The class *Shape* defined in the Example 14-1 supports only two features: the color and number of sides of a shape. The *Circle* and *Polygon* classes both extend the base *Shape* class: the *Circle* constructor function always sets the number of sides to 1,* while the *Polygon* class allows an arbitrary number of sides and defines the member function *angles( )* that returns the number of angles the shape makes.

The *Polygon* class is extended by the *Triangle* and *Rectangle* classes, and each defines a constructor function that sets the appropriate number of sides. The relationship between the classes defined in Example 14-1 is shown in the class diagram in Figure 14-1.

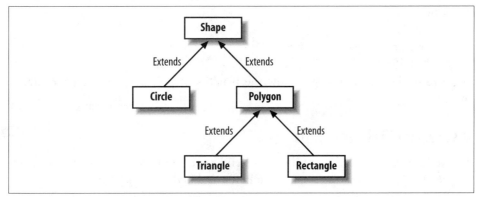

Figure 14-1. Class hierarchy for the Shape classes

The classes defined in Example 14-1 aren't particularly useful—we kept the functionality to a minimum to illustrate how a hierarchy is formed. A real application that deals with shapes would define member variables and functions to support the

---

* The number of sides of a circle depends on your definition of side—some definitions lead to no sides, some to an infinite number. By our definition, a circle has one side.

application requirements. For example, if you were interested in the size of a shape, you could add member variables to record the dimensions, and functions that calculate the area.

Polymorphism

While a class hierarchy can help you to develop modular code, most of the power of object-oriented programming comes from the ability to use an object differently in different circumstances, a capability known as *polymorphism*. Consider the objects that we can create from the classes defined in Example 14-1. The following fragment creates an array of objects using the *Circle*, *Triangle*, and *Rectangle* classes; and then prints information about each shape using a foreach loop.

```
// Create an array of objects
$shapes = array(
    new Triangle("blue"),
    new Circle("green"),
    new Rectangle("red"));

foreach ($shapes as $s)
    print "I have a {$s->color()} shape with {$s->sides()} sides\n";
```

We can call the *color()* and *sides()* member functions on each of the objects in the previous example because each object, through inheritance, is a *Shape*. We can't call the *angles()* function on each object because not all of the objects are *Polygons* and only instances of *Polygons* have the *angles()* member function. The previous example prints:

```
I have a blue shape with 3 sides
I have a green shape with 1 sides
I have a red shape with 4 sides
```

We give further examples that show the benefits of polymorphic behavior later in this chapter.

Discovering Relationships

The instanceof keyword is available in PHP5, and the is_a(), get_class(), and get_parent_class() functions are available in PHP4 and PHP5.

When you're dealing with an object in a PHP script, it's not always obvious what type of object it is. For example, while all the objects we created in the previous example are *Shapes*, only the *Triangle* and *Rectangle* objects can be used as *Polygon* objects. PHP5 supports the instanceof operator that allows you to write scripts that can test the capabilities of an object before using it. The following fragment shows how each shape object is tested before an attempt is made to call the *Polygon* member function:

```
// Create an array of objects
$shapes = array(
```

```
    new Triangle("blue"),
    new Circle("green"),
    new Rectangle("red"));

foreach ($shapes as $s)
{
    if ($s instanceof Polygon)
        print "I have a {$s->color()} polygon with {$s->sides()}
            sides and {$s->angles()} internal angles\n";
    else
        print "I have a {$s->color()} shape with {$s->sides()} sides\n";
}
```

The previous example prints the longer *Polygon* message for the *Triangle* and *Rectangle* objects, and the shorter *Shape* message for the *Circle* object:.

```
I have a blue polygon with 3
            sides and 3 internal angles
I have a green shape with 1 sides
I have a red polygon with 4
            sides and 4 internal angles
```

Functions

The instanceof keyword performs a similar function to the PHP library function *is_a()*. Both evaluate to true if the object is an instance of the test class, or an ancestor class. Here's an example that uses *is_a()* to perform the same function as in the previous example:

```
    if (is_a($s "Polygon"))
        print "I have a {$s->color()} polygon with {$s->sides()}
            sides and {$s->angles()} internal angles\n";
    else
        print "I have a {$s->color()} shape with {$s->sides()} sides\n";
```

PHP provides several related functions that return information about the class hierarchy of an object:

boolean is_subclass_of(object obj, string classname)
string get_class(object obj)
string get_parent_class(object obj)

The function *is_subclass_of()* returns true if the class of object *obj* is a descendant of *classname*. The *get_class()* function returns the name of the class for the object *obj*, and *get_parent_class()* returns the parent class name. Both *get_class()* and *get_parent_class()* normalize the name of the class to lower case as demonstrated in the following fragment:

```
// Create a new Triangle object
$shape = new Triangle("orange");

// prints "triangle"
print get_class($shape);
```

```
// prints "polygon"
print get_parent_class($shape);
```

Class Type Hints

The class type hint feature is available in PHP5.

PHP is a loosely typed language, and this allows different types of data to be passed as parameters into functions. When user-defined functions or class member functions are designed to work with object parameters, it is often useful to check the type of object before it is used. PHP5 allows you to specify the type of object parameter with a *class type hint*. Consider the following example that defines a function to return information about *Shape* objects:

```
// User-defined function that returns information about a Shape
// object
function shapeInfo(Shape $shape)
{
    return "I have a {$s->color()} shape with {$s->sides()} sides";
}
```

The definition of the function *shapeInfo()* includes the class type hint Shape before the parameter $shape. This instructs PHP to check the class of $shape when the script is run. If the function is called with an object that is not a *Shape*, or even a value that was not an object, PHP causes the script to terminate with a fatal error.

Using class type hints is the equivalent of checking the parameter with the instanceof keyword. Using this approach, the *shapeInfo()* function could be rewritten as:

```
// User-defined function that returns information about a Shape
// object
function shapeInfo($shape)
{
    if (not $shape instanceof Shape)
        die ("Parameter not a Shape object");

    return "I have a {$s->color()} shape with {$s->sides()} sides";
}
```

Abstract Classes and Interfaces

When developing class hierarchies, it's often useful to insert extra classes to help logically organize code or to provide a base for polymorphic behavior.

The abstract keyword

Abstract classes are available in PHP5.

In Example 14-1, we defined a set of related classes to describe shapes that includes a base class *Shape* and its two member functions *color()* and *sides()*. Let's suppose we want to add a function *area()* that calculates the area of a shape. If we want to allow the area to be calculated for all *Shape* objects, then the function must be made available in the *Shape* class.

However, unlike the *color()* and *sides()* functions, the *area()* function can only be implemented in the descendant classes because area calculations vary from shape to shape. The area of a circle is calculated using the radius, while a rectangle uses height and width, and so on. Using the abstract keyword, PHP5 allows you to define member functions without having to define an implementation. However, a class that contains an abstract function can't be used to create objects, and must also be defined as abstract. Example 14-2 shows how the *Shapes* class is redefined to include the abstract *area()* function.

Example 14-2. An abstract base class

```php
<?php

abstract class Shape
{
    var $color;
    var $sides;

    function color()
    {
        return $this->color;
    }

    function sides()
    {
        return $this->sides;
    }

    abstract function area();

    function __construct($color, $sides)
    {
        $this->color = $color;
        $this->sides = $sides;
    }
}

class Circle extends Shape
{
    var $radius;

    function area()
    {
        return pi() * $this->radius * $this->radius;
    }
```

Example 14-2. An abstract base class (continued)

```php
    function __construct($color, $radius)
    {
        $this->radius = $radius;
        parent::__construct($color, 1);
    }
}

class Rectangle extends Shape
{
    var $width;
    var $height;

    function area()
    {
        return $this->width * $this->height;
    }

    function __construct($color, $width, $height)
    {
        $this->width = $width;
        $this->height = $height;
        parent::__construct($color, 4);
    }
}

class Triangle extends Shape
{
    // The length of each side
    var $a;
    var $b;
    var $c;

    function area()
    {
        // Area using Heron's formula
        $s = ($this->a + $this->b + $this->c)/2;
        $area = sqrt(
            $s * ($s - $this->a) * ($s - $this->b) * ($s - $this->c)
            );

        return $area;
    }

    function __construct($color, $a, $b, $c)
    {
        $this->a = $a;
        $this->b = $b;
        $this->c = $c;
        parent::__construct($color, 3);
    }
}
?>
```

Example 14-2 includes three classes—*Circle*, *Rectangle*, and *Triangle*—that extend the abstract *Shape* class and provide shape specific implementations of the abstract function *area()*. (We have also removed the *Polygon* class and the *angles()* function to help simplify the example.)

The following fragment shows which classes from Example 14-2 can be used:

```
require 'example.14-2.php';

$t = new Triangle("yellow", 2, 3, 4);
$c = new Circle("blue", 5);
$r = new Rectangle("green", 2, 4);

print "Area of our triangle = {$t->area()} sq units\n";
print "Area of our circle = {$c->area()} sq units\n";
print "Area of our rectangle = {$r->area()} sq units\n";

// The following line causes a fatal error because Shape is abstract
$s = new Shape("green", 5);
```

Before the fatal error caused by the attempt to create an object from the abstract class *Shape*, the previous example prints:

```
Area of our triangle = 2.9047375096556 sq units
Area of our circle = 31.415926535898 sq units
Area of our rectangle = 8 sq units
```

There are a few rules to observe when defining abstract classes and functions:

- An abstract member function can't contain a body definition.
- A class must be declared as abstract if it contains any abstract functions.
- You can declare protected and public functions as abstract, however, it is an error to declare a private function as abstract.
- Any descendant classes that don't implement an abstract function defined in a base class must also be declared as abstract.

Interfaces

Interfaces are available in PHP5.

Interfaces provide another way of describing functionality in a class hierarchy. An *interface* defines member functions without providing any implementation, and class definitions *implement* those functions. Interfaces are defined using the `interface` keyword, and class definitions use interfaces with the `implements` keyword. An example is shown in Example 14-3:

Example 14-3. Using Interfaces

```
<?php

interface Audible
```

Example 14-3. Using Interfaces (continued)

```php
{
    function sound( );
}

class Animal implements Audible
{
    var $name;
    var $says;
    var $legs;

    function sound( )
    {
        return $this->says;
    }

    function name( )
    {
        return $this->name;
    }

    function numberOfLegs( )
    {
        $this->legs;
    }

    function __construct($name, $says, $legs)
    {
        $this->name = $name;
        $this->says = $says;
        $this->legs = $legs;
    }
}
?>
```

The *Audible* interface defined in Example 14-3 acts like an abstract base class for the *Animal* class: you can't create *Audible* objects directly, but an *Animal* object can be used as if it were an *Audible* object. Classes that specify an interface with the `implements` keyword must implement all the functions from the interface.

Interfaces are useful for implementing polymorphic behavior and are commonly used to relate classes that otherwise would not be related. For example, a *Trumpet* class wouldn't necessarily be related to the *Animal* class, however we may want to generically process objects from both classes as *Audible*:

```php
// access to the Audible interface
require "example.14-3.php";

class Trumpet implements Audible
{
    function sound( )
    {
        return "Toot";
```

```
        }

        // Other functions that support a Trumpet
        // ...
        function orchestraSection()
        {
            return "Brass";
        }
    }
```

To further illustrate the point, we can implement the *sound()* function for the *Triangle* class we defined earlier:

```
// access to the Shape class
require "example.14-1.php";

// access to the Audible interface
require "example.14-3.php";

class Triangle extends Shape implements Audible
{
    // The length of each side
    var $a;
    var $b;
    var $c;

    function sound()
    {
        return "Ding";
    }

    function area()
    {
        // Area using Heron's formula
        $s = ($this->a + $this->b + $this->c)/2;
        $area = sqrt(
            $s * ($s - $this->a) * ($s - $this->b) * ($s - $this->c)
            );

        return $area;
    }

    function __construct($color, $a, $b, $c)
    {
        $this->a = $a;
        $this->b = $b;
        $this->c = $c;
        parent::__construct($color, 3);
    }
}
```

Now *Animal*, *Trumpet*, and *Triangle* objects can all be treated as *Audible* objects:

```
// Create an empty array to hold some objects
$things = array();
```

```
// Add some objects

// An Animal is constructed with a name, sound, and leg count
$things[] = new Animal("Cow", "Moo", 4);

// A Trumpet is constructed without any parameters
$things[] = new Trumpet;

// A Triangle is constructed with a color, and the
// length of the three sides
$things[] = new Triangle("Silver", 3, 3, 3);

// A Circle is constructed with a color and a radius
$things[] = new Circle("Blue", 5);

// Check out the sound
foreach ($things as $t)
{
    if ($t instanceof Audible)
        print $t->sound( );
}
```

Interfaces also provide a mechanism for exposing subsets of a class's functionality. When a *Triangle* is being used as an *Audible* object, we only care about the *sound()* member function. The code in the above example would still work even if we change the names of the other *Triangle* member functions: because *Triangle* implements *Audible*, we can be sure that a *Triangle* can be used as an *Audible* object.

Functions can intentionally limit how an object is used using class type hints. Consider a function that works with *Audible* objects:

```
// return a formatted string to represent sound
function showSound(Audible $obj)
{
    return "!! {$obj->sound( )} !!";
}
```

The function *showSound()* can only use $obj parameter if it's an *Audible* object because the parameter is declared as *Audible*. An interface acts like a contract: classes that implement an interface are guaranteed to support a defined set of functions, while users of an interface warrant only to use those functions.

PHP allows multiple interfaces to be implemented in a class definition by including a comma-separated list of interface names after the `implements` keyword. This allows a class definition to use interfaces to formally describe how it can be used in different circumstances. We have shown how several different classes can implement the *Audible* interface; we can just as easily add other interfaces such as a *WebDisplayable* interfaces that defines functions for rendering the object as HTML. Of course, each class that implements an interface must support the functions it describes.

Freight Calculator Example

The examples we have shown so far in this chapter have been contrived to help illustrate the features of PHP. In this section, we apply these techniques and features discussed in this chapter to improve the freight calculator example we introduced in Chapter 4.

Review of the FreightCalculator

The *FreightCalculator* class defined in Example 4-9 is used to calculate the cost of delivering an online order. Example 4-9 also define the *AirFreightCalculator* class that redefines the two protected member functions that do the work of calculating the cost components: *perKgTotal()* and *perCaseTotal()*.

FreightCalculator objects, including *AirFreightCalculator* objects, are constructed with two parameters, the total weight and the number of cases that make up a delivery:

```php
function __construct($numberOfCases, $totalWeight)
{
    $this->numberOfCases = $numberOfCases;
    $this->totalWeight = $totalWeight;
}
```

We also defined the *CaseCounter* class in Example 4-8 that extends the simple *UnitCounter* class defined in Example 4-4. A *CaseCounter* object can be used to accumulate units that make up a delivery and calculate the total weight and number of cases required to pack the order. The following example shows how a *CaseCounter* is created and used:

```php
// Access to the CaseCounter class definition
require "example.4-8.php";

// Create a CaseCounter object where there are
// 12 units to a case, and each unit weights 1.2 Kg.
$myOrder = new CaseCounter(12, 1.2);

// Add 5 bottles
$myOrder->add(5);

// Add 11 bottles
$myOrder->add(11);

// Add a case
$myOrder->addCase();

// Now show me how many cases are required and the total weight
print "My order can be packed in {$myOrder->caseCount()} and
        weighs {$myOrder->totalWeight()} Kg.";
```

The *CaseCounter* object is constructed with two parameters: the number of units that fit into a case, and the weight per unit. Once constructed, we can add units or cases to the counter. We describe how the *CaseCounter* works in Chapter 4.

To calculate the cost of delivering an order, we can create an *AirFreightCalculator* object using the output from the *caseCount()* and *totalWeight()* functions. Here's how it's done:

```php
// Access to the CaseCounter class definition
require "example.4-8.php";

// Access to the AirFreightCalculator class definition
require "example.4-9.php";

// Create a CaseCounter object where there are 12 units to
// a case, and each unit weights 1.2 Kg.
$myOrder = new CaseCounter(12, 1.2);

// Add 28 bottles
$myOrder->add(28);

// Create an AirFreightCalculator
$air = new AirFreightCalculator($myOrder->caseCount(),
                                $myOrder->totalWeight())

// Now show me the cost
print "The cost of delivering $myOrder->numberOfUnits() bottles
       is $ {$air->totalFreight()}.";
```

We can simplify the use of *FreightCalculator* objects by redefining the *FreightCalculator* class to use a *CaseCounter* object rather than passing in individual numeric values. However, a better solution is to use an interface that defines the functions that are required to calculate freight costs—an interface that can be used with classes other than *CaseCounter*.

Deliverable Interface

Example 14-4 shows the definition of the *Deliverable* interface that specifies the *caseCount()* and *totalWeight()* functions.

Example 14-4. Delivery interface

```php
<?php

interface Deliverable
{
    function caseCount();
    function totalWeight();
}
?>
```

The *CaseCounter* class already supports the *caseCount()* and *totalWeight()* functions —*caseCount()* is implemented in the *CaseCounter* definition, while the *totalWeight()* implementation is inherited from the base class *UnitCounter*—so the only change required is to use the *Deliverable* interface. This is shown in Example 14-5.

Example 14-5. The CaseCounter class implementing Deliverable

```php
<?php

// Access to the UnitCounter class definition
require_once "example.4-4.php";

// Access to the Deliverable interface definition
require_once "example.14-4.php";


class CaseCounter extends UnitCounter implements Deliverable
{
    private $unitsPerCase;

    function addCase()
    {
        $this->add($this->unitsPerCase);
    }

    function caseCount()
    {
        return ceil($this->numberOfUnits()/$this->unitsPerCase);
    }

    function __construct($caseCapacity, $unitWeight)
    {
        parent::__construct($unitWeight);
        $this->unitsPerCase = $caseCapacity;
    }
}
```

Improving the FreightCalculator

We now turn our attention to improving the *FreightCalculator* class. Improvements are made in two ways: we modify the class to use objects that support the *Deliverable* interface—thus simplifying the use of *FreightCalculator* objects—and we make the class abstract. The improved *FreightCalculator* class is shown in Example 14-6.

Example 14-6. The improved FreightCalculator class

```php
<?php

// Access to the Deliverable interface definition
require_once "example.14-4.php";

abstract class FreightCalculator
{
```

Example 14-6. The improved FreightCalculator class (continued)

```
    // The Deliverable item
    protected $item;

    function totalFreight( )
    {
        return $this->perCaseTotal() + $this->perKgTotal( );
    }

    abstract protected function perCaseTotal( );
    abstract protected function perKgTotal( );

    function __construct(Deliverable $item)
    {
        $this->item = $item;
    }
}

?>
```

While the *FreightCalculator* class defined in Example 4-9 implements a default pricing scheme, real schemes are implemented in descendant classes that redefine the protected *perCaseTotal()* and *perKgTotal()* functions. We designed the *FreightCalculator* class to be extended, creating a descendant class for each freight option that is offered by an online store. For example, the *AirFreightCalculator* class shown in Example 4-9 provides a pricing scheme appropriate for airfreight.

By defining the *FreightCalculator* class as abstract, we can prevent accidental creation of *FreightCalculator* objects. We can also remove the misleading implementation that doesn't correspond to any real pricing scheme by declaring the *perCaseTotal()* and *perKgTotal()* functions as abstract:

```
    abstract protected function perCaseTotal( );
    abstract protected function perKgTotal( );
```

PHP 5 allows the abstract and protected keywords to be used in either order.

The improved *FreightCalculator* class in Example 14-6 also replaces the protected member variables $numberOfCases and $totalWeight with the single protected variable $item. The *__construct()* function has also been modified to accept one parameter: a class type hint allowing only *Deliverable* objects to be passed:

```
    function __construct(Deliverable $item)
    {
        $this->item = $item;
    }
```

Descendant classes of *FreightCalculator* must also be modified to use the protected *Deliverable* member variable $item. Example 14-7 shows two descendant classes: a modified version of the *AirFreightCalculator* and a *RoadFreightCalculator*.

Example 14-7. AirFreightCalculator and RoadFreightCalculator

```php
<?php

// Access to the FreightCalculator class
require_once "example.14-6.php";

class AirFreightCalculator extends FreightCalculator
{
    protected function perCaseTotal()
    {
        return 15 + $this->item->caseCount() * 1.00;
    }

    protected function perKgTotal()
    {
        return $this->item->totalWeight() * 0.40;
    }
}

class RoadFreightCalculator extends FreightCalculator
{

    protected function perCaseTotal()
    {
        $numcases = $this->item->caseCount();

        if ($numcases < 5)
            return 15;
        else
            return 15 + ($numcases - 5) * 1.50;
    }

    protected function perKgTotal()
    {
        $weight = $this->item->totalWeight();

        if ($weight < 50)
            return 0;
        else
            return ($weight - 50) * 0.10;
    }
}

?>
```

The class *AirFreightCalculator* calculates freight costs for a single delivery as $15 plus $1 per case and $0.40 per kilogram, while *RoadFreightCalculator* is a little more complicated with stepped rates for both case counts and total weight.

The member variables and functions that are available from $item can be accessed by chaining together -> access operators. For example, in the *RoadFreightCalculator* class definition, the number of cases is determined with the following code:

```php
    $numcases = $this->item->caseCount();
```

Summary of Improvements

The classes we have defined in this section to calculate freight costs have real advantages over the *FreightCalculator* we presented in Chapter 4:

- The *FreightCalculator* class is now defined as abstract, eliminating the risk of accidentally writing code that generate misleading freight costs.
- We use the *Deliverable* interface allowing us to safely modify *CaseCounter* in the future without risk of breaking the *FreightCalculator* class.
- Using the *Deliverable* interface, the *FreightCalculator* class can now be used with other, non-*CaseCounter* objects.

To illustrate the last point, consider the *ChristmasHamper* class in Example 14-8.

Example 14-8. A ChristmasHamper class

```php
<?php

// access to the Deliverable interface
require_once "example.14-4.php";

class ChristmasHamper implements Deliverable
{
    function caseCount( )
    {
        return 1;
    }

    function totalWeight ( )
    {
        return 26.5;
    }

    function description( )
    {
        return "A hamper chock-full of Christmas goodies";
    }
}
?>
```

The *ChristmasHamper* class implements the *Deliverable* interface, so we can calculate the freight costs of *ChristmasHamper* objects using a *FreightCalculator* object. The following fragment shows how *AirFreightCalculator* objects can be created using *CaseCounter* and *ChristmasHamper* objects:

```php
$wineOrder = new CaseCounter(12, 1.2);
$hamperOrder = new ChristmasHamper;
```

```
$wineOrder->add(10);

// Create two AirFreightCalculator objects
$a = new AirFreightCalculator($wineOrder);
$b = new AirFreightCalculator($hamperOrder);

// prints "Air freight on Christmas Hamper = 26.6"
print "Air freight on Christmas Hamper = {$b-> totalFreight( )}";
```

Using the Improved Freight Calculator

Example 14-9 demonstrates how the classes developed in this section can be used to build a simple application. The template that works with the script is shown in Example 14-10.

The application is a single web page that shows a table that compares the freight costs for different sized orders. This page might be included with an online store to help a customer choose delivery options when it comes time to purchase an order.

Example 14-9. Freight comparison table

```php
<?php
require_once "HTML/Template/ITX.php";

// Access to the FreightCalculator classes
require_once"example.14-7.php";

// Access to the CaseCounter class
require_once"example.14-5.php";

// Access to the ChristmasHamper class
require_once"example.14-8.php";

$template = new HTML_Template_ITX("./templates");
$template->loadTemplatefile("example.14-10.tpl", true, true);

$exampleOrder = new CaseCounter(12, 1.2);

$air = new AirFreightCalculator($exampleOrder);
$road = new RoadFreightCalculator($exampleOrder);

for ($i = 0; $i < 10; $i++)
{
    $exampleOrder->add(6);

    $template->setCurrentBlock("order");
    $template->setVariable("UNITS", $exampleOrder->numberOfUnits( ));
    $template->setVariable("CASES", $exampleOrder->caseCount( ));
    $template->setVariable("WEIGHT", $exampleOrder->totalWeight( ));
```

Example 14-9. Freight comparison table (continued)

```php
    $template->setVariable("AIR", $air->totalFreight());
    $template->setVariable("ROAD", $road->totalFreight());
    $template->parseCurrentBlock();
}

// Create a ChristmasHamper object
$hamper = new ChristmasHamper;
$air = new AirFreightCalculator($hamper);
$road = new RoadFreightCalculator($hamper);

// output the last row for the ChristmasHamper
$template->setCurrentBlock("order");
$template->setVariable("UNITS", "A Christmas hamper");
$template->setVariable("CASES", $hamper->caseCount());
$template->setVariable("WEIGHT", $hamper->totalWeight());
$template->setVariable("AIR", $air->totalFreight());
$template->setVariable("ROAD", $road->totalFreight());
$template->parseCurrentBlock();

$template->show();
?>
```

Example 14-10. The template used with Example 14-9

```html
<!DOCTYPE HTML PUBLIC "-//W3C//DTD HTML 4.01 Transitional//EN"
                      "http://www.w3.org/TR/html401/loose.dtd">
<html>
<head>
  <meta http-equiv="Content-Type" content="text/html; charset=iso-8859-1">
  <title>Freight Costs</title>
</head>
<body>
<h2>Freight Cost Comparison: Air vs. Road</h2>
<table border='1'>
    <tr>
      <th>Order size</th><th>Cases</th><th>Total Weight (kg)</th>
      <th>Air Freight</th><th>Road Freight</th>
    </tr>
<!-- BEGIN order -->
    <tr>
        <td>{UNITS}</td>
        <td>{CASES}</td>
        <td>{WEIGHT}</td>
        <td>${AIR}</td>
        <td>${ROAD}</td>
    </tr>
<!-- END order -->
</table>
</body>
</html>
```

To calculate the freight costs for the wine order, *AirFreightCalculator* and *RoadFreightCalculator* objects are constructed using the $exampleOrder *CaseCounter* object. Rates for different-sized orders can be calculated by adding units to the $exampleOrder object—we don't need to create new *FreightCalculator* objects for each order size. We do this inside the for loop that creates the table rows by adding 6 bottles to the $exampleOrder object:

```
$exampleOrder->add(6);
```

The result of Example 14-9 is shown in Figure 14-2.

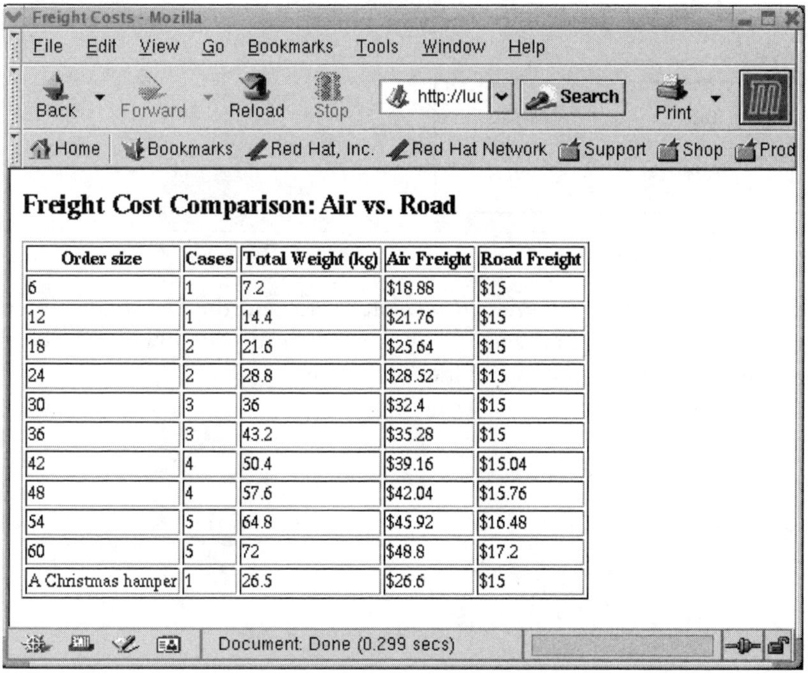

Freight Cost Comparison: Air vs. Road

Order size	Cases	Total Weight (kg)	Air Freight	Road Freight
6	1	7.2	$18.88	$15
12	1	14.4	$21.76	$15
18	2	21.6	$25.64	$15
24	2	28.8	$28.52	$15
30	3	36	$32.4	$15
36	3	43.2	$35.28	$15
42	4	50.4	$39.16	$15.04
48	4	57.6	$42.04	$15.76
54	5	64.8	$45.92	$16.48
60	5	72	$48.8	$17.2
A Christmas hamper	1	26.5	$26.6	$15

Figure 14-2. Freight comparison table

Class Diagram

The freight calculation example now uses six classes, and one interface definition. Figure 14-3 shows how these definitions are related in a class diagram.

As with Figure 14-1, inheritance is shown with connecting lines and solid arrowheads. In Figure 14-3 we've used additional notation to represent the *Deliverable* interface and the abstract class *FreightCalculator*.

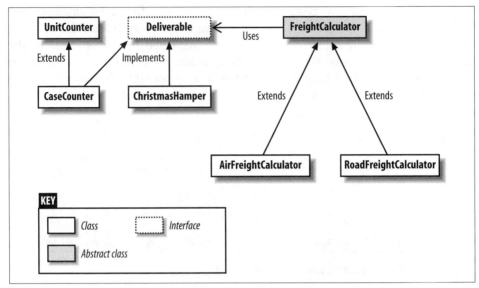

Figure 14-3. Class diagram

The relationship between the *FreightCalculator* class and the *Deliverable* interface is shown with a connecting line with an open arrowhead. The open arrowhead indicates where one class *uses* the capabilities of another.

CHAPTER 15

Advanced SQL

The SQL shown in Chapter 5 was sufficient for the scripts in earlier chapters and for the winestore application that's described in the next five chapters. However, SQL is extremely powerful and provides many other capabilities, some of which we'll cover in this chapter. Examples of these useful features include advanced join types, nested queries, and aliases.

Many of the features shown in this chapter are specific to MySQL's version of SQL. For example, MySQL's functions are useful tools for working with strings, dates and times, and math. Also, we'll show some ways to tune MySQL in order to improve application performance. It's important to know how to choose and design indexes for fast querying, and how to use MySQL's query cache for fast results.

We cover the following topics in this chapter:

- Exploring your database, tables, indexes, and performance with SHOW
- More on SELECT queries, including advanced join types, aliases, nested queries, user variables, and the limitations of MySQL
- More on manipulating data and databases, including finding out about tables and databases, creating tables with queries, altering tables, more on the UPDATE and DELETE statements, and bulk loading and exporting data
- Functions and operators in SQL and MySQL
- Automatically running queries
- MyISAM, InnoDB, and Heap table types
- Backup and recovery, and transferring data between database servers
- Managing database server users and privileges, and creating users for web database applications
- Basic tuning of MySQL, including index design, using the query cache, and, miscellaneous tips for speed

This chapter contains advanced concepts. If you're keen to continue working with PHP and MySQL and study our example web database application, you can jump to Chapter 16. However, if you do skip this chapter, return later when you're ready to know more about how to improve your application. If you are proceeding with this chapter, refresh your memory about our *winestore* database that's discussed in Chapter 5 as it's used in most examples in this chapter.

Exploring with SHOW

The SHOW command is useful for exploring the details of databases, tables, indexes, and MySQL. It's a handy tool when you're writing new queries, modifying database structure, creating reports, or understanding how your MySQL server is performing. The SHOW command isn't part of the SQL standard and is MySQL-specific. It can be used in several ways:

SHOW DATABASES
> Lists the databases that are accessible by the MySQL server. You will only see those databases that you have access to, unless you have the SHOW DATABASES privilege; privileges and user rights are discussed later in this chapter.

SHOW TABLES
> Shows the tables in the database, after a database has been selected with the use command.

SHOW TABLE STATUS
> Provides information about all tables in the current database, including the table type, number of rows, how the rows are stored, average row length, size of the datafile, next auto_increment value (if applicable), creation time, last modification time, and any extra options used with CREATE TABLE.

SHOW CREATE TABLE *tablename*
> Shows the CREATE TABLE statement that was used to create the table *tablename*. The output always includes any additional information automatically added or changed by MySQL during the creation process, such as the table type and character set used.

SHOW OPEN TABLES
> Shows which tables the server currently has open and which tables are locked.

SHOW COLUMNS FROM *tablename*
> Shows the attributes, types of attributes, key information, whether NULL is permitted, defaults, and other information for a table *tablename*. The alias DESCRIBE table produces the same output.

SHOW INDEX FROM *tablename*
> Presents the details of all indexes on the table *tablename*, including the PRIMARY KEY. It shows (amongst other information) what the attributes are that form each index, whether values in the index uniquely identify rows, how many different

values there are in the index (the cardinality), and the index data structure used (usually a B-tree).

SHOW PRIVILEGES

Lists the access privileges that can be given or denied to users of the version of MySQL server that you've installed. Privileges are discussed in the section "Managing Users and Privileges."

SHOW PROCESSLIST

Lists the current MySQL processes (or threads) that are running, and what query they're carrying out on which database.

SHOW STATUS

Reports details of the MySQL server performance and statistics. Selected statistics and their use in database tuning is discussed later in this chapter.

SHOW TABLE TYPES

Lists the possible table types that are available in the version of the MySQL server that you have installed, and notes alongside each whether you have compiled-in support for that table type. Table types are discussed in "Table Types."

SHOW VARIABLES

Reports the values of most MySQL system variables.

SHOW WARNING *and* SHOW ERRORS

Reports warnings or errors from the last command or statement that was run on a table.

Advanced Querying

In Chapter 5, we covered most of the querying techniques you'll need to develop web database applications. In this section, we show you selected advanced techniques including shortcuts for joins, other join types, how to use aliases, using MySQL's new nested query support, working with user variables, and obtaining subtotals using WITH ROLLUP. This section concludes with a list of what we've omitted, and what MySQL doesn't yet include.

Advanced Join Types

This section introduces you to the INNER JOIN, LEFT JOIN, RIGHT JOIN, and UNION statements. The INNER JOIN statement is a shortcut that can save you some typing (and we use it throughout many examples in this chapter), LEFT JOIN and RIGHT JOIN add new functionality to find rows that don't have a match in another table, and UNION brings together the results from two separate queries.

Natural and inner joins

In the Chapter 5, we showed you how to perform a join between two or more tables. For example, to join the *customer* and *orders* tables, with the goal of displaying customers who've placed orders, you would type:

```
SELECT DISTINCT surname, firstname, customer.cust_id FROM customer, orders
  WHERE customer.cust_id = orders.cust_id;
```

The join condition in the WHERE clause limits the output to only those rows where there's a matching customer and order (and the DISTINCT clause presents each customer's details once).

We've referred to our example query as a natural join, but this isn't strictly correct. A natural join (which is also introduced in the Chapter 5) produces the same results, but doesn't actually require you to specify what the join condition is. Consider an example:

```
SELECT DISTINCT surname, firstname, customer.cust_id
  FROM customer NATURAL JOIN orders;
```

The MySQL server determines what attributes have the same name in the tables *orders* and *customer*, and creates the WHERE clause behind the scenes to join those attributes. For readable queries, we recommend you make your joins explicit by adding the WHERE clause and listing the attributes.

Just to make querying more confusing, the previous examples are also an example of an *inner join*. You can express the same query using the INNER JOIN syntax and the USING clause:

```
SELECT DISTINCT surname, firstname, customer.cust_id
  FROM customer INNER JOIN orders USING (cust_id);
```

This query matches rows between the *customer* and *orders* tables using the cust_id attribute that's common to both tables. It's required that the attribute (or comma-separated attributes) listed in the USING clause are enclosed in brackets. If you leave out the USING clause, you'll get a Cartesian product and that's not what you want.

The join in the previous example is an inner join because only the rows that match between the two tables are output. Customers that haven't placed orders aren't output, and nor are orders that don't have a matching customer. The INNER JOIN with a USING clause can be used interchangeably with the comma-based syntax of the first example in this section (and, for that matter, all joins of two or more tables in Chapter 5). We use the INNER JOIN syntax frequently throughout this chapter.

The USING clause is a handy shortcut when two tables share a join attribute with the same name. When they don't, you can use the ON clause to achieve the same result. Consider an example that joins the *wine* and *wine_type* tables to discover the type of wine #100:

```
SELECT wine_type.wine_type
  FROM wine INNER JOIN wine_type ON wine.wine_type=wine_type.wine_type_id
  WHERE wine.wine_id=100;
```

In general, you should use the ON clause only to specify a join condition. You should use a WHERE clause to specify which rows should be output.

You can have several conditions in an ON clause. For example, to find all of the wines in customer #20's first order, use:

```
SELECT wine_id FROM orders INNER JOIN items
  ON orders.order_id=items.order_id AND orders.cust_id=items.cust_id
  WHERE orders.cust_id=20 AND orders.order_id=1;
```

In this case, since the attributes have the same name in the two tables, the shortcut with USING works too:

```
SELECT wine_id FROM orders INNER JOIN items USING (cust_id,order_id)
  WHERE orders.cust_id=20 AND orders.order_id=1;
```

Left and right joins

The queries in the previous section output rows that match between tables. But what if you want to output data from a table, even if it doesn't have a matching row in the other table? For example, suppose you want to output a list of all countries and the customers who live in that country, and you want to see a country listed even if it has no customers. You can do this with a LEFT JOIN query:

```
SELECT country, surname, firstname, cust_id
  FROM countries LEFT JOIN customer USING (country_id);
```

In part, this outputs the results:

```
| Australia        | Stribling  | Michelle  |  646 |
| Australia        | Skerry     | Samantha  |  647 |
| Australia        | Cassisi    | Betty     |  648 |
| Australia        | Krennan    | Jim       |  649 |
| Australia        | Woodburne  | Lynette   |  650 |
| Austria          | NULL       | NULL      | NULL |
| Azerbaijan       | NULL       | NULL      | NULL |
| Bahamas          | NULL       | NULL      | NULL |
| Bahrain          | NULL       | NULL      | NULL |
| Bangladesh       | NULL       | NULL      | NULL |
```

The LEFT JOIN clause outputs all rows from the table listed to the left of the clause. In this example, all countries are listed because the countries is on the left in the clause countries LEFT JOIN customer. When there are no matching rows in the *customer* table then NULL values are output for the *customer* attributes. So, for example, none of our customers live in Austria. The syntax of the LEFT JOIN is the same as the INNER JOIN clause, except that a USING or ON clause is required.

The RIGHT JOIN clause is identical, except that it outputs all rows from the table listed to the right of the clause, and NULL values are shown for the table on the left of the clause when there's no matching data. It's included in MySQL for convenience, so that you can write joins with the tables in the order you want in a query. However, we use only LEFT JOIN in our queries to keep things simple.

There's also a variation of NATURAL JOIN that does the same thing as LEFT JOIN:

```
SELECT country, surname, firstname, cust_id
  FROM countries NATURAL LEFT JOIN customer;
```

This just allows you to omit the USING and ON clauses, and to rely on the MySQL server figuring it out instead. Of course, there's NATURAL RIGHT JOIN too. Again, we recommend not using either and instead including an ON or USING clause to make the join condition explicit.

As we've seen, the LEFT JOIN clause outputs NULL values when there's no matching row in the table listed to the right of the clause. You can use this to limit your output to only those rows in the left table that don't have matching rows in the right table. For example, suppose you want to find all customers who've never placed an order. You can do this with the query:

```
SELECT surname, firstname, orders.cust_id
  FROM customer LEFT JOIN orders USING (cust_id)
  WHERE orders.cust_id IS NULL;
```

The query performs a left join, and then only outputs those rows where the cust_id in the *orders* table has been set to NULL in the join process. In part, the output is:

```
+------------+-----------+---------+
| surname    | firstname | cust_id |
+------------+-----------+---------+
| Sorrenti   | Caitlyn   |    NULL |
| Mockridge  | Megan     |    NULL |
| Krennan    | Samantha  |    NULL |
| Dimitria   | Melissa   |    NULL |
| Oaton      | Mark      |    NULL |
| Cassisi    | Joshua    |    NULL |
```

Unions

The UNION clause allows you to combine the results of two or more queries. Most of the time you won't need it because a WHERE clause, GROUP BY, or HAVING clause provides the features you need to extract rows. However, there are occasions where it's not possible to write one query that'll do a task, and UNION sometimes saves you merging results manually after two queries have been executed.

To use UNION, you need to have attributes of the same type listed in the same order in the SELECT statement. Consider a simple example where we want to list the three oldest and three newest customers from the *customer* table:

```
(SELECT cust_id, surname, firstname
   FROM customer ORDER BY cust_id LIMIT 3)
UNION
(SELECT cust_id, surname, firstname
   FROM customer ORDER BY cust_id DESC LIMIT 3);
```

The query produces the following results:

```
+---------+-----------+-----------+
| cust_id | surname   | firstname |
+---------+-----------+-----------+
|       1 | Rosenthal | Joshua    |
|       2 | Serrong   | Martin    |
|       3 | Leramonth | Jacob     |
|     650 | Woodburne | Lynette   |
|     649 | Krennan   | Jim       |
|     648 | Cassisi   | Betty     |
+---------+-----------+-----------+
6 rows in set (0.01 sec)
```

You can also combine queries from different tables, with different attributes of the same type. When you do this, the output is labeled with the attribute names from the first query. As an example, suppose you want to produce a list of regions and wineries. You could do this with:

```
(SELECT winery_name FROM winery)
UNION
(SELECT region_name FROM region);
```

The first and last four rows from the output are wineries and regions respectively:

```
+--------------------------------+
| winery_name                    |
+--------------------------------+
| Anderson and Sons Premium Wines |
| Anderson and Sons Wines        |
| Anderson Brothers Group        |
| Anderson Creek Group           |
...
| Riverland                      |
| Rutherglen                     |
| Swan Valley                    |
| Upper Hunter Valley            |
+--------------------------------+
310 rows in set (0.01 sec)
```

Aliases

To save typing, add additional functionality, or just improve the labeling of columns, aliases are sometimes used for attribute and table names in querying. Attribute aliases are particularly useful in PHP as they can help you rename duplicate attribute names as discussed in Chapter 6. Table aliases add functionality when you want to join a table with itself and they're essential in some aspects of nested queries as discussed later in the "Nested Queries" section.

Consider an example query that uses table aliases:

```
SELECT * FROM inventory i, wine w
  WHERE i.wine_id = 183 AND i.wine_id = w.wine_id;
```

In this query, the `FROM` clause specifies aliases for the table names. The alias `inventory i` means than the *inventory* table can be referred to as i elsewhere in the query. For example, `i.wine_id` is the same as `inventory.wine_id`. This just saves typing in this example.

Aliases are very useful for complex queries that need to use the same table twice but in different ways. For example, to find any two customers with the same `surname`, you can use:

```
SELECT c1.cust_id, c2.cust_id FROM customer c1, customer c2
    WHERE c1.surname = c2.surname AND c1.cust_id != c2.cust_id;
```

Here we used the `customer` table twice but gave it two aliases (c1 and c2) so we can compare two customers. The final clause, `c1.cust_id != c2.cust_id`, is essential because, without it, all customers are reported as answers; this would occur because all customers are rows in tables *c1* and *c2*, and each customer row would match itself.

Attribute aliases are similar to table aliases. Consider an example:

```
SELECT surname AS s, firstname AS f FROM customer
    WHERE surname = "Krennan" ORDER BY s, f;
```

In part, this outputs:

```
+---------+----------+
| s       | f        |
+---------+----------+
| Krennan | Andrew   |
| Krennan | Betty    |
| Krennan | Caitlyn  |
| Krennan | Caitlyn  |
| Krennan | Dimitria |
```

An attribute alias can be used in the `ORDER BY`, `GROUP BY`, and `HAVING` clauses, but not in the `WHERE` clause; it can't be used in a `WHERE` clause (or `USING` or `ON`) because an attribute may not be known when the `WHERE` clause is executed. The alias is also used for the column headings in the output (and, as discussed in Chapter 6, you'll find this useful when you're working with PHP's *mysql_fetch_array()* function or PEAR DB's *DB::fetchRow()*).

Attribute aliases can also be used with functions. In the next example, we're finding out how many customers are resident in each city (but only for cities that have more than five customers):

```
SELECT count(*) AS residents, city FROM customer
    GROUP BY city HAVING residents>5 ORDER by residents DESC;
```

Here, `residents` is an alias that refers to the count function. In part, the query outputs:

```
+-----------+---------------+
| residents | city          |
+-----------+---------------+
|        16 | Portsea       |
|        14 | Alexandra     |
|        13 | Kidman        |
|
```

```
|    13 | Montague  |
|    13 | Doveton   |
|    13 | Mohogany  |
```

Nested Queries

MySQL 4.1 supports nested queries, solving MySQL's most frequently discussed weakness. *Nested queries* are those that contain another query—they are both elegant and powerful but, unfortunately, can be difficult to learn to use. This section presents an overview of nested queries, but you'll find much longer discussions in the relational database texts listed in Appendix G.

Introduction

Consider an example nested query that finds the names of the wineries that are in the Margaret River region:

```
SELECT winery_name FROM winery WHERE region_id
  = (SELECT region_id FROM region WHERE region_name = "Margaret River");
```

The *inner query* (the one in brackets) returns the region_id value of the Margaret River region. The *outer query* (the one listed first) finds the winery_name values from the *winery* table where the region_id matches the result of the inner query.

You can nest to any level, as long as you get the brackets right. Here's another example that finds the name of the region that makes wine #17:

```
SELECT region_name FROM region WHERE region_id =
  (SELECT region_id FROM winery WHERE winery_id =
    (SELECT winery_id FROM wine WHERE wine_id = 17));
```

Both of our previous examples can be easily rewritten as a single query with a WHERE clause and an AND operator. Indeed, you should always try to write join queries where possible and avoid nesting unless you need it; MySQL isn't good at optimizing nested queries and they are therefore usually slower to run. However, sometimes, you need a nested query.

Here's an example where a nested query is the only practical solution. Suppose you want to find which customers have made the largest single purchase of a wine. You can find which wine was sold for the highest total price using:

```
SELECT MAX(price) FROM items;
```

This reports the maximum price:

```
+------------+
| MAX(price) |
+------------+
|     329.12 |
+------------+
1 row in set (0.01 sec)
```

You could then write a second query to find the customers who bought the wine:

```
SELECT customer.cust_id FROM customer INNER JOIN items USING (cust_id)
  WHERE price = 329.12;
```

However, with nesting you can put the queries together into a single step:

```
SELECT DISTINCT customer.cust_id FROM customer
  INNER JOIN items USING (cust_id)
  WHERE price = (SELECT MAX(price) FROM items);
```

It's not possible to write this query in one step without nesting. As we discussed in Chapter 8, using the output of a SELECT query as the input to an UPDATE, INSERT, or DELETE can cause concurrency problems and, therefore, nested queries allow you to avoid locking for many (but not all) queries.

Nesting can also be used in the HAVING clause. We don't discuss this in detail here.

In the examples so far, we've used the equals = operator. You can also use other comparison operators, including <, >, <=, >=, and !=. These operators are discussed in more detail later in "Functions." Also, all of our examples return single values from the inner query, and only one attribute or aggregate. If the inner query returns more than one value or attribute, MySQL reports an error; this can be solved using the IN clause we discuss next.

The IN clause

Suppose you want to find the wines that have been purchased by customers who've placed at least six orders. You can't use the techniques we've discussed in the previous section because the inner query (which finds the customers who've made more than six purchases) is likely to return more than one cust_id value. However, you can still use a nested query for the task by using the IN clause.

Let's consider how you'd find customers who've placed six or more orders. You'd use a query such as this:

```
SELECT customer.cust_id FROM customer
  INNER JOIN orders USING (cust_id)
  GROUP BY cust_id HAVING count(order_id) >= 6;
```

When you test this query on the *winestore* database, you'll find there are 107 customers returned as answers. However, to make things easy, let's look only for the three customers returned with cust_id values of 7, 14, and 107.

You could find all of the wines purchased by those three customers using the following query:

```
SELECT DISTINCT wine_id FROM items
  WHERE cust_id = 7 OR cust_id = 14 OR cust_id = 107;
```

Of course, you could extend this to find all wines for all 107 customers, but that requires a lot of typing!

Here's how you can do it with a nested query and the IN clause:

```
SELECT DISTINCT wine_id FROM items WHERE cust_id IN
  (SELECT customer.cust_id FROM customer
```

```
    INNER JOIN orders USING (cust_id)
    GROUP BY cust_id HAVING count(order_id) >= 6);
```

The outer query finds all wine_id values from the *items* table where the cust_id is in the set of values returned from the inner query. The inner query finds all customers who've made at least six orders. If you run this query on your MySQL installation, you'll find it's very slow to execute because MySQL isn't yet that good at optimizing nested queries. However, the result is exactly what you want.

You can compare several attributes in the nesting condition by listing more than one attribute before an IN clause, as long as the attributes are of the same type and order as those listed in the nested query. This isn't a common requirement, because most of the time you can do this with a WHERE clause and a join query. But to illustrate the syntax, suppose we had a table that contained a list of contacts, and we wanted to find out which of our contacts had the same name as a customer. A possible query would be:

```
SELECT * FROM contacts WHERE (surname, firstname) IN
    (SELECT surname, firstname FROM customer);
```

The query would return the set of people whose surnames and firstnames are the same in the *contacts* and *customer* tables. Of course, this query could be rewritten as:

```
SELECT * FROM contacts INNER JOIN
    customer USING (surname, firstname);
```

With MySQL, the join query runs much faster, and should be used in preference.

Nested queries can also use the NOT IN clause. This has the opposite effect to IN, and is analogous to the != operator but is applied to more than one row. Here's an example, where we want to find those customers who've not made at least five orders:

```
SELECT customer.cust_id, surname, firstname FROM customer
    WHERE customer.cust_id NOT IN
      (SELECT customer.cust_id FROM customer
       INNER JOIN orders USING (cust_id)
       GROUP BY cust_id HAVING count(*) >= 5);
```

The EXISTS clause

Perhaps the least intuitive (and most complicated) of the nested querying tools is the EXISTS clause. However, it's very useful. The EXISTS clause is used to return output from the outer query if the inner query returns any results. Consider an example:

```
SELECT region_name FROM region WHERE EXISTS
    (SELECT region_id FROM winery GROUP BY region_id HAVING count(*) > 35);
```

MySQL first runs the inner query which, if you run it yourself, returns the following regions that contain at least 35 wineries:

```
+-----------+
| region_id |
+-----------+
|         4 |
```

```
|          5 |
|          9 |
+-----------+
3 rows in set (0.00 sec)
```

Because the inner query returns a result, the outer query is executed, and so the overall output of the nested query is:

```
+---------------------+
| region_name         |
+---------------------+
| All                 |
| Barossa Valley      |
| Coonawarra          |
| Goulburn Valley     |
| Lower Hunter Valley |
| Margaret River      |
| Riverland           |
| Rutherglen          |
| Swan Valley         |
| Upper Hunter Valley |
+---------------------+
10 rows in set (0.01 sec)
```

This perhaps isn't what you expected: it's a list of all regions, and it has nothing to do with those regions that have at least 35 wineries!

You're probably wondering now whether EXISTS is actually useful. It is, but only when the inner query contains an *outer reference*. An outer reference creates a relationship between the inner query and the outer query, in the same way as IN or a comparison operator such as = does in the previous sections. Consider an example that corrects our previous one:

```
SELECT region_name FROM region WHERE EXISTS
  (SELECT * FROM winery WHERE region.region_id = winery.region_id
   GROUP BY region_id HAVING count(*) > 35);
```

The query returns the following results:

```
+---------------------+
| region_name         |
+---------------------+
| Coonawarra          |
| Upper Hunter Valley |
| Margaret River      |
+---------------------+
3 rows in set (0.00 sec)
```

The query is now returning the results we expected: a list of regions that contain more than 35 wineries. You'll notice that the *region* table's region_id attribute is referenced in the inner query but the *region* table isn't listed in its FROM clause. This is the outer reference, and it causes MySQL to run the inner query for every value returned from the outer query and output is only produced when the inner query returns a result. The *region* table's region_id is used in the inner query in the WHERE

---

and GROUP BY clauses, and the count(*) in the HAVING clause therefore refers to the number of wineries in a region.

Figure 15-1 shows how MySQL evaluates the previous query using the EXISTS clause. For each region_name that's in the *region* table, MySQL runs an inner query. If the inner query produces results, the region_name from the outer query is added to the results; if it doesn't produce results, the outer result isn't shown. As the figure illustrates, MySQL evaluates an inner query for every outer result, and this can be slow.

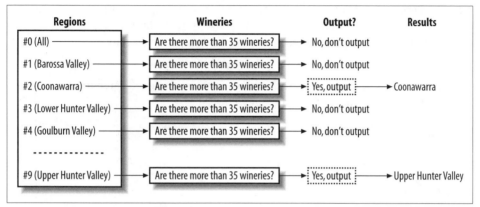

Figure 15-1. Evaluating a nested query that uses EXISTS

Whether you use the IN clause or the EXISTS clause is almost always a personal preference. You'll recall this query from the previous section:

```
SELECT DISTINCT wine_id FROM items WHERE cust_id IN
  (SELECT customer.cust_id FROM customer
   INNER JOIN orders USING (cust_id)
   GROUP BY cust_id HAVING count(order_id) >= 6);
```

This query revolves around the use of cust_id in both the inner and outer queries. The inner query joins tables using cust_id and groups results by cust_id. Therefore, the outer query finds the cust_id associated with six or more orders.

It can be rewritten using the EXISTS clause as follows:

```
SELECT DISTINCT wine_id FROM items WHERE EXISTS
  (SELECT * FROM orders WHERE orders.cust_id = items.cust_id
   GROUP BY cust_id HAVING count(order_id) >= 6);
```

This query revolves around orders in the inner query and items in the outer query. We group all orders by cust_id to find the count of six or greater. The items are irrelevant to this inner SELECT, but we refer to the items attribute so that we can search for items in the outer query (items is the outer reference).

Interestingly, while the EXISTS version is much slower than a typical join, the IN version is more than fives times slower again in our test environment. This again illustrates how poor MySQL is at optimizing nested queries, and this is hopefully something that will change soon. However, when you can, you should always write a join query in preference to a nested query.

One final note: there's also a NOT EXISTS clause that has the opposite function to EXISTS. Using NOT EXISTS, the outer query is executed if the inner query doesn't return any results.

Nested queries in the FROM clause

Nested queries can also be used in the FROM clause of a query to create an artificial table. Consider a (contrived) example where you want to find the alphabetically last customer. The following query outputs consolidated customer names:

```
SELECT concat(surname, " ", firstname) AS name FROM customer;
```

The *concat()* function joins together strings, and is discussed later in "Functions." The first few lines of output from the query are:

```
+----------------------+
| name                 |
+----------------------+
| Rosenthal Joshua     |
| Serrong Martin       |
| Leramonth Jacob      |
| Keisling Perry       |
```

Adding the nesting to the query allows you to find the maximum (alphabetically last) customer:

```
SELECT max(cust.name) FROM
    (SELECT concat(surname, " ", firstname) AS name FROM customer) AS cust;
```

This outputs:

```
+-------------------+
| max(cust.name)    |
+-------------------+
| Woodestock Sandra |
+-------------------+
1 row in set (0.01 sec)
```

You'll notice that we've aliased concat(surname, " ", firstname) as name so that it's easily referenced in the outer query. Also, you'll notice we've aliased the inner query using a table alias as cust. It's mandatory to alias the results returned from the inner query using a table alias, otherwise MySQL doesn't know how to reference the results in the outer query.

Of course, more simply, the previous query could have been accomplished using an unnested query and MySQL's proprietary LIMIT clause:

```
SELECT surname, firstname FROM customer
    ORDER BY surname DESC, firstname DESC LIMIT 1;
```

User Variables

User variables are used to store intermediate results and use them in later statements. We explain how to use them and discuss their advantages and limitations in this section.

Consider an example. In Chapter 8, we showed you the following sequence of statements as an example of when to use locking:

```
mysql> LOCK TABLES items READ, temp_report WRITE;

mysql> SELECT sum(price) FROM items WHERE cust_id=1;
+------------+
| sum(price) |
+------------+
|     438.65 |
+------------+
1 row in set (0.04 sec)

mysql> UPDATE temp_report SET purchases=438.65
    WHERE cust_id=1;
mysql> UNLOCK TABLES;
```

The example is a little clumsy. It requires that you write down or copy the value 438.65, and then use type it in or paste it into the UPDATE statement. In contrast, if you were executing the statements using PHP, you would retrieve the row produced by the SELECT statement using *mysql_fetch_array()*, save the value in a PHP variable, and then execute the UPDATE statement and include the value of the PHP variable in its WHERE clause.

A better approach than recording the value or using PHP variables is to save the value in a MySQL user variable. MySQL user variables allow you to save results for a connection without using PHP and, therefore, without transferring results to the web server. Here's the previous example rewritten to use this approach:

```
mysql> LOCK TABLES items READ, temp_report WRITE;

mysql> SELECT @total:=sum(price) FROM items WHERE cust_id=1;
+--------------------+
| @total:=sum(price) |
+--------------------+
|             438.65 |
+--------------------+
1 row in set (0.14 sec)

mysql> UPDATE temp_report SET purchases=@total
    WHERE cust_id=1;
mysql> UNLOCK TABLES;
```

User variables are prefixed with an @ character and the assignment operator is :=. In this example, the result of the SELECT statement is saved in the MySQL variable @total. In the UPDATE statement, the value of the variable @total is assigned to the attribute purchases. The benefit is that you don't have to remember (or cut and paste) the result of the SELECT statement.

Consider another example. Suppose you want to find which customers bought the most expensive wine (or wines). First, you run a query that finds the price of the most expensive wine and save the result in a MySQL variable @max_cost:

```
mysql> SELECT @max_cost:=max(cost) FROM inventory;
+----------------------+
| @max_cost:=max(cost) |
+----------------------+
|                29.92 |
+----------------------+
1 row in set (0.01 sec)
```

Now that the maximum cost is saved, you can use it in the WHERE clause of a query to find the names of the customers who've bought the most expensive wine. To do this, you join together the *customer*, *items*, and *inventory* tables in the following query:

```
mysql> SELECT customer.cust_id, surname, firstname FROM
    -> customer INNER JOIN items USING (cust_id)
    -> INNER JOIN inventory USING (wine_id)
    -> WHERE cost = @max_cost;
+---------+------------+-----------+
| cust_id | surname    | firstname |
+---------+------------+-----------+
|      32 | Archibald  | Joshua    |
|      33 | Galti      | Lynette   |
|      44 | Mellili    | Michelle  |
|      54 | Woodestock | George    |
|      71 | Mellaseca  | Lynette   |
|     144 | Nancarral  | Joshua    |
|     156 | Cassisi    | Joshua    |
|     236 | Mockridge  | Megan     |
|     274 | Eggelston  | Melissa   |
|     320 | Mellaseca  | Craig     |
|     334 | Serrong    | Caitlyn   |
|     408 | Patton     | Joshua    |
|     510 | Sorrenti   | Joel      |
|     531 | Nancarral  | Michelle  |
|     551 | Skerry     | Joel      |
|     622 | Serrong    | Peter     |
+---------+------------+-----------+
16 rows in set (0.08 sec)
```

The WHERE clause uses the MySQL user variable saved from the previous SELECT query.

There are three issues you need to remember with MySQL user variables:

- They only work for a connection. You can't see or use them from other connections, and they're lost when the connection closes.

- They can only contain alphanumeric characters, the underscore character, the dollar sign, or a period.

- They usually only work when you assign the variable in one statement and use its value in another. To avoid unexpected behavior, do not assign and use the variable in the same statement.

In general, we recommend using MySQL variables where possible in preference to saving intermediate values in your PHP scripts.

ROLLUP with GROUP BY

MySQL 4.1.1 and later versions support the WITH ROLLUP modifier that provides sub-totaling of grouped columns in output. To show you how it works, first consider a simple example without WITH ROLLUP, where we want to find the sales of wines made in each year:

```
SELECT year, sum(price) FROM wine
  INNER JOIN items USING (wine_id)
  GROUP BY year;
```

In part, this reports:

```
+------+------------+
| year | sum(price) |
+------+------------+
| 1970 |   20562.89 |
| 1971 |   16273.73 |
...
| 1997 |   18009.39 |
| 1998 |   20739.53 |
| 1999 |   18890.10 |
+------+------------+
30 rows in set (0.13 sec)
```

Now, consider what happens if you add WITH ROLLUP to the query:

```
SELECT year, sum(price) FROM wine INNER JOIN items USING (wine_id)
  GROUP BY year WITH ROLLUP;
```

You get one extra row in the results:

```
| 1997 |   18009.39 |
| 1998 |   20739.53 |
| 1999 |   18890.10 |
| NULL |..577975.66 |
+------+------------+
31 rows in set (0.13 sec)
```

The extra row has a NULL value for the year, and the sum(price) column is the sum of all sales in all years. It's a shortcut that saves you running the following extra query:

```
SELECT sum(price) FROM items INNER JOIN wine USING (wine_id);
```

Now, consider a more sophisticated example that finds the total sales of each wine. In the example, we've included the *region* and *winery* tables so that we can use WITH ROLLUP to get a subtotal of wines sold by each winery and region. The key to obtaining the subtotal is to use unique values from the *region* and *winery* tables (in addition to the wine_id) in the GROUP BY clause. Here's the query:

```
SELECT region_name, winery_name, wine.wine_id, sum(price) FROM region
  INNER JOIN winery USING (region_id)
  INNER JOIN wine USING (winery_id)
  INNER JOIN items USING (wine_id)
  GROUP BY region_name, winery_name, wine.wine_id WITH ROLLUP;
```

The output reports, in part, the following:

```
+----------------+---------------------+---------+------------+
| region_name    | winery_name         | wine_id | sum(price) |
+----------------+---------------------+---------+------------+
| Barossa Valley | Anderson Daze Wines |     214 |     978.25 |
| Barossa Valley | Anderson Daze Wines |     215 |      31.62 |
| Barossa Valley | Anderson Daze Wines |     216 |     576.25 |
| Barossa Valley | Anderson Daze Wines |     217 |     225.39 |
| Barossa Valley | Anderson Daze Wines |     218 |     190.26 |
| Barossa Valley | Anderson Daze Wines |    NULL |    2001.77 |
...
| Barossa Valley | NULL                |    NULL |   68403.90 |
...
| NULL           | NULL                |    NULL |  577975.66 |
+----------------+---------------------+---------+------------+
```

The sixth row shows that the total sales of the Anderson Daze Wines winery (which equals the sum of rows one to five) is $2001.77. Similarly, a total for each winery is listed immediately after that winery. After all wines for all wineries in the Barossa Valley are listed, the total for the Barossa Valley region of $68403.90 is shown using NULL values for winery_name and wine_id. Again, a region subtotal is shown immediately after each region. The last row in the table has NULL values for all attributes, and is the total sales of $577,975.66 for all regions, wineries, and wines.

The WITH ROLLUP modifier has a few peculiarities. First, the ORDER BY clause cannot be used with WITH ROLLUP. Second, the LIMIT clause is applied after the output is produced, and so it includes the subtotal rows that have NULL values. Other limitations are discussed in the MySQL manual.

Other MySQL Topics

We've gone as far as we're going with querying, and further than you'll need for most web database applications that you'll develop. There are topics that we've left out, including optimizing queries, using procedures, and full-text searching. Some of these topics are discussed in books dedicated solely to MySQL that are listed in Appendix E.

You'll find more about optimizing queries by diagnosis with the EXPLAIN statement in Section 5.2.1 of the MySQL manual, and we briefly discuss it in the section Tuning MySQL. Section 5 of the MySQL manual also includes an explanation of how MySQL optimizes most join queries, but it doesn't yet discuss nested queries. Forcing MySQL to use or ignore an index is discussed in Section 6.4.1 of the MySQL manual. Other general ideas about improving the performance of MySQL are also discussed in the section "Tuning MySQL."

MySQL procedures are C++ code that can be called within a SELECT statement to post-process data. Writing procedures is discussed in Section 12 of the MySQL manual. If you're familiar with other database servers, you might also be familiar with stored procedures, which aren't the same thing. Stored procedures are SQL statements that are precompiled and stored in the server so that the client application can call the procedure instead of re-running the query, with the result that performance is substantially improved. Stored procedure support is planned for MySQL 5. *Triggers* are another common database server component; they are similar to stored procedures but triggers are invoked by the server when a condition is met. Triggers support is also planned for MySQL 5.

Views aren't supported in MySQL, but support is planned in MySQL 5.1. *Views* consolidate read-only access to several tables based on a join condition. For example, a view might allow a user to browse the sales made up to April without the need to create a temporary table. Other limitations that we don't discuss here include the lack of support for foreign keys in some table types and the lack of cursor support. Both are planned for MySQL 5.

Manipulating Data and Databases

In this section, we show you how to alter a database's structure after you've created it. We also expand on the topics of creating, inserting, deleting, and updating data, including how to work with external files and multiple tables, and optimizing queries.

Altering Databases

Altering a table is unusual: most of the time, you'll define the structure of a table before you create it and you won't change it during its lifetime. However, indexes, attributes, modifiers, and other features of a table can be changed after creation, and this is sometimes a useful feature when you want to add a new index that supports a new query, modify an attribute type or length when needed, or tune your database.

Adding indexes is a popular use of the ALTER TABLE statement. For example, to add an index to the *customer* table, you can run:

```
ALTER TABLE customer ADD INDEX cities (city);
```

The label cities is the name of the new index and the attribute that's indexed is city.

To remove the same index from the *customer* table, use:

```
ALTER TABLE customer DROP INDEX cities;
```

This removes the index, not the attribute.

The `DROP` statement discussed in Chapter 5 can also be used to remove an index. For example:

```
DROP INDEX cities ON customer;
```

Behind the scenes, MySQL converts this to an `ALTER TABLE` statement.

The `ALTER TABLE` statement can also be used to add, remove, and alter all other aspects of the table, such as attributes and the primary index. For example, to add a new fax attribute to the *customer* table, you can use:

```
ALTER TABLE customer ADD fax varchar(15);
```

To remove the attribute fax, use:

```
ALTER TABLE customer DROP fax;
```

To change the `cust_id` attribute from type `int` to `smallint`, you can use:

```
ALTER TABLE customer MODIFY cust_id smallint;
```

You can use a similar syntax to rename an attribute `cust_id` to `id`:

```
ALTER TABLE customer CHANGE cust_id id smallint;
```

You can also change attribute lengths using a similar syntax:

```
ALTER TABLE customer MODIFY surname char(10);
```

You can even rename the *customer* table to *clients*:

```
ALTER TABLE customer RENAME clients;
```

This isn't an exhaustive list of things you can do with `ALTER TABLE`: for example, as we show in "Table Types," you can use it to alter the table type after creation. The complete syntax of the examples we've shown and many more examples can be found in Section 6.5.4 of the MySQL manual.

Be careful when altering your tables. For example, if you rename attributes then your associative access to those attributes in PHP will need modification. If you reduce the maximum length of an attribute, then values that exceed the new length will be truncated to fit; for numbers, this means that if the old value exceeds the new maximum value then the new maximum value is stored, while for other types it means that they are right truncated.

More on Inserting Data

In this section, we show you how to insert data from one or more tables into another table, create a new table using a query, replace existing data with new data, bulk load data from a text file into a database, and cache insertions in a buffer so that they can be optimized.

Using INSERT with SELECT

In the previous chapter, we showed you how to insert data using three different techniques. In this section, we show you how insertion and querying can be closely tied together using a nested querying approach with the INSERT INTO ... SELECT statement. This is useful for copying data and, if needed, modifying the data as it is copied.

Consider an example where you want to create a permanent record of the total sales to each customer. First of all, let's create a simple table to store the customer and sales details:

```
CREATE TABLE salesuntilnow
(
  cust_id int(5) NOT NULL,
  surname varchar(50),
  firstname varchar(50),
  totalsales decimal(5,2),
  PRIMARY KEY (cust_id)
) type=MyISAM;
```

Now, you can issue a nested INSERT INTO ... SELECT statement to populate the new table with the customer details and the total sales:

```
INSERT INTO salesuntilnow (cust_id, surname, firstname, totalsales)
  SELECT customer.cust_id, surname, firstname, SUM(price)
    FROM customer INNER JOIN items USING (cust_id)
    GROUP BY items.cust_id;
```

The four attributes listed in the SELECT statement are mapped to the four attributes listed in the INSERT INTO statement. For example, the customer.cust_id in the SELECT statement is mapped into cust_id in the *salesuntilnow* table. Note that unlike other nested queries, the SELECT statement isn't surrounded by brackets (and MySQL will complain if you try to include them). Note also that the VALUES keyword isn't used with the INSERT statement.

Here's a query on the new table:

```
SELECT * from salesuntilnow;
```

It output the following results in part:

```
+---------+-----------+-----------+------------+
| cust_id | surname   | firstname | totalsales |
+---------+-----------+-----------+------------+
|       1 | Rosenthal | Joshua    |     925.80 |
|       2 | Serrong   | Martin    |    1535.07 |
|       3 | Leramonth | Jacob     |     896.27 |
|       4 | Keisling  | Perry     |     979.17 |
|       5 | Mockridge | Joel      |     240.70 |
|       6 | Ritterman | Richard   |     448.72 |
|       7 | Morfooney | Sandra    |     972.74 |
|       8 | Krennan   | Betty     |      69.98 |
```

There are two sensible limitations when inserting with a SELECT statement: first, the query can't contain an ORDER BY, and second, the FROM clause can't contain the target table of the INSERT INTO.

Using CREATE TABLE with SELECT

You can create a table and insert data from one or more other tables in a single step. For example, you can create the *salesuntilnow* table we created in the previous section and insert the sales data in one query. Here's how it's done:

```
CREATE TABLE salesuntilnow
    SELECT customer.cust_id, surname, firstname, SUM(price)
    FROM customer INNER JOIN items USING (cust_id) GROUP BY items.cust_id;
```

The result is exactly the same as in the previous section, except that you don't have explicit control over the definition of the attribute names and types, and the indexes. Instead, the attribute names are copied from the SELECT statement, and the types are chosen by MySQL (though they are usually the same as the source attributes). No indexes are created; you need to add indexes afterwards using ALTER TABLE. In this example, the table has the following structure (as shown by running SHOW COLUMNS FROM salesuntilnow):

```
+------------+--------------+-------------------+------+-----+---------+-------+
| Field      | Type         | Collation         | Null | Key | Default | Extra |
+------------+--------------+-------------------+------+-----+---------+-------+
| cust_id    | int(5)       | binary            |      |     | 0       |       |
| surname    | char(50)     | latin1_swedish_ci | YES  |     | NULL    |       |
| firstname  | char(50)     | latin1_swedish_ci | YES  |     | NULL    |       |
| SUM(price) | double(19,2) | binary            | YES  |     | NULL    |       |
+------------+--------------+-------------------+------+-----+---------+-------+
4 rows in set (0.00 sec)
```

This isn't ideal: an attribute with the name SUM(price) is difficult to reference (because it's confused by MySQL with the aggregate function SUM).

In MySQL 4.1, you can explicitly choose attribute names, types, and lengths using a variation of the previous approach, and you can create indexes. Using this method, you provide a comma-separated list of attribute names, types, lengths, and modifiers. You then add any index definitions. Here's the previous example rewritten using this approach:

```
CREATE TABLE salesuntilnow (cust_id int(5) NOT NULL,
                            surname varchar(50),
                            firstname varchar(50),
                            totalsales decimal(5,2),
                            primary key (cust_id))
    SELECT customer.cust_id, surname, firstname, SUM(price) AS totalsales
    FROM customer INNER JOIN items USING (cust_id) GROUP BY items.cust_id;
```

In this example, the table that's created has the following structure (again as shown by running SHOW COLUMNS FROM salesuntilnow):

```
+------------+-------------+-------------------+------+-----+---------+-------+
| Field      | Type        | Collation         | Null | Key | Default | Extra |
+------------+-------------+-------------------+------+-----+---------+-------+
| cust_id    | int(5)      | binary            |      | PRI | 0       |       |
| surname    | varchar(50) | latin1_swedish_ci | YES  |     | NULL    |       |
| firstname  | varchar(50) | latin1_swedish_ci | YES  |     | NULL    |       |
| totalsales | decimal(5,2)| binary            | YES  |     | NULL    |       |
+------------+-------------+-------------------+------+-----+---------+-------+
4 rows in set (0.00 sec)
```

Note that in the SELECT query, you must alias attributes so that they match the attribute names in the new table (if the attribute names aren't the same). In our example, we alias SUM(price) AS totalsales, so that it is stored in the totalsales attribute in the new table. If you don't include an alias, an extra attribute is added to the new table; you can use this as a feature if you want to add an attribute without defining it.

MySQL 4.1 also allows you to create a new table with exactly the same structure as an existing table. For example, to create the *salesuntilyesterday* table, with the exact structure of *salesuntilnow* (including any indexes), use:

```
CREATE TABLE salesuntilyesterday LIKE salesuntilnow;
```

This doesn't copy any data.

Replacing data

The INSERT INTO ... SELECT statement inserts new data. If you want to change existing data, REPLACE or UPDATE should be used instead. If you get a complaint about duplicate primary key insertion, the problem is that you tried to INSERT where there was already a row with that key.

You can tell MySQL to ignore errors when using INSERT by including the IGNORE modifier. Consider an example, where we want to write data into the *salesuntilnow* table:

```
INSERT IGNORE INTO salesuntilnow (cust_id, surname, firstname, totalsales)
  SELECT customer.cust_id, surname, firstname, SUM(price)
    FROM customer INNER JOIN items USING (cust_id)
    GROUP BY items.cust_id;
```

This query runs without complaint, but won't insert any new row that has the same primary key as a row that's already in the *salesuntilnow* table. So, for example, if there's a row that has a cust_id value of 1 in the *salesuntilnow* table, any data returned from the SELECT statement for that customer will be silently ignored.

But what about if you want to override data using a simple INSERT statement? Let's suppose you've loaded the *winestore* database, and now you want to repeat the insertion of the first customer with some amended details:

```
INSERT INTO customer VALUES (1,'Rosenthal','John','B',1,
  '34 Mellili Cres','Earlwood','VIC','6750',12, '(613)83008461',
  '1969-01-26');
```

If you execute the statement, MySQL complains (as it should) about a duplicate key value being used. In this example, you can solve the problem by writing an UPDATE statement to change values, or you can use the REPLACE statement instead of UPDATE:

```
REPLACE INTO customer VALUES (1,'Rosenthal','John','B',1,
  '34 Mellili Cres','Earlwood','VIC','6750',12, '(613)83008461',
  '1969-01-26');
```

The REPLACE statement reports:

```
Query OK, 2 rows affected (0.00 sec)
```

Two rows are reported as changed because the old row is first deleted, and then the new row is inserted. This shows you the difference between UPDATE and REPLACE: you can use UPDATE only when a row exists, but you can use REPLACE even if the row hasn't yet been created (and MySQL will just silently skip the deletion step). If you do use REPLACE instead of INSERT into an empty table, you'll find that REPLACE works the same as INSERT and reports that only one row was affected.

The REPLACE statement supports the same syntax as INSERT: all different approaches to insertion that are described in Chapter 5 work with REPLACE.

Bulk loading a file into a database

A common need is to load data from a formatted ASCII text file into a database. A formatted text file is usually a comma-delimited (also known as a comma-separated) or tab-delimited file, where the values to be inserted are separated by comma or tab characters, respectively. Lines, which map to rows in a table, are usually terminated with a carriage return. For example, consider the following winery information that has been exported from a legacy spreadsheet program:

```
1, "Hanshaw Estates Winery", 2
2, "De Morton and Sons Wines", 5
3, "Jones's Premium Wines", 3
4, "Borg Daze Premium Wines", 5
5, "Binns Group", 6
6, "Davie Brook Vineyard", 3
7, "Eglington Creek Premium Wines", 4
8, "McKay Station Vineyard", 4
9, "Dennis and Sons Wines", 5
10, "Beard Brothers Vineyard", 4
```

The data in this example is saved in the file *winery.csv*. We've organized the attribute values into the same order as the attributes in the winestore *winery* table. Most spreadsheet software allows data to be reorganized and manipulated as it is exported. We've also used the spreadsheet to create unique primary key values for each row as the first attribute. If you're using a Unix platform, or avoiding spreadsheets, you'll find *awk* is almost the only tool you'll ever need for line-by-line data manipulation; there's also a Microsoft Windows version available.

The MySQL statement LOAD DATA INFILE is used to load formatted data from a file into a database. This is nonstandard SQL. The *winery.csv* file can be inserted into the *winery* table using the statement:

```
LOAD DATA INFILE 'winery.csv' INTO TABLE winery
   FIELDS TERMINATED BY ',' ENCLOSED BY '"' LINES TERMINATED BY '\n';
```

If quotation marks form part of an attribute, they must be escaped using backslashes. For example:

```
"Smith's \"Lofty Heights\" Winery"
```

Spreadsheet software usually automatically escapes quotation marks in strings when data is exported.

More detail on the LOAD DATA INFILE statement, including other options to specify data formats and techniques to control its priority, are discussed in Section 6.4.9 of the MySQL manual.

Delayed insertion

If your application is under heavy load, you can use the MySQL-specific DELAYED modifier for insertion. It works only with the default MyISAM table type that's discussed in "Table Types." Here's an example:

```
INSERT DELAYED INTO customer VALUES (1,'Rosenthal','John','B',1,
   '34 Mellili Cres','Earlwood','VIC','6750',12, '(613)83008461',
   '1969-01-26');
```

This modifier causes an INSERT statement to be stored in a buffer at the database server so that it can be run later together with any other statements that are in the insert buffer for that table. This has two advantages: first, it allows the client to continue without waiting for the query to execute; and, second, it allows MySQL to optimize the insertion process by working with many rows at once. The main drawback is that you can't get sensible information about the result of the insertion process. For example, if you execute the previous example and you already have a row with a cust_id value of 1, you'll still receive a message that indicates the process worked (even though it didn't):

```
Query OK, 1 row affected (0.01 sec)
```

In addition, this modifier is faster only if the application is under heavy load; if it isn't, don't use DELAYED because your insertion will run slower.

More on Deleting Data

Our discussion of the DELETE statement in Chapter 5 focused on simple examples with one table. In this section, we show you how to delete using a join query and how to delete from more than one table with a single query. We also show you a few tricks to speed up your deletes.

As with the SELECT statement, you can include a join condition in the WHERE clause of a DELETE, and you can delete rows from more than one table in a single statement. For example, suppose you want to remove all *orders* and related *items* rows, if the order was placed prior to 1 March 2000. You can do this with the following query:

```
DELETE orders, items FROM orders, items WHERE orders.cust_id=items.cust_id
    AND orders.order_id=items.order_id AND orders.date < "2000/03/01";
```

The syntax is a little different from a SELECT statement: the table names from which rows should be deleted are listed after the DELETE statement and the tables that are used in the join condition are listed after the FROM statement. Another example shows why this is needed: let's suppose you want to delete all wineries from the Barossa Valley region (but not the region itself). Here's the query:

```
DELETE winery FROM region, winery WHERE winery.region_id=region.region_id
    AND region_name = "Barossa Valley";
```

The query only affects the *winery* table, but it uses both the *winery* and *region* tables to discover which rows should be deleted.

You can also use the advanced join operators in DELETE statements. For example, our first query in this section can be rewritten using the INNER JOIN syntax as:

```
DELETE orders, items FROM orders INNER JOIN items
    USING (cust_id, order_id) WHERE orders.date < "2000/03/01";
```

You can also use nested queries (as long as the inner query doesn't reference data that's being deleted), GROUP BY, and HAVING in DELETE statements. You can also use ORDER BY in a single-table DELETE, but that doesn't make much sense unless you're combining it with the LIMIT modifier so that only some rows are removed; ORDER BY and LIMIT can't be used with multi-table deletes.

If you're deleting all of the data from one table, there's a faster alternative than using DELETE. The TRUNCATE statement drops a table (deleting the data and the table structure), and then recreates the table structure. Here's an example:

```
TRUNCATE customer;
```

Its only significant limitation is that it doesn't report how many rows were deleted from the table. Also, it works on only one table.

You can add a QUICK modifier to a DELETE statement, but this works only with tables of the default MyISAM table type. For example:

```
DELETE QUICK FROM customer WHERE cust_id < 100;
```

The QUICK option causes lazy deletion of index entries, and this can speed up large or frequent delete operations.

If you use the MyISAM table type, an occasional clean up of the table after deletion will reduce file size and speed up subsequent queries. You can do this with the OPTIMIZE TABLE statement:

```
OPTIMIZE TABLE customer;
```

More on Updating Data

Our UPDATE examples in Chapter 5 are simple. In this section, we show you how to include a join condition in an update and how to avoid errors that can occur.

You can use joins in UPDATE statements. For example, here's a query that adds a note to the end of the order delivery instructions for all customers who live in the state of Western Australia (WA):

```
UPDATE customer, orders
    SET instructions = CONCAT(instructions, " Ship using rail.")
    WHERE customer.cust_id = orders.cust_id AND customer.state = "WA";
```

The *CONCAT()* function joins two or more strings together, and is used in this example to add the additional instruction to the end of the current instruction; it's discussed later in "Functions."

You can also use the INNER JOIN and LEFT JOIN clauses with an UPDATE. For example, our previous query could be rewritten as:

```
UPDATE customer INNER JOIN orders USING (cust_id)
    SET instructions = CONCAT(instructions, " Ship using rail.")
    WHERE customer.state = "WA";
```

You can also use nested queries for updates, with the limitation that the inner query can't read data that's being updated by the outer query. There's also no problem in using GROUP BY and HAVING. What's more, you can also use ORDER BY to update rows in a specific order, but that's useful only if you're combining it with the LIMIT modifier so that only some rows are affected.

Last of all, you can add the keyword IGNORE to an update so that MySQL won't abort even if an error is encountered: this is useful if you're preparing a set of SQL statements, and want them all to run even if something goes wrong. Here's an example:

```
UPDATE IGNORE customer SET cust_id = 1 WHERE cust_id = 2;
```

In this case, because there's already another row with this unique cust_id, MySQL shows it hasn't done anything but doesn't complain either:

```
Query OK, 0 rows affected (0.00 sec)
Rows matched: 1  Changed: 0  Warnings: 0
```

Functions

As you've seen in many examples so far, functions and operators can be used in SQL statements. In this section, we show you selected functions and operators and provide more examples. We've chosen to show you only those functions and operators that we regularly use in web database applications, but there are many others that you may find useful for mathematical operations, date and time comparisons, and string processing. A full list with examples is available in Section 6.3 of the MySQL manual.

Arithmetic and Comparison Operators

Table 15-1 shows examples of the basic arithmetic and comparison operators and their output when tested with a SELECT statement. The basic arithmetic operators are *, +, /, and -, as well as the parentheses ( ) that are used to control the order of evaluation of an expression.

Table 15-1. Using the arithmetic and comparison operators

Statement	Output
SELECT 8+3*2;	14
SELECT (8+3)*2;	22
SELECT 2=2;	1
SELECT 1!=2;	1
SELECT 2<=2;	1
SELECT 3<=2;	0
SELECT 'Apple' = 'Apple';	1
SELECT 'Apple' < 'Banana';	1
SELECT 'Banana' BETWEEN 'Apple' AND 'Carrot';	1
SELECT 7 NOT BETWEEN 2 AND 5;	1
SELECT 6 IN (6, 'cat', 3.14);	1
SELECT 6 NOT IN (6, 'cat', 3.14);	0
SELECT NULL IS NULL;	1
SELECT 0 IS NULL;	0
SELECT 0 IS NOT NULL;	1
SELECT NULL = 0;	NULL
SELECT NULL <=> NULL;	1
SELECT NULL <=> 0;	0

The comparison operators include =, !=, <, >, <=, >=, and <=>. If an expression evaluates as true, the output is 1; if an expression evaluates as false, the output is 0. When you compare values of the same type, they are compared using that type of comparison; for example, when you compare integers to integers, they are compared numerically as integer values, and when you compare two strings they're compared alphabetically as strings. For string comparison, case is ignored and so is any trailing whitespace.

To test for equality, a single equals sign = is used; this is different from PHP, where the double equals == is used for equality tests, and a single equals sign = is used for assignment. However, if you compare NULL to any other value (including NULL) with the single equals sign = then the result is NULL. MySQL therefore includes a NULL-safe equality comparison operator <=> that returns 1 when two NULL values are compared and 0 when a NULL value is compared to any other value. You can also explicitly test whether a value is NULL by using IS NULL, and not NULL using IS NOT NULL. The other basic operators work the same as in PHP as discussed in Chapter 2.

The BETWEEN operator returns 1 if a value lies in the range defined by the following two parameters, inclusive. The NOT BETWEEN operator does the opposite. The IN operator returns 1 if a the value preceding the operator is in the set that's listed after the operator, and NOT IN does the opposite.

String functions

Table 15-2 shows examples using the MySQL string functions. There are also functions for converting integers to strings, strings to integers, and integers to different numbering schemes such as octal, hexadecimal, and binary; we've omitted these, but you'll find more details in the MySQL manual. Regular expressions can also be used through the function *regexp( )*; for more on regular expressions, see Chapter 3.

Table 15-2. Using string comparison functions and operators

Statement	Output
SELECT 'Apple' LIKE 'A%';	1
SELECT 'Apple' LIKE 'App%';	1
SELECT 'Apple' LIKE 'A%l%';	1
SELECT 'Apple' LIKE 'Appl_';	1
SELECT 'Apple' LIKE 'Appl__';	0
SELECT concat('con','cat');	concat
SELECT concat('con','c','at');	concat
SELECT concat_ws(",", "Williams", "Lucy");	Williams,Lucy
SELECT length('Apple');	5
SELECT locate('pp','Apple');	2
SELECT locate('pp','Apple',3);	0
SELECT lower('Apple');	apple
SELECT ltrim(' Apple');	Apple
SELECT rtrim('Apple ');	Apple
SELECT quote("Won't");	'Won\'t'
SELECT replace('The Web', 'Web', 'WWW');	The WWW
SELECT strcmp('a','a');	0
SELECT strcmp('a','b');	-1
SELECT strcmp('b','a');	1
SELECT strcmp('A','a');	0
SELECT substring('Apple',2,3);	ppl
SELECT trim(' Apple ');	Apple
SELECT upper('Apple');	APPLE

The string functions work as follows:

LIKE

A useful way to compare a string with an approximate representation of a string. For example, you can use it to find all rows that begin with a character or prefix. The % character is a wildcard that represents any number of unspecified characters. So, for example, the comparison of the string 'Apple' LIKE 'A%' returns 1, as does the comparison of 'Apple' LIKE 'App%'. The underscore character can be used to match a single wildcard character. For example, 'Apple' LIKE 'Appl_' returns 1, while 'Appl' LIKE 'Appl_' returns 0.

concat( )

Joins (concatenates) two or more strings together and returns a single string consisting of the parameters.

concat_ws( )

Joins two or more strings together using the first parameter as a separator and returns a single string. It ignores any parameters that are NULL.

length( )

Returns the length of the string in characters.

locate( )

Returns the location of the first string parameter in the second string parameter. If the string doesn't occur, the result is 0. If the optional third parameter is provided, the search begins at that offset.

replace( )

Replaces all occurrences of the second parameter in the first parameter with the third parameter, and returns the modified string.

substring( )

Returns part of the string passed as the first parameter. The string that is returned begins at the offset supplied as the second parameter and is of the length supplied as the third parameter.

ltrim( )

Removes any left-padding space characters from the string parameter and returns the left-trimmed string.

rtrim( )

Removes any right-padding space characters from the string parameter and returns the right-trimmed string.

trim( )

Performs the function of both *ltrim( )* and *rtrim( )*. Any leading or trailing spaces are removed, and the trimmed string is returned.

quote( )

Puts quotation marks around a string, and escapes any characters that need to be escaped. This is useful for preparing a string to be used in an SQL statement.

strcmp( )

Compares two string parameters, and returns a case-sensitive value that indicates the alphabetic ordering of the strings. If they are identical, it returns 0. If the first string is alphabetically less than the second, it returns a negative number. If the first string is alphabetically greater than the second, it returns a positive number. Uppercase characters are less than lowercase characters.

lower( )

Converts the string parameter to lowercase and returns the lowercase string.

upper( )

Converts the string parameter to uppercase and returns the uppercase string.

Mathematical functions

We make little use of the mathematical functions provided by MySQL in this book, and that's true of most web database applications. However, Table 15-3 shows selected key MySQL mathematical functions you can use and their output.

Table 15-3. Using the MySQL mathematical functions

Statement	Output
SELECT abs(-33);	33
SELECT abs(33);	33
SELECT ceiling(3.14159);	4
SELECT cos(pi( ));	-1.000000
SELECT floor(3.14159);	3
SELECT format(12345.23,0);	12,345
SELECT format(12345.23, 1);	12,345.2
SELECT ln(10);	2.302585
SELECT log(100,3);	0.238561
SELECT log10(100);	2
SELECT mod(10,3);	1
SELECT 10 % 3;	1
SELECT pow(4,2);	16.000000
SELECT rand( );	0.88605689619301
SELECT round(3.14159);	3
SELECT sin(pi( ));	0.000000
SELECT sqrt(36);	6.000000
SELECT tan(pi( ));	-0.000000
SELECT truncate(3.14159,3);	3.141

Several of the functions in Table 15-3 require some explanation:

abs( )

> Returns the absolute value of a number: it removes the negative sign from negative numbers.

% and mod( )

> Modulo has two syntaxes with identical effects. These divide the first number by the second number and output the remainder.

floor( ) and ceiling( )

> These are complementary: *floor( )* returns the largest integer not greater than the parameter, while *ceiling( )* returns the smallest integer not less than the parameter.

round( )

> Rounds to the nearest integer and returns the result.

ln( ), log( ), and log10( )

> These are natural, parameterizable, and base-10 logarithm functions respectively. The second parameter to the *log( )* function is the base to use, and if the parameter is omitted it behaves the same as *ln( )*. All return the result of the operation.

pow( )

> Raises the first number to the power of the second and returns the result.

sqrt( )

> Takes the square root of the parameter and returns the result.

sin( ), cos( ), and tan( )

> These trigonometry functions take values expressed in radians as parameters, and return the sine, cosine, and tangent of the parameter as a result. The complementary arc sine, arc cosine, and arc tangent are available as *asin( )*, *acos( )*, and *atan( )*.

pi( )

> Returns the value of Pi.

rand( )

> Returns a pseudo-random number in the range 0 to 1.

truncate( )

> Removes decimal places without rounding and returns the result.

format( )

> This isn't really a mathematical function but is instead used for returning numbers in a predefined format. The first parameter is the number, and the second parameter is the number of decimal places to return. The first parameter is rounded so that, for example, 123.56 formatted to one decimal place is 123.6.

Date and time functions

Table 15-4 shows sample uses of selected time and date functions available in MySQL. However, you'll find that most of your date and time manipulation in a web database application occurs in your PHP scripts, and for that reason, we've kept this section brief; we discuss PHP date and time manipulation in Chapters 3 and 9. MySQL functions for date and time manipulation are described in detail in Section 6.3.4 of the MySQL manual.

Table 15-4. Using the date and time functions

Statement	Output
SELECT curdate( );	2002-01-01
SELECT curtime( );	11:27:20
SELECT date('2005-10-10 12:22:54');	2005-10-10
SELECT date_add('2005-05-03', INTERVAL 1 DAY);	2005-05-04
SELECT date_format(now( ), "%W, %e %M, %Y.");	Tuesday, 30 September, 2003.
SELECT dayofweek('2000-05-03');	3
SELECT dayname('2000-05-03');	Wednesday
SELECT dayofyear('2000-05-03');	124
SELECT monthname('2000-05-03');	May
SELECT extract(YEAR FROM '2005-01-01 11:27:20');	2005
SELECT now( );	2005-01-01 11:27:20
SELECT quarter('2000-05-03');	2
SELECT time('2005-10-10 12:22:54');	12:22:54
SELECT timestamp('2005-10-10');	2005-10-10 12:35:10
SELECT week('2000-05-03');	18
SELECT weekday('2000-05-03');	2

Here are some the key issues related to MySQL data and time functions:

date_add( )

We've provided only one example of using this function. This function can add over 20 different types of values (including seconds, minutes, hours, days, months, years, and combinations of these) to a variety of different date and time formats. It's described in detail in the MySQL manual, with many examples. There's also a complementary *date_sub( )* function for subtraction.

curdate( ), curtime( ), and *now()*

The *curdate()* and *curtime()* functions return the current date and time respectively, and *now( )* returns both. These functions are evaluated before a query begins, and so multiple calls to them in the same query will return the same result.

extract( )

We've provided only one example of using this function, showing how it retrieves a component from a date or combined date and time. It supports the same wide range of parameters as *date_add( )*.

date_format( )

This can take over 20 different parameters to control the output of a date in almost any desired format. We've only shown one example, but the parameters and many more examples are in the MySQL manual.

week( )

Returns the number of the week in the year in the range 0 to 53. You can provide a second parameter that controls whether a week begins on Sunday or Monday, and whether the function returns values from 0 to 53 or 1 to 53. With 0 (the default) you get a Sunday start, and 0 to 53 as a result. With 1, it's Monday and 0 to 53; with 2, Sunday and 1 to 53; and, with 3, Monday and 1 to 53.

timestamp( )

Converts a date into a timestamp that includes a date and time. You can extract a Unix timestamp (the number of seconds since 1 January 1970) using *unix_timestamp( )*.

Miscellaneous operators and functions

Miscellaneous operators and functions are shown in Table 15-5.

Table 15-5. Miscellaneous functions

Statement	Output
Control flow functions	
SELECT if(1<0,"yes","no")	no
Encryption functions	
SELECT decode('"|2 1~','shhh')	secret
SELECT encode('secret','shhh')	"|2 1~
SELECT md5('secret');	5ebe2294ecd0e0f08eab7690d2a6ee69
SELECT password('secret')	*aace71a608b0b77c141250293c9f9b5b7ec75c970ea7
Other functions	
SELECT database( )	winestore
SELECT user( )	*dimitria@localhost*

Here's a short discussion of these functions:

if

This conditional function outputs the first string if the expression is true and the second if it is false. This can be used in complex ways. For example, it could be used in an UPDATE statement for intelligent changes to an attribute:

```
UPDATE orders SET instructions =
    if(trim(instructions)='','None specified',instructions);
```

In this case, the SQL statement replaces blank instructions attributes with a string and leaves already filled instructions unaltered.

decode( ) and *encode( )*

These functions are related two way functions that can be used to encrypt and decrypt data using a password. Encryption is discussed in Chapter 11.

password( )

This is a one way encryption function that converts a plain-text string into an encoded string; it's also used internally by MySQL to store passwords in the *users* table that's discussed in the section "Managing Users and Privileges." Encryption is discussed in Chapter 11.

md5( )

This function produces an MD5 hash or digest of the string parameter. Encryption is discussed in Chapter 11.

database( ) and *user( )*

These functions provide the names of the current database and user, respectively.

Automating Querying

Sometimes automated queries are useful for producing periodic reports, updating data, or deleting temporary data. As we show you later in "Backup and Recovery," they're also useful tools to produce database backups.

Consider an example from the *winestore* database where query automation is useful. The shopping cart in the online winestore is implemented using the database. As we discuss in detail later in Chapter 18, when an anonymous user adds a wine to their shopping basket, a row is added to the *orders* table. The row is for a dummy customer with a cust_id=-1. A related *items* row is then created for each item in the shopping cart. For the moment, the details of how this works and why we do it this way aren't important.

Our system requirements in Chapter 16 specify that if a customer doesn't purchase the wines in their shopping cart within one day, the shopping cart should be emptied. This is similar to most online stores, and it's necessary to prevent the database being filled with abandoned carts. In this case, it's a DELETE query that should be automated.

The following instructions assume you've followed our installation instructions in Appendixes A through C.

If you're using a Unix environment, the following query can be run from the shell to remove all shopping cart rows from the *orders* and *items* tables that are more than one day old:

```
% /usr/local/mysql/bin/mysql -uusername -ppassword -e 'USE winestore;
  DELETE orders, items FROM orders INNER JOIN items
  USING (cust_id, order_id) WHERE date < date_sub(now( ), interval 1 day)
  AND orders.cust_id = -1;'
```

In a Microsoft Windows environment you can do the same thing using the Run dialog box that's accessible from the Start menu. Type the following and then click OK:

```
"C:\Program Files\EasyPHP1-7\mysql\bin\mysql.exe" -uusername -ppassword
  -D winestore -e "DELETE orders, items FROM orders INNER JOIN items
  USING (cust_id, order_id) WHERE date < date_sub(now( ), interval 1 day)
  AND orders.cust_id = -1;"
```

The MySQL time and date functions *date_sub()* and *now()* are described in "Functions." The next two sections show how to install a command so it runs regularly.

Unix

Having designed and tested a query, it can be inserted into a *cron* table (or *crontab*) to automate the operation. The *crond* daemon is a process that runs by default in a Unix installation and continually checks the time. If any of the entries in user tables match the current time, the commands in the entries are executed. Consider an example from a user cron table:

```
30 17 * * 1-5 echo 'Go home!'
```

This instructs *crond* to print the string at 5:30 p.m. each day from Monday (day 1) to Friday (day 5). The two asterisks mean every day of the month, and every month of the year respectively. The string 1-5 means the days Monday to Friday inclusive.

A cron entry has six parts: a time in minutes from 0 to 59, a time in hours using the 24-hour clock, a day of the month from 1 to 31, a month of the year from 1 to 12, a day of the week from 0 to 7 (Sunday is both 0 and 7), and the command to execute. For each of the first five parts, you can set an integer value (for example, 1), a comma-separated list of values (for example, 1,3,5), a range of values (for example, 1-3), a combination or a list and a range (for example, 1-3,5), or a stepped value (for example, 0-23/2 could be used to mean every second hour). You can also replace any value with an asterisk * meaning all values.

Under Linux, you can replace integer day numbers with the shortcut names mon to sun, and numeric months with the shortcuts jan to dec. More details about cron can be found by typing **man crontab** in a shell to read the manual page. Note that crontabs in some other Unix variants also have a slightly different format.

You can add the housekeeping query discussed in the previous section to the *cron* table by typing the following at a shell prompt:

```
% crontab -e
```

This edits your *cron* table. Let's decide that the system should check for old shopping carts every 30 minutes. To do so, add the following line to the file (it must be on one line):

```
0,30 * * * * /usr/local/mysql/bin/mysql -uusername -ppassword
  -e 'USE winestore; DELETE orders, items FROM orders INNER JOIN items
  USING (cust_id, order_id) WHERE date < date_sub(now( ), interval 1 day)
  AND orders.cust_id = -1;'
```

After you save the file, the shopping cart `DELETE` query runs every 30 minutes.

Reports and other tasks can be added to the *cron* table in a similar way. For example, you can output a simple report of the number of bottles purchased yesterday and send this to your email address each morning. Here's how you might do it:

```
0 8 * * * mon-fri /usr/local/mysql/bin/mysql -uusername -ppassword
  -e 'USE winestore; SELECT sum(qty) FROM orders INNER JOIN items
  USING (cust_id, order_id) WHERE date > date_sub(now( ), interval 1 day)
  AND orders.cust_id != -1;' | /bin/mail hugh@hughwilliams.com
```

We could also have automatically written the information to a log file or to a table in the database.

There are other ways to automate queries or housekeeping in a Unix environment, including with the commands *at* and *batch*. We don't discuss these here, but you can find out more by typing **man at** or **man batch** at a shell prompt. A Mac OS X-focused article (that's also mostly relevant to other Unix users) can be found at *http://www.macdevcenter.com/pub/a/mac/2002/07/02/terminal_5.html*.

Microsoft Windows

Having designed and tested a query, it can be scheduled to run automatically by Microsoft Windows. The Windows task scheduler is a process that runs by default and continually checks the time. If any of the scheduled entries match the current date and time, the commands in the entries are executed.

Suppose you want to check for old shopping carts once every day. To do this, click on the Start Menu, then on Settings, and then on the Control Panel menu option. Now, double-click on the Scheduled Tasks icon. In the window, you'll see an icon labeled Add Scheduled Task. Double click the icon, and a wizard that guides you through setting up a task will start. We discuss the steps for Windows 2000 next and assume you've followed our installation instructions in Appendixes A through C.

To use the wizard, click Next to begin. Then, click the Browse button and locate the *mysql.exe* program in the directory *C:\Program Files\EasyPHP1-7\mysql\bin*. Click Open to select the program. Now, because we want to run the task daily, click on the Daily radio button and click on Next. On the next screen, you can accept the default start time, interval (Every Day), and start Date, and click Next again. The following screen asks for your Windows username and password: enter these and press Next. You're now on the final screen of the wizard, but you still need to modify exactly what the task will do. So, click the Open Advanced Properties checkbox and click on Finish. A mysql task dialog box should appear containing three tabs.

You've now completed working with the wizard, but you need to add extra details to the command that will run. In the Run text box shown in the Task tab, alter the text so that it is as follows:

```
"C:\Program Files\EasyPHP1-7\mysql\bin\mysql.exe"-uusername -ppassword
  -D winestore -e "DELETE orders, items FROM orders INNER JOIN items
  USING (cust_id, order_id) WHERE date < date_sub(now( ), interval 1 day)
  AND orders.cust_id = -1;"
```

Click on Apply, and then on OK. After the dialog window closes, the shopping cart DELETE query runs every day.

You can schedule tasks to run once or more frequently than daily by changing the settings in the Schedule tab for the task. You can access this by selecting Settings from the Start Menu, then Control Panel, double-clicking on Scheduled Tasks, and then on the task you want to edit. The Advanced button allows you to customize when a task repeats. For example, suppose you want a task to run every 10 minutes. To do this, you select the Repeat Task checkbox, change the Every option to 10 minutes, select the Duration radio button, and change the hour(s) setting to 24. Then, click on OK.

The Settings tab lets you adjust other conditions that determine if a task should be run, such as whether your notebook is running on batteries, whether the computer is sleeping, or if the computer is idle.

You can find out more about the Task Scheduler using the Microsoft Windows Help system. Click on Help in the Start Menu, and typing **Scheduled Tasks** into the Index tab. Double-click the Overview sub-entry.

Table Types

As we've discussed previously, when you create a table, its default type is MyISAM. There are other choices you can make, including Merge, Heap, InnoDB, and BDB (Berkeley DB), and you're free to make different choices for the tables in a single database. This section discusses the choices, the advantages and disadvantages of each table type, and how to use them in practice.

Overview

The main choice you need to make when deciding on a table type is whether you want a *transaction-safe* (TST) or *not-transaction-safe* (NTST) table; if you don't make a choice, then the default is MyISAM.

InnoDB and BDB tables are transaction-safe tables, and the MyISAM, Merge, and Heap types are non-transaction-safe tables. We describe the MyISAM, Heap, and InnoDB tables in this section; details of the BDB and Merge (which is a variant of MyISAM) tables, which aren't often used in web database applications, can be found in Section 7 of the MySQL manual.

Transaction-safe tables have the following advantages:

- They look after your data, and you'll be able to restore your data if MySQL or your system crashes (this'll either happen automatically, or you'll be able to do it using a backup you've put aside and using the log that a transaction-safe table stores; see the section "Backup and Recovery" for more information).

- You can batch together a set of SQL statements as a *transaction* and treat them as a distinct, atomic operation. This means you can either do all of the statements or none of them. This allows you to easily rollback out of a situation where the user presses the Cancel button, a step fails, or the user doesn't complete their interaction with the web database application. We show you an example later in this section.

Transaction-safe tables sound good, but nontransaction-safe tables also have their advantages:

- They're much faster, because looking after and managing data in a transaction-safe table has a substantial overhead.

- They use less resources (both disk space and memory) because of the reduced overhead.

- They're conceptually simpler: compare the size of the manual entries in the MySQL manual!

In general, you don't need transaction-safe tables in web database applications. Commit and rollback processing is useful, but it's less interesting in the stateless HTTP environment, in which operations aren't usually complex and need to be as independent as possible. For most practical purposes in web database applications, transactional processing isn't required. If it is required, it's normally part of the logic of your PHP scripts.

After you've decided to use a table type, you need to create or change a table to have that type. When you create a table, you can optionally add the table type you require (it defaults to MyISAM). For example, to make the *winery* table an InnoDB table type, you can create it as follows:

```
CREATE TABLE winery (
    winery_id int(4) NOT NULL,
    winery_name varchar(100) NOT NULL,
    region_id int(4) NOT NULL,
    PRIMARY KEY (winery_id),
    KEY name (winery_name),
    KEY region (region_id)
) type=InnoDB;
```

The MyISAM, Merge, Heap, and InnoDB table types are available as choices in all MySQL 4 installations. If you want BDB support, you need to compile it in. If you try and create a table of a type that isn't supported by your installation, MySQL will silently create a MyISAM table instead; this was done to improve portability of databases between installations but can be annoying.

You can also change a table's type after it has been created using the ALTER TABLE statement described previously in this chapter. For example, to change the *winery* table to an InnoDB table, type:

```
ALTER TABLE winery type=InnoDB;
```

MyISAM

The MyISAM table type is the default. It's nontransaction-safe but is instead designed for very fast querying, and also has low overheads for data modifications that are common in web database applications. What's more, it has three underlying storage methods that allow it to adapt to different table designs and requirements. Most of the time, it's the ideal tool for a web database application.

One of the key features of MyISAM is that it has *table locking*. We discuss locking in detail in Chapter 8, but it's important only in situations where there's more than one simultaneous user (*concurrency*), and one user needs to read data from a database and then use that data in modifying the database (or the user writes data and then reads the same data back). Table locking means that one or more tables are wholly or partially unavailable to other users in only those situations.

Table locking works particularly well for most web database applications that have concurrency issues. This is because:

- Locks are needed only for a short time. DELETE and UPDATE operations are on specific rows (most often accessed by the primary key value) and the rows are accessed through an index, so the commands are fast.

- Locks are used infrequently. There are usually many more read operations than write operations, and concurrency issues are rare anyway.

- Table locking is the only option for some operations. Examples include GROUP BY operations, updates of sets of rows, and reading in most rows in a table.

- MyISAM tables automatically manage concurrent updates in a clever way. When a mix of read and write operations occur on a MyISAM table, MySQL automatically creates a new copy of the data to be changed and carries out the write operation on the copy. Other SELECT statements being run by other users read the unchanged data and, when they are no longer reading the unchanged data, the modified copy is written back to the database. This technique is known as *data versioning*.

Although table locking sounds heavy handed, it's typically beneficial in a web database application. However, there are advantages and disadvantages in comparison with other finer-grain locking paradigms, and these are discussed in "InnoDB."

Technical details of MyISAM tables and indexes are discussed in Section 7.1 of the MySQL manual. However, one major point is that MyISAM is clever in its choice of disk storage structure. If your table has only fixed-length attributes (because it doesn't use varchar, blob, or text types), MySQL stores rows in a fixed-length format on disk. This makes access to the data extremely fast, and it'll stay that way even if the data changes frequently. What's more, it's easy to recover in the event of a crash.

If your table has variable-length attributes, MyISAM automatically switches to a dynamic table, which is slower but more compact on disk. There's also a third type, a compressed table, that's read-only, fast, and compact, and can be created using the *myisampack* tool by an administrator; we don't discuss this further here.

InnoDB

The InnoDB table type is a general-purpose alternative to MyISAM. It's transaction-safe, enforces FOREIGN KEY constraints, and offers commit, rollback, data recovery, and row-level locking. It's a powerful table type, but its benefits usually don't outweigh its drawbacks for a web database application. Most of the time, you can stick with MyISAM.

In detail, the advantages of InnoDB are:

- COMMIT and ROLLBACK support. This allows you to treat a set of SQL statements as one block, and to ensure either all or none of them affect the database. We show you an example later in this section.

- Flexible, fast, row-level locking. This means InnoDB locks affect only the rows being queried and updated, rather than the whole table as in MyISAM. This works better than MyISAM's table locking when many users are writing to a database concurrently, or locks are held for a long time.

- FOREIGN KEY constraint support. This is a tool that protects the structure and integrity of your data, ensuring that you can't add rows to one table unless there's a valid matching row in another table. For example, you could use this to ensure that you can't create a row in the *orders* table that has a cust_id value for which there isn't a matching row in the *customer* table. Also, it'll ensure you can't delete a customer if they still have an order in the *orders* table.

  For most web database applications, foreign key constraints are unnecessary. They add overhead to the data modification process, and your application logic in PHP should implement the controls and manage the constraints anyway. Writing data with PHP is discussed in Chapter 8.

  In MySQL, if a table type doesn't support foreign keys constraints, then the FOREIGN KEY constraint is silently ignored.

- Checkpoints for recovery. A checkpoint is a log file entry that allows an InnoDB table to recover quickly in the event of database or system failure.

- Flexible transaction isolation. In Chapter 9, we describe common concurrency problems. You can relax the InnoDB transaction model so that queries are faster, but all of the transaction properties aren't enforced (and so there is less guarantee of correct results within a transaction).

- Flexible indexing. InnoDB decides when a table needs a fast hash index (similar to that used in the Heap table type discussed next) and creates one automatically.

The disadvantages of InnoDB tables are:

- They require much more space than MyISAM tables.
- Foreign key constraints, if used, add overhead to table management.
- Data versioning and transactions add overhead to table management.
- They are much slower than MyISAM for most web database applications.
- They can lead to high memory requirements to manage large numbers of locks used in row locking.
- Locking can cause relatively slow performance, because row locking involves much more locking and unlocking activity. In particular, operations that require locks on a whole table, such as GROUP BY operations, are very slow.
- Indexes are slow to build when they're added after a table has been created. Indexes should therefore be created when the data is bulk-loaded.

Transactions using COMMIT and ROLLBACK

Transactions allow you to treat a series of SQL statements as an indivisible group: either all of the statements in the group succeed and affect the database, or none do. Transactions can only be used with transaction-safe table types such as InnoDB.

By default, InnoDB transactions offer repeatable reads. As discussed in Chapter 8, this allows you to reread data from a database and get consistent results, regardless of what data other users change. For example, if you check the amount of stock available in the inventory using a SELECT that's part of a transaction, and another user adds more stock through an update, you'll still see the original value if you re-run the SELECT until you issue either a ROLLBACK or COMMIT statement. You can learn about other transaction isolation options in Section 6.7.4 of the MySQL manual.

When using transactions, writes to the database don't occur until you issue a COMMIT.* Therefore, other users can't see any changes you're making until the end of the transaction. However, you can see the changes as if they've been written: if you change the database and then read your change as part of a transaction, the database will appear to you as if it's changed.

---

* Or another statement that implicitly ends a transaction such as START TRANSACTION, ALTER TABLE, DROP DATABASE, LOCK TABLES, UNLOCK TABLES, DROP TABLE, CREATE INDEX, and other major database structural changes or transaction-related statements.

There are two methods you can use to work with transactions. The first is to use the START TRANSACTION, COMMIT, and ROLLBACK statements. The second is to turn off MySQL's auto-commit feature, and to manually issue COMMIT or ROLLBACK statements as required.

Consider an example of using START TRANSACTION and COMMIT that's entered into the MySQL command interpreter:

```
mysql> START TRANSACTION;
Query OK, 0 rows affected (0.01 sec)

mysql> SELECT SUM(on_hand) FROM inventory;
+--------------+
| SUM(on_hand) |
+--------------+
|       513275 |
+--------------+
1 row in set (0.01 sec)

mysql> INSERT INTO report VALUES (1, "December 2004", 513275);
Query OK, 1 row affected (0.00 sec)

mysql> COMMIT;
Query OK, 0 rows affected (0.00 sec)
```

In this example, a transaction is started and then a value is read from the *inventory* table. This value is then used to update an InnoDB *report* table that stores a primary key value, a description of the report, and the total from the previous query. After that, the transaction is committed, which writes the insert to the database.

If you don't want to proceed with changes to the database, you can replace the COMMIT with ROLLBACK in the previous example as follows:

```
mysql> INSERT INTO report VALUES (1, "December 2004", 513275);
Query OK, 1 row affected (0.00 sec)

mysql> ROLLBACK;
Query OK, 0 rows affected (0.01 sec)
```

After the rollback is complete, all statements issued since the most-recent START TRANSACTION are undone. In both our previous examples, there's no need to LOCK TABLES because your transaction is correctly isolated from other transactions.

The second method you can use to work with transactions is to disable the auto-commit mode. You do this as follows:

```
mysql> set autocommit=0;
Query OK, 0 rows affected (0.00 sec)
```

With auto-commit disabled, data isn't written to the database until you issue a COMMIT statement. If you issue a ROLLBACK, all writes to the database are rolled-back until immediately after the last COMMIT statement. You can turn auto-commit on by issuing:

```
mysql> set autocommit=1;
Query OK, 0 rows affected (0.00 sec)
```

When auto-commit is on and you're not in a transaction, MySQL behaves as though it does not have transaction support.

If you use transaction statements with a table type that doesn't support them, your transaction statements will be silently ignored. This applies to the Heap and MyISAM table types we discuss in this section.

Heap

Heap tables are used for special purposes and have significant limitations. They're stored in memory (not on disk) and use a *hash index* to access the rows. They're ideal for temporary tables or for frequently used lookup tables. However, they have several limitations that prevent them being used for a wide range of purposes. The most significant limitation is that when MySQL is shutdown and restarted, the data in your Heap tables is not loaded.

Hash indexing is the fastest search method when you want to find an exact match using = or <=>, but it can't be used if you want to find values using the other comparison operators. Moreover, you can't use the hash index to do an ORDER BY. Therefore, a Heap table's primary use is as a lookup table where you want to find a row associated with a key value.

Heap tables are limited in the features they support. They don't support TEXT or BLOB types, and they don't support MySQL's auto_increment feature. Of course, because they're memory-resident they take up memory just by existing, and should therefore be restricted to small tables and used sparingly. Last of all, they offer locking only on the table level.

If MySQL crashes, you'll lose the data in any Heap tables since they're never written to disk. In addition, the data in Heap tables is only kept while the MySQL server is running. When you stop and restart MySQL, you need to manually reload your Heap tables with data. To do this, you can follow the steps in "Restore" for only your Heap tables.

Backup and Recovery

It's happened to all of us: your hard disk crashes, your machine dies, somebody steals your box, or you get horribly hacked. In these cases, the only way to recover your application is to restore a backup copy of your database (after you've reinstalled MySQL!). There are also less catastrophic events that can occur from which you need to recover: indexes and tables can become corrupt because of a power failure or MySQL unexpectedly dying, your operating system might crash, or a disk may become unreliable.

To protect against catastrophic events, you should make regular backups and store these offsite. There are many different ways you can backup your MySQL installation, and different ways you can automate the process. The simplest technique is to automate the dumping of your database as SQL statements into a file using the *mysqldump* utility, and this is the approach we focus on in this section.

In a Unix environment, you can also use *mysqlhotcopy* to do backups; it's a Perl script that works only for MyISAM tables and is described in more detail in Section 4.8.7 of the MySQL manual. Other approaches you can use in all environments are the BACKUP TABLE and RESTORE TABLE statements from within the command interpreter or a PHP script, and simply copying the database files when the database is offline. We don't discuss these approaches here.

All backup techniques have in common that they result in one or more files that are the backup of the database. You could burn these files onto a CD or other media (if they'll fit), copy them across a network to a backup server, or use a tape or removable disk backup unit to make a copy (and perhaps also backup other user data and the operating system). Ideally, you should then take the backup offsite.

To recover from less catastrophic events, such as a power failure, MySQL has utilities for repairing tables. We also discuss these in this section.

Backup

The simplest way to backup all of your databases is to run the following command in a Unix environment from a shell prompt:

```
% /usr/local/mysql/bin/mysqldump -uroot -ppassword --all-databases
    --opt > /tmp/backup
```

This writes the backup to the file */tmp/backup*.

In Microsoft Windows, choose the Run option in the Start menu and type:

```
"C:\Program Files\EasyPHP1-7\mysql\bin\mysqldump.exe" -uroot -ppassword
    --all-databases --opt > c:\windows\temp\backup
```

This writes the backup to the file *C:\windows\temp\backup*.

Leave your MySQL server running while you issue these commands. Both commands assume you've followed our installation instructions in Appendixes A through C.

These commands write everything you need into the backup file and you can then copy this file elsewhere for safe keeping; you could automate the backup and copying process using the techniques discussed in "Automating Querying." If you inspect the backup file, you'll find it's the SQL statements that create and insert all of the databases, tables, and data that's in your MySQL installation.

The --opt option to *mysqldump* writes a file that's fast to load when restored, and it also locks all tables in a database before dumping it (and so avoids concurrency issues within a database). If you want to lock all tables across all databases then add the --first-slave option to the *mysqldump* command; we don't recommend this if your application is online, and it isn't necessary if your applications have only one database each.

Selective Backups

The *winestore* database that you've loaded into your MySQL installation is stored in the file *winestore.database*. The file was created by dumping the data from our MySQL server using *mysqldump* (and then neatening up the file so it's organized a little better). We dumped it initially with MySQL 3.23, and we've maintained it manually since.

You can dump individual databases using the *mysqldump* command line utility. For example, to dump the *winestore* database to the file *ws-dump* in a Unix environment, you can use:

```
% /usr/local/mysql/bin/mysqldump --opt -uroot -ppassword
  --databases winestore > /tmp/ws-dump
```

To do the same thing in Microsoft Windows, type the following in the Run dialog that's accessible from the Start menu:

```
"C:\Program Files\EasyPHP1-7\mysql\bin\mysqldump.exe" --opt -uroot
  -ppassword --databases winestore > C:\windows\temp\ws-dump
```

The --databases option automatically adds a CREATE DATABASE IF NOT EXISTS winestore and USE winestore to the beginning of the file. These statements make loading of the file straightforward using the techniques we discuss next.

Leave MySQL running while you issue these commands. Both commands assume you've followed our installation instructions in Appendixes A through C.

Restore

You can load a backup produced with *mysqldump* into MySQL to restore a database. On any platform, run the command interpreter and then type:

```
mysql> SOURCE filename
```

For example, on a Unix-based MySQL, if the file is stored as */tmp/ws-dump* use:

```
mysql> SOURCE /tmp/ws-dump
```

For Microsoft Windows, if the file is stored as *c:\windows\temp\ws-dump*, you can use:

```
mysql> SOURCE C:\windows\temp\ws-dump
```

Be careful: this will overwrite the database or databases in your MySQL installation. Also, make sure your application is offline when you do this, as it's likely to result in unpredictable results for unsuspecting users.

As an alternative, you can pipe a file to the command interpreter. This has the advantage that it can be added to a script file. For example, on a Unix system, you could type:

```
% /usr/local/mysql/bin/mysql -uroot -ppassword < /tmp/ws-dump
```

In a command window on a Microsoft Windows machine you can use:

```
C:\> type c:\windows\temp\ws-dump | c:\progra~1\easyph~1\mysql\bin\mysql -uroot -ppassword
```

These commands assume you've followed our installation instructions in Appendixes A through C.

Checking and Fixing Tables

Sometimes, your MySQL server may stop without being able to carry out its normal shutdown processes. Possible causes include machine and power failures, operating system errors, and MySQL internal problems. If your MySQL server does die, you should take two basic steps: first, check the error log to see if information has been recorded that can help you fix the problem; and, second, check your databases and tables for errors.

The error log is a text file and you can open it in your text editor to inspect it; to do this, you usually need to log in as the root or administrator user. The file has a *.err* extension and is found in the *var* or *data* subdirectory of your MySQL installation. The name of your machine usually precedes the *.err* extension. If you've followed our Linux installation instructions, you'll find the error file in */usr/local/mysql/var*. On Mac OS X, it is in */usr/local/mysql/data*, and on Microsoft Windows in *C:\ Program Files\EasyPHP1-7\mysql\var*. You'll find that the textual explanations usually explain clearly what problem has caused your MySQL to stop or fail to start, and it's obvious what actions to take to rectify the problem.

There are other situations in which you should check your databases and tables. You should check your tables if strange results begin appearing from queries, such as unexpected end of file, can't find file, or table handler errors. It's possible that tables haven't been closed properly, that the indexes are corrupted, or that data modifications to tables weren't completed. It's also possible that a component in your system is about to fail, such as a hard disk. If so, you'll need to carry out repairs. If your system is about to fail, after this you should attempt to backup using the techniques we've discussed so far.

The CHECK TABLE statement checks a table, and works for MyISAM and InnoDB tables; since Heap tables are an in-memory structure, they don't need to be checked and repaired. For example, to check the *customer* table, use:

```
CHECK TABLE customer;
```

It'll report a message such as:

```
+--------------------+-------+----------+----------+
| Table              | Op    | Msg_type | Msg_text |
+--------------------+-------+----------+----------+
| winestore.customer | check | status   | OK       |
+--------------------+-------+----------+----------+
1 row in set (0.06 sec)
```

Everything is fine if the Msg_Type reported is status and the Msg_text is one of OK or Table is already up to date. If an error is found through CHECK TABLE, it'll probably report more than one row in the results, and the rows will list information, warnings, and errors in the Msg_type column and explanatory text in the Msg_text column. If this happens, you need to repair the table as discussed later in this section.

The CHECK TABLE statement has an optional parameter that adjusts how quick and superficial, or slow and thorough, the checks are. By default, it uses the MEDIUM setting, but you can specify QUICK, FAST, MEDIUM, EXTENDED, or CHANGED. We recommend using the default of MEDIUM, and then rerunning the EXTENDED option if the default reports errors. EXTENDED does a slow and thorough test of the table and its indexes. For example, to use EXTENDED on the *customer* table, type:

```
CHECK TABLE customer EXTENDED;
```

If you find an error in a MyISAM table, you can use the REPAIR TABLE statement to attempt a repair. Here's an example that repairs the *customer* table:

```
REPAIR TABLE customer;
```

You can also use a more thorough EXTENDED option that recreates the indexes in a slow but careful manner:

```
REPAIR TABLE customer EXTENDED;
```

In almost all cases, this should repair a MyISAM table. If it doesn't, or errors keep occurring, you should look elsewhere for the problem: perhaps your hard disk has become unreliable and is about to crash. Section 4.4.6.9 of the MySQL manual discusses table repair in more detail, and discusses what to do in the unlikely event that REPAIR TABLE doesn't fix your problem.

You can't use REPAIR TABLE on an InnoDB table. However, they don't usually have errors. Because of InnoDB's transactions and logging (and checkpointing) discussed in the section "Table Types," it's very robust in recovering from power and database server failures, and this is a key feature of InnoDB. However, in the unlikely event that something does go wrong and an error is reported by CHECK TABLE, Section 7.5.4.1 of the MySQL manual shows you how to get InnoDB to boot safely. This'll maximize the chances of you being able to export your data from the database before (probably) your hard disk crashes or system fails.

Exporting Data to Other Environments

Data can also be dumped from a database using SQL. MySQL supports the SELECT ... INTO OUTFILE statement that allows you to write out data in a regular format, such as a comma-delimited file that can be read into a spreadsheet program. Consider an example query that exports a report on customer orders into the file */tmp/ orders-file*:

```
SELECT customer.cust_id, surname, firstname, orders.order_id, sum(price)
  INTO OUTFILE "/tmp/orders-file"
  FIELDS TERMINATED BY "," OPTIONALLY ENCLOSED BY '"' ESCAPED BY '\\'
  LINES TERMINATED BY "\n"
  FROM customer INNER JOIN orders USING (cust_id)
  INNER JOIN items USING (cust_id, order_id)
  GROUP BY cust_id, order_id;
```

On Microsoft Windows, you could replace */tmp/orders-file* with a Windows path and file such as *c:\windows\temp\orders-file*.

In part, the output file contains the following output:

```
1,"Rosenthal","Joshua",1,11.56
1,"Rosenthal","Joshua",2,375.58
1,"Rosenthal","Joshua",3,51.31
1,"Rosenthal","Joshua",4,487.35
2,"Serrong","Martin",1,367.04
2,"Serrong","Martin",2,532.12
2,"Serrong","Martin",3,251.62
2,"Serrong","Martin",4,75.57
2,"Serrong","Martin",5,308.72
```

The statement is complementary to the LOAD DATA INFILE statement discussed in "More on Inserting Data." More detail on both statements can be found in Sections 6.4.1 and 6.4.9 of the MySQL manual.

Managing Users and Privileges

MySQL has complex, flexible account and database access management. It supports multiple accounts (known as *users*), and each has an optional password and a set of privileges that define what the user can do. For example, you can allow a database administrator to startup, shutdown, and manage MySQL. You can allow an application administrator to create, drop, and alter tables and databases. In a web database application, you might limit a user to only altering data in tables, or give them read-only access. You can also control which databases, tables, and attributes a user can access, and from where they can access the server.

This section explains how user and privilege management is supported in MySQL, and recommends how to manage it for a web database application.

Creating Users and Privileges

When you installed MySQL by following our instructions in Appendixes A through C, you set up two users (the root user and a web database application user) and created passwords for each. The root user has more privileges than should be used with an application: it can create other users and privileges, view and manipulate all databases, and control and manage MySQL. We recommend that you use the additional user you created for your application and that you create an additional user for each application that you build. We also recommend you keep it to one simple user per application: extra users or complex privileges slow down MySQL since there's more information to check before an operation can proceed.

Suppose you want to create a new user, lucy, who has control over the *application* database and can access MySQL from the machine that hosts the MySQL server. You can create this user by logging in as the root user and typing the following statement into the command interpreter:

```
GRANT SELECT, INSERT, UPDATE, DELETE, LOCK TABLES ON application.* TO
    lucy@127.0.0.1 IDENTIFIED BY 'password';
```

This statement grants the same privileges as the statement you executed in Appendixes A through C to create a *winestore* database user.

The new user can then run the command interpreter from the Unix shell with the command:

```
% /usr/local/mysql/bin/mysql -ulucy -ppassword
```

Or, for Microsoft Windows from the Run dialog in the Start menu, type:

```
"C:\Program Files\EasyPHP1-7\mysql\bin\mysql.exe" -ulucy -ppassword
```

The user in our online winestore application in Chapters 16 through 20 has these privileges.

Privileges and scope

Table 15-6 shows the privileges you can grant to a user; we've omitted a few privileges that involve advanced applications and future MySQL features. We've granted the basic privileges you need to work with a database to the user lucy in the previous section. To that list, depending on your requirements, you might add CREATE, CREATE TEMPORARY TABLES, DROP, INDEX, and FILE.

Unless you want to give the user administrator-style privileges, there's no need to use PROCESS, RELOAD, SHOW DATABASES, SHUTDOWN, SUPER, or GRANT OPTION. Be careful with GRANT OPTION: it allows a user to pass on their privileges to another user, and users can get together to grant each other privileges (perhaps leading to a security hole).

Also, we don't recommend using ALL: for better security, think about what privileges are needed and explicitly list them.

Table 15-6. Privileges

Privilege	Function
ALL	Every privilege except GRANT OPTION
ALTER	Allows ALTER TABLE
CREATE	Allows CREATE TABLE
CREATE TEMPORARY TABLES	Allows CREATE TEMPORARY TABLE
DELETE	Allows DELETE
DROP	Allows DROP TABLE
FILE	Allows SELECT...INTO OUTFILE and LOAD DATA INFILE
INDEX	Allows CREATE INDEX and DROP INDEX
INSERT	Allows INSERT
LOCK TABLES	Allows LOCK TABLES and UNLOCK TABLES on those tables that have the SELECT privilege
PROCESS	Allows SHOW FULL PROCESSLIST
RELOAD	Allows FLUSH
SELECT	Allows SELECT
SHOW DATABASES	Allows SHOW DATABASES to show all databases (including those the user can't access)
SHUTDOWN	Allows *mysqladmin shutdown*
SUPER	Overrides connection limitations, and allows the user to kill database threads, and set MySQL options
UPDATE	Allows UPDATE
USAGE	The same as no privileges
GRANT OPTION	Allows the user to pass on their privileges using GRANT

In our examples so far, we've granted privileges to application.*. This means that the privileges apply to the *application* database, and all tables within the database. For a database, you can grant ALTER, CREATE, CREATE TEMPORARY TABLES, DELETE, DROP, FILE, INDEX, INSERT, LOCK TABLES, FLUSH, SELECT, and UPDATE. Some privileges can be applied to complete databases, some to individual tables, and some even to attributes (columns) within tables.

If you want to grant a global privilege for all databases and tables, use *.*. For example, to allow lucy to SELECT from all databases and tables:

```
GRANT SELECT ON *.* TO lucy@127.0.0.1 IDENTIFIED BY 'password';
```

For the privileges PROCESS, RELOAD, SHOW DATABASES, SHUTDOWN, and SUPER, it only makes sense to grant these to *.* since they aren't specific to a database.

If you want to grant the INSERT privilege for only the *customer* table in the *winestore* database, you can do that with:

```
GRANT INSERT ON winestore.customer TO lucy@127.0.0.1
  IDENTIFIED BY 'password';
```

For tables, you can grant the SELECT, INSERT, UPDATE, DELETE, CREATE, DROP, GRANT OPTION, INDEX, and ALTER privileges.

You can even go a step further and allow a user only to INSERT into the attributes cust_id and surname in the *customer* table:

```
GRANT INSERT (cust_id, surname) ON winestore.customer TO lucy@127.0.0.1
  IDENTIFIED BY 'password';
```

For attributes, you can grant the SELECT, INSERT, and UPDATE privileges.

Privileges take precedence by their level in the hierarchy. If the user lucy has SELECT access to *.*, she can access all databases and tables; it doesn't matter whether she has SELECT access for the *winestore* database. The same applies to a database: if you can SELECT from a database, you can SELECT from all its tables and attributes. Similarly, if you have table privileges, you have all attribute privileges for that table.

Network access

There is usually no need to allow network access for a web database application if the middle-tier components (the web server and PHP scripting engine) are installed on the same machine as the MySQL server. However, if you want to allow access, you can do so in a broad or selective manner. Thus, to give user lucy access over a network from the server *hugh.hughinvy.com*, you can replace *127.0.0.1* with the IP address of the server or its domain name:

```
GRANT SELECT, INSERT, UPDATE, DELETE, LOCK TABLES ON winestore.*
  TO lucy@hugh.hughinvy.com IDENTIFIED BY 'password';
```

If you want to allow access from all hosts in the *hughinvy.com* domain, you can use the wildcard %:

```
GRANT SELECT, INSERT, UPDATE, DELETE, LOCK TABLES ON winestore.*
  TO lucy@"%.hughinvy.com" IDENTIFIED BY 'password';
```

You can use the % wildcard anywhere in a domain or IP address. Note that when you use a wildcard, you need to enclose the domain string in quotes. If you want to allow access from anywhere, grant privileges to lucy without the @ suffix:

```
GRANT SELECT, INSERT, UPDATE, DELETE, LOCK TABLES ON winestore.*
  TO lucy IDENTIFIED BY 'password';
```

As discussed previously, we don't recommend using wildcards. Instead, we recommend that you explicitly list the servers so that you minimize the chance of creating a security hole.

Revoking Privileges

The REVOKE statement removes privileges. In contrast, executing a second or subsequent GRANT statement for a user doesn't revoke their previous privileges. For example, if you type:

```
GRANT SELECT ON winestore.* TO lucy@127.0.0.1 IDENTIFIED by 'password';
GRANT INSERT ON winestore.* TO lucy@127.0.0.1;
```

then the user lucy can now SELECT and INSERT into the *winestore* database.

To revoke one or more privileges, use REVOKE. For example, to remove the INSERT privilege we've just granted, use:

```
REVOKE INSERT ON winestore.* FROM lucy@127.0.0.1;
```

The REVOKE statement has much the same syntax as GRANT. You can revoke global, databases, table, and attribute privileges, and you use the same method of specifying databases and tables. For example, to remove all global privileges from lucy, use:

```
REVOKE ALL ON *.* FROM lucy@127.0.0.1;
```

Beware: this doesn't remove the user's privileges on all databases, tables, or attributes! You need to explicitly remove privileges that you've granted from each level of the hierarchy.

Here's one final example. To remove an attribute privilege from the *customer* table, use:

```
REVOKE INSERT (cust_id) ON winestore.customer FROM lucy@127.0.0.1;
```

How MySQL manages privileges

The user and privilege information is stored in the *mysql* database, and you can explore and maintain that database in the same way as any other. The *user* table contains the global privilege settings. It contains one row for each user and host combination, and each attribute value in the row is set to Y or N, depending on whether the user has the privilege described by the attribute name. The encrypted password of the user is also stored in the row (it's encrypted with the *password()* function described in "Functions").

Similarly to the *user* table, the *db* table in the *mysql* database contains database-level settings for all databases, the *tables_priv* contains table-level settings for all tables, and the *columns_priv* table contains attribute-level settings for all attributes. If a table doesn't contain a row for a user, that user has no privileges for that level of setting. If you revoke all privileges in a row, the row is deleted.

Exploring these tables is an excellent way to check what settings you've created, and to remove or change settings quickly using UPDATE, INSERT, or DELETE. However, if you do adjust privileges manually, issue a FLUSH PRIVILEGES statement afterwards so that MySQL rereads the tables and updates itself.

Tuning MySQL

To conclude this chapter, we show you selected techniques for improving the performance of your databases, queries, and MySQL server. We focus on how to choose and design indexes, tips for querying and database design, how to tune the server parameters, and how to use MySQL's query cache.

Index Design

As discussed in Chapter 5, each table should have a PRIMARY KEY definition as part of its CREATE TABLE statement. A primary key is an attribute (or set of attributes) that uniquely identifies a row in a table. Storing two rows with the same primary key isn't permitted and an attempt to INSERT duplicate primary keys produces an error (unless you use the IGNORE modifier).

The attribute values of the primary key are stored in an *index* to allow fast access to a row using the primary key values. The default index type for a MyISAM table type is fast for queries that find a specific row, a range of rows, for joins between tables, grouping data, ordering data, and finding minimum and maximum values. Indexes don't provide any speed improvement for retrieving all the rows in a table or for other query types.

As discussed briefly in Chapter 5, indexes are also useful for fast access to rows by values other than those in the primary key. For example, in the *customer* table, you might define an index by adding it using:

```
ALTER TABLE customer ADD INDEX namecity (surname,firstname,city);
```

After you define this index, some queries that select a particular customer through a WHERE clause automatically use it. Consider an example:

```
SELECT * FROM customer WHERE surname = 'Marzalla'
  AND firstname = 'Dimitria' AND city = 'St Albans';
```

This query can use the new index to quickly locate the row that matches the search criteria. Without the index, the server must scan all the rows in the *customer* table and compare each row to the WHERE clause. This might be quite slow and certainly requires significantly more disk activity than the index-based approach (assuming the table has more than a few rows).

A particular feature of database servers is that they develop a query evaluation strategy and optimize it without any interaction from the user or programmer. If an index is available, and it makes sense to use it in the context of a query, the server does this automatically. All you need to do is identify which queries are common, and make an index available for those common queries by adding the KEY clause to the CREATE TABLE statement or using ALTER TABLE on an existing table.

If you've created the namecity index, and you want to check that MySQL will use it for the previous query, you can do so with the EXPLAIN statement:

```
EXPLAIN SELECT * FROM customer WHERE surname = 'Marzalla'
  AND firstname = 'Dimitria' AND city = 'St Albans';
```

This reports that:

```
+----+-------------+----------+------+---------------+----------+---------+----------
---------+------+-------------+
| id | select_type | table    | type | possible_keys | key      | key_len | ref
| rows | Extra       |
+----+-------------+----------+------+---------------+----------+---------+----------
---------+------+-------------+
|  1 | SIMPLE      | customer | ref  | namecity      | namecity |     153 |
const,const,const |    1 | Using where |
+----+-------------+----------+------+---------------+----------+---------+----------
---------+------+-------------+
1 row in set (0.06 sec)
```

You can see that the namecity index is listed as a possible choice in the possible_keys column and, as expected, it's the index that'll be used to evaluate the query as shown in the key column. The EXPLAIN statement is a useful diagnostic tool for understanding and optimizing complex queries but we don't discuss it in detail here; you can find out more about it in Section 5.2.1 of the MySQL manual.

Careful index design is important. The namecity index we have defined can also speed queries other than those that supply a complete surname, firstname, and city. For example, consider a query:

```
SELECT * FROM customer WHERE surname = 'LaTrobe' AND
  firstname = 'Anthony';
```

This query can also use the index namecity, because the index permits access to rows in sorted order first by surname, then firstname, and then city. With this sorting, all "LaTrobe, Anthony" index entries are clustered together in the index. Indeed, the index can also be used for the query:

```
SELECT * FROM customer WHERE surname LIKE 'Mar%';
```

Similarly, all surnames beginning with "Mar" are clustered together in the index. You can use EXPLAIN to check that the index is being used.

However, the index can't be used for a query such as:

```
SELECT * FROM customer WHERE firstname = 'Dimitria' AND
  city = 'St Albans';
```

The index can't be used because the leftmost attribute named in the index, surname, isn't part of the WHERE clause. In this case, all rows in the *customer* table must be scanned and the query is much slower (again assuming there are more than a few rows in the *customer* table, and assuming there is no other index that could be used).

Careful choice of the order of attributes in a KEY clause is important. For an index to be usable in a query, the leftmost attribute must appear in a WHERE clause.

There are other cases in which an index can't be used, such as when a query contains an OR that isn't on an indexed attribute:

```
SELECT * FROM customer WHERE surname = 'Marzalla' OR zipcode = "3001";
```

Again, the *customer* table must be completely scanned, because the second condition, zipcode="3001", requires all rows to be retrieved as there is no index available on the attribute zipcode. Also, the attributes that are combined together with OR must be the leftmost attributes in the index; otherwise the query requires a complete scan of the *customer* table. The following example requires a complete scan:

```
SELECT * FROM customer WHERE firstname = 'Dimitria' OR
   surname = 'Marzalla';
```

If all the attributes in the index are used in all the queries, to optimize index size, the leftmost attribute in the KEY clause should be the attribute with the highest number of duplicate entries.

Because indexes speed up queries, why wouldn't you create indexes on all the attributes you can possibly search on? The answer is that while indexes are fast for searching, they consume space and require updates each time rows are added or deleted, or key attributes are changed. So, if a database is largely static, additional indexes have low overheads, but if a database changes frequently, each additional index slows down the update process significantly. In either case, indexes consume additional space on disk and in memory, and unnecessary indexes should be avoided.

One way to reduce the size of an index and speed updates is to create an index on a prefix of an attribute. Our namecity index uses considerable space: for each row in the *customer* table, an index entry is up to 150 characters in length because it is created from the combined values of the surname, firstname, and city attributes.*

To reduce space, you can define the index as:

```
ALTER TABLE customer ADD INDEX namecity
   (surname(10),firstname(3),city(2));
```

This uses only the first 10 characters of surname, 3 of firstname, and 2 of city to distinguish index entries. This is quite reasonable, because 10 characters from a sur-

---

* This isn't the space actually required by an index entry, because the data is compressed for storage. However, even with compression, the fewer characters that are indexed, the more compact is the representation, the more space is saved, and (depending on the usability of the index) the faster searching and updates are.

name distinguishes between most surnames, and the addition of a few characters from a first name and the prefix of their city should be sufficient to uniquely identify almost all customers. Having a smaller index with less information can also mean that queries are actually faster, because more index information can be retrieved from disk per second, more of the index can fit into spare memory, and disk retrieval speed is almost always the bottleneck in query performance.

The space saving is significant with a reduced index. A new index entry requires only 15 characters, a savings of up to 135 characters, so index insertions, deletions, and modifications are now likely to be much faster. Note that for TEXT and BLOB attribute types, a prefix must be taken when indexing, because indexing the entire attribute is impractical and isn't permitted by the MySQL server.

Design Tips

Careful index design is one technique that improves speed and reduces resource requirements. However, design of your database, tables, attributes, and queries is also important. As discussed previously, accessing a hard disk is slow and is usually the bottleneck in database server performance. Therefore, most techniques described in this section improve performance by minimizing disk space and disk use.

Reducing disk space requirements improves both disk seek and read performance. Disk read performance is improved because less data is required to be transferred, while seek performance is improved because the disk head has to move less on average when randomly accessing a smaller file than when accessing a larger file.

Here are some simple ways to improve database server performance:

- Carefully choose attribute types and lengths. Where possible, use small variants such as SMALLINT or MEDIUMINT rather than the regular choice INT. When using fixed-length attributes, such as CHAR, specify a length that is as short as possible.

- Use fixed-length attributes: try to avoid the types VARCHAR, BLOB, and TEXT. While fixed-length text attributes may waste space, scanning fixed-length rows is much faster than scanning variable-length rows (and, as discussed in "Table Types," the MyISAM table type adjusts its structure for speed when variable-length types aren't used).

- MySQL can't join tables using an index if the attributes are different types or (in some cases) have different lengths. You should use ALTER TABLE to change the attribute types and lengths so that they match. However, MySQL can join char and varchar attributes, as long as they have the same declared length. You can check what's happening with the EXPLAIN statement.

- Create a statistics table if aggregate functions such as COUNT( ) or SUM( ) are frequently used in queries that contain WHERE clauses and are on large tables. A statistics table usually stores only one row that is manually updated with the aggregate values of another table.

For example, suppose you want to create a statistics table that tracks the number of rows in the *customer* table. You would create it with the following statement:

```
CREATE TABLE custCount (custCount int(5));
```

It doesn't need a primary key because there's only going to be one row of data in the table. You would then initialize the statistics table to the current count of customers using:

```
INSERT INTO custCount SELECT count(*) FROM customer;
```

From then on, you'd use the new table to check the count of customers. For example:

```
SELECT custCount from custCount;
```

If a row is deleted from the *customer* table, you need to update the statistics table:

```
UPDATE custCount SET custCount = custCount - 1;
```

Similarly, if a new row is added, you add one to the counter. For large tables, this technique is often faster than calculating aggregate functions with the slow built-in functions that require complete processing of all rows.

- If you're inserting large numbers of rows, list the values in one (or few) insert statements as this is much faster to process. For example, convert:

```
INSERT INTO table (1, "cat");
INSERT INTO table (2, "dog");
```

into:

```
INSERT INTO table (1, "cat"), (2, "dog");
```

- If large numbers of rows are deleted from a table, or a table containing variable-length attributes is frequently modified, disk space may be wasted. MySQL doesn't usually remove deleted or modified data; it only marks the location as being no longer in use. Wasted space can affect access speed.

  To reorganize a table, use the OPTIMIZE TABLE command discussed in "More on Deleting Data." It should be used periodically (perhaps once per month).

- MySQL uses statistics about a table to make decisions about how to optimize each query. You can update these statistics by running:

```
ANALYZE TABLE customer;
```

You don't need to do this often.

- Use the Heap table type discussed in "Table Types" for small tables that are searched only for exact matches using = or <=>.

- Section 5.2.13 of the MySQL manual includes other excellent ideas for simple performance improvement.

Server Tuning Tips

Comprehensive database tuning is a complex topic that fills many books. We include in this section only a few practical ideas to help you to begin to improve the performance of a database system. You can refer to the books in Appendix G for more information and also read Section 5.5 of the MySQL manual.

MySQL includes is the *mysqladmin* tool for database administration. Details of the system setup can be found by running the following command in a Unix shell:

```
% /usr/local/mysql/bin/mysqladmin -uroot -ppassword variables
```

In Microsoft Windows, type the following into the Run dialog that's accessible through the Start menu:

```
"C:\Program Files\EasyPHP1-7\mysql\bin\mysqladmin.exe" -uroot
    -ppassword variables
```

Both commands assume you've followed our installation instructions in Appendixes A through C.

This shows, in part, the following selected system parameters:

```
join_buffer          current value: 131072
key_buffer           current value: 8388600
net_buffer_length    current value: 16384
record_buffer        current value: 131072
sort_buffer          current value: 2097144
table_cache          current value: 64
```

Some of the important parameters are those that impact disk use. MySQL has several main-memory buffer parameters that control how much data is kept in memory for processing. These include:

- The `record_buffer` for scanning all rows in a table
- The `sort_buffer` for `ORDER BY` and `GROUP BY` operations
- The `key_buffer` for storing indexes in main memory
- The `join_buffer` for joins that don't use indexes

In general, the larger these buffers, the more data from disk is *cached* or stored in memory and the fewer disk accesses are required. However, if the sum of these parameters is near to exceeding the size of the memory installed in the server, the operating system will start to swap data between disk and memory, and the MySQL server will be slow. In any case, careful experimentation based on the application is likely to improve server performance.

Section 5.5.2 of the MySQL manual suggests parameter settings when starting the MySQL server. First, for machines with more than 256 MB of free memory, large tables in the database, and a moderate number of users, start your MySQL in Unix with:

```
% /usr/local/mysql/bin/mysqld_safe -O key_buffer=64M -O table_cache=256 \
    -O sort_buffer=4M -O read_buffer_size=1M &
```

The following setting is appropriate for an application such as the online winestore, because many users are expected, the queries are largely index-based, and the database is small:

```
mysqld_safe -O key_buffer=512k -O sort_buffer=16k \
-O table_cache=32 -O read_buffer_size=8k -O net_buffer_length=1K &
```

There are two other parameters used in this example that we've not discussed. The table_cache parameter manages the maximum number of open tables per user connection, while the net_buffer parameter sets the minimum size of the network query buffer in which incoming queries are kept before they are executed.

The SHOW STATUS and SHOW VARIABLES commands that are described at the beginning of this chapter can be used to report on MySQL's use and behavior. SHOW VARIABLES does the same thing as the *mysqladmin* command at the beginning of this section. SHOW STATUS gives a brief point-in-time summary of the server status and can help find more about the number of user connections, queries, and table use. This is useful input into changing the startup parameters we've just described.

Query Caching

MySQL 4 features an optional query cache. When you activate it, the results of queries are stored in a memory buffer. If an identical query arrives later, the results are returned from the cache rather than the query being rerun. This is an excellent feature if your application runs many identical queries and your database doesn't change too often. Typically, this makes it an ideal tool for web database applications, and we recommend you use it for your applications; if you followed our Unix installation instructions in Appendixes A through C, you've already enabled the query cache with default parameters.

Consider an example. In our online winestore, the following query is executed every time any user visits the homepage. The query finds the latest three wines that have been stocked at the winestore and have been reviewed by a wine writer:

```
SELECT wi.winery_name, w.year, w.wine_name, w.wine_id, w.description
  FROM wine w, winery wi, inventory i WHERE w.winery_id = wi.winery_id
  AND w.wine_id = i.wine_id AND w.description IS NOT NULL
  GROUP BY w.wine_id ORDER BY i.date_added DESC LIMIT 3;
```

The query isn't fast to run: it uses three tables, two join conditions, a conditional check for a description, a GROUP BY clause, an ORDER BY clause, and the LIMIT modifier. However, it's an ideal candidate for query caching: the homepage is popular and new wines, wine reviews, and inventory are infrequently added. From simple experiments with our online winestore from the first edition of this book, we've found that adding query caching makes visiting the homepage almost three times faster.

Query caching has several features:

- It's configurable so that you can control which queries are cached when you write the queries (more later in this section).

- It can be tuned: you can control how much memory is used in total, the maximum size of a result set in the cache, and the size of memory blocks that are allocated in the cache (more on this next).

- It's sensitive to data or table structure changes: if they change, any query that uses them is automatically flushed from the cache.

However, there are some situations in which it isn't useful and you need to be careful:

- If you rarely execute the same query, most queries are first checked against the cache and then executed anyway. This adds an overhead to most queries.

- If your data changes frequently, the cached queries have to be frequently flushed from the cache, and this slows querying down. If any row changes in a table, a query using that table is flushed (even if it doesn't access the row).

- To use the cache, a query must be identical byte for byte with a query that's in the cache. So, for example, SELECT * FROM customer and SELECT * FROM CUSTOMER are treated as different queries, and the latter won't find the former in the cache. Even additional whitespace renders two queries different.

- Queries that use functions that could return different results don't use the cache. Most of these are obvious: system time functions, system date functions, locking functions, and so on. A complete list is in Section 6.9.1 of the MySQL manual.

Configuring query caching

Query caching is off by default when you install MySQL 4.1. To turn it on, you need to edit your MySQL configuration file that you installed when following the installation procedure in Appendixes A through C. In a Unix environment, edit the file */etc/my.cnf*, and in Microsoft Windows edit the *my.ini* file in *C:\winnt* for Windows 2000/2003/NT or *C:\windows* for Windows XP. Find the section that beings with the heading:

```
# The MySQL server
[mysqld]
```

Add the following statements to the end of that section:

```
query_cache_size = 16M
query_cache_type = 1
query_cache_min_res_unit = 4K
query_cache_limit = 1M
```

You need to add the first parameter query_cache_size that defines how much memory the cache uses (we've decided on 16 MB): the default is 0, which disables caching. The remaining three statements are optional, but we've included them with their default settings anyway. The query_cache_type parameter defines whether caching is off (0), on (1), or only used when you ask for it (2); we discuss how to control which queries are cached in the next section. The third parameter `query_cache_min_res_unit` defines the minimum memory block size for a cached result set, and the default of 4 KB. works well. The last parameter `query_cache_limit` defines the maximum size of a result set that can be cached, and the 1 MB default is a sensible choice.

After you've made the changes, save the file, and restart your MySQL using the method described for your platform in Appendixes A through C. Alternatively, reboot your machine.

You now have caching enabled. If you repeat a query such as `SELECT * FROM customer` twice or more, you can check that the cache is in action by using the `SHOW STATUS` command from the command interpreter. This outputs, in part, the following:

```
| Qcache_queries_in_cache | 1        |
| Qcache_inserts          | 1        |
| Qcache_hits             | 3        |
| Qcache_lowmem_prunes    | 0        |
| Qcache_not_cached       | 0        |
| Qcache_free_memory      | 16709128 |
| Qcache_free_blocks      | 1        |
| Qcache_total_blocks     | 4        |
```

In our example, you can see that our system has just started up: there's one query in the cache, only one query has ever been inserted, it's been re-run three times, and no queries that couldn't be cached have ever been run. There's also plenty of memory free.

Controlling query caching

After you've got caching turned on, you can control whether an individual query is cached or not. If you don't prevent caching, and the `query_cache_type` parameter is set to its default of 1, all queries are cached (with the exception of those queries that it doesn't make sense to cache, as discussed previously). If the `query_cache_type` parameter is set to 2, only those queries you ask to be cached will be cached.

Here's an example of how to explicitly cache a query:

```
SELECT SQL_CACHE * FROM customer;
```

Here's an example of how not to cache a query:

```
SELECT SQL_NO_CACHE * FROM customer;
```

Caching only works with `SELECT` queries. It doesn't make sense to cache dynamic `DELETE`, `INSERT`, or `UPDATE` queries (or their variants such as `TRUNCATE`).

CHAPTER 16

Hugh and Dave's Online Wines: A Case Study

This chapter is the first of five that outline the major case study for this book, *Hugh and Dave's Online Wines*. It contains an overview of the system requirements, a walk-through of the complete application, and a pointer to where the fundamentals of each component are explained in the book. It also explains most of the components we've developed for reuse throughout the application.

The material presented in the winestore chapters doesn't fully explain the application. Also, we avoid duplicating our discussions of the principles and basic techniques for building web database applications. Chapters 2 through 13 are required background reading to fully understand the implementations.

To make implementing the winestore a little simpler, we've developed two template classes. They inherit from PEAR's ITX templates and are designed to give every winestore page a generic framework. In particular, our form class includes code for creating form widgets that can report errors and display previously entered data. We explain how we use these classes in this chapter, and list the code and the templates. We also discuss our functions for general-purpose validation, our custom error handler, database settings, and general-purpose functions and constants.

Before you begin this chapter, we recommend downloading and installing the online winestore on a local machine following the instructions in Appendixes A to C. The best way to understand the code is to have a local copy of the application, to open the scripts in an editor, and to walk through the scripts while using the application with a browser. Modifications of the scripts are encouraged. Suggestions are welcome by email to *hugh@hughwilliams.com*.

The source code to the winestore application (and all other code in this book) can be redistributed as long as it continues to include a statement that it's from Hugh E. Williams and David Lane, *Web Database Application with PHP and MySQL*, Second Edition, published by O'Reilly & Associates. You're welcome to use it for any purpose with one exception: it cannot be included in any other book, publication, or educational product without permission from O'Reilly & Associates. No warranty is attached, and we can't take responsibility for errors or fitness for use.

Functional and System Requirements

Before we built the winestore, our fictional client told us what it should do and what features they wanted. Let's take a look at the scope and aims of the winestore that would typically be gathered from interviews, studying workflow, and so on.

Hugh and Dave's Online Wines is a fictional online wine retailer. The winestore sells wines from wineries that are located in regions throughout Australia. The winestore is open to the public: anonymous users have limited access to the application, and users can make purchases if they become members.

Any user with a web browser can access the site, browse or search for wines, and view wine details. The winestore carries thousands of wines, and the details of each wine include its name, vintage (year of release), the winery that makes it, grape varieties, and, in some cases, an expert review of the wine.

An anonymous user can search for wines and add selected wines to a shopping cart. However, to purchase wines, a user must be a member and log in using their username and password. Membership is open to all users and the membership application process collects details about the customer in the same way as at most online sites. When placing an order, the member must provide their credit card details, as well as any shipping instructions. An order is shipped immediately and a confirmation sent by email.

The winestore doesn't do much more than manage members, wines, and ordering. It doesn't have a reporting module, an administration interface, or any content management features. It is not designed to be a fully functional application but only to illustrate most of the fundamental techniques discussed throughout the book.

The next section outlines the requirements of the winestore in more detail.

Requirements List

Here's a summary of the functional and system requirements:

- The online winestore is an e-commerce site to sell wine.
- The application doesn't manage accounting, stock control, payroll, ordering, and other tasks.
- Users may select wines and add them to a shopping cart. Users may purchase the items in their shopping cart for up to one day after the first item is added to the basket.
- Shopping carts are maintained for 24 hours, after which they're emptied. If a user quits their web browser or logs out, then the cart is emptied.

- Users have only one shopping cart each and may empty their carts at any time.

- Users of the site may be anonymous and can remain anonymous until they decide to purchase the items in the shopping cart.

- To purchase items in a shopping basket, the user must log in to the system. To log in, a user must be a member.

- To get a membership, a user must provide at least his surname, first name, a title, an address line, a city, a Zip Code, a country, his birth date, an email address, and a password. The email address is used as the user's login name. The user may also optionally provide a middle initial, a state, and a telephone number.

- When a member purchases wines, she must provide credit card details. The card details are associated with the order. An order may also have a delivery note that is directed to the delivery company; for example, a note might indicate to "leave the wines at the back door of the house."

- When a member purchases wines, his order is kept in the database.

- Wines are classified into broad types of red, white, sparkling, sweet, and fortified. Wines also have a name, a vintage (year of release), and a description; descriptions are optional free-form text that are typically a review of the wine similar to that found on the label.

- Wines are made with different grape varieties, including Chardonnay, Semillon, Merlot, and so on. A wine can be made of any number of grape varieties, and the ordering of these grape varieties is important. For example, for a wine made of two varieties, Cabernet and Merlot, a Cabernet Merlot is different from a Merlot Cabernet.

- Users may browse wines at the winestore by broad type (red, white, and so on) or wine region.

- Wines are produced by one winery. Each winery has a name.

- Wineries are located in a region. A region is an area (for example, the Barossa Valley in South Australia).

- A shopping cart is an order that isn't yet associated with a customer. Each order contains items. It can be converted to a completed order after the user logs in.

- Each item in an order is for a particular wine, a quantity of that wine to be purchased, and a price per bottle. The price of the wine is always the cheapest available inventory price.

- The quantities of wines in the shopping cart can be updated by the user, and items can be removed from the shopping cart by setting their quantity to zero.

- The wines available for sale are stored in an inventory. Each inventory record is unique to a particular wine. The inventory record contains the arrival date of the stock, the quantity available, and a per-bottle price. There can be several inventory records for a wine, representing different shipments that arrived at the winestore on different dates or that have a different price.

- The user will always be given the lowest advertised prices for each wine. When a user adds a wine to her shopping cart, she is guaranteed this price.

- A user can purchase only wines that are in stock.

- When a user converts his shopping cart to an order, the application checks for sufficient inventory to complete the order. If insufficient wine is available, the user is alerted, and the quantities in the shopping basket are updated; this situation can occur if a user adds more wine to his basket than is available, and this can happen when many users shop for the same wine at the same time.

- When sufficient inventory is available to complete an order, the quantity of wine in the inventory is reduced as the order is finalized. The inventory reduced is always the oldest inventory of that wine.

The process of modeling these requirements with relational database entity-relationship (ER) modeling and converting this model to SQL statements is the subject of Appendix E. The winestore ER model can be found in Chapter 5.

Application Overview

The winestore application was developed to meet the requirements outlined in the previous section. It is a complete PHP and MySQL web database application, and uses PEAR ITX templates and PEAR DB to abstract HTML presentation and the database layer. It was developed on a Linux platform using the MySQL 4.1 DBMS and PHP 4.3, but works in the Microsoft Windows and Mac OS X environments.

It has been tested with PHP 5.0.0 beta (b2). At the time of writing, PEAR DB does not work with PHP5 and MySQL 4.1. This will likely be fixed when PHP5 is released, and we'll provide updated code on our book's web site *http://www.webdatabasebook.com*.

The winestore has many components of a typical web database application, including:

- Maintainable web pages generated with templates, and populated with data from a database.

- User-driven querying and browsing, in which the user provides the parameters that limit the searching or browsing of the database. This includes one-component querying.

- Data entry and validation.

- User tracking with session management techniques.

- User authentication and management.

- SQL querying that requires table locking.

- Receipt pages that avoid the reload problem.

- Robust error handling with a custom error module.

- Email- and browser-based receipts.

The application has five separate modules that we discuss in the next four chapters:

Customer management
>   Becoming a member and amending membership details. The scripts that imple-
>   ment this functionality are in Chapter 17.

Shopping cart
>   Adding wines to a shopping cart, deleting items from the cart, adjusting quanti-
>   ties, and emptying the cart. The shopping cart is discussed in Chapter 18.

Ordering and shipping
>   Processing the cart so that it becomes an order, validating a credit card, confirm-
>   ing shipping details by email, and confirming shipping details with an HTML
>   receipt. These scripts are the subject of Chapter 19.

Browsing and searching
>   Searching and browsing the wines using user-supplied parameters. Outlined in
>   Chapter 20.

Authentication
>   Logging in, logging out, and changing passwords. Also discussed in Chapter 20.

The application also has a set of common components, including PEAR ITX template extensions, authentication functions, a custom error handler, validation functions, and general purpose functions and constants. With the exception of the
authentication functions, these common components are discussed later in this
chapter. The general-purpose authentication functions are discussed in Chapter 20.

Winestore Scripts

Figure 16-1 and Figure 16-2 show the scripts developed for the winestore application and how they interact. Scripts are shown as boxes. Solid boxes indicate scripts
that generate HTML, while dashed boxes don't produce output but instead redirect
to other scripts. Lines with arrows show how the scripts call each other, and dashed
lines indicate the path is followed when validation fails or an error occurs. The three
key user interface scripts, *index.php*, *customer/details.php*, and *cart/showcart.php*, are
shown in both figures.

Functional overview

The main or home page of the online winestore is shown in Figure 16-1 and
Figure 16-2 and is labeled *index.php*. This page allows the user to add bottles and
cases of the three selected "hot new wines" to his shopping cart and to access the
other parts of the application. The shopping cart functionality is shown by the double-
ended arrow to the add-to-cart script labeled *cart/addtocart.php*. The *cart/addtocart.
php* script is shown as a dashed rectangle in Figure 16-1, indicating that it's a one-
component query module that has no output and instead redirects to the calling page.

The home page also allows the user to view his shopping cart by clicking on the cart
icon at the top of the page or the View Cart button at the bottom of the page. View-

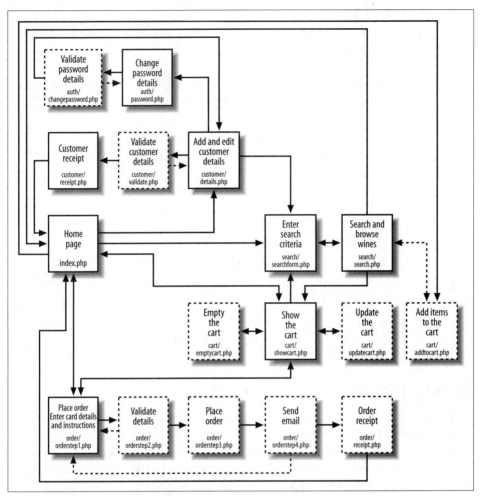

Figure 16-1. The winestore application architecture

the-cart functionality is provided by the *cart/showcart.php* script introduced later in this section. Three other actions are also possible from the home page:

- Searching the wines using the script *search/searchform.php*
- Becoming a member or changing customer details using the *customer/details.php* script
- Logging in or logging out using the scripts *auth/login.php* and *auth/logout.php*, respectively

Figure 16-1 and Figure 16-2 show the cart, customer, authentication, password change, searching, ordering, and shipping scripts. In detail, the features are:

Customer details management

This is provided by the *customer/details.php*, *customer/validate.php*, and *customer/receipt.php* scripts that implement the become-a-member and change details features. The scripts show how to build a real-world data entry, validation, and receipt module using the techniques we discuss in Chapters 6 through 9.

The script *customer/details.php* presents an empty customer form to new customers. The form allows entry of all customer details, including an email address that is used as the login name of the user and a password for future visits to the site. The *customer/validate.php* script validates customer data and, on success, writes to the database and redirects to the customer receipt script *customer/receipt.php*.

On validation failure, *customer/validate.php* redirects to *customer/details.php*, where the validation errors are reported as batch errors that are interleaved with the form widgets.

For customers who are amending their details, the password and email input widgets are omitted from the customer form.

Password management

This is provided by the *auth/password.php* and *auth/changepassword.php* scripts. The scripts show how to build part of a real-world authentication module using the techniques discussed in Chapters 10 and 11, in conjunction with the basic techniques of Chapters 6 through 9.

Logged in users can change their passwords by clicking on the Change Password button at the bottom of the Change Details page which then calls the *auth/password.php* script.

To change their password, users are required to enter their current password to reduce the risk of an unauthorized change, and then to enter the new password twice to minimize the chance of a typing error. The password change is validated by the authorization script *auth/changepassword.php*. A receipt is shown for a successful change by redirecting the user to the customer details page *customer/details.php*, which then displays a confirmation message; we chose not to add a receipt page to this module because it's unnecessary when there's no information that the user needs to record.

An unsuccessful password change attempt redirects the user to *auth/password.php* where error messages are displayed.

Authentication

The remaining three authorization scripts *auth/login.php*, *auth/logincheck.php*, and *auth/logout.php* are shown in Figure 16-2. These scripts continue our real-world examples of building an authentication module.

The *auth/login.php* script produces a form for the user to enter their email address and password. The *auth/logincheck.php* script validates the email address and password, and checks if a matching user is a member. If so, the script logs the user into the application and redirects the user to the *index.php* main page script, where their login status is displayed at the top of the page. If the login process fails, they're returned to *auth/login.php* and errors are displayed.

The script *auth/logout.php* logs the user out of the application and redirects her to the main page *index.php*; the logout script doesn't produce output. Figure 16-2 also shows the three scripts from Figure 16-1 that interact with the login and logout process.

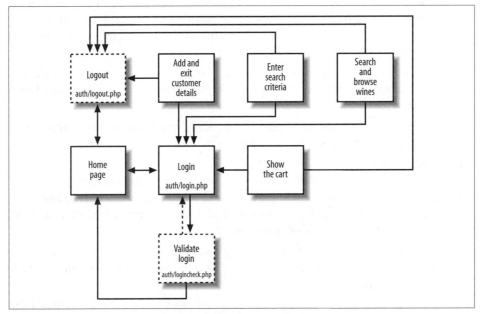

Figure 16-2. More winestore application architecture

Shopping Cart

The shopping cart scripts *cart/showcart.php*, *cart/updatecart.php*, and *cart/emptycart.php* are shown in Figure 16-1. These scripts show you how to build a scalable database-based shopping cart using the techniques described in Chapters 5 and 8, along with the sessions techniques in Chapter 10 and the basic web database querying techniques of Chapter 6.

The script *cart/showcart.php* shows the user the contents of his shopping cart. If the cart contains items, the quantities are presented in a form environment that allows the user to change them. The view cart script *cart/showcart.php* also allows the user to return to the home page, search, log in, and log out.

To update changes in quantities, the *cart/updatecart.php* script is requested by clicking the Update Quantities button; this script redirects to *cart/showcart.php*, and either shows the user the correctly updated quantities or reports an error describing why the update failed.

The user can also empty his cart completely by clicking on a button that requests the *cart/emptycart.php* script.

Ordering and Shipping

The ordering and shipping processes are implemented in the scripts *order/order-step1.php*, *order/order-step2.php*, *order/order-step3.php*, *order/order-step4.php*, *order/order-step5.php*, and *order/receipt.php*. These scripts show all aspects of data entry, querying, writing to databases using locks, validation, and receipts, and they make use of most of the techniques discussed in Chapters 5 through 10.

Users who are logged in place orders by clicking on the Make Purchase button in the view cart screen. When the button is clicked, the script *order/order-step1.php* is requested and a form is presented that requires the user to enter their credit card number and expiration date, as well as any optional delivery instructions. The application supports the fictional SurchargeCard credit card, which is validated according to the Luhn algorithm discussed in Chapter 9.

When the user submits the credit card form, the script *order/order-step2.php* is requested to perform validation. If the card validates, then the script redirects to *order/order-step3.php* otherwise the script returns to *order/order-step1.php* and shows error messages.

The complex database processing used to finalize an order is performed by *order/order-step3.php*. If the ordering process fails, the script redirects to *order-step1.php,* where errors are reported. If the ordering process succeeds, it redirects to *order/order-step4.php*. This script sends the user an email receipt of his order and redirects to *order/receipt.php* which shows the user the same receipt as an HTML page. From *order/receipt.php*, the user can return to the home page.

Searching and Browsing

Searching and browsing is implemented in the scripts *search/searchform.php* and *search/search.php*. These scripts show an advanced example of embedding links in an HTML document and creating drop-down lists using the techniques from Chapter 6. They also show how to add validation and sessions to a querying module with the techniques of Chapters 9 and 10.

The *search/searchform.php* script shows a form that allows the user to enter wine search criteria. The users can choose to browse a specific wine type (such as red or white) and a specific region (such as Margaret River). They can also choose to browse all wine types or all regions. When the user submits the form, the script *search/search.php* is requested. The search criteria are saved using sessions for when the user revisits the page.

The *search/search.php* script shows the wines that match the search criteria in pages of 12 wines each, and the user can traverse the pages using previous and next links, or click on a page number link to jump to a specific page. Bottles or cases of wine can be added to the shopping cart by clicking on a link that requests and passes parameters to the *cart/addtocart.php* script.

As on the other main pages, the user can also click on buttons to view his cart, login or logout, return to the home page, or start a new search with different criteria.

Using and accessing the source code

The winestore application can be used at this book's web site or on your local server, if you have followed the instructions to install the examples in Appendixes A to C. The source code can also be viewed at the book's web site and (if the installation instructions have been followed) can be edited and viewed in the directory */usr/local/ apache2/htdocs/wda2-winestore/* on your local Unix server, in *C:\Program Files\ EasyPHP1-7\www\wda2-winestore* under Microsoft Windows, or in */Library/ WebServer/Documents/wda2-winestore* on Mac OS X. A summary of the winestore scripts, and functions is shown in Table 16-1.

Table 16-1. The winestore scripts and functions

Script	Function
index.php	Main page and hot new wines panel
templates/index.tpl	Main page template
VERSION	Application version information for developers
license.txt	Application licensing information
includes/authenticate.inc	Authentication functions
auth/login.php	User login form
auth/logincheck.php	User login authentication
auth/logout.php	User logout
auth/password.php	User password change form
auth/changepassword.php	Password change validation and update
cart/addtocart.php	Add an item to the shopping cart
cart/empty.php	Empty the shopping cart
cart/showcart.php	Show the user the cart contents
templates/showcart.tpl	Cart template
cart/updatecart.php	Update cart quantities
customer/details.php	Enter or amend user details
customer/validate.php	Validate and update amended user details
customer/receipt.php	User update receipt
templates/custreceipt.tpl	User update receipt template
order/order-step1.php	Collect credit card details and delivery instructions

Table 16-1. The winestore scripts and functions (continued)

Script	Function
order/order-step2.php	Validate credit card details
order/order-step3.php	Finalize order
order/order-step4.php	Send email receipt
order/receipt.php	Show HTML order receipt
search/searchform.php	Collect search criteria
search/search.php	Browse wines
templates/search.tpl	Browse wines template
includes/customHandler.inc	Custom error handler
templates/winestore.tpl	Skeleton template for all winestore pages
templates/details.tpl	Template for most winestore form pages
includes/validate.inc	Validation functions
includes/winestore.inc	General-purpose functions and define( ) statements
includes/db.inc	DBMS credentials

Common Components

This section describes the components of the winestore that are used by all parts of the application. We discuss our extensions of the PEAR ITX templates that provide a framework for all winestore pages and special-purpose tools for building form pages. We also discuss our validation functions, database parameters, custom error handler, and general-purpose constants and functions. The authentication module is discussed in Chapter 20.

Application Templates

The winestore application uses the PEAR ITX template class discussed in Chapter 7 to abstract presentation from code structure. Templates make the code easier to modify and the HTML presentation easy to change. For example, if you want to change the look and feel of the application, you only need to edit the template files in the *templates* directory.

We don't use the ITX templates directly. Instead, because we populate the same placeholders with similar data in each script, we've extended them to create two new child classes with the reusable features we need. This saves coding in script files, and leads to a simpler application that's easy to adapt. These two new classes are stored in the *includes/template.inc* file discussed later.

The first class we've created is the winestoreTemplate class that has a basic skeleton structure used throughout the winestore. It's associated with the generic template *templates/winestore.tpl* that's shown later in Example 16-1 and uses the template to show error messages to the user, optionally show a shopping cart icon and the total items in the cart, display the user login status, and present a configurable set of buttons at the bottom of the page.

The second class we've built extends the `winestoreTemplate` class to provide form data entry and error reporting features. This class is called `winestoreFormTemplate`. It includes features to create mandatory text widgets, optional text widgets, drop-down lists, and password entry widgets. The template that's used with it is *templates/detail.tpl*; it is included at runtime into the body of the parent *templates/winestore.tpl* template.

Both classes are discussed in more detail throughout this section.

The winestoreTemplate Class

The `winestoreTemplate` class provides a generic framework for all winestore pages. We've developed it to include the features we want on all winestore pages, and to save writing and maintaining different pages in the winestore. This is a practical example of how the templates discussed in Chapter 7 make application development easier.

The class works as follows. When the class constructor is called, the skeleton template *templates/winestore.tpl* that is shown in Example 16-1 is loaded and its placeholder `PAGE_BODY` is replaced with the page passed as a parameter to the constructor. Part of the class's function is also to add buttons, messages, the login status, and an optional cart icon to the page. We decide in each script what combination of these should be displayed. When we've finished working with the page body, the method *winestoreTemplate::showWinestore()* outputs the page.

The template page ends with a link to the W3C HTML validator. If you host the winestore scripts on a web server that's accessible over the Web, then you can click on the link and the HTML in the page will be validated. If your web server isn't externally accessible, clicking on the link won't work.

Example 16-1. The templates/winestore.tpl generic winestore template

```
<!DOCTYPE HTML PUBLIC
                "-//W3C//DTD HTML 4.01 Transitional//EN"
                "http://www.w3.org/TR/html401/loose.dtd">
<html>
<head>
  <meta http-equiv="Content-Type" content="text/html; charset=iso-8859-1">
  <title>{TITLE}</title>
</head>
<body bgcolor="white">
<p align="right"><b>{LOGIN_STATUS}</b></p>
<!-- BEGIN cartheader -->
<table>
  <tr>
```

Example 16-1. The templates/winestore.tpl generic winestore template (continued)

```
        <td><a href="{S_SHOWCART}" onMouseOut="cart.src='{I_CART_OFF}'"
                                 onMouseOver="cart.src='{I_CART_ON}'">
            <img src="{I_CART_OFF}" vspace=0 border=0
                    alt="cart picture" name="cart"></a>
        </td>

        <td>Total in cart: ${TOTAL} ({COUNT} items)
          </td>

      </tr>
</table>
<!-- END cartheader -->
<!-- BEGIN message -->
<br><b><font color="red">{INFO_MESSAGE}</font></b>
<!-- END message -->
{PAGE_BODY}
<!-- BEGIN buttons -->
<table>
<tr>
<!-- BEGIN form -->
  <td><form action="{ACTION}" method="GET">
    <input type="submit" name="{NAME}" value="{VALUE}">
  </form></td>
<!-- END form -->
</tr>
</table>
<!-- END buttons -->
<br><a href="http://validator.w3.org/check/referer">
  <img src="http://www.w3.org/Icons/valid-html401" height="31" width="88"
        align="right" border="0" alt="Valid HTML 4.01!"></a>
</body>
</html>
```

Let's consider an example. Suppose we want to write a very simple HTML page for the winestore that says that the user has received an order discount; we don't actually use this page in the winestore, it's only an example to illustrate how to reuse our template. Here's the HTML body that we want to include in the page:

```
<h1>Hugh and Dave's Online Wines<h1>
Congratulations! You've received a discount of ${AMOUNT}
off your cart total!
```

Let's assume this fragment is stored in the file *templates/discount.tpl*.

Now, to create a winestore page, we need to decide if we want to show the user a cart icon that they can click on to show their shopping cart. Let's do that because the page is about their cart. We also need to decide what buttons we want to show. In this case, let's assume we want two buttons: one to return to the main page of the store and another to visit the cart. We discuss the buttons more later.

Here's the very short but complete code to create our page:

```php
<?php
require_once "../includes/template.inc";

set_error_handler("customHandler");

$template = new winestoreTemplate("discount.tpl");
$template->setCurrentBlock( );
$template->setVariable("AMOUNT", "5.00");

// Don't show a cart icon, and show only the "home" button
// Then, output the page
$template->showWinestore(SHOW_ALL, B_HOME | B_SHOW_CART);
?>
```

The output of the example in a Mozilla browser is shown in Figure 16-3.

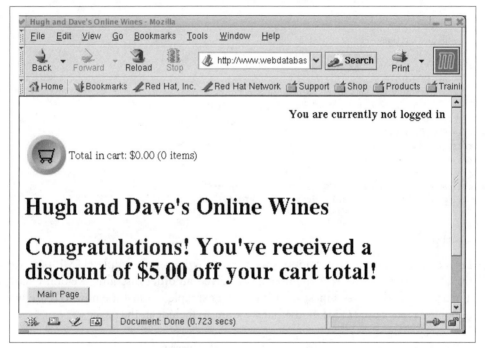

Figure 16-3. The winestoreTemplate class in action

How the class works

The code for the winestoreTemplate class is shown in Example 16-2.

Example 16-2. The includes/template.inc file that shows the winestoreTemplate class

```php
<?php
// ITX template class extensions for the winestore
// -- winestoreTemplate is a generic page
// -- winestoreFormTemplate is a <form> page (and extends winestoreTemplate)
```

```php
require_once "DB.php";
require_once "HTML/Template/ITX.php";
require_once "winestore.inc";

define("P_TITLE", "Hugh and Dave's Online Wines");

// An extension of HTML_Template_ITX for the winestore pages
class winestoreTemplate extends HTML_Template_ITX
{
   // Class constructor
   // Loads the winestore.tpl skeleton, and a named page
   // Sets the page title
   function winestoreTemplate($pageBody, $pageTitle = P_TITLE)
   {
      $this->template = $this->HTML_Template_ITX(D_TEMPLATES);
      $this->loadTemplatefile(T_SKELETON, true, true);
      $this->setVariable("TITLE", $pageTitle);
      $this->addBlockFile("PAGE_BODY", "pageBody", "{$pageBody}");
   }

   // Completes the page, and outputs with show()
   function showWinestore($options = NO_CART, $buttons = B_HOME)
   {
      $this->setCurrentBlock();

      // Show the user login status
      $this->showLogin();

      if ($options & ~NO_CART)
         // Show the dollar and item total of the cart
         $this->showCart();

      // Display any messages to the user
      $this->showMessage();

      // Set up the buttons
      if ($buttons != 0)
         $this->showButtons($buttons);

      $this->setCurrentBlock();
      $this->parseCurrentBlock();
      $this->show();
   }

   // Show the total number of items and dollar value of the shopping
   // cart, as well as a clickable cart icon
   function showCart()
   {
      global $dsn;

      $connection = DB::connect($dsn, true);

      if (DB::isError($connection))
```

```
    trigger_error($connection->getMessage( ), E_USER_ERROR);

// initialize an empty cart
$cartAmount = 0;
$cartCount = 0;

// If the user has added items to their cart, then
// the variable order_no will be registered
if (isset($_SESSION["order_no"]))
{
    $cartQuery = "SELECT qty, price FROM items
                    WHERE cust_id = -1
                    AND order_id = {$_SESSION["order_no"]}";

    // Find out the number and the dollar value of
    // the items in the cart. To do this, we run the
    // cartQuery through the connection on the database
    $result = $connection->query($cartQuery);

    if (DB::isError($result))
        trigger_error($result->getMessage( ), E_USER_ERROR);

    while ($row = $result->fetchRow(DB_FETCHMODE_ASSOC))
    {
        $cartAmount += $row["price"] * $row["qty"];
        $cartCount += $row["qty"];
    }
}

$this->setCurrentBlock("cartheader");
$this->setVariable("I_CART_OFF", I_CART_OFF);
$this->setVariable("I_CART_ON", I_CART_ON);
$this->setVariable("S_SHOWCART", S_SHOWCART);
$this->setVariable("TOTAL", sprintf("%-.2f", $cartAmount));
$this->setVariable("COUNT", sprintf("%d", $cartCount));
$this->parseCurrentBlock("cartheader");
}


// Display any messages that are set, and then
// clear the message
function showMessage( )
{
    // Is there an error message to show the user?
    if (isset($_SESSION["message"]))
    {
        $this->setCurrentBlock("message");
        $this->setVariable("INFO_MESSAGE", $_SESSION["message"]);
        $this->parseCurrentBlock("message");

        // Clear the error message
        unset($_SESSION["message"]);
```

```
        }
    }

    // Show whether the user is logged in or not
    function showLogin()
    {
        // Is the user logged in?
        if (isset($_SESSION["loginUsername"]))
            $this->setVariable("LOGIN_STATUS",
                        "You are currently logged in as {$_SESSION["loginUsername"]}");
        else
            $this->setVariable("LOGIN_STATUS",
                        "You are currently not logged in");
    }

    // Output the buttons for a winestore page
    function showButtons($buttons)
    {
        $this->setCurrentBlock("buttons");

        // If the cart has contents, offer the opportunity to view the cart
        // or empty the cart.
        if (isset($_SESSION["order_no"]))
        {
            if ($buttons & B_EMPTY_CART)
            {
                $this->setCurrentBlock("form");
                $this->setVariable("ACTION", S_EMPTYCART);
                $this->setVariable("NAME", "empty");
                $this->setVariable("VALUE", "Empty Cart");
                $this->parseCurrentBlock("form");
            }

            if ($buttons & B_SHOW_CART)
            {
                $this->setCurrentBlock("form");
                $this->setVariable("ACTION", S_SHOWCART);
                $this->setVariable("NAME", "view");
                $this->setVariable("VALUE", "View Cart");
                $this->parseCurrentBlock("form");
            }

            // Must be logged in and have items in cart
            if (($buttons & B_PURCHASE) &&
                isset($_SESSION["loginUsername"]) &&
                isset($_SESSION["order_no"]))
            {
                $this->setCurrentBlock("form");
                $this->setVariable("ACTION", S_ORDER_1);
                $this->setVariable("NAME", "purchase");
                $this->setVariable("VALUE", "Make Purchase");
                $this->parseCurrentBlock("form");
            }
```

```
  }

  if ($buttons & B_SEARCH)
  {
    $this->setCurrentBlock("form");
    $this->setVariable("ACTION", S_SEARCHFORM);
    $this->setVariable("NAME", "search");
    $this->setVariable("VALUE", "Search Wines");
    $this->parseCurrentBlock("form");
  }

  if ($buttons & B_HOME)
  {
    $this->setCurrentBlock("form");
    $this->setVariable("ACTION", S_MAIN);
    $this->setVariable("NAME", "home");
    $this->setVariable("VALUE", "Main Page");
    $this->parseCurrentBlock("form");
  }

  if ($buttons & B_DETAILS)
  {
    $this->setCurrentBlock("form");
    $this->setVariable("ACTION", S_DETAILS);
    if (isset($_SESSION["loginUsername"]))
    {
      $this->setVariable("NAME", "account");
      $this->setVariable("VALUE", "Change Details");
    }
    else
    {
      $this->setVariable("NAME", "account");
      $this->setVariable("VALUE", "Become a Member");
    }
    $this->parseCurrentBlock("form");
  }

  if ($buttons & B_LOGINLOGOUT)
  {
    $this->setCurrentBlock("form");
    if (isset($_SESSION["loginUsername"]))
    {
      $this->setVariable("ACTION", S_LOGOUT);
      $this->setVariable("NAME", "logout");
      $this->setVariable("VALUE", "Logout");
    }
    else
    {
      $this->setVariable("ACTION", S_LOGIN);
      $this->setVariable("NAME", "login");
      $this->setVariable("VALUE", "Login");
    }
    $this->parseCurrentBlock("form");
```

```
    }

    if (($buttons & B_PASSWORD) && isset($_SESSION["loginUsername"]))
    {
        $this->setCurrentBlock("form");
        $this->setVariable("ACTION", S_PASSWORD);
        $this->setVariable("NAME", "password");
        $this->setVariable("VALUE", "Change Password");
        $this->parseCurrentBlock("form");
    }

    $this->setCurrentBlock("buttons");
    $this->parseCurrentBlock("buttons");
  }
}
?>
```

The skeleton of *templates/winestore.tpl* shown in Example 16-1 and the methods in Example 16-2 provide the features in the template. The *winestoreTemplate:: showLogin()* method populates the LOGIN_STATUS placeholder in the template and informs the user whether they're logged in. The *winestoreTemplate::showMessage()* method populates the INFO_MESSAGE placeholder with any messages that have been set in the $_SESSION["message"] session variable; this is used throughout the winestore for displaying errors. The *winestoreTemplate::showButtons()* and *winestoreTemplate::showCart()* methods show optional buttons at the bottom of the page and an optional cart icon at the top, depending on the parameters that are passed to the *winestoreTemplate::showWinestore()* method. The *winestoreTemplate:: showWinestore()* method itself outputs the template.

The *winestoreTemplate::showWinestore()* method takes two parameters: whether or not to show the cart icon, and what buttons to display at the base of the page. The list of possible buttons is defined in the *includes/winestore.inc* file that's listed later in this chapter:

```
// Button definitions
define("B_EMPTY_CART", 1);
define("B_SHOW_CART", 2);
define("B_UPDATE_CART", 4);
define("B_PURCHASE", 8);
define("B_SEARCH", 16);
define("B_HOME", 32);
define("B_DETAILS", 64);
define("B_LOGINLOGOUT", 128);
define("B_PASSWORD", 256);
define("B_ALL", 511);
```

The buttons and the button parameter

Let's take a detour for a moment and explain the technique used for displaying buttons. If you don't need the details, skip to the next section.

To create a page that shows the cart, and the search and home buttons, the method *winestoreTemplate::showWinestore()* can be called as follows:

```
$template->showWinestore(SHOW_ALL, B_SEARCH | B_HOME);
```

In turn, the *winestoreTemplate::showWinestore()* method calls *winestoreTemplate:: showButtons()* and passes through the B_SEARCH | B_HOME value.

Several buttons are selected by a logical OR between them using the | operator. The option B_ALL means all buttons, and it can be combined with the AND operator & and NOT operator ~ to unselect one or more buttons. For example, everything but the purchase button can be shown with:

```
$template->showWinestore(SHOW_ALL, B_ALL & ~B_PURCHASE);
```

The button parameter passing implements a useful feature: it allows you to pass through several options without having several parameters. It's the same technique used in other parts of PHP such as, for example, the method of setting the error reporting level with the *error_reporting()* library function.

The selection of buttons works as follows. When you OR button values, you get a unique number that is equal to the sum of the values. For example, consider the first three button settings B_EMPTY_CART which has a value of 1, B_SHOW_CART which has a value of 2, and B_UPDATE_CART which has a value of 4. If you evaluate the expression B_EMPTY_CART | B_UPDATE_CART you get 5; there's no other combination of buttons that can give you that value. Similarly, if you OR all three values you get 7, and there's no other combination that arrives at that value.

Notice that the button values are all power of 2. The first button is 1, the second is 2, the third is 4, the fourth is 8, the fifth 16, and so on. This is what guarantees there's only one combination of buttons that can lead to each possible summed value. Notice also that B_ALL is 511, which is the same value you'll obtain if you OR (or sum) together all of the other button values.

To test if a button is set, a code fragment such as the following is used in the method *winestoreTemplate::showButtons()*:

```
if ($buttons & B_EMPTY_CART)
{
```

The $buttons variable contains the value for the button setting that has been passed to *winestoreTemplate::showWinestore()*. The result of the & operation in the if statement is only true if the value in $buttons was created using the value for B_EMPTY_CART. For example, suppose the $buttons value is 5. Because B_EMPTY_CART is 1, the if expression evaluates as true because 4+1=5 and there's no other way to arrive a value of 5. In contrast, if we AND B_SHOW_CART which has a value of 2 and the $buttons value of 5, the expression evaluates as false because 2 isn't part of the sum

4+1=5. (If you want to understand the detail of how this works, you need to be familiar with binary arithmetic.)

The *winestoreTemplate::showButtons()* method outputs the buttons as separate forms in the HTML page. For example, the code for the empty cart in our previous example outputs the following:

```
<td>
  <form action="/wda2-winestore/cart/emptycart.php" method="GET">
    <input type="submit" name="empty" value="Empty Cart">
  </form>
</td>
```

When the user clicks on the button, the form submits, and the script that's requested is the *cart/emptycart.php* script. The action attribute of the form element is set in the code to the constant S_EMPTYCART. As we show later, this is a constant that's defined in the *includes/winestore.inc* file and its value is *cart/emptycart.php*.

The winestoreFormTemplate Class

The winestoreFormTemplate class is an extension of the winestoreTemplate class with the specific purpose of displaying a data entry form that supports pre-filled inputs, error reporting, and several different types of widget. Unlike the winestoreTemplate class, the body of the page inserted into the placeholder PAGE_BODY is always the *templates/details.tpl* template shown in Example 16-3.

Example 16-3. The templates/details.tpl template for displaying a form

```
<!-- BEGIN inputform -->
<form method="{METHOD}" action="{S_VALIDATE}">
<h1>{FORMHEADING}</h1>
<b>{INSTRUCTIONS}  Fields shown in <font color="red">red</font>
   are mandatory.</b>
<p>
<table>
<col span="1" align="right">
<!-- BEGIN widget -->
<!-- BEGIN select -->
   <tr>
      <td><font color="red">{SELECTTEXT}</font></td>
      <td><select name="{SELECTNAME}">
<!-- BEGIN option -->
      <option{SELECTED} value="{OPTIONVALUE}">{OPTIONTEXT}
<!-- END option -->
      </select></td>
   </tr>
<!-- END select -->
<!-- BEGIN mandatoryinput -->
   <tr>
      <td><font color="red">{MINPUTTEXT}</font></td>
      </td>
```

```
        <td>
<!-- BEGIN mandatoryerror -->
        <font color="red">{MERRORTEXT}</font><br>
<!-- END mandatoryerror -->
            <input type="text" name="{MINPUTNAME}"
            value="{MINPUTVALUE}" size={MINPUTSIZE}>
        </td>
    </tr>
<!-- END mandatoryinput -->
<!-- BEGIN optionalinput -->
    <tr>
        <td>{OINPUTTEXT}
        </td>
        <td>
<!-- BEGIN optionalerror -->
        <font color="red">{OERRORTEXT}</font><br>
<!-- END optionalerror -->
            <input type="text" name="{OINPUTNAME}"
            value="{OINPUTVALUE}" size={OINPUTSIZE}>
        </td>
    </tr>
<!-- END optionalinput -->
<!-- BEGIN passwordinput -->
    <tr>
        <td><font color="red">{PINPUTTEXT}</font>
        </td>
        <td>
<!-- BEGIN passworderror -->
        <font color="red">{PERRORTEXT}</font><br>
<!-- END passworderror -->
            <input type="password" name="{PINPUTNAME}"
            value="{PINPUTVALUE}" size={PINPUTSIZE}>
        </td>
    </tr>
<!-- END passwordinput -->
<!-- END widget -->
<tr>
    <td><input type="submit" value="Submit"></td>
</tr>
</table>
</form>
<!-- END inputform -->
```

Consider an example that uses this class. Suppose we want to create a form with a widget for the user to enter their password; again, this is just an example to illustrate how to use the class, and it isn't part of the online winestore application. Here's a short code fragment that's stored in the file *passwordform.php* that does the whole job:

```php
<?php
require_once "../includes/template.inc";
```

```
    set_error_handler("customHandler");

    // Takes form heading, instructions, action,
    // session array storing previously-entered values,
    // and session array storing error messages
    // as parameters
    $template = new winestoreFormTemplate("Enter Password",
                    "Please enter your password.",
                    "check.php, "variables", "errors");

    // Create the widget
    $template->passwordWidget("password", "Password:", 8);

    // Add buttons and messages, and show the page
    $template->showWinestore(NO_CART, B_HOME);
    ?>
```

The output of the code fragment is shown in Figure 16-4 in a Mozilla browser.

Figure 16-4. Output of the winestoreFormTemplate class example shown in a Mozilla browser

How the class works

The code for the class is shown in Example 16-4. It's stored in the file *includes/template.inc*, along with the `winestoreTemplate` class from Example 16-2. The constructor takes several parameters including headings and instructions, the target action script when the form is submitted, two session array names that store data and error messages from previously failed validation attempts, and optional parameters to set the form method and page title.

Example 16-4. The second half of the includes/template.inc file that shows the winestoreFormTemplate class

```php
<?php
// An extension of winestoreTemplate for pages that contain a form
class winestoreFormTemplate extends winestoreTemplate
{
  // The formVars array associated with this page of widgets
  var $formVars = null;

  // The errors array associated with this page of widgets
  var $formErrors = null;

  // Class constructor
  // Parameters:
  // (1) Heading in <h1> above the <form>
  // (2) Instructions in <b> above the <form>
  // (3) <form action=""> value
  // (4) formVars $_SESSION array name for storing widget values
  // (5) formErrors $_SESSION array name for storing widget errors
  // (6) [optional] form method type
  // (7) [optional] <title> for the page
  function winestoreFormTemplate($formHeading, $instructions,
                                 $action, $formVars, $formErrors,
                                 $method = "POST", $pageTitle = P_TITLE)
  {
    $this->template = $this->winestoreTemplate(T_DETAILS, $pageTitle);

    // Set up the <form> headings and target
    $this->setVariable("FORMHEADING", $formHeading);
    $this->setVariable("INSTRUCTIONS", $instructions);
    $this->setVariable("S_VALIDATE", $action);
    $this->setVariable("METHOD", $method);

    // Save formVars and formErrors
    $this->formVars = $formVars;
    $this->formErrors = $formErrors;
  }

  // Produces a mandatory <form> widget
  // Parameters are:
  // (1) The HTML widget name and matching table attribute name
  // (2) The text to show next to the widget
  // (3) The size of the widget
  function mandatoryWidget($name, $text, $size)
  {
    // Are there any errors to show for this widget?
    // If so, show them above the widget
    if (isset($_SESSION["{$this->formErrors}"]["{$name}"]))
    {
```

```
        $this->setCurrentBlock("mandatoryerror");
        $this->setVariable("MERRORTEXT",
          $_SESSION["{$this->formErrors}"]["{$name}"]);
        $this->parseCurrentBlock("mandatoryerror");
    }

    // Setup the widget
    $this->setCurrentBlock("mandatoryinput");
    $this->setVariable("MINPUTNAME", "{$name}");
    if (isset($_SESSION["{$this->formVars}"]["{$name}"]))
        $this->setVariable("MINPUTVALUE",
          $_SESSION["{$this->formVars}"]["{$name}"]);
    $this->setVariable("MINPUTTEXT", "{$text}");
    $this->setVariable("MINPUTSIZE", $size);
    $this->parseCurrentBlock("mandatoryinput");
    $this->setCurrentBlock("widget");
    $this->parseCurrentBlock("widget");
}


// Produces an optional <form> widget
// Parameters are:
// (1) The HTML widget name and matching table attribute name
// (2) The text to show next to the widget
// (3) The size of the widget
function optionalWidget($name, $text, $size)
{
    // Are there any errors to show for this widget?
    // If so, show them above the widget
    if (isset($_SESSION["{$this->formErrors}"]["{$name}"]))
    {
        $this->setCurrentBlock("optionalerror");
        $this->setVariable("OERRORTEXT",
          $_SESSION["{$this->formErrors}"]["{$name}"]);
        $this->parseCurrentBlock("optionalerror");
    }

    // Setup the widget
    $this->setCurrentBlock("optionalinput");
    $this->setVariable("OINPUTNAME", "{$name}");
    if (isset($_SESSION["{$this->formVars}"]["{$name}"]))
        $this->setVariable("OINPUTVALUE",
          $_SESSION["{$this->formVars}"]["{$name}"]);
    $this->setVariable("OINPUTTEXT", "{$text}");
    $this->setVariable("OINPUTSIZE", $size);
    $this->parseCurrentBlock("optionalinput");
    $this->setCurrentBlock("widget");
    $this->parseCurrentBlock("widget");
}


// Produces a password <form> widget
// Parameters are:
// (1) The HTML widget name and matching table attribute name
```

Example 16-4. The second half of the includes/template.inc file that shows the winestoreFormTemplate class (continued)

```
// (2) The text to show next to the widget
// (3) The size of the widget
function passwordWidget($name, $text, $size)
{
    // Are there any errors to show for this widget?
    // If so, show them above the widget
    if (isset($_SESSION["{$this->formErrors}"]["{$name}"]))
    {
        $this->setCurrentBlock("passworderror");
        $this->setVariable("PERRORTEXT",
          $_SESSION["{$this->formErrors}"]["{$name}"]);
        $this->parseCurrentBlock("passworderror");
    }

    // Setup the widget
    $this->setCurrentBlock("passwordinput");
    $this->setVariable("PINPUTNAME", "{$name}");
    if (isset($_SESSION["{$this->formVars}"]["{$name}"]))
        $this->setVariable("PINPUTVALUE",
          $_SESSION["{$this->formVars}"]["{$name}"]);
    $this->setVariable("PINPUTTEXT", "{$text}");
    $this->setVariable("PINPUTSIZE", $size);
    $this->parseCurrentBlock("passwordinput");
    $this->setCurrentBlock("widget");
    $this->parseCurrentBlock("widget");
}

// Produces a <select> <form> widget.
// Unlike others, this doesn't support error display
// Parameters are:
// (1) The table attribute that fills the <option> value. Also used as
//     the <select> name
// (2) The text to show next to the widget
// (3) The table attribute that is displayed with the <option>
// (3) The PEAR DB Result to get the data from
function selectWidget($name, $text, $optiontext, $data)
{
    while ($row = $data->fetchRow(DB_FETCHMODE_ASSOC))
    {
        $this->setCurrentBlock("option");
        $this->setVariable("OPTIONTEXT", $row["{$optiontext}"]);
        $this->setVariable("OPTIONVALUE", $row["{$name}"]);
        if (isset($_SESSION["{$this->formVars}"]["{$name}"]) &&
            $_SESSION["{$this->formVars}"]["{$name}"] == $row["{$name}"])
          $this->setVariable("SELECTED", " selected");
        $this->parseCurrentBlock("option");
    }
    $this->setCurrentBlock("select");
    $this->setVariable("SELECTNAME", "{$name}");
    $this->setVariable("SELECTTEXT", "{$text}");
    $this->parseCurrentBlock("select");
```

Example 16-4. The second half of the includes/template.inc file that shows the winestoreFormTemplate class (continued)

```
    $this->setCurrentBlock("widget");
    $this->parseCurrentBlock("widget");
  }
}
?>
```

The code can produce as many widget blocks using the template as are required, and each block can contain one of the four data entry widgets that are supported. The four template fragments that create form widgets each have a similar structure and are used to create mandatoryinput widgets (input elements of type="text" with red-colored labels), optionalinput widgets (with normal, black text), passwordinput widgets (which are shown with red-colored labels because they're always mandatory), and selectinput drop-down select lists. With the exception of the select lists, the widgets can display error messages in a red font. All of the widgets can display previously-entered data.

For example, a mandatoryinput widget is created with the following template fragment:

```
<!-- BEGIN mandatoryinput -->
  <tr>
    <td><font color="red">{MINPUTTEXT}</font>
    </td>
    <td>
<!-- BEGIN mandatoryerror -->
    <font color="red">{MERRORTEXT}</font><br>
<!-- END mandatoryerror -->
      <input type="text" name="{MINPUTNAME}"
        value="{MINPUTVALUE}" size={MINPUTSIZE}>
    </td>
  </tr>
<!-- END mandatoryinput -->
```

The code in the *winestoreFormTemplate::mandatoryWidget()* method populates the template fragment by setting the text to display into the placeholder MINPUTTEXT, the name of the input into MINPUTNAME, and the size of the input into MINPUTSIZE. These three values are passed as parameters. We've prefixed the mandatory widget placeholders with an M to indicate they're associated with a mandatory widget; the password widget placeholders are prefixed with a P, and optional ones with an O.

The value shown in the widget and any error message are displayed from session arrays that are created during the validation process; this is the same approach as advocated in Chapter 10. If the session variable that stores previously-entered data isn't empty, the previously-entered data is shown in the MINPUTVALUE placeholder. If an error has occurred in previous validation, the session array variable that stores error messages is used to display an error in MERRORTEXT.

To show how these session arrays might be populated during validation, let's continue our previous example of the simple password page; again, this script isn't part of the winestore, it's just used as a simple illustration in this section. Consider the script *check.php* that's requested when the form is submitted:

```php
<?php
// Register and clear an error array - just in case!
$_SESSION["errors"] = array();

// Set up a session array for the POST variables
$_SESSION["variables"] = array();

// Validate password
if ($_POST["password"] == "password")
{
  $_SESSION["errors"]["password"] = "Password too obvious!";
  $_SESSION["variables"]["password"] = $_POST["password"];
}

// Now the script has finished the validation,
// check if there were any errors
if (count($_SESSION["errors"]) > 0)
{
    // There are errors.  Relocate back to the password form
    header("Location: passwordform.php");
    exit;
}

// Everything is ok...

// Empty the session arrays
unset($_SESSION["errors"]);
unset($_SESSION["variables"]);

// go to receipt
header("Location: ok.php");
?>
```

The script is straightforward: it creates two session arrays to store form values and possible error messages. If an error occurs, the value in the widget is stored in one session array and an error message in the other, and the name of the input widget is used as the element name in both arrays. These two session array names are then supplied as parameters to the *winestoreFormTemplate::winestoreFormTemplate()* constructor method.

The $_SESSION["error"] array has data in it only if an error occurs, so its size is checked to see if an error has occurred. If so, the script redirects to the form (where the session data is displayed). If not, the session arrays are emptied and the script redirects to the receipt page.

We've omitted untainting the data to keep the example short. We do this properly in the winestore scripts.

Database Parameters

The database parameters are stored in their own include file *includes/db.inc*. This file has the same content as the *db.inc* file explained in Chapter 6:

```php
<?php
    $hostname = "127.0.0.1";
    $databasename = "winestore";
    $username = "fred";
    $password = "shhh";
?>
```

The $username and $password must be modified to match your local settings as explained in the installation instructions in Appendixes A to C. These parameters are used to create the data source name (DSN) used to connect to the database server with PEAR DB. The $dsn global variable is defined in the *includes/winestore.inc* file discussed later in this chapter.

Validation

The validation functions are stored in the file *includes/validate.inc*, which is shown in Example 16-5. Almost all of these functions are discussed in Chapter 9, and the remainder are simple combinations of the fundamental techniques that are described there.

Example 16-5. The includes/validate.inc functions for form validation

```php
<?php
// General-purpose validation functions

// Test if a mandatory field is empty
function checkMandatory($field, $errorString, $errors, $formVars)
{
   if (!isset($_SESSION["{$formVars}"]["{$field}"]) ||
       empty($_SESSION["{$formVars}"]["{$field}"]))
   {
      $_SESSION["{$errors}"]["{$field}"] =
         "The {$errorString} field cannot be blank.";
      return false;
   }
   return true;
}

// Test if a field is less than a min or greater than a max length
function checkMinAndMaxLength($field, $minlength, $maxlength,
                      $errorString, $errors, $formVars)
{
   if (isset($_SESSION["{$formVars}"]["{$field}"]) &&
      (strlen($_SESSION["{$formVars}"]["{$field}"]) < $minlength ||
       strlen($_SESSION["{$formVars}"]["{$field}"]) > $maxlength))
   {
      $_SESSION["{$errors}"]["{$field}"] =
```

```
                "The {$errorString} field must be greater than or equal to" .
                "{$minlength} and less than or equal to {$maxlength} " .
                "characters in length.";
        return false;
    }
    return true;
}

// Simple zipcode validator -- there's a better one in Chapter 9!
function checkZipcode($field, $errorString, $errors, $formVars)
{
    if (isset($_SESSION["{$formVars}"]["{$field}"]) &&
        !ereg("^([0-9]{4,5})$", $_SESSION["{$formVars}"]["{$field}"]))
    {
        $_SESSION["{$errors}"]["{$field}"] =
            "The zipcode must be 4 or 5 digits in length";
        return false;
    }
    return true;
}

// Check a phone number
function checkPhone($field, $errorString, $errors, $formVars)
{
    $validPhoneExpr = "^([0-9]{2,3}[ ]?)?[0-9]{4}[ ]?[0-9]{4}$";

    if (isset($_SESSION["{$formVars}"]["{$field}"]) &&
        !ereg($validPhoneExpr, $_SESSION["{$formVars}"]["{$field}"]))
    {
        $_SESSION["{$errors}"]["{$field}"] =
            "The {$field} field must be 8 digits in length, " .
            "with an optional 2 or 3 digit area code";
        return false;
    }
    return true;
}

// Check a birth date and that the user is 18+ years
function checkDateAndAdult($field, $errorString, $errors, $formVars)
{
    if (!ereg("^([0-9]{2})/([0-9]{2})/([0-9]{4})$",
            $_SESSION["{$formVars}"]["{$field}"], $parts))
    {
        $_SESSION["{$errors}"]["{$field}"] =
            "The date of birth is not a valid date " .
            "in the format DD/MM/YYYY";
        return false;
    }

    if (!checkdate($parts[2],$parts[1],$parts[3]))
    {
        $_SESSION["{$errors}"]["{$field}"] =
```

```
         "The date of birth is invalid. Please " .
         "check that the month is between 1 and 12, " .
         "and the day is valid for that month.";
      return false;
   }

   if (intval($parts[3]) < 1902 ||
       intval($parts[3]) > intval(date("Y")))
   {
      $_SESSION["{$errors}"]["{$field}"] =
         "You must be alive to use this service.";
      return false;
   }

   $dob = mktime(0, 0, 0, $parts[2], $parts[1], $parts[3]);

   // Check whether the user is 18 years old
   // See Chapter 9 for an MS Windows version
   if ((float)$dob > (float)strtotime("-18years"))
   {
      $_SESSION["{$errors}"]["{$field}"] =
         "You must be 18+ years of age to use this service";
      return false;
   }
   return true;
}

// Check an email address
function emailCheck($field, $errorString, $errors, $formVars)
{
   // Check syntax
   $validEmailExpr =  "^[0-9a-z~!#$%&_-]([.]?[0-9a-z~!#$%&_-])*" .
                      "@[0-9a-z~!#$%&_-]([.]?[0-9a-z~!#$%&_-])*$";

   if (!eregi($validEmailExpr, $_SESSION["{$formVars}"]["{$field}"]))
   {
      $_SESSION["{$errors}"]["{$field}"] =
         "The email must be in the name@domain format.";
      return false;
   }

   // See Chapter 7 for an MS Windows version
   if (function_exists("getmxrr") &&
       function_exists("gethostbyname"))
   {
     // Extract the domain of the email address
     $maildomain =
       substr(strstr($_SESSION["{$formVars}"]["{$field}"], '@'), 1);

     if (!(getmxrr($maildomain, $temp) ||
           gethostbyname($maildomain) != $maildomain))
     {
       $_SESSION["{$errors}"]["{$field}"] =
```

```
          "The email domain does not exist.";
        return false;
      }
    }

    return true;
}

// Check a credit card using Luhn's algorithm
function checkCard($field, $errors, $formVars)
{
  if (!ereg("^[0-9 ]*$", $_SESSION["{$formVars}"]["{$field}"]))
  {
    $_SESSION["{$errors}"]["{$field}"] =
      "Card number must contain only digits and spaces.";
    return false;
  }

  // Remove spaces
  $_SESSION["{$formVars}"]["{$field}"] = ereg_replace('[ ]', '', $_
SESSION["{$formVars}"]["{$field}"]);

  // Check first four digits
  $firstFour = intval(substr($_SESSION["{$formVars}"]["{$field}"], 0, 4));
  $type = "";
  $length = 0;

  if ($firstFour >= 8000 && $firstFour <= 8999)
  {
    // Try: 8000 0000 0000 1001
    $type = "SurchargeCard";
    $length = 16;
  }

  if (empty($type))
  {
    $_SESSION["{$errors}"]["{$field}"] =
      "Please check your card details.";
    return false;
  }

  if (strlen($_SESSION["{$formVars}"]["{$field}"]) != $length)
  {
    $_SESSION["{$errors}"]["{$field}"] =
      "Card number must contain {$length} digits.";
    return false;
  }

  $check = 0;

// Add up every 2nd digit, beginning at the right end
  for($x=$length-1;$x>=0;$x-=2)
    $check += intval(substr($_SESSION["{$formVars}"]["{$field}"], $x, 1));
```

```
  // Add up every 2nd digit doubled, beginning at the right end - 1.
  // Subtract 9 where doubled value is greater than 10
  for($x=$length-2;$x>=0;$x-=2)
  {
    $double = intval(substr($_SESSION["{$formVars}"]["{$field}"], $x, 1)) * 2;
    if ($double >= 10)
      $check += $double - 9;
    else
      $check += $double;
  }

  // Is $check not a multiple of 10?
  if ($check % 10 != 0)
  {
    $_SESSION["{$errors}"]["{$field}"] =
      "Credit card invalid. Please check number.";
    return false;
  }
  return true;
}

// Check a credit card expiry date
function checkExpiry($field, $errors, $formVars)
{
  if (!ereg("^([0-9]{2})/([0-9]{2})$",
          $_SESSION["{$formVars}"]["{$field}"], $parts))
  {
    $_SESSION["{$errors}"]["{$field}"] =
      "The expiry date is not a valid date " .
      "in the format MM/YY";
    return false;
  }

  // Check the month
  if (!is_numeric($parts[1]) ||
      intval($parts[1]) < 1 ||
      intval($parts[1]) > 12)
  {
    $_SESSION["{$errors}"]["{$field}"] =
      "The month is invalid.";
    return false;
  }

  // Check the date
  if (!is_numeric($parts[2]) ||
      // Year has passed?
      intval($parts[2]) < intval(date("y")) ||
      // This year, but the month has passed?
      (intval($parts[2]) == intval(date("y")) &&
       intval($parts[1]) < intval(date("n"))) ||
      // More than 10 years in the future?
      intval($parts[2]) > (intval(date("y")) + 10))
```

Example 16-5. The includes/validate.inc functions for form validation (continued)

```
  {
    $_SESSION["{$errors}"]["{$field}"] =
      "The date is invalid.";
    return false;
  }

  return true;
}
?>
```

Custom Error Handler

Example 16-6 shows our implementation of a custom error handler that's used with the winestore. The code is almost identical to that presented in Chapter 12, with three exceptions: first, you can choose the error file that's used for logging; second, you can set whether to log events to a file or screen; and, third, when the error requires that the application is stopped, the script cleans up session variables to log the user out and empty their cart. The logging is managed by three constants that are set in the *includes/winestore.inc* that we describe later.

Example 16-6. The includes/customHandler.inc error handler

```php
<?php
require_once "winestore.inc";

// Back trace an error
function backTrace($context)
{
  $calls = "";

  // Get a backtrace of the function calls
  $trace = debug_backtrace();

  $calls = "\nBacktrace:";

  // Start at 2 -- ignore this function (0) and the customHandler() (1)
  for($x=2; $x < count($trace); $x++)
  {
    $callNo = $x - 2;
    $calls .= "\n  {$callNo}: {$trace[$x]["function"]} ";
    $calls .= "(line {$trace[$x]["line"]} in {$trace[$x]["file"]})";
  }

  $calls .= "\nVariables in {$trace[2]["function"]} ():";

  // Use the $context to get variable information for the function
  // with the error
  foreach($context as $name => $value)
  {
    if (!empty($value))
```

Example 16-6. The includes/customHandler.inc error handler (continued)

```php
        $calls .= "\n  {$name} is {$value}";
      else
        $calls .= "\n  {$name} is NULL";
    }
  return ($calls);
}

// Custom error handler function -- reproduced from Chapter 12
function customHandler($number, $string, $file, $line, $context)
{
  $error = "";

  switch ($number)
  {
    case E_USER_ERROR:
      $error .= "\nERROR on line {$line} in {$file}.\n";
      $stop = true;
      break;
    case E_WARNING:
    case E_USER_WARNING:
      $error .= "\nWARNING on line {$line} in {$file}.\n";
      $stop = false;
      break;
    case E_NOTICE:
    case E_USER_NOTICE:
      $error .= "\nNOTICE on line {$line} in {$file}.\n";
      $stop = false;
      break;
    default:
      $error .= "UNHANDLED ERROR on line {$line} in {$file}.\n";
      $stop = false;
  }
  $error .= "Error: \"{$string}\" (error #{$number}).";
  $error .= backTrace($context);
  $error .= "\nClient IP: {$_SERVER["REMOTE_ADDR"]}";

  $prepend = "\n[PHP Error " . date("YmdHis") . "]";
  $error = ereg_replace("\n", $prepend, $error);

  if (SCREEN_ERRORS)
    print "<pre>{$error}</pre>";

  if (FILE_ERRORS)
    error_log($error, 3, ERROR_FILE);

  if ($stop == true)
  {
    if (isset($_SESSION["order_no"]))
      unset($_SESSION["order_no"]);

    if (isset($_SESSION["loginUsername"]))
      unset($_SESSION["loginUsername"]);
```

Example 16-6. The includes/customHandler.inc error handler (continued)

```
  if (isset($_SESSION["loginIP"]))
    unset($_SESSION["loginIP"]);

  die();
  }
}

?>
```

General-Purpose Functions

The *includes/winestore.inc* file shown in Example 16-7 stores the common constants and functions used throughout the winestore application. It is included in almost all scripts and in the other include files.

The constants at the beginning of the script are designed so that you can flexibly change the directories in which the scripts or templates are stored, and rename the files, without making changes in more than one place. Our aim is to make it easy for you to extract one or more modules that you want to reuse in another application.

If you've followed our installation instructions in Appendixes A to C, you should find that the main directory settings don't need to be changed. Directory setting are those prefixed with D_ at the beginning of the file. The installation path D_INSTALL_ PATH is set to the same value as the Apache DocumentRoot setting and D_WEB_PATH is set to the directory *wda2-winestore* that's been created in the document root. All other directory, script, and template locations are prefixed by the D_INSTALL_PATH and D_ WEB_PATH definitions. The list of locations of scripts can be found earlier in this chapter in Table 16-1.

The buttons definitions (which are prefixed with B_) are described earlier in our template discussion. The cart icon settings NO_CART and SHOW_CART control whether the cart icon is hidden or shown, respectively. The constant SEARCH_ROWS defines how many search results are presented per page, to support functionality discussed in Chapter 20. The constants ERROR_FILE, FILE_ERRORS, and SCREEN_ERRORS control how errors are logged as discussed in the previous section. The string $dsn is the data source name that's used to create a PEAR DB connection in all winestore scripts.

Example 16-7. The includes/winestore.inc file

```
<?php
require_once 'db.inc';
require_once 'customHandler.inc';

// Choose or adjust one of the following
// NOTE: do not add a trailing slash
// define("D_INSTALL_PATH", "c:/progra~1/easyph~1/www");
  define("D_INSTALL_PATH", "/Library/WebServer/Documents");
```

Example 16-7. The includes/winestore.inc file (continued)

```
//define("D_INSTALL_PATH", "/usr/local/apache2/htdocs");

// Paths -- for these, add trailing slash
define("D_WEB_PATH", "/wda2-winestore/");
define("D_CART", D_WEB_PATH . "cart/");
define("D_CARTIMAGES", D_CART . "images/");
define("D_CUSTOMER", D_WEB_PATH . "customer/");
define("D_AUTH", D_WEB_PATH . "auth/");
define("D_ORDER", D_WEB_PATH . "order/");
define("D_SEARCH", D_WEB_PATH . "search/");
define("D_TEMPLATES", D_INSTALL_PATH . D_WEB_PATH . "templates/");

// No slash at beginning
// S - scripts
define("S_MAIN", D_WEB_PATH . "index.php");
define("S_ADDTOCART", D_CART . "addtocart.php");
define("S_EMPTYCART", D_CART . "emptycart.php");
define("S_SHOWCART", D_CART . "showcart.php");
define("S_UPDATECART", D_CART . "updatecart.php");
define("S_ORDER_1", D_ORDER . "order-step1.php");
define("S_ORDER_2", D_ORDER . "order-step2.php");
define("S_ORDER_3", D_ORDER . "order-step3.php");
define("S_ORDER_4", D_ORDER . "order-step4.php");
define("S_ORDERRECEIPT", D_ORDER . "receipt.php");
define("S_SEARCH", D_SEARCH . "search.php");
define("S_SEARCHFORM", D_SEARCH . "searchform.php");
define("S_DETAILS", D_CUSTOMER . "details.php");
define("S_VALIDATE", D_CUSTOMER . "validate.php");
define("S_CUSTRECEIPT", D_CUSTOMER . "receipt.php");
define("S_LOGOUT", D_AUTH . "logout.php");
define("S_LOGIN", D_AUTH . "login.php");
define("S_LOGINCHECK", D_AUTH . "logincheck.php");
define("S_PASSWORD", D_AUTH . "password.php");
define("S_CHANGEPASSWORD", D_AUTH . "changepassword.php");
define("S_PASSWORDRECEIPT", D_AUTH . "receipt.php");

// T - templates
define("T_SKELETON", "winestore.tpl");
define("T_HOME", "index.tpl");
define("T_SHOWCART", "showcart.tpl");
define("T_DETAILS", "details.tpl");
define("T_CUSTRECEIPT", "custreceipt.tpl");
define("T_LOGIN", "login.tpl");
define("T_PASSWORD", "password.tpl");
define("T_PASSWORDRECEIPT", "passwordreceipt.tpl");
define("T_EMAIL", "email.tpl");
define("T_ORDERRECEIPT", "orderreceipt.tpl");
define("T_SEARCH", "search.tpl");
define("T_SOURCE", "source.tpl");

// I - images
define("I_CART_OFF", D_CARTIMAGES . "cart_off.jpg");
define("I_CART_ON", D_CARTIMAGES . "cart_on.jpg");
```

Example 16-7. The includes/winestore.inc file (continued)

```php
// B - Buttons
define("B_EMPTY_CART", 1);
define("B_SHOW_CART", 2);
define("B_UPDATE_CART", 4);
define("B_PURCHASE", 8);
define("B_SEARCH", 16);
define("B_HOME", 32);
define("B_DETAILS", 64);
define("B_LOGINLOGOUT", 128);
define("B_PASSWORD", 256);
define("B_ALL", 511);

// Show the cart icon?
define("NO_CART", 1);
define("SHOW_ALL", 2);

// Search rows per page
define("SEARCH_ROWS", 12);

// Custom error handler controls
// File to log errors to
define("ERROR_FILE", "/tmp/php_error_log");

// Save errors to a file?
define("FILE_ERRORS", true);

// Show errors to the screen?
define("SCREEN_ERRORS", true);


// The database connection string
$dsn = "mysql://{$username}:{$password}@{$hostname}/{$databasename}";

// Untaint user data
function pearclean($array, $index, $maxlength, $connection)
{
  if (isset($array["{$index}"]))
  {
    $input = trim(substr($array["{$index}"], 0, $maxlength));
    $input = mysql_real_escape_string($input);
    return ($input);
  }
  return NULL;
}

// Find the cust_id using the user_name
function getCust_id($user_name, $connection = null)
{
  global $dsn;

  // If a connection parameter is not passed, then
  // use our own connection
  if (!isset($connection))
  {
```

Example 16-7. The includes/winestore.inc file (continued)

```
      $connection = DB::connect($dsn, false);
      if (DB::isError($connection))
        trigger_error($connection->getMessage( ), E_USER_ERROR);
   }

   $query = "SELECT cust_id FROM users WHERE
             user_name = '{$user_name}'";

   $result = $connection->query($query);
   if (DB::isError($result))
      trigger_error($result->getMessage( ), E_USER_ERROR);

   $row = $result->fetchRow(DB_FETCHMODE_ASSOC);
   return($row["cust_id"]);
}

// Show the user the details of one wine in their cart
function showWine($wineId, $connection = null)
{
   global $dsn;

   $wineQuery = "SELECT year, winery_name, wine_name
                 FROM winery, wine
                 WHERE wine.winery_id = winery.winery_id
                 AND wine.wine_id = {$wineId}";

   // If a connection parameter is not passed, then
   // use our own connection to avoid any locking problems
   if (!isset($connection))
   {
      $connection = DB::connect($dsn, false);
      if (DB::isError($connection))
        trigger_error($connection->getMessage( ), E_USER_ERROR);
   }

   $result = $connection->query($wineQuery);

   if (DB::isError($result))
      trigger_error($result->getMessage( ), E_USER_ERROR);

   $row = $result->fetchRow(DB_FETCHMODE_ASSOC);

   // Print the wine details
   $output = "{$row["year"]} {$row["winery_name"]} {$row["wine_name"]}";

   // Print the varieties for this wine
   $output .= showVarieties($connection, $wineId);

   return $output;
}
```

Example 16-7. The includes/winestore.inc file (continued)

```
// Find the varieties for a wineID
function showVarieties($connection, $wineID)
{
   // Find the varieties of the current wine,
   // and order them by id
   $query = "SELECT gv.variety
           FROM grape_variety gv, wine_variety wv, wine w
           WHERE w.wine_id = wv.wine_id
           AND wv.variety_id = gv.variety_id
           AND w.wine_id = {$wineID}
           ORDER BY wv.id";

   $result = $connection->query($query);

   if (DB::isError($result))
      trigger_error($result->getMessage( ), E_USER_ERROR);

   $varieties = "";

   // Retrieve and print the varieties
   while ($row = $result->fetchRow(DB_FETCHMODE_ASSOC))
      $varieties .= " {$row["variety"]}";

   return $varieties;
}

// Find the cheapest bottle price for a wineID
function showPricing($connection, $wineID)
{
   // Find the price of the cheapest inventory
   $query = "SELECT min(cost) FROM inventory
           WHERE wine_id = {$wineID}";

   $result = $connection->query($query);

   if (DB::isError($result))
      trigger_error($result->getMessage( ), E_USER_ERROR);

   // Retrieve the oldest price
   $row = $result->fetchRow(DB_FETCHMODE_ASSOC);

   $price = $row["min(cost)"];

   return $price;
}

// Lookup the country_id in the countries lookup table
// and return the country name
function showCountry($country_id, $connection)
{
  $query = "SELECT country FROM countries WHERE
           country_id = {$country_id}";
```

Example 16-7. The includes/winestore.inc file (continued)

```
  $result = $connection->query($query);

  if (DB::isError($result))
     trigger_error($result->getMessage( ), E_USER_ERROR);

  $countryRow = $result->fetchRow(DB_FETCHMODE_ASSOC);

  return($countryRow["country"]);
}

// Lookup the title in the titles lookup table
// and return the title string
function showTitle($title_id, $connection)
{
  $query = "SELECT title FROM titles WHERE
             title_id = {$title_id}";

  $result = $connection->query($query);

  if (DB::isError($result))
     trigger_error($result->getMessage( ), E_USER_ERROR);

  $titleRow = $result->fetchRow(DB_FETCHMODE_ASSOC);

  return($titleRow["title"]);
}
?>
```

The *includes/winestore.inc* file also stores several functions that are used throughout the winestore. The function *pearclean()* untaints user data and is a variation of the *mysqlclean()* function discussed in Chapter 6. The function *getCust_id()* takes as a parameter the username of a logged-in user (and an optional open database connection), and returns their unique cust_id identifier by querying the *users* table; this function is used throughout the winestore in, for example, customer detail changes and the ordering process.

The *getCust_id()* function (and the *showWine()* function that we discuss next) has an optional database connection for three reasons. First, if you've already got a connection handle, there's usually no reason to open another and so it's useful to be able to pass it as a parameter. Second, if you don't have a connection open, the function can open one itself. Third, if you do have a connection open but you don't want to use it because you've locked some tables, then if don't pass a parameter to the function it'll open a new, distinct connection and avoid any locking problems.

The functions *showWine()*, *showVarieties()*, and *showPricing()* are utilities to retrieve details about a specific wine that's identified by a wine_id. The *showWine()* function returns a string that includes the vintage, wine name, and winery for the wine. The *showVarieties()* function returns a string that lists the grape varieties of the wine, and the *showPricing()* function returns the cheapest price in the inventory for the wine.

The *showCountry()* and *showTitle()* functions are utilities that return a string from a lookup table. The *showCountry()* function takes as a parameter a country identifier and returns a country name from the *countries* table. The *showTitle()* function does the same thing for titles from the *titles* table. Both are used in the customer processes discussed in the next chapter.

CHAPTER 17

Managing Customers

This chapter is the second of five that outline our winestore case study application. The scripts that are discussed here concern the customer management processes, and include moderately complex data entry, validation, error reporting, and receipt scripts. The module uses most of the basic web database application techniques discussed in Chapters 6 through 10. It also makes extensive use of the generic winestore templates and other reusable components that are discussed in Chapter 16.

The scripts that are discussed perform the following functions:

Becoming a member
> A customer form that allows users to join the online winestore by providing their name, address, email address, password, and other details. The form collects mandatory and optional fields, and makes use of all of the features of the winestoreFormTemplate class discussed in Chapter 16.
>
> The customer form is based on the phonebook details insert example in Chapter 8.

Updating customer details
> A customer form that allows users to update the details they provided when they joined the online winestore. This functionality is integrated into the script used for becoming a member, and is based on the phonebook details update example in Chapter 8.

Checking customer details
> The complete validation and database management processes for updating and creating new customers. These processes extend the form processing techniques introduced in Chapter 8 by applying the validation techniques from Chapter 9. The process includes creating and storing passwords using the encryption techniques discussed in Chapter 11.

Providing a customer receipt
> A receipt page that presents the results of the customer membership processing and avoids the reload problem discussed in Chapter 6.

Code Overview

The customer management process is provided by the *customer/details.php*, *customer/validate.php*, and *customer/receipt.php* scripts.

The script *customer/details.php* presents a form to both new customers and members who are updating their details. The form collects and inserts or updates data that is stored by *customer/validate.php* into the *customer* table. The *customer* table was created with the following statement:

```
CREATE TABLE customer (
    cust_id int(5) NOT NULL,
    surname varchar(50),
    firstname varchar(50),
    initial char(1),
    title_id int(3),
    address varchar(50),
    city varchar(50),
    state varchar(20),
    zipcode varchar(10),
    country_id int(4),
    phone varchar(15),
    birth_date char(10),
    PRIMARY KEY (cust_id)
) type=MyISAM;
```

The form is initially empty if the user isn't logged in, and hasn't previously attempted and failed validation. If the user is logged in and validation hasn't previously failed, the form is pre-filled with her details from the *customer* table. Finally, regardless of whether a user is logged in or not, if data has failed validation, the invalid data is displayed for amendment. The customer form, showing errors from failed validation, is shown rendered in a Mozilla browser in Figure 17-1.

For new members, the form requires an email address that is used as the login name of the user and a password for future visits to the site. This information is stored in the *users* table that was created with the following statement:

```
CREATE TABLE users (
    cust_id int(5) NOT NULL,
    user_name varchar(50) NOT NULL,
    password varchar(32) NOT NULL,
    PRIMARY KEY (user_name),
    KEY password (password),
    KEY cust_id (cust_id)
) type=MyISAM;
```

The table is identical to the *users* table discussed in Chapter 11, except we've added two extra indexes for fast searching by password and cust_id.

Two lookup tables are used for displaying and selecting the user's country and title. The *customer* table stores the identifiers title_id and country_id, and these identifiers are the primary keys of the *titles* and *countries* lookup tables, respectively. The

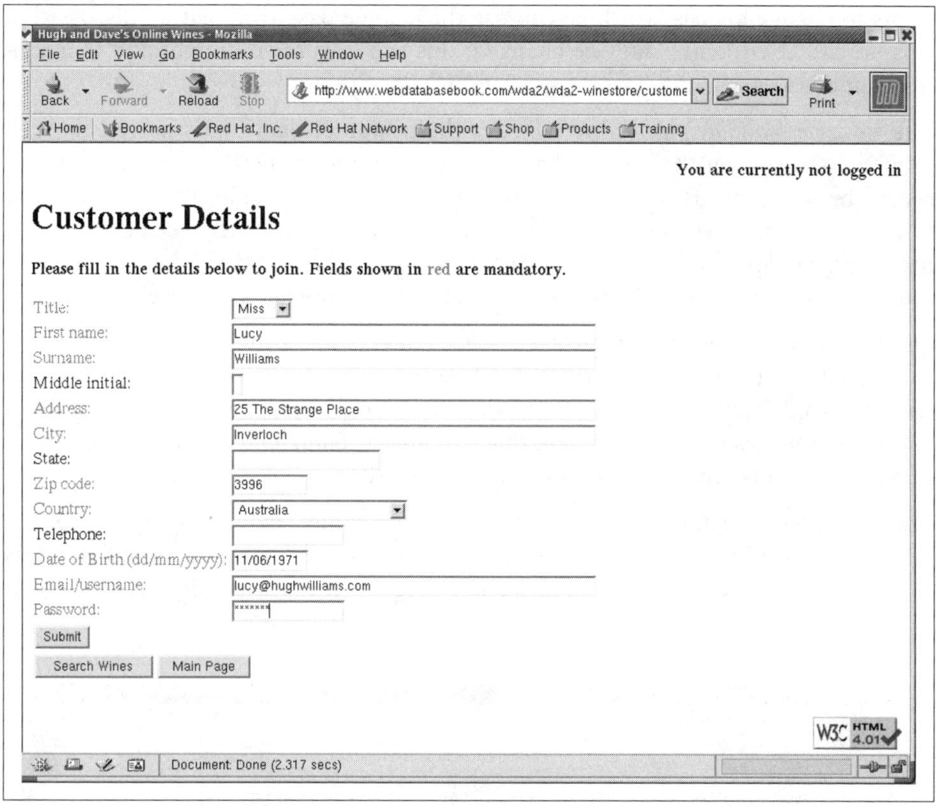

Figure 17-1. The customer form rendered in a Mozilla browser

contents of both lookup tables are displayed as drop-down lists using the HTML `<select>` element and make use of our `winestoreFormTemplate select` blocks. The tables were created with the following statements:

```
CREATE TABLE titles (
  title_id int(2) NOT NULL,
  title char(10),
  PRIMARY KEY (title_id)
) type=MyISAM;

CREATE TABLE countries (
  country_id int(4) NOT NULL,
  country char(30) NOT NULL,
  PRIMARY KEY (country_id),
  KEY (country)
) type=MyISAM;
```

Passwords are digested so as not to be stored in plaintext anywhere; they're between 6 and 8 characters in length when entered by the user, but the digest process generates a string of 32 characters. For customers who are amending their details, the password and email input widgets are omitted from the customer form. If the user wants to change his password, he can use the change password feature discussed in Chapter 20. User names can't be changed; this is a feature you might add to a real-world application.

The *customer/validate.php* script validates the customer data that's passed through from the form using the POST method. If the customer is new and validation succeeds, the script inserts the new customer into the *customer* table, adds the new user to the *users* table, logs the user in, and redirects to the customer receipt script *customer/receipt.php*. If the customer is amending her details and validation succeeds, the script updates her row in the *customer* table and redirects to the receipt script.

On validation failure, *customer/validate.php* redirects to *customer/details.php,* where the validation errors are reported as batch errors that are interleaved with the form widgets. To display errors and the previously entered data, the script makes use of two session arrays that are populated by *customer/validate.php* as part of the validation process. This process is discussed in Chapter 10.

The *customer/receipt.php* script displays the customer details by querying the *customer* table and retrieving the details for the user who's currently logged in. Users can't view customer receipts if they're not logged in. An example receipt page is shown in Figure 17-2.

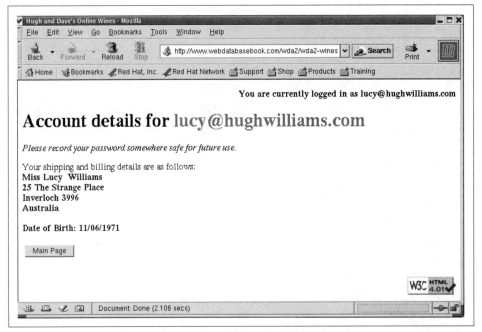

Figure 17-2. A customer receipt page rendered in the Mozilla browser

We reuse this template-based data entry process, validation, and receipt framework in other parts of the winestore. For example, the code is adapted for password changing and credit card data entry. The framework is explained in Chapter 16.

Customer Validation

Example 17-1 lists the *customer/validate.php* script. It is based on Example 10-4 and has the same structure with four exceptions:

- It validates a larger set of fields.
- It manages the creation of digests from passwords and user account allocation.
- It uses the *includes/validate.inc* include file, which contains general-purpose validation functions based on those in Chapter 9. The file is discussed in Chapter 16.
- If the validation succeeds and the member isn't logged in, the user is authenticated and logged in using functions in *includes/authenticate.inc*, which is discussed in Chapter 20.

Example 17-1. The winestore customer validation script, customer/validate.php

```php
<?php
require_once "DB.php";
require_once "../includes/winestore.inc";
require_once "../includes/validate.inc";
require_once "../includes/authenticate.inc";

set_error_handler("customHandler");

session_start();

$connection = DB::connect($dsn, true);
if (DB::isError($connection))
   trigger_error($connection->getMessage(), E_USER_ERROR);

// Clear and register an error array - just in case!
$_SESSION["custErrors"] = array();

// Set up a custFormVars array for the POST variables
$_SESSION["custFormVars"] = array();

// Clean and load the POST variables
foreach($_POST as $varname => $value)
   $_SESSION["custFormVars"]["{$varname}"] =
     pearclean($_POST, $varname, 50, $connection);

// Validate the firstname
checkMandatory("firstname", "first name", "custErrors", "custFormVars");

// Validate the Surname
```

Example 17-1. The winestore customer validation script, customer/validate.php (continued)

```
checkMandatory("surname", "surname", "custErrors", "custFormVars");

// Validate the Address
checkMandatory("address", "address", "custErrors", "custFormVars");

// Validate the Initial
if (!empty($_SESSION["custFormVars"]["initial"]) &&
    !eregi("^[[:alpha:]]{1}$", $_SESSION["custFormVars"]["initial"]))
  $_SESSION["custErrors"]["initial"] =
    "The initial field must be empty or one " .
    "alphabetic character in length.";

// Validate the City
checkMandatory("city", "city", "custErrors", "custFormVars");

// Validate Zipcode
if (checkMandatory("zipcode", "Zip code", "custErrors", "custFormVars"))
  checkZipcode("zipcode", "Zip code", "custErrors", "custFormVars");

// Phone is optional, but if it is entered it must have correct format
if (!empty($_SESSION["custFormVars"]["phone"]))
  checkPhone("phone", "telephone", "custErrors", "custFormVars");

// Validate Date of Birth
if (checkMandatory("birth_date", "date of birth", "custErrors",
            "custFormVars"))
  checkDateAndAdult("birth_date", "date of birth", "custErrors",
              "custFormVars");

// Only validate email if this is an INSERT
if (!isset($_SESSION["loginUsername"]))
{
  if (checkMandatory("loginUsername", "email/username",
              "custErrors", "custFormVars") &&
      emailCheck("loginUsername", "email/username",
              "custErrors", "custFormVars"))
  {
    // Check if the email address is already in use in
    //  the winestore
    $query = "SELECT * FROM users WHERE user_name =
              '{$_SESSION["custFormVars"]["loginUsername"]}'";

    $result = $connection->query($query);
    if (DB::isError($result))
      trigger_error($result->getMessage( ), E_USER_ERROR);

    if ($result->numRows( ) == 1)
      $_SESSION["custErrors"]["loginUsername"] =
        "A customer already exists with this " .
        "email address.";
  }
```

```
    // Validate password - between 6 and 8 characters
    if (checkMandatory("loginPassword", "password",
                "custErrors", "custFormVars"))
       checkMinAndMaxLength("loginPassword", 6, 8, "password",
                    "custErrors", "custFormVars");
}

// Now the script has finished the validation,
// check if there were any errors
if (count($_SESSION["custErrors"]) > 0)
{
    // There are errors.  Relocate back to the client form
    header("Location: " . S_DETAILS);
    exit;
}

// Is this an update?
if (isset($_SESSION["loginUsername"]))
{
    // Check the user is properly logged in
    sessionAuthenticate(S_DETAILS);

    $cust_id = getCust_id($_SESSION["loginUsername"], $connection);

    $query = "UPDATE customer SET
            title_id =    {$_SESSION["custFormVars"]["title_id"]},
            surname =     '{$_SESSION["custFormVars"]["surname"]}',
            firstname =   '{$_SESSION["custFormVars"]["firstname"]}',
            initial =     '{$_SESSION["custFormVars"]["initial"]}',
            address =     '{$_SESSION["custFormVars"]["address"]}',
            city =        '{$_SESSION["custFormVars"]["city"]}',
            state =       '{$_SESSION["custFormVars"]["state"]}',
            zipcode =     '{$_SESSION["custFormVars"]["zipcode"]}',
            country_id =   {$_SESSION["custFormVars"]["country_id"]},
            phone =       '{$_SESSION["custFormVars"]["phone"]}',
            birth_date =  '{$_SESSION["custFormVars"]["birth_date"]}'
            WHERE cust_id = {$cust_id}";

    $result = $connection->query($query);
    if (DB::isError($result))
       trigger_error($result->getMessage( ), E_USER_ERROR);
}
else
{
    // Lock to get the next available customer ID
    $result = $connection->query("LOCK TABLES customer WRITE");
    if (DB::isError($result))
       trigger_error($result->getMessage( ), E_USER_ERROR);

    // Find the max cust_id
    $result = $connection->query("SELECT max(cust_id) FROM customer");
    if (DB::isError($result))
```

```
            trigger_error($result->getMessage( ), E_USER_ERROR);
        $row = $result->fetchRow(DB_FETCHMODE_ASSOC);

        // Work out the next available ID
        $cust_id = $row["max(cust_id)"] + 1;

        // Insert the new customer
        $query = "INSERT INTO customer VALUES ({$cust_id},
                '{$_SESSION["custFormVars"]["surname"]}',
                '{$_SESSION["custFormVars"]["firstname"]}',
                '{$_SESSION["custFormVars"]["initial"]}',
                 {$_SESSION["custFormVars"]["title_id"]},
                '{$_SESSION["custFormVars"]["address"]}',
                '{$_SESSION["custFormVars"]["city"]}',
                '{$_SESSION["custFormVars"]["state"]}',
                '{$_SESSION["custFormVars"]["zipcode"]}',
                 {$_SESSION["custFormVars"]["country_id"]},
                '{$_SESSION["custFormVars"]["phone"]}',
                '{$_SESSION["custFormVars"]["birth_date"]}')";

        $result = $connection->query($query);
        if (DB::isError($result))
            trigger_error($result->getMessage( ), E_USER_ERROR);

        // Unlock the customer table
        $result = $connection->query("UNLOCK TABLES");
        if (DB::isError($result))
            trigger_error($result->getMessage( ), E_USER_ERROR);

        // As this was an INSERT, we need to INSERT into the users table too
        newUser($_SESSION["custFormVars"]["loginUsername"],
                $_SESSION["custFormVars"]["loginPassword"],
                $cust_id, $connection);

        // Log the user into their new account
        registerLogin($_SESSION["custFormVars"]["loginUsername"]);
}

// Clear the custFormVars so a future form is blank
unset($_SESSION["custFormVars"]);
unset($_SESSION["custErrors"]);

// Now show the customer receipt
header("Location: " . S_CUSTRECEIPT);
?>
```

The presence of the session variable $_SESSION["loginUsername"] indicates whether or not the user is logged in. The script adds a new customer to the *customer* table and a row to the *users* table if the user isn't logged in, because the user must be applying for membership (otherwise, she's updating details of her membership). We don't use MySQL's auto_increment feature to obtain the next available cust_id, but

---

instead use locking to figure out the maximum value and reserve the next value for this customer. We've avoided auto_increment because it's proprietary and you'd have to change it if you migrated the winestore to a different database server. We could have used an auxiliary table to manage the key fields (as discussed in Chapter 8), but we decided to keep things simple.

If the user is logged in, the member must be updating her details. In this case, before updating the row, the external function calls *getCust_id( )* to get the customer cust_id associated with the $_SESSION["loginUsername"] session variable. The function is defined in the *winestore.inc* file discussed in Chapter 16.

If validation fails in Example 17-1, the script redirects the browser to the *customer/details.php* script shown in Example 17-2. Any validation error messages are recorded in the array $_SESSION["custErrors"] and this array is used to display the messages interleaved with the customer form widgets. The values that are passed from the form in the $_POST superglobal are themselves stored in the $_SESSION["custFormVars"] array so that they can be returned to the form for redisplay. This process of using session arrays to store intermediate data is discussed in Chapter 10.

If validation and the database write succeed, the session variables are emptied and the script redirects to the *customer/receipt.php* script shown in Example 17-3. Also, if it's a new user that's been created, they're logged in using the *registerLogin( )* function that's discussed in Chapter 20.

The Customer Form

The script *customer/details.php* is shown in Example 17-2. If the user is logged in and validation has not previously failed, the customer data is retrieved from the *customer* table and used to populate the form widgets. If the user isn't logged in, and validation has not previously failed, a blank form is shown to collect new member details. If data has failed validation, the form is repopulated and the error messages are displayed. Error messages and previously entered form values are stored by the *customer/validate.php* script in the session array variables $_SESSION["custFormVars"] and $_SESSION["custErrors"] respectively.

The customer form and its widgets are displayed using our winestoreFormTemplate class that's derived from the PEAR ITX template class. It's discussed in detail in Chapter 16.

Example 17-2. The customer form script customer/details.php

```php
<?php
require_once "DB.php";
require_once "../includes/winestore.inc";
require_once "../includes/authenticate.inc";
require_once "../includes/template.inc";
```

Example 17-2. The customer form script customer/details.php (continued)

```php
set_error_handler("customHandler");

// Show meaningful instructions for UPDATE or INSERT
if (isset($_SESSION["loginUsername"]))
   $instructions = "Please amend your details below as required.";
else
   $instructions = "Please fill in the details below to join.";

// Takes <form> heading, instructions, action, formVars name,
// and formErrors name as parameters
$template = new winestoreFormTemplate("Customer Details",
               $instructions, S_VALIDATE, "custFormVars", "custErrors");

session_start();

$connection = DB::connect($dsn, true);
if (DB::isError($connection))
  trigger_error($connection->getMessage(), E_USER_ERROR);

// Is the user logged in and are there no errors from previous
// validation?  If so, look up the customer for editing
if (isset($_SESSION["loginUsername"]) &&
    !isset($_SESSION["custErrors"]))
{
   // Check the user is properly logged in
   sessionAuthenticate(S_MAIN);

   $query = "SELECT title_id, surname, firstname, initial, address,
                     city, state, zipcode, country_id, phone,
                     birth_date
             FROM users, customer
             WHERE users.cust_id = customer.cust_id
             AND user_name = '{$_SESSION["loginUsername"]}'";

   $result = $connection->query($query);
   if (DB::isError($result))
      trigger_error($result->getMessage(), E_USER_ERROR);
   $row = $result->fetchRow(DB_FETCHMODE_ASSOC);

   // Reset $_SESSION["custFormVars"], since we're loading
   // from the customer table
   $_SESSION["custFormVars"] = array();

   // Load all the <form> widgets with customer data
   foreach($row as $variable => $value)
      $_SESSION["custFormVars"]["{$variable}"] = $value;
}

// Load the titles from the title table
$titleResult = $connection->query("SELECT * FROM titles");
if (DB::isError($titleResult))
   trigger_error($titleResult->getMessage(), E_USER_ERROR);
```

Example 17-2. The customer form script customer/details.php (continued)

```php
// Load the countries from the country table
$countryResult = $connection->query("SELECT * FROM countries");
if (DB::isError($countryResult))
   trigger_error($countryResult->getMessage( ), E_USER_ERROR);

// Create widgets for each of the customer fields
$template->selectWidget("title_id", "Title:",
                        "title", $titleResult);
$template->mandatoryWidget("firstname", "First name:", 50);
$template->mandatoryWidget("surname", "Surname:", 50);
$template->optionalWidget("initial", "Middle initial:", 1);
$template->mandatoryWidget("address", "Address:", 50);
$template->mandatoryWidget("city", "City:", 50);
$template->optionalWidget("state", "State:", 20);
$template->mandatoryWidget("zipcode", "Zip code:", 10);
$template->selectWidget("country_id", "Country:",
                        "country", $countryResult);
$template->optionalWidget("phone", "Telephone:", 15);
$template->mandatoryWidget("birth_date",
                           "Date of Birth (dd/mm/yyyy):", 10);

// Only show the username/email and password widgets to new users
if (!isset($_SESSION["loginUsername"]))
{
   $template->mandatoryWidget("loginUsername", "Email/username:", 50);
   $template->passwordWidget("loginPassword", "Password:", 15);
}

// Add buttons and messages, and show the page
$template->showWinestore(NO_CART, B_ALL & ~B_EMPTY_CART & ~B_UPDATE_CART &
                ~B_PURCHASE & ~B_DETAILS & ~B_LOGINLOGOUT)
?>
```

The Customer Receipt Page

Example 17-3 shows the customer receipt script, *customer/receipt.php*, that is called after a database write to insert or update a customer. The script is a receipt page that can be bookmarked and the script only reads details from the database. Reloading of the page therefore has no undesirable side effects.

Example 17-3. The customer/receipt.php customer receipt page

```php
<?php
// This script shows the user a receipt for their customer
// UPDATE or INSERT. It carries out no database writes and
// can be bookmarked.
// The user must be logged in to view it.

require_once "DB.php";
require_once "../includes/winestore.inc";
require_once "../includes/authenticate.inc";
```

Example 17-3. The customer/receipt.php customer receipt page (continued)

```
require_once "../includes/template.inc";

set_error_handler("customHandler");

// Show the user a customer INSERT or UPDATE receipt
function show_HTML_receipt($cust_id, $connection, &$template)
{
  // Retrieve the customer details
  $query = "SELECT * FROM customer WHERE cust_id = {$cust_id}";
  $result = $connection->query($query);
  if (DB::isError($result))
     trigger_error($result->getMessage(), E_USER_ERROR);
  $row = $result->fetchRow(DB_FETCHMODE_ASSOC);

  // Is there an optional phone field? If so, add it to the output
  if (!empty($row["phone"]))
  {
     $template->setCurrentBlock("phone");
     $template->setVariable("PHONE", $row["phone"]);
     $template->parseCurrentBlock("address");
  }

  // Now, add all the mandatory fields to the output
  $template->setCurrentBlock();
  $template->setVariable("EMAIL", $_SESSION["loginUsername"]);
  $template->setVariable("FIRSTNAME", $row["firstname"]);
  $template->setVariable("SURNAME", $row["surname"]);
  $template->setVariable("INITIAL", $row["initial"]);
  $template->setVariable("ADDRESS", $row["address"]);
  $template->setVariable("CITY", $row["city"]);
  $template->setVariable("STATE", $row["state"]);
  $template->setVariable("ZIPCODE", $row["zipcode"]);
  $template->setVariable("DOB", $row["birth_date"]);
  $template->setVariable("CUSTTITLE", showTitle($row["title_id"],
                         $connection));
  $template->setVariable("COUNTRY", showCountry($row["country_id"],
                         $connection));
}

// -----

session_start();

$connection = DB::connect($dsn, true);
if (DB::isError($connection))
  trigger_error($connection->getMessage(), E_USER_ERROR);

// Check the user is properly logged in
sessionAuthenticate(S_MAIN);

// Find out the cust_id of the user
$cust_id = getCust_id($_SESSION["loginUsername"]);
```

Example 17-3. The customer/receipt.php customer receipt page (continued)

```
// Start a new page
$template = new winestoreTemplate(T_CUSTRECEIPT);

// Show the customer confirmation
show_HTML_receipt($cust_id, $connection, $template);

// Add buttons and messages, and show the page
$template->showWinestore(NO_CART, B_HOME);
?>
```

Customers can view their receipts only when logged in. The cust_id of the customer is again retrieved using the function *getCust_id( )* that's discussed in Chapter 16.

The receipt script populates the *templates/custreceipt.tpl* template shown in Example 17-4. The receipt page uses the winestoreTemplate class that's discussed in Chapter 16 to provide the HTML framework for displaying the page and to show messages to the user. The *templates/custreceipt.tpl* template is therefore only part of the body of the page.

Example 17-4. The templates/custreceipt.tpl customer receipt template

```
h1>Account details for <font color="red">{EMAIL}</font></h1>

<p><i>Please record your password somewhere safe for future use.</i>

<p>Your shipping and billing details are as follows:
<br><b>{CUSTTITLE} {FIRSTNAME} {INITIAL} {SURNAME}
<br>{ADDRESS}
<br>{CITY} {STATE} {ZIPCODE}
<br>{COUNTRY}</b>
<br>
<!-- BEGIN phone -->
<br><b>Telephone: {PHONE}
<!-- END phone -->
<br><b>Date of Birth: {DOB}</b>
<br>
<br>
```

CHAPTER 18
The Shopping Cart

In this chapter, we introduce the shopping cart developed for the online winestore. The shopping cart is typical of those used in online stores: the user can add items to the cart and manage the quantities of the different items. However, it's also a little different: unlike many other implementations, the cart data is stored in database tables, and one session variable per user tracks the cart's identity.

This chapter is the third of five that outline the complete winestore application. We present here the four scripts that manage the shopping cart and a fifth script that produces the home page of the winestore. The scripts in this chapter perform the following functions:

Display the home page
> Shows new wines that have recently been reviewed. The script also includes embedded links that allow the user to add items to their cart; this is one part of the one-component querying strategy discussed in Chapter 6, and the other part is a feature of the script that adds items to the cart, discussed next.

Add items to the cart
> Adds a quantity of a specific wine to the user's shopping cart. This illustrates database writing and locking techniques discussed in Chapter 8 and one component querying discussed in Chapter 6.

View the shopping cart
> Queries the database and displays the contents of the user's shopping cart. This demonstrates basic querying techniques from Chapter 6, combined with the winestoreFormTemplate class discussed in Chapter 16.

Empty the cart
> Deletes all the items in the cart and removes the cart. This illustrates one component querying as discussed in Chapter 6.

Update quantities of items

> Manages changes to the number of bottles of wines in the cart, including deletion of one or more wines. This illustrates database writing techniques discussed in Chapter 8 and one component querying discussed in Chapter 6.

The process of converting a shopping cart into an order, and adjusting the inventory as the stock is sold, is discussed in Chapter 19. The process of emptying the database of unused carts is discussed in Chapter 15.

Code Overview

This section outlines the functions of the scripts that implement the shopping cart and winestore home page. The cart is implemented in the *cart/showcart.php*, *cart/addtocart.php*, *cart/emptycart.php*, and *cart/updatecart.php* scripts. The home page is implemented as *index.php*. The database-based cart management process is discussed later in the section "The Shopping Cart Implementation."

The script *cart/showcart.php* is the only shopping cart script that presents output to the user. It shows the cart's current contents using a form in an HTML table environment that allows the user to modify the quantity of any of the items. If the cart contains no items, a message is shown instead. Figure 18-1 shows an example of a cart containing four items.

If the user modifies any quantity in the cart, then he must click on the *Update Quantities* button to write the change to the database. This submits the form and requests the script *cart/updatecart.php*, which processes the variables and values passed with the GET method and updates the quantities. Setting a quantity to zero deletes the item. If the user wants to completely empty the cart, he can click on *Empty Cart* which requests the *cart/emptycart.php* script. *cart/updatecart.php* and *cart/emptycart.php* don't produce any HTML output, but instead redirect the browser back to *cart/showcart.php*.

The *cart/addtocart.php* scripts adds a quantity of a wine to the cart. It can be requested from both the home page and the *search/search.php* script discussed in Chapter 20. The script expects two parameters to be passed: the wine to be added (referenced by its wine_id) and the quantity to add. The script handles the three different cases that can occur when adding a wine item to the cart:

1. The item is the first to be added to an empty cart, and a new cart needs to be created before the item is added.

2. The item is a new item being added to an existing cart.

3. The item is already in the cart and the user is adding an additional quantity.

When a wine is added for the first time to the cart, the script also discovers the cheapest price of that wine in the inventory (as per the requirements in Chapter 16).

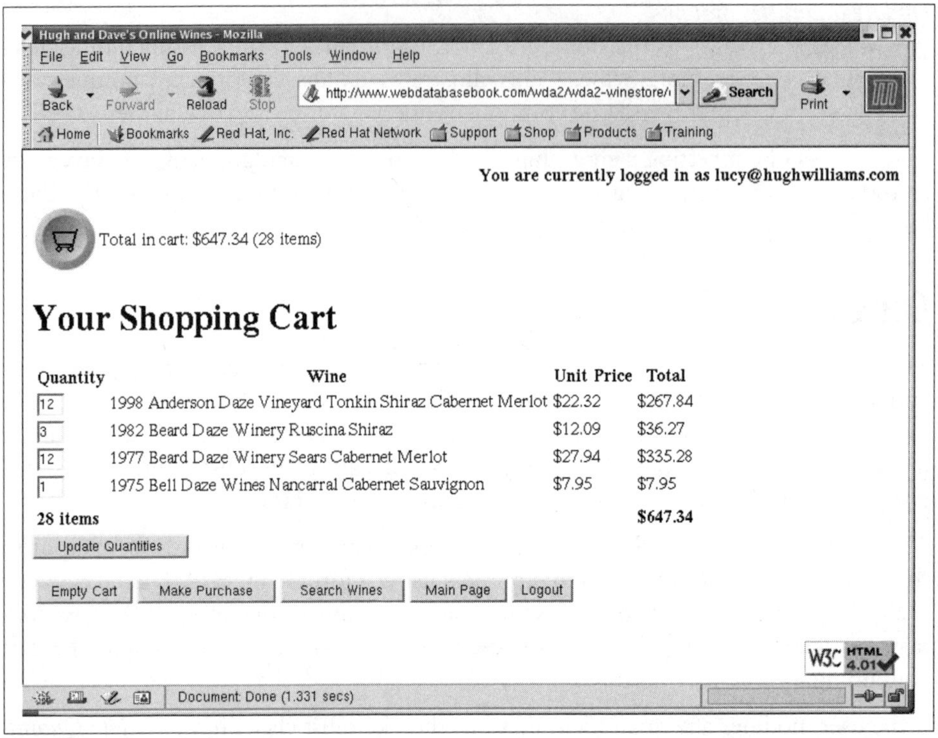

Figure 18-1. A shopping cart containing four items

The homepage script *index.php* displays the three wines that have most-recently been reviewed by a wine writer. With each of these wines, it includes embedded links that can be clicked on to add one or a dozen bottles to the shopping cart using the *cart/ addtocart.php* script. The home page also displays a welcome message, and buttons that allow the user to search the wines, become a member or amend member details, and login or logout. The home page is shown in Figure 18-2.

The Winestore Home Page

Example 18-1, later in this section, lists the code for the home page of the online winestore. The code outputs the following from the *winestore* database:

- Information about the three most-recently added wines that have been reviewed, including the vintage year, the winery, the wine name, and the varieties.
- A review of the wine that's been written by a wine writer.
- The price of a bottle and of a dozen bottles of the wine.

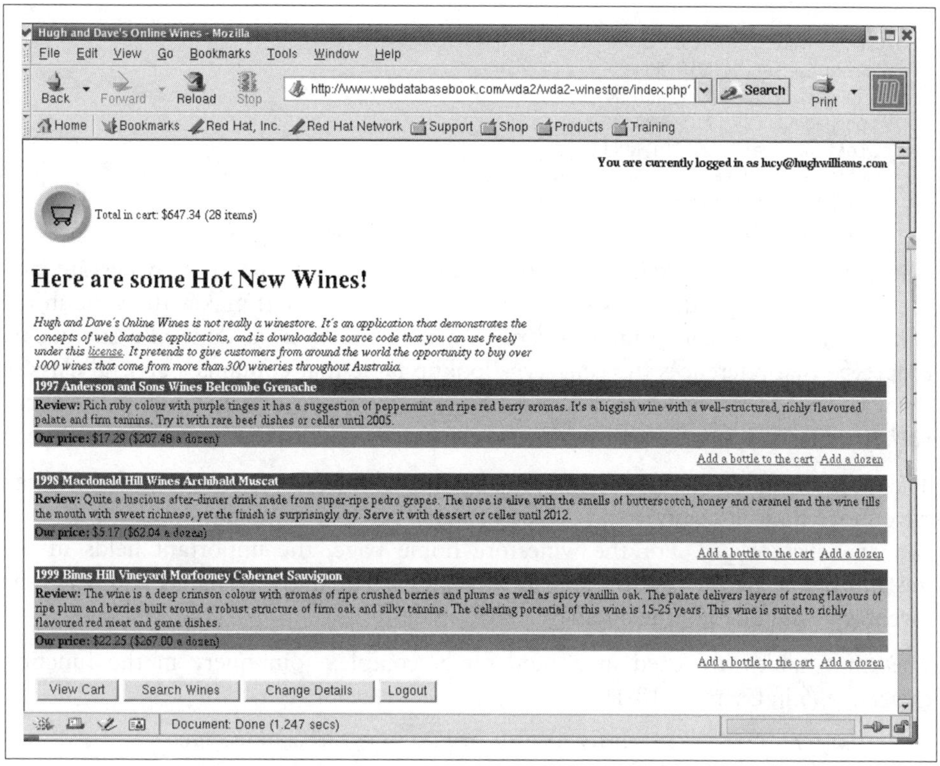

Figure 18-2. The winestore home page

To produce this information, the script queries the *wine*, *winery*, and *inventory* tables. These tables were created using the following statements:

```
CREATE TABLE wine (
  wine_id int(5) NOT NULL,
  wine_name varchar(50) NOT NULL,
  wine_type int(2) NOT NULL,
  year int(4) NOT NULL,
  winery_id int(4) NOT NULL,
  description blob,
  PRIMARY KEY (wine_id),
  KEY name (wine_name),
  KEY winery (winery_id)
) type=MyISAM;

CREATE TABLE winery (
  winery_id int(4) NOT NULL,
  winery_name varchar(100) NOT NULL,
  region_id int(4) NOT NULL,
  PRIMARY KEY (winery_id),
  KEY name (winery_name),
  KEY region (region_id)
) type=MyISAM;
```

```
CREATE TABLE inventory (
    wine_id int(5) NOT NULL,
    inventory_id int(3) NOT NULL,
    on_hand int(5) NOT NULL,
    cost decimal(5,2) NOT NULL,
    date_added date,
    PRIMARY KEY (wine_id,inventory_id)
) type=MyISAM;
```

The *wine* table stores details about the wines that are available in the winestore, and includes a winery_id that's used to reference the winery that makes the wine in the *winery* table. The *winery* table describes wineries. The *wine* table also includes a wine_type that references the *wine_type* lookup table that contains a general class of the wine such as red or white. It's also related to the *grape_variety* table via the *wine_variety* table, and this is used to maintain the grape varieties that make up the wine.

The *inventory* table stores information about stock at the winestore. Each wine can have more than one entry, and so the primary key is a combination of the wine_id and an inventory_id. For the winestore home page, the important fields in the *inventory* table are the cost of the wine, the on_hand quantity available, and when the inventory was added to the database (date_added).

The three tables are used in a moderately complex join query in the function *showPanel()* in Example 18-1:

```
$query = "SELECT  wi.winery_name, w.year, w.wine_name, w.wine_id,
                  w.description
          FROM wine w, winery wi, inventory i
          WHERE w.winery_id = wi.winery_id
          AND w.wine_id = i.wine_id
          AND w.description IS NOT NULL
          GROUP BY w.wine_id
          ORDER BY i.date_added DESC LIMIT 3";
```

The query finds the details of the three most-recently stocked wines that have been reviewed by a wine writer. The query uses table aliases, as discussed in Chapter 15, so that the query is more compact.

The WHERE clause joins together the *wine*, *winery*, and *inventory* tables, and ensures only reviewed wines—those with a description that isn't NULL—are returned. The GROUP BY clause is needed because, without it, the query returns one row for each inventory of a wine and so, if a wine had multiple inventories, the wine would appear multiple times. The ORDER BY clause uses the DESC modifier. The date_added isn't an attribute of the *wine*, it is a value from the latest-added *inventory*, and the LIMIT 3 ensures only the three latest-added inventories are retrieved.

Two external functions are called in the *showPanel()* function. The function *showVarieties()* displays the varieties of a specific wine and *showPricing()* is used to discover the cheapest bottle price of a wine. Both are part of the *winestore.inc* file discussed in Chapter 16.

Example 18-1. The index.php script that displays the winestore home page

```php
<?php
// This is the home page of the online winestore
require_once "DB.php";
require_once "includes/winestore.inc";
require_once "includes/template.inc";

set_error_handler("customHandler");

function showPanel($connection, &$template)
{
   // Find the hot new wines
   $query = "SELECT  wi.winery_name, w.year, w.wine_name, w.wine_id,
                     w.description
            FROM wine w, winery wi, inventory i
            WHERE w.winery_id = wi.winery_id
            AND w.wine_id = i.wine_id
            AND w.description IS NOT NULL
            GROUP BY w.wine_id
            ORDER BY i.date_added DESC LIMIT 3";

   // Run the query on the database through
   // the connection
   $result = $connection->query($query);
   if (DB::isError($result))
      trigger_error($result->getMessage( ), E_USER_ERROR);

   // Process the three new wines
   while ($row = $result->fetchRow(DB_FETCHMODE_ASSOC))
   {
      // Add the wine details to the template
      $template->setCurrentBlock("row");
      $template->setVariable("YEAR", $row["year"]);
      $template->setVariable("WINERY", $row["winery_name"]);
      $template->setVariable("WINE", $row["wine_name"]);
      $template->setVariable("DESCRIPTION", $row["description"]);
      $template->setVariable("VARIETIES",
                              showVarieties($connection, $row["wine_id"]));
      $price = showPricing($connection, $row["wine_id"]);
      $template->setVariable("BOTTLE_PRICE", sprintf("%.2f", $price));
      $template->setVariable("DOZEN_PRICE", sprintf("%.2f", ($price*12)));

      // Add a link to add one wine to the cart
      $template->setCurrentBlock("link");
      $template->setVariable("SCRIPT", S_ADDTOCART);
      $template->setVariable("QTY", "1");
      $template->setVariable("WINE_ID", $row["wine_id"]);
      $template->setVariable("STRING", "Add a bottle to the cart");
      $template->parseCurrentBlock("link");

      // Add a link to add a dozen wines to the cart
      $template->setVariable("SCRIPT", S_ADDTOCART);
      $template->setVariable("QTY", "12");
```

```
      $template->setVariable("WINE_ID", $row["wine_id"]);
      $template->setVariable("STRING", "Add a dozen");
      $template->parseCurrentBlock("link");

      $template->setCurrentBlock("row");
      $template->parseCurrentBlock("row");
  }
}

// ---------

session_start();

$template = new winestoreTemplate(T_HOME);

$connection = DB::connect($dsn, true);
if (DB::isError($connection))
  trigger_error($connection->getMessage(), E_USER_ERROR);

showPanel($connection, $template);

// Add buttons and messages, and show the page
$template->showWinestore(SHOW_ALL, B_ALL & ~B_UPDATE_CART &
                        ~B_HOME & ~B_PASSWORD &
                        ~B_PURCHASE & ~B_EMPTY_CART);
?>
```

The home page is produced using the template shown in Example 18-2. As explained in Chapter 16, winestore templates are included at runtime in the template *winestore.tpl* skeleton that's used for all winestore pages; this functionality is part of the constructor of the winestoreTemplate class that's also discussed in Chapter 16.

Example 18-2. The index.tpl home page template

```
<h1>Here are some Hot New Wines!</h1>
<table width="60%">
  <tr>
    <td><i>Hugh and Dave's Online Wines is not really a winestore.
    It's an application that demonstrates the concepts of web database
    applications, and is downloadable source code that you can use freely
    under this <a href="license.txt">license</a>. It pretends to
    give customers from around the world the opportunity to buy over
    1000 wines that come from more than 300 wineries throughout
    Australia.</i>
    </td>
  </tr>
</table>
<table border=0>
<!-- BEGIN row -->
  <tr>
```

Example 18-2. The index.tpl home page template (continued)

```
    <td bgcolor="maroon"><b><font color="white">
    {YEAR} {WINERY} {WINE} {VARIETIES}</font></b>
    </td>
  </tr>

  <tr>
    <td bgcolor="silver"><b>Review: </b>{DESCRIPTION}
    </td>
  </tr>

  <tr>
    <td bgcolor="gray">
    <b>Our price: </b>${BOTTLE_PRICE} (${DOZEN_PRICE} a dozen)
    </td>
  </tr>

  <tr>
    <td align="right">
<!-- BEGIN link -->
    <a href="{SCRIPT}?qty={QTY}&amp;wineId={WINE_ID}">{STRING}</a> 
<!-- END link -->
    </td>
  </tr>
  <tr>
    <td></td>
  </tr>
<!-- END row -->
</table>
```

The template page is structured using an HTML table environment to achieve distinct presentation of the three components for each wine: the details, the review, and the price. It has the following features:

- The information for a wine is represented over three table rows using three `<tr>` tags.

- Different background colors—maroon, silver, and gray—are set for each table row.

- The color attribute of the `<font>` tag is set to white for the heading of the wine.

- A blank row follows the wine for spacing in the presentation.

- An embedded link follows each wine that supports parameters being passed to the *cart/addtocart.php* script.

The row block in the template contains the placeholders that describe the wine and this is output three times by the script. It also contains a link block that produces an embedded link to the one-component querying script *cart/addtocart.php* that adds wines to the shopping cart. The link block is output twice by the script for each wine: once to produce a link to add one bottle to the shopping cart, and again to produce a link to add a dozen bottles to the cart.

The link block itself has four placeholders: SCRIPT is for the name of the script to request, QTY is the quantity of wine to add, WINE_ID is the unique identifier of the wine, and STRING is the textual link description to show the user.

The Shopping Cart Implementation

In Chapter 16, we introduced the requirements of the winestore shopping cart. A shopping cart is analogous to an incomplete order, in which each item in the cart is one or more bottles of a particular wine. Users can select any wine that is in stock to add to the cart, and wines in the cart can be purchased for up to one day after they have been added. The quantities of the wines can be updated by the user, and items in the cart can be deleted. In addition, the entire cart can be emptied.

We use the *orders* and *items* tables in the *winestore* database to manage the shopping cart. The *orders* table stores the date and time that the cart was created and a unique identifier for the cart. The *items* table stores the wine identifiers (wine_id values) of the wines in the cart, the quantity of each wine, and the price that the user has been offered (which is the cheapest price from any of the inventories for that wine). The tables have the following structure:

```
CREATE TABLE items (
  cust_id int(5) NOT NULL,
  order_id int(5) NOT NULL,
  item_id int(3) NOT NULL,
  wine_id int(4) NOT NULL,
  qty int(3),
  price decimal(5,2),
  PRIMARY KEY (cust_id,order_id,item_id)
) type=MyISAM;

CREATE TABLE orders (
  cust_id int(5) NOT NULL,
  order_id int(5) NOT NULL,
  date timestamp(12),
  PRIMARY KEY (cust_id,order_id)
) type=MyISAM;
```

We've omitted three attributes from the *orders* table that are only used in the ordering and shipping module discussed in Chapter 19. Also, for the shopping cart, the cust_id attribute is ignored: we set it to -1 for all shopping carts in both the *orders* and *items* tables so that we can distinguish shopping carts from actual customers. (In Chapter 19, we explain how to convert a shopping cart into an order, a process that involves a customer taking ownership of a shopping cart.) An alternative way to implement a shopping cart would have been to have two additional tables, say, *cart* and *cart_items*, but this isn't necessary if you set the cust_id to -1.

We use the *orders* and *items* tables as follows. When a user adds an item to his initially empty shopping cart, a new row is inserted into the *orders* table with a unique order_id. The order_id allocated to the user's cart is stored as a session variable. The existence of the session variable is used throughout the cart scripts to indicate that the shopping cart has contents, and the value of the variable is used as a key to retrieve its contents.

Shopping carts can be inspected using the MySQL command interpreter. First, you can inspect how many active shopping carts there are by checking the *orders* tables:

```
mysql> SELECT order_id, date FROM orders WHERE cust_id = -1;
+----------+--------------+
| order_id | date         |
+----------+--------------+
|        1 | 011210060918 |
|        2 | 011210061534 |
|        3 | 011210061817 |
|        4 | 011210063249 |
+----------+--------------+
4 rows in set (0.00 sec)
```

Having found that there are four shopping carts active in the system, you can inspect any cart to check its contents. Consider, for example, the contents of the fourth shopping cart with an order_id of 4:

```
mysql> SELECT item_id, wine_id, qty, price
       FROM items
       WHERE cust_id = -1 AND order_id = 4;
+---------+---------+------+-------+
| item_id | wine_id | qty  | price |
+---------+---------+------+-------+
|       1 |     624 |    4 | 22.25 |
|       2 |     381 |    1 | 20.86 |
+---------+---------+------+-------+
2 rows in set (0.00 sec)
```

From this simple inspection, we know there are four shopping carts, and the owner of the fourth cart has a total quantity (qty) of five bottles of two different wines in her cart.

Using database tables for shopping cart management is a good solution. Alternative approaches to managing shopping carts include using only PHP sessions and Java-Script on the client. The JavaScript approach is the least desirable because (as discussed in Chapter 9) JavaScript and the client should be considered unreliable. PHP sessions are a practical, simple solution, but storing data in disk files results in unnecessary disk activity and relies on the operating system to manage I/O efficiently. The default disk file session store can be replaced with a MySQL session store, as discussed in Appendix F, but the approach is still likely to be less efficient than dedicated database tables.

Throughout the rest of this section, we outline how the cart is implemented. Automatic emptying of the cart if the user doesn't proceed with the order within 24 hours is discussed in Chapter 15.

Viewing the Shopping Cart

Example 18-3 shows the *cart/showcart.php* script, which displays the contents of the shopping cart.

Example 18-3. The cart/showcart.php script that displays the cart's contents

```php
<?php
// This script shows the user the contents of their shopping cart

require_once "DB.php";
require_once "../includes/winestore.inc";
require_once "../includes/template.inc";

set_error_handler("customHandler");

// Show the user the contents of their cart
function displayCart($connection, &$template)
{
    // If the user has added items to their cart, then
    // the variable order_no will be registered
    if (isset($_SESSION["order_no"]))
    {
        // Set the action of the <form>
        $template->setVariable("S_UPDATECART", S_UPDATECART);

        // Find the items in the cart
        $cartQuery = "SELECT qty, price, wine_id, item_id
                      FROM items WHERE cust_id = -1
                      AND order_id = {$_SESSION["order_no"]}";
        $result = $connection->query($cartQuery);
        if (DB::isError($result))
            trigger_error($result->getMessage(), E_USER_ERROR);

        $cartAmount = 0;
        $cartCount = 0;

        // Go through each of the wines in the cart
        while ($row = $result->fetchRow(DB_FETCHMODE_ASSOC))
        {
            // Keep a running total of the number of items
            // and dollar-value of the items in the cart
            $cartCount += $row["qty"];
            $lineTotal = $row["price"] * $row["qty"];
            $cartAmount += $lineTotal;

            $template->setCurrentBlock("item");
            $template->setVariable("QUANTITY_NAME", $row["item_id"]);
            $template->setVariable("QUANTITY_VALUE", $row["qty"]);
            $template->setVariable("WINE",
                                   showWine($row["wine_id"], $connection));
            $template->setVariable("ITEM_PRICE",
                                   sprintf("%-.2f", $row["price"]));
```

```
        $template->setVariable("TOTAL_VALUE",
                            sprintf("%-.2f", $lineTotal));
        $template->parseCurrentBlock("item");
      }
      $template->setCurrentBlock("cart");
      $template->setVariable("TOTAL_ITEMS", $cartCount);
      $template->setVariable("TOTAL_COST", sprintf("%-.2f", $cartAmount));
      $template->parseCurrentBlock("cart");
    }
    else
    {
      // The user has not put anything in the cart
      $template->setCurrentBlock("emptycart");
      $template->setVariable("TEXT", "Your cart is empty");
      $template->parseCurrentBlock("emptycart");
    }
}

session_start();

$template = new winestoreTemplate(T_SHOWCART);

$connection = DB::connect($dsn, true);
if (DB::isError($connection))
  trigger_error($connection->getMessage(), E_USER_ERROR);

// Show the contents of the shopping cart
displayCart($connection, $template);

$template->showWinestore(SHOW_ALL, B_ALL & ~B_SHOW_CART &
                         ~B_PASSWORD & ~B_DETAILS);
?>
```

The body of the script is the *displayCart()* function, which queries and displays the contents of the shopping cart. The function checks if the cart has contents by testing for the presence of the session variable $_SESSION["order_no"]. If it's registered, its value is the order_id associated with the shopping cart, and the following query is executed:

```
$cartQuery = "SELECT qty, price, wine_id, item_id
              FROM items WHERE cust_id = -1
              AND order_id = {$_SESSION["order_no"]}";
```

The query retrieves the items in the user's cart, and the items are then displayed in an HTML table using the *showcart.tpl* template shown in Example 18-4. The function *showWine()* that returns the textual details of a wine is part of the *winestore.inc* include file and is discussed in Chapter 16.

Example 18-4. The showcart.tpl template for displaying the shopping cart

```
<!-- BEGIN cart -->
<h1>Your Shopping Cart</h1>
<form action="{S_UPDATECART}" method="GET">
<table border="0" cellpadding="0" cellspacing="5">
    <tr>
        <th>Quantity</th>
        <th>Wine</th>
        <th>Unit Price</th>
        <th>Total</th>
    </tr>
<!-- BEGIN item -->
    <tr>
        <td><input type="text" size=3 name="{QUANTITY_NAME}"
             value="{QUANTITY_VALUE}"></td>
        <td>{WINE}</td>
        <td>${ITEM_PRICE}</td>
        <td>${TOTAL_VALUE}</td>
    </tr>
<!-- END item -->
    <tr></tr>
    <tr>
        <td><b>{TOTAL_ITEMS} items</b></td>
        <td></td>
        <td></td>
        <td><b>${TOTAL_COST}</b></td>
    </tr>
</table>
<input type="submit" name="update" value="Update Quantities">
</form>
<!-- END cart -->
<!-- BEGIN emptycart -->
<h1><font color="red">{TEXT}</font></h1>
<!-- END emptycart -->
```

The quantities of each item in the cart are displayed within the table as input elements of a form. For example, consider the following HTML fragment that represents the second item in a user's cart:

```
<tr>
    <td><input type="text" size=3 name="2" value="12"></td>
    <td>1998 Macdonald Hill Wines Archibald Muscat</td>
    <td>$5.17</td>
    <td>$62.04</td>
</tr>
```

When rendered in a browser, this item displays a quantity of 12 bottles that can be edited by the user. The name of the input element is name="2", which means it's the second item in the cart. This matches the value of the item_id for the wine that's stored in the shopping cart's *items* table.

The input widget supports updates to the wine quantities as follows. If the user changes the quantity to 13 bottles and requests the *cart/updatecart.php* script to update the quantities, then the name and new value are passed to the script with the GET method as the string 2=13. This is then used to update the cart's second item to a quantity of 13 bottles. We discuss this process in more detail later in "Updating the Shopping Cart Quantities."

Adding Items to the Shopping Cart

Example 18-5 shows the *cart/addtocart.php* script, which adds items to the shopping cart. The script expects two parameters: a wineId that matches a wine_id in the *wine* table and a qty (quantity) of the wine to add to the cart. These parameters are supplied by clicking on embedded links on the homepage or the search page discussed in Chapter 19. For example, the homepage discussed earlier in this chapter contains links such as:

```
<a href="/wda2-winestore/cart/addtocart.php?qty=1&amp;wineId=191">
    Add a bottle to the cart</a>
```

When the user clicks on the link, the *cart/addtocart.php* script adds a bottle of the wine to the cart, database processing occurs, and the user is redirected to the calling page; the redirection doesn't work on all browsers (such as old versions of Internet Explorer) and we've included a work-around that redirects to the home page only when this problem occurs. This use of one-component querying for adding wines to the cart is discussed in more detail in Chapter 6.

The script in Example 18-5 has several steps:

1. It checks whether the shopping cart exists. If it does exist, it locks the *items* table for writing and the *inventory* table for reading. If the cart doesn't exist, the *orders* table is also locked for writing.

2. Locking is required because the script may suffer from the dirty read and lost update concurrency problems discussed in Chapter 8. These problems can occur if, for example, another user is simultaneously creating a shopping cart (without locking, both users may obtain the same cart number).

3. After locking the required tables, the script tests whether a cart already exists. If it doesn't exist, it is created as a new row in the *orders* table with the next available order_id. The order_id is then assigned to the session variable $_SESSION["order_no"]. If the cart does exist, the script checks if the item being added to the cart is already one of the items in the cart. If it is, the item_id is saved so that the quantity of the item can be updated. If it isn't in the cart, the next available item_id is assigned to the new wine.

4. If this is a new item being added to the cart, the script queries to find the cheapest inventory price for the wine. An error is reported if the wine has sold out by registering a message as a session variable; messages are displayed by all scripts that interact with the user through a call to the *showMessage()* method discussed in Chapter 12. It's unusual for wines to sell out: that occurs only if

another user purchases all the remaining stock of a wine before this user clicks on the embedded link.

5. After all checks of the cart and the inventory, the cart item is updated or inserted.

6. The table locks are released.

7. Finally, the script redirects to the calling page (or to the home page if the calling page can't be found), completing the one-component add-to-cart script.

Example 18-5. The cart/addtocart.php script that adds a quantity of a specific wine to the shopping cart

```php
<?php
// This script adds an item to the shopping cart
// It expects a WineId of the item to add and a
// quantity (qty) of the wine to be added

require_once "DB.php";
require_once "../includes/winestore.inc";

set_error_handler("customHandler");

// Have the correct parameters been provided?
if (empty($_GET["wineId"]) || empty($_GET["qty"]))
{
    $_SESSION["message"] = "Incorrect parameters to addtocart.php";
    header("Location: {$_SERVER["HTTP_REFERER"]}");
    exit;
}

session_start();

$connection = DB::connect($dsn, true);
if (DB::isError($connection))
  trigger_error($connection->getMessage(), E_USER_ERROR);

$wineId = pearclean($_GET, "wineId", 5, $connection);
$qty = pearclean($_GET, "qty", 3, $connection);

$update = false;

// If the user has added items to their cart, then
// the variable $_SESSION["order_no"] will be registered

// First, decide on which tables to lock
// We don't touch orders if the cart already exists
if (isset($_SESSION["order_no"]))
    $query = "LOCK TABLES inventory READ, items WRITE";
else
    $query = "LOCK TABLES inventory READ, items WRITE, orders WRITE";

// LOCK the tables
```

```
$result = $connection->query($query);
if (DB::isError($result))
   trigger_error($result->getMessage( ), E_USER_ERROR);

// Second, create a cart if we don't have one yet
// or investigate the cart if we do
if (!isset($_SESSION["order_no"]))
{
   // Find out the maximum order_id, then
   // register a session variable for the new order_id
   // A cart is an order for the customer with cust_id = -1
   $query = "SELECT max(order_id) FROM orders WHERE cust_id = -1";
   $result = $connection->query($query);
   if (DB::isError($result))
      trigger_error($result->getMessage( ), E_USER_ERROR);

   // Save the cart number as order_no
   // This is used in all cart scripts to access the cart
   $row = $result->fetchRow(DB_FETCHMODE_ASSOC);
   $_SESSION["order_no"] = $row["max(order_id)"] + 1;

   // Now, create the shopping cart
   $query = "INSERT INTO orders SET cust_id = -1,
             order_id = {$_SESSION["order_no"]}";

   $result = $connection->query($query);
   if (DB::isError($result))
      trigger_error($result->getMessage( ), E_USER_ERROR);

   // Default the item_id to 1
   $item_id = 1;
}
else
{
   // We already have a cart. Check if the customer already
   // has this item in their cart
   $query = "SELECT item_id, qty FROM items WHERE cust_id = -1
             AND order_id = {$_SESSION["order_no"]}
             AND wine_id = {$wineId}";
   $result = $connection->query($query);
   if (DB::isError($result))
      trigger_error($result->getMessage( ), E_USER_ERROR);

   // Is the item in the cart already?
   if ($result->numRows( ) > 0)
   {
      $update = true;
      $row = $result->fetchRow(DB_FETCHMODE_ASSOC);

      // Save the item number
      $item_id = $row["item_id"];
```

Example 18-5. The cart/addtocart.php script that adds a quantity of a specific wine to the shopping cart (continued)

```
   }

   // If this is not an update, find the next available item_id
   if ($update == false)
   {
      // We already have a cart, find the maximum item_id
      $query = "SELECT max(item_id) FROM items WHERE cust_id = -1
                AND order_id = {$_SESSION["order_no"]}";
      $result = $connection->query($query);
      if (DB::isError($result))
         trigger_error($result->getMessage( ), E_USER_ERROR);

      $row = $result->fetchRow(DB_FETCHMODE_ASSOC);

      // Save the item number of the new item
      $item_id = $row["max(item_id)"] + 1;
   }
}

// Third, add the item to the cart or update the cart
if ($update == false)
{
   // Get the cost of the wine
   // The cost comes from the cheapest inventory
   $query = "SELECT count(*), min(cost) FROM inventory
             WHERE wine_id = {$wineId}";
   $result = $connection->query($query);
   if (DB::isError($result))
      trigger_error($result->getMessage( ), E_USER_ERROR);

   $row = $result->fetchRow(DB_FETCHMODE_ASSOC);

   // This wine could have just sold out - check this
   // (this happens if another user buys the last bottle
   //  before this user clicks "add to cart")
   if ($row["count(*)"] == 0)
      // Register the error as a session variable
      // This message will then be displayed back on
      // page where the user adds wines to their cart
      $_SESSION["message"] =
        "Sorry! We just sold out of this great wine!";
   else
   {
      // We still have some of this wine, so save the
      // cheapest available price
      $cost = $row["min(cost)"];
      $query = "INSERT INTO items SET cust_id = -1,
                order_id = {$_SESSION["order_no"]},
                item_id = {$item_id}, wine_id = {$wineId}, qty = {$qty},
                price = {$cost}";
   }
}
```

Example 18-5. The cart/addtocart.php script that adds a quantity of a specific wine to the shopping cart (continued)

```
else
   $query = "UPDATE items SET qty = qty + {$qty}
                         WHERE cust_id = -1
                         AND order_id = {$_SESSION["order_no"]}
                         AND item_id = {$item_id}";

// Either UPDATE or INSERT the item
// (Only do this if there wasn't an error)
if (empty($_SESSION["message"]))
{
   $result = $connection->query($query);
   if (DB::isError($result))
      trigger_error($result->getMessage( ), E_USER_ERROR);
}

$result = $connection->query("UNLOCK TABLES");
if (DB::isError($result))
   trigger_error($result->getMessage( ), E_USER_ERROR);

// HTTP_REFERER isn't set by some browsers. If it isn't, then
// redirect to the main page.
if (isset($_SERVER["HTTP_REFERER"]))
  header("Location: {$_SERVER["HTTP_REFERER"]}");
else
  header("Location: " . S_MAIN);
?>
```

Emptying the Shopping Cart

Example 18-6 lists the *cart/emptycart.php* script that empties the shopping cart. The script is again a one-component module that carries out its actions, produces no output, and then redirects to the calling page. The script removes the row in the *orders* table and any rows in the *items* table that have an order_id equal to the value of the session variable $_SESSION["order_no"]. It then deletes the session variable itself, thus completing the emptying of the cart.

Example 18-6. The cart/emptycart.php script that empties the cart

```
<?php
// This script empties the cart and deletes the session variable

require_once "DB.php";
require_once "../includes/winestore.inc";

set_error_handler("customHandler");

// Initialise the session - this is needed before
// a session can be destroyed
session_start( );
```

Example 18-6. The cart/emptycart.php script that empties the cart (continued)

```php
// Is there a cart in the database?
if (isset($_SESSION["order_no"]))
{
   $connection = DB::connect($dsn, true);
   if (DB::isError($connection))
     trigger_error($connection->getMessage( ), E_USER_ERROR);

   // First, delete the order
   $query = "DELETE FROM orders WHERE cust_id = -1
             AND order_id = {$_SESSION["order_no"]}";
   $result = $connection->query($query);
   if (DB::isError($result))
     trigger_error($result->getMessage( ), E_USER_ERROR);

   // Now, delete the items
   $query = "DELETE FROM items WHERE cust_id = -1
             AND order_id = {$_SESSION["order_no"]}";
   $result = $connection->query($query);
   if (DB::isError($result))
     trigger_error($result->getMessage( ), E_USER_ERROR);

   // Finally, destroy the session variable
   unset($_SESSION["order_no"]);
}
else
   $_SESSION["message"] = "There is nothing in your cart.";

// HTTP_REFERER isn't set by some browsers. If it isn't, then
// redirect to the main page.
if (isset($_SERVER["HTTP_REFERER"]))
  header("Location: {$_SERVER["HTTP_REFERER"]}");
else
  header("Location: " . S_MAIN);
?>
```

Updating the Shopping Cart Quantities

The *cart/updatecart.php* script, which updates the quantities of items in the shopping cart, is shown in Example 18-7. The script is requested by the *cart/showcart.php* script and expects GET method parameters of item_id and update quantity pairs. For example, consider the following request for the script:

```
http://localhost/updatecart.php?1=12&2=13&3=6&update=Update+Quantities
```

This requests that the quantity of the first item in the cart be updated to 12 bottles, the second item to 13 bottles, and the third item to 6 bottles. The update parameter at the end of the URL is ignored.

The script works as follows:

1. It untaints the user data using the *pearclean()* function and assigns the results into the array parameters.

2. It uses the foreach loop statement to iterate through each parameter. For each parameter, it checks to ensure that the item_id and the quantity are both numbers of less than four or three digits in length, respectively. If this test fails, a message is registered as a session variable and displayed after the script redirects back to the *cart/showcart.php* script.

3. If the final quantity of the wine is zero, the item is deleted from the cart.

4. If the final quantity is non-zero, the quantity is updated to the value passed as a parameter.

5. If the cart is now empty (which happens if all items are set to zero quantities) the cart is deleted by removing the *cart* row from the *orders* table.

6. The script redirects to the *cart/showcart.php* script.

Example 18-7. The cart/updatecart.php script that updates the quantities of wines in the shopping cart

```php
<?php
// This script updates quantities in the cart
// It expects parameters of the form XXX=YYY
// where XXX is a wine_id and YYY is the new
// quantity of that wine that should be in the
// cart

require_once "DB.php";
require_once "../includes/winestore.inc";

set_error_handler("customHandler");

session_start();

$connection = DB::connect($dsn, true);
if (DB::isError($connection))
  trigger_error($connection->getMessage(), E_USER_ERROR);

// Clean up the data, and save the results in an array
foreach($_GET as $varname => $value)
    $parameters[$varname] = pearclean($_GET, $varname, 4, $connection);

// Did they want to update the quantities?
// (this should be true except if the user arrives here unexpectedly)
if (empty($parameters["update"]))
{
    $_SESSION["message"] = "Incorrect parameters to " . S_UPDATECART;
    header("Location: " . S_SHOWCART);
    exit;
}

// If the user has added items to their cart, then
// the session variable order_no will be registered

// Go through each submitted value and update the cart
```

```php
foreach($parameters as $itemName => $itemValue)
{
   // Ignore the update variable
   if ($itemName != "update")
   {
      // Does this item's name look like a wine_id?
      if (ereg("^[0-9]{1,4}$", $itemName))
      {
         // Is the update value a number?
         if (ereg("^[0-9]{1,3}$", $itemValue))
         {
            // If the number is zero, delete the item
            if ($itemValue == 0)
               $query = "DELETE FROM items WHERE cust_id = -1
                       AND order_id = {$_SESSION["order_no"]}
                       AND item_id = {$itemName}";
            else
              // otherwise, update the value
              $query = "UPDATE items SET qty = {$itemValue}
                      WHERE cust_id = -1
                      AND order_id = {$_SESSION["order_no"]}
                      AND item_id = {$itemName}";
            $result = $connection->query($query);
            if (DB::isError($result))
               trigger_error($result->getMessage( ), E_USER_ERROR);

         } // if (ereg("^[0-9]{1,3}$", $itemValue))
         else
           $_SESSION["message"] =
             "A quantity is non-numeric or an incorrect length.";
      } // if (ereg("^[0-9]{1,4}$", $itemName))
      else
        $_SESSION["message"] =
          "A wine identifier is non-numeric or an incorrect length.";
   } // if ($itemName != "update")
} // foreach($parameters as $itemName => $itemValue)

// The cart may now be empty. Check this.
$query = "SELECT count(*) FROM items WHERE cust_id = -1
        AND order_id = {$_SESSION["order_no"]}";
$result = $connection->query($query);
if (DB::isError($result))
   trigger_error($result->getMessage( ), E_USER_ERROR);

$row = $result->fetchRow(DB_FETCHMODE_ASSOC);

// Are there no items left?
if ($row["count(*)"] == 0)
{
   // Delete the order
   $query = "DELETE FROM orders WHERE cust_id = -1
```

```
            AND order_id = {$_SESSION["order_no"]}";
  $result = $connection->query($query);
  if (DB::isError($result))
     trigger_error($result->getMessage( ), E_USER_ERROR);

  unset($_SESSION["order_no"]);
}

// Go back to the cart
header("Location: " . S_SHOWCART);
?>
```

CHAPTER 19

Ordering and Shipping at the Online Winestore

This chapter is the fourth of five that outline the complete winestore application. In this chapter, we complete our description of the shopping components of the winestore by explaining the ordering and shipping modules. The ordering module collects and validates credit card details and manages the conversion of the shopping cart discussed in Chapter 18 to an order. In this process, the module manages the most complex database interactions in the winestore and uses locking to address concurrency problems.

The scripts discussed in this chapter perform the following functions:

Collect credit card and delivery details
> Collects a credit card number, expiration date, and optional delivery instructions. These are validated using the techniques discussed in Chapter 9.

Finalize orders
> Converts a shopping cart to an order and manages the sale of wine from the *inventory* table. This illustrates complex database processing that requires the locking techniques discussed in Chapter 8.

Email receipts
> Sends a confirmation email to the user using the PEAR Mail package and a template that illustrates how the templates described in Chapter 7 can be used for non-HTML applications. Code that uses the PHP *mail()* library function is also included, but is not enabled by default.

HTML order receipts
> Completes the ordering process with an HTML receipt that avoids the reload problem discussed in Chapter 6.

Code Overview

The ordering and shipping processes are implemented in the following scripts: *order/order-step1.php*, *order/order-step2.php*, *order/order-step3.php*, *order/order-step4.php*, and *order/receipt.php*.

The scripts work with the *orders*, *items*, and *inventory* tables discussed in Chapter 18:

```
CREATE TABLE orders (
    cust_id int(5) NOT NULL,
    order_id int(5) NOT NULL,
    date timestamp(12),
    instructions varchar(128),
    creditcard char(16),
    expirydate char(5),
    PRIMARY KEY (cust_id,order_id)
) type=MyISAM;

CREATE TABLE items (
    cust_id int(5) NOT NULL,
    order_id int(5) NOT NULL,
    item_id int(3) NOT NULL,
    wine_id int(4) NOT NULL,
    qty int(3),
    price float(5,2),
    date timestamp(12),
    PRIMARY KEY (cust_id,order_id,item_id)
) type=MyISAM;

CREATE TABLE inventory (
    wine_id int(5) NOT NULL,
    inventory_id int(3) NOT NULL,
    on_hand int(5) NOT NULL,
    cost decimal(5,2) NOT NULL,
    date_added date,
    PRIMARY KEY (wine_id,inventory_id)
) type=MyISAM;
```

The *orders* table includes the attributes instructions, creditcard, and expirydate that were omitted from our discussions in Chapter 18. These are used to store delivery and credit card details for each order that's shipped to a customer.

The script *order/order-step1.php* presents a form to the user that collects credit card and delivery details. The script is implemented using the same approach as the customer membership module in Chapter 17, and is based on the winestoreFormTemplate class discussed in detail in Chapter 16. Figure 19-1 shows the page rendered in a Mozilla browser.

The credit card details are validated using the script *order/order-step2.php*. This script makes use of the validation functions in the include file *validate.inc* that's discussed in Chapter 16. On validation failure, the script redirects back *order/order-step1.php*, which redisplays the erroneous data and error messages. On validation success, the script continues to the script *order/order-step3.php*. This process is discussed later in "Credit Card and Shipping Instructions."

Step three of the process, which is implemented in the script *order/order-step3.php*, performs the database processing that converts a shopping cart to an order that's owned by a customer. The script updates the *customer*, *order*, and *inventory* tables,

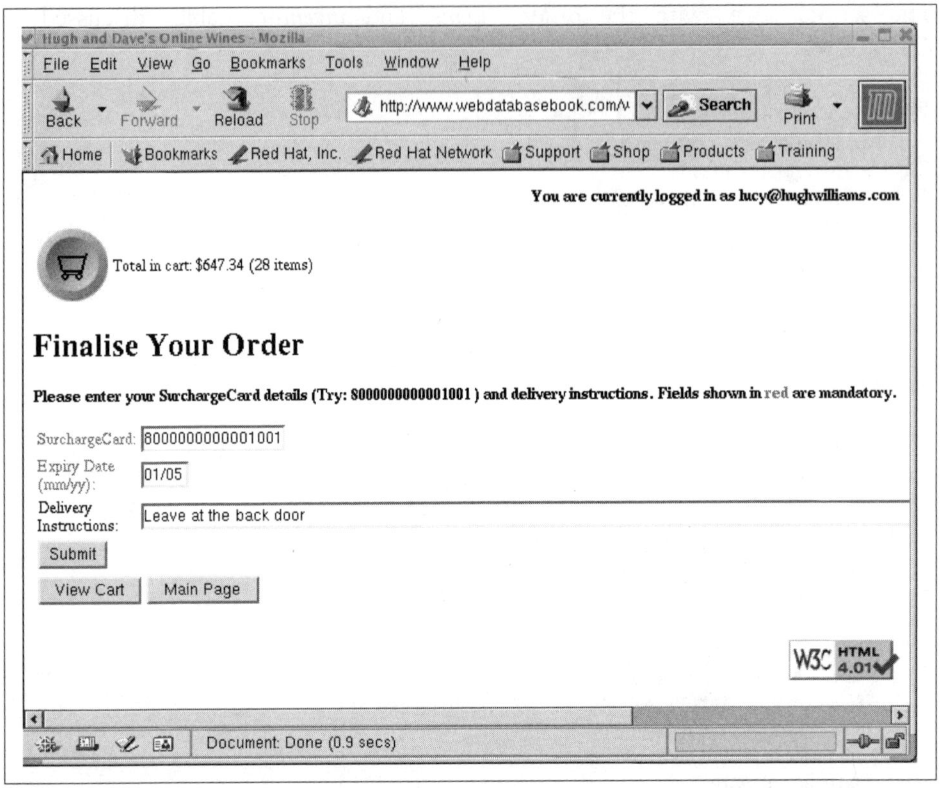

Figure 19-1. The form that collects credit card and delivery details

and checks for several error conditions that can occur, such as there being insufficient inventory to fulfill the order; details of this process are discussed later in "Finalizing Orders." On error, the script redirects back to *cart/showcart.php* script discussed in Chapter 18, and on success it redirects to *order/order-step4.php*. The script itself produces no output.

After the order has been finalized, two receipts are produced. The first is an email receipt output by the script *order/order-step4.php*. The email is produced using the same template approach used to prepare a HTML page, and sent with the PEAR Mail package; we also include alternative code that uses the PHP *mail()* library function. The script then redirects to the final script in this chapter, *order/receipt.php*, that shows the user their receipt as an HTML page as shown in Figure 19-2.

Credit Card and Shipping Instructions

When a user finishes adding items to his cart, he usually proceeds to a purchase. In the winestore, the first step after clicking on the *Make Purchase* button is entering credit card details and optional shipping instructions.

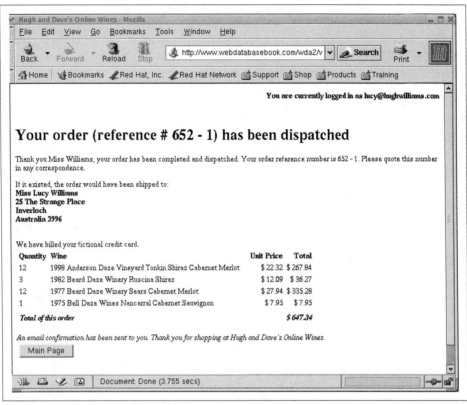

Figure 19-2. An HTML order receipt

The first steps of the ordering process are encapsulated in the *order/order-step1.php* and *order/order-step2.php* scripts shown in Example 19-1 and Example 19-2 respectively. The *order/order-step1.php* script collects credit card details and delivery instructions, and the *order/order-step2.php* script validates these and writes them to the *orders* table if they're valid. On validation failure, *order/order-step1.php* is re-requested and error messages are displayed above the data entry widgets and the widgets are repopulated with the erroneous data.

The scripts are implemented using the same approach as the customer management processes discussed in Chapter 17. The winestoreFormTemplate class that's described in Chapter 16 is used to display the form, and two session arrays are used to manage previously-entered data and error messages. The validation of credit card details is performed by functions that are discussed in detail in Chapter 9, and stored in the *validate.inc* include file that's listed in Chapter 16.

The credit card number is stored unencrypted. You can encrypt it using the two-way *mcrypt* library functions, which aren't installed on most platforms by default and are briefly discussed in Chapter 9. These functions are discussed at *http://www.php.net/ manual/en/ref.mcrypt.php*.

Example 19-1. The order/order-step1.php credit card and delivery details form

```php
<?php
// This script allows a user to enter their credit card number
// and delivery instructions.
// The user must be logged in to view it.

require_once "../includes/template.inc";
require_once "../includes/winestore.inc";
require_once "../includes/authenticate.inc";

set_error_handler("customHandler");

session_start();

// Check the user is properly logged in
sessionAuthenticate(S_SHOWCART);

// Takes form heading, instructions, action, formVars name, and
// formErrors name as parameters
$template = new winestoreFormTemplate("finalize Your Order",
            "Please enter your SurchargeCard details " .
            "(Try: 8000000000001001 ) and delivery instructions.",
            S_ORDER_2, "ccFormVars", "ccErrors");

// Create the credit card widgets
$template->mandatoryWidget("creditcard", "SurchargeCard:", 16);
$template->mandatoryWidget("expirydate", "Expiry Date (mm/yy):", 5);
$template->optionalWidget("instructions", "Delivery Instructions:", 128);

$template->showWinestore(SHOW_ALL, B_SHOW_CART | B_HOME);
?>
```

Example 19-2. The order/order-step2.php credit card validation and writing script

```php
<?php
require_once "DB.php";
require_once "../includes/winestore.inc";
require_once "../includes/authenticate.inc";
require_once "../includes/validate.inc";

set_error_handler("customHandler");

session_start();

// Connect to a authenticated session
sessionAuthenticate(S_SHOWCART);

// Check that the cart isn't empty
if (!isset($_SESSION["order_no"]))
{
    $_SESSION["message"] = "Your cart is empty!";

    header("Location: " . S_SHOWCART);
```

Example 19-2. The order/order-step2.php credit card validation and writing script (continued)

```php
   exit;
}

$connection = DB::connect($dsn, true);
if (DB::isError($connection))
   trigger_error($connection->getMessage( ), E_USER_ERROR);

// Register an error array - just in case!
$_SESSION["ccErrors"] = array( );

// Set up a formVars array for the POST variables
$_SESSION["ccFormVars"] = array( );

foreach($_POST as $varname => $value)
   $_SESSION["ccFormVars"]["{$varname}"] =
     pearclean($_POST, $varname, 128, $connection);

// Check if mandatory credit card entered
if (checkMandatory("creditcard", "SurchargeCard",
              "ccErrors", "ccFormVars"))
   // Validate credit card using Luhn algorithm
   checkCard("creditcard", "ccErrors", "ccFormVars");

// Check if mandatory credit card expiry entered
if (checkMandatory("expirydate", "expiry date",
              "ccErrors", "ccFormVars"))
   // Validate credit card expiry date
   checkExpiry("expirydate", "ccErrors", "ccFormVars");

// Now the script has finished the validation,
// check if there were any errors
if (count($_SESSION["ccErrors"]) > 0)
{
   // There are errors.  Relocate back to step #1
   header("Location: " . S_ORDER_1);
   exit;
}

// OK to update the order
$query = "UPDATE orders SET
         creditcard = '{$_SESSION["ccFormVars"]["creditcard"]}',
         expirydate = '{$_SESSION["ccFormVars"]["expirydate"]}',
         instructions = '{$_SESSION["ccFormVars"]["instructions"]}'
         WHERE cust_id = -1 AND
               order_id = {$_SESSION["order_no"]}";

$result = $connection->query($query);

if (DB::isError($result))
   trigger_error($result->getMessage( ), E_USER_ERROR);

// Clear the formVars so a future <form> is blank
```

Example 19-2. The order/order-step2.php credit card validation and writing script (continued)

```
unset($_SESSION["ccFormVars"]);
unset($_SESSION["ccErrors"]);

// Relocate to the order processing
header("Location: " . S_ORDER_3);
?>
```

Finalizing Orders

After entering valid credit card details and optional delivery instructions, the next step in the ordering process is to turn the shopping cart into an order that's owned by a customer. This requires several steps that include checking that sufficient inventory is available to complete the order and deducting the wines sold from the inventory.

The order finalization requires locking of the database and is an example of the moderately complex query processing that described in Chapter 8. Locking prevents several undesirable problems. For example, locking prevents the same inventory being purchased by two users at the same time. It also prevents unlikely problems such as the same user finalizing two separate orders at the same time in two browser windows and confusing the application.

The script *order/order-step3.php* shown in Example 19-3, later in this section, performs the ordering process. The script works as follows:

1. It tests that the user is logged in (using the *sessionAuthenticate()* function discussed in Chapter 20) and that the cart has contents. These tests should never fail, as the *Make Purchase* button is shown only when the user is viewing the cart, is logged in, and the cart has contents. If either test fails, an error message is registered, and the script redirects to the *cart/showcart.php* script.

2. The *inventory*, *items*, and *orders* tables are locked for writing, and the *users* and *customer* tables are locked for reading. The *inventory*, *items*, and *orders* tables are all updated in the purchasing process, and they must be locked because the inventory is first checked to ensure that sufficient quantities of wine are available and then later updated.

   Without locking, it's possible for another user to purchase the wine while this script is running, resulting in more wine being sold than is in stock. This is an example of the dirty read concurrency problem discussed in Chapter 8, and locking must be used to avoid the problem.

3. Each item in the cart is then processed, and the inventory is checked to ensure that enough wine is available. If no wine is available (the *count()* of the matching inventory rows is zero) an error message is registered. Similarly, if less wine is available than the user wants (the *sum()* of the on_hand quantity of the matching rows is less than the shopping cart qty) an error message is also registered. On error, the script also updates the shopping cart so that the quantity (qty) of wine in the cart matches the quantity that is on_hand.

4. In the case of an error, the script uses the function *showWine()* to find the details of the wine. It opens its own connection to the DBMS so that the *wine*, *wine_variety*, *winery*, and *grape_variety* tables don't need to be locked for reading in the *order/order-step3.php* script. The function is part of *winestore.inc* and is discussed in Chapter 16.

5. If the inventory checks succeed, the script proceeds to convert the shopping cart to be a customer order. This process is straightforward, and is encapsulated in the next three steps.

6. The first step of converting a cart to an order is to determine the customer's cust_id from the $_SESSION["loginUsername"] variable using the function *getCust_id()* that's described in Chapter 16.

7. The second step is to find the maximum order_id for this customer so that the next order_id can be assigned to the new order.

8. The third and final step is to update the *orders* and *items* rows by replacing the cust_id of -1 with the customer's cust_id (obtained in Step 5) and the order_id with the next available order_id (obtained in Step 6) for this customer.

9. After the database has been updated, the cart is emptied using unset($_SESSION["order_no"]); to remove the session variable.

10. Having completed the order and checked the inventory, the script finishes the ordering process by reducing the inventory. This can never fail, because all required tables are locked and we've checked that sufficient quantities are available.

    The process is similar to checking the cart as described in Step 3: we iterate through each item and, for each one, we update the inventory. The inventories are processed from oldest to newest. Consider an example in which the user wants to purchase 24 bottles of a wine. Suppose there are two inventories of this wine: the first has 13 bottles and was added in May 2000; the second has 25 bottles and was added in September 2001. To satisfy the order, the oldest inventory of 13 bottles is emptied and deleted, and the second inventory is reduced by 11 bottles.

11. With the process complete, the tables are unlocked. If there are no errors, the script redirects to the *order/order-step4.php* script to confirm the order, and the cust_id and order_id are passed as GET method parameters. If there are errors, the user is returned to the cart view page, *cart/showcart.php*.

Example 19-3. The order/order-step3.php script that finalizes the user's purchase

```
<?php
// This script finalizes a purchase
// It expects that a cart has contents and that the
// user is logged in

require_once "DB.php";
require_once "../includes/winestore.inc";
```

Example 19-3. The order/order-step3.php script that finalizes the user's purchase (continued)

```
require_once "../includes/authenticate.inc";

set_error_handler("customHandler");

session_start();

// Connect to a authenticated session
sessionAuthenticate(S_SHOWCART);

// Check that the cart isn't empty
if (!isset($_SESSION["order_no"]))
{
   $_SESSION["message"] = "Your cart is empty!";

   header("Location: " . S_SHOWCART);
   exit;
}

$connection = DB::connect($dsn, true);
if (DB::isError($connection))
   trigger_error($connection->getMessage(), E_USER_ERROR);

// Several tables must be locked to finalize a purchase.
$query = "LOCK TABLES inventory WRITE,
                      orders WRITE,
                      items WRITE,
                      users READ,
                      customer READ";

$result = $connection->query($query);
if (DB::isError($result))
   trigger_error($result->getMessage(), E_USER_ERROR);

// Process each wine in the cart and find out if there is sufficient
// stock available in the inventory
$query = "SELECT * FROM items
         WHERE cust_id = -1
         AND order_id = {$_SESSION["order_no"]}";

// initialize an empty error message
$_SESSION["message"] = "";

$result = $connection->query($query);
if (DB::isError($result))
   trigger_error($result->getMessage(), E_USER_ERROR);

// Get the next wine in the cart
for ($winesInCart = 0;
     $winesInCart < $result->numRows();
     $winesInCart++)
{
   $cartRow[$winesInCart] = $result->fetchRow(DB_FETCHMODE_ASSOC);
```

```php
    // Is there enough of this wine on hand?
    $query = "SELECT COUNT(on_hand), SUM(on_hand)
              FROM inventory
              WHERE wine_id = {$cartRow[$winesInCart]["wine_id"]}";

    $stockResult = $connection->query($query);
    if (DB::isError($stockResult))
       trigger_error($stockResult->getMessage( ), E_USER_ERROR);

    $on_hand = $stockResult->fetchRow(DB_FETCHMODE_ASSOC);

    if ($on_hand["COUNT(on_hand)"] == 0)
       $available = 0;
    else
       $available = $on_hand["SUM(on_hand)"];

    // Is there more wine in the cart than is for sale?
    if ($cartRow[$winesInCart]["qty"] > $available)
    {

       if ($available == 0)
          $_SESSION["message"] = "Sorry! We just sold out of " .
                    showWine($cartRow[$winesInCart]["wine_id"], NULL) .
                    "\n<br>";
       else
          $_SESSION["message"] .=
                    "Sorry! We only have {$on_hand["SUM(on_hand)"]}
                    bottles left of " .
                    showWine($cartRow[$winesInCart]["wine_id"], NULL) .
                    "\n<br>";

       // Update the user's quantity to match the available amount
       $query = "UPDATE items
                 SET qty = {$available}
                 WHERE cust_id = -1
                 AND order_id = {$_SESSION["order_no"]}
                 AND item_id = {$cartRow[$winesInCart]["item_id"]}";

       $result = $connection->query($query);
       if (DB::isError($result))
          trigger_error($result->getMessage( ), E_USER_ERROR);
    }
} // for $winesInCart < $result->numRows( )

// We have now checked if there is enough wine available.
// If there is, we can proceed with the order. If not, we
// send the user back to the amended cart to consider whether
// to proceed with the order.

if (empty($_SESSION["message"]))
{
    // Everything is ok - let's proceed then!
```

Example 19-3. The order/order-step3.php script that finalizes the user's purchase (continued)

```
// First of all, find out the user's cust_id and
// the next available order_id for this customer.
$cust_id = getCust_id($_SESSION["loginUsername"], $connection);

$query = "SELECT max(order_id)
           FROM orders
           WHERE cust_id = {$cust_id}";
$result = $connection->query($query);
if (DB::isError($result))
   trigger_error($result->getMessage( ), E_USER_ERROR);

$row = $result->fetchRow(DB_FETCHMODE_ASSOC);

$newOrder_no = $row["max(order_id)"] + 1;

// Now, change the cust_id and order_id of their cart!
$query = "UPDATE orders SET
           cust_id = {$cust_id},
           order_id = {$newOrder_no}
           WHERE order_id = {$_SESSION["order_no"]}
           AND cust_id = -1";

$result = $connection->query($query);
if (DB::isError($result))
   trigger_error($result->getMessage( ), E_USER_ERROR);

$query = "UPDATE items SET
           cust_id = {$cust_id},
           order_id = {$newOrder_no}
           WHERE order_id = {$_SESSION["order_no"]}
           AND cust_id = -1";

$result = $connection->query($query);
if (DB::isError($result))
   trigger_error($result->getMessage( ), E_USER_ERROR);

// Empty the cart
unset($_SESSION["order_no"]);

// Now we have to update the inventory.
// We do this one cart item at a time.
// For all items, we know that there *is*
// sufficient inventory, since we've checked earlier
foreach($cartRow as $currentRow)
{
   // Find the inventory rows for this wine, oldest first
   $query = "SELECT inventory_id, on_hand
             FROM inventory
             WHERE wine_id = {$currentRow["wine_id"]}
             ORDER BY date_added";

   $result = $connection->query($query);
```

```php
        if (DB::isError($result))
           trigger_error($result->getMessage( ), E_USER_ERROR);

        // While there are still bottles to be deducted
        while($currentRow["qty"] > 0)
        {
            // Get the next-oldest inventory
            $row = $result->fetchRow(DB_FETCHMODE_ASSOC);

            // Is there more wine in this inventory than the user wants?
            if ($row["on_hand"] > $currentRow["qty"])
            {
                // Reduce the inventory by the amount the user ordered
                $query = "UPDATE inventory SET
                        on_hand = on_hand - {$currentRow["qty"]}
                        WHERE wine_id = {$currentRow["wine_id"]}
                        AND inventory_id = {$row["inventory_id"]}";

                // The user doesn't need any more of this wine
                $currentRow["qty"] = 0;
            }
            else
            {
                // Remove the inventory - we sold the remainder to
                // this user
                $query = "DELETE FROM inventory
                        WHERE wine_id = {$currentRow["wine_id"]}
                        AND inventory_id = {$row["inventory_id"]}";

                // This inventory reduces the customer's required
                // amount by at least 1, but we need to process more
                // inventory
                $currentRow["qty"] -= $row["on_hand"];
            }

            // UPDATE or DELETE the inventory
            $result = $connection->query($query);
            if (DB::isError($result))
                trigger_error($result->getMessage( ), E_USER_ERROR);
        }
    }
}
else
    $_SESSION["message"] .=
      "\n<br>The quantities in your cart have been updated\n.";

// Last, UNLOCK the tables
$result = $connection->query("UNLOCK TABLES");
if (DB::isError($result))
   trigger_error($result->getMessage( ), E_USER_ERROR);

// Redirect to the email confirmation page if everything is ok
// (supply the cust_id and order_id to the script)
```

Example 19-3. The order/order-step3.php script that finalizes the user's purchase (continued)

```
// otherwise go back to the cart page and show a message
if (empty($_SESSION["message"]))
{
   header("Location: " . S_ORDER_4 .
          "?cust_id={$cust_id}&order_id={$newOrder_no}");
   exit;
}
else
   header("Location: " . S_SHOWCART);
?>
```

HTML and Email Receipts

After an order has been processed, the winestore application confirms the shipping of the wines through both an email and an HTML receipt. The *order/order-step4.php* script sends the user an email. In turn, the *order/order-step4.php* script redirects to the *order/receipt.php* script which produces the HTML receipt.

The HTML receipt can be visited again at a later time by bookmarking the URL. As it carries out no database updates, it doesn't suffer from the reload problem described in Chapter 6. The receipt functionality is separated into two scripts so that returning to the HTML receipt doesn't cause an additional email receipt to be sent to the customer.

Email Receipt

Example 19-4 shows the *order/order-step4.php* script that sends an email receipt to the user. The function *send_confirmation_email()* creates the email body, destination address, subject, and additional headers of an email message, and then sends that email message. To do so, it uses the template that's shown in Example 19-5 and stored in the file *templates/email.tpl*.

Example 19-4. The order/order-step4.php script sends an order confirmation as an email

```
<?php
// This script sends the user a confirmation email for their order
// and then redirects to an HTML receipt version

// By default, this script uses PEAR's Mail package.
// To use PHP's internal mail() function instead, change "true" to "false"
// in the following line
define("USE_PEAR", true);

require_once "DB.php";
require_once "HTML/Template/ITX.php";
require_once "../includes/winestore.inc";
require_once "../includes/authenticate.inc";
```

```php
// Use the PEAR Mail package if USE_PEAR is defined
if (USE_PEAR == true)
  require_once "Mail.php";

set_error_handler("customHandler");

// Send the user an email that summarises their purchase
function send_confirmation_email($custID, $orderID, $connection)
{
    $template = new HTML_Template_ITX(D_TEMPLATES);
    $template->loadTemplatefile(T_EMAIL, true, true);

    // Find customer information
    $query = "SELECT * FROM customer, users
            WHERE customer.cust_id = {$custID}
            AND users.cust_id = customer.cust_id";

    $result = $connection->query($query);
    if (DB::isError($result))
        trigger_error($result->getMessage( ), E_USER_ERROR);
    $row = $result->fetchRow(DB_FETCHMODE_ASSOC);

    // Start by setting up the "To:" email address
    $to = "{$row["firstname"]} {$row["surname"]} <{$row["user_name"]}>";

    // Now setup all the customer fields
    $template->setVariable("TITLE", showTitle($row["title_id"],
                            $connection));
    $template->setVariable("SURNAME", $row["surname"]);
    $template->setVariable("CUST_ID", $custID);
    $template->setVariable("ORDER_ID", $orderID);
    $template->setVariable("FIRSTNAME", $row["firstname"]);
    $template->setVariable("INITIAL", $row["initial"]);
    $template->setVariable("ADDRESS", $row["address"]);
    $template->setVariable("CITY", $row["city"]);
    $template->setVariable("STATE", $row["state"]);
    $template->setVariable("COUNTRY", showCountry($row["country_id"],
                            $connection));
    $template->setVariable("ZIPCODE", $row["zipcode"]);

    $orderTotalPrice = 0;

    // list the particulars of each item in the order
    $query = "SELECT  i.qty, w.wine_name, i.price,
                    w.wine_id, w.year, wi.winery_name
            FROM    items i, wine w, winery wi
            WHERE   i.cust_id = {$custID}
            AND     i.order_id = {$orderID}
            AND     i.wine_id = w.wine_id
            AND     w.winery_id = wi.winery_id
            ORDER BY item_id";
```

```php
$result = $connection->query($query);
if (DB::isError($result))
   trigger_error($result->getMessage( ), E_USER_ERROR);

// Add each item to the email
while ($row = $result->fetchRow(DB_FETCHMODE_ASSOC))
{
  // Work out the cost of this line item
  $itemsPrice = $row["qty"] * $row["price"];

  $orderTotalPrice += $itemsPrice;

  $wineDetail = showWine($row["wine_id"], $connection);

  $template->setCurrentBlock("row");
  $template->setVariable("QTY", str_pad($row["qty"],9));
  $template->setVariable("WINE",
                          str_pad(substr($wineDetail, 0, 53), 55));
  $template->setVariable("PRICE",
                          str_pad(sprintf("$%4.2f" ,
                          $row["price"]), 11));
  $template->setVariable("TOTAL",
                          str_pad(sprintf("$%4.2f", $itemsPrice), 12));
  $template->parseCurrentBlock("row");
}

$template->setCurrentBlock("items");
$template->setVariable("ORDER_TOTAL",
                        sprintf("$%4.2f\n", $orderTotalPrice));
$template->parseCurrentBlock("items");
$template->setCurrentBlock( );
$template->parseCurrentBlock( );

$out = $template->get( );

if (USE_PEAR == false)
{
  // ------------------------------------------
  // The internal PHP mail( ) function is used only if USE_PEAR is false

  // Now, setup the "Subject:" line
  $subject = "Hugh and Dave's Online Wines: Order Confirmation";

  // And, last (before we build the email), set up some mail headers
  $headers  = "From: Hugh and Dave's Online Wines " .
             "<help@webdatabasebook.com>\r\n";
  $headers .= "X-Sender: <help@webdatabasebook.com>\r\n";
  $headers .= "X-Mailer: PHP\r\n";
  $headers .= "Return-Path: <help@webdatabasebook.com>\r\n";

  // Send the email!
  mail($to, $subject, $out, $headers);
```

Example 19-4. The order/order-step4.php script sends an order confirmation as an email (continued)

```
    // -------------------------------------------
  }
  else
  {
    // -------------------------------------------
    // Use the PEAR Mail package and SMTP since USE_PEAR is true

    // Now, setup the "Subject:" line
    $headers["Subject"] =
      "Hugh and Dave's Online Wines: Order Confirmation";

    // And, last (before we build the email), set up some mail headers
    $headers["From"] = "Hugh and Dave's Online Wines " .
                        "<help@webdatabasebook.com>";
    $headers["X-Sender"] = "<help@webdatabasebook.com>";
    $headers["X-Mailer"] = "PHP";
    $headers["Return-Path"] = "<help@webdatabasebook.com>";

    $smtpMail =& Mail::factory("smtp");
    $smtpMail->send($to, $headers, $out);
    // -------------------------------------------
  }
}

// ----------

session_start();

// Connect to a authenticated session
sessionAuthenticate(S_SHOWCART);

// Check the correct parameters have been passed
if (!isset($_GET["cust_id"]) || !isset($_GET["order_id"]))
{
  $_SESSION["message"] =
    "Incorrect parameters to order-step4.php";
  header("Location: " . S_SHOWCART);
  exit;
}

// Check this customer matches the $cust_id
$connection = DB::connect($dsn, true);

if (DB::isError($connection))
  trigger_error($connection->getMessage(), E_USER_ERROR);

$cust_id = pearclean($_GET, "cust_id", 5, $connection);
$order_id = pearclean($_GET, "order_id", 5, $connection);

$real_cust_id = getCust_id($_SESSION["loginUsername"]);

if ($cust_id != $real_cust_id)
  $_SESSION["message"] = "You can only view your own receipts!";
```

Example 19-4. The order/order-step4.php script sends an order confirmation as an email (continued)

```
    header("Location: " . S_HOME);
    exit;
}

// Send the user a confirmation email
send_confirmation_email($cust_id, $order_id, $connection);

// Redirect to a receipt page (this can't be the receipt page,
// since the reload problem would cause extra emails).
header("Location: " . S_ORDERRECEIPT .
      "?cust_id={$cust_id}&order_id={$order_id}");
?>
```

Example 19-5. The template templates/email.tpl that's used to compose an email receipt

```
Dear {TITLE} {SURNAME},

Thank you for placing an order at Hugh and Dave's Online Wines. This email
is best viewed in a fixed-width font such as Courier.

Your fictional order (reference # {CUST_ID} - {ORDER_ID}) has been
dispatched. Please quote this number in any correspondence.

If it existed, the order would have been shipped to:
{TITLE} {FIRSTNAME} {INITIAL} {SURNAME}
{ADDRESS}
{CITY} {STATE}
{COUNTRY} {ZIPCODE}

We have billed your fictional SurchargeCard credit card.

Your fictional order contains:
<!-- BEGIN items -->
Quantity Wine                                    Unit Price Total
<!-- BEGIN row -->
{QTY}{WINE}{PRICE}{TOTAL}
<!-- END row -->
Total of this order: {ORDER_TOTAL}
<!-- END items -->

Thank you for shopping at Hugh and Dave's Online Wines!

Kind Regards,


Hugh and Dave, http://www.webdatabasebook.com/
```

The destination $to address is created using the firstname, surname, and user_name (which is the email address) attributes of the customer that are retrieved from the *customer* and *users* tables. For example, with a surname value of Smith, a firstname of Michael, and a user_name of mike@webdatabasebook.com, it has the following format:

```
Michael Smith <mike@webdatabasebook.com>
```

The additional email headers are static and always have the following format:

```
From: "Hugh and Dave's Online Wines" <help@webdatabasebook.com>
X-Sender: <help@webdatabasebook.com>
X-Mailer: PHP
Return-Path: <help@webdatabasebook.com>
```

The subject of the email is always:

```
Hugh and Dave's Online Wines: Order Confirmation
```

The body of the message is created by querying and retrieving the details of the *customer*, *orders*, and *items* tables and setting variables in the template. The following is an example of the body of a confirmation email:

```
Dear Dr Smith,

Thank you for placing an order at Hugh and Dave's Online Wines. This email
is best viewed in a fixed-width font such as Courier.

Your fictional order (reference # 651 - 12) has been
dispatched. Please quote this number in any correspondence.

If it existed, the order would be shipped to:

Dr Michael Smith
12 Hotham St.
Collingwood Victoria 3066
Australia

We have billed your fictional SurchargeCard credit card.

Your fictional order contains:

Quantity  Wine                        Unit Price  Total
12        1999 Smith's Chardonnay     $22.25      $267.00

Total: $267.00

Thank you for shopping at Hugh and Dave's Online Wines!

Kind Regards,


Hugh and Dave, http://www.webdatabasebook.com/
```

In our template examples so far, the *HTML_Template_IT::show()* method is used to output data to the browser. However, in this case, we don't want to output the data to the browser and so we use the *HTML_Template_IT::get()* method instead. This method returns the template as a string after all placeholder replacements have been made, and we assign the return value to the variable $out. The variable is used as a parameter to the mailing method. The *HTML_Template_IT::get()* method is described in Chapter 7.

The email itself is sent using the PEAR Mail package with the following fragment:

```
$smtpMail =& Mail::factory("smtp");
$smtpMail->send($to, $headers, $out);
```

The Mail class supports three different ways of sending email, and we use a Simple Mail Transfer Protocol (SMTP) server in this example to send the email. The class is discussed in the next section.

The body of the script also checks that the user is logged in, that the correct parameters of a cust_id and an order_id have been provided, and that the user viewing the receipt is the owner of the receipt. If any of the checks fail, the user is redirected so that an error message can be displayed.

The PEAR Mail package

The PEAR Mail package is used to send the order confirmation receipt by connecting to an SMTP server. PEAR Mail works well, but requires that you install the Mail package by following the package installation instructions in Chapter 7. If you don't want to use the PEAR Mail package, then change the *define()* at beginning of the file *order/order-step4.php* shown in Example 19-4 to:

```
define("USE_PEAR", false);
```

When PEAR Mail isn't used, the PHP library function *mail()* is used instead. Without additional configuration, *mail()* only works on Unix platforms.

After installation, using PEAR's Mail package requires only two simple steps: first, create an instance of a mailer backend; and, second, send the email. There are three choices of backends:

Simple Mail Transfer Protocol (SMTP) server
> This is most generic approach, as it doesn't rely on having specific software installed on the web server, and is portable across all PHP platforms. The disadvantage is that it requires an SMTP server, and these sometimes require username and password credentials, or can be configured in a non-standard way.

The internal PHP mail() function
> Without additional configuration, this only works on Unix platforms. Under Microsoft Windows, it needs to be configured to use an SMTP-based approach.

The Unix sendmail program
> This only works on Unix platforms. (It also supports other mail sending programs that have a wrapper that makes them look like sendmail).

We create the backend in our code using:

```
$smtpMail =& Mail::factory("smtp");
```

However, the *Mail::factory()* method for the SMTP mailer also supports an optional second array parameter $params that can contain the following associative elements:

`$params["host"]`

The *host* name of the SMTP server. It's set to localhost by default.

`$params["post"]`

The *port* number of the SMTP server. Set to 25 by default.

`$params["auth"]`

Whether to use SMTP authentication. Set to false by default.

`$params["username"]`

The *username* to use for authentication. No default value.

`$params["password"]`

The *password* to use for authentication. No default value.

In general, the defaults work for most Unix installations. If you don't have a mailer installed on your server or you're using Microsoft Windows, then try setting `$params["host"]` to your ISP's mail server. For example, if you were a customer of *bigpond.com*, you would use:

```
$params["host"] = "mail.bigpond.com";
$smtpMail =& Mail::factory("smtp", $params);
```

If you want to use PHP's internal *mail( )* function with PEAR Mail, then use:

```
$smtpMail =& Mail::factory("mail");
$smtpMail->send($to, $headers, $out);
```

It has no additional parameters.

If you want to use the Unix sendmail backend, then use:

```
$smtpMail =& Mail::factory("sendmail");
$smtpMail->send($to, $headers, $out);
```

The *factory( )* method for the sendmail mailer also supports the optional second array parameter $params that can contain the following associative elements:

`$params["sendmail_path"]`

The path to the sendmail program. By default it's */usr/bin/sendmail*.

`$params["sendmail_args"]`

Additional arguments to the sendmail program. There's none by default.

HTML Receipts

Example 19-6 shows the *order/receipt.php* script that confirms the shipping of an order using HTML. The script has an identical structure to *order/order-step4.php* and executes the same queries. The only difference is that the script outputs HTML rather than creating a template that's emailed to the customer. The template that's used with the script is shown in Example 19-7; as with other templates in the winestore, the `winestoreTemplate` class that's explained in Chapter 16 is used to display the page.

Example 19-6. The order/receipt.php script confirms an order as an HTML receipt

```php
<?php
// This script shows the user an HTML receipt

require_once "DB.php";
require_once "../includes/template.inc";
require_once "../includes/winestore.inc";
require_once "../includes/authenticate.inc";

set_error_handler("customHandler");

function show_HTML_receipt($custID, $orderID, $connection)
{
   $template = new winestoreTemplate(T_ORDERRECEIPT);

   // Find customer information
   $query = "SELECT * FROM customer, users
            WHERE customer.cust_id = {$custID}
            AND users.cust_id = customer.cust_id";
   $result = $connection->query($query);
   if (DB::isError($result))
      trigger_error($result->getMessage( ), E_USER_ERROR);

   $row = $result->fetchRow(DB_FETCHMODE_ASSOC);

   // Now setup all the customer fields
   $template->setVariable("CUSTTITLE", showTitle($row["title_id"],
                        $connection));
   $template->setVariable("SURNAME", $row["surname"]);
   $template->setVariable("CUST_ID", $custID);
   $template->setVariable("ORDER_ID", $orderID);
   $template->setVariable("FIRSTNAME", $row["firstname"]);
   $template->setVariable("INITIAL", $row["initial"]);
   $template->setVariable("ADDRESS", $row["address"]);
   $template->setVariable("CITY", $row["city"]);
   $template->setVariable("STATE", $row["state"]);
   $template->setVariable("COUNTRY", showCountry($row["country_id"],
                        $connection));
   $template->setVariable("ZIPCODE", $row["zipcode"]);

   $orderTotalPrice = 0;

   // list the particulars of each item in the order
   $query = "SELECT  i.qty, w.wine_name, i.price,
                  w.wine_id, w.year, wi.winery_name
            FROM    items i, wine w, winery wi
            WHERE   i.cust_id = {$custID}
            AND     i.order_id = {$orderID}
            AND     i.wine_id = w.wine_id
            AND     w.winery_id = wi.winery_id
            ORDER BY item_id";

   $result = $connection->query($query);
```

```
   if (DB::isError($result))
     trigger_error($result->getMessage( ), E_USER_ERROR);

   // Add each item to the page
   while ($row = $result->fetchRow(DB_FETCHMODE_ASSOC))
   {
     // Work out the cost of this line item
     $itemsPrice = $row["qty"] * $row["price"];

     $orderTotalPrice += $itemsPrice;

     $wineDetail = showWine($row["wine_id"], $connection);

     $template->setCurrentBlock("row");
     $template->setVariable("QTY", $row["qty"]);
     $template->setVariable("WINE", $wineDetail);
     $template->setVariable("PRICE",
                            sprintf("$%4.2f" , $row["price"]), 11);
     $template->setVariable("TOTAL", sprintf("$%4.2f", $itemsPrice));
     $template->parseCurrentBlock("row");
   }

   $template->setCurrentBlock("items");
   $template->setVariable("ORDER_TOTAL",
                          sprintf("$%4.2f\n", $orderTotalPrice));
   $template->parseCurrentBlock("items");
   $template->setCurrentBlock( );

   $template->showWinestore(NO_CART, B_HOME);
}

// ----------

session_start( );

// Connect to a authenticated session
sessionAuthenticate(S_SHOWCART);

// Check the correct parameters have been passed
if (!isset($_GET["cust_id"]) || !isset($_GET["order_id"]))
{
   $_SESSION["message"] =
     "Incorrect parameters to order-step4.php";
   header("Location: " . S_SHOWCART);
   exit;
}

// Check this customer matches the $cust_id
$connection = DB::connect($dsn, true);

if (DB::isError($connection))
   trigger_error($connection->getMessage( ), E_USER_ERROR);
```

Example 19-6. The order/receipt.php script confirms an order as an HTML receipt (continued)

```
$cust_id = pearclean($_GET, "cust_id", 5, $connection);
$order_id = pearclean($_GET, "order_id", 5, $connection);

$real_cust_id = getCust_id($_SESSION["loginUsername"]);

if ($cust_id != $real_cust_id)
{
    $_SESSION["message"] = "You can only view your own receipts!";
    header("Location: " . S_HOME);
    exit;
}

// Show the confirmation HTML page
show_HTML_receipt($cust_id, $order_id, $connection);
?>
```

Example 19-7. The templates/orderreceipt.tpl order receipt template

```
<h1>Your order (reference # {CUST_ID} - {ORDER_ID}) has
been dispatched</h1>
Thank you {CUSTTITLE} {SURNAME},
your order has been completed and dispatched.
Your order reference number is {CUST_ID} - {ORDER_ID}.
Please quote this number in any correspondence.
<br>
<p>If it existed, the order would have been shipped to:
<br><b>
{CUSTTITLE} {FIRSTNAME} {INITIAL} {SURNAME}
<br>
{ADDRESS}
<br>{CITY} {STATE}
<br>{COUNTRY} {ZIPCODE}
</b>
<br>
<br>
<p>We have billed your fictional credit card.
<!-- BEGIN items -->
<table border=0 width=70% cellpadding=0 cellspacing=5>
<tr>
    <td><b>Quantity</b></td>
    <td><b>Wine</b></td>
    <td align="right"><b>Unit Price</b></td>
    <td align="right"><b>Total</b></td>
</tr>
<!-- BEGIN row -->
<tr>
    <td>{QTY}</td>
    <td>{WINE}</td>
    <td align="right">{PRICE}</td>
    <td align="right">{TOTAL}</td>
</tr>
<!-- END row -->
<tr></tr>
```

```
<tr>
    <td colspan=2 align="left"><i><b>Total of this order</b></td>
    <td></td>
    <td align="right"><b><i>{ORDER_TOTAL}</b></td>
</tr>
</table>
<!-- END items -->
<p><i>An email confirmation has been sent to you.
Thank you for shopping at Hugh and Dave's Online Wines.</i>
```

CHAPTER 20

Searching and Authentication in the Online Winestore

This chapter completes our discussion of the online winestore. We present here the wine searching and browsing module, and the authentication module that logs users in and out, checks whether they're authenticated, and allows them to change their passwords. The searching and browsing module is a moderately complex implementation of the querying techniques discussed in Chapter 6, and includes embedded links for browsing between pages of results. The authentication code is an adaptation of the code presented in Chapter 11.

The scripts we outline in this chapter cover the following topics:

Searching and browsing

Allows the user to search the wines in the winestore using optional search criteria, and displays matching wines in pages of twelve wines each. The querying techniques are discussed in Chapter 6, and the code makes use of the PEAR templates from Chapter 7 and our custom extension in Chapter 16. This module is an example of using embedded links to control the querying processes.

Logging in and logging out

Checks the user's credentials against a database, and registers the user as logged in by setting a session variable. It also allows the user to log out by destroying the session variable. Sessions are explained in Chapter 10, and the authentication implementation is almost identical to that described in Chapter 11.

Checking login status

Tests whether the user is authorized to access a script. This is identical to the approach explained in Chapter 11.

Changing passwords

Allows the user to change their password by supplying their old password and two copies of the new one. The techniques used are based on the template class developed in Chapter 16, and use the same approach as customer management in Chapter 17 and order finalization in Chapter 19. A receipt page isn't used because it's unlikely the user would want to bookmark a password change confirmation.

Code Overview

The searching and browsing module is implemented in the *search/searchform.php* and *search/search.php* scripts. Authentication is implemented in the *auth/login.php*, *auth/logincheck.php*, *auth/logout.php*, *auth/password.php*, and *auth/changepassword. php* scripts. The authentication process also uses general-purpose functions stored in *includes/authenticate.inc*.

Searching and Browsing

The searching and browsing scripts work with the *wine, winery, inventory, region,* and *wine_type* tables. These tables are created with the following statements:

```
CREATE TABLE wine (
   wine_id int(5) NOT NULL,
   wine_name varchar(50) NOT NULL,
   wine_type int(2) NOT NULL,
   year int(4) NOT NULL,
   winery_id int(4) NOT NULL,
   description blob,
   PRIMARY KEY (wine_id),
   KEY name (wine_name),
   KEY winery (winery_id)
) type=MyISAM;

CREATE TABLE winery (
   winery_id int(4) NOT NULL,
   winery_name varchar(100) NOT NULL,
   region_id int(4) NOT NULL,
   PRIMARY KEY (winery_id),
   KEY name (winery_name),
   KEY region (region_id)
)  type=MyISAM;

CREATE TABLE inventory (
   wine_id int(5) NOT NULL,
   inventory_id int(3) NOT NULL,
   on_hand int(5) NOT NULL,
   cost decimal(5,2) NOT NULL,
   date_added date,
   PRIMARY KEY (wine_id,inventory_id)
) type=MyISAM;

CREATE TABLE region (
   region_id int(4) NOT NULL,
   region_name varchar(100) NOT NULL,
   PRIMARY KEY (region_id),
   KEY region (region_name)
) type=MyISAM;

CREATE TABLE wine_type(
   wine_type_id int(2) NOT NULL,
```

```
    wine_type varchar(32) NOT NULL,
    PRIMARY KEY (wine_type_id)
) type=MyISAM;
```

The *wine* table stores details of wines that are for sale. Each wine is produced by a winery that's stored in the *winery* table, and each winery is located in a region that's stored in the *region* table. The available stock of a wine is stored in the *inventory* table: a wine has one row in the *inventory* table for each date it was received or for each different sale price. Wines also have a wine type (such as red or white) that's stored in the *wine_type* table. The *grape_variety* and *wine_variety* tables are also used in the searching process to display details of each wine through the *showVarieties()* function that's discussed in Chapter 16.

The script *search/searchform.php* presents a form to the user that collects search criteria. The user can choose to browse wines in all regions and of all wine types, or they can narrow their search to a specific wine type or region. The script is implemented using the same approach as the customer membership form in Chapter 17, and is based on the `winestoreFormTemplate` class discussed in detail in Chapter 16. Figure 20-1 shows the page rendered in a Mozilla browser.

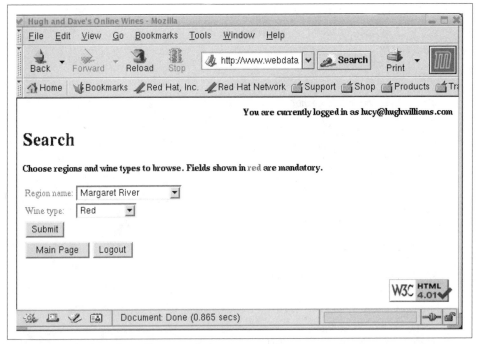

Figure 20-1. The form that collects search criteria

When the user submits the search form, the script *search/search.php* is requested. This script finds the wines that match the search criteria, and displays them in one or more pages of twelve wines per page. On each page, hypertext links are provided for the user to move to the previous or next page, or jump to a specific page. When the user clicks on these links, the *search/search.php* script is re-requested, and an additional offset parameter is provided that's used to retrieve the new page of results. An example of a search to find all wines in the Margaret River region is shown in Figure 20-2.

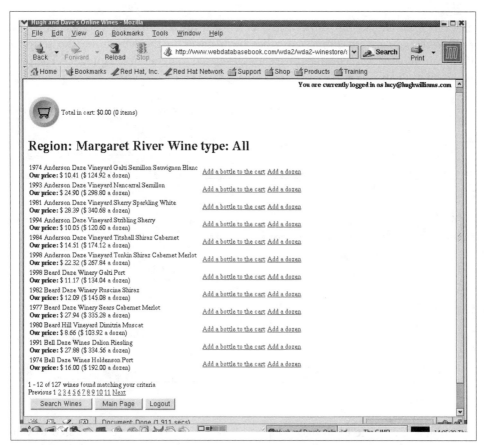

Figure 20-2. The results of a search for all wines in the Margaret River region

Authentication

Authentication is discussed in detail in Chapter 11. This section provides only a brief overview of the winestore authentication process.

The authentication scripts work only with the *users* table:

```
CREATE TABLE users (
    cust_id int(5) NOT NULL,
    user_name varchar(50) NOT NULL,
    password varchar(32) NOT NULL,
    PRIMARY KEY (user_name),
```

```
        KEY password (password),
        KEY cust_id (cust_id)
) type=MyISAM;
```

The *users* table stores the user_name of the customer (which is their email address), their digested password, and their cust_id (which is used to reference their data in other tables).

The script *auth/login.php* shows the user a form for entering their login name and password. Similarly to almost all other form pages in the winestore, the script is based on the winestoreFormTemplate class discussed in detail in Chapter 16. The page is shown in Figure 20-3.

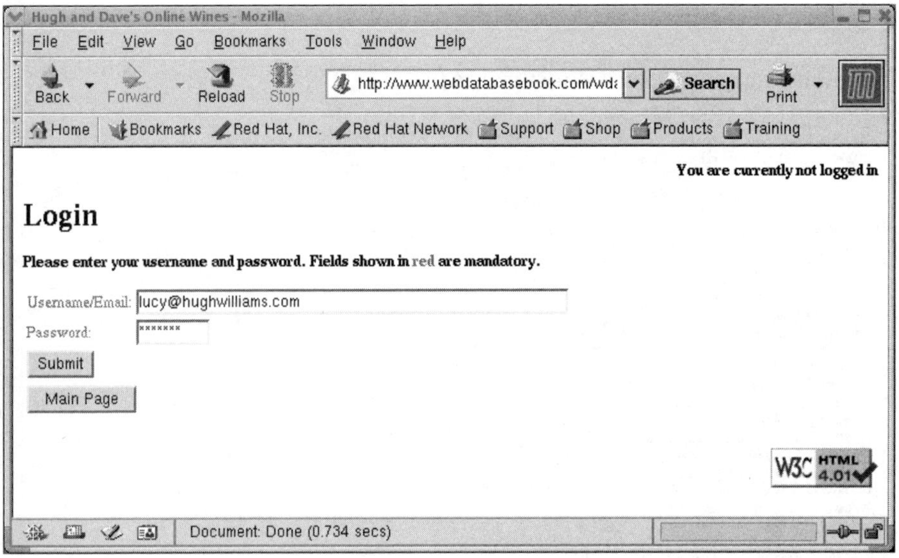

Figure 20-3. The login form

On submission of the login page, the *auth/logincheck.php* script is requested to validate the user's credentials. The script digests the user-supplied password, and compares the username and digested password credentials against those in the *users* table. On error (where the username and digested password don't match a row in the table) it redirects to the *auth/login.php* script and displays error messages. On success, the script registers a session variable $_SESSION["loginUsername"] that signifies that the user has logged in, and then the script redirects to the winestore homepage. The processes of registering the session variable and validating the credentials are performed respectively by the *registerLogin()* and *authenticateUser()* functions that are part of the *includes/authenticate.inc* include file.

The *auth/logout.php* script deletes the entire session, doesn't produce any output, and redirects to the winestore homepage. Our rationale for deleting more than the $_SESSION["loginUsername"] variable is that a user who logs out doesn't want to use the

---

application further, and therefore would also want their shopping cart emptied. This is a particularly useful feature for users who share a web browser on a machine in, for example, an Internet cafe.

The script *auth/password.php* displays the password change form shown in Figure 20-4. To change their password, the user must supply their existing password (to minimize tampering) and two copies of the new password (to minimize the chances of a typing error). The script is based on the winestoreFormTemplate class discussed in detail in Chapter 16.

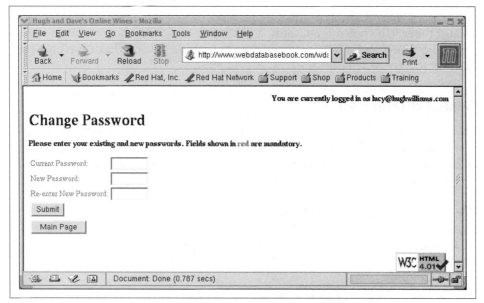

Figure 20-4. The password change form

On submission of the form, the browser requests *auth/changepassword.php*. This script validates the password change, and updates the *users* table when validation succeeds. The script produces no output: on validation success, it redirects to the customer details page and displays a confirmation message to the user; on failure, it redirects back to the password change form and displays validation errors.

The *includes/authenticate.inc* file contains the *authenticateUser()* and *registerLogin()* functions described earlier. In addition, it also contains three other functions:

newUser()

   This function adds a new user to the *users* table and digests their password using the *md5()* function described in Chapter 11.

unregisterLogin()

   This function removes the session variables associated with a login without removing the session. This function is called whenever a user fails the authentication process.

sessionAuthenticate( )

> This function checks whether a user is logged in, and also ensures that they're accessing the application from the same IP address. On failure it redirects to the page that's supplied as a parameter. The function is called at the top of any script that requires the user to be logged in.

Searching and Browsing

This section describes the searching and browsing module in the winestore. As the scripts are complex, we've divided the discussions into three parts: a short description of the search criteria input form; a discussion of the SQL query used to retrieve matching wines; and, an longer overview of the code that produces the browsable results.

Search Criteria Form

Example 20-1 lists the search input criteria *search/searchform.php* script. The script is a straightforward use of the winestoreFormTemplate class discussed in Chapter 16. It allows users to choose a region and a wine type to browse, and uses the *winestoreFormTemplate::selectWidget( )* method to present these as drop-down lists.

Example 20-1. Thesearch/searchform.php script that displays a search criteria entry form

```php
<?php
// This is the script that allows the to search and browse wines, and
// to select wines to add to their shopping cart

require_once "../includes/template.inc";
require_once "../includes/winestore.inc";

set_error_handler("customHandler");

session_start();

// Takes <form> heading, instructions, action, formVars name, and
// formErrors name as parameters
$template = new winestoreFormTemplate("Search",
                "Choose regions and wine types to browse.",
                S_SEARCH, "searchFormVars", NULL, "GET");

$connection = DB::connect($dsn, true);
if (DB::isError($connection))
   trigger_error($connection->getMessage( ), E_USER_ERROR);

// Create the drop-down search widgets for the page

// Load the regions from the region table
$regionResult = $connection->query("SELECT * FROM region");
if (DB::isError($regionResult))
```

```
    trigger_error($regionResult->getMessage( ), E_USER_ERROR);

// Load the wine types from the wine_type table
$wineTypeResult = $connection->query("SELECT * FROM wine_type");
if (DB::isError($wineTypeResult))
    trigger_error($wineTypeResult->getMessage( ), E_USER_ERROR);

$template->selectWidget("region_name", "Region name:",
                        "region_name", $regionResult);

$template->selectWidget("wine_type", "Wine type:",
                        "wine_type", $wineTypeResult);

$template->showWinestore(NO_CART, B_HOME | B_SHOW_CART | B_LOGINLOGOUT);
?>
```

Querying and Displaying Results

Example 20-2 lists the complex *search/search.php* script that performs the search. The script retrieves wines that match the user-supplied combination of wine region name and wine type, and displays the results in pages of twelve wines each. For example, the script can be used to browse the Red wines from the Margaret River region, and to view the 38 matching wines over 4 result pages.

Example 20-2. The search/search.php script that displays wines in pages

```
<?php
// This is the script that allows the to search and browse wines, and
// to select wines to add to their shopping cart

require_once "DB.php";
require_once "../includes/template.inc";
require_once "../includes/winestore.inc";

set_error_handler("customHandler");

// Construct the query
function setupQuery($region_name, $wine_type)
{
    // Show the wines stocked at the winestore that match
    // the search criteria
    $query = "SELECT DISTINCT wi.winery_name,
                    w.year,
                    w.wine_name,
                    w.wine_id
            FROM wine w, winery wi, inventory i, region r, wine_type wt
            WHERE w.winery_id = wi.winery_id
            AND w.wine_id = i.wine_id";

    // Add region_name restriction if they've selected anything
    // except "All"
```

```
    if ($region_name != "All")
        $query .= " AND r.region_name = '{$region_name}'
                    AND r.region_id = wi.region_id";

    // Add wine type restriction if they've selected anything
    // except "All"
    if ($wine_type != "All")
        $query .= " AND wt.wine_type = '{$wine_type}'
                    AND wt.wine_type_id = w.wine_type";

    // Add sorting criteria
    $query .= " ORDER BY wi.winery_name, w.wine_name, w.year";

    return ($query);
}

// Show the user the wines that match their query
function showWines($connection, &$template)
{
    // Produce a heading for the top of the page
    $template->setCurrentBlock();
    $template->setVariable("SEARCHCRITERIA",
                "Region: {$_SESSION["searchFormVars"]["region_name"]} " .
                "Wine type: {$_SESSION["searchFormVars"]["wine_type"]}");

    // Encode the search parameters for embedding in links to other pages
    // of results
    $browseString = "wine_type=" .
                    urlencode($_SESSION["searchFormVars"]["wine_type"]) .
                    "&amp;region_name=" .
                    urlencode($_SESSION["searchFormVars"]["region_name"]);

    // Build the query using the search criteria
    $query = setupQuery($_SESSION["searchFormVars"]["region_name"],
                        $_SESSION["searchFormVars"]["wine_type"]);

    $result = $connection->query($query);
    if (DB::isError($result))
        trigger_error($result->getMessage(), E_USER_ERROR);

    $numRows = $result->numRows();

    // Is there any data?
    if ($numRows > 0)
    {
        // Yes, there is data.

        // Check that the offset is sensible and, if not, fix it.

        // Offset greater than the number of rows?
        // Set it to the number of rows LESS SEARCH_ROWS
        if ($_SESSION["searchFormVars"]["offset"] > $numRows)
```

```
    $_SESSION["searchFormVars"]["offset"] = $numRows - SEARCH_ROWS;

  // Offset less than zero? Set it to zero
  if ($_SESSION["searchFormVars"]["offset"] < 0)
    $_SESSION["searchFormVars"]["offset"] = 0;

  // The "Previous" page begins at the current
  // offset LESS the number of SEARCH_ROWS per page
  $previousOffset =
    $_SESSION["searchFormVars"]["offset"] - SEARCH_ROWS;

  // The "Next" page begins at the current offset
  // PLUS the number of SEARCH_ROWS per page
  $nextOffset = $_SESSION["searchFormVars"]["offset"] + SEARCH_ROWS;

  // Fetch one page of results (or less if on the
  // last page, starting at $_SESSION["searchFormVars"]["offset"])
  for ( $rowCounter = 0;
        $rowCounter < SEARCH_ROWS &&
        $rowCounter + $_SESSION["searchFormVars"]["offset"] <
        $result->numRows( ) &&
        $row = $result->fetchRow(DB_FETCHMODE_ASSOC,
               $_SESSION["searchFormVars"]["offset"] + $rowCounter);
        $rowCounter++)
  {
    $template->setCurrentBlock("row");
    $template->setVariable("YEAR", $row["year"]);
    $template->setVariable("WINERY", $row["winery_name"]);
    $template->setVariable("WINE", $row["wine_name"]);
    $template->setVariable("VARIETIES",
               showVarieties($connection, $row["wine_id"]));

    $price = showPricing($connection, $row["wine_id"]);
    $template->setVariable("BOTTLE_PRICE",
                           sprintf("$%4.2f", $price));
    $template->setVariable("DOZEN_PRICE",
                           sprintf("$%4.2f", ($price*12)));

    $template->setVariable("ONEHREF", S_ADDTOCART .
                           "?qty=1&amp;wineId={$row["wine_id"]}");
    $template->setVariable("DOZENHREF", S_ADDTOCART .
                           "?qty=12&amp;wineId={$row["wine_id"]}");
    $template->parseCurrentBlock("row");
  } // end for rows in the page

  // Show the row numbers that are being viewed
  $template->setCurrentBlock( );
  $template->setVariable("BEGINROW",
                         $_SESSION["searchFormVars"]["offset"] + 1);
  $template->setVariable("ENDROW", $rowCounter +
                         $_SESSION["searchFormVars"]["offset"]);
  $template->setVariable("ROWS", $result->numRows( ));
```

```php
    // Are there any previous pages?
    if ($_SESSION["searchFormVars"]["offset"] >= SEARCH_ROWS)
    {
      // Yes, so create a previous link
      $template->setCurrentBlock("link");
      $template->setVariable("HREF", S_SEARCH . "?offset=" .
                             rawurlencode($previousOffset) .
                             "&amp;{$browseString}");
      $template->setVariable("HREFTEXT", "Previous");
      $template->parseCurrentBlock("link");
    }
    else
    {
      // No, there is no previous page so don't
      // print a link
      $template->setCurrentBlock("outtext");
      $template->setVariable("OUTTEXT", "Previous");
      $template->parseCurrentBlock("outtext");
    }

    $template->setCurrentBlock("links");
    $template->parseCurrentBlock("links");

    // Output the page numbers as links
    // Count through the number of pages in the results
    for($x=0, $page=1; $x<$result->numRows( ); $x+=SEARCH_ROWS, $page++)
    {
      // Is this the current page?
      if ($x < $_SESSION["searchFormVars"]["offset"] ||
          $x > ($_SESSION["searchFormVars"]["offset"] +
              SEARCH_ROWS - 1))
      {
        // No, so print a link to that page
        $template->setCurrentBlock("link");
        $template->setVariable("HREF",
          S_SEARCH . "?offset=" . rawurlencode($x) .
          "&amp;{$browseString}");
        $template->setVariable("HREFTEXT", $page);
        $template->parseCurrentBlock("link");
      }
      else
      {
        // Yes, so don't print a link
        $template->setCurrentBlock("outtext");
        $template->setVariable("OUTTEXT", $page);
        $template->parseCurrentBlock("outtext");
      }

      $template->setCurrentBlock("links");
      $template->parseCurrentBlock("links");
    }
```

Example 20-2. The search/search.php script that displays wines in pages (continued)

```
      // Are there any Next pages?
      if (isset($row) && ($result->numRows( ) > $nextOffset))
      {
         // Yes, so create a next link
         $template->setCurrentBlock("link");
         $template->setVariable("HREF",
             S_SEARCH . "?offset=" . rawurlencode($nextOffset) .
             "&amp;{$browseString}");
         $template->setVariable("HREFTEXT", "Next");
         $template->parseCurrentBlock("link");
      }
      else
      {
         // No, there is no next page so don't
         // print a link
         $template->setCurrentBlock("outtext");
         $template->setVariable("OUTTEXT", "Next");
         $template->parseCurrentBlock("outtext");
      }

      $template->setCurrentBlock("links");
      $template->parseCurrentBlock("links");
   } // end if numRows( )
   else
   {
      $template->setCurrentBlock("outtext");
      $template->setVariable("OUTTEXT",
                             "No wines found matching your criteria.");
      $template->parseCurrentBlock("outtext");
      $template->setCurrentBlock("links");
      $template->parseCurrentBlock("links");
   }
}


// ---------

session_start( );

$template = new winestoreTemplate(T_SEARCH);

$connection = DB::connect($dsn, true);
if (DB::isError($connection))
   trigger_error($connection->getMessage( ), E_USER_ERROR);

// Store the search parameters so the <form> redisplays the
// previous search
$_SESSION["searchFormVars"]["region_name"] =
   pearclean($_GET, "region_name", 100, $connection);

$_SESSION["searchFormVars"]["wine_type"] =
   pearclean($_GET, "wine_type", 32, $connection);
```

Example 20-2. The search/search.php script that displays wines in pages (continued)

```
// If an offset isn't provided, set it to 0
if (isset($_GET["offset"]))
   $_SESSION["searchFormVars"]["offset"] =
     pearclean($_GET, "offset", 5, $connection);
else
   $_SESSION["searchFormVars"]["offset"] = 0;

// Show the user their search
showWines($connection, $template);

$template->showWinestore(SHOW_ALL, B_HOME | B_SHOW_CART | B_SEARCH |
                         B_LOGINLOGOUT);
?>
```

Finding the wines

The query that retrieves the matching wines is implemented in the *setupQuery()* function in Example 20-2. The query performs a natural join between the *wine*, *winery*, and *inventory* tables, and displays the winery_name, year, wine_name, and wine attributes from those tables:

```
SELECT DISTINCT wi.winery_name,
                w.year,
                w.wine_name,
                w.wine
FROM wine w, winery wi, inventory i, region r, wine_type wt
WHERE w.winery_id = wi.winery_id
AND w.wine_id = i.wine_id
```

The query includes the *inventory* table in the FROM clause because the user can only purchase wines that are in stock. The *region* and *wine_type* tables are included because they are the source of the user-supplied search criteria.

The *inventory* table can have more than one row for each wine. Because it's included in the join, a wine can be returned from the query more than once, in the case where it's available at two or more prices or it arrived at the warehouse on two or more days. However, because we only want to see the details of each wine once in the browse screen, the query uses the DISTINCT clause to remove any duplicates.

Depending on whether the user has supplied a wine type or a region as a search criteria, additional clauses are added to the query. For example, if the user supplies the region name **Margaret River,** the following is added:

```
AND r.region_name = 'Margaret River'
AND r.region_id = wi.region_id
```

This restricts the answer set to only those wines that are from the **Margaret River** region, and includes the *region* table in the natural join. If the user supplies a wine type of **Red,** a similar clause is added for the *wine_type* table:

```
AND wt.wine_type = 'Red'
AND wt.wine_type_id = w.wine_type
```

The additional clauses are omitted if the user selects **All** regions or **All** wine types.

After adding the additional clauses as required, the last step in forming the query is to add sorting criteria. We sort the wines by winery_name, then by wine_name, and last by vintage year:

```
ORDER BY wi.winery_name, w.wine_name, w.year
```

Displaying the wines

The results of the query are shown in pages of twelve wines each. Previous and Next page links are shown so that the user can move between pages, as well as page numbers shown as links that allow direct access to any page in the results. This is a useful technique to display large result sets in pages and it works as follows:

- When the user inputs their search criteria for the first time, only the first 12 rows (with indexes 0 to 11) of matching wines are shown.

- An embedded Next link is shown that allows the user to move to the next page of rows. If the user is accessing the first page, the Next link runs a query that shows the second page of results, that is, with indexes of 12 to 23.

- When the user reaches the last page of results (which usually has less than 12 rows) the Next link is hidden.

- An embedded Previous link is shown that moves backward through the pages. The Previous link is hidden when the first page is displayed.

- Page numbers are displayed that allow direct access to other pages without repeatedly clicking on the previous or next links. The current page isn't shown as a link.

- For each wine on the page, an embedded link is shown that allows the user to add one or a dozen bottles of the wine to the shopping cart using the *cart/addto-cart.php* script discussed in Chapter 18.

The main body of the script stores the search criteria region_name and wine_type in the session array searchFormVars. They're saved so that when the user revisits the *search/searchform.php* script, their previously entered search criteria are redisplayed. In addition, if an offset is supplied, it's saved. The offset is used to indicate which row should be the first row displayed on the page, and this is used to display pages when the user clicks on Next, Previous, or a page number. When the user runs their first search, the offset isn't supplied and it's set to zero.

The *showWines()* function displays the search results. To do this, it uses the template *templates/search.tpl* shown in Example 20-3. The template has several blocks and placeholders that are used as follows:

- The SEARCHCRITERIA placeholder displays the parameters that have been used in the search process. For example, if the user is browsing Margaret River Red wines, it is set to <h1>Region: Margaret River Wine type: Red</h1>.

- The row block displays each of the wines that match the search criteria. The wine details are shown in the YEAR, WINERY, WINE, and VARIETIES placeholders, the prices in BOTTLE_PRICE and DOZEN_PRICE, and the links that are used to add wines to the shopping cart in ONEHREF and DOZENHREF.

- At the base of the list of wines, the placeholders BEGINROW, ENDROW, and ROWS show information about the range of wines that are displayed on the pages. For example, on the first page of results, this may show *1 - 12 of 38 wines found matching your criteria.*

- The links block is output once for the Previous and Next text, and once for each page number that's needed at the base of a results page. It contains the link and outtext blocks, and each time a links block is output, only one of the nested link or outtext blocks are shown.

- The link block is used for a hypertext link that points at HREF and is labeled with HREFTEXT. For example, the link text could be set to *Next* and the hypertext link to */wda2-winestore/search/search.php?offset=12&wine_type=Red&region_name=Margaret+River.* Alternatively, the link text might be set to a page number or Previous.

- The outtext block is used to display text that isn't a hypertext link. This is used when there's no previous or next page, or to show the page number of the current page.

Example 20-3. The templates/search.tpl template that's used to display search results

```
<h1>{SEARCHCRITERIA}</h1>
<table border="0">
<!-- BEGIN row -->
<tr>
  <td>{YEAR} {WINERY} {WINE} {VARIETIES}
  <br><b>Our price: </b>{BOTTLE_PRICE} ({DOZEN_PRICE} a dozen)
  </td>
  <td><a href="{ONEHREF}">Add a bottle to the cart</a>
  </td>
  <td><a href="{DOZENHREF}">Add a dozen</a>
  </td>
</tr>
<!-- END row -->
</table>
<br>{BEGINROW} - {ENDROW} of {ROWS} wines found matching your criteria
<br>
<!-- BEGIN links -->
<!-- BEGIN link -->
<a href="{HREF}">{HREFTEXT}</a>
<!-- END link -->
<!-- BEGIN outtext -->
{OUTTEXT}
<!-- END outtext -->
<!-- END links -->
```

The *showWines()* function itself carries out the following steps:

1. It outputs the heading using the SEARCHCRITERIA placeholder.

2. It creates a $browseString that includes the current search parameters. This is used as part of any embedded links at the base of the results page. For example, if the user wants Margaret River Red wines, the $browseString is:

```
wine_type=Red&amp;region_name=Margaret+River
```

The *urlencode()* function is used to convert strings to text suitable for a URL by, for example, converting spaces to plus signs. You'll also notice that we've converted the & to an & entity reference as required by the HTML recommendation.

3. The *setupQuery()* function discussed previously is used to formulate the query, and the query is executed.

4. If any results are returned, they're displayed as discussed next. If no wines are found that match the criteria, a message is output using the OUTTEXT placeholder that states *No wines found matching your criteria*.

5. The relative offsets of Previous and Next links are calculated. For example, if the current page begins at row 0, the $nextOffset is set to 12 and the $previousOffset to -12. If the $previousOffset is less than 0, a previous link isn't shown. If the $nextOffset is greater than the number of rows in the result set, a next link isn't shown.

6. The for loop outputs the rows on the page. The for loop continues to retrieve rows and increment $rowCounter while three conditions hold: first, the $rowCounter is less than 12; second, the offset plus the $rowCounter is less than the number of rows in the result set; and, last, fetching the row that is the sum of the $rowCounter and the offset succeeds. The final two conditions are only important on the last page of results when there are less than 12 results to display. To read a specific row in the result set, the optional second parameter to the PEAR *DB::fetchRow()* method is used; this is discussed in Chapter 7.

7. For each row that's output, the helper functions *showVarieties()* and *showPricing()* are used to find the grape varieties and the cheapest price of the wine. These are part of the *winestore.inc* include file that's discussed in Chapter 16.

8. After the rows are output, the BEGINROW, ENDROW, and ROWS placeholders are populated as discussed previously.

9. To conclude the function, the script produces the Previous, Next, and page number links. The previous link is created with the following code fragment:

```
// Are there any previous pages?
if ($_SESSION["searchFormVars"]["offset"] > SEARCH_ROWS)
{
  // Yes, so create a previous link
  $template->setCurrentBlock("link");
  $template->setVariable("HREF", S_SEARCH . "?offset=" .
```

```
          rawurlencode($previousOffset) .
          "&amp;{$browseString}");
    $template->setVariable("HREFTEXT", "Previous");
    $template->parseCurrentBlock("link");
}
else
{
    // No, there is no previous page so don't
    // print a link
    $template->setCurrentBlock("outtext");
    $template->setVariable("OUTTEXT", "Previous");
    $template->parseCurrentBlock("outtext");
}

$template->setCurrentBlock("links");
$template->parseCurrentBlock("links");
```

A Previous link is produced only if the first row displayed on the page is greater than SEARCH_ROWS (which is set to 12); this is true if we've just produced the second or a later page. The link itself points to the *search/search.php* script with the offset variable set to the value of $previousOffset calculated earlier, and the parameter $browseString provides the region name and wine type criteria for the next search.

The *rawurlencode()* function isn't strictly needed here (we are only coding a number) but consistently using it to create URLs with correctly encoded characters is good practice. The Next link is created with similar logic.

10. The page number links are output using a similar approach to the previous and next links. A for loop counts through the rows in the result set, one page of 12 wines at a time. When the counter is set to a row number on the page we've just displayed, a textual page number is produced. If the counter isn't on the current page, the page number is output as a link that has its offset set to the first row on that page. As previously, the $browseString stores the search criteria.

Authentication

The authentication module consists of the *includes/authenticate.inc* include file, the login and logout scripts, and the password change scripts. The code is closely based on that presented in Chapter 11 and we describe it only briefly here.

General-Purpose Functions

Example 20-4 shows the helper functions stored in the *includes/authenticate.inc* include file. The function *newUser()* creates a new row in the *users* table, and digests the password that's passed as a parameter using the *md5()* hash function. This is discussed in detail in Chapter 11.

The function *authenticateUser()* checks whether a row in the *users* table matches the supplied username and password (the supplied password is digested prior to comparison with those stored in the database). It returns true when there's a match and false otherwise.

The *registerLogin()* function saves the user's username as a session variable, and also stores the IP address from which they've accessed the winestore. The presence of the $_SESSION["loginUsername"] variable indicates the user has logged in successfully. The function *unregisterLogin()* deletes the same two session variables.

The function *sessionAuthenticate()* checks whether a user is logged in (by testing for the presence of $_SESSION["loginUsername"]) and that they're returning from the same IP address. If either test fails, the script calls *unregisterLogin()* and redirects to the script supplied as a parameter. This approach won't work for all situations—for example, if a user's ISP accesses the winestore through different web proxy servers, their IP address may change. It's up to you to decide whether this additional security step is needed in your applications. This is discussed in more detail in Chapter 11.

Example 20-4. The includes/authenticate.inc include file

```php
<?php
// Add a new user to the users table
function newUser($loginUsername, $loginPassword, $cust_id, $connection)
{
   // Create the encrypted password
   $stored_password = md5(trim($loginPassword));

   // Insert a new user into the users table
   $query = "INSERT INTO users SET
             cust_id = {$cust_id},
             password = '{$stored_password}',
             user_name = '{$loginUsername}'";

   $result = $connection->query($query);

   if (DB::isError($result))
      trigger_error($result->getMessage(), E_USER_ERROR);
}

// Check if a user has an account that matches the username and password
function authenticateUser($loginUsername, $loginPassword, $connection)
{
   // Create a digest of the password collected from the challenge
   $password_digest = md5(trim($loginPassword));

   // Formulate the SQL to find the user
   $query = "SELECT password FROM users
             WHERE user_name = '$loginUsername'
             AND password = '$password_digest'";

   $result = $connection->query($query);

   if (DB::isError($result))
      trigger_error($result->getMessage(), E_USER_ERROR);
```

Example 20-4. The authentication.inc include file (continued)

```
    // exactly one row? then we have found the user
    if ($result->numRows( ) != 1)
        return false;
    else
        return true;
}

// Register that user has logged in
function registerLogin($loginUsername)
{
    // Register the loginUsername to show the user is logged in
    $_SESSION["loginUsername"] = $loginUsername;

    // Register the IP address that started this session
    $_SESSION["loginIP"] = $_SERVER["REMOTE_ADDR"];
}

// Logout (unregister the login)
function unregisterLogin( )
{
    // Ensure login is not registered
    if (isset($_SESSION["loginUsername"]))
        unset($_SESSION["loginUsername"]);

    if (isset($_SESSION["loginIP"]))
        unset($_SESSION["loginIP"]);
}

// Connects to a session and checks that the user has
// authenticated and that the remote IP address matches
// the address used to create the session.
function sessionAuthenticate($destinationScript)
{
  // Check if the user hasn't logged in
  if (!isset($_SESSION["loginUsername"]))
  {
    // The request does not identify a session
    $_SESSION["message"] = "You are not authorized to access the URL
                        {$_SERVER["REQUEST_URI"]}";

    unregisterLogin( );
    header("Location: {$destinationScript}");
    exit;
  }

  // Check if the request is from a different IP address to previously
  if (isset($_SESSION["loginIP"]) &&
     ($_SESSION["loginIP"] != $_SERVER["REMOTE_ADDR"]))
  {
    // The request did not originate from the machine
    // that was used to create the session.
    // THIS IS POSSIBLY A SESSION HIJACK ATTEMPT
```

Example 20-4. The authentication.inc include file (continued)

```
    $_SESSION["message"] = "You are not authorized to access the URL
                           {$_SERVER["REQUEST_URI"]} from the address
                           {$_SERVER["REMOTE_ADDR"]}";

    unregisterLogin( );
    header("Location: {$destinationScript}");
    exit;
  }
}
?>
```

Logging In and Out

The *auth/login.php* and *auth/logincheck.php* scripts are shown in Example 20-5 and
Example 20-6 respectively. The *auth/login.php* script is a straightforward use of the
winestoreFormTemplate class described in Chapter 16, and it simply collects the user's
login name (their email address) and their password. The *auth/logincheck.php* script
validates the username and password using functions from *validate.inc* discussed in
Chapter 16, and then uses the helper functions discussed in the previous section to
check the user's credentials and complete the login process.

The *auth/logout.php* script that logs the user out is shown in Example 20-7.

Example 20-5. The auth/login.php script that collects the user's credentials

```php
<?php
// Show the login page

require_once "../includes/template.inc";
require_once "../includes/winestore.inc";
require_once "../includes/validate.inc";

set_error_handler("customHandler");

session_start( );

// Takes <form> heading, instructions, action, formVars name, and
// formErrors name as parameters
$template = new winestoreFormTemplate("Login",
               "Please enter your username and password.",
               S_LOGINCHECK, "loginFormVars", "loginErrors");


$template->mandatoryWidget("loginUsername", "Username/Email:", 50);
$template->passwordWidget("loginPassword", "Password:", 8);

// Add buttons and messages, and show the page
$template->showWinestore(NO_CART, B_HOME);
?>
```

Example 20-6. The auth/logincheck.php that validates and checks the user's credentials

```php
<?php
// This script manages the login process.
// It should only be called when the user is not logged in.
// If the user is logged in, it will redirect back to the calling page.
// If the user is not logged in, it will show a login <form>

require_once "DB.php";
require_once "../includes/winestore.inc";
require_once "../includes/authenticate.inc";
require_once "../includes/validate.inc";

set_error_handler("customHandler");

function checkLogin($loginUsername, $loginPassword, $connection)
{

  if (authenticateUser($loginUsername, $loginPassword, $connection))
  {
     registerLogin($loginUsername);

     // Clear the formVars so a future <form> is blank
     unset($_SESSION["loginFormVars"]);
     unset($_SESSION["loginErrors"]);

     header("Location: " . S_MAIN);
     exit;
  }
  else
  {
     // Register an error message
     $_SESSION["message"] = "Username or password incorrect. " .
                            "Login failed.";

     header("Location: " . S_LOGIN);
     exit;
  }
}

// ------

session_start();

$connection = DB::connect($dsn, true);

if (DB::isError($connection))
  trigger_error($connection->getMessage(), E_USER_ERROR);

// Check if the user is already logged in
if (isset($_SESSION["loginUsername"]))
{
     $_SESSION["message"] = "You are already logged in!";
     header("Location: " . S_HOME);
     exit;
```

Example 20-6. The auth/logincheck.php that validates and checks the user's credentials (continued)

```php
}

// Register and clear an error array - just in case!
if (isset($_SESSION["loginErrors"]))
   unset($_SESSION["loginErrors"]);
$_SESSION["loginErrors"] = array();

// Set up a formVars array for the POST variables
$_SESSION["loginFormVars"] = array();

foreach($_POST as $varname => $value)
   $_SESSION["loginFormVars"]["{$varname}"] =
   pearclean($_POST, $varname, 50, $connection);

// Validate password -- has it been provided and is the length between
// 6 and 8 characters?
if (checkMandatory("loginPassword", "password",
              "loginErrors", "loginFormVars"))
  checkMinAndMaxLength("loginPassword", 6, 8, "password",
                   "loginErrors", "loginFormVars");

// Validate email -- has it been provided and is it valid?
if (checkMandatory("loginUsername", "email/username",
              "loginErrors", "loginFormVars"))
  emailCheck("loginUsername", "email/username",
              "loginErrors", "loginFormVars");

// Check if this is a valid user and, if so, log them in
checkLogin($_SESSION["loginFormVars"]["loginUsername"],
           $_SESSION["loginFormVars"]["loginPassword"],
           $connection);
?>
```

Example 20-7. The auth/logout.php script that logs the user out

```php
<?php
// This script logs a user out and redirects
// to the calling page.

require_once '../includes/winestore.inc';
require_once '../includes/authenticate.inc';

set_error_handler("customHandler");

// Restore the session
session_start();

// Check they're logged in
sessionAuthenticate(S_LOGIN);

// Destroy the login and all associated data
session_destroy();
```

```
// Redirect to the main page
header("Location: " . S_MAIN);
exit;
?>
```

Changing Passwords

The password change feature is implemented in the *auth/password.php* script shown in Example 20-8 and the *auth/changepassword.php* script in Example 20-9. The password change form that's output by *auth/password.php* is based on the winestoreFormTemplate class described in Chapter 16, and requires the user to enter their current password and two copies of their new password.

Example 20-8. The auth/password.php script that collects the user's old and new passwords

```
<?php
// This script shows the user a <form> to change their password
// The user must be logged in to view it.

require_once "../includes/template.inc";
require_once "../includes/winestore.inc";
require_once "../includes/authenticate.inc";

set_error_handler("customHandler");

session_start();

// Check the user is properly logged in
sessionAuthenticate(S_MAIN);

// Takes <form> heading, instructions, action, formVars name,
// and formErrors name as parameters
$template = new winestoreFormTemplate("Change Password",
                "Please enter your existing and new passwords.",
                S_CHANGEPASSWORD, "pwdFormVars", "pwdErrors");

// Create the password change widgets
$template->passwordWidget("currentPassword", "Current Password:", 8);
$template->passwordWidget("newPassword1", "New Password:", 8);
$template->passwordWidget("newPassword2", "Re-enter New Password:", 8);

// Add buttons and messages, and show the page
$template->showWinestore(NO_CART, B_HOME);
?>
```

The *auth/changepassword.php* script checks that all three passwords are supplied and that each is between 6 and 8 characters in length. It then checks that the two copies of the new password are identical, that the new password is different to the old one, and that the old password matches the one stored in the *users* table. If all the checks pass, the new password is digested with the *md5()* hash function, and the *users* table updated with the new value. The script then redirects to the winestore home page, where a success message is displayed. If any check fails, the script redirects to *auth/password.php*.

Example 20-9. The auth/changepassword.php script that validates a password change and updates the database

```php
<?php
require_once "DB.php";
require_once "../includes/winestore.inc";
require_once "../includes/authenticate.inc";
require_once "../includes/validate.inc";

set_error_handler("customHandler");

session_start();

// Connect to a authenticated session
sessionAuthenticate(S_MAIN);

$connection = DB::connect($dsn, true);

if (DB::isError($connection))
   trigger_error($connection->getMessage(), E_USER_ERROR);

// Register and clear an error array - just in case!
if (isset($_SESSION["pwdErrors"]))
   unset($_SESSION["pwdErrors"]);
$_SESSION["pwdErrors"] = array();

// Set up a formVars array for the POST variables
$_SESSION["pwdFormVars"] = array();

foreach($_POST as $varname => $value)
   $_SESSION["pwdFormVars"]["{$varname}"] =
     pearclean($_POST, $varname, 50, $connection);

// Validate passwords - between 6 and 8 characters
if (checkMandatory("currentPassword", "current password",
            "pwdErrors", "pwdFormVars"))
  checkMinAndMaxLength("loginPassword", 6, 8, "current password",
                "pwdErrors", "pwdFormVars");

if (checkMandatory("newPassword1", "first new password",
            "pwdErrors", "pwdFormVars"))
  checkMinAndMaxLength("newPassword1", 6, 8, "first new password",
                "pwdErrors", "pwdFormVars");

if (checkMandatory("newPassword2", "second new password",
            "pwdErrors", "pwdFormVars"))
  checkMinAndMaxLength("newPassword2", 6, 8, "second new password",
                "pwdErrors", "pwdFormVars");

// Did we find no errors? Ok, check the new passwords are the
// same, and that the current password is different.
```

```php
// Then, check the current password.
if (count($_SESSION["pwdErrors"]) == 0)
{
   if ($_SESSION["pwdFormVars"]["newPassword1"] !=
       $_SESSION["pwdFormVars"]["newPassword2"])
     $_SESSION["pwdErrors"]["newPassword1"] =
       "The new passwords must match.";

   elseif ($_SESSION["pwdFormVars"]["newPassword1"] ==
           $_SESSION["pwdFormVars"]["currentPassword"])
     $_SESSION["pwdErrors"]["newPassword1"] =
       "The password must change.";

   elseif (!authenticateUser($_SESSION["loginUsername"],
                             $_SESSION["pwdFormVars"]["currentPassword"],
                             $connection))
     $_SESSION["pwdErrors"]["currentPassword"] =
       "The current password is incorrect.";
}

// Now the script has finished the validation,
// check if there were any errors
if (count($_SESSION["pwdErrors"]) > 0)
{
    // There are errors.  Relocate back to the password form
    header("Location: " . S_PASSWORD);
    exit;
}

// Create the encrypted password
$stored_password = md5(trim($_SESSION["pwdFormVars"]["newPassword1"]));

// Update the user row
$query = "UPDATE users SET password = '$stored_password'
          WHERE user_name = '{$_SESSION["loginUsername"]}'";

$result = $connection->query($query);
if (DB::isError($result))
   trigger_error($result->getMessage(), E_USER_ERROR);

// Clear the formVars so a future <form> is blank
unset($_SESSION["pwdFormVars"]);
unset($_SESSION["pwdErrors"]);

// Set a message that says that the page has changed
$_SESSION["message"] = "Your password has been successfully changed.";

// Relocate to the customer details page
header("Location: " . S_DETAILS);
?>
```

Linux Installation Guide

This appendix is a guide to installing the software used in the book on a Linux platform. The instructions were written for the RedHat distribution, but work for most other distributions; they have not been tested for other Unix variants, but should work. Specific instructions for Mac OS X can be found in Appendix C.

The instructions are designed for administrators: you'll need to be able to log in as the root user. The first section shows how to find out what's already installed. We then show you how to install the components that you need and optionally how to install a secure web server.

After showing you how to get PHP, Apache, and MySQL running, we present a short guide to downloading and installing the PHP script and database examples used in this book. We also show you how to set up tools that are needed for the examples in the book but aren't included in the default Apache, PHP, and MySQL installations.

The Linux environment, PHP, Apache, MySQL, and our code examples can all change over time. This means that this guide may not work perfectly when you use it. To get the latest installation guide in HTML and PDF formats, along with changes and corrections to this guide, visit *http://www.webdatabasebook.com/install-guides*.

Finding Out What's Installed

This section shows you how to find out what's already installed on your Linux server.

The Apache web server with the PHP module is usually installed with most common Linux distributions (such as, for example, most default RedHat installs). MySQL has also become a commonly-distributed component in many distributions. However, this doesn't mean you don't need to reinstall them or that you won't need to have the source code available.

There are many common distributions that have insecure, buggy, and old versions of the software. Moreover, many don't have support for some of the modules you'll need and aren't compatible with many of the advanced features discussed in this book. To test what you've got, follow the instructions in this section, and then decide whether you need to re-install your software.

The instructions in this section assume standard directories where tools are installed. For example, you'll typically find MySQL in */usr/local/mysql/*, Apache in */usr/local/apache2*, and Apache's document root directory is */usr/local/apache2/htdocs*. However, that's not true for all distributions: for example, another common place you'll find the document root is in */var/www*. If you know where the standard directories are on your system, use those instead of the ones listed in our instructions.

MySQL

To check whether you have MySQL installed, follow these steps. If you know that MySQL is installed and which directory it's in, but you're not sure what version you have, skip to Step 4.

1. Get a shell prompt (by running a terminal) and log in as the root user. You can log in as root by typing *su* and then supplying the root user password.

2. Let's see if you have MySQL installed. You can find the *mysqld* server binary by typing the following at the shell prompt (the shell prompt is represented by a %):

   ```
   % cd /
   % find . -name mysqld -print
   ```

   Be patient, this could take a very long time.

   This prints out a full path if it finds the server. For example, you might see:

   ```
   ./usr/local/mysql/bin/mysqld
   ```

   If it's found, make a note of MySQL's directory location as you'll need it later (in this example, it's */usr/local/mysql/*). If it's not found, it isn't installed and you should skip to the section "Apache and PHP."

3. If you've found MySQL, in the terminal window type:

   ```
   % ps -e | grep mysql
   ```

   If you've got MySQL running, you'll see two or more lines containing references to MySQL:

   ```
    996 ?        00:00:00 mysqld_safe
   1073 ?        00:00:01 mysqld
   ```

   If it is running, use Step 4; if it's not, use Step 5.

4. To find out what version is running, use the following:

   ```
   % /usr/local/mysql/bin/mysqladmin version
   ```

   If MySQL was installed in a different directory, replace */usr/local/mysql/bin* with the directory you discovered in Step 2.

   You should see output as follows:

   ```
   mysqladmin Ver 8.40 Distrib 4.0.17, for intel-linux on i686
   Copyright (C) 2000 MySQL AB & MySQL Finland AB & TCX DataKonsult AB
   ```

```
This software comes with ABSOLUTELY NO WARRANTY. This is free software,
and you are welcome to modify and redistribute it under the GPL license

Server version        4.0.17-log
Protocol version      10
Connection            Localhost via UNIX socket
UNIX socket           /tmp/mysql.sock
Uptime:               8 hours 57 min 39 sec
```

If you have Server version 3, you should install a new version.

If you have Server version 4.0, you can use all of the book except some of the new features of MySQL 4.1 that are discussed in Chapter 15. At the time of writing, this is the best, most-stable choice.

If you have Server version 4.1 or later, the material in this book that relies on the standard MySQL library can't be used at the time of writing. The standard library is discussed in Chapter 6, and the standard library supports the PEAR DB package described in Chapter 7 and used in the example application in Chapters 16 through 20. It's likely that this problem will be remedied in the future; see Appendix H for more information.

To install or upgrade, follow the instructions in "Installing MySQL."

5. If MySQL isn't running, follow the instructions in "Starting MySQL" to get it started.

Apache and PHP

This section shows you how to check if you have an Apache web server with a PHP module, whether it's a suitable version for use with this book, and if it's currently running. If you know Apache is installed and you know what directory it's in, then skip Step 2. Follow these steps:

1. Get a shell prompt (by running a terminal) and login in as the root user. You can log in as root by typing *su* and then supplying the root user password.

2. Now, let's see if you have the Apache web server installed. You can find the *httpd* server binary by typing the following at the shell prompt:

   ```
   % cd /
   % find . -name httpd -print
   ```

   Be patient, this could take a very long time.

   This prints out a full path if it finds the server. For example, you might see:

   ```
   ./usr/local/apache2/bin/httpd
   ```

   If it's found, make a note of Apache's directory location as you'll need it later (in this example, it's */usr/local/apache2/*). If it's not found, it isn't installed and you should skip to "Installation Overview."

3. If you've found the web server, check whether it is running. To do this, type:

   ```
   % ps -e | grep httpd
   ```

If you see several lines similar to the following, you have Apache running:

```
1324 ?        00:00:00 httpd
1325 ?        00:00:00 httpd
1326 ?        00:00:00 httpd
1327 ?        00:00:00 httpd
1328 ?        00:00:00 httpd
1329 ?        00:00:00 httpd
```

If Apache isn't running, follow the instructions in "Installing Apache" to get it started.

4. Now that Apache is running, check that the Apache web server is responding to HTTP requests. Load the URL *http://127.0.0.1/* in a web browser on the same machine as the web server. If Apache is serving correctly, a web page will be shown.

5. To test the PHP module, change directory to the Apache document root:

```
% cd /usr/local/apache2/htdocs
```

If this directory doesn't exist, you'll need to find the document root *htdocs* directory elsewhere on your server. You can do this with:

```
% cd /
% find . -name htdocs -print
```

Be patient, this might take a very long time. When you've found the directory, use *cd* to change directory to it.

6. Create a file with the name *phpinfo.php* using a text editor. In the file, type the following, save the script, and exit the editor:

```
<?php phpinfo(); ?>
```

7. You may need to make the file readable by your web server using:

```
% chmod a+r /usr/local/apache2/htdocs/phpinfo.php
```

8. Test the newly created PHP script by retrieving the URL *http://127.0.0.1/ phpinfo.php* in a web browser.

If you see a page full of information, your Apache has functioning PHP support. The version of PHP you're working with is shown at the top of the web page.

If you have PHP4, you can use most of the material in this book with the exception of the advanced object-oriented features described in Chapter 14.

If you have PHP5, you can use all of the material in this book.

To check the version of Apache you're working with, look for the setting of the Server API, which is usually the fourth row in the first table. If it says `Apache 2.0 Handler`, you're using Apache 2. If it says Apache 1.3, you're using an older version, but that's also fine for working with this book.

9. You now need to check whether your PHP has the support you need for MySQL. Look for the Configure Command row in the first table on the web page. Check if it includes:

```
--with-mysql=/usr/local/mysql/
```

If the `--with-mysql` directive is included and it specifies a path to your MySQL installation (as described in the previous section), your Apache and PHP has the basic setup needed to work with this book, and you can move on to the next section.

If the directive isn't there or doesn't point to your MySQL distribution, scroll down until you find a `mysql` section. If you don't find it, your PHP doesn't have MySQL support and you'll need to add it. If you find the heading and you're working with MySQL 4.0, you have basic setup needed to work with this book.

At the time of writing, if you're working with MySQL 4.1 or later, you'll need the improved MySQL library instead of the standard library. Instructions to install this on a Linux platform are in Appendix H.

If your PHP doesn't meet the criteria above for MySQL 4.0, then you'll need to reinstall Apache and PHP by following the instructions in the "Installing Apache" and "Installing PHP" sections. If you've previously installed Apache 2 with shared module support, you only need to reinstall PHP.

Installation Overview

There are three approaches to installing MySQL, Apache, and PHP:

- Install a distribution of Linux that includes the software as precompiled packages. This is the easiest approach, but is prone to the problem of the software being out-of-date.
- Obtain an installation package or packages. Again, the software is often out of date.
- Obtain and build the software from source code. This is the most difficult approach, but it has the advantage that the latest software is installed and the configuration layout and options are controlled in the process.

This section focuses on the third approach.

Installing MySQL

This section shows you how to install and configure your MySQL 4 DBMS server. When you've completed this section, continue on to "Starting MySQL" and "Configuring MySQL."

1. Get a shell prompt (by running a terminal) and log in as the root user. You can log in as root by typing **su** and then supplying the root user password.
2. If you determined earlier in "Finding Out What's Installed" that a MySQL server is already running, stop it using:

```
% /usr/local/mysql/bin/mysqladmin -uroot -ppassword shutdown
```

If your MySQL isn't installed in this directory, replace the directory with the correct one you noted earlier. If this doesn't work, try omitting -*ppassword* from the command.

3. Download MySQL. At the time of writing, we recommend MySQL 4.0 for the reasons discussed in "Finding Out What's Installed."

To download MySQL, visit *http://www.mysql.com/downloads/*. Under the heading *MySQL database server & standard clients*, click on the link that's marked as the production release. From the release page, choose the option under "Source Downloads" marked "tarball (.tar.gz)". Download the file into a directory where files can be created and there is sufficient disk space. A good location is */tmp*.

The *mysql.com* web site recommends you use their precompiled versions of MySQL, rather than creating one yourself. You can do this, and it usually works, but occasionally you'll find you don't have all of the support libraries and versions you need for a successful installation. We therefore recommend that the most reliable option, despite the warning, is to build your own version from source code.

4. Move the MySQL source code file to the base directory of the desired installation. The most common location is */usr/local/src* and, assuming the distribution downloaded is MySQL 4.0.17, and it was downloaded in the first step into the */tmp* directory, the command is:

```
% mv /tmp/mysql-4.0.17.tar.gz /usr/local/src
```

5. After moving the distribution to the desired location, change the directory to that location using:

```
% cd /usr/local/src
```

6. Uncompress the package in the new installation directory by running:

```
% gzip -d mysql-version.tar.gz
```

If MySQL 4.0.17 has been downloaded, the command is:

```
% gzip -d mysql-4.0.17.tar.gz
```

7. Un-*tar* the tape archive file by running:

```
% tar xvf mysql-version.tar
```

A list of files that are extracted is shown. If the version downloaded is MySQL 4. 0.17, the command is:

```
% tar xvf mysql-4.0.17.tar
```

8. Change directory to the MySQL distribution directory:

```
% cd mysql-version
```

If the version is MySQL 4.0.17, type:

```
% cd mysql-4.0.17
```

9. Add a new Linux group account for the MySQL files:

```
% groupadd mysql
```

10. Add a new Linux user who is a member of the newly created group `mysql`:

    ```
    % useradd -g mysql mysql
    ```

11. Decide on an installation directory. Later, we recommend that PHP and Apache be installed in */usr/local/*, so a good choice is */usr/local/mysql/*. We assume throughout these steps that */usr/local/mysql/* is used.

12. Configure the MySQL installation by running the *configure* script. This detects the available Linux tools and the installation environment for the MySQL configuration:

    ```
    % ./configure --prefix=/usr/local/mysql
    ```

13. Compile the MySQL DBMS:

    ```
    % make
    ```

14. Install MySQL by running the command:

    ```
    % make install
    ```

15. MySQL is now installed but isn't yet configured. Now, run the *mysql_install_db* script to initialize the system databases used by MySQL:

    ```
    % ./scripts/mysql_install_db
    ```

16. Change the owner of the MySQL program files to be the root user:

    ```
    % chown -R root /usr/local/mysql
    ```

17. Change the owner of the MySQL databases and log files to be the `mysql` user:

    ```
    % chown -R mysql /usr/local/mysql/var
    ```

18. Change the group of the MySQL installation files to be the `mysql` group:

    ```
    % chgrp -R mysql /usr/local/mysql
    ```

19. Copy the default medium-scale parameter configuration file to the default location of */etc*. These parameters are read when MySQL is started. The copy command is:

    ```
    % cp support-files/my-medium.cnf /etc/my.cnf
    ```

20. Edit the configuration file and adjust the default number of maximum connections to match the default value for the maximum Apache web server connections. Also, activate the query cache. Using a text editor, edit the file */etc/my.cnf*, and find the section beginning with the following text:

    ```
    # The MySQL server
    [mysqld]
    ```

    In this section, add the following lines, save the file, and exit the editor:

    ```
    set-variable = max_connections=150
    query_cache_type = 1
    ```

The installation of MySQL is now complete, but it isn't completely configured and the server isn't running. The steps in the next two sections start the DBMS, and set it up further.

Starting MySQL

In the previous section, you installed MySQL. Now, you need to get it running. Follow these steps:

1. If you're not logged in as the root user, get a shell prompt (by running a terminal) and log in as the root user. You can do this by typing **su** and then supplying the root user password.

2. Now that MySQL is installed, you can start it with the following command:

   ```
   % /usr/local/mysql/bin/mysqld_safe --user=mysql &
   ```

3. Check that the MySQL DBMS is running with the *mysqladmin* utility. The following command reports statistics about the MySQL DBMS version and usage:

   ```
   % /usr/local/mysql/bin/mysqladmin version
   ```

   If you have already defined a password *secret*, you'll need to insert -p*secret* before the version parameter; adding a password is discussed in the next section.

4. When the machine is rebooted, MySQL doesn't restart automatically. After reboot, you can use the previous step to restart MySQL or, alternatively, this process can be made automatic. If you know the standard method to add an automatically-started service on your system, add the startup command.

   One common standard method to make the process automatic is to add commands to the file *rc.local* (normally either in or below the directory */etc*). The *rc.local* file is used to list locally installed software that should be run on startup. Using an editor, add the following line to the bottom of the *rc.local* file, save the file, and exit your editor:

   ```
   /usr/local/mysql/bin/safe_mysqld --user=mysql &
   ```

5. If you need to stop MySQL, use the following command:

   ```
   % /usr/local/mysql/bin/mysqladmin shutdown
   ```

   If you have already defined a password *secret*, you'll need to insert -p*secret* before the shutdown parameter; adding a password is discussed in the next section.

Configuring MySQL

The following steps set a password for the root user and create a new user for the MySQL installation that is used in PHP scripts to access the server. The steps assume you're logged in as the root user and that MySQL is running; see the previous section if this isn't true.

The new user can carry out all actions required from Chapter 6 to Chapter 20 on the *winestore* database but has no access to other databases and can't change database access privileges. The new user also can't access the DBMS from a remote server. If you're creating your own application, replace *winestore* with the name of your database. More information on user privileges can be found in Chapter 15.

The steps are as follows:

1. Choose and set a password for root user access to the MySQL DBMS. To set a password of *secret*, use:

   ```
   % /usr/local/mysql/bin/mysqladmin -uroot password secret
   ```

   Record the password for later use.

2. Start the MySQL command line interpreter using the password defined in the previous step:

   ```
   % /usr/local/mysql/bin/mysql -uroot -psecret
   ```

3. Add a new user. Choose a username to replace *username* and a password to replace *password* in the following command:

   ```
   GRANT SELECT, INSERT, UPDATE, DELETE, LOCK TABLES ON winestore.* TO
       username@127.0.0.1 IDENTIFIED BY 'password';
   ```

   It doesn't matter that the *winestore* database doesn't exist yet.

   MySQL responds with:

   ```
   Query OK, 0 rows affected (0.00 sec)
   ```

   Record the username and password.

   If the statement doesn't work for your release, try it again but omit the , LOCK TABLES component.

4. Quit the MySQL command interpreter with the command:

   ```
   mysql> quit
   ```

   MySQL responds with:

   ```
   Bye
   ```

5. Test the user by running the MySQL command interpreter using the *username* and *password*:

   ```
   % /usr/local/mysql/bin/mysql -uusername -psecret
   ```

6. MySQL responds with a message beginning:

   ```
   Welcome to the MySQL monitor.
   ```

7. Quit the MySQL interpreter again with:

   ```
   mysql> quit
   ```

The MySQL DBMS is now configured with a user who can access the *winestore* database from the database server machine 127.0.0.1. The *winestore* database can't be tested yet as it isn't loaded. The database is loaded in "What's Needed for This Book."

Installing Apache

This section explains how to install the Apache 2 web server. We also show you how to optionally install and configure a secure web server that can serve *https://* requests, including how to create a private key, a certificate request, and a simple self-signed certificate.

Installing a Secure Apache Server

This section describes how to prepare to install a secure version of the Apache web server so that you can support *https://* URLs. If you don't need a secure server, skip this section and continue the basic Apache 2 install in "Installing a Regular Apache Server." You can find out more about secure web servers in Chapter 11.

There are two major differences encountered when installing Apache to use SSL versus installing Apache normally:

Secure Sockets Layer software is required.
> There are several sources of Secure Sockets Layer software. The OpenSSL is probably the most-commonly used with Apache, and we show you how to obtain and install it in this section.

A site certificate needs to be obtained and configured.
> A free, self-signed certificate can be created (and that's what we do in this section). You need to replace it with a purchased certificate from a Certification Authority when an application goes live.

Installing OpenSSL

To start your secure install, you need to set up the secure tools as follows:

1. Get the latest version of OpenSSL from *http://www.openssl.org/source/*. Download the Unix *tar*-ed and *gzip*-ed file under the heading "Tarball." For example, download the file *openssl-0.9.7c.tar.gz*.

2. Run a terminal program and login as the root user.

3. Store the distribution file in a directory that can be used to build the OpenSSL libraries. To move the file to */usr/local/src*, use:

   ```
   % mv openssl-0.9.7c.tar.gz /usr/local/src
   ```

   Then, change directory to where the file is stored:

   ```
   % cd /usr/local/src
   ```

4. Uncompress and un-tar the distribution file in the new installation directory using gzip and tar. If the version downloaded was 0.9.7c, the commands are:

   ```
   % gzip -d openssl-0.9.7c.tar.gz
   % tar xvf openssl-0.9.7c.tar
   ```

   The distribution files are listed as they are extracted from the tar file.

5. Change the directory to the *openssl* source directory, run the *config* script, and then *make* the installation. Assuming the version downloaded is 0.9.7c, the commands are:

   ```
   % cd openssl-0.9.7c
   % ./config
   % make
   % make test
   ```

To install OpenSSL in a *directory-path* of your choice instead of */usr/local/ssl*, run *config* with the `openssldir=directory-path` directive.

6. Build the install binaries of SSL:

   ```
   % make install
   ```

   This creates an installation of SSL in the directory */usr/local/ssl*.

7. Now continue with the section "Installing a Regular Apache Server." You need to complete the regular install before you can continue with the next section.

Creating a key and a certificate

For Apache to use SSL, it needs to be configured with a private key and a certificate. Once the key and certificate have been created, they need to be configured into Apache. These steps show you how:

1. First, complete the steps in the previous section and in the section "Installing a Regular Apache Server." You need to complete these before you can continue with these steps.

2. Log in as the root user, and change directory to the location of the *openssl* binary and create the key:

   ```
   % cd /usr/local/ssl/bin
   % ./openssl genrsa -des3 1024 > /usr/local/apache2/conf/localhost.key
   ```

   If you have an actual domain for your server, replace *localhost* with the full domain name. Supply a password, and record it for future use. You've now created the private key.

3. Create the certificate request by typing:

   ```
   % ./openssl req -new -key /usr/local/apache2/conf/localhost.key > \
     /usr/local/apache2/conf/localhost.csr
   ```

   If you have an actual domain for your server, replace *localhost* with the full domain name. The process asks for several fields including country, state, organization name, and email address. The script produces a file that contains the certificate signing request.

4. Now, create the self-signed certificate by typing:

   ```
   % ./openssl req -x509 -days 90 -key \
     /usr/local/apache2/conf/localhost.key \
     -in /usr/local/apache2/conf/localhost.csr > \
     /usr/local/apache2/conf/localhost.crt
   ```

   You need to provide the password you used to create your private key.

5. Modify the *ssl.conf* file with a text editor so that it uses your certificate. The configuration file is found in the directory */usr/local/apache2/conf/*. Using a text editor, find the following lines in the *ssl.conf* file:

   ```
   DocumentRoot "/usr/local/apache2/htdocs"
   ServerName new.host.name:443
   SSLCertificateFile /usr/local/apache2/conf/ssl.crt/server.crt
   SSLCertificateKeyFile /usr/local/apache2/conf/ssl.key/server.key
   ```

Change the lines so that they are as follows:

```
DocumentRoot "secure-document-root"
ServerName localhost:443
SSLCertificateFile /usr/local/apache2/conf/localhost.crt
SSLCertificateKeyFile /usr/local/apache2/conf/localhost.key
```

Replace *secure-document-root* with the directory from which you want to serve secure files. You could use */usr/local/apache2/htdocs-secure*. If you have an actual domain for your server, also replace `localhost` with the full domain name.

6. Create the directory from which you want to serve secure files. For example, if you replaced *secure-document-root* with */usr/local/apache2/htdocs-secure* in the previous step, use:

```
% mkdir /usr/local/apache2/htdocs-secure
```

Now, for testing, create a simple *index.html* file in the new directory with a text editor that contains:

```
<html>Secure hello!</html>
```

Save the file, and ensure it's world-readable using:

```
% chmod a+rx /usr/local/apache2/htdocs-secure/
% chmod a+r /usr/local/apache2/htdocs-secure/index.html
```

7. Start Apache. Use the following command:

```
% /usr/local/apache2/bin/apachectl startssl
```

You need to provide your password again. A secure Apache is now running and serving requests on port 443 (the default HTTPS port) via SSL and also serving regular HTTP requests on post 80. You can test it by requesting the resources *https://127.0.0.1/* and *http://127.0.0.1/* with a web browser running on the same machine as the web server. You should see your sample page, and your regular pages respectively.

When a resource such as *https://127.0.0.1/* is requested with a browser, the browser alerts the user to an unknown certificate. To obtain a certificate that will be trusted by users, you need to send your certificate request to a Certification Authority to be signed using their authoritative certificates. There is a fee for this service. While the Apache configuration allows both the key and the certificate to be placed in a single file, the private key should not be sent to anyone, not even the Certification Authority. More documentation can be found at *http://www.openssl.org/docs/apps/openssl.html*.

Installing a Regular Apache Server

This section explains how to install a regular Apache 2 web server that supports HTTP requests. Here are the steps to install Apache 2:

1. If you determined earlier in "Finding Out What's Installed" that an Apache web server is already running, stop the web server using:

```
% /usr/local/apache2/bin/apachectl stop
```

- If your Apache isn't installed in this directory, replace the directory with the correct one you noted earlier.

2. Get the latest version of the Apache HTTP Server from *http://httpd.apache.org/*. Scroll down the page until you see a heading such as *Apache 2.0.48 is the best available version*. Form beneath the heading, choose the latest source code version ending in the suffix *.tar.gz* and save the file in the */tmp* directory.

3. Move the Apache distribution file to the desired installation directory. The most common location is */usr/local/src*. Assuming the distribution downloaded is Apache 2.0.47, and it was downloaded in the first step into the */tmp* directory, the command is:

```
% mv httpd-2.0.47.tar.gz /usr/local/src
```

4. After moving the distribution to the desired location, change the directory to that location using:

```
% cd /usr/local/src
```

5. Uncompress the package in the new installation directory by running:

```
% gzip -d httpd-version_number.tar.gz
```

If the distribution downloaded is Apache 2.0.47, the command is:

```
% gzip -d httpd-2.0.47.tar.gz
```

6. Un-*tar* the archive file by running:

```
% tar xvf httpd-version_number.tar
```

The list of files extracted is shown. If the version downloaded was Apache 2.0. 47, the command is:

```
% tar xvf httpd-2.0.47.tar
```

7. Change directory to the Apache installation:

```
% cd httpd-version_number
```

If the Apache version is 2.0.47, type:

```
% cd httpd-2.0.47
```

8. Configure the Apache installation by running the *configure* script. This detects the available tools, the installation environment, and other details for the Apache configuration:

```
% ./configure --enable-so --with-layout=Apache
```

Respectively, the two parameters enable the shared module support (PHP can then be loaded as a shared module) and set up the standard directory layout.

If you are planning on serving HTTPS requests, and you've installed OpenSSL following our instructions in "Installing a Secure Apache Server", add --enable-ssl to the list of parameters:

```
% ./configure --enable-so --with-layout=Apache --enable-ssl
```

9. Compile the Apache web server using the command:

```
% make
```

10. Install the Apache server using the command:

    ```
    % make install
    ```

11. If the installation of Apache with PHP support has been successful, you'll be returned to a shell prompt without any error messages appearing. The last line of the install should be similar to this:

    ```
    make[1]: Leaving directory `/usr/local/src/httpd-2.0.47'
    ```

12. Start the Apache web server by running the command:

    ```
    % /usr/local/apache2/bin/apachectl start
    ```

13. Check that the server is responding to HTTP requests by accessing it using a web browser. The simplest way to check is to use a web browser to load the URL *http://127.0.0.1/*. If Apache is serving correctly, a web page is displayed.

14. You can now create and serve HTML pages from the directory *usr/local/apache2/htdocs/* and these will be accessible using the base URL *http://127.0.0.1/* or using the domain name of your server. Record this directory for later use.

    For example, you could create the file *usr/local/apache2/htdocs/hello.html* using a text editor and this is then accessible as *http://127.0.0.1/hello.html*. If you find that a Forbidden error appears when you try and retrieve a new page, you'll need to make the file readable by everyone using, for example, **chmod a+r /usr/local/apache2/htdocs/hello.html**.

15. When the machine is rebooted, Apache will not be restarted automatically. After reboot, you can manually restart Apache using *apachectl* or, alternatively, this process can be made automatic. If you know the standard method to add an automatically-started service on your system, add the startup command.

    One common standard method to make the process automatic is to add commands to the file *rc.local* (normally either in or below the directory */etc*). The *rc.local* file is used to list locally installed software that should be run on startup. You'll typically find the file *rc.local* either in or below the directory */etc*. Using an editor, add the following line to the bottom of the *rc.local* file:

    ```
    /usr/local/apache2/bin/apachectl start
    ```

16. If Apache needs to be stopped at any time, this can by achieved by executing:

    ```
    % /usr/local/apache2/bin/apachectl stop
    ```

Installing PHP

This section explains how to install PHP 4 (versions later than 4.3) or PHP 5 as a shared module in Apache 2:

1. Once you have installed Apache, you can install the shared PHP module as part of the web server. Login in as the root user.

2. Get the latest version of PHP from *http://www.php.net/downloads.php*. Download the "Complete Source Code" version into the */tmp* directory. Do not down-

load any version earlier than PHP 4.3.0, as this will not work with the latest version of Apache 2. This book uses PHP 4.3.3 and PHP 5.0.0 beta, and we recommend installing the latest stable version at the time of writing.

3. Choose an installation directory. If the Apache installation was begun in */usr/local/*, the same location can also be used for PHP. Move the PHP source code file to the base directory of the desired installation. Assuming this is */usr/local/src* and, assuming the distribution downloaded is PHP 4.3.3 and it was downloaded into the */tmp* directory, the command is:

```
% mv php-4.3.3.tar.gz /usr/local/src
```

4. After moving the distribution to the desired location, change directory to that location using:

```
% cd /usr/local/src
```

5. Uncompress the package in the new installation directory by running:

```
% gzip -d php-version_number.tar.gz
```

If the version downloaded is PHP 4.3.3, the command is:

```
% gzip -d php-4.3.3.tar.gz
```

6. Un-*tar* the distribution by running:

```
% tar xvf php-version_number.tar
```

A list of files extracted is displayed. If the version downloaded is PHP 4.3.3, the command is:

```
% tar xvf php-4.3.3.tar
```

7. Change directory to the PHP installation:

```
% cd php-version_number
```

If the version is PHP 4.3.3, type:

```
% cd php-4.3.3
```

8. Configure the PHP installation by running the *configure* script. This detects the available tools and the installation environment, adds MySQL support, and prepares for Apache 2 integration. It assumes that MySQL has been installed previously in the directory */usr/local/mysql* and that Apache 2 has been installed in */usr/local/apache2*.

If you've installed MySQL 4.0, then use the following command:

```
% ./configure --with-apxs2=/usr/local/apache2/bin/apxs \
  --with-mysql=/usr/local/mysql/
```

If you've installed MySQL 4.1, then the regular PHP MySQL library won't work at the time of writing. Instead, you need to use the improved MySQL library that's discussed in Appendix H (and you need to be aware that the functions described in Chapter 6 are replaced by new functions discussed in Appendix H). To use the improved library, type:

```
% ./configure --with-apxs2=/usr/local/apache2/bin/apxs \
  --without-mysql --with-mysqli=/usr/local/mysql/bin/mysql_config
```

A common problem that occurs with PHP 5 is that the script complains that you need a newer version of libxml2. If this occurs, visit *ftp://xmlsoft.org/* and obtain and install the latest version of libxml2. The installation process is straightforward: choose the *.tar.gz* version, extract it using the *gzip* and *tar* utilities, and then run *./configure*, *make*, and *make install*.

9. Compile the PHP scripting engine by running:

    ```
    % make
    ```

10. Now that the PHP scripting engine is built, install the PHP engine using:

    ```
    % make install
    ```

11. The PHP installation is almost complete. Now copy across the default PHP configuration file to the default location, This file, *php.ini*, contains the settings that control the behavior of PHP and includes, for example, how variables are initialized, how sessions are managed, and what scripting tags can be used. The command to copy the file is:

    ```
    % cp php.ini-dist /usr/local/lib/php.ini
    ```

12. Edit the Apache configuration file and enable PHP script engine support for files that have the suffix *.php*. To do this, edit the file */usr/local/apache2/conf/httpd.conf* and add the following line to the AddType section (at approximately line 850):

    ```
    AddType application/x-httpd-php .php
    ```

    For PHP 5 installs, check that the following line has automatically been added to the file:

    ```
    LoadModule php5_module    modules/libphp5.so
    ```

    If the line is not present, add it.

    For PHP 4 installs, check that the following line has automatically been added to the file:

    ```
    LoadModule php4_module    modules/libphp4.so
    ```

    If the line is not present, add it. Save the file and exit the editor.

13. Restart the Apache web server by running the command

    ```
    % /usr/local/apache2/bin/apachectl restart
    ```

14. To test the PHP module, change the directory to the Apache document root:

    ```
    % cd /usr/local/apache2/htdocs
    ```

15. Create a file with the name *phpinfo.php* using a text editor. In the file, type the following, save the script, and exit the editor:

    ```
    <?php phpinfo(); ?>
    ```

16. Test the newly created PHP script by retrieving with a browser the following URL *http://127.0.0.1/phpinfo.php*. You should see a page full of information.

Apache is now running and serving both static HTML and PHP scripts. The installation of Apache, PHP, and MySQL is now complete, and you've also successfully installed PEAR, as it's now a default component of PHP.

What's Needed for This Book

This section shows you how to download and install our example database, all of the book code examples, the sample online winestore application, and the additional packages that are used throughout the book.

Installing PEAR Packages

The following optional PEAR package is required:

HTML_Template_IT
    This is needed to work with Chapter 7 and all later chapters.

Detailed instructions to install optional packages can be found in Chapter 7. You'll also find a discussion there about how to find about, install, and upgrade packages.

In brief, to install and upgrade the packages you need for this book do the following:

1. Log in as the root user.
2. If you're not already, connect to the Internet.
3. Type the following to install the optional package:

    ```
    % pear install HTML_Template_IT
    ```

4. Type the following to check if upgrades of the core packages used in this book are available:

    ```
    % pear upgrade PEAR
    % pear upgrade Date
    % pear upgrade DB
    % pear upgrade Mail
    ```

Installing the Code Examples

The example PHP scripts in this book are available from our book's web site, *http://www.webdatabasebook.com*. In this section, we show you how to install them for use on your machine. The winestore application isn't installed in this section; see "Installing the Winestore Application" for instructions.

We assume you've already followed the instructions in this chapter to install MySQL, PHP, and Apache. We also assume you've installed these tools in the locations we recommend; if you haven't, replace the directory */usr/local/apache2/htdocs* with your document root location during the following steps.

To install the example scripts, follow these steps:

1. Using a browser, download the file *http://www.webdatabasebook.com/examples.zip* into the */tmp* directory.
2. To start, you need to configure your Apache web server so that it won't show users the content of the *.inc* include files if they're retrieved with a web browser.

There are several ways to do this, but the simplest is to edit your *httpd.conf* configuration file. You'll find the file in */usr/local/apache2/conf/*. To edit the file, you'll need to login as the root user.

Now, open the *httpd.conf* file in an editor, and add this to the end of the file:

```
<Files ~ "\.inc$">
    Order allow,deny
    Deny from all
    Satisfy All
</Files>
```

Save the file and exit the editor. You now need to restart your Apache server. You can do this by typing:

```
% /usr/local/apache2/bin/apachectl restart
```

3. Now, create a directory in your Apache document root to store the examples, and copy the downloaded file to that location:

```
% mkdir /usr/local/apache2/htdocs/wda
% cp /tmp/examples.zip /usr/local/apache2/htdocs/wda
```

4. Unzip the *wda.zip* examples in their new directory by doing this:

```
% cd /usr/local/apache2/htdocs/wda
% unzip examples.zip
```

5. Edit the file *db.inc* in the *wda* directory and modify the lines beginning with $username and $password so that *fred* and *shhh* are replaced with the username and password you chose for your user when installing MySQL:

```
<?php
    $hostName = "127.0.0.1";
    $databaseName = "winestore";
    $username = "fred";
    $password = "shhh";
```

Save the file and exit the editor.

6. You may also need to set the file permissions so that examples are accessible through your web browser. To do this, use:

```
% chmod a+rx /usr/local/apache/htdocs/wda
% chmod a+r /usr/local/apache/htdocs/wda/*
```

7. You should now be able to load the example list by requesting the following URL with a web browser running on the same machine as the web server: *http://127.0.0.1/wda/*. Test the examples from Chapters 2 through 4—they should work.

You'll find that some of the examples from Chapter 6 onward run only if the *winestore* database has been loaded into the MySQL DBMS by following the instructions in the next section. In addition, most examples from Chapter 7 onward work only if you've installed the PEAR package HTML_Template_IT.

Installing the PDF PHP Library

To work with the PDF PHP library in Chapter 13, you need to download the class files. To do this, follow these steps:

1. Visit the web site *http://ros.co.nz/pdf/*.

2. From the Downloads section, choose the link to the Zip file that contains the class, sample, and the required font metric files. Save the file in */tmp*.

3. Change directory to the temporary directory and unzip the download file. into an install directory.

   If you're only planning to use the library with our examples, first install the code examples as described in the previous section, and then use:

   ```
   % unzip pdfClassesAndFonts_009e.zip -d /usr/local/apache2/htdocs/wda
   ```

   This installs the class files and fonts in the examples directory.

   An alternative approach is to install the files into a shared file location such as */usr/local/src/pdf-php*. Then, edit your *php.ini* file and include the directory at the end of the include_path directive. This allows you to include the path in a PHP script using only the class name and without specifying the directory.

Loading the Winestore Database

A local copy of the *winestore* database is required to test the SQL examples in Chapter 5, to test some of the web database application examples in Chapters 6 through 13, and to use the sample winestore application described in Chapters 16 through 20. In addition, MySQL must be installed and configured before the *winestore* database can be loaded.

We assume you've installed MySQL in the location we recommend; if you haven't, replace the directory */usr/local/mysql* with your MySQL installation directory in the following steps.

The steps to load the *winestore* database are as follows:

1. Using a web browser, download the file *http://www.webdatabasebook.com/database.zip* into the */tmp* directory.

2. Uncompress the winestore database in any directory by typing the following in a shell window:

   ```
   % unzip database.zip
   ```

3. Run the MySQL command-line interpreter using the root username and the *password* you set, and load the *winestore* database:

   ```
   % /usr/local/mysql/bin/mysql -uroot -ppassword < /tmp/winestore.data
   ```

   Be patient, this may take a while. Exit the command interpreter by typing **quit**.

4. After the loading is complete (it may take a while) the database can be tested by running a query. To do this, use the *username* and *password* you created when installing and configuring MySQL:

```
% /usr/local/mysql/bin/mysql -uusername -ppassword
```

Now type:

```
mysql> SELECT * FROM region;
```

This should produce the following list of wine regions as output:

```
+-----------+--------------------+
| region_id | region_name        |
+-----------+--------------------+
|         1 | All                |
|         2 | Goulburn Valley    |
|         3 | Rutherglen         |
|         4 | Coonawarra         |
|         5 | Upper Hunter Valley |
|         6 | Lower Hunter Valley |
|         7 | Barossa Valley     |
|         8 | Riverland          |
|         9 | Margaret River     |
|        10 | Swan Valley        |
+-----------+--------------------+
```

The *winestore* database has now been loaded and tested.

Installing the Winestore Application

The sample online winestore application is available from our book's web site, *http://www.webdatabasebook.com*. In this section, we show you how to install it on your machine.

We assume you've installed the *winestore* database by following the instructions in the previous section. We also assume you've already followed the instructions in this chapter to install MySQL, PHP, and Apache, and that you've installed these tools in the locations we recommend; if you haven't, replace the directory */usr/local/apache2/htdocs* with your document root location in the following steps.

Follow these steps:

1. Using a browser, download the file *http://www.webdatabasebook.com/wda2-winestore.zip* into the */tmp* directory.

2. If you haven't configured your Apache web server so that it won't show users the content of the *.inc* include files, follow Step 2 in the section "Installing the Code Examples."

3. Log in as the root user and move the application into your Apache document root:

```
% cp /tmp/wda2-winestore.zip /usr/local/apache2/htdocs/
```

4. Unzip the *wda2-winestore.zip* code in the document root directory. This will create the subdirectory *wda2-winestore*:

```
% cd /usr/local/apache2/htdocs/
% unzip wda2-winestore.zip
```

5. Edit the file *wda2-winestore/includes/db.inc* and modify the lines beginning with $username and $password so that *fred* and *shhh* are replaced with the username and password you selected when configuring MySQL:

```
<?php
    $hostname = "127.0.0.1";
    $databasename = "winestore";
    $username = "fred";
    $password = "shhh";
```

Save the file and exit the editor.

6. You may also need to set the file permissions so that examples are accessible through your web browser. To do this, use:

```
% chmod a+rx /usr/local/apache2/htdocs/wda2-winestore
% chmod a+r /usr/local/apache2/htdocs/wda2-winestore/*
```

7. You should now be able to load the application index by requesting the following URL with a web browser running on the same machine as the web server: *http://127.0.0.1/wda2-winestore/*. Click on the Use the Application link and you should be able to use the application.

APPENDIX B

Microsoft Windows Installation Guide

This appendix is a guide to installing the software used in the book under the Microsoft Windows 2000, 2003, and XP environments. You'll need to be able to log in as the administrator in Microsoft Windows to follow these instructions.

We assume that PHP, MySQL, and Apache aren't installed. We show you how to get them installed and running, and we then present a short guide to downloading and installing the PHP script and database examples used in this book.

We don't cover installing a secure Apache web server or the improved MySQL library under Microsoft Windows.

The Windows environment, PHP, Apache, MySQL, and our code examples can all change over time. This means that this guide may not work perfectly when you use it. To get the latest installation guide in HTML and PDF formats, along with changes and corrections to this guide, visit *http://www.webdatabasebook.com/install-guides*.

Installation Overview

There are two approaches to installing MySQL, Apache, and PHP under Microsoft Windows:

- Obtain an installation package or packages. This is the best choice because it's the simplest. The disadvantage is that packages don't always contain the latest software.

- Obtain and build the software from source code. This isn't possible unless you've previously installed a C compiler and other support tools that are needed to compile software. The advantage is you always get the latest versions.

Most Windows users don't have a C compiler, so this section focuses on using a package.

In addition to a working Windows 2000 or 2003 installation, you'll need a Zip program to extract files. If you don't have one, a good choice is InfoZIP's free program

Wiz from *http://www.info-zip.org/pub/infozip/WiZ.html*. Windows XP comes with Zip software installed.

We don't cover installation on Microsoft Windows 98 or earlier versions.

Installing with EasyPHP

The best integrated Apache, PHP, and MySQL package for Microsoft Windows is EasyPHP. It's frequently updated, carefully maintained, and reasonably easy to install. However, unless you're a French speaker, it does have the minor disadvantage that some of the documentation and instructions are in French.

Here are the steps to installing EasyPHP under Microsoft Windows. In all steps, make sure you use upper or lowercase characters as shown:

1. Using a web browser, visit the *http://www.easyphp.org/* web site. Click on the language icon at the top of the page that best suits you (the U.S. flag means English).

2. Under the Main Menu heading on the left of the page, click on Downloads and then click on the current version to start the download; at the time of writing, this was EasyPHP1.7 which contains Apache 1.3.27, PHP 4.3.3, and MySQL 4.0.15, and we assume this version in these steps.

   Save the downloaded file in a temporary directory such as *C:\temp*.

   When using EasyPHP 1.7, you'll find that some of the features of MySQL 4.1 discussed in Chapter 15 and the features of PHP5 discussed in Chapter 14 can't be used. However, the rest of the material (including the online winestore) works without modification.

3. Run the downloaded file using the Run option in the Start menu. If you downloaded EasyPHP 1.7, the file that's downloaded is *easyphp1-7_setup.exe*. and you can run it by typing:

   ```
   c:\temp\easyphp1-7_setup.exe
   ```
   Click OK. This will begin the EasyPHP installation process.

4. Now, click Next to start, read the agreements and then check the option that accepts the agreement and click Next. Then, if your French is good, read the advice and click Next again; the advice suggests that the EasyPHP environment works well for development but isn't for application deployment. Our advice—for security and performance reasons—is to use a Unix environment such as Linux for application deployment.

5. The installer asks where you want to install the software, and defaults to *c:\ Program Files\EasyPHP1-7*. Unless you want to change it, click Next and answer Yes to creating the new directory. We assume this directory in the rest of this appendix.

6. Now, choose where you want the EasyPHP menu option to be in your Start Menu launcher. Unless you don't want it in the Programs menu, just accept the default by clicking Next. We assume it's in the Programs menu in the following steps.

7. You've now made all the choices that are needed. Click Install and wait as the install process completes. When it's finished, click Finish.

8. You can now run your Apache and MySQL servers. Click on the Start menu, Programs, Easy PHP 1.7, and on the Easy PHP program. A window should appear; if it doesn't, Apache is already running, and you should see a large E in your taskbar that you can double-click to make the window appear.

9. In the EasyPHP window, choose the language from the drop down that suits you. Then, assuming you've chosen English, select the options *Start on Windows Startup* and *Start Apache and MySQL as Services*. Then click on Apply, and minimize the window. You should now see a large E with a blinking red dot in your taskbar that signifies EasyPHP is running.

10. To test your Apache and PHP, create the file *phpinfo.php* in the directory *C:\ Program Files\EasyPHP1-7\www* and type in the following contents:

    ```
    <?php phpinfo(); ?>
    ```

    If you don't have a special-purpose text editor, use Notepad or WordPad, but make sure the file is saved with the extension *.php* and not *.php.txt*.

    Now, load the URL *http://127.0.0.1/phpinfo.php* with a web browser on the same machine as your EasyPHP installation. You should see a screen containing information about your Apache and PHP installation.

    Make a note that your Apache Document Root is *C:\Program Files\EasyPHP1-7\ www*.

11. Let's configure your MySQL. To begin, test that you can access the MySQL server using the command interpreter. To do this, select the Run option in the Start Menu and enter:

    ```
    "C:\Program Files\EasyPHP1-7\mysql\bin\mysql.exe" -uroot
    ```

    Click OK, and a window containing the command interpreter should appear. This means your MySQL server is running. Quit the MySQL command interpreter with the command:

    ```
    mysql> quit
    ```

    The window should close automatically.

12. Choose and set a password for **root** user access to the MySQL DBMS. To set a password of *secret*, choose the Run option in the Start Menu and enter:

    ```
    "C:\Program Files\EasyPHP1-7\mysql\bin\mysqladmin.exe" -uroot
        password secret
    ```

    Click OK and a window will rapidly open and close, and you shouldn't hear a beep if you've typed the command correctly. Record the password for later use.

13. Start the MySQL command line interpreter using the password defined in the previous step by clicking on Run in the Start Menu and entering:

```
"C:\Program Files\EasyPHP1-7\mysql\bin\mysql.exe" -uroot -psecret
```

Click OK.

Record this step for later use—you'll need it whenever you want to access the command interpreter as the root user.

14. Let's create a new user for the MySQL installation that can carry out all actions required for a typical application (such as accessing our *winestore* database examples in the book), but has no access to other databases and can't change database access privileges. The new user also can't access the DBMS from a remote server.

To add the user, choose a username to replace *username* and a password to replace *password* in the following command:

```
GRANT SELECT, INSERT, UPDATE, DELETE, LOCK TABLES ON winestore.* TO
   username@127.0.0.1 IDENTIFIED BY 'password';
```

MySQL responds with:

```
Query OK, 0 rows affected (0.00 sec)
```

Record the username and password. Quit the MySQL command interpreter with the command:

```
mysql> quit
```

The window should close automatically.

15. Start the MySQL command line interpreter using the *username* and *password* you defined in the previous step by clicking on Run in the Start Menu and entering:

```
"C:\Program Files\EasyPHP1-7\mysql\bin\mysql.exe" -uusername -ppassword
```

Record this step for later use—you'll need it whenever you want to access the command interpreter using your user account *username*. Quit the MySQL interpreter again with:

```
mysql> quit
```

16. Your Apache, PHP, and MySQL setup is now functioning. To finish installation, you now need to set up PEAR and your mail services. Let's start with PEAR, and for this you'll need an Internet connection.

17. Edit the file *C:\Program Files\EasyPHP1-7\php\go-pear.bat*. To do this, you can use Notepad or WordPad. Change:

```
set PHP_BIN=cli/php.exe
```

to

```
set PHP_BIN=php.exe
```

Save the file and quit the editor.

18. Click on Run in the Start Menu and enter:

```
"C:\Program Files\EasyPHP1-7\php\go-pear.bat"
```

Click OK. Press Enter to proceed, and then either type in your web proxy server details or press Enter (for most installations, you can just press Enter).

19. You'll now be presented with a list of 7 options, and option 1 should show *c:\ Program Files\EasyPHP1-7\php\PEAR*. If it doesn't press **1**, Enter, and type in the path:

```
c:\progra~1\easyph~1\php\PEAR
```

Press Enter and the path should update next to option 1.

20. Option 7 may not show the path to your *php.exe* correctly. If it's blank or is not set to *C:\Program Files\EasyPHP1-7\php* then type **7** and press Enter, and then type:

```
C:\progra~1\easyph~1\php\
```

The trailing backslash is necessary. When you press Enter, you should see that option 7 has updated to the correct path.

21. Press Enter to continue the installation. Check that you're still connected to the Internet, and then press Enter to choose to install the bundled packages. This will start the install process and you'll see packages being installed.

22. At the conclusion of the install, there may be a warning about your *php.ini* not containing the correct path to the PEAR include files. Ignore this by pressing Enter, and we'll fix it manually in the next step.

23. Using an editor such as Notepad or WordPad, edit the file:

```
C:\Program Files\EasyPHP1-7\apache\php.ini
```

Find the line beginning:

```
include_path =
```

and change it so the complete line is:

```
include_path = ".;c:\Program Files\EasyPHP1-7\php\pear\pear"
```

24. While we're editing the *php.ini* file, we'll update the mail sending settings. Find the line beginning:

```
SMTP =
```

and adjust this to be the name of your outgoing SMTP mail server. Generally, this is your ISP's domain name prefixed by *mail*. For example, for users of *bigpond.com*, it's:

```
SMTP = mail.bigpond.com
```

Now find the line beginning:

```
sendmail_from =
```

and update it to your email address *me@myaddress.com*:

```
sendmail_from = me@myaddress.com
```

Now, save the file and exit the editor. The mail configuration allows both PHP's internal *mail()* function and the PEAR Mail package to work.

25. To re-read the *php.ini* file, you need to restart your Apache web server. To do this, double-click on the E in the taskbar, press the button labeled "Apache," click on Restart, and then press Close to minimize the window.

26. You've now completed the installation process. Make a note that your PHP configuration *php.ini* file is located in *C:\Program Files\EasyPHP1-7\apache*.

   Your MySQL configuration *my.ini* file (this is known as *my.cnf* in Unix) is in stored in *C:\winnt* or *C:\windows* depending on your Windows version. To check where it is, click on the Start menu, then on Search, and then on For Files or Folders. Type **my.ini** and press the Enter key. The folder that contains the file will be shown after the search is complete. Make a note of the folder.

   If need to edit these files, you can do so using Notepad, WordPad, or another editor, or you can edit them by double-clicking on the large E in the taskbar, and then single-clicking the E in the top-left of the window, selecting the Configuration option, and selecting the file you want to edit. You can also use the EasyPHP window to start and stop Apache and MySQL; clicking on the MySQL and Apache buttons shows all of the options.

   This completes the Microsoft Windows install. If you want to install the book sample code, continue on to the next section.

What's Needed for This Book

This section shows you how to download and install our example database, all of the book code examples, the sample online winestore application, and the additional packages that are used throughout the book.

Installing PEAR Packages

The optional PEAR package *HTML_Template_IT* is required. It is needed to work with Chapter 7 and all later chapters.

Detailed instructions to install optional packages can be found in Chapter 7. You'll also find a discussion there about how to find about, install, and upgrade packages.

In brief, after you've installed EasyPHP, carry out the following steps:

1. If you're not already, connect to the Internet.

2. Run a command window. Do this by selecting the Run option from the Start Menu and typing **command** and then pressing OK. A window will appear that shows a prompt.

3. Into the command window, type:

```
C:\> C:\progra~1\easyph~1\php\pear\pear.bat install HTML_Template_IT
```

   Press Enter. The package will download and install. If something goes wrong, check that you've completed Steps 18 to 24 in "Installing with EasyPHP."

4. Now, check if upgrades of the core packages used in this book are available. Into the command window, type:

```
C:\> C:\progra~1\easyph~1\php\pear\pear.bat upgrade PEAR
```

Press Enter and the package will be downloaded if required.

5. Repeat Step 4, but type:

```
C:\> C:\progra~1\easyph~1\php\pear\pear.bat upgrade Date
```

6. Repeat Step 4, but type:

```
C:\> C:\progra~1\easyph~1\php\pear\pear.bat upgrade DB
```

7. Repeat Step 4, but type:

```
C:\> C:\progra~1\easyph~1\php\pear\pear.bat upgrade Mail
```

Installing the Code Examples

The example PHP scripts from this book are available from our book's web site, *http://www.webdatabasebook.com*. In this section, we show you how to install them for use on your machine. The winestore application isn't installed in this section; see the "Installing the Winestore Application" section for instructions.

To install the example scripts, follow these steps:

1. Using a browser, download the file *http://www.webdatabasebook.com/examples.zip* into a temporary directory such as *C:\windows\temp*.

2. To start, you need to configure your Apache web server so that it won't show users the content of the *.inc* include files if they're retrieved with a web browser. There are several ways to do this, but the simplest is to edit your *httpd.conf* configuration file in *C:\Program Files\EasyPHP1-7\apache\conf*.

   Open the *httpd.conf* file in an editor such as Notepad or WordPad, and add this to the end of the file:

   ```
   <Files ~ "\.inc$">
       Order allow,deny
       Deny from all
       Satisfy All
   </Files>
   ```

   Save the file and exit the editor. You now need to restart your Apache server by double-clicking the E icon in the taskbar, pressing the Apache button, and selecting Restart from the drop-down list.

3. Now, create a directory in your Apache document root to store the examples, and copy the downloaded file to that location.

   To do this, use Windows Explorer to create a new folder below *C:\Program Files\EasyPHP1-7\www* with the name *wda*, and then copy and paste the file *C:\windows\temp\wda.zip* into that folder.

4. Unzip the *wda.zip* examples in their new directory using your Zip program.

You can do this with a double-click on the *wda.zip* icon and then using your Zip program to extract the files into *C:\Program Files\EasyPHP1-7\www\wda*.

5. Edit the file *db.inc* in the *wda* directory and modify the lines beginning with $username and $password so that *fred* and *shhh* are replaced with the username and password you chose for your user when installing MySQL:

```php
<?php
    $hostName = "127.0.0.1";
    $databaseName = "winestore";
    $username = "fred";
    $password = "shhh";
```

Save the file and exit the editor.

6. You should now be able to load the example list by requesting the following URL with a web browser running on the same machine as the web server: *http://127.0.0.1/wda/*.

7. Test the examples from Chapters 2 to 4, and they should work.

You'll find that some of the examples from Chapter 6 onwards run only if the *winestore* database has been loaded into the MySQL DBMS by following the instructions in the next section. In addition, most examples from Chapter 7 onwards work only if you've installed the PEAR package HTML_Template_IT.

Installing the PDF PHP Library

To work with the PDF PHP library in Chapter 13, you need to download the class files. To do this, follow these steps:

1. Visit the web site *http://ros.co.nz/pdf/*.

2. From the Downloads section, choose the link to the Zip file that contains the class, sample, and the required font metric files. Save the file in a temporary directory such as *c:\windows\temp*.

3. Unzip the download file into an install directory using your Zip program. If you're only planning to use the library with this book, then a good location is *C:\Program Files\EasyPHP1-7\www\wda*. This is a directory that's used in the previous section for the code examples.

An alternative approach is to install the files into a shared file location such as *C:\Program Files\EasyPHP1-7\PDF PHP*. Then, edit your *php.ini* file and include the directory at the end of the include_path directive. This allows you to include the path in a PHP script using only the class name and without specifying the directory.

Loading the Winestore Database

A local copy of the *winestore* database is required to test the SQL examples in Chapter 5, to test some of the web database application examples in Chapters 6 to

13, and to use the sample winestore application described in Chapters 16 to 20. MySQL must be installed and configured before the *winestore* database can be loaded.

The steps to load the *winestore* database are as follows:

1. Using a web browser, download the file *http://www.webdatabasebook.com/database.zip* into a temporary directory such as *C:\windows\temp*.

2. Uncompress the winestore database in any directory. You can do this with your Zip utility and save the file in the *C:\windows\temp* directory.

3. Run the MySQL command-line interpreter using the root username and the *password* you set, and load the *winestore* database.

   You do this by choosing the Run option in the Start menu and typing:

   ```
   "C:\Program Files\EasyPHP1-7\mysql\bin\mysql.exe" -uroot -ppassword
   ```

   Then, load the database using:

   ```
   mysql> source C:\windows\temp\winestore.data
   ```

   Be patient, this may take a while.

4. After the loading is complete (it may take a while) the database can be tested by running a query. To do this, type:

   ```
   mysql> SELECT * FROM region;
   ```

   This should produce the following list of wine regions as output:

   ```
   +-----------+---------------------+
   | region_id | region_name         |
   +-----------+---------------------+
   |         1 | All                 |
   |         2 | Goulburn Valley     |
   |         3 | Rutherglen          |
   |         4 | Coonawarra          |
   |         5 | Upper Hunter Valley |
   |         6 | Lower Hunter Valley |
   |         7 | Barossa Valley      |
   |         8 | Riverland           |
   |         9 | Margaret River      |
   |        10 | Swan Valley         |
   +-----------+---------------------+
   ```

The *winestore* database has now been loaded and tested.

Installing the Winestore Application

The sample online winestore application is available from our book's web site, *http://www.webdatabasebook.com*. In this section, we show you how to install it on your machine.

We assume you've installed the *winestore* database by following the instructions in the previous section. We also assume you've already followed the instructions in this chapter to install EasyPHP.

Follow these steps:

1. Using a browser, download the file *http://www.webdatabasebook.com/wda2-winestore.zip* into the directory *C:\Program Files\EasyPHP1-7\www*.

2. If you haven't configured your Apache web server so that it won't show users the content of the *.inc* include files, follow Step 2 in the section "Installing the Code Examples."

3. Unzip the *wda2-winestore.zip* code in the document root directory using your Zip program. This will create the subdirectory *wda2-winestore*. You can usually do this by double-clicking on the *wda2-winestore.zip* icon and using your Zip program to extract the files into *c:\Program Files\EasyPHP1-7\www*.

4. Edit the file *wda2-winestore/includes/db.inc* and modify the lines beginning with $username and $password so that *fred* and *shhh* are replaced with the username and password you selected when configuring MySQL:

   ```
   <?php
     $hostname = "127.0.0.1";
     $databasename = "winestore";
     $username = "fred";
     $password = "shhh";
   ```

   Save the file and exit the editor.

5. Edit the file *wda2-winestore/includes/winestore.inc* and locate the following three lines:

   ```
   // define("D_INSTALL_PATH", "c:/progra~1/easyph~1/www");
   // define("D_INSTALL_PATH", "/Library/WebServer/Documents");
   define("D_INSTALL_PATH", "/usr/local/apache2/htdocs");
   ```

   Uncomment the first line and comment-out the third so that you have the following:

   ```
   define("D_INSTALL_PATH", "c:/progra~1/easyph~1/www");
   // define("D_INSTALL_PATH", "/Library/WebServer/Documents");
   // define("D_INSTALL_PATH", "/usr/local/apache2/htdocs");
   ```

   Save the file and quit the editor.

   Note that forward slashes are used in the Microsoft Windows path.

6. You should now be able to load the application index by requesting the following URL with a web browser running on the same machine as the web server: *http://127.0.0.1/wda2-winestore/*. Click on the Use the Application link and you should be able to use the application.

Mac OS X Installation Guide

This appendix is a guide to installing the software used in the book on an Apple Macintosh OS X platform. The instructions are designed for administrators, so you'll need to be able to log in as the root user. The instructions were written and tested on Mac OS X Panther (Version 10.3.1) with kernel version Darwin 7.0.0.

After showing you how to get PHP, Apache, and MySQL running, we then present a short guide to downloading and installing the PHP script and database examples used in this book. We also show you how to set up tools that are needed by examples in the book but aren't included in the default Apache, PHP, and MySQL installations.

The Mac OS X environment, PHP, Apache, MySQL, and our code examples can all change over time. This means that this guide may not work perfectly when you use it. To get the latest installation guide in HTML and PDF formats, along with changes and corrections to this guide, visit *http://www.webdatabasebook.com/install-guides*.

Getting Started

There are two approaches to working with MySQL, Apache, and PHP:

- Use the software that's installed with Mac OS X and add the missing components. Panther includes Apache 1.3.28 and PHP, but not MySQL. This is the easiest approach, but is prone to the problem of the software being out-of-date and, of course, you still need to install and configure some components.

- Obtain and build the software from source code. This is the most difficult approach, but it has the advantage that the latest software is installed and the configuration layout and options are controlled in the process.

This appendix focuses on the first approach: we use the Apache that comes with Mac OS X, upgrade PHP, and add MySQL.

Before we can begin, you need to unlock your root user. Do the following:

1. Open NetInfo Manager, which is located in Applications → Utilities.

2. Click on the Security menu, and then on Enable Root User. Enter a password and record it for later use.

3. Quit NetInfo manager.

When you've finished the installation steps in this appendix, you can choose to disable the root user by repeating the steps above but clicking on Disable Root User instead.

Installing MySQL

This section shows you how to install and configure your MySQL 4 DBMS server. When you've completed this section, continue on to "Configuring MySQL."

1. Download MySQL. Using a web browser, visit *http://www.mysql.com/ downloads/*. Under the heading *MySQL database server & standard clients*, click on the link that's marked as the production release. On the release page, find the heading *Mac OS X Package Installer downloads* (not Mac OS X downloads!). Click on download next to the Standard option. Save the file to the desktop.

   At the time of writing, choosing which release to use is difficult. We recommend Server version 4.0, as you can use all of the book except some of the new features of MySQL 4.1 that are discussed in Chapter 15.

   If you choose Server version 4.1 or later, then the material in this book that relies on the standard MySQL library can't be used at the time of writing. The standard library is discussed in Chapter 6, and the standard library supports the PEAR DB package described in Chapter 7 and used in the example application in Chapters 16 to 20. It's likely that this will be remedied in the future, and that downloading 4.1 will become a good option. See Appendix H for more information.

2. After the download completes, double-click on the downloaded file that's stored on the desktop; the file has a name such as *mysql-standard-4.0.17.dmg*. This mounts the image file: a dialog will show progress and then the Finder will appear showing two packages and a *ReadMe.txt* file.

3. Double-click the install package in the Finder. This is the package named, for example, *mysql-standard-4.0.17.pkg*. The Installer will run.

4. The first step in the installation is an Introduction page. Click Continue.

5. The second step is viewing the Read Me file. This has few useful hints, so you might find it useful to save the file somewhere for later reference but there's no requirement to do so. Click on Continue.

6. The third step is the license. Click Continue.

7. The fourth step is to select a destination volume (it defaults to Mac OS X). Unless you have a reason to change it, click Continue.

8. The fifth step is the Easy Install page. Click Install. You may then need to enter the root user password you set up in the previous section. Now, wait while the software installs.

9. The final step is the Finish up page. Click Close.

10. Install the StartupItem package. This configures your machine so that the MySQL server will start when your machine is turned on. To do this, double click the StartupItem package in the Finder; this is the package named, for example, *MySQLStartupItem.pkg*. The Installer will run. Now repeat the six steps from Steps 6 to 11 for the StartUpItem.

11. MySQL is now installed but isn't yet configured. To configure it, start by opening Terminal, which is located in Applications → Utilities. This opens a terminal window which we recommend maximizing. In the following steps that require the Terminal, we show commands that are entered next to a prompt, %. To enter these commands, type them into your Terminal window and press Enter.

12. Log in as the root user. You can login as root by typing:

    `% su`

    and then supplying the root user password that you set when enabling the root user in the previous section.

13. Run the *mysql_install_db* script to initialize the system databases used by MySQL. To do this, change directory to where MySQL is installed:

    `% cd /usr/local/mysql`

    Type the following to run the installation script:

    `% ./scripts/mysql_install_db`

14. Change the owner of the MySQL program files to be the root user:

    `% chown -R root /usr/local/mysql`

15. Change the owner of the MySQL databases and log files to be the mysql user:

    `% chown -R mysql /usr/local/mysql/data`

    This user already exists in your Panther installation.

16. Change the group of the MySQL installation files to be the mysql group:

    `% chgrp -R mysql /usr/local/mysql`

    This group already exists in your Panther installation.

17. Copy the default medium-scale parameter configuration file to the default location of */etc*. These parameters are read when MySQL is started. The copy command is:

    `% cp support-files/my-medium.cnf /etc/my.cnf`

18. Edit the configuration file and adjust the default number of maximum connections to match the default value for the maximum Apache web server connections. Also, let's turn on the query cache. To do this, we'll use the pico editor that comes installed with Mac OS X; we don't use the popular TextEdit editor

because it has trouble saving files when you're the root user and when the file exists.

To edit the configuration file with pico, type:

```
% pico /etc/my.cnf
```

Using the down arrow key, scroll down through the file until you find section beginning with the following text:

```
# The MySQL server
[mysqld]
```

In this section, type the following lines:

```
set-variable = max_connections=150
query_cache_type = 1
```

Save the file by holding down the ctrl (Control) key and pressing the **o** key (we refer to this as **ctrl-o** throughout this appendix). Then press Enter. Quit pico by holding ctrl and pressing **x** (**ctrl-x**).

19. The installation of MySQL is now complete, but it isn't running. To get it running, restart your machine by clicking on the Apple menu and then Restart.

MySQL isn't completely configured. The steps in the next section set it up further.

Configuring MySQL

The following steps set a password for the root user and create a new user for the MySQL installation that is used in PHP scripts to access the DBMS. The steps assume you've run Terminal, logged in as the root user, and that MySQL is running; see the previous section for more information.

The new user can carry out all actions required from Chapter 6 to Chapter 20 on the *winestore* database but has no access to other databases and can't change database access privileges. The new user also can't access the DBMS from a remote server. If you're creating your own application, replace *winestore* with the name of your database. More information on user privileges can be found in Chapter 15.

The steps are as follows:

1. Choose and set a password for root user access to the MySQL DBMS. To set a password of *secret*, type into your Terminal window:

```
% /usr/local/mysql/bin/mysqladmin -uroot password secret
```

Record the password for later use.

2. Start the MySQL command line interpreter using the password defined in the previous step:

```
% /usr/local/mysql/bin/mysql -uroot -psecret
```

This displays a mysql> prompt.

3. Add a new user by typing the following into the command interpreter. Choose a username to replace *username* and a password to replace *password* in the following command:

```
mysql> GRANT SELECT, INSERT, UPDATE, DELETE, LOCK TABLES ON winestore.* TO
    username@127.0.0.1 IDENTIFIED BY 'password';
```

It doesn't matter that the *winestore* database doesn't exist yet.

MySQL responds with:

```
Query OK, 0 rows affected (0.00 sec)
```

Record the username and password.

If the statement doesn't work for your release, try it again but omit the , LOCK TABLES component.

4. Quit the MySQL command interpreter with the command:

```
mysql> quit
```

MySQL responds with:

```
Bye
```

5. Test the user by running the MySQL command interpreter using the *username* and *password*:

```
% /usr/local/mysql/bin/mysql -uusername -psecret
```

6. MySQL responds with a message beginning:

```
Welcome to the MySQL monitor.
```

7. Quit the MySQL interpreter again with:

```
mysql> quit
```

The MySQL DBMS is now configured with a user who can access the *winestore* database from the database server machine 127.0.0.1. The *winestore* database can't be tested yet because it isn't loaded. The database is loaded in "What's Needed for This Book."

Setting Up Apache and PHP

Apache Version 1 is already installed under Panther and doesn't need to be upgraded to use this book; you don't need the latest version, Apache 2. However, by default, it isn't running, it won't serve PHP requests, and it only serves standard, non-secure requests. In this section, we discuss how it's set up on your machine, how to get it started, and how to modify it so that it can serve secure and PHP requests.

PHP 4.3.2 is installed with Panther. It includes most of the features you need to work with this book, except that the PEAR installer doesn't work without an additional step. In this section, we show you how to upgrade to the latest stable release using a package. Fixing the PEAR installer is discussed in "What's Needed for This Book."

Starting Apache

Let's start by getting Apache running. To get it started, you can do one of two things:

Automatically start Apache each time your machine starts.
> To do this, launch System Preferences from Applications → System Preferences. Then, select Sharing from beneath the *Internet & Network* heading. At the left of the window, select Personal Web Sharing by ticking the box. Quit System Preferences. Apache will now start and will also start each time you start up your computer.

Manually start Apache using Terminal.
> Start by opening Terminal, which is located in Applications → Utilities. In the Terminal window, log in as the root user and start Apache using:
>
> ```
> % su
> % apachectl start
> ```
> You should see a message such as:
>
> ```
> /usr/sbin/apachectl start: httpd started
> ```
> Quit the Terminal program. When you restart your machine, you need to repeat this process to restart Apache.

To test that your Apache is running, use a web browser to retrieve the URL *http:// 127.0.0.1/*. You should see an Apache test page.

The Apache and PHP Setup

Your Apache is installed differently from most other Unix variants:

- You'll find the Document Root (where the documents are stored that are retrieved when you request *http://127.0.0.1/*) in the directory */Library/ WebServer/Documents*. (On other Unix variants, the directory is */usr/local/ apache2/htdocs/*.)

- You'll find the Apache configuration file *httpd.conf* in the directory */etc/httpd*. (On other Unix variants, it's usually in */usr/local/apache2/conf*.)

- The script used to start and stop Apache, *apachectl*, is located in */usr/sbin*. (On other Unix variants, it's usually in */usr/local/apache2/bin/*.)

- You'll find the PHP *php.ini* configuration file in the directory */usr/local/php/lib*.

In addition, while your Apache does have the PHP module available to it, it isn't configured to serve PHP requests. To set it up so that it will serve PHP requests you can do one of two things:

Upgrade your PHP module
> By using Marc Liyanage's upgrade package to get the latest release of PHP, your Apache will be automatically configured to serve PHP requests. If you plan to do this, then follow the instructions in the next section now and, when you've done that, return to Step 9 in this section to test that everything is working correctly.

Modify the httpd.conf configuration

If you don't want to upgrade your PHP module, you can manually modify the configuration of your Apache so that it serves PHP requests. This is outlined in the steps described next.

We recommend upgrading your PHP module to the latest release.

To manually set up your Apache to serve PHP requests, do the following:

1. Start by opening Terminal, which is located in Applications → Utilities. Maximize the Terminal window. In the Terminal window, log in as the root user by typing:

   ```
   % su
   ```

   Supply the password you set when unlocking the root user.

2. In the Terminal window, type:

   ```
   % pico /etc/httpd/httpd.conf
   ```

   This launches the pico editor and opens the *httpd.conf* file.

3. Search in the file for the string php. You can do this by holding the ctrl (Control) key and pressing the **w** key (**ctrl-w**), typing **php**, and pressing Enter. You should see the following line:

   ```
   #LoadModule php4_module    libexec/httpd/libphp4.so
   ```

4. From the line in Step 3, remove the # so that it reads:

   ```
   LoadModule php4_module    libexec/httpd/libphp4.so
   ```

5. Search again for the string php by pressing **ctrl-w** and then Enter. You should see the following line:

   ```
   #AddModule mod_php4.c
   ```

6. From the line in Step 5, remove the # so that it reads:

   ```
   AddModule mod_php4.c
   ```

7. Save the file by **ctrl-o** and Enter. Quit pico by typing **ctrl-x**.

8. Restart your Apache so that it rereads its configuration by typing into your Terminal window:

   ```
   % /usr/sbin/apachectl stop
   % /usr/sbin/apachectl start
   ```

   (For some reason, **/usr/sbin/apachectl restart** doesn't work.)

9. To test the PHP module, change the directory to the Apache document root using your Terminal window:

   ```
   % cd /Library/WebServer/Documents
   ```

10. Create a file with the name *phpinfo.php* using pico. Type the following into your Terminal window:

    ```
    % pico phpinfo.php
    ```

    The pico editor runs and an empty window appears. Into the window, type:

    ```
    <?php phpinfo( ); ?>
    ```

Save the file using **ctrl-o** and pressing Enter. Then quit pico using **ctrl-x**.

11. Test the newly created PHP script by retrieving with a browser the following URL *http://127.0.0.1/phpinfo.php*. You should see a page of information about Apache and PHP.

Upgrading PHP

PHP 4.3.2 is installed with Panther. To upgrade your PHP to the latest stable release, do the following:

1. Using a web browser, visit Marc Liyanage's web site, *http://www.entropy.ch/ software/macosx/php/*.

2. Scroll down to the *Installation Instructions* heading. Next to item 1 in the list, click on the link to the installation package. This is labelled, for example, *PHP 4.3.4 (entropy.ch Release 1)*. Save the downloaded file.

3. After the download is complete, double-click on the disk image file that's been downloaded. It has a file name such as *Entropy-PHP-4.3.4-1.dmg*. This mounts the disk image file and the Finder appears.

4. In the Finder, double-click on the package and the Installer runs; the package has a name such as *php-4.3.4.pkg*. On the Installer welcome screen, click Continue. On the Destination screen, click on the destination volume that is home to your Apache server and click Continue. On the Easy Install screen, click Upgrade; you may need to then provide your root user password. The package will install. On the Finish Up screen, click Close.

The PHP upgrade is complete—you don't even need to restart your Apache!

Installing a Secure Apache Server

This section describes how to configure a secure version of the Apache web server so that you can support *https://* requests. If you don't need a secure server, skip this section. You can find out more about secure web servers in Chapter 11.

There are two major differences encountered when configuring Apache to use SSL versus using Apache normally:

Secure Sockets Layer software is required.
 There are several sources of Secure Sockets Layer software. The OpenSSL is probably the most-commonly used with Apache, and it's already installed with Panther. We use it in this section.

A site certificate needs to be obtained and configured.
 A free, self-signed certificate can be created (and that's what we do in this section). You need to replace it with a purchased certificate from a Certification Authority when an application goes live.

Creating a key and certificate

For Apache to use SSL, it needs a private key and a certificate. Once the key and certificate have been created, they need to be configured into Apache. These steps show you how to do this:

1. Start by opening Terminal, which is located in Applications → Utilities. Maximize the Terminal window. In the Terminal window, login as the root user by typing:

   ```
   % su
   ```

   Supply the password you set when unlocking the root user.

2. Create the key. Into the Terminal window, type:

   ```
   % openssl genrsa -des3 1024 > /etc/httpd/localhost.key
   ```

   If you have an actual domain for your server, replace *localhost* with the full domain name. Decide on a password and enter it twice; record it for future use. You've now created the private key.

3. Create the certificate request by typing:

   ```
   % openssl req -new -key /etc/httpd/localhost.key > \
     /etc/httpd/localhost.csr
   ```

   If you have an actual domain for your server, replace *localhost* with the full domain name. The process asks for several fields including country, state, organization name, and email address; answer these as best you can, but it doesn't matter if you omit some answers by pressing Enter. The script produces a file that contains the certificate signing request.

4. Now, create the self-signed certificate by typing:

   ```
   % openssl req -x509 -days 90 -key \
     /etc/httpd/localhost.key \
     -in /etc/httpd/localhost.csr > \
     /etc/httpd/localhost.crt
   ```

   You need to provide the password you used to create your private key.

5. Activate your SSL module in your Apache installation. To do this, type:

   ```
   % apxs -e -a -n ssl /usr/libexec/httpd/libssl.so
   ```

6. You need to instruct Apache how to process secure requests. In the Terminal window, type:

   ```
   % pico /etc/httpd/httpd.conf
   ```

   This launches the pico editor and opens a window containing the *httpd.conf* file.

7. Scroll to the end of the file using the down arrow key. At the end of the *httpd.conf* file, add the following lines:

   ```
   <IfModule mod_ssl.c>

       Listen 80
       Listen 443
   ```

```
SSLRandomSeed startup builtin
SSLRandomSeed connect builtin

<VirtualHost _default_:443>
  SSLEngine on
  DocumentRoot "/Library/WebServer/SecureDocuments"

  SSLCertificateFile /etc/httpd/localhost.crt
  SSLCertificateKeyFile /etc/httpd/localhost.key
</VirtualHost>
```

```
</IfModule>
```

These instructions configure Apache to serve secure documents from the directory */Library/WebServer/SecureDocuments*. If you don't want to use that directory, you can replace it with your choice; we assume our choice in the next few steps. If you have an actual domain for your server, also replace localhost with the full domain name.

Save the file using **ctrl-o** and pressing Enter, and quit using **ctrl-x**.

8. Create the directory from which you want to serve secure files. Type:

```
% mkdir /Library/WebServer/SecureDocuments
```

9. For testing, create a simple *index.html* file in the new directory. Type:

```
% pico /Library/WebServer/SecureDocuments/index.html
```

Into the file, type:

```
<html>Secure hello!</html>
```

Save the file using **ctrl-o** and pressing Enter. Quit pico using **ctrl-x**. Ensure the file can be accessed by typing:

```
% chmod a+rx /Library/WebServer/SecureDocuments/
% chmod a+r /Library/WebServer/SecureDocuments/index.html
```

10. Stop and start Apache so it rereads its configuration. Use the following commands:

```
% apachectl stop
% apachectl start
```

You need to provide the password you used in creating your key. A secure Apache is now running and serving requests on port 443 (the default HTTPS port) via SSL and also serving regular HTTP requests on post 80. You can test it by requesting the resources *https://127.0.0.1/* and *http://127.0.0.1/* with a web browser running on the same machine as the web server. You should see the sample page you created in Step 7, and your regular pages respectively.

When a resource such as *https://127.0.0.1/* is requested with a browser, the browser alerts the user to an unknown certificate. To obtain a certificate that will be trusted by users, you need to send your certificate request to a Certification Authority to be signed using their authoritative certificates. There is a fee for this service. While the Apache configuration allows both the key and the certificate to be placed in a single file, the private key should not be sent to anyone, not even the Certification Authority. More documentation can be found at *http://www.openssl.org/docs/apps/openssl.html*.

What's Needed for This Book

This section shows you how to download and install our example database, all of the book code examples, the sample online winestore application, and the additional packages that are used throughout the book.

Installing PEAR Packages

The following optional PEAR package is required:

HTML_Template_IT
    This is needed to work with Chapter 7 and all later chapters.

Detailed instructions to install optional packages can be found in Chapter 7. You'll also find a discussion there about how to find out about, install, and upgrade packages.

Panther has a problem: the PEAR installer doesn't work and you need to carry out an extra step to get it going. We show you how to install, upgrade, and fix the problem in the following steps:

1. Start by opening Terminal, which is located in Applications → Utilities. Maximize the Terminal window. In the Terminal window, log in as the root user by typing:

    ```
    % su
    ```

    Supply the password you set when unlocking the root user.

2. Let's fix the PEAR installer's configuration. To do this, you need to set the environment variable PHP_PEAR_INSTALL_DIR to point to the PEAR directory */usr/local/php/lib/php*. However, when you use Terminal to type commands, you're using a shell program, and how you set environment variables is dependent on the shell you use.

    Most users use the bash shell. To set an environment variable in bash, type into your Terminal window:

    ```
    % set PHP_PEAR_INSTALL_DIR /usr/local/php/lib/php
    ```

    If you know you're using the csh or tcsh shell, then type:

    ```
    % setenv PHP_PEAR_INSTALL_DIR /usr/local/php/lib/php
    ```

    If you know how to add environment settings to your shell resource file (such as *.bashrc* or *.cshrc*), then add the command you just typed to the end of that file. If you don't do this, then each time you want to use the PEAR installer, you need to repeat this step first.

3. If you're not already, connect to the Internet.

4. Type the following to install the optional package:

```
% pear install HTML_Template_IT
```

5. Type the following to check if upgrades of the core packages used in this book are available:

```
% pear upgrade PEAR
% pear upgrade Date
% pear upgrade DB
% pear upgrade Mail
```

Installing the Code Examples

The example PHP scripts in this book are available from our book's web site, *http://www.webdatabasebook.com*. In this section, we show you how to install them for use on your machine. The winestore application isn't installed in this section; see "Installing the Winestore Application" for instructions.

To install the example scripts, follow these steps:

1. Using a browser, download the file *http://www.webdatabasebook.com/examples.zip* into the */tmp* directory.

2. Open Terminal, which is located in Applications → Utilities. Maximize the Terminal window. In the Terminal window, login as the root user by typing:

```
% su
```

Supply the password you set when unlocking the root user.

3. You need to configure your Apache web server so that it won't show users the content of the *.inc* include files if they're retrieved with a web browser. There are several ways to do this, but the simplest is to edit your *httpd.conf* configuration file. You'll find the file in */etc/httpd/*.

To edit the file, login as the root user and edit the file by typing the following into a Terminal window:

```
% su
% pico /etc/http/httpd.conf
```

Scroll to the end of the file using the down arrow key. To the end of the file, add:

```
<Files ~ "\.inc$">
    Order allow,deny
    Deny from all
    Satisfy All
</Files>
```

Save the file by pressing **ctrl-o** and then Enter. Quit pico using **ctrl-x**. You now need to restart your Apache server. You can do this by typing:

```
% apachectl stop
% apachectl start
```

4. Create a directory in your Apache document root to store the examples, and copy the downloaded file to that location:

```
% mkdir /Library/WebServer/Documents/wda
% cp /tmp/examples.zip /Library/WebServer/Documents/wda
```

5. Unzip the *wda.zip* examples in their new directory by doing this:

```
% cd /Library/WebServer/Documents/wda
% unzip examples.zip
```

6. Edit the file *db.inc* in the *wda* directory. Type:

```
% pico db.inc
```

7. Modify the lines beginning with $username and $password so that *fred* and *shhh* are replaced with the username and password you chose for your user when installing MySQL.

```
<?php
    $hostName = "127.0.0.1";
    $databaseName = "winestore";
    $username = "fred";
    $password = "shhh";
```

Save the file by pressing **ctrl-o** and Enter. Quit pico using **ctrl-x.**

8. You may also need to set the file permissions so that examples are accessible through your web browser. To do this, use:

```
% chmod a+rx /Library/WebServer/Documents/wda
% chmod a+r /Library/WebServer/Documents/wda/*
```

9. You should now be able to load the example list by requesting the following URL with a web browser running on the same machine as the web server: *http://127.0.0.1/wda/*. Test the examples from Chapters 2 to 4, and they should work.

You'll find that some of the examples from Chapter 6 onward run only if the *winestore* database has been loaded into the MySQL DBMS by following the instructions in the next section. In addition, most examples from Chapter 7 onward work only if you've installed the PEAR package HTML_Template_IT.

Installing the PDF PHP Library

To work with the PDF PHP library in Chapter 13, you need to download the class files. To do this, follow these steps:

1. Visit the web site *http://ros.co.nz/pdf/*.

2. From the Downloads section, choose the link to the Zip file that contains the class, sample, and the required font metric files. Save the file in */tmp*.

3. Change directory to the temporary directory and unzip the download file. into an install directory.

If you're only planning to use the library with our examples, first install the code examples as described in the next section, and then use:

```
% cd /tmp
% unzip pdfClassesAndFonts_009e.zip -d /Library/WebServer/Documents/wda
```

This installs the class files and fonts in the examples directory.

An alternative approach is to install the files into a shared file location such as */usr/local/src/pdf-php*. Then, edit your *php.ini* file with pico and include the directory at the end of the include_path directive. This allows you to include the path in a PHP script using only the class name and without specifying the directory.

Loading the Winestore Database

A local copy of the *winestore* database is required to test the SQL examples in Chapter 5, to test some of the web database application examples in Chapters 6 to 13, and to use the sample winestore application described in Chapters 16 to 20. In addition, MySQL must be installed and configured before the winestore database can be loaded.

The steps to load the *winestore* database are as follows:

1. Using a web browser, download the file *http://www.webdatabasebook.com/database.zip* into the */tmp* directory.

2. Open Terminal, which is located in Applications → Utilities. Maximize the Terminal window. In the Terminal window, log in as the root user by typing:

   ```
   % su
   ```

   Supply the password you set when unlocking the root user.

3. Uncompress the *winestore* database by typing the following

   ```
   % cd /tmp
   % unzip database.zip
   ```

4. Run the MySQL command-line interpreter using the root username and the *password* you set, and load the *winestore* database:

   ```
   % /usr/local/mysql/bin/mysql -uroot -ppassword < /tmp/winestore.data
   ```

   Be patient, this may take a while.

5. After the loading is complete the database can be tested by running a query. To do this, use the *username* and *password* you created when installing and configuring MySQL:

   ```
   % /usr/local/mysql/bin/mysql -uusername -ppassword
   ```

   Now type:

   ```
   mysql> SELECT * FROM region;
   ```

   This should produce the following list of wine regions as output:

   ```
   +-----------+--------------------+
   | region_id | region_name        |
   +-----------+--------------------+
   |         1 | All                |
   |         2 | Goulburn Valley    |
   |         3 | Rutherglen         |
   |         4 | Coonawarra         |
   |         5 | Upper Hunter Valley |
   |         6 | Lower Hunter Valley |
   ```

```
|         7 | Barossa Valley    |
|         8 | Riverland         |
|         9 | Margaret River    |
|        10 | Swan Valley       |
+-----------+-------------------+
```

The *winestore* database has now been loaded and tested.

Installing the Winestore Application

The sample online winestore application is available from our book's web site, *http://www.webdatabasebook.com*. In this section, we show you how to install it on your machine. We assume you've installed the *winestore* database by following the instructions in the previous section.

Follow these steps:

1. Using a browser, download the file *http://www.webdatabasebook.com/wda2-winestore.zip* into the */tmp* directory.

2. If you haven't configured your Apache web server so that it won't show users the content of the *.inc* include files, follow Steps 2 and 3 in the section "Installing the Code Examples."

3. Open Terminal, which is located in Applications → Utilities. Maximize the Terminal window. In the Terminal window, login as the root user by typing:

   ```
   % su
   ```

   Supply the password you set when unlocking the root user.

4. Move the application into your Apache document root by typing into your Terminal window:

   ```
   % mv /tmp/wda2-winestore.zip /Library/WebServer/Documents
   ```

5. Unzip the *wda2-winestore.zip* code in the document root directory. This will create the subdirectory *wda2-winestore:*

   ```
   % cd /Library/WebServer/Documents
   % unzip wda2-winestore.zip
   ```

6. Edit the file *wda2-winestore/includes/db.inc* using pico by typing:

   ```
   % pico wda2-winestore/includes/db.inc
   ```

7. Modify the lines beginning with $username and $password so that *fred* and *shhh* are replaced with the username and password you selected when configuring MySQL:

   ```
   <?php
       $hostname = "127.0.0.1";
       $databasename = "winestore";
       $username = "fred";
       $password = "shhh";
   ```

   Save the file by pressing **ctrl-o** and Enter. Exit pico using **ctrl-x**.

8. Edit the file *wda2-winestore/includes/winestore.inc* by typing:

```
% pico wda2-winestore/includes/winestore.inc
```

Locate the following three lines:

```
// define("D_INSTALL_PATH", "c:/progra~1/easyph~1/www");
// define("D_INSTALL_PATH", "/Library/WebServer/Documents");
define("D_INSTALL_PATH", "/usr/local/apache2/htdocs");
```

Uncomment the second line and comment-out the third so that you have the following:

```
// define("D_INSTALL_PATH", "c:/progra~1/easyph~1/www");
define("D_INSTALL_PATH", "/Library/WebServer/Documents");
// define("D_INSTALL_PATH", "/usr/local/apache2/htdocs");
```

Save the file by pressing **ctrl-o** and Enter. Quit the editor using **ctrl-x**.

9. You may also need to set the file permissions so that examples are accessible through your web browser. To do this, use:

```
% chmod a+rx /Library/WebServer/Documents/wda2-winestore
% chmod a+r /Library/WebServer/Documents/wda2-winestore/*
```

10. You should now be able to load the application index by requesting the following URL with a web browser running on the same machine as the web server: *http://127.0.0.1/wda2-winestore/*. Click on the Use the Application link and you should be able to use the application.

APPENDIX D
Web Protocols

In this appendix, we introduce some of the protocols and standards of the Web. We cover the following topics:

- Network basics, including IP addresses and ports.
- The structure of URLs (Uniform Resource Locators).
- When to use the GET and POST methods.
- The HTTP request and response model, including response code classes.

Network Basics

This section briefly introduces the function of the TCP and IP protocols, and explains how IP addresses and ports are used for communication on the Internet.

TCP/IP

The Transmission Control Protocol (TCP) and the Internet Protocol (IP) manage the sending and receiving of messages over the Internet.

The Web is a network application that uses the services of TCP and IP. When a web browser requests a page from a web server, the TCP/IP services provide a virtual connection—a virtual circuit—between the two communicating systems. (The connection is virtual because the Internet doesn't operate like an old telephone network. It doesn't create an actual circuit dedicated to a particular call.)

Once a connection is established and acknowledged, the two systems can communicate by sending messages. These messages can be large, such as the binary representation of an image, and TCP may fragment the data into a series of IP *datagrams*. An IP datagram is like a postage envelope: it holds all or part of a message and it's labeled with a destination address and other fields that manage its transmission from the sender to the receiver.

Each node in the network runs IP software, and the software moves the datagrams through the network. When an IP node receives a datagram, it inspects the address and other header fields, looks up a table of routing information, and sends it on to the next node. Often these nodes are dedicated routers—systems that form interconnections between networks—but the nodes can also include standard machines. IP datagrams are totally independent of each other: the IP software just moves them from node to node through a network.

TCP software performs the function of gluing the fragments in IP datagrams together at the destination. For example, if a large image is broken into ten parts that are each stored in a datagram, then TCP reassembles those parts into a whole. TCP also makes sure the process is robust: if an IP datagram goes missing, a datagram is corrupted, duplicate datagrams arrive, or datagrams arrive out of order, then TCP looks after requesting, throwing away duplicates or erroneous data, or sorting out ordering.

IP Addresses

To allow communication over heterogeneous networks, each with its own addressing standard, every location in a network needs a globally unique IP address. A computer that is connected to the Internet needs at least one IP address; a node that interconnects two networks needs two.

IP (version 4) addresses are 32-bit numbers that are usually represented as a series of four decimal numbers between 0 and 255, separated by a period. An example IP address is 134.148.250.28. Some IP addresses have special meanings. For example, the IP addresses 127.0.0.0 and 127.0.0.1 are reserved for loopback testing on a host. If a connection is to be made from a client to server, both running on the same machine, the address 127.0.0.1 can be used. This address loops back to 127.0.0.0, the localhost.

If you've got your own private network at home or at work, then it's likely you're using addresses such as 192.168.1.1 and 192.168.1.2. Addresses in the range 192.168.0.0 to 192.168.255.255 are reserved for this purpose and are never used on the Internet. (There are also other ranges that are not used on the Internet, but we don't discuss this in detail here.)

It's inconvenient to remember IP addresses. For example, it's much easier for Hugh to remember that *hugh.cs.rmit.edu.au* is his machine at work than to remember its IP address is 131.170.27.120. For this reason, most IP addresses have one or more equivalent domain names that we use to log in, access web sites, and so on. The mapping of IP addresses to names and back again is managed by domain name servers. When you set up a new domain and host it on a server, the domain name servers responsible for finding the system are usually informed about the mapping between the machine's IP address and your new domain name.

Ports

When a virtual connection is set up between two communicating systems, each end is tied to a *port*. The port is an identifier used by the TCP software rather than an actual physical device, and it allows multiple network connections to be made on one machine by different applications.

When a message is received by the TCP software running on a host computer, the data is sent to the correct application based on the port number. By convention, a *well-known port* is normally used by a server providing a service that has seen widespread adoption. A list of well-known ports for various applications is maintained by Internet Assigned Number Authority (IANA) and can be found at *http://www.iana.org/assignments/port-numbers*. For example, the File Transfer Protocol (FTP) uses port 21, and a web server uses port 80.

Systems with TCP/IP software installed have a services file that lists the ports used on that machine. This file is often preconfigured for common applications and is maintained by the system administrator to reflect the actual port usage on the machine. For example, this file is usually */etc/services* on a Unix system.

Hypertext Transfer Protocol

As discussed in Chapter 1, HTTP is the standard that allows documents to be communicated and shared over the Web. From a network perspective, HTTP is an *application-layer* protocol that is built on top of TCP/IP. Since the original version, HTTP/0.9, there have only been two revisions of the HTTP standard. HTTP/1.0 was released as RFC-1945* in May 1996 and HTTP/1.1 as RFC-2616 in June 1999.

In Chapter 1, we told you that HTTP is very simple: a client—most conspicuously a web browser—sends a request for some resource to a web (HTTP) server, and the server sends back a response. The HTTP response carries the resource—the HTML document or image or whatever—as its payload back to the client.

Continuing our analogy from the previous section, HTTP is a kind of cover letter—like a fax cover sheet—that is stored in an envelope and tells the receiver what language the document is in, instructions on how to read the letter, and how to reply.

---

* Request for Comments, or RFCs, are submitted to the RFC editor (*http://www.rfc-editor.org*) usually by authors attached to organizations such as the Internet Engineering Task Force (IETF at *http://www.ietf.org*). RFCs date back to the early ARPAnet days and are used to present networking protocols, procedures, programs, and concepts. They also include meeting notes, opinions, bad poems, and other humor: RFC-2324 describes the Hypertext Coffee Pot Control Protocol.

Uniform Resource Locators

Uniform resource locators—more commonly known as URLs—are used as the primary naming and addressing method of the Web. URLs belong to the larger class of *uniform resource identifiers*; both identify resources, but URLs include specific host details that allow connection to a server that holds the resource.

A URL can be broken into three basic parts: first, the protocol identifier; second, the host and service identifier; and, last, a resource identifier that contains a path with optional parameters and an optional query that identifies the resource. The following example shows a URL that identifies an HTTP resource:

```
http://host_domain_name:8080/absolute_path?query
```

The HTTP standard doesn't place any limit on the length of a URL, but some older browsers and proxy servers do. The structure of a URL is formally described by RFC-2396: Uniform Resource Identifiers (URI): Generic Syntax.

Protocol

The first part of the URL identifies the application protocol. HTTP URLs start with the familiar *http://*. Other applications that use URLs to locate resources identify different protocols; for example, URLs used with the File Transfer Protocol (FTP) begin with *ftp://*. URLs that identify HTTP resources served over connections that are encrypted using the Secure Sockets Layer start with *https://*. We discuss the use of the Secure Sockets Layer to protect data transmitted over the Internet in Chapter 11.

Host and service identification

The next part of the HTTP URL identifies the host on which the web server is running, and the port on which the server listens for HTTP requests. The domain name or the IP address can identify the host component. Using the domain name allows user-friendly web addresses such as:

```
http://www.w3.org/Protocols/
```

The equivalent URL using the IP address is:

```
http://18.29.1.35/Protocols/
```

Domain names are not case sensitive.

Nonstandard TCP ports

By default, a HTTP server listens for requests on port 80. So, for example, requests for the URL *http://www.oreilly.com* are made to the host machine *www.oreilly.com* on port 80. When a nonstandard port is used, the URL must include the port number so the browser can successfully connect to the service. For example, the URL *http://example.com:8080* connects to the web server running on port 8080 on the host *example.com*.

Resource identification

The remaining URL components help locate a specific resource. The path, with optional parameters, and an optional query are processed by the web server to locate or compute a response.

The path often corresponds to an actual file path on the host's filesystem. For example, an Apache web server running on a Unix machine that hosts *example.com* may store all the web content under the directory */usr/local/apache2/htdocs* and be configured to use the path component of the URL relative to that directory. In this case, the HTTP response to the URL *http://example.com/marketing/home.html* contains the file */usr/local/apache2/htdocs/marketing/home.html*.

In contrast to domain names, the resource identification component is usually case sensitive. This is because it refers to a directory or file on the web server, and Unix servers (which host the majority of web sites) are case sensitive.

Parameters and queries

The path component of a URL can include parameters and queries that are used by the web server. A common example is to include a query as part of the URL that runs a search script. The following example shows the string q=red as a query that the script *search.php* can use:

```
http://example.com/search.php?q=red
```

Multiple query terms can be encoded using the & character as a separator:

```
http://example.com/search.php?q=red&r=victoria
```

Parameters allow other information not related to a query to be encoded. For example, consider the parameter lines=10 in the URL:

```
http://example.com/search.php;lines=10?q=red
```

This can be used by the *search.php* script to modify the number of lines to display in a result screen.

HTTP provides the distinction between parameters and queries, but parameters are more complex than described here and are not commonly used in practice. We discussed how PHP can use query variables encoded into URLs in Chapter 6.

Fragment identifiers

A URL can include a *fragment identifier* that is interpreted by the client once a requested resource has been received. A fragment identifier is included at the end of a URL separated from the path by the # character. The meaning of the fragment identifier depends on the type of the resource. For example, the following URL includes the fragment identifier tannin for a HTML document:

```
http://example.com/documents/glossary.html#tannin
```

When a web browser receives the HTML resource, it then positions the rendered document in the display to start at the anchor element <a name="tannin"> if the named anchor exists.

Absolute and relative URLs

The URL general syntax allows a resource to be specified as an absolute or a relative URL. Absolute URLs identify the protocol *http://*, the host, and the path of the resource, and can be used alone to locate a resource. Here's an example absolute URL:

```
http://example.com/documents/glossary.html
```

Relative URLs don't contain all the components and are always considered with respect to a *base URL*. A relative URL is resolved to an absolute URL, with respect to the base URL. Typically, a relative URL contains the path components of a resource and allows related sets of resources to reference each other in a relative way. This allows path hierarchies to be readily changed without the need to change every URL embedded in a set of documents.

A web browser has two ways to set base URLs when resolving relative URLs. The first method allows a base URL to be encoded into the HTML using the <base> element. The second method sets the base URL to that of the current document; this is done in the absence of a <base> element. For example, the following HTML document contains three relative URLs embedded into <a> elements:

```
<p>Read my <a href="cv.html">Curriculum Vitae</a>
<p>Read my <a href="work/emp.html">employment history</a>
<p>Visit <a href="/admin/fred.html">Fred's home page</a>
```

Consider what happens if the page that contains the example is requested with the following URL:

```
http://example.com/development/dave/home.html
```

The three relative URLs are resolved to the following absolute URLs by the browser:

```
http://example.com/development/dave/cv.html
http://example.com/development/dave/work/emp.html
http://example.com/admin/fred.html
```

Table D-1 shows several relative URLs and how they are resolved to the corresponding absolute URLs given the base URL *http://example.com/a/b/c.html?foo=bar*.

Table D-1. Example relative URLs resolved to absolute URLs

Relative URL	Absolute URL with respect to *http://example.com/a/b/c.html?foo=bar*
d.html	*http://example.com/a/b/d.html*
e/d.html	*http://example.com/a/b/e/d.html*
/d.html	*http://example.com/d.html*
../d.html	*http://example.com/a/d.html*

Relative URL	Absolute URL with respect to *http://example.com/a/b/c.html?foo=bar*
#xyz	*http://example.com/a/b/c.html?foo=bar#xyz*
/	*http://example.com/a/b/*
../	*http://example.com/a/*

URL encoding

The characters used in resource names, query strings, and parameters must not conflict with the characters that have special meanings or aren't allowed in a URL. For example, a question mark character identifies the beginning of a query, and an ampersand (&) character separates multiple terms in a query.

The meanings of these characters can be escaped using a hexadecimal encoding consisting of the percent character (%) followed by the two hexadecimal digits representing the ASCII encoded of the character. For example, an ampersand (&) character is encoded as %26.

The characters that need to be escape-encoded are the control, space, and reserved characters:

```
; / ? : @ & = + $ ,
```

Delimiter characters must also be encoded:

```
< > # % "
```

The following characters can cause problems with gateways and network agents, and should also be encoded:

```
{ } | \ ^ [ ] `
```

PHP provides the *rawurlencode()* function to encode special characters. For example, *rawurlencode()* can build the href attribute of an embedded link:

```
echo '<a href="search.php?q=' . rawurlencode("100% + more") . '">';
```

The result is an <a> element with an embedded URL correctly encoded:

```
<a href="search.php?q=100%25%20%2B%20more">
```

HTTP Requests

The model used for HTTP requests is to apply *methods* to identified *resources*. A HTTP request message contains a method name, a URL to which the method is to be applied, and header fields. Some requests can include a body—for example, the data collected in a form—that is referred to in the HTTP standard as the entity-body.

The following is the example HTTP request we showed you in Chapter 1:

```
GET /~hugh/index.html HTTP/1.1
Host: goanna.cs.rmit.edu.au
```

```
From: hugh@hughwilliams.com (Hugh Williams)
User-agent: Hugh-fake-browser/version-1.0
Accept: text/plain, text/html
```

The request applies the GET method to the */~hugh/index.html* resource. The action is to retrieve the HTML document stored in the file *index.html*.

The first line of the message is the request and contains the method name GET, the request URL */~hugh/index.html*, and the HTTP version HTTP/1.1, each separated by a space character. The request is followed by a list of header fields. Each field is represented as a name and value pair separated with a colon character, and each field is on a separate line.

The header fields are followed by a blank line and then by the optional body of the message. A POST method request usually contains a body of text, as we discuss in the next section.

Request methods

There are six request methods, but only three are used in practice:

GET

Retrieves a resource. A query can be used to add extra information to the GET request and, as we discussed in our introduction to URLs, these are appended to the URL itself. A database search is a good example of an application of the GET request: the resource is likely to be a web script, and the query component of the URL is the search conditions.

POST

Sends data to a server. Rather than appending data to the URL, the data is sent in the body of the HTTP request.

HEAD

Requests only the header fields as a response, not the resource itself. This can be used for lightweight retrieval, so that the modification date of a resource can be checked before the full resource is retrieved with GET.

DELETE

Allows a resource identified by the URL to be deleted from a server. This is the counterpart to the PUT method discussed next and it allows an author to remove a resource from the specified URL. It's usually not implemented by web servers.

PUT

Similar to the POST method, this method is designed to put a resource onto a server. Some HTML editors and web servers support the PUT methods allowing authors to put resources onto a web site at the specified URL. However, it's usually not implemented by web servers.

TRACE

Produces diagnostic information.

The HTTP standard divides these methods into those that are safe and those that aren't. The safe methods—GET and HEAD—don't have any persistent side effects on the server. The unsafe methods—POST, PUT, and DELETE—are designed to have persistent effects on the server. The standard allows for clients to warn users that a request may be unsafe and, for example, most browsers won't resend a request with the POST method without user confirmation.

The HTTP standard further classifies methods as *idempotent* when a request can be repeated many times and have the same effect as if the method was called once. The GET, HEAD, PUT, and DELETE methods are classified as idempotent. The POST method isn't.

GET versus POST

Both the GET and POST methods send data to the server, but which method should you use?

The HTTP standard includes the two methods to achieve different goals. The POST method was intended to create a resource. The contents of the resource would be encoded into the body of the HTTP request. For example, an order form might be processed and a new row in a database created.

The GET method is used when a request has no side effects (such as performing a search) and the POST method is used when a request has side effects (such as adding a new row to a database). A more practical issue is that the GET method may result in long URLs, and may even exceed some browser and server limits on URL length.

Use the POST method if any of the following are true:

- The result of the request has persistent side effects such as adding a new database row.
- The data collected on the form is likely to result in a long URL if you used the GET method.
- The data to be sent is in any encoding other than seven-bit ASCII.

Use the GET method if all the following are true:

- The request is to find a resource, and HTML form data is used to help that search.
- The result of the request has no persistent side effects.
- The data collected and the input field names in a HTML form are in total less than 1,024 characters in size.

HTTP Responses

When a web server processes a request from a browser, it attempts to apply the method to the identified resource and create a response. The action of the request may succeed or fail, but the web server always sends a response message back to the browser.

A HTTP response message contains a status line, header fields, and (usually) the requested entity as the body of the message. For example, the following is the result of a GET method request for a small HTML file:

```
HTTP/1.1 200 OK
Date: Sun, 19 Dec 2004 02:54:37 GMT
Server: Apache/2.0.48
Last-Modified: Fri, 19 Dec 2003 02:53:08 GMT
ETag: "4445f-bf-39f4f994"
Content-Length: 321
Accept-Ranges: bytes
Connection: close
Content-Type: text/html

<!DOCTYPE HTML PUBLIC
    "-//W3C//DTD HTML 4.0 Transitional//EN"
    "http://www.w3.org/TR/html4/loose.dtd" >
<html>
<head><title>Grapes and Glass</title></head>
<body>
<img src="http://example.com/grapes.gif">
<p>Welcome to my simple page
<p><img src="http://example.com/glass.gif">
</body>
</html>
```

The first, status line begins with the protocol version of the message, followed by a status code and a reason phrase, each separated by a space character. The status code is a number and the reason phrase describes its meaning; these are discussed in the next section. The status line is then followed by the header fields. As with the request, each field is represented as a name and value pair separated with a colon character. A blank line separates the header fields from the body of the response, in this case an HTML document.

Status codes

HTTP status codes are used to classify responses to requests. The HTTP status code system is extensible, with a set of codes described in the standard that are "generally recognized in current practice". HTTP defines a status code as a three-digit number, where the first digit is the class of response. The following list shows the five classes of codes defined by HTTP:

1xx

Informational. HTTP 1.1 uses codes in this class to indicate the request has been received by the server and that processing is continuing.

2xx

Success. The request was successfully received, and the action successfully performed.

3xx

> Redirection. When a response has a redirection code, the client needs to make a further request to get the specified resource. The URL of the actual resource is included in the response header field Location. When the status code is set to 301, the browser automatically makes the request for the URL specified in the Location header field. The use of the Location header field is discussed further in Chapter 6, and used in many examples throughout this book.

4xx

> Client error. The request can't be processed because of bad syntax of the message, the sender is unauthorized or forbidden to access the resource, or the resource can't be found.

5xx

> Server error. The server failed to fulfill a valid request.

Caching

Most user agents, such as web browsers, allow HTTP responses to be cached. HTTP responses are cached by saving a response to a request in memory. When a browser considers a request, it first looks to its local cache to see if it has an up-to-date copy of the response before sending the request to the web server. This can significantly reduce the number of requests sent to a web server, improving the performance of the web application and responsiveness to users.

Consider a web site that includes a company logo on the top of each HTML page:

```
<img src="/images/logo.gif">
```

When the browser requests a page that contains the image, a separate request is sent to retrieve the image */images/logo.gif*. If the image resource is *cacheable*, and browser caching is enabled, the browser saves the response. A subsequent request for the image is recognized, and the local copy from the cache is used rather than sending another request to the web server.

A browser uses a cached response until the response becomes *stale*, or the cache becomes full and the response is displaced by the resources from other requests. The primary mechanism for determining if a response is stale is comparing the date and time set in the Expires header field with the date and time of the machine running the browser. If the date and time are incorrectly set on the machine, a cached response may expire immediately or be cached longer than intended.

HTTP describes the conditions that allow a user agent to cache a response. However, there are many situations in which an application may wish to prevent a page from being cached, particularly when the content of a response is dynamically generated, such as in a web database application.

HTTP/1.1 uses the Cache-Control header field as its basic caching control mechanism. For example, setting the Cache-Control header field to no-cache in a HTTP response prevents the response from being cached by a HTTP/1.1 user agent. The header can be used in requests and responses, but we consider only responses here.

Some HTTP/1.1 Cache-Control settings are directed to user agents that maintain caches for more that one user, such as proxy servers. Proxy servers are used to achieve several goals, the most important of which is to provide caching of responses for a group of users. A local network, such as that found in a university department, can be configured to send all HTTP requests to a proxy server. The proxy server forwards requests to the destination web server and passes back the responses to the originating client.

Proxy servers can cache responses and thus reduce requests sent outside the local network. Setting the Cache-Control header field to public allows a user agent to make the cached response available to any request. Setting the Cache-Control header field to private allows a user agent to make the cached response available only to the client who made the initial request.

Setting the Cache-Control header to no-store prevents a user agent from storing the response on disk. This prevents sensitive information from being inadvertently saved beyond the life of a browser session. HTTP/1.1 defines several other Cache-Control header fields not described here.

Modeling and Designing Relational Databases

Designing a database is the essential first step to developing a web database application. In this appendix, we introduce database modeling and the techniques to convert a model into the SQL statements needed to create a database. We assume you've worked your way through Chapter 5, and are familiar with the basic database terminology and SQL statements.

This appendix isn't intended to replace a course or book on relational databases. Modeling requirements with an entity-relationship model requires both patience and experience. Instead, we detail our thought processes in a case study that models the winestore requirements and converts them to SQL CREATE TABLE statements. Pointers to resources on modeling and database design are included in Appendix G.

The Relational Model

Relational database management systems maintain, enforce, and use relationships between data to answer complex queries. To illustrate the principles of relational databases, we use the winestore system requirements and descriptions from Chapter 16 as the basis for our examples.

Case Study: Relationships in the Winestore

There are three essential types of data or *entities* that form the basis of the winestore. First, there is the wine itself: each wine has characteristics or attributes such as a name, a type, and a variety. Second, there is the customer, who has attributes such as a name and an address. Last (and importantly in selling wine!) is a customer purchase order. It's the order that forms a relationship between customers and wines.

An order is made when a customer purchases a quantity of wine, and this creates a relationship between a customer, a wine, and an order. Consider an example. One of our customers, customer #37 (we give our customers a number, so as not to confuse two customers who have the same name) purchases two bottles of wine #168, our

1996 Cape Mentelle Cabernet Merlot. The database stores this relationship as an order: customer #37 placed their fifth order with us, ordered wine #168, and required a quantity of two bottles. Figure E-1 shows a simple representation of this relationship.

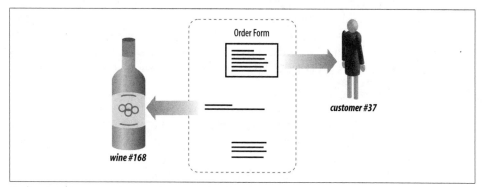

Figure E-1. Customer #37 purchases two bottles of wine #168

There are several constraints in the order that may be obvious but are worth stating: there is only one customer #37, there is one wine we refer to as #168, and the next time the customer orders with us, it will be their sixth order. Relational databases can enforce many constraints on data stored, including ensuring that an order can be made only by a valid customer and that only wines we stock can be ordered.

When you represent data in a database, entities such as wine, customers, and orders need to be represented as tables or relations that group together related data. It's important that you make the right choices in deciding whether to add tables, relationships, or attributes to your database. If you get it wrong, then your application will be inflexible: you'll have trouble updating data, adding new information, or keeping the data consistent.

Suppose, after thinking about our example in Figure E-1, that we decide to create two tables, *customer* and *order*. Let's assume customers only have a customer identifier, a name, and an address. Let's also assume that orders have a customer identifier, an order identifier, a wine identifier, and a quantity. Here's the statements we use:

```
CREATE TABLE customer (
  cust_id int(5) NOT NULL,
  name varchar(50),
  address varchar(50),
  PRIMARY KEY (cust_id)
);

CREATE TABLE order (
  cust_id int(5) NOT NULL,
  order_id int(5) NOT NULL,
  wine_id int(5),
  quantity int(3),
```

```
    PRIMARY KEY (order_id)
  );
```

To illustrate the problem of database design, consider a serious limitation of our simple model: an order has only one `wine_id` and so it consists of bottles of only one wine. There are several ways this problem can be resolved. Perhaps the most obvious approach is to add additional attributes to the *order* table, such as `wine_id2`, `quantity2`, `wine_id3`, `quantity3`, and so on. The problem is where to stop: what is the maximum number of wines per order? And, if an order contains only one wine, how are the unused attributes processed? To work with this design, you'll need lots of `if` clauses in your PHP scripts.

Another solution to the problem is to introduce a new table that stores the items that make up an order. This approach is subtle but solves the problems with the initial approach and we discuss it in detail later. How, then, do you know when to add attributes or when to add tables? Traditionally, this answer has been the somewhat technical explanation that the database should be *normalized* according to a set of rules. Fortunately, with the advent and refinement of simpler modeling techniques for designing databases—such as entity-relationship (ER) modeling—a well-designed database can be achieved by carefully following simple rules and some trial and error. You don't need to know anything about normalization.

We discuss ER modeling in the next section, as we focus on designing a workable winestore.

Entity-Relationship Modeling

Entity-relationship (ER) modeling is a simple and clear method of expressing the design of database. ER modeling isn't new—it was first proposed by Chen in 1976—but it has emerged as the dominant modeling technique only in the past 15 years.

Figure E-2 shows a partial model of the winestore. In this diagram, you can see the relationship between a *wine*, a *winery*, and a wine-growing *region*. Each *wine* has attributes such as a `wine_name`, `year`, and a `description`. A *wine* is made by a *winery*, and each *winery* has a `winery_name`. Many *wineries* are located in a *region*, where a *region* has a `region_name`.

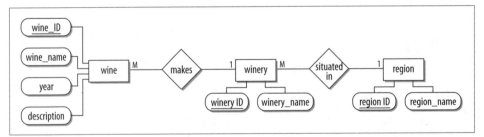

Figure E-2. A simple ER model showing the relationship between wines, wineries, and regions

ER diagrams aren't complicated, and we have already illustrated most of the features of ER modeling in Figure E-2. These features include:

Rectangles
Represent entities, the objects being modeled. Each entity is labeled.

Diamonds
Represent relationships between entities; a relationship is labeled with a descriptive title that explains how the entities interact.

Ellipses
Represent attributes that describe an entity. Underlined attributes are primary keys that uniquely identify instances of the entity.

Lines between rectangles and diamonds
Connect entities to relationships. Lines may be *annotated*, which means that the two ends can be marked with an M and an N, an M and a 1, an N and a 1, or a 1 and a 1. Annotations indicate the cardinality of the relationship, discussed later in this section.

Lines between rectangles and ellipses
Connect attributes to entities. These lines are never labeled.

Other ER modeling tools include *double ellipses*, *dashed ellipses*, and *double lines*; we use some of these advanced features later in this appendix.

Case Study: Modeling the Online Winestore

To illustrate how ER modeling can be used to effectively design a database, we return to our online winestore.

Identifying entities in ER modeling

The first step in developing a web database application is to consider the requirements of the system. The requirements for the online winestore are described in Chapter 16 and are typically gathered from a scope document, customer interviews, user requirements documents, and so on. Having identified the general requirements of the system, the first phase in the ER modeling process is to identify the entities from those requirements.

Entities are objects or things that can be described by their characteristics. As you identify entities, you list the attributes that describe the entity. For example, a *customer* is an entity that has a *name*, an *address*, a *phone*, and other details.

 Be careful when choosing entities. A *customer* or a *wine* is an entity. Reducing the stock in the inventory and adding it to a shopping cart is a function or process, not an entity. The basic rule is that an entity is an object or thing.

Five entities and their attributes have already been identified previously in this appendix. Four are easy to determine from the winestore requirements:

- The *wine* entity has the attributes wine_name, year, and description. Wines also have a type (such as red or white), but we'll return to this later.
- The *customer* entity has the attributes surname, firstname, initial, address, city, state, zipcode, phone, and birth_date. Customers also have a title (such as Mr. or Mrs.) and reside in a country, but we'll return to this later.
- The *winery* entity has the attribute winery_name.
- The *region* entity has the attribute region_name.

We add a *users* entity to maintain user account details at the winestore:

- The *users* entity has the attributes user_name and password. The user_name is the customer's email address.

The remaining entities—and, in two cases, the distinction between the entities—are harder to identify. This is where experience, and trial and error come into play.

We have earlier identified the *orders* entity in our introduction to ER modeling, but an order is hard to precisely define. One description might be:

> An order is an object created by a customer when they agree to purchase one or more (possibly different) bottles of wine.

We can then say that *orders* are created on a date, and the system requirements in Chapter 16 identify that an *order* has an associated creditcard, card expirydate, and delivery instructions. The credit card details aren't associated with a customer because we want to know with which credit card each order was purchased.

We can also say that this model of *orders* consists of one or more different *wines* and, for each different *wine*, a quantity of that wine is purchased. The subparts in each order—the different wines—are the *items* that make up the *order*. But is the *wine* itself part of an *item*? The distinction is hard, but the correct answer is probably no: this is a relationship, in which the *items* that make up *orders* are related to *wines*.

There are now two more entities—*orders* and *items*—and two relationships, which illustrates how difficult it is to reason about entities without considering how they are related. Determining entities isn't always easy, and many different drafts of an ER model are often required before a final, correct model is achieved. The ER model for the winestore took us several attempts to get right.

Here are the *items* and *orders* entities:

- The *items* entity—which is related to *orders*—has the attributes qty (quantity) and price. In turn, the items entity is related to the *wine* entity.
- The *orders* entity has attributes date, instructions, creditcard, and expirydate.

The system requirements in Chapter 16 also describe how *wine* is delivered to the store in shipments. Each shipment is on a particular date and consists of a number of bottles at a particular price. How is this to be incorporated into the model? Perhaps the most obvious solution is to add `quantity` and `price` attributes to the *wine* entity.

Adding a quantity and price to the *wine* entity doesn't work well. Shipments arrive at different times and the price of a wine can change over time. We therefore need to maintain different prices for different shipments so that we can charge the user the correct price for the bottles in that shipment. In Australia, for example, it's illegal to sell an old shipment at a higher price than you've previously advertised when a new shipment arrives.

A good solution to the inventory problem is an *inventory* entity. This entity is related to the *wine*, and maintains different data for each shipment of each *wine*:

- The *inventory* entity has an `on_hand` quantity, a per bottle `cost`, and a `date_added`.

The last major entity is somewhat of an oddity. If a wine is a Cabernet Merlot, you can simply store the string Cabernet Merlot in an attribute in the *wine* entity. Another approach is to have a *grape_variety* entity, where each different grape variety is described individually and you can combine them to create wine blends. So, for example, *Cabernet* is one instance of a *grape_variety* entity, and *Merlot* is another. The *grape_variety* entity is then related to the *wine* entity. This approach does seem overly complicated, but let's opt for it anyway because it introduces an instructive twist to our modeling, a many-to-many relationship discussed in the next section.

Here's the *grape_variety* entity:

- The *grape_variety* entity has the attribute `variety` (which is a grape type such as Merlot).

There are other possible entities. For example, the shopping basket could be an entity: the shopping cart is an object that contains items that will later be ordered. However, in our application we've built the shopping cart by using the *orders* entity in a different way and adding some logic in our code to distinguish between completed orders and shopping carts. Including a shopping cart as an entity would perhaps be a valid choice, and depends on how the entities are interpreted from the requirements.

There are also other entities that are outside the scope of our requirements. For example, a county or state might contain many regions, but there is no requirement for these to be modeled in our system. Also, the winestore itself is an entity, but we are actually interested in the entities that make up the winestore, not the whole concept itself. Selecting entities is all about getting the granularity and scope of choice right.

Another common type of entity are lookup tables that store lists of commonly used values. For example, a lookup table that stores Zip Codes and city names is a common entity in many designs. In the winestore application, there's four possible lookup tables: a *countries* lookup for customers, a *titles* lookup (for values such as Dr., Mr., Miss, Mrs., or Ms.) for customers, a *wine_type* lookup (such as red or white) for wines, and the *grape_variety* entity that we've previously discussed. Let's define these as new entities:

- The *countries* entity has country names
- The *wine_type* entity has wine_type values
- The *titles* entity has customer title values

It's a good idea to include lookup tables as entities. The alternative is to define them as attributes of another table; for example, country could be an attribute of *customer*. However, if they're defined as attributes of another entity, this doesn't force the user to pick from a list of possible values, leading to possible inconsistencies between values (such as Australia, australia, aust, AUS, and so on) unless you add complex validation to your PHP script. Inconsistency in values makes it difficult to write reports and run queries: for example, it'd be hard to figure out how many customers live in Australia if it's represented in several different ways.

We have hinted at but not explicitly identified the relationships between the entities. For example, a *winery* is part of a *region*, a *wine* is made by a *winery*, and an *item* is related to a *wine*. The first step is to identify the entities and their attributes; the second step is to identify how the entities are related.

Identifying relationships in ER modeling

Before identifying the relationships between entities, let's explore the possible types of relationship or *cardinalities* that can exist. *Cardinality* refers to the three possible relationships between two entities:[*]

One-to-one
> A one-to-one relationship is represented by a line labeled with a 1 at each end that joins two entities. One-to-one means that for the two entities connected by the line, there is exactly one instance of the first entity for each one instance of the second entity. An example might be *customers* and *user* details: each *customer* has exactly one set of *user* details (a username and a password), and those *user* details are for only that *customer*.

One-to-many (or many-to-one)
> A one-to-many relationship is represented by a line annotated with a 1 and an M (or a 1 and an N). One-to-many means that for the two entities connected by the

---

[*] Actually, relationships can exist between as many entities as there are in the model. We have deliberately omitted the distinction with relationships that are optional, that is, where one instance of an entity—such as a *customer*—can exist without a related entity, such as an *order*. We avoid complex relationships in this appendix; more detail can be found in the books listed in Appendix G

line, there are one or more instances of the second entity for each one instance of the first entity. From the perspective of the second entity, any instance of the second entity is related to only one instance of the first entity. An example is *wineries* and *wines*: each *winery* sells many *wines*, but each *wine* is made by exactly one *winery*. Many-to-one relationships are the most common relationships between entities.

Many-to-many

A many-to-many relationship is represented by a line annotated with an M and an N. Many-to-many means that for the two entities connected by the line, each instance of the first entity is related to one or more instances of the second entity and, from the other perspective, each instance of the second entity is related to one or more instances of the first entity. An example is the relationship between wineries and delivery firms: a winery may use many delivery firms to freight wine to customers, while a delivery firm may work for many different wineries.

It isn't surprising that many database modelers make mistakes with cardinalities. Determining the cardinalities of the relationships between the entities is the most difficult skill in ER modeling, but one that, when performed correctly, results in a well-designed database. To illustrate how cardinality is determined, let's consider the relationships between the entities in the winestore and present arguments for their cardinalities.

Correctly assigning cardinalities is essential. Mistakes in cardinalities of relationships lead to duplicated data, inconsistencies, and redundancy in the database. All lead to poor performance and a hard-to-maintain database.

Relationships in the winestore ER model

Before considering cardinalities, you need to consider what entities are related. You know from previous discussion that a *region* is related to a *winery*, and that a *winery* is related to a *wine*. There are other relationships that are implicitly identified: *orders* contains *items*, a *customer* places *orders*, *users* have *customer* details, and a *wine* has an *inventory*. Also, *titles* and *countries* are lookups related to the *customer* entity, and the *wine_type* lookup is related to *wine*.

There is also one crucial relationship that links the *wine* sold to the *customer*, that is, the relationship between an *items* and the *inventory*. Last, a *wine* contains one or more different *grape_variety* entities.

To assign cardinalities, let's start with the relationship of *wine* to *winery*. To begin, you need to decide what sort of relationship these entities have and assign a descriptive term. A good description of the relationship between *wine* and *winery* is that a winery *makes* wine. Now draw a diamond labeled *makes* between the entities *wine* and *winery*, and connect the relationship to the two entities with an unannotated line. This process is shown in Figure E-3 (A).

The next step is to determine what cardinality to assign to this relationship. The most effective approach to determining cardinality is to consider the relationship from the perspective of both entities. From the perspective of a *winery*, the question to ask is: Does a *winery* make exactly one *wine* or one or more *wine* objects? The answer is the latter, so you write M at the *wine* end of the relationship. From the other perspective—that of the *wine*—you can ask a second simple question: Is a *wine* made by exactly one or more than one *winery*? This answer is the former—that limitation is noted in the system requirements—and you can write a 1 at the *winery* end of the relationship. The annotated, one-to-many relationship is shown in Figure E-3 (B).

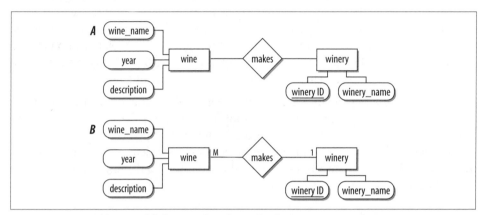

Figure E-3. A partial ER model showing the relationship between wines and wineries

Dealing with the relationship between *winery* and *region* involves similar arguments. You begin by describing the relationship. In this case, an appropriate label might be that a *winery* is *situated* in a *region*. After drawing the diamond and labeling it, now consider the cardinalities. A *winery* belongs in exactly one *region*, so label the *region* end with a 1. A *region* can contains more than one *winery*, so you label the *winery* end with an M.

There are six more relationships that can be completed using the same one-to-many arguments:

- The *consists-of* relationship between *orders* and *items*
- The *purchase* relationship between *customer* and *orders*
- The *stocked* relationship between *wine* and *inventory*
- The *classed-as* relationship between *wine* and the *wine_type* lookup
- The *lives-in* relationship between *customer* and the *countries* lookup
- The *titled* relationship between *customer* and the *titles* lookup

You can label all six with a 1 and an M (or N). These relationships are shown as part of Figure E-4.

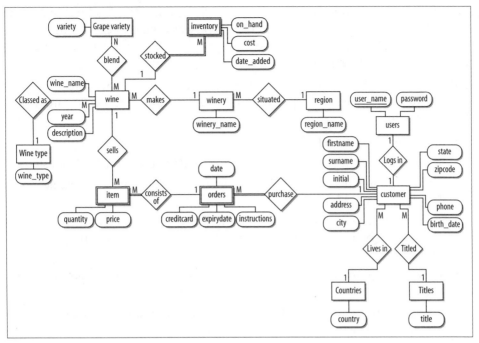

Figure E-4. An almost-complete ER model for the winestore

You know that the *users* and *customer* have a one-to-one relationship. So, let's draw a line between the two entities and label it with a 1 at each end. Label the relationship as *logs-in*.

The final two relationships are a more difficult to identify and annotate.

The first is the relationship between an order's *items* and a *wine*. The one-to-many cardinality isn't a difficult proposition, but determining that this relationship actually exists is harder. When considering what makes up *orders*, there are two possibilities: *items* can be related to a specific *inventory* entry, or *items* can be related to a *wine*. The former is possibly more intuitive because the *items* that are delivered are bottles from our *inventory*. However, the latter works better when modeling the system's data requirements. So, let's settle on *items* being related to *wine* and label the relationship *sells*.

The second difficult—and final—relationship is that between *wine* and *grape_variety*. Naming the relationship is easy: let's call this relationship *blend*. Determining the cardinality is harder. First, consider the relationship from the *wine* perspective. A *wine* can contain more than one *grape variety* when it is a blend, so you label the *grape variety* end of the relationship with an M. Now consider the relationship from the *grape variety* perspective. A *grape variety*, such as *semillon*, may be in many different *wines*. So, let's settle on a many-to-many relationship and label the *wine* end with an N.

Our ER model is almost complete, and Figure E-4 shows it with all its entities and relationships. What remains is to consider the key attributes in each of the entities, which are discussed in the next section. As you consider these, you can adjust the types of relationships slightly.

Before we move on, let's summarize what we've done so far. There are a few rules that determine what relationships, entities, and attributes are, and what cardinalities should be used:

- Expect to draft a model several times.
- Begin modeling with entities, add attributes, and then determine relationships.
- Include an entity only when it can be described with attributes that are needed in the model.
- Some entities can be modeled as attributes. For example, a state can be an entity, but it might be better modeled as one of the attributes that is part of an customer.
- Avoid unnecessary relationships. Create only those relationships that are needed in the system.
- One-to-one relationships are uncommon. If two entities participate in a one-to-one relationship, check that they aren't actually the same entity.
- Many-to-many relationships are complex. Use one-to-many relationships in preference where possible.

Identifying key attributes in ER modeling

In our introduction to ER modeling, we noted some of the implicit constraints of our model, including that there is only one customer #37 and one wine that we refer to as #168. However, in the modeling so far, we haven't considered how to uniquely identify each entity with a primary key.

Uniqueness is an important constraint. When a *customer* places an *order*, you must be able to uniquely identify that *customer* and associate the unique *order* with that unique *customer*. You also need to be able to uniquely identify the *wine* that a *customer* purchases. In fact, all entities must be uniquely identifiable, and this is true for all relational databases.

So, the next step in ER modeling is to identify the attributes or sets of attributes that uniquely identify an entity. Let's begin with the *customer*. A surname (or any combination of names) doesn't uniquely identify a customer. A surname, firstname, initial, and a complete address may work, although there are some cases where children and parents share the same name and address.

A less complicated approach for unique identification—and a common one that's guaranteed to work—is to add an identifier number (ID) attribute to the entity. Identifiers are used in all aspects of life—not just databases—and include such things as phone, passport, and street numbers, and Zip codes and IP addresses. A short unique identifier also leads to better database performance than using several string attributes, as discussed in Chapter 15.

Using this approach, we can create a cust_id attribute and assign ID #1 to the first customer, ID #2 to the second customer, and so on. In the modeling process, this new attribute is underlined to indicate that it uniquely identifies the customer, as shown later in Figure E-5.

You can take the same approach with *wine* and add an ID attribute, wine_id. For *winery* and *region*, the name attribute is most likely unique or, at least, it can be made so. However, for simplicity, you can still use the ID attribute approach to prevent any ambiguity or need for the winestore administrator to carefully choose unique names. The same argument can be applied to the *grape_variety*, *titles*, *wine_type*, and *countries* entities.

The *orders* entity can also be dealt with by a unique ID, as can *items* and *inventory*. However, there are two ways to tackle the problem. First, you can uniquely number each of the *orders* across the whole database, beginning with the application's first order_id #1. Alternatively, you can begin each of the customer's *orders* with order_id #1. The combination of cust_id and order_id is still unique: for example, cust_id #37, order_id #1 is different from cust_id #15, order_id #1.

An advantage of combining a customer and order number is that the number is more meaningful to the user. For example, a user can tell from the combined number how many *orders* they've placed, and the order_id provides a convenient counting tool for reporting. We use this approach in the winestore application.

Because *orders* can't exist without a *customer*, they're *weak entities* that are involved in a *full participation* relationship. Full participation means that *orders* aren't possible without a related *customer* and, because the cust_id forms part of the *orders* entity's unique identifier, *orders* are a weak entity. Participation is discussed briefly in the next section and weak entities are discussed in more detail later in this chapter.

You can follow the same argument about unique identification for *items*. The *items* can be uniquely numbered across the whole database or can be numbered from #1 within an *order*. Again, we follow the latter approach. The same applies for *inventory*, which is numbered within a *wine* since there are potentially many different shipments of each wine.

The only entity remaining is *users*. The user_name attribute must be unique, so we can choose it to uniquely identify the rows.

Other ER modeling tools

Other ER modeling tools include double ellipses, double lines, and double rectangles. These tools permit the representation of other constraints, multivalued attributes, and the specification of full participation. In addition, it's possible for a relationship to have an attribute, that is, for a diamond to have attributes that are part of the relationship, not part of the entities. Useful references for more advanced ER modeling—and enhanced ER (EER) modeling—are provided in Appendix G.

Double lines between a relationship diamond and an entity indicate full participation and represent cases where an instance of one entity can't exist without a corresponding instance of the entity that it is related to. An example is the *orders* entity in the winestore model. An instance of *orders* can't exist without a *customer* to make that order. Therefore, the relationship between *orders* and *customer* should be represented as a double line. The same constraints apply in the model to *items* and *inventory*.

Double rectangles represent weak entities. A weak entity isn't uniquely identifiable without including the key of the entity it's related to. For example, in the previous section, we explained how *orders* are uniquely identified by a combination of the *customer* ID and the *orders* ID. Without a customer, an order isn't uniquely identifiable and so it's a weak entity. The same applies to *items* and *inventory*.

Dashed ellipses represent multivalued attributes, attributes that may contain more than one instance. For example, the attribute address can be multivalued, because there could be a business address, a postal address, and a home address. Multivalued attributes aren't used in our model.

In addition, there are other extensions to the modeling techniques that have already been applied. For example, more than two entities can be related in a relationship (that is, more than two entities can be connected to a diamond). For example, the sale of a wine can be described as a three-way relationship between a *wine*, a *customer*, and *orders*. A second complex technique is the composite attribute; for example, an attribute of *customer* is address and the attribute address has its own attributes, a street, city, and zipcode. We don't explore complex relationships in this book.

Completing the ER model

Figure E-5 shows the final ER model with the unique key constraints shown. Notice that for *items, orders,* and *inventory,* the attributes from other entities aren't included. They are instead indicated as weak entities with a double rectangle and they participate fully in the related entities as indicated by double lines.

If *items, orders,* and *inventory* were numbered across the whole system, you could omit the double rectangles. The double lines can be omitted if any entity can exist without the related entity.

A summary of ER notation tools is shown in Figure E-6.

Converting an Entity-Relationship Model to SQL

There are five steps to convert an ER model to SQL CREATE TABLE statements.

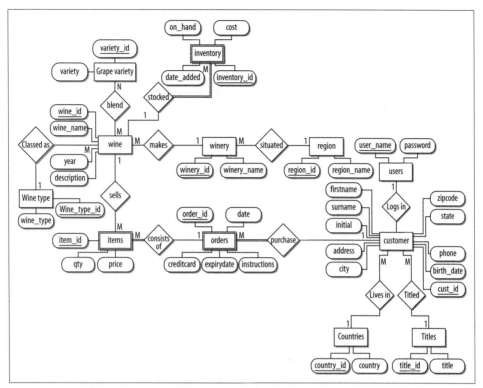

Figure E-5. The complete ER model for the winestore database

Step 1: Convert regular entities to tables

The first step is the simplest. Here's what you do:

1. For each non-weak entity in the ER model, write out a CREATE TABLE statement with the same name as the entity.

2. Include all attributes of the entity and assign appropriate types to the attributes.

3. Include as table attributes all of the ER model attributes that uniquely identify the entity and add the NOT NULL modifier to them. Include a PRIMARY KEY clause that lists the attributes.

To perform this step, you need to make decisions about attribute types in the SQL CREATE TABLE statements. Attribute types are discussed in Chapter 5.

There are several non-weak entities in the model. Let's begin with the *region* entity, which has the attributes region_id and region_name. You might anticipate no more than 100 different regions, but let's be cautious in case more than 1,000 regions need to be stored. So, let's decide that region_id is an int (integer) type and that it has a width of 4 digits. Let's assume that a region name can be at most 100 characters in length and define region_name as a varchar(100).

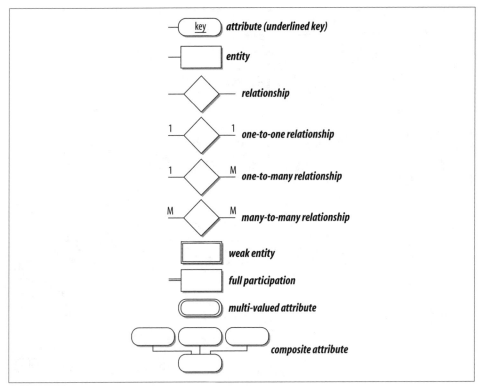

Figure E-6. Tools used in ER modeling

As decided earlier in the appendix, the unique key of the *region* table is an ID, which is now called region_id. Accordingly, you define a PRIMARY KEY of region_id. A requirement of all primary keys is that they are specified as NOT NULL, and this is added to the attribute.

The resulting definition for the *region* table is as follows:

```
CREATE TABLE region (
  region_id int(4) NOT NULL,
  region_name varchar(100) NOT NULL,
  PRIMARY KEY (region_id),
  KEY region (region_name)
) type=MyISAM;
```

Notice an additional KEY on the region_name named region. By adding this key, we're anticipating that a common query is a search by region_name. Also, a region must have a name, so a NOT NULL is added to the region_name attribute. Last, we've added a table type of MyISAM to the end of the definition; table types are discussed in Chapter 15.

The CREATE TABLE statements for the other non-weak entities are listed next. Remember, however, that this is only the first step: some of these CREATE TABLE statements are altered by the processes in later steps. Here they are:

```
CREATE TABLE countries (
   country_id int(4) NOT NULL,
   country char(30) NOT NULL,
   PRIMARY KEY (country_id),
   KEY (country)
) type=MyISAM;

CREATE TABLE customer (
   cust_id int(5) NOT NULL,
   surname varchar(50),
   firstname varchar(50),
   initial char(1),
   address varchar(50),
   city varchar(50),
   state varchar(20),
   zipcode varchar(10),
   phone varchar(15),
   birth_date char(10),
   PRIMARY KEY (cust_id)
) type=MyISAM;

CREATE TABLE grape_variety (
   variety_id int(3) NOT NULL,
   variety varchar(50) DEFAULT '' NOT NULL,
   PRIMARY KEY (variety_id),
   KEY var (variety)
) type=MyISAM;

CREATE TABLE titles (
   title_id int(2) NOT NULL,
   title char(10),
   PRIMARY KEY (title_id)
) type=MyISAM;

CREATE TABLE users (
   user_name varchar(50) NOT NULL,
   password varchar(32) NOT NULL,
   PRIMARY KEY (user_name),
   KEY password (password)
) type=MyISAM;

CREATE TABLE wine (
   wine_id int(5) NOT NULL,
   wine_name varchar(50) NOT NULL,
   year int(4) NOT NULL,
   description blob,
   PRIMARY KEY (wine_id),
   KEY name (wine_name),
) type=MyISAM;
```

```
CREATE TABLE winery (
  winery_id int(4) NOT NULL,
  winery_name varchar(100) NOT NULL,
  PRIMARY KEY (winery_id),
  KEY name (winery_name),
) type=MyISAM;
```

Step 2: Convert weak entities to tables

The second step is almost identical to the first but is used for weak entities. Here's what you do:

1. For each weak entity in the model—there are three: *inventory*, *orders*, and *items*—translate the entity directly to a CREATE TABLE statement as in Step 1.

2. Include all attributes as in Step 1.

3. Include as attributes the primary key attributes of the *owning* entity, the entity the weak entity is related to. Then, include these attributes as part of the primary key of the weak entity.

For example, for the *inventory* entity, create the following:

```
CREATE TABLE inventory (
  wine_id int(5) NOT NULL,
  inventory_id int(3) NOT NULL,
  on_hand int(5) NOT NULL,
  cost decimal(5,2) NOT NULL,
  date_added date,
  PRIMARY KEY (wine_id,inventory_id)
) type=MyISAM;
```

The wine_id is included from the *wine* table and forms part of the PRIMARY KEY definition. However, just because we've done this, it doesn't mean that our SQL queries can automatically discover the relationship between *wine* and *inventory* or that the numbering in the identifiers will be synchronized. You need to maintain the relationships using SQL queries that specify the join attributes in WHERE clauses. This is discussed in Chapter 5.

Note that all attributes can't be NULL in the *inventory* table, so NOT NULL is used liberally.

A similar approach is taken with *orders*, in which cust_id is included from the *customer* table as an attribute and as part of the PRIMARY KEY definition:

```
CREATE TABLE orders (
  cust_id int(5) NOT NULL,
  order_id int(5) NOT NULL,
  date timestamp(12),
  instructions varchar(128),
  creditcard char(16),
  expirydate char(5),
  PRIMARY KEY (cust_id,order_id)
) type=MyISAM;
```

The *items* table is slightly more complex, but made easier because *orders* has already been defined. The *items* table includes the PRIMARY KEY attributes of the entity it is related to (that is, *orders*). Because the PRIMARY KEY of *orders* is already resolved, the *items* table is as follows:

```
CREATE TABLE items (
  cust_id int(5) NOT NULL,
  order_id int(5) NOT NULL,
  item_id int(3) NOT NULL,
  qty int(3),
  price decimal(5,2),
  PRIMARY KEY (cust_id,order_id,item_id)
) type=MyISAM;
```

Step 3: One-to-one relationships

If two entities have a one-to-one relationship, check that your modeling is correct. If the entities totally participate in each other (where an instance of either entity can't exist without a matching instance in the other entity) and neither participates in another relationship, consider removing one of the tables and merging the attributes into a single table.

If you can't remove one of the entities, follow this process for conversion:

1. Choose one of the two tables that's involved in the relationship (this table has already been identified and written out as part of Steps 1 or 2). If the relationship involves total participation, choose the entity that totally participates.

2. In the chosen table, include as an attribute (or attributes) the primary key of the other table.

There is a one-to-one relationship between *customer* and *users* in our model. The rule in the first step isn't a constraint, so we arbitrarily choose the *users* table. Then, we add the identifier cust_id from *customer* to it:

```
CREATE TABLE users (
  cust_id int(5) NOT NULL,
  user_name varchar(50) NOT NULL,
  password varchar(32) NOT NULL,
  PRIMARY KEY (user_name),
  KEY password (password),
  KEY cust_id (cust_id)
) type=MyISAM;
```

Step 4: One-to-many relationships

For a one-to-many relationship, here's the procedure:

1. Identify the table representing the many (M or N) side of the relationship.

2. Add to the many-side (M or N) table the primary key of the 1-side table.

3. Optionally, add NOT NULL to any attributes added.

In the model, this means adding a `winery_id` and a `wine_type` identifier to the *wine* table:

```
CREATE TABLE wine (
    wine_id int(5) NOT NULL,
    wine_name varchar(50) NOT NULL,
    wine_type int(2) NOT NULL,
    year int(4) NOT NULL,
    winery_id int(4) NOT NULL,
    description blob,
    PRIMARY KEY (wine_id),
    KEY name (wine_name),
    KEY winery (winery_id)
) type=MyISAM;
```

For the *winery* table, it means adding a `region_id`:

```
CREATE TABLE winery (
    winery_id int(4) NOT NULL,
    winery_name varchar(100) NOT NULL,
    region_id int(4) NOT NULL,
    PRIMARY KEY (winery_id),
    KEY name (winery_name),
    KEY region (region_id)
) type=MyISAM;
```

For the *items* table, it means adding a `wine_id`:

```
CREATE TABLE items (
    cust_id int(5) NOT NULL,
    order_id int(5) NOT NULL,
    item_id int(3) NOT NULL,
    wine_id int(4) NOT NULL,
    qty int(3),
    price decimal(5,2),
    PRIMARY KEY (cust_id,order_id,item_id)
) type=MyISAM;
```

For the *customer* table, it means adding a `country_id` and a `title_id`:

```
CREATE TABLE customer (
    cust_id int(5) NOT NULL,
    surname varchar(50),
    firstname varchar(50),
    initial char(1),
    title_id int(3),
    address varchar(50),
    city varchar(50),
    state varchar(20),
    zipcode varchar(10),
    country_id int(4),
    phone varchar(15),
    birth_date char(10),
    PRIMARY KEY (cust_id)
) type=MyISAM;
```

In cases where you wish to prevent a row being inserted without a corresponding value in the related table, you can add a NOT NULL to the newly added attribute.

Step 5: Many-to-many relationships

For many-to-many relationships—there is one in our model between *wine* and *grape_variety*—the following procedure is used:

1. Create a new table with a composite name made of the two entities that are related.
2. Add the primary keys of the two related entities to this new table.
3. Add an ID attribute if the order of relationship is important. For example, in the winestore, a Cabernet Merlot Shiraz is different from a Shiraz Merlot Cabernet, so an ID is required.
4. Define the primary key of the new table to be the primary keys of the two related entities.

For the winestore, this leads to creating the following table:

```
CREATE TABLE wine_variety (
  wine_id int(5) NOT NULL,
  variety_id int(3) NOT NULL,
  id int(1) NOT NULL,
  PRIMARY KEY (wine_id,variety_id),
) type=MyISAM;
```

The table contains the primary keys of *wine* and *grape_variety* and defines these as the PRIMARY KEY. No change is required to the *wine* or *grape_variety* tables.

Our conversion of the model to SQL is now complete, and the database is ready to be created and loaded with data.

Managing Sessions in the Database Tier

In Chapter 10, we discussed the development of session-based applications using the PHP session management features. In this appendix, we briefly explain how to create your own, alternative session storage functions that store session variables in a database. Specifically, this appendix covers:

- Why you might want to replace the default PHP session storage layer with customized functions using the database tier
- How to write user-defined PHP session storage handlers
- How to create and install a fully functional set of PHP handlers that use a table in a MySQL database to store session variables

Using a Database to Keep State

The demand on popular web sites is sometimes more than can be met by a single web server. When this happens, there are two approaches you can follow: take steps to lighten the load on the server, or share the processing load across several servers. In the latter approach, each different HTTP request can be sent to a different web server, even if the requests come from the same user.

The stateless nature of HTTP permits load balancing, but PHP's session handler undermines it. Sessions maintain variables across several HTTP requests: the variables that are written by one request are retrieved and updated by subsequent requests. By default, PHP stores session variables in files on the web server and, therefore, the web server that begins a session must process all subsequent requests that belong to that session.

If you want the benefits of load balancing with sessions, you need to store session variables in a common area that all your web servers can access. A natural candidate for such storage is your database, because you are already using it in your applications. What's more, storing the sessions in the database tier should lighten the load on your web server, because reading and writing to a database should be much faster than reading and writing disk files.

Taking the trouble to code your own storage solution can pay off substantially on heavily loaded web sites. In many applications, the middle tier—the layer that implements most of the application logic—is the performance bottleneck. By deploying multiple web servers, HTTP load balancing can be achieved and the database server better utilized.

As shown in Figure F-1, moving the session data to the database allows an application to scale horizontally at the middle tier. The web server doesn't have to keep session variables; so more than one web server can be employed to process HTTP requests. The PHP scripts on each web server still implement the application logic, but session variables are retrieved from a central database. However, this isn't an infinitely scalable solution: there's a point at which the performance of the DBMS becomes the bottleneck. Also, allowing multiple web servers to access a central database server requires strategies to control concurrent access, a topic we discuss in Chapter 8.

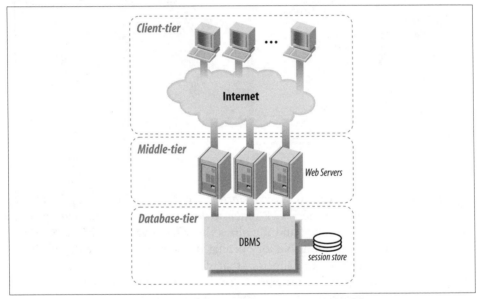

Figure F-1. Three-tier architecture using a database to store session variables

PHP Session Management

In Chapter 10, we described the three characteristics of session management: storing session variables, matching these session variables to HTTP requests using a session identifier, and removing timed-out sessions with garbage collection. PHP session management largely takes care of these issues, and with the default configuration, you needn't worry how storage, session identification, and garbage collection are performed.

To understand what we accomplish in this appendix, you should know a bit about what PHP does behind the scenes. You should also understand the layers within the PHP session support and how you can hook your own functions in.

Figure F-2 shows how session variables are stored and retrieved when PHP runs an application script that uses session support. PHP session support is divided into two layers: the PHP session management layer provides the interface to session-based scripts, and the storage layer is responsible for reading and writing session variables in the session store. The storage layer in the default configuration works with files in a directory designated for PHP session storage.

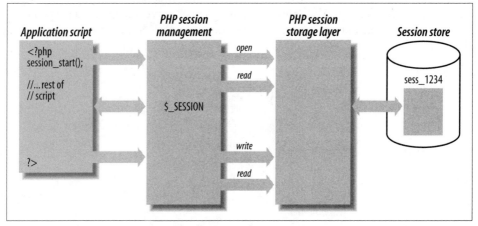

Figure F-2. PHP session management

When a script makes a call to *session_start()*, the PHP session management layer reads the session ID from the HTTP request, starts a session by making open and read calls to the storage layer, and initializes the session variables in the $_SESSION array. The open call is responsible for opening the session store: the default implementation simply identifies the directory that stores the session file. The read call is responsible for finding and returning the *serialized* session variables associated with the session ID; we discuss serialization later in this section.

When the script ends, the session management layer calls write and close functions to write the contents of the array $_SESSION back to the session store and close the session. The write function is responsible for finding the session file and writing the serialized session variables to that file. The close function formally closes the session store: in the default implementation, the close operation does nothing, as no close operation is required on a file system.

The session management layer is responsible for serializing and deserializing the session variables. Serialization means that the variables are converted to strings that describe the variable name, its type, length, and value. When a script ends, the session variables in the array $_SESSION are serialized and passed as a single string to the write function to be saved in the session store. For example, if the array $_SESSION contains a string variable name, a float variable height, and an integer variable age; the serialized string might look like this:

```
name|s:4:"Dave";height|d:1.86;age|i:38;
```

When the read function identifies a session file, it simply returns the serialized string back to the session management layer to be deserialized into the $_SESSION array.

The PHP session storage layer also implements functions that destroy a session when a script calls *session_destroy()*. It also performs garbage collection to remove timed-out sessions. Unlike the other storage functions, garbage collection is not tied directly to an event in the application script. Instead the session management layer calls garbage collection randomly when a call is made to *session_start()*. The probability that garbage collection is called is defined by the configuration parameters session.gc_probability and session.gc_dividend. For a more detailed discussion about garbage collection see Chapter 10.

PHP Session Management Storage Methods

Different storage strategies can be used for session management. PHP can be configured to store session variables in files on disk (the default method), in memory, or in a user-defined way. The storage method used is configured by the session.save_handler parameter in the *php.ini* file. The values the session.save_handler parameter can take are:

files

> This is the default storage method for PHP, where session variables are serialized and written to a session disk file.

mm

> The memory management storage method allows session variables to be stored in Apache's runtime memory. Using memory has the advantage of better performance than files on disk. However, if many sessions must be supported, and each session uses a large volume of data, the memory used by the Apache process may be high. To use memory to store session variables, PHP must be configured and compiled to use an installed memory management module (--with-mm). The memory management module is not available for Microsoft Windows systems.

user

> The user-defined method allows an application to save session variables to systems other than file or memory, such as to a table in a database. By defining sev-

eral handler prototypes, PHP allows the developer to define the behavior of the low-level session storage. A full explanation is given in the next section.

Building User-Defined Storage Handlers

By implementing user-defined storage handlers, a developer can modify how PHP sessions are stored without needing to change any application logic. The only modification required in a PHP script is an additional require directive that specifies the use of the user-defined session management handlers.

When the PHP session.save_handler parameter is set to user, you are basically writing your own replacement for the right-hand side of Figure F-2 shown earlier. Everything from the column showing the *open* through *close* calls to the Session Store is up to you. PHP must be provided with a set of functions that provide the low-level session storage support. These functions replace the default storage layer illustrated in Figure F-2. The functions that you need to write, and the prototypes they must conform to, are listed below:

Boolean open(string save_path, string session_name)
> Called by PHP to open the session store when a script calls *session_start( )*. PHP passes the values of the parameters session.save_path and session.name defined in *php.ini* as arguments to this function, and these arguments can be used to locate the session store. By default, session.save_path is set to */tmp* to indicate the directory for the files storage method, and session.name is set to PHPSESSID as the name of the session ID cookie. The function should return true on success and false on failure.
>
> Later, when we implement the handlers to store session variables in a MySQL database, we use these parameters to select a database and a table.

mixed read(string session_id)
> Called by PHP to read the variables for the session identified by *session_id* when a session is initialized. The function returns a string that contains the serialized session variables. The PHP session management converts the string to the individual session variables and sets up the $_SESSION array. If no session is found, the function should return a blank string. The function should return false if an error occurs during the read operation.

Boolean write(string session_id, string values)
> Called by PHP at the end of a script to save the session variables managed in the $_SESSION array to the session store. This function is passed the ID of the session, and the session variables serialized into a single string by PHP. The implementation of *write()* must store the serialized string associated with the session, and record the time the session was last accessed. The function should return false if an error occurs during the write operation and true on success.

Boolean close()

Called by PHP at the end of a script and can be used to perform tasks required to close the session store. The function should return false if an error occurs during the close operation and true on success.

Boolean destroy(string session_id)

Called by PHP when a script calls *session_destroy()*. The function should use the session_id parameter to identified a session and remove the associated storage. The function should return false if an error occurs during the destroy operation and true on success.

Boolean gc(int max_lifetime)

The garbage collection function called by PHP to identify and remove sessions that have not been accessed within max_lifetime seconds. The value of the max_lifetime parameter is the value of session.gc_maxlifetime defined in *php.ini*. When a script calls *session_start()*, PHP randomly calls the garbage collection function with a probability defined by the parameters session.gc_probability and session.gc_dividend. If the garbage collection handler is executed without error, it should return true, and false otherwise. For a more detailed discussion about garbage collection see Chapter 10.

The return types and the parameters passed to the functions must conform to the prototypes listed here, but you can set the actual function names to whatever you like. However, these functions need to be registered with PHP using *session_set_save_handler()*:

void session_set_save_handler(string open, string close, string read, string write, string destroy, string gc)

Registers PHP function names as the handler functions for user-defined session management. The arguments to this function are the names of the functions. The six parameters passed to *session_set_save_handler()* are interpreted as the names of the *open*, *close*, *read*, *write*, *destroy*, and *gc* functions described previously in this section.

MySQL Session Store

In this section we develop a set of user-defined handlers that store session variables in a MySQL table.

Session Table Structure

For the session handler code that stores session variables, a table is needed to hold sessions. You can create the table as part of your application database (for example, as a table in the *winestore* database), or create a new database to store only sessions. We follow the former approach, but it doesn't matter what you choose in practice;

the database is accessed using its own connection, so you won't have any trouble accessing the table even when other tables are locked.

The following SQL CREATE TABLE statement creates a table to hold the session ID, the serialized session variables, and a timestamp to indicate when the session was last accessed. If you want to add it to the *winestore* database, login to the MySQL command interpreter as root user and type the following:

```
mysql> use winestore;
Database changed
mysql> CREATE TABLE PHPSESSION(
    ->    session_id varchar(50) NOT NULL,
    ->    session_variable text,
    ->    last_accessed decimal(15,3) NOT NULL,
    ->    PRIMARY KEY (session_id),
    ->    KEY last_acc (last_accessed)
    -> ) type=MyISAM;
Query OK, 0 rows affected (0.05 sec)
```

The session_id attribute is the primary key and the last_accessed attribute is indexed to allow fast deletion of dormant sessions using custom garbage-collection code described later.

When the code is up and running, the *PHPSESSION* table can be examined to see the current sessions. The following example shows that two sessions are held in the table (we have truncated the values in the session_id column to fit on the page):

```
mysql> SELECT * FROM PHPSESSION;
+--------------------+----------------------------+--------------+
| session_id         | session_variable           | last_updated |
+--------------------+----------------------------+--------------+
| ee83912e13b11a8c042 | count|i:39;start|i:90900585; | 90900661.575 |
| 6e721f8557df77b7b6d | count|i:0;start|i:90900677;  | 90900678.705 |
+--------------------+----------------------------+--------------+
2 rows in set (0.02 sec)
```

Handler Implementations

We store the session handlers in a support file. By placing the functions shown in Examples F-1 through F-8 in the one file, you can require that file at the beginning of any PHP script that uses sessions. If the file is saved as *mysql_sessions.inc*, then it's required as shown in the following example:

```
<?php
  require "mysql_sessions.inc";
  start_session();

  //... rest of the script ...
?>
```

Support functions

The MySQL-based session handlers can use the simple *showerror()* function discussed in Chapter 6 or the custom error handler developed in Chapter 12. To keep the examples simple, we use the *showerror()* function that's stored in the *db.inc* require file. Using this approach, when an error occurs, the function reports a MySQL error message and stops the script. If you use a custom handler instead and replace the calls to *showerror()* with calls to *trigger_error()*, then you can handle errors more gracefully by logging them to a file and presenting an error message to the user that has a look and feel that's consistent with the application.

The *db.inc* file that contains *showerror()* also maintains the database credentials, stored in the $hostName, $username, and $password variables.

Example F-1 shows the function *getMicroTime()*, which generates a timestamp. The timestamp records the last session access by the *sessionWrite()* handler and creates a query that identifies idle sessions in the *sessionGC()* handler. The *sessionWrite()* handler and the *sessionGC()* handler are developed later in this section.

Example F-1. The support function getMicroTime()

```php
<?php
require "db.inc";

// Returns current time as a number. Used for recording the
// last session access.

function getMicroTime()
{
  // microtime() returns the number of seconds since
  // 0:00:00 January 1, 1970 GMT as a  microsecond part
  // and a second part. e.g.: 0.08344800 1000952237

  // Convert the two parts into an array
  $mtime = explode(" ", microtime());

  // Return the addition of the two parts e.g.: 1000952237.08344800
  return($mtime[1] + $mtime[0]);
}
```

Session open handler

Example F-2 shows the first of the session handlers required by PHP session management. When PHP calls the *sessionOpen()* function, the values of session.save_path and session.name defined in the *php.ini* file, are passed as parameters and these values can be used however you choose. In the *sessionOpen()* function defined here, these two parameters identify the database and table used to store session variables.

The $database_name parameter—the value of session.save_path—is used to select a database after a connection to a MySQL server is established. The $table_name parameter—the value of session.name—is stored in the global variable $session_ table. The global variables `$session_table` and `$connection` appear in subsequent session store handlers, where they are used to execute SELECT, INSERT, UPDATE, and DELETE queries.

Example F-2. The sessionOpen( ) handler

```
// The database connection
$connection = NULL;

// The global variable that holds the table name
$session_table = NULL;

// The session open handler called by PHP whenever
// a session is initialized. Always returns true.

function sessionOpen($database_name, $table_name)
{
  // Save the database connection in a global variable
  global $connection;

  // Save the session table name in a global variable
  global $session_table;

  // Database credentials
  global $hostName;
  global $username;
  global $password;

  if (!($connection = @ mysql_connect($hostName, $username, $password)))
     showerror( );

  if (!mysql_select_db($database_name, $connection))
     showerror( );

  $session_table = $table_name;

  return true;
}
```

With the handler shown in Example F-2, the database and table names can be configured in the *php.ini* file. For example, with the following *php.ini* file settings:

```
session.save_path = winestore
session.name = PHPSESSION
```

the *openSession()* function selects the *winestore* database and identifies the *PHPSESSION* table. If you want to use our session handler, you need to modify your *php.ini* to have these settings and restart your Apache.

Session read handler

The *sessionRead( )* handler function shown in Example F-3 is called by PHP to read session variables. The handler returns the serialized string that holds the session vari-

---

ables for the session ID $sess_id. The function executes a query to find the row with a session_id equal to $sess_id and, if the row is found, the session_variable attribute is returned. If no session is found, *sessionRead()* returns a blank string.

The *sessionRead()* handler uses the global variables $session_table and $connection, set up by the *sessionOpen()* handler, to formulate and execute the query. The function returns all the session variables as a serialized string and PHP's session management layer automatically deserializes the string to set up the $_SESSION array; you don't have to worry about serialization and deserialization in your code.

Example F-3. The sessionRead() handler

```
// This function is called whenever a session_start() call is
// made and reads the session variables associated with the session
// identified by the $sess_id parameter. Returns "" when a session
// is not found and the session variables as a serialized string
// when the session exists.

function sessionRead($sess_id)
{
  // Access the DBMS connection
  global $connection;

  // Access the sessions table
  global $session_table;

  // Formulate a query to find the session identified by $sess_id
  $search_query = "SELECT * FROM {$session_table}
                   WHERE session_id = '{$sess_id}'";

  // Execute the query
  if (!($result = @ mysql_query($search_query, $connection)))
    showerror();

  if(mysql_num_rows($result) == 0)
    // No session found - return an empty string
    return "";
  else
  {
    // Found a session - return the serialized string
    $row = mysql_fetch_array($result);
    return $row["session_variable"];
  }
}
```

Session write handler

The *sessionWrite()* handler function is called by PHP at the end of a script that calls *session_start()*, and is responsible for writing variables to the session store and for recording when a session was last accessed. It's important that the last_access timestamp is updated each time the *sessionWrite()* handler is called, even if the session variables haven't changed. If the last access time isn't updated, a session may be seen as dormant by the garbage collection handler and destroyed even though the variables have recently been read.

Example F-4 starts by executing a SELECT query to determine if a session exists. If a session is found, an UPDATE query is executed; otherwise a new session row is created with an INSERT query. Both the INSERT and UPDATE queries set the last_accessed field with the timestamp created by the support function *getMicroTime( )* shown in Example F-1.

Example F-4. The sessionWrite() handler

```
function sessionWrite($sess_id, $val)
{
  // Access the DBMS connection
  global $connection;

  // Access the sessions table
  global $session_table;

  $time_stamp = getMicroTime( );

  $search_query = "SELECT session_id FROM {$session_table}
                WHERE session_id = '{$sess_id}'";

  // Execute the query
  if (!($result = @ mysql_query($search_query, $connection)))
     showerror( );

  if(mysql_num_rows($result) == 0)
  {
     // No session found, insert a new one
     $insert_query = "INSERT INTO {$session_table}
                  (session_id, session_variable, last_accessed)
                  VALUES ('{$sess_id}', '{$val}', {$time_stamp})";

     if (!mysql_query($insert_query, $connection))
        showerror( );
  }
  else
  {
     // Existing session found - Update the session variables
     $update_query = "UPDATE {$session_table}
                  SET session_variable = '{$val}',
                     last_accessed = {$time_stamp}
                  WHERE session_id = '{$sess_id}'";

     if (!mysql_query($update_query, $connection))
        showerror( );
  }
}
```

Session close handler

The *sessionClose()* handler is called by PHP when a session-based script ends, and can be used to perform any housekeeping functions needed to close a session store. The handler implementation shown in Example F-5, accomplishes the minimum, just returning true.

Example F-5. The sessionClose() handler

```
// This function is executed on shutdown of the session.
// Always returns true.

function sessionClose()
{
    return true;
}
```

Session destroy handler

When *session_destroy()* is called, PHP calls the *sessionDestroy()* handler shown in Example F-6. This function deletes the row identified by the $sess_id argument from the table that holds the session variables.

Example F-6. The sessionDestroy() handler

```
// This is called whenever the session_destroy() function
// call is made. Returns true if the session  has successfully
// been deleted.

function sessionDestroy($sess_id)
{
  // Access the DBMS connection
  global $connection;

  // Access the sessions table
  global $session_table;

  $delete_query = "DELETE FROM {$session_table}
                  WHERE session_id = '{$sess_id}'";

  if (!($result = @ mysql_query($delete_query, $connection)))
    showerror();

  return true;
}
```

Garbage collection handler

The last handler to be defined is the garbage collection function. Example F-7 shows the implementation of *sessionGC()*, which queries for all session rows that have been dormant for $max_lifetime seconds. When PHP session management calls this function, the value of the session.gc_maxlifetime parameter is passed as $max_lifetime.

The time a session has been dormant is calculated by subtracting the last update time held in the session row from the current time.

Example F-7. The sessionGC() garbage collection handler

```
// This function is called on a session's start up with the
// probability specified in session.gc_probability.  Performs
// garbage collection by removing all sessions that haven't been
// updated in the last $max_lifetime seconds as set in
// session.gc_maxlifetime.
// Returns true if the DELETE query succeeded.

function sessionGC($max_lifetime)
{
  // Access the DBMS connection
  global $connection;

  // Access the sessions table
  global $session_table;

  $current_time = getMicroTime();

  $delete_query = "DELETE FROM {$session_table}
            WHERE last_accessed < ({$current_time} - {$max_lifetime})";

  if (!($result = @ mysql_query($delete_query, $connection)))
     showerror();

  return true;
}
```

Registering session handlers

Finally, the handlers implemented in Examples F-2 through Example F-7 need to be registered as callback functions with PHP. Example F-8 shows the call to *session_set_save_handler()* with the names of each handler function.

Example F-8. Registering the user-defined session handlers with PHP

```
// Call to register user call back functions.

session_set_save_handler("sessionOpen",
                         "sessionClose",
                         "sessionRead",
                         "sessionWrite",
                         "sessionDestroy",
                         "sessionGC");
?>
```

Using the User-Defined Session Handler Code

Once the user-defined session handler code is implemented, it can be used by setting up the session configuration in the *php.ini* file and including the library at the top of

PHP scripts that use sessions. The session.save_handler parameter needs to be set to user, indicating that user-defined handlers are used; the session.save_path parameter is set to the name of the database; and, session.name parameter is set to the name of the table. The following example settings are used if session variables are stored in the *PHPSESSION* table of the *winestore* database:

```
session.save_handler = user
session.save_path = winestore
session.name = PHPSESSION
```

After changing *php.ini*, you need to restart Apache for the settings to take effect.

Example F-9 shows how application scripts are modified to use the MySQL session store; the script is a copy of Example 10-1, with the addition of the directive to require *mysql_session.inc*.

Example F-9. A simple PHP script that uses the MySQL session store

```php
<?php
  require_once "HTML/Template/ITX.php";
  require "mysql_sessions.inc";

  // This call either creates a new session or finds an existing one.
  session_start();

  // Check if the value for "count" exists in the session store
  // If not, set a value for "count" and "start"
  if (!isset($_SESSION["count"]))
  {
    $_SESSION["count"] = 0;
    $_SESSION["start"] = time();
  }

  // Increment the count
  $_SESSION["count"]++;

  $template = new HTML_Template_ITX("./templates");
  $template->loadTemplatefile("example.d-10.tpl", true, true);

  $template->setVariable("SESSION", session_id());
  $template->setVariable("COUNT", $_SESSION["count"]);
  $template->setVariable("START", $_SESSION["start"]);
  $duration = time() - $_SESSION["start"];
  $template->setVariable("DURATION", $duration);

  $template->parseCurrentBlock();

  $template->show();
?>
```

The script uses the template shown in Example F-10.

Example F-10. The template used with Example F-9

```
<!DOCTYPE HTML PUBLIC "-//W3C//DTD HTML 4.01 Transitional//EN"
                      "http://www.w3.org/TR/html401/loose.dtd">
<html>
<head>
  <meta http-equiv="Content-Type" content="text/html; charset=iso-8859-1">
  <title>Session State Test</title>
</head>
<body>
    <p>This page points at a session {SESSION}
    <br>count = {COUNT}
    <br>start = {START}
    <p>This session has lasted {DURATION} seconds.
</body>
</html>
```

PEAR's HTTP_Session Package

The PEAR HTTP_Session module is another example of PHP session handlers that implement a MySQL based session store. We introduce PEAR in Chapter 10.

The module has been developed to define an HTTP_Session class that provides a higher-level API to the PHP session management than the code we've developed here. The HTTP_Session class includes functions that not only access session variables, but also provide control over the session parameters such as cookies. HTTP_Session includes a database container method *HTTP_Session::setContainer()* that sets up PHP to use MySQL session handlers.

Resources

This appendix contains lists of books and online resources that cover many of the topics discussed in this book. The appendix is divided into four sections:

Client-tier resources
   HTML, XML, XHTML, CSS, and JavaScript resources

Middle-tier resources
   Web server, web technology, and PHP resources

Database-tier resources
   Database theory, SQL, and DBMS-specific resources

Security and cryptography resources
   More information on security, authentication, and privacy

Client Tier Resources

More information on HTML, the related topic of CSS, JavaScript, and directions in the standards that web browsers support can be found in the following resources:

- The W3C web site *http://www.w3.org* has links to many of the web standards, including HTML 4.01 (*http://www.w3.org/TR/html4/*), Cascading Style Sheets, XML, and XHTML. The HTML validator—which is linked into the bottom of each of the pages of the online winestore—can be found at *http://validator.w3.org*.

- The HTML Writer's Guild (HWG) is an organization that provides many useful resources to web developers, including links to lists of browser features and HTML validators. Trial membership is free for the first year. The HWG web site is *http://www.hwg.org*.

- *HTML and XHTML: The Definitive Guide*, C. Musciano and B. Kennedy (O'Reilly). This book is a comprehensive guide to writing HTML web pages. It covers HTML 4 features, including Cascading Style Sheets.

- *Cascading Style Sheets: The Definitive Guide*, E. A. Meyer (O'Reilly). Besides presenting the CSS material with many examples and case studies, this book provides a CSS support chart that shows which browsers support which features.
- *JavaScript: The Definitive Guide*, D. Flanagan (O'Reilly). Provides an in-depth reference to JavaScript with selected code examples; this book is ideal for the intermediate audience who can program and understand the requirements of JavaScript for a web database application.
- The original cookie specification was developed by Netscape and can be found at *http://www.netscape.com/newsref/std/cookie_spec.html*.

Middle-Tier Resources

This section lists resources that contain more information on the Apache web server, web performance tuning, networking, PHP programming, and third-party PHP add-ons including Integrated Development Environments (IDEs), script optimization tools, and commercially supported installation packages.

Web Server and Web Technology Resources

More information on the Apache web server can be found in the following resources:

- The Apache documentation. You can find this online at *http://httpd.apache.org/docs-project/*.
- *Apache: The Definitive Guide*, B. Laurie and P. Laurie (O'Reilly). Oriented around the directives that can be used in the *httpd.conf* file.
- *Apache Cookbook*, K. Coar and R. Bowen (O'Reilly). A collection of problems, solutions, and examples for webmasters.

More information on web performance tuning, and web performance modeling and traffic characteristics can be found in the following resources:

- *Web Performance Tuning*, P. Killelea (O'Reilly).
- *Capacity Planning for Web Performance: Metrics, Models, and Methods*, D. A. Menasce and V. A. F. Almeida (Prentice-Hall).

Networking and Web Resources

- The W3C web site: *http://www.w3.org/History.html*. This URL provides a good starting point that includes pages containing many links, time lines, growth statistics, and other useful resources.
- *Internet Core Protocols*, E. Hall and V. Cerf (O'Reilly). This book offers a good introduction to the protocols of the Web.
- *HTTP: The Definitive Guide*, D. Gourley and B. Totty (O'Reilly). Covers all of the technical details of HTTP.

- The HTTP/1.1 specification is contained in RFC-2616 and is found on the IETF web site at *http://www.ietf.org/rfc/rfc2616.txt*.
- The Uniform Resource Identifiers (URI): Generic Syntax specification is contained in RFC-2396 and is found on the IETF web site at *http://www.ietf.org/rfc/rfc2396.txt*.
- RFC-1180: *TCP/IP Tutorial*, T. Socolofsky and C. Kale. This RFC provides a tutorial on how data is passed through a TCP/IP network and can be found at: *http://www.ietf.org/rfc/rfc1180.txt*.

PHP resources

The best place to start is to check the list of links at the official PHP site, *http://www.php.net/links.php*.

Here are some resources we frequently use:

http://www.php.net/manual/
> The annotated online PHP manual at the official PHP site. Includes many comments for each library and function and tips on use and common problems encountered.

http://pear.php.net/
> The PEAR package home page. Includes a package searcher and browser.

http://www.zend.com/
> Site of the commercial company held by long-term developers of PHP. Includes articles, resources, free code, and tutorials.

http://www.phpbuilder.com/
> Articles, documentation, and code fragments.

http://www.devshed.com/Server_Side/PHP/
> Tutorial-style articles on a range of PHP topics.

http://px.sklar.com/
> A simple, low-bandwidth site that contains PHP code fragments and some complete applications.

Zend Optimizer
> A freely available code optimizer that improves the performance of the intermediate code generated by the Zend scripting engine. The Zend web site is *http://www.zend.com*.

DBG: PHP Debugger
> A free interactive debugger for PHP that includes a code profiler that finds code bottlenecks. Available for Microsoft Windows and many Unix platforms (including Linux and Mac OS X), and licensed under the same license as PHP. Available from: *http://dd.cron.ru/dbg/*.

Zend Cache
  A tool that integrates with the Zend engine to better cache scripts, prevent some scripts being cached, and reduce latency. If high-throughput of a web database application is required, Zend Cache is a useful tool. This is a commercial product.

http://www.php-editors.com/
  A list of development environments for PHP, most of which include syntax highlighting and debugging tools.

Database Tier Resources

Many excellent general database texts are available that cover the broad fields of relational databases, ER modeling, and SQL. Among the best are:

- *An Introduction to Database Systems,* C.J. Date (Addison Wesley).
- *Database System Concepts,* A. Silberschatz, H.F. Korth, and S. Sudarshan (McGraw-Hill).
- *Fundamentals of Database Systems*, R. Elmasri and S.B. Navathe (Addison Wesley).
- *Database Management Systems*, R. Ramakrishnan and J. Gehrke (McGraw-Hill).

For a coverage of SQL, several good books exist, but many are out of print. Currently available books include:

- *A Guide to the SQL Standard: A User's Guide to the Standard Database Language SQL*, C.J. Date and H. Darwen (Addison Wesley). This book isn't for the beginner but does an excellent job of covering the standard in detail.
- *SQL-99 Complete, Really,* P. Gulutzan and T. Pelzer (CMP Books). At present, MySQL almost supports the SQL-92 standard, but this book is an excellent and long introduction to SQL with many worked examples.

For MySQL, the *manual.html* file distributed with the installation is an excellent resource. Other books include:

- *Managing and Using MySQL*, R.J. Yarger, G. Reese, and T. King (O'Reilly).
- *MySQL*, P. DuBois (New Riders Publishing).

Security and Cryptography Resources

Many books on Web security and cryptography are available. We recommend the following books:

- *Web Security,* L. Stein (Addison Wesley). An excellent, comprehensive book with both technical and nontechnical depth.

- *Applied Cryptography: Protocols, Algorithms, and Source Code in C,* B. Schneier (John Wiley and Sons). Covers the field of cryptography in technical depth.
- *The Code Book,* S. Singh (Anchor Books). An enjoyable popular science book.
- *Building Secure Servers with Linux,* M. Bauer (O'Reilly).
- *Security Engineering,* R.J. Anderson (Wiley). An excellent all-round book.
- *Web security, privacy and Commerce,* S. Garfinkel, (O'Reilly).
- The RSA encryption web site, *http://www.rsa.com.*

The Improved MySQL Library

A new improved MySQL function library is being developed for applications that use PHP5 and MySQL 4.1. It gives you access to new features that are available in MySQL 4.1, including preparing and executing queries, load balancing, and encrypted and compressed connections. These features, along with others that are discussed in this appendix, allow you to improve the performance of your web database application.

At the time of writing, the library is experimental, meaning that names of functions and parameters may change. However, it's likely that the library will remain in roughly its current form and that it'll soon be a stable component of PHP. It won't replace the regular library; it will be an additional tool that's available for you to use.

If you're using MySQL 4.1, you need to know about this new improved library. At the time of writing, you can't use the MySQL library that's discussed in Chapter 6 or the PEAR DB package described in Chapter 7 with MySQL 4.1. However, it's likely that in the future, both the standard library and PEAR DB may work with MySQL 4.1; there'll be pressure on the PHP developers to offer backward compatibility for legacy code.

In this appendix, we briefly introduce some of the new concepts in the improved MySQL library and show you simple code examples. For more detailed information and function prototypes, refer to the PHP manual at *http://www.php.net/manual/en/ ref.mysqli.php*. This appendix assumes you've read up to and including Chapter 8.

New Features

The improved MySQL library adds new features, remove old features, improves performance, and offers more flexibility compared to the standard MySQL library. These changes include:

Prepared statements and parameter binding
  This feature allows you to speed-up the processing of repeated queries that perform the same function. For example, it's a fast way to insert hundreds or thousands of rows into the same table.

Compressed and encrypted connections

You now have more flexibility over how you communicate between your web and database servers. By using compression, you can reduce the amount of data transferred between the servers; this will speed up your communications if the servers are installed on different machines that communicate over a network. With SSL encryption, you can secure a connection between your servers; this is of benefit only if the connection between your web and database server is susceptible to the security problems discussed in Chapter 11.

Object-oriented methods

You can now choose whether to use the traditional procedural style to call the functions (as described in Chapter 6) or to use an object-oriented style that's similar to that used by PEAR DB.

Transaction control

You can turn MySQL's autocommit feature on or off, and also call functions that start, commit, and roll back transactions. Transactions are discussed in detail in Chapter 15.

Replication and distribution support

For high-end applications, MySQL databases can now be replicated across many machines. In this configuration, a master server manages slave servers, and the new library supports functions that allow you to control how the master and slaves are used to evaluate queries. We don't discuss replication in this book.

Profiling

The profiler tracks all MySQL function calls and writes information about these to the stderr device on Unix servers, to a file, or to a Unix network socket. The information written includes the file and line number of each MySQL function that's called, the execution time of the function, the output of the EXPLAIN statement for that query, and any error messages or warnings. The EXPLAIN statement is discussed briefly in Chapter 15.

Code cleanups and optimizations

Functions have been removed, changed, and added in an effort to improve how scripts can access the MySQL server. For example, the *mysqli_connect()* function includes an optional parameter to select a database, and executing queries and buffering results have been logically separated. Annoyingly, many parameter orderings have been changed; in particular, the connection handle is almost always the first parameter to most functions.

Removed functions

Many of the functions we listed as those we don't use in Chapter 6 have been removed in the new library. Also, persistent connections are no longer available.

Getting Started

This section explains how to install the improved MySQL library and the basics of migrating existing code to the new functions.

Installing the Library

This section discusses installation on only Unix platforms. We assume you have followed our installation instructions in Appendixes A through C, and that you have installed MySQL 4.1, PHP, and Apache and now want to enable the new library. We also assume that you've kept the source code for the components, and stored it in the subdirectories of */usr/local/src/* that are recommended in Appendixes A through C.

To configure the improved MySQL library, you need to reconfigure, recompile, and reinstall PHP. You also need to restart your Apache 2 server. To do this, follow these steps:

1. Log in as the Unix root user.
2. Change directory to your PHP source directory location using:

   ```
   % cd /usr/local/src/php-version_number
   ```

   For example, if the version is PHP 5.0.0, type:

   ```
   % cd /usr/local/src/php-5.0.0
   ```

3. Configure the PHP installation by running the *configure* script. Add improved MySQL support and disable regular MySQL support. This step assumes that MySQL 4.1 has been installed previously in the directory */usr/local/mysql* and that Apache 2 has been installed in */usr/local/apache2*:

   ```
   % ./configure --with-apxs2=/usr/local/apache2/bin/apxs \
       --without-mysql --with-mysqli=/usr/local/mysql/bin/mysql_config
   ```

   If your *configure* script complains, then try removing *mysql_config* from the second line:

   ```
   % ./configure --with-apxs2=/usr/local/apache2/bin/apxs \
       --without-mysql --with-mysqli=/usr/local/mysql/bin/
   ```

4. Compile the PHP scripting engine by running:

   ```
   % make
   ```

5. Now that the PHP scripting engine is built, install the PHP engine using:

   ```
   % make install
   ```

6. Restart the Apache web server by running the command:

   ```
   % /usr/local/apache2/bin/apachectl restart
   ```

Migrating to the New Library

Migrating legacy code to the new library is typically straightforward but requires that all MySQL function calls be modified. The function names in the regular and improved MySQL libraries are different and so are most of the parameter orders.

Renaming your functions is easy. Almost all functions in the regular library have an equivalent in the improved library, and the improved library function simply has mysqli_ as its prefix instead of mysql_. For example, *mysql_query()* is replaced by *mysqli_query()*.

The other significant difference in migrating code is that the connection resource parameter is mandatory to almost all functions and is the first parameter. For example, for *mysqli_query()* the first parameter is the connection handle and the second the SQL query; this is the opposite of *mysql_query()*.

Consider an example. Example H-1 is a copy of Example 6-1 from Chapter 6. that uses the regular library. It's been rewritten to use the improved library in Example H-2. The changes required are to globally replace mysql_ with mysqli_ and to move the connection handle parameter to be the first parameter in all function calls. Also, the constant MYSQL_NUM is changed to MYSQLI_NUM.

Example H-1. A code example that uses the regular MySQL library

```
<!DOCTYPE HTML PUBLIC
                "-//W3C//DTD HTML 4.01 Transitional//EN"
                "http://www.w3.org/TR/html401/loose.dtd">
<html>
<head>
  <meta http-equiv="Content-Type" content="text/html; charset=iso-8859-1">
  <title>Wines</title>
</head>
<body>
<pre>
<?php
    // (1) Open the database connection
    $connection = mysql_connect("localhost","hugh","drum");

    // (2) Select the winestore database
    mysql_select_db("winestore", $connection);

    // (3) Run the query on the winestore through the connection
    $result = mysql_query ("SELECT * FROM wine", $connection);

    // (4) While there are still rows in the result set, fetch the current
    // row into the array $row
    while ($row = mysql_fetch_array($result, MYSQL_NUM))
    {
      // (5) Print out each element in $row, that is, print the values of
      // the attributes
      foreach ($row as $attribute)
        print "{$attribute} ";

      // Print a carriage return to neaten the output
      print "\n";
    }
?>
</pre>
</body>
</html>
```

Example H-2. A modified version of Example H-1 that uses the improved MySQL library

```html
<!DOCTYPE HTML PUBLIC
                "-//W3C//DTD HTML 4.01 Transitional//EN"
                "http://www.w3.org/TR/html401/loose.dtd">
<html>
<head>
  <meta http-equiv="Content-Type" content="text/html; charset=iso-8859-1">
  <title>Wines</title>
</head>
<body>
<pre>
<?php
  // (1) Open the database connection
  $connection = mysqli_connect("localhost","hugh","drum");

  // (2) Select the winestore database
  mysqli_select_db($connection, "winestore");

  // (3) Run the query on the winestore through the connection
  $result = mysqli_query($connection, "SELECT * FROM wine");

  // (4) While there are still rows in the result set, fetch the current
  // row into the array $row
  while ($row = mysqli_fetch_array($result, MYSQLI_NUM))
  {
    // (5) Print out each element in $row, that is, print the values of
    // the attributes
     foreach ($row as $attribute)
        print "{$attribute} ";

     // Print a carriage return to neaten the output
     print "\n";
  }
?>
</pre>
</body>
</html>
```

The following popular functions aren't available in the improved library:

mysql_escape_string()
> Replace with calls to *mysqli_real_escape_string()*.

mysql_pconnect()
> Replace with calls to *mysqli_connect()*.

mysql_unbuffered_query()
> Replace with a call to *mysqli_real_query()* and then *mysql_use_result()*. These are discussed in the next section.

Using the New Features

This section explains some of the new features and illustrates them with short examples. We show you:

- How to use the new basic features
- Basic examples of how to prepare and execute statements
- How to profile your MySQL function calls

We don't discuss features for working with replicated servers, the new transaction features, or how to set up compressed or encrypted connections

Basic Features

With the regular library, you connect to a server and select a database using a fragment such as the following:

```
$connection = mysql_connect("localhost", "fred", "shhh");
mysql_select_db("winestore", $connection);
```

With the improved library, you can combine these two steps as follows:

```
$connection = mysqli_connect("localhost", "fred", "shhh", "winestore");
```

As shown in Example H-2, you can still use the old approach if you want to.

Both the regular and improved libraries have two query functions. The regular library has *mysql_query()* and *mysql_unbuffered_query()*, while the improved library has *mysqli_query()* and *mysql_real_query()*. As we showed in the previous section, *mysql_query()* and *mysqli_query()* are equivalent.

The *mysqli_real_query()* function can be used for either buffered or unbuffered output; it can provide normal output or the same features as *mysql_unbuffered_query()*. After you've called *mysql_real_query()*, you need to call either *mysql_use_result()* or *mysql_store_result()* to specify how results are to be retrieved. If you call *mysql_use_result()*, then rows are buffered on demand and the behavior is the same as *mysql_unbuffered_query()*. If you call *mysql_store_result()*, then all rows are buffered and the behavior is the same as *mysql_query()*.

Consider an example that uses the regular library and *mysql_query()*:

```
$result = mysql_query("SELECT * FROM customer", $connection);
```

This example runs the query and buffers all result rows. To do the same thing with the improved library, you can do either of the following:

```
// Simplified version
$result = mysqli_query($connection, "SELECT * FROM customer");

// Two-step version
if (mysqli_real_query($connection, "SELECT * FROM customer"))
  $result = mysqli_store_result($connection);
```

With the regular library, use *mysql_unbuffered_query()* as follows:

```
$result = mysql_unbuffered_query("SELECT * FROM customer", $connection);
```

To do the same thing with the improved library, do the following:

```
if (mysqli_real_query($connection, "SELECT * FROM customer"))
   $result = mysqli_use_result($connection);
```

If you prefer the object-oriented style of PEAR DB over the procedural style of the regular library, then you'll enjoy using the improved library. Here's an example fragment that uses the new object-oriented style:

```
<?php
$connection = mysqli_connect("localhost", "fred", "drum", "winestore");

$result = $connection->query("SELECT * FROM wine");

while ($row = $result->fetch_array())
{
  foreach($row as $element)
    print "$element ";
  print "\n";
}

$connection->close();
?>
```

Preparing and Executing Queries

With the improved library, you can separate query preparation from query execution. This means that if you need to repeat the same query many times, but with different values, you can improve your application's performance.

To use this approach, write an SQL query that contains placeholders instead of values. Then issue a prepare statement that asks MySQL to do as much parsing and preparation of the statement as possible in advance. Then, repeatedly replace the placeholders with values and execute the prepared query.

Inserting data

Consider an example of inserting data with prepare and execute. Suppose you want to insert more than one row into the *items* table from the *winestore* database. The table was created with the following statement:

```
CREATE TABLE items (
  cust_id int(5) NOT NULL,
  order_id int(5) NOT NULL,
  item_id int(3) NOT NULL,
  wine_id int(4) NOT NULL,
  qty int(3),
  price decimal(5,2),
  PRIMARY KEY (cust_id,order_id,item_id)
) type=MyISAM;
```

Without prepare and execute, you'd insert two rows into the table using a fragment such as the following:

```
// first row to be inserted
$cust_id = 14;
$order_id = 3;
$item_id = 1;
$wine_id = 770;
$qty = 2;
$price = 16.95;

$result = mysqli_query($connection,
  "INSERT INTO items VALUES ({$cust_id}, {$order_id}, {$item_id},
  {$wine_id}, {$qty}, {$price})");

if (mysqli_affected_rows($connection) != 1)
  die("Had a problem");

// Change the variables
$cust_id = 14;
$order_id = 3;
$item_id = 2;
$wine_id = 184;
$qty = 12;
$price = 12.90;

// Insert the second row
$result = mysqli_query($connection,
  "INSERT INTO items VALUES ({$cust_id}, {$order_id}, {$item_id},
  {$wine_id}, {$qty}, {$price})");

if (mysqli_affected_rows($connection) != 1)
  die("Had a problem");
```

Using the prepare and execute approach, you insert the same rows using the following fragment:

```
// Create a query with placeholders
$query = "INSERT INTO items VALUES (?,?,?,?,?,?)";

// Prepare the query
$stmt = mysqli_prepare($connection, $query);

// first row to be inserted
$cust_id = 14;
$order_id = 3;
$item_id = 1;
$wine_id = 770;
$qty = 2;
$price = 16.95;

// Bind the variables to the placeholders
mysqli_bind_param($stmt,
  array(MYSQLI_BIND_INT, MYSQLI_BIND_INT, MYSQLI_BIND_INT,
        MYSQLI_BIND_INT, MYSQLI_BIND_INT, MYSQLI_BIND_DOUBLE),
```

```
    $cust_id, $order_id, $item_id, $wine_id, $qty, $price);

// Insert the first row
mysqli_execute($stmt);
if (mysqli_stmt_affected_rows($stmt) != 1)
  die("Had a problem");

// Change the variables
$cust_id = 14;
$order_id = 3;
$item_id = 2;
$wine_id = 184;
$qty = 12;
$price = 12.90;

// Insert the second row
mysqli_execute($stmt);
if (mysqli_stmt_affected_rows($stmt) != 1)
  die("Had a problem");

// Close the statement
mysqli_stmt_close($stmt);
```

This approach requires more steps, but it can tremendously improve performance when scaled up to large numbers of queries. The code just shown starts by creating and preparing a query with the following lines of code:

```
// Create a query with placeholders
$query = "INSERT INTO items VALUES (?,?,?,?,?,?)";

// Prepare the query
$stmt = mysqli_prepare($connection, $query);
```

The question mark characters ? represent where values will be placed when the query is executed. The *mysqli_prepare()* function returns a prepared query statement that's saved in the variable $stmt.

After you create variables and assign them the values to be inserted, you bind the variables to the placeholders in the prepared statement using the following fragment:

```
// Bind the variables to the placeholders
mysqli_bind_param($stmt,
  array(MYSQLI_BIND_INT, MYSQLI_BIND_INT, MYSQLI_BIND_INT,
        MYSQLI_BIND_INT, MYSQLI_BIND_INT, MYSQLI_BIND_DOUBLE),
  $cust_id, $order_id, $item_id, $wine_id, $qty, $price);
```

The first parameter is the prepared statement. The second parameter is an array that specifies the types of each of the variables that are bound to the statement. In this example, there are six variables, where the first five are integers and the last is a double precision number. You can also specify MYSQL_BIND_STRING to bind a string variable and MYSQL_SEND_DATA to bind a very large amount of data. The remaining parameters are the variables themselves, and they must match the elements in the second parameter, both in the number of elements and their order.

Once the variables are bound to the query, you can execute the statement. In the fragment, this is done with:

```
// Insert the first row
mysqli_execute($stmt);

if (mysqli_stmt_affected_rows($stmt) != 1)
  die("Had a problem");
```

The function *mysqli_stmt_affected_rows()* is the same as *mysqli_affected_rows()*, but works for statements instead of regular queries.

Now that the query is prepared and the variables are bound, to insert another row, all you need to do is change the values of the variables and reexecute the statement:

```
// Change the variables
$cust_id = 14;
$order_id = 3;
$item_id = 2;
$wine_id = 184;
$qty = 12;
$price = 12.90;

// Insert the second row
mysqli_execute($stmt);

if (mysqli_stmt_affected_rows($stmt) != 1)
  die("Had a problem");
```

Once you've finished with a prepared statement, you can free the resources that are associated with it using:

```
// Close the statement
mysqli_stmt_close($stmt);
```

The code we've shown is somewhat artificial. Normally, you'd do the preparation and binding, and then run a loop that creates the input, assigns the values to the placeholders, and executes the query.

Retrieving data

You can also repeat a SELECT query using the prepare and execute approach. This is useful if you want to run the same query, but want to use different values each time in the WHERE clause. For example, this would be a useful tool in our online winestore search feature, where wine prices are repeatedly retrieved for different wines.

Let's start by showing the old way of doing things. Wine prices can be retrieved using the following function (which is based on the *showPricing()* function described in Chapter 16 but rewritten to use the improved MySQL library):

```
function showPricing($connection)
{
  global $wineID;
```

```
// Find the price of the cheapest inventory
$query = "SELECT min(cost) FROM inventory
            WHERE wine_id = {$wineID}";

// Run the query
$result = mysqli_query($connection, $query);

// Retrieve and return the price
$row = mysqli_fetch_array($result, MYSQLI_BOTH);

return $row["min(cost)"];
}
```

To modify the function to use the prepare and execute approach, you need to have an extra variable that stores a prepared statement. If the statement isn't yet prepared, the function will prepare it. If it is prepared, then it'll use that statement. Here's the rewritten code:

```
function showPricing($connection)
{
  global $statement, $wineID;

  if (empty($statement))
  {
    // Find the price of the cheapest inventory
    $query = "SELECT min(cost) FROM inventory
                WHERE wine_id = ?";

    // Prepare the query
    $statement = mysqli_prepare($connection, $query);

    // Bind the $wineID to the placeholder
    mysqli_bind_param($statement, array(MYSQLI_BIND_INT), $wineID);
  }

  // Run the query
  mysqli_execute($statement);

  $cost = "";

  // Bind the output -- links min(cost) to $cost
  mysqli_bind_result($statement, $cost);

  // Retrieve and return the price
  mysqli_fetch($statement);

  return $cost;
}
```

The code is a little longer than the old way of doing things, but it's much faster when prices are retrieved many times. The following fragment checks if the statement has been prepared and, if not, it prepares it and binds the $wineID to the placeholder:

```
if (empty($statement))
{
```

```
// Find the price of the cheapest inventory
$query = "SELECT min(cost) FROM inventory
          WHERE wine_id = ?";

// Prepare the query
$statement = mysqli_prepare($connection, $query);

// Bind the $wineID to the placeholder
mysqli_bind_param($statement, array(MYSQLI_BIND_INT), $wineID);
}
```

This process is explained in the previous section. However, in this example, we've declared the $wineID as global in the function; at the time of writing, passing the variable as a parameter by reference didn't work.

Once the statement is prepared, it is executed with:

```
// Run the query
mysqli_execute($statement);
```

Now that the query has been run, we need to retrieve the results. To do this, you need to bind the output to one or more variables. In our example, there's only one attribute retrieved by the query, min(cost). This is bound to the variable $cost using the following fragment:

```
// Bind the output -- links min(cost) to $cost
mysqli_bind_result($statement, $cost);
```

If there were instead two attributes returned by the query, you'd bind both using two variables:

```
mysqli_bind_result($statement, $var1, $var2);
```

Once the variable has been bound to the output, you can retrieve the row of data and the value of $cost:

```
// Retrieve and return the price
mysqli_fetch($statement);

return $cost;
```

Note that you must use *mysqli_fetch()* to retrieve rows from an executed query and that it takes the statement as its parameter.

Profiling Queries

The new query profiler allows you to collect information about how the improved MySQL library is functioning. Once configured, it reports information including:

Source file data
    The name and line number of each improved MySQL function library call.

Timings
    The total script execution time, and the execution time of each MySQL function call.

Parameters and warnings
> Information such as the machine host name, database server user name, and warnings about missing statements (for example, warning you that you didn't call *mysqli_close()*).

Query data
> For each MySQL function call, the report lists information such as the function called, its return value, the query string passed as a parameter, the output of the EXPLAIN statement for that query (which shows how the query was evaluated), and the number of affected rows.

You can use this information to correct bugs and warnings and check the query speed (and take corrective action if it isn't acceptable). The information is output in an XML format.

To use the profiler, call the *mysqli_profiler()* function at the beginning of each script you want to profile. The easiest option is to write the report to a file. You can do this with:

```
mysqli_profiler(MYSQLI_PR_REPORT_FILE, "/tmp/report");
```

Replace */tmp/report* with the directory and file you want to write the report to. You can also write to the stderr device on a Unix platform by using:

```
mysqli_profiler(MYSQLI_PR_REPORT_STDERR);
```

You can also write to a network socket, but we don't discuss this here.

In part, the output of a report has the following example format:

```
<query>
<functionname>mysqli_query</functionname>
<fileinfo>
<filename>/usr/local/apache2/htdocs/test.php</filename>
<line>7</line>
</fileinfo>
<timeinfo>
<execution_time>0.000636</execution_time>
</timeinfo>
<query_string>SELECT * FROM wine</query_string>
<explain>
<id>1</id>
<select_type>SIMPLE</select_type>
<table>wine</table>
<type>ALL</type>
<possible_keys>(null)</possible_keys>
<key>(null)</key>
<key_len>(null)</key_len>
<ref>(null)</ref>
<rows>1048</rows>
<Extra></Extra>
</explain>
<affected_rows>-1</affected_rows>
```

Index

Symbols

Numbers

A

date_add( ) function (MySQL), 511
date_format( ) function (MySQL), 512
DB::affectedRows( ) function, 226
DB::connect( ) function, 225, 226
DB::createSequence( ) function, 227
DB::dropSequence( ) function, 227
DB::fetchRow( ) function, 225
db.inc require file, 183
db.inc (winestore database), 569
DB::isError( ) function, 225, 228
DBMSs (database management systems), 3,
    11–15, 135, 138
  MySQL, 14
DB::nextId( ) function, 228
DB::nextId( ) method, 282
DB.php, inclusion in path, 224
DB::query( ) function, 225, 228
DB::quote( ) function, 228
DB_Result::fetchRow( ) function, 227
DB_Result::numRows( ) function, 228
DB_Result::tableInfo( ) function, 229
debug_backtrace( ) function (PHP), 416
decbin( ) function (PHP), 104
dechex( ) function (PHP), 104
decoct( ) function (PHP), 104
decode( ) function (MySQL), 513
DEFAULT modifier, 146
DELAYED modifier, 503
DELETE request (HTTP), 721
DELETE statement, 151, 503
descendant classes, 127
destroy( ) function (PHP), 751
destructors, 115
details.php (winestore database), 546, 547,
    584, 586, 591–593
die( ) function (MySQL), 176
digests, 380
dirty reads, 271
displayCart( ) function (winestore
    database), 607
DISTINCT clause, 165, 167
Document Object Model (see DOM)
DOM (Document Object Model), 314–316
dot (.) operator, 27
double-equal (==) operator, 31
doublevalue( ) function (PHP), 49
DROP statement, 147

E

EasyPHP, 689–693
echo statement, 20

ECMA-SCRIPT
  (see also JavaScript)
ECMA-Script, 307
elementary natural joins, 162
elements, 57
else clause, 29
email address validation, 292–295
empty( ) language construct, 42
encode( ) function (MySQL), 513
encoding standards, 23
  web sites, 24
encryption functions (MySQL), 512
encryption of passwords, 379–382
end anchors ($) (regular expressions), 89
entities, 137, 726
  identifying, 729
entity-relationship (ER) modeling, 137, 138
entity-relationship modeling (see ER
    modeling)
equality operator
  assignment operator, compared to, 32
  SQL compared to PHP, 506
equal-to or greater-than (=>) operator, 60
ER (entity-relationship) modeling, 137, 138,
    728–740
  converting to SQL, 738–745
  entities, 726
    identifying, 729
  ER diagrams, 729
  identifying relationships, 732
  key attributes, identifying, 736
  multivalues attributes, 738
  tools, 729, 737, 738
  weak entities, 737, 738
ereg( ) function (PHP), 88, 94
eregi( ) function (PHP), 94
eregi_replace ( ) function (PHP), 95
ereg_replace( ) function (PHP), 95
error handling of MySQL
    functions, 176–178
errors, 402–412
  basic custom handlers, 412–415
    disadvantages, 415
  common programming errors, 407–410
    partial or no page output, 407
    variables, 408–410
  custom error handlers, 412–421
  less common problems, 410
    header complaints, 410
    missing semicolons, braces, and
      quotes, 411
    source shown in browsers, 411

getFile( ) function (PHP), 132
gethostbyname( ) function (PHP), 294
getLine( ) function (PHP), 132
getMessage( ) function (PHP), 132
getmxrr( ) function (PHP), 294
get_parent_class( ) function (PHP), 461
getrandmax( ) function (PHP), 107
gettype( ) function (PHP), 41
ghostview, 424
global variables, 47
gmdate( ) function (PHP), 100
gmmktime( ) function (PHP), 97
gmstrftime( ) function (PHP), 101
GRANT OPTION statement, 528
GROUP BY clause, 156, 496
Gtk packages, 220

H

hash arrays, 60
hash indexes, 522
HAVING clause, 157
HEAD request (HTTP), 721
header( ) function (PHP), 206
headers, 5
heap tables, 522
heterogenous arrays, 61
hexadecimal encoding sequences, 23
hexdec( ) function (PHP), 104
high-bit characters, 23
homepage (winestore database), 598–604
home.php script, 392
home.tpl template, 393
htaccess file, 373
HTML forms for user input, 252–255
HTML Integrated Templates (IT) package
    (see IT package)
HTML PEAR packages, 248
HTML report output format, 425
HTML_Template_IT package (see IT
    package)
HTML_Template_ITX package (see ITX
    package)
HTML_ToPDF, 425
HTTP (Hypertext Transfer Protocol), 4,
    716–725
    authentication, 369–373
        PHP, 373–385
    GET method, 191
    HTTP requests, 720–722
        GET versus POST, 722
        request methods, 721

HTTP responses, 722–724
    caching, 724
    status codes, 723
    PEAR packages for, 249
    POST method, 191
    request, 5
    response, 5
    URLs (see URLs)
httpd.conf configuration file, 372

I

identifiers table, 280
if function (MySQL), 512
if statement, 28
if...else statement, 28–30
implode( ) function (PHP), 66
IN clause, 488
in_array( ) function (PHP), 67
include files, 51–53
    defining classes with, 112
    managing, 52
    tagging requirements, 51
includes/authenticate.inc (winestore
    database), 646, 647
includes/customHandler.inc (winestore
    database), 574–576
includes/db.inc (winestore database), 569
includes/template.inc file (winestore
    database), 563
includes/validate.inc (winestore
    database), 569–574
includes/winestore.inc (winestore
    database), 576, 576–582
incorrect summary problem, 272
indexes, 58, 138
    design, 532–536
    tips, 535
index.php (winestore database), 545, 598,
    601
index.tpl (winestore database), 602
inheritance, 124–131, 457
inner queries, 487
InnoDB tables, 519
    COMMIT and ROLLBACK
        transactions, 520
    disadvantages, 520
INSERT DELAYED statement, 276
INSERT statement, 148–151
    using with SELECT, 499
instanceof keyword (PHP 5), 461
instances, 110

POST request (HTTP), 721
postcode validation, 290–292
PostScript, 425
post-validation, 286
pow( ) function (MySQL), 510
<pre> tags, 59
precedence, 28
primary keys, 136, 138, 736
print statement, 20
printf( ) function (PHP), 77
    supported conversion types, 78
printing reports (see reporting)
print_r( ) function (PHP), 41
    including output in web page, 59
private member functions, 117
private member variables, 116
privileges
    granting, 528
    management in MySQL, 531
    network access, 530
    revoking, 531
    scope and, 528
protected functions, 129
protected member variables, 129
pseudo-random numbers, 106
PUT request (HTTP), 721

Q

queries, 166
    automating, 513–516
        Unix, 514
        Windows, 515
    indexes and, 532
    join queries (see join queries)
    locks, avoiding through design, 275
    nested queries, 487–492
    on MySQL with PHP, 172–188
        error handling, 176–178
        formatting results, 180–183
        mysql_fetch_array( ) function, 175
        opening a database
          connection, 172–175
        security concerns, 198–202
        select lists on HTML forms, 184–188
        table structures, 178–180
    one-component querying, 189, 205–207
    user input, generating from, 203–207
    user-driven querying, 188
query caching, 538–540
QUICK modifier, 504
quote( ) function (MySQL), 508

R

rand( ) function (MySQL), 510
rand( ) function (PHP), 106
random numbers
    generating seeds for, 99
range( ) function (PHP), 66
rawurlencode( ) function (PHP), 658, 720
read( ) function (PHP), 750
realm, 371
receipt.php (winestore database), 547
records, 136
redefined functions
    object-oriented programming
        redefined functions, 127–129
regular expressions, 87–97
    \ (backslash), 92
    { } (braces), 90
    [x12] (brackets), 88
    $ (end anchor), 89
    * (matching operator), 90
    + (matching operator), 90
    ? (matching operator), 90
    ^ (not operator), 89
    ^ (start anchor), 89
    alternative patterns, 92
    anchors, 89
    character lists, 88
        using, 92
    character ranges, specifying, 88
    functions, 94–97
    groups, 91
    metacharacters, 93
    POSIX character classes, 94
    special characters, escaping, 92
    syntax, 87
relational databases, 135, 726–745
    constraints, 727
    entities, 726
    ER modeling (see ER modeling)
    many-to-many relationships, 733, 735, 745
    one-to-many relationships, 732, 735, 743
    one-to-one relationships, 732, 735, 743
    winestore example, 726–728
relational models, 138
relative URLs, 719
reload problem, 255–260
replace( ) function (MySQL), 508
reporting, 422–456
    "Hello, world", 427
    output formats, 423–426
        choosing, 422

About the Authors

Hugh E. Williams is the Associate Professor in Information Retrieval in the School of Computer Science and IT at RMIT University in Melbourne, Australia. He teaches in all areas of computer science and began teaching databases in 1995 and PHP programming in 2000. His research interests include building better web search engines, retrieving multimedia and genomic information, and designing fast data structures. When not at work, Hugh likes to go running, watch Richmond play footy, follow the cricket, and write books. Hugh has a PhD from RMIT University.

David Lane works as a software engineer and IT manager with the Multimedia Database Systems group at RMIT University in Melbourne, Australia. In that group, he has helped to develop and commercialize the TeraText Database System, a large-scale SGML/XML document repository. David has also worked in areas as diverse as Satellite Communications, Human Factors Research, and Electronic Document Interchange (EDI). Away from work, David enjoys running and building sand castles with his two children. David has a bachelor's degree in Applied Science (majoring in mathematics and computer science) from Swinburne University.

Colophon

Our look is the result of reader comments, our own experimentation, and feedback from distribution channels. Distinctive covers complement our distinctive approach to technical topics, breathing personality and life into potentially dry subjects.

The animal on the cover of *Web Database Applications with PHP and MySQL, Second Edition* is a platypus. The platypus (*Ornithorhynchus anatinus*) of Australia and Tasmania has been described as a living fossil. Its earliest known remains date back 100,000 years, and it combines mammalian and reptilian features. It is aquatic, furry, warm-blooded, and lays eggs. It sports webbed feet, a beaverlike tail, and a ducklike bill.

The preferred plural of platypus is either "platypus" or "platypuses," and a baby platypus has been referred to as a "platapup."

The platypus was first described by Dr. George Shaw, a British scientist. He thought the animal was a hoax and took a pair of scissors to the pelt, expecting to find stitches attaching appendages to skin.

The platypus is an air-breathing mammal that spends most of its day resting in an underground burrow. However, it feeds only in the water and is rarely observed on land. The platypus hunts mostly at night for such food as shrimp, worms, and aquatic insects. Because the animal doesn't need to hear or see its intended food, a platypus protects its eyes and ears by automatically closing them underwater and relies on its bill to locate prey. While diving, the platypus temporarily stores food in special cheek pouches. When the animal returns to the surface to breathe, the food is ground up between rough pads located inside the bill.

A female platypus produces a clutch of one to three eggs in late winter or spring. The mother is believed to incubate them between her lower belly and curled-up tail for about 10 days as she rests in an underground nest made of vegetation collected from the water. She doesn't have nipples; her milk is instead secreted from two patches of skin midway along her belly. It's believed that a platypup feeds by slurping up milk with sweeps of its stubby bill. When juveniles enter the water at about four months, they are nearly as long as an adult.

The platypus is the only Australian mammal known to be venomous. Adult males have a pointed spur located above the heel of each hind leg that can inject poison produced by a gland in the thigh. Platypus venom isn't considered life-threatening to humans. However, spurring is painful, because platypus spurs are sharp and can be driven in with great force; the poison itself triggers severe pain in the affected limb.

The platypus is officially classified as "common but vulnerable" in Australia. As a species, it isn't currently considered endangered. However, platypus populations are believed to have declined or disappeared, particularly in urban and agricultural settings; the specific underlying reasons for this decline are unknown.

Darren Kelly was the production editor, and Nancy Reinhardt was the copyeditor for *Web Database Applications with PHP and MySQL*, Second Edition. Jamie Peppard, Claire Cloutier, and Philip Dangler provided quality control. Mary Agner provided production assistance. John Bickelhaupt wrote the index.

Ellie Volckhausen and Emma Colby designed the cover of this book, based on a series design by Edie Freedman. The cover image is a 19th-century engraving from the Dover Pictorial Archive. Emma Colby produced the cover layout with Quark-XPress 4.1 using Adobe's ITC Garamond font.

Melanie Wang designed the interior layout, based on a series design by David Futato. This book was converted by Andrew Savikas to FrameMaker 5.5.6 with a format conversion tool created by Erik Ray, Jason McIntosh, Neil Walls, and Mike Sierra that uses Perl and XML technologies. The text font is Linotype Birka; the heading font is Adobe Myriad Condensed; and the code font is LucasFont's TheSans Mono Condensed. The illustrations that appear in the book were produced by Robert Romano and Jessamyn Read using Macromedia FreeHand 9 and Adobe Photoshop 6. The tip and warning icons were drawn by Christopher Bing. This colophon was compiled by Mary Anne Weeks Mayo.